THE SUMMA THEOLOGICA

VOLUME 6

SAINT THOMAS AQUINAS

AETERNA PRESS

PUBLISHED BY AETERNA PRESS.
COVER DESIGN BY AETERNA PRESS.

9 VOLUMES

TRANSLATED BY THE FATHERS OF THE ENGLISH DOMINICAN PROVINCE

NIHIL OBSTAT:
RT. REV. MSGR. JOHN M. FEARNS, S.T.D
CENSOR DEPUTATUS

IMPRIMATUR:
FRANCIS CARDINAL SPELLMAN,
ARCHBISHOP OF NEW YORK

ISBN-13: 978-1-78516-373-9

AVAILABLE AS AN E-BOOK:
WWW.AETERNAPRESS.COM

CONTENTS

TREATISE ON FORTITUDE AND TEMPERANCE (QQ[123]-170)

OF FORTITUDE (TWELVE ARTICLES)

After considering justice we must in due sequence consider fortitude. We must (1) consider the virtue itself of fortitude; (2) its parts; (3) the gift corresponding thereto; (4) the precepts that pertain to it.

Concerning fortitude three things have to be considered: (1) Fortitude itself; (2) its principal act, viz. martyrdom; (3) the vices opposed to fortitude.

Under the first head there are twelve points of inquiry:

(1) Whether fortitude is a virtue?

(2) Whether it is a special virtue?

(3) Whether fortitude is only about fear and daring?

(4) Whether it is only about fear of death?

(5) Whether it is only in warlike matters?

(6) Whether endurance is its chief act?

(7) Whether its action is directed to its own good?

(8) Whether it takes pleasure in its own action?

(9) Whether fortitude deals chiefly with sudden occurrences?

(10) Whether it makes use of anger in its action?

(11) Whether it is a cardinal virtue?

(12) Of its comparison with the other cardinal virtues.

Whether fortitude is a virtue?

Objection 1: It seems that fortitude is not a virtue. For the Apostle says (2 Cor. 12:9): "Virtue is perfected in infirmity." But fortitude is contrary to infirmity. Therefore fortitude is not a virtue.

Objection 2: Further, if it is a virtue, it is either theological, intellectual, or moral. Now fortitude is not contained among the theological virtues, nor among the intellectual virtues, as may be gathered from what we have said above ([3281]FS, Q[57], A[2]; [3282]FS, Q[62], A[3]). Neither, apparently, is it contained among the moral virtues, since according to the Philosopher (Ethic. iii, 7,8): "Some seem to be brave through ignorance; or through experience, as soldiers," both of which cases seem to pertain to act rather than to moral virtue, "and some are called brave on account of certain passions"; for instance, on account of fear of threats, or of dishonor, or again on account of sorrow, anger, or hope. But moral virtue does not act from passion but from choice, as stated above ([3283]FS, Q[55], A[4]). Therefore fortitude is not a virtue.

Objection 3: Further, human virtue resides chiefly in the soul, since it is a "good quality of the mind," as stated above (Ethic. iii, 7,8). But fortitude, seemingly, resides in the body, or at least results from the temperament of the body. Therefore it seems that fortitude is not a virtue.

On the contrary, Augustine (De Morib. Eccl. xv, xxi, xxii) numbers fortitude among the virtues.

I answer that, According to the Philosopher (Ethic. ii, 6) "virtue is that which makes its possessor good, and renders his work good." Hence human virtue, of which we are speaking now, is that which makes a man good, and renders his work good. Now man's good is to be in accordance with reason, according to Dionysius (Div. Nom. iv, 22). Wherefore it belongs to human virtue to make man good, to make his work accord with reason. This happens in three ways: first, by rectifying reason itself, and this is done by the intellectual virtues; secondly, by establishing the rectitude of reason in human affairs, and this belongs to justice; thirdly, by removing the obstacles to the establishment of this rectitude in human affairs. Now the human will is hindered in two ways from following the rectitude of reason. First, through being drawn by some object of pleasure to something other than what the rectitude of reason requires; and this obstacle is removed by the virtue of temperance. Secondly, through the will being disinclined to follow that which is in accordance with reason, on account of some difficulty that presents itself. In order to remove this obstacle fortitude of the mind is requisite, whereby to resist the aforesaid difficulty even as a man, by fortitude of body, overcomes and removes bodily obstacles.

Hence it is evident that fortitude is a virtue, in so far as it conforms man to reason.

Reply to Objection 1: The virtue of the soul is perfected, not in the infirmity of the soul, but in the infirmity of the body, of which the Apostle was speaking. Now it belongs to fortitude of the mind to bear bravely with infirmities of the flesh, and this belongs to the virtue of patience or fortitude, as also to acknowledge one's own infirmity, and this belongs to the perfection that is called humility.

Reply to Objection 2: Sometimes a person performs the exterior act of a virtue without having the virtue, and from some other cause than virtue. Hence the Philosopher (Ethic. iii, 8) mentions five ways in which people are said to be brave by way of resemblance, through performing acts of fortitude without having the virtue. This may be done in three ways. First, because they tend to that which is difficult as though it were not difficult: and this again happens in three ways, for sometimes this is owing to ignorance, through not perceiving the greatness of the danger; sometimes it is owing to the fact that one is hopeful of overcoming dangers—when, for instance, one has often experienced escape from danger; and sometimes this is owing to a certain science and art, as in the case of soldiers who, through skill and practice in the use of arms, think little of the dangers of battle, as they reckon themselves capable of defending themselves against them; thus Vegetius says (De Re Milit. i), "No man fears to do what he is confident of having learned to do well." Secondly, a man performs an act of fortitude without having the virtue, through the impulse of a passion, whether of sorrow that he wishes to cast off, or again of anger. Thirdly, through choice, not indeed of a due end, but of some temporal advantage to be obtained, such as honor, pleasure, or gain, or of some disadvantage to be avoided, such as blame, pain, or loss.

Reply to Objection 3: The fortitude of the soul which is reckoned a virtue, as explained in the Reply to the First Objection, is so called from its likeness to fortitude of the body. Nor is it inconsistent with the notion of virtue, that a man should have a natural inclination to virtue by reason of his natural temperament, as stated above ([3284]FS, Q[63], A[1]).

Whether fortitude is a special virtue?

Objection 1: It seems that fortitude is not a special virtue. For it is written (Wis. 7:7): "She teacheth temperance, and prudence, and justice, and fortitude," where the text has "virtue" for "fortitude." Since then the term "virtue" is common to all virtues, it seems that fortitude is a general virtue.

Objection 2: Further, Ambrose says (De Offic. i): "Fortitude is not lacking in courage, for alone she defends the honor of the virtues and guards their behests. She it is that wages an inexorable war on all vice, undeterred by toil, brave in face of dangers, steeled against pleasures, unyielding to lusts, avoiding covetousness as a deformity that weakens virtue"; and he says the same further on in connection with other vices. Now this cannot apply to any special virtue. Therefore fortitude is not a special virtue.

Objection 3: Further, fortitude would seem to derive its name from firmness. But it belongs to every virtue to stand firm, as stated in Ethic. ii. Therefore fortitude is a general virtue.

On the contrary, Gregory (Moral. xxii) numbers it among the other virtues.

I answer that, As stated above ([3285]FS, Q[61], AA[3],4), the term "fortitude" can be taken in two ways. First, as simply denoting a certain firmness of mind, and in this sense it is a general virtue, or rather a condition of every virtue, since as the Philosopher states (Ethic. ii), it is requisite for every virtue to act firmly and immovably. Secondly, fortitude may be taken to denote firmness only in bearing and withstanding those things wherein it is most difficult to be firm, namely in certain grave dangers. Therefore Tully says (Rhet. ii), that "fortitude is deliberate facing of dangers and bearing of toils." In this sense fortitude is reckoned a special virtue, because it has a special matter.

Reply to Objection 1: According to the Philosopher (De Coelo i, 116) the word virtue refers to the extreme limit of a power. Now a natural power is, in one sense, the power of resisting corruptions, and in another sense is a principle of action, as stated in Metaph. v, 17. And since this latter meaning is the more common, the term "virtue," as denoting the extreme limit of such a power, is a common term, for virtue taken in a general sense is nothing else than a habit whereby one acts well. But as denoting the extreme limit of power in the first sense, which sense is more specific, it is applied to a special virtue, namely fortitude, to which it belongs to stand firm against all kinds of assaults.

Reply to Objection 2: Ambrose takes fortitude in a broad sense, as denoting firmness of mind in face of assaults of all kinds. Nevertheless even as a special virtue with a determinate matter, it helps to resist the assaults of all vices. For he that can stand firm in things that are most difficult to bear, is prepared, in consequence, to resist those which are less difficult.

Reply to Objection 3: This objection takes fortitude in the first sense.

Whether fortitude is about fear and dying?

Objection 1: It seems that fortitude is not about fear and daring. For Gregory says (Moral. vii): "The fortitude of the just man is to overcome the flesh, to withstand self-indulgence, to quench the lusts of the present life." Therefore fortitude seems to be about pleasures rather than about fear and daring.

Objection 2: Further, Tully says (De Invent. Rhet. ii), that it belongs to fortitude to face dangers and to bear toil. But this seemingly has nothing to do with the passions of fear and daring, but rather with a man's toilsome deeds and external dangers. Therefore fortitude is not about fear and daring.

Objection 3: Further, not only daring, but also hope, is opposed to fear, as stated above ([3286]FS, Q[45], A[1], ad 2) in the treatise on passions. Therefore fortitude should not be about daring any more than about hope.

On the contrary, The Philosopher says (Ethic. ii, 7; iii, 9) that fortitude is about fear and daring.

I answer that, As stated above [3287](A[1]), it belongs to the virtue of fortitude to remove any obstacle that withdraws the will from following the reason. Now to be withdrawn from something difficult belongs to the notion of fear, which denotes withdrawal from an evil that entails difficulty, as stated above ([3288]FS, Q[42], AA[3],5) in the treatise on passions. Hence fortitude is chiefly about fear of difficult things, which can withdraw the will from following the reason. And it behooves one not only firmly to bear the assault of these difficulties by restraining fear, but also moderately to withstand them, when, to wit, it is necessary to dispel them altogether in order to free oneself therefrom for the future, which seems to come under the notion of daring. Therefore fortitude is about fear and daring, as curbing fear and moderating daring.

Reply to Objection 1: Gregory is speaking then of the fortitude of the just man, as to its common relation to all virtues. Hence he first of all mentions matters pertaining to temperance, as in the words quoted, and then adds that which pertains properly to fortitude as a special virtue, by saying: "To love the trials of this life for the sake of an eternal reward."

Reply to Objection 2: Dangers and toils do not withdraw the will from the course of reason, except in so far as they are an object of fear. Hence fortitude needs to be immediately about fear and daring, but mediately about dangers and toils, these being the objects of those passions.

Reply to Objection 3: Hope is opposed to fear on the part of the object, for hope is of good, fear of evil: whereas daring is about the same object, and is opposed to fear by way of approach and withdrawal, as stated above ([3289]FS, Q[45], A[1]). And since fortitude properly regards those temporal evils that withdraw one from virtue, as appears from Tully's definition quoted in the Second Objection, it follows that fortitude properly is about fear and daring and not about hope, except in so far as it is connected with daring, as stated above ([3290]FS, Q[45], A[2]).

Whether fortitude is only about dangers of death?

Objection 1: It seems that fortitude is not only about dangers of death. For Augustine says (De Morib. Eccl. xv) that "fortitude is love bearing all things readily for the sake of the object beloved": and (Music. vi) he says that fortitude is "the love which dreads no hardship, not even death." Therefore fortitude is not only about danger of death, but also about other afflictions.

Objection 2: Further, all the passions of the soul need to be reduced to a mean by some virtue. Now there is no other virtue reducing fears to a mean. Therefore fortitude is not only about fear of death, but also about other fears.

Objection 3: Further, no virtue is about extremes. But fear of death is about an extreme, since it is the greatest of fears, as stated in Ethic. iii. Therefore the virtue of fortitude is not about fear of death.

On the contrary, Andronicus says that "fortitude is a virtue of the irascible faculty that is not easily deterred by the fear of death."

I answer that, As stated above [3291](A[3]), it belongs to the virtue of fortitude to guard the will against being withdrawn from the good of reason through fear of bodily evil. Now it behooves one to hold firmly the good of reason against every evil whatsoever, since no bodily good is equivalent to the good of the reason. Hence fortitude of soul must be that which binds the will firmly to the good of reason in face of the greatest evils: because he that stands firm against great things, will in consequence stand firm against less things, but not conversely. Moreover it belongs to the notion of virtue that it should regard something extreme: and the most fearful of all bodily evils is death, since it does away all bodily goods. Wherefore Augustine says (De Morib. Eccl. xxii) that "the soul is shaken by its fellow body, with fear of toil and pain, lest the body be stricken and harassed with fear of death lest it be done away and destroyed." Therefore the virtue of fortitude is about the fear of dangers of death.

Reply to Objection 1: Fortitude behaves well in bearing all manner of adversity: yet a man is not reckoned brave simply through bearing any kind of adversity, but only through bearing well even the greatest evils; while through bearing others he is said to be brave in a restricted sense.

Reply to Objection 2: Since fear is born of love, any virtue that moderates the love of certain goods must in consequence moderate the fear of contrary evils: thus liberality, which moderates the love of money, as a consequence, moderates the fear of losing it, and the same is the case with temperance and other virtues. But to love one's own life is natural: and hence the necessity of a special virtue modifying the fear of death.

Reply to Objection 3: In virtues the extreme consists in exceeding right reason: wherefore to undergo the greatest dangers in accordance with reason is not contrary to virtue.

Whether fortitude is properly about dangers of death in battle?

Objection 1: It seems that fortitude is not properly about dangers of death in battle. For martyrs above all are commended for their fortitude. But martyrs are not commended in connection with battle. Therefore fortitude is not properly about dangers of death in battle.

Objection 2: Further, Ambrose says (De Offic. i) that "fortitude is applicable both to warlike and to civil matters": and Tully (De Offic. i), under the heading, "That it pertains to fortitude to excel in battle rather than in civil life," says: "Although not a few think that the business of war is of greater importance than the affairs of civil life, this opinion must be qualified: and if we wish to judge the matter truly, there are many things in civil life that are more important and more glorious than those connected with war." Now greater fortitude is about greater things. Therefore fortitude is not properly concerned with death in battle.

Objection 3: Further, war is directed to the preservation of a country's temporal peace: for Augustine says (De Civ. Dei xix) that "wars are waged in order to insure peace." Now it does not seem that one ought to expose oneself to the danger of death for the temporal peace of one's country, since this same peace is the occasion of much license in morals. Therefore it seems that the virtue of fortitude is not about the danger of death in battle.

On the contrary, The Philosopher says (Ethic. iii) that fortitude is chiefly about death in battle.

I answer that, As stated above [3292](A[4]), fortitude strengthens a man's mind against the greatest danger, which is that of death. Now fortitude is a virtue; and it is essential to virtue ever to tend to good; wherefore it is in order to pursue some good that man does not fly from the danger of death. But the dangers of death arising out of sickness, storms at sea, attacks from robbers, and the like, do not seem to come on a man through his pursuing some good. on the other hand, the dangers of death which occur in battle come to man directly on account of some good, because, to wit, he is defending the common good by a just fight. Now a just fight is of two kinds. First, there is the general combat, for instance, of those who fight in battle; secondly, there is the private combat, as when a judge or even private individual does not refrain from giving a just judgment through fear of the impending sword, or any other danger though it threaten death. Hence it belongs to fortitude to strengthen the mind against dangers of death, not only such as arise in a general battle, but also such as occur in singular combat, which may be called by the general name of battle. Accordingly it must be granted that fortitude is properly about dangers of death occurring in battle.

Moreover, a brave man behaves well in face of danger of any other kind of death; especially since man may be in danger of any kind of death on account of virtue: thus may a man not fail to attend on a sick friend through fear of deadly infection, or not refuse to undertake a journey with some godly object in view through fear of shipwreck or robbers.

Reply to Objection 1: Martyrs face the fight that is waged against their own person, and this for the sake of the sovereign good which is God; wherefore their fortitude is praised above all. Nor is it outside the genus of fortitude that regards warlike actions, for which reason they are said to have been valiant in battle. [*Office of Martyrs, ex. Heb. xi. 34.]

Reply to Objection 2: Personal and civil business is differentiated from the business of war that regards general wars. However, personal and civil affairs admit of dangers of death arising out of certain conflicts which are private wars, and so with regard to these also there may be fortitude properly so called.

Reply to Objection 3: The peace of the state is good in itself, nor does it become evil because certain persons make evil use of it. For there are many others who make good use of it; and many evils prevented by it, such as murders and sacrileges, are much greater than those which are occasioned by it, and which belong chiefly to the sins of the flesh.

Whether endurance is the chief act of fortitude?

Objection 1: It seems that endurance is not the chief act of fortitude. For virtue "is about the difficult and the good" (Ethic. ii, 3). Now it is more difficult to attack than to endure. Therefore endurance is not the chief act of fortitude.

Objection 2: Further, to be able to act on another seems to argue greater power than not to be changed by another. Now to attack is to act on another, and to endure is to persevere unchangeably. Since then fortitude denotes perfection of power, it seems that it belongs to fortitude to attack rather than to endure.

Objection 3: Further, one contrary is more distant from the other than its mere negation. Now to endure is merely not to fear, whereas to attack denotes a movement contrary to that of fear, since it implies pursuit. Since then fortitude above all withdraws the mind from fear, it seems that it regards attack rather than endurance.

On the contrary, The Philosopher says (Ethic. iii, 9) that "certain persons are" said to be brave chiefly because they endure affliction.

I answer that, As stated above [3293](A[3]), and according to the Philosopher (Ethic. iii, 9), "fortitude is more concerned to allay fear, than to moderate daring." For it is more difficult to allay fear than to moderate daring, since the danger which is the object of daring and fear, tends by its very nature to check daring, but to increase fear. Now to attack belongs to fortitude in so far as the latter moderates daring, whereas to endure follows the repression of fear. Therefore the principal act of fortitude is endurance, that is to stand immovable in the midst of dangers rather than to attack them.

Reply to Objection 1: Endurance is more difficult than aggression, for three reasons. First, because endurance seemingly implies that one is being attacked by a stronger person, whereas aggression denotes that one is attacking as though one were the stronger party; and it is more difficult to contend with a stronger than with a weaker. Secondly, because he that endures already feels the presence of danger, whereas the aggressor looks upon danger as something to come; and it is more difficult to be unmoved by the present than by the future. Thirdly, because endurance implies length of time, whereas aggression is consistent with sudden movements; and it is more difficult to remain unmoved for a long time, than to be moved suddenly to something arduous. Hence the Philosopher says (Ethic. iii, 8) that "some hurry to meet danger, yet fly when the danger is present; this is not the behavior of a brave man."

Reply to Objection 2: Endurance denotes indeed a passion of the body, but an action of the soul cleaving most resolutely [fortissime] to good, the result being that it does not yield to the threatening passion of the body. Now virtue concerns the soul rather than the body.

Reply to Objection 3: He that endures fears not, though he is confronted with the cause of fear, whereas this cause is not present to the aggressor.

Whether the brave man acts for the sake of the good of his habit?

Objection 1: It seems that the brave man does not act for the sake of the good of his habit. For in matters of action the end, though first in intention, is last in execution. Now the act of fortitude, in the order of execution, follows the habit of fortitude. Therefore it is impossible for the brave man to act for the sake of the good of his habit.

Objection 2: Further, Augustine says (De Trin. xiii): "We love virtues for the sake of happiness, and yet some make bold to counsel us to be virtuous," namely by saying that we should desire virtue for its own sake, "without loving happiness. If they succeed in their endeavor, we shall surely cease to love virtue itself, since we shall no longer love that for the sake of which alone we love virtue." But fortitude is a virtue. Therefore the act of fortitude is directed not to fortitude but to happiness.

Objection 3: Further, Augustine says (De Morib. Eccl. xv) that "fortitude is love ready to bear all things for God's sake." Now God is not the habit of fortitude, but something better, since the end must needs be better than what is directed to the end. Therefore the brave man does not act for the sake of the good of his habit.

On the contrary, The Philosopher says (Ethic. iii, 7) that "to the brave man fortitude itself is a good": and such is his end.

I answer that, An end is twofold: proximate and ultimate. Now the proximate end of every agent is to introduce a likeness of that agent's form into something else: thus the end of fire in heating is to introduce the likeness of its heat into some passive matter, and the end of the builder is to introduce into matter the likeness of his art. Whatever good ensues from this, if it be intended, may be called the remote end of the agent. Now just as in things made, external matter is fashioned by art, so in things done, human deeds are fashioned by prudence. Accordingly we must conclude that the brave man intends as his proximate end to reproduce in action a likeness of his habit, for he intends to act in accordance with his habit: but his remote end is happiness or God.

This suffices for the Replies to the Objections: for the First Objection proceeds as though the very essence of a habit were its end, instead of the likeness of the habit in act, as stated. The other two objections consider the ultimate end.

Whether the brave man delights in his act?

Objection 1: It seems that the brave man delights in his act. For "delight is the unhindered action of a connatural habit" (Ethic. x, 4,6,8). Now the brave deed proceeds from a habit which acts after the manner of nature. Therefore the brave man takes pleasure in his act.

Objection 2: Further, Ambrose, commenting on Gal. 5:22, "But the fruit of the Spirit is charity, joy, peace," says that deeds of virtue are called "fruits because they refresh man's mind with a holy and pure delight." Now the brave man performs acts of virtue. Therefore he takes pleasure in his act.

Objection 3: Further, the weaker is overcome by the stronger. Now the brave man has a stronger love for the good of virtue than for his own body, which he exposes to the danger of death. Therefore the delight in the good of virtue banishes the pain of the body; and consequently the brave man does all things with pleasure.

On the contrary, The Philosopher says (Ethic. iii, 9) that "the brave man seems to have no delight in his act."

I answer that, As stated above ([3294]FS, Q[31], AA[3],4,5) where we were treating of the passions, pleasure is twofold; one is bodily, resulting from bodily contact, the other is spiritual, resulting from an apprehension of the soul. It is the latter which properly results from deeds of virtue, since in them we consider the good of reason. Now the principal act of fortitude is to endure, not only certain things that are unpleasant as apprehended by the soul—for instance, the loss of bodily life, which the virtuous man loves not only as a natural good, but also as being necessary for acts of virtue, and things connected with them—but also to endure things unpleasant in respect of bodily contact, such as wounds and blows. Hence the brave man, on one side, has something that affords him delight, namely as regards spiritual pleasure, in the act itself of virtue and the end thereof: while, on the other hand, he has cause for both spiritual sorrow, in the thought of losing his life, and for bodily pain. Hence we read (2 Macc. 6:30) that Eleazar said: "I suffer grievous pains in body: but in soul am well content to suffer these things because I fear Thee."

Now the sensible pain of the body makes one insensible to the spiritual delight of virtue, without the copious assistance of God's grace, which has more strength to raise the soul to the Divine things in which it delights, than bodily pains have to afflict it. Thus the Blessed Tiburtius, while walking barefoot on the burning coal, said that he felt as though he were walking on roses.

Yet the virtue of fortitude prevents the reason from being entirely overcome by bodily pain. And the delight of virtue overcomes spiritual sorrow, inasmuch as a man prefers the good of virtue to the life of the body and to whatever appertains thereto. Hence the Philosopher says (Ethic. ii, 3; iii, 9) that "it is not necessary for a brave man to delight so as to perceive his delight, but it suffices for him not to be sad."

Reply to Objection 1: The vehemence of the action or passion of one power hinders the action of another power: wherefore the pain in his senses hinders the mind of the brave man from feeling delight in its proper operation.

Reply to Objection 2: Deeds of virtue are delightful chiefly on account of their end; yet they can be painful by their nature, and this is principally the case with fortitude. Hence the Philosopher says (Ethic. iii, 9) that "to perform deeds with pleasure does not happen in all virtues, except in so far as one attains the end."

Reply to Objection 3: In the brave man spiritual sorrow is overcome by the delight of virtue. Yet since bodily pain is more sensible, and the sensitive apprehension is more in evidence to man, it follows that spiritual pleasure in the end of virtue fades away, so to speak, in the presence of great bodily pain.

Whether fortitude deals chiefly with sudden occurrences?

Objection 1: It seems that fortitude does not deal chiefly with sudden occurrences. For it would seem that things occur suddenly when they are unforeseen. But Tully says (De Invent. Rhet. ii) that "fortitude is the deliberate facing of danger, and bearing of toil." Therefore fortitude does not deal chiefly with sudden happenings.

Objection 2: Further, Ambrose says (De Offic. i): "The brave man is not unmindful of what may be likely to happen; he takes measures beforehand, and looks out as from the conning-tower of his mind, so as to encounter the future by his forethought, lest he should say afterwards: This befell me because I did not think it could possibly happen." But it is not possible to be prepared for the future in the case of sudden occurrences. Therefore the operation of fortitude is not concerned with sudden happenings.

Objection 3: Further, the Philosopher says (Ethic. iii, 8) that the "brave man is of good hope." But hope looks forward to the future, which is inconsistent with sudden occurrences. Therefore the operation of fortitude is not concerned with sudden happenings.

On the contrary, The Philosopher says (Ethic. iii, 8) that "fortitude is chiefly about sudden dangers of death."

I answer that, Two things must be considered in the operation of fortitude. One is in regard to its choice: and thus fortitude is not about sudden occurrences: because the brave man chooses to think beforehand of the dangers that may arise, in order to be able to withstand them, or to bear them more easily: since according to Gregory (Hom. xxv in Evang.), "the blow that is foreseen strikes with less force, and we are able more easily to bear earthly wrongs, if we are forearmed with the shield of foreknowledge." The other thing to be considered in the operation of fortitude regards the display of the virtuous habit: and in this way fortitude is chiefly about sudden occurrences, because according to the Philosopher (Ethic. iii, 8) the habit of fortitude is displayed chiefly in sudden dangers: since a habit works by way of nature. Wherefore if a person without forethought does that which pertains to virtue, when necessity urges on account of some sudden danger, this is a very strong proof that habitual fortitude is firmly seated in his mind.

Yet is it possible for a person even without the habit of fortitude, to prepare his mind against danger by long forethought: in the same way as a brave man prepares himself when necessary. This suffices for the Replies to the Objections.

Whether the brave man makes use of anger in his action?

Objection 1: It seems that the brave man does not use anger in his action. For no one should employ as an instrument of his action that which he cannot use at will. Now man cannot use anger at will, so as to take it up and lay it aside when he will. For, as the Philosopher says (De Memoria ii), when a bodily passion is in movement, it does not rest at once just as one wishes. Therefore a brave man should not employ anger for his action.

Objection 2: Further, if a man is competent to do a thing by himself, he should not seek the assistance of something weaker and more imperfect. Now the reason is competent to achieve by itself deeds of fortitude, wherein anger is impotent: wherefore Seneca says (De Ira i): "Reason by itself suffices not only to make us prepared for action but also to accomplish it. In fact is there greater folly than for reason to seek help from anger? the steadfast from the unstaid, the trusty from the untrustworthy, the healthy from the sick?" Therefore a brave man should not make use of anger.

Objection 3: Further, just as people are more earnest in doing deeds of fortitude on account of anger, so are they on account of sorrow or desire; wherefore the Philosopher says (Ethic. iii, 8) that wild beasts are incited to face danger through sorrow or pain, and adulterous persons dare many things for the sake of desire. Now fortitude employs neither sorrow nor desire for its action. Therefore in like manner it should not employ anger.

On the contrary, The Philosopher says (Ethic. iii, 8) that "anger helps the brave."

I answer that, As stated above ([3295]FS, Q[24], A[2]), concerning anger and the other passions there was a difference of opinion between the Peripatetics and the Stoics. For the Stoics excluded anger and all other passions of the soul from the mind of a wise or good man: whereas the Peripatetics, of whom Aristotle was the chief, ascribed to virtuous men both anger and the other passions of the soul albeit modified by reason. And possibly they differed not in reality but in their way of speaking. For the Peripatetics, as stated above ([3296]FS, Q[24], A[2]), gave the name of passions to all the movements of the sensitive appetite, however they may comport themselves. And since the sensitive appetite is moved by the command of reason, so that it may cooperate by rendering action more prompt, they held that virtuous persons should employ both anger and the other passions of the soul, modified according to the dictate of reason. On the other hand, the Stoics gave the name of passions to certain immoderate emotions of the sensitive appetite, wherefore they called them sicknesses or diseases, and for this reason severed them altogether from virtue.

Accordingly the brave man employs moderate anger for his action, but not immoderate anger.

Reply to Objection 1: Anger that is moderated in accordance with reason is subject to the command of reason: so that man uses it at his will, which would not be the case were it immoderate.

Reply to Objection 2: Reason employs anger for its action, not as seeking its assistance, but because it uses the sensitive appetite as an instrument, just as it uses the members of the body. Nor is it unbecoming for the instrument to be more imperfect than the principal agent, even as the hammer is more imperfect than the smith. Moreover, Seneca was a follower of the Stoics, and the above words were aimed by him directly at Aristotle.

Reply to Objection 3: Whereas fortitude, as stated above [3297](A[6]), has two acts, namely endurance and aggression, it employs anger, not for the act of endurance, because the reason by itself performs this act, but for the act of aggression, for which it employs anger rather than the other passions, since it belongs to anger to strike at the cause of sorrow, so that it directly cooperates with fortitude in attacking. On the other hand, sorrow by its very nature gives way to the thing that hurts; though accidentally it helps in aggression, either as being the cause of anger, as stated above ([3298]FS, Q[47], A[3]), or as making a person expose himself to danger in order to escape from sorrow. In like manner desire, by its very nature, tends to a pleasurable good, to which it is directly contrary to withstand danger: yet accidentally sometimes it helps one to attack, in so far as one prefers to risk dangers rather than lack pleasure. Hence the Philosopher says (Ethic. iii, 5): "Of all the cases in which fortitude arises from a passion, the most natural is when a man is brave through anger, making his choice and acting for a purpose," i.e. for a due end; "this is true fortitude."

Whether fortitude is a cardinal virtue?

Objection 1: It seems that fortitude is not a cardinal virtue. For, as stated above [3299](A[10]), anger is closely allied with fortitude. Now anger is not accounted a principal passion; nor is daring which belongs to fortitude. Therefore neither should fortitude be reckoned a cardinal virtue.

Objection 2: Further, the object of virtue is good. But the direct object of fortitude is not good, but evil, for it is endurance of evil and toil, as Tully says (De Invent. Rhet. ii). Therefore fortitude is not a cardinal virtue.

Objection 3: Further, the cardinal virtues are about those things upon which human life is chiefly occupied, just as a door turns upon a hinge [cardine]. But fortitude is about dangers of death which are of rare occurrence in human life. Therefore fortitude should not be reckoned a cardinal or principal virtue.

On the contrary, Gregory (Moral. xxii), Ambrose in his commentary on Lk. 6:20, and Augustine (De Moribus Eccl. xv), number fortitude among the four cardinal or principal virtues.

I answer that, As stated above ([3300]FS, Q[61], AA[3],4), those virtues are said to be cardinal or principal which have a foremost claim to that which belongs to the virtues in common. And among other conditions of virtue in general one is that it is stated to "act steadfastly," according to Ethic. ii, 4. Now fortitude above all lays claim to praise for steadfastness. Because he that stands firm is so much the more praised, as he is more strongly impelled to fall or recede. Now man is impelled to recede from that which is in accordance with reason, both by the pleasing good and the displeasing evil. But bodily pain impels him more strongly than pleasure. For Augustine says (QQ[83], qu. 36): "There is none that does not shun pain more than he desires pleasure. For we perceive that even the most untamed beasts are deterred from the greatest pleasures by the fear of pain." And among the pains of the mind and dangers those are mostly feared which lead to death, and it is against them that the brave man stands firm. Therefore fortitude is a cardinal virtue.

Reply to Objection 1: Daring and anger do not cooperate with fortitude in its act of endurance, wherein its steadfastness is chiefly commended: for it is by that act that the brave man curbs fear, which is a principal passion, as stated above ([3301]FS, Q[25], A[4]).

Reply to Objection 2: Virtue is directed to the good of reason which it behooves to safeguard against the onslaught of evils. And fortitude is directed to evils of the body, as contraries which it withstands, and to the good of reason, as the end, which it intends to safeguard.

Reply to Objection 3: Though dangers of death are of rare occurrence, yet the occasions of those dangers occur frequently, since on account of justice which he pursues, and also on account of other good deeds, man encounters mortal adversaries.

Whether fortitude excels among all other virtues?

Objection 1: It seems that fortitude excels among all other virtues. For Ambrose says (De Offic. i): "Fortitude is higher, so to speak, than the rest."

Objection 2: Further, virtue is about that which is difficult and good. But fortitude is about most difficult things. Therefore it is the greatest of the virtues.

Objection 3: Further, the person of a man is more excellent than his possessions. But fortitude is about a man's person, for it is this that a man exposes to the danger of death for the good of virtue: whereas justice and the other moral virtues are about other and external things. Therefore fortitude is the chief of the moral virtues.

Objection 4: On the contrary, Tully says (De Offic. i): "Justice is the most resplendent of the virtues and gives its name to a good man."

Objection 5: Further, the Philosopher says (Rhet. i, 19): "Those virtues must needs be greatest which are most profitable to others." Now liberality seems to be more useful than fortitude. Therefore it is a greater virtue.

I answer that, As Augustine says (De Trin. vi), "In things that are great, but not in bulk, to be great is to be good": wherefore the better a virtue the greater it is. Now reason's good is man's good, according to Dionysius (Div. Nom. iv) prudence, since it is a perfection of reason, has the good essentially: while justice effects this good, since it belongs to justice to establish the order of reason in all human affairs: whereas the other virtues safeguard this good, inasmuch as they moderate the passions, lest they lead man away from reason's good. As to the order of the latter, fortitude holds the first place, because fear of dangers of death has the greatest power to make man recede from the good of reason: and after fortitude comes temperance, since also pleasures of touch excel all others in hindering the good of reason. Now to be a thing essentially ranks before effecting it, and the latter ranks before safeguarding it by removing obstacles thereto. Wherefore among the cardinal virtues, prudence ranks first, justice second, fortitude third, temperance fourth, and after these the other virtues.

Reply to Objection 1: Ambrose places fortitude before the other virtues, in respect of a certain general utility, inasmuch as it is useful both in warfare, and in matters relating to civil or home life. Hence he begins by saying (De Offic. i): "Now we come to treat of fortitude, which being higher so to speak than the others, is applicable both to warlike and to civil matters."

Reply to Objection 2: Virtue essentially regards the good rather than the difficult. Hence the greatness of a virtue is measured according to its goodness rather than its difficulty.

Reply to Objection 3: A man does not expose his person to dangers of death except in order to safeguard justice: wherefore the praise awarded to fortitude depends somewhat on justice. Hence Ambrose says (De Offic. i) that "fortitude without justice is an occasion of injustice; since the stronger a man is the more ready is he to oppress the weaker."

The Fourth argument is granted.

Reply to Objection 5: Liberality is useful in conferring certain particular favors: whereas a certain general utility attaches to fortitude, since it safeguards the whole order of justice. Hence the Philosopher says (Rhet. i, 9) that "just and brave men are most beloved, because they are most useful in war and peace."

OF MARTYRDOM (FIVE ARTICLES)

We must now consider martyrdom, under which head there are five points of inquiry:

(1) Whether martyrdom is an act of virtue?

(2) Of what virtue is it the act?

(3) Concerning the perfection of this act;

(4) The pain of martyrdom;

(5) Its cause.

Whether martyrdom is an act of virtue?

Objection 1: It seems that martyrdom is not an act of virtue. For all acts of virtue are voluntary. But martyrdom is sometimes not voluntary, as in the case of the Innocents who were slain for Christ's sake, and of whom Hillary says (Super Matth. i) that "they attained the ripe age of eternity through the glory of martyrdom." Therefore martyrdom is not an act of virtue.

Objection 2: Further, nothing unlawful is an act of virtue. Now it is unlawful to kill oneself, as stated above ([3302]Q[64], A[5]), and yet martyrdom is achieved by so doing: for Augustine says (De Civ. Dei i) that "during persecution certain holy women, in order to escape from those who threatened their chastity, threw themselves into a river, and so ended their lives, and their martyrdom is honored in the Catholic Church with most solemn veneration." Therefore martyrdom is not an act of virtue.

Objection 3: Further, it is praiseworthy to offer oneself to do an act of virtue. But it is not praiseworthy to court martyrdom, rather would it seem to be presumptuous and rash. Therefore martyrdom is not an act of virtue.

On the contrary, The reward of beatitude is not due save to acts of virtue. Now it is due to martyrdom, since it is written (Mat. 5:10): "Blessed are they that suffer persecution for justice' sake, for theirs is the kingdom of heaven." Therefore martyrdom is an act of virtue.

I answer that, As stated above ([3303]Q[123], AA[1],3), it belongs to virtue to safeguard man in the good of reason. Now the good of reason consists in the truth as its proper object, and in justice as its proper effect, as shown above ([3304]Q[109], AA[1],2;[3305] Q[123], A[12]). And martyrdom consists essentially in standing firmly to truth and justice against the assaults of persecution. Hence it is evident that martyrdom is an act of virtue.

Reply to Objection 1: Some have said that in the case of the Innocents the use of their free will was miraculously accelerated, so that they suffered martyrdom even voluntarily. Since, however, Scripture contains no proof of this, it is better to say that these babes in being slain obtained by God's grace the glory of martyrdom which others acquire by their own will. For the shedding of one's blood for Christ's sake takes the place of Baptism. Wherefore just as in the case of baptized children the merit of Christ is conducive to the acquisition of glory through the baptismal grace, so in those who were slain for Christ's sake the merit of Christ's martyrdom is conducive to the acquisition of the martyr's palm. Hence Augustine says in a sermon on the Epiphany (De Diversis lxvi), as though he were addressing them: "A man that does not believe that children are benefited by the baptism of Christ will doubt of your being crowned in suffering for Christ. You were not old enough to believe in Christ's future sufferings, but you had a body wherein you could endure suffering of Christ Who was to suffer."

Reply to Objection 2: Augustine says (De Civ. Dei i) that "possibly the Church was induced by certain credible witnesses of Divine authority thus to honor the memory of those holy women [*Cf.[3306] Q[64], A[1], ad 2]."

Reply to Objection 3: The precepts of the Law are about acts of virtue. Now it has been stated ([3307]FS, Q[108], A[1], ad 4) that some of the precepts of the Divine Law are to be understood in reference to the preparation of the mind, in the sense that man ought to be prepared to do such and such a thing, whenever expedient. In the same way certain things belong to an act of virtue as regards the preparation of the mind, so that in such and such a case a man should act according to reason. And this observation would seem very much to the point in the case of martyrdom, which consists in the right endurance of sufferings unjustly inflicted. Nor ought a man to give another an occasion of acting unjustly: yet if anyone act unjustly, one ought to endure it in moderation.

Whether martyrdom is an act of fortitude?

Objection 1: It seems that martyrdom is not an act of fortitude. For the Greek {martyr} signifies a witness. Now witness is borne to the faith of Christ. according to Acts 1:8, "You shall be witnesses unto Me," etc. and Maximus says in a sermon: "The mother of martyrs is the Catholic faith which those glorious warriors have sealed with their blood." Therefore martyrdom is an act of faith rather than of fortitude.

Objection 2: Further, a praiseworthy act belongs chiefly to the virtue which inclines thereto, is manifested thereby, and without which the act avails nothing. Now charity is the chief incentive to martyrdom: Thus Maximus says in a sermon: "The charity of Christ is victorious in His martyrs." Again the greatest proof of charity lies in the act of martyrdom, according to Jn. 15:13, "Greater love than this no man hath, that a man lay down his life for his friends." Moreover without charity martyrdom avails nothing, according to 1 Cor. 13:3, "If I should deliver my body to be burned, and have not charity, it profiteth me nothing." Therefore martyrdom is an act of charity rather than of fortitude.

Objection 3: Further, Augustine says in a sermon on St. Cyprian: "It is easy to honor a martyr by singing his praises, but it is a great thing to imitate his faith and patience." Now that which calls chiefly for praise in a virtuous act, is the virtue of which it is the act. Therefore martyrdom is an act of patience rather than of fortitude.

On the contrary, Cyprian says (Ep. ad Mart. et Conf. ii): "Blessed martyrs, with what praise shall I extol you? Most valiant warriors, how shall I find words to proclaim the strength of your courage?" Now a person is praised on account of the virtue whose act he performs. Therefore martyrdom is an act of fortitude.

I answer that, As stated above ([3308]Q[123], A[1], seqq.), it belongs to fortitude to strengthen man in the good of virtue, especially against dangers, and chiefly against dangers of death, and most of all against those that occur in battle. Now it is evident that in martyrdom man is firmly strengthened in the good of virtue, since he cleaves to faith and justice notwithstanding the threatening danger of death, the imminence of which is moreover due to a kind of particular contest with his persecutors. Hence Cyprian says in a sermon (Ep. ad Mart. et Conf. ii): "The crowd of onlookers wondered to see an unearthly battle, and Christ's servants fighting erect, undaunted in speech, with souls unmoved, and strength divine." Wherefore it is evident that martyrdom is an act of fortitude; for which reason the Church reads in the office of Martyrs: They "became valiant in battle" [*Heb. 11:34].

Reply to Objection 1: Two things must be considered in the act of fortitude. one is the good wherein the brave man is strengthened, and this is the end of fortitude; the other is the firmness itself, whereby a man does not yield to the contraries that hinder him from achieving that good, and in this consists the essence of fortitude. Now just as civic fortitude strengthens a man's mind in human justice, for the safeguarding of which he braves the danger of death, so gratuitous fortitude strengthens man's soul in the good of Divine justice, which is "through faith in Christ Jesus," according to Rom. 3:22. Thus martyrdom is related to faith as the end in which one is strengthened, but to fortitude as the eliciting habit.

Reply to Objection 2: Charity inclines one to the act of martyrdom, as its first and chief motive cause, being the virtue commanding it, whereas fortitude inclines thereto as being its proper motive cause, being the virtue that elicits it. Hence martyrdom is an act of charity as commanding, and of fortitude as eliciting. For this reason also it manifests both virtues. It is due to charity that it is meritorious, like any other act of virtue: and for this reason it avails not without charity.

Reply to Objection 3: As stated above ([3309]Q[123], A[6]), the chief act of fortitude is endurance: to this and not to its secondary act, which is aggression, martyrdom belongs. And since patience serves fortitude on the part of its chief act, viz. endurance, hence it is that martyrs are also praised for their patience.

Whether martyrdom is an act of the greatest perfection?

Objection 1: It seems that martyrdom is not an act of the greatest perfection. For seemingly that which is a matter of counsel and not of precept pertains to perfection, because, to wit, it is not necessary for salvation. But it would seem that martyrdom is necessary for salvation, since the Apostle says (Rom. 10:10), "With the heart we believe unto justice, but with the mouth confession is made unto salvation," and it is written (1 Jn. 3:16), that "we ought to lay down our lives for the brethren." Therefore martyrdom does not pertain to perfection.

Objection 2: Further, it seems to point to greater perfection that a man give his soul to God, which is done by obedience, than that he give God his body, which is done by martyrdom: wherefore Gregory says (Moral. xxxv) that "obedience is preferable to all sacrifices." Therefore martyrdom is not an act of the greatest perfection.

Objection 3: Further, it would seem better to do good to others than to maintain oneself in good, since the "good of the nation is better than the good of the individual," according to the Philosopher (Ethic. i, 2). Now he that suffers martyrdom profits himself alone, whereas he that teaches does good to many. Therefore the act of teaching and guiding subjects is more perfect than the act of martyrdom.

On the contrary, Augustine (De Sanct. Virgin. xlvi) prefers martyrdom to virginity which pertains to perfection. Therefore martyrdom seems to belong to perfection in the highest degree.

I answer that, We may speak of an act of virtue in two ways. First, with regard to the species of that act, as compared to the virtue proximately eliciting it. In this way martyrdom, which consists in the due endurance of death, cannot be the most perfect of virtuous acts, because endurance of death is not praiseworthy in itself, but only in so far as it is directed to some good consisting in an act of virtue, such as faith or the love of God, so that this act of virtue being the end is better.

A virtuous act may be considered in another way, in comparison with its first motive cause, which is the love of charity, and it is in this respect that an act comes to belong to the perfection of life, since, as the Apostle says (Col. 3:14), that "charity . . . is the bond of perfection." Now, of all virtuous acts martyrdom is the greatest proof of the perfection of charity: since a man's love for a thing is proved to be so much the greater, according as that which he despises for its sake is more dear to him, or that which he chooses to suffer for its sake is more odious. But it is evident that of all the goods of the present life man loves life itself most, and on the other hand he hates death more than anything, especially when it is accompanied by the pains of bodily torment, "from fear of which even dumb animals refrain from the greatest pleasures," as Augustine observes (QQ[83], qu. 36). And from this point of view it is clear that martyrdom is the most perfect of human acts in respect of its genus, as being the sign of the greatest charity, according to Jn. 15:13: "Greater love than this no man hath, that a man lay down his life for his friends."

Reply to Objection 1: There is no act of perfection, which is a matter of counsel, but what in certain cases is a matter of precept, as being necessary for salvation. Thus Augustine declares (De Adult. Conjug. xiii) that a man is under the obligation of observing continency, through the absence or sickness of his wife. Hence it is not contrary to the perfection of martyrdom if in certain cases it be necessary for salvation, since there are cases when it is not necessary for salvation to suffer martyrdom; thus we read of many holy martyrs who through zeal for the faith or brotherly love gave themselves up to martyrdom of their own accord. As to these precepts, they are to be understood as referring to the preparation of the mind.

Reply to Objection 2: Martyrdom embraces the highest possible degree of obedience, namely obedience unto death; thus we read of Christ (Phil. 2:8) that He became "obedient unto death." Hence it is evident that martyrdom is of itself more perfect than obedience considered absolutely.

Reply to Objection 3: This argument considers martyrdom according to the proper species of its act, whence it derives no excellence over all other virtuous acts; thus neither is fortitude more excellent than all virtues.

Whether death is essential to martyrdom?

Objection 1: It seems that death is not essential to martyrdom. For Jerome says in a sermon on the Assumption (Epist. ad Paul. et Eustoch.): "I should say rightly that the Mother of God was both virgin and martyr, although she ended her days in peace": and Gregory says (Hom. iii in Evang.): "Although persecution has ceased to offer the opportunity, yet the peace we enjoy is not without its martyrdom, since even if we no longer yield the life of the body to the sword, yet do we slay fleshly desires in the soul with the sword of the spirit." Therefore there can be martyrdom without suffering death.

Objection 2: Further, we read of certain women as commended for despising life for the sake of safeguarding the integrity of the flesh: wherefore seemingly the integrity of chastity is preferable to the life of the body. Now sometimes the integrity of the flesh has been forfeited or has been threatened in confession of the Christian faith, as in the case of Agnes and Lucy. Therefore it seems that the name of martyr should be accorded to a woman who forfeits the integrity of the flesh for the sake of Christ's faith, rather than if she were to forfeit even the life of the body: wherefore also Lucy said: "If thou causest me to be violated against my will, my chastity will gain me a twofold crown."

Objection 3: Further, martyrdom is an act of fortitude. But it belongs to fortitude to brave not only death but also other hardships, as Augustine declares (Music. vi). Now there are many other hardships besides death, which one may suffer for Christ's faith, namely imprisonment, exile, being stripped of one's goods, as mentioned in Heb. 10:34, for which reason we celebrate the martyrdom of Pope Saint Marcellus, notwithstanding that he died in prison. Therefore it is not essential to martyrdom that one suffer the pain of death.

Objection 4: Further, martyrdom is a meritorious act, as stated above (A[2], ad 1; A[3]). Now it cannot be a meritorious act after death. Therefore it is before death; and consequently death is not essential to martyrdom.

On the contrary, Maximus says in a sermon on the martyrs that "in dying for the faith he conquers who would have been vanquished in living without faith."

I answer that As stated above [3310](A[2]), a martyr is so called as being a witness to the Christian faith, which teaches us to despise things visible for the sake of things invisible, as stated in Heb. 11. Accordingly it belongs to martyrdom that a man bear witness to the faith in showing by deed that he despises all things present, in order to obtain invisible goods to come. Now so long as a man retains the life of the body he does not show by deed that he despises all things relating to the body. For men are wont to despise both their kindred and all they possess, and even to suffer bodily pain, rather than lose life. Hence Satan testified against Job (Job 2:4): "Skin for skin, and all that a man hath he will give for his soul" [Douay: 'life'] i.e. for the life of his body. Therefore the perfect notion of martyrdom requires that a man suffer death for Christ's sake.

Reply to Objection 1: The authorities quoted, and the like that one may meet with, speak of martyrdom by way of similitude.

Reply to Objection 2: When a woman forfeits the integrity of the flesh, or is condemned to forfeit it under pretext of the Christian faith, it is not evident to men whether she suffers this for love of the Christian faith, or rather through contempt of chastity. Wherefore in the sight of men her testimony is not held to be sufficient, and consequently this is not martyrdom properly speaking. In the sight of God, however, Who searcheth the heart, this may be deemed worthy of a reward, as Lucy said.

Reply to Objection 3: As stated above ([3311]Q[123], AA[4],5), fortitude regards danger of death chiefly, and other dangers consequently; wherefore a person is not called a martyr merely for suffering imprisonment, or exile, or forfeiture of his wealth, except in so far as these result in death.

Reply to Objection 4: The merit of martyrdom is not after death, but in the voluntary endurance of death, namely in the fact that a person willingly suffers being put to death. It happens sometimes, however, that a man lives for some time after being mortally wounded for Christ's sake, or after suffering for the faith of Christ any other kind of hardship inflicted by persecution and continued until death ensues. The act of martyrdom is meritorious while a man is in this state, and at the very time that he is suffering these hardships.

Whether faith alone is the cause of martyrdom?

Objection 1: It seems that faith alone is the cause of martyrdom. For it is written (1 Pet. 4:15,16): "Let none of you suffer as a murderer, or a thief, or a railer, or a coveter of other men's things. But if as a Christian, let him not be ashamed, but let him glorify God in this name." Now a man is said to be a Christian because he holds the faith of Christ. Therefore only faith in Christ gives the glory of martyrdom to those who suffer.

Objection 2: Further, a martyr is a kind of witness. But witness is borne to the truth alone. Now one is not called a martyr for bearing witness to any truth, but only for witnessing to the Divine truth, otherwise a man would be a martyr if he were to die for confessing a truth of geometry or some other speculative science, which seems ridiculous. Therefore faith alone is the cause of martyrdom.

Objection 3: Further, those virtuous deeds would seem to be of most account which are directed to the common good, since "the good of the nation is better than the good of the individual," according to the Philosopher (Ethic. i, 2). If, then, some other good were the cause of martyrdom, it would seem that before all those would be martyrs who die for the defense of their country. Yet this is not consistent with Church observance, for we do not celebrate the martyrdom of those who die in a just war. Therefore faith alone is the cause of martyrdom.

On the contrary, It is written (Mat. 5:10): "Blessed are they that suffer persecution for justice' sake," which pertains to martyrdom, according to a gloss, as well as Jerome's commentary on this passage. Now not only faith but also the other virtues pertain to justice. Therefore other virtues can be the cause of martyrdom.

I answer that, As stated above [3312](A[4]), martyrs are so called as being witnesses, because by suffering in body unto death they bear witness to the truth; not indeed to any truth, but to the truth which is in accordance with godliness, and was made known to us by Christ: wherefore Christ's martyrs are His witnesses. Now this truth is the truth of faith. Wherefore the cause of all martyrdom is the truth of faith.

But the truth of faith includes not only inward belief, but also outward profession, which is expressed not only by words, whereby one confesses the faith, but also by deeds, whereby a person shows that he has faith, according to James 2:18, "I will show thee, by works, my faith." Hence it is written of certain people (Titus 1:16): "They profess that they know God but in their works they deny Him." Thus all virtuous deeds, inasmuch as they are referred to God, are professions of the faith whereby we come to know that God requires these works of us, and rewards us for them: and in this way they can be the cause of martyrdom. For this reason the Church celebrates the martyrdom of Blessed John the Baptist, who suffered death, not for refusing to deny the faith, but for reproving adultery.

Reply to Objection 1: A Christian is one who is Christ's. Now a person is said to be Christ's, not only through having faith in Christ, but also because he is actuated to virtuous deeds by the Spirit of Christ, according to Rom. 8:9, "If any man have not the Spirit of Christ, he is none of His"; and again because in imitation of Christ he is dead to sins, according to Gal. 5:24, "They that are Christ's have crucified their flesh with the vices and concupiscences." Hence to suffer as a Christian is not only to suffer in confession of the faith, which is done by words, but also to suffer for doing any good work, or for avoiding any sin, for Christ's sake, because this all comes under the head of witnessing to the faith.

Reply to Objection 2: The truth of other sciences has no connection with the worship of the Godhead: hence it is not called truth according to godliness, and consequently the confession thereof cannot be said to be the direct cause of martyrdom. Yet, since every lie is a sin, as stated above ([3313]Q[110], AA[3],4), avoidance of a lie, to whatever truth it may be contrary, may be the cause of martyrdom inasmuch as a lie is a sin against the Divine Law.

Reply to Objection 3: The good of one's country is paramount among human goods: yet the Divine good, which is the proper cause of martyrdom, is of more account than human good. Nevertheless, since human good may become Divine, for instance when it is referred to God, it follows that any human good in so far as it is referred to God, may be the cause of martyrdom.

OF FEAR* (FOUR ARTICLES)

[*St. Thomas calls this vice indifferently 'fear' or 'timidity.' The translation requires one to adhere to these terms on account of the connection with the passion of fear. Otherwise 'cowardice' would be a better rendering.]

We must now consider the vices opposed to fortitude: (1) Fear; (2) Fearlessness; (3) Daring.

Under the first head there are four points of inquiry:

(1) Whether fear is a sin?

(2) Whether it is opposed to fortitude?

(3) Whether it is a mortal sin?

(4) Whether it excuses from sin, or diminishes it?

Whether fear is a sin?

Objection 1: It seems that fear is not a sin. For fear is a passion, as stated above ([3314]FS, Q[23], A[4]; Q[42]). Now we are neither praised nor blamed for passions, as stated in Ethic. ii. Since then every sin is blameworthy, it seems that fear is not a sin.

Objection 2: Further, nothing that is commanded in the Divine Law is a sin: since the "law of the Lord is unspotted" (Ps. 18:8). Yet fear is commanded in God's law, for it is written (Eph. 6:5): "Servants, be obedient to them that are your lords according to the flesh, with fear and trembling." Therefore fear is not a sin.

Objection 3: Further, nothing that is naturally in man is a sin, for sin is contrary to nature according to Damascene (De Fide Orth. iii). Now fear is natural to man: wherefore the Philosopher says (Ethic. iii, 7) that "a man would be insane or insensible to pain, if nothing, not even earthquakes nor deluges, inspired him with fear." Therefore fear is not a sin. .

On the contrary, our Lord said (Mat. 10:28): "Fear ye not them that kill the body," and it is written (Ezech. 2:6): "Fear not, neither be thou afraid of their words."

I answer that, A human act is said to be a sin on account of its being inordinate, because the good of a human act consists in order, as stated above ([3315]Q[109], A[2];[3316] Q[114], A[1]). Now this due order requires that the appetite be subject to the ruling of reason. And reason dictates that certain things should be shunned and some sought after. Among things to be shunned, it dictates that some are to be shunned more than others; and among things to be sought after, that some are to be sought after more than others. Moreover, the more a good is to be sought after, the more is the opposite evil to be shunned. The result is that reason dictates that certain goods are to be sought after more than certain evils are to be avoided. Accordingly when the appetite shuns what the reason dictates that we should endure rather than forfeit others that we should rather seek for, fear is inordinate and sinful. On the other hand, when the appetite fears so as to shun what reason requires to be shunned, the appetite is neither inordinate nor sinful.

Reply to Objection 1: Fear in its generic acceptation denotes avoidance in general. Hence in this way it does not include the notion of good or evil: and the same applies to every other passion. Wherefore the Philosopher says that passions call for neither praise nor blame, because, to wit, we neither praise nor blame those who are angry or afraid, but only those who behave thus in an ordinate or inordinate manner.

Reply to Objection 2: The fear which the Apostle inculcates is in accordance with reason, namely that servants should fear lest they be lacking in the service they owe their masters.

Reply to Objection 3: Reason dictates that we should shun the evils that we cannot withstand, and the endurance of which profits us nothing. Hence there is no sin in fearing them.

Whether the sin of fear is contrary to fortitude?

Objection 1: It seems that the sin of fear is not contrary to fortitude: because fortitude is about dangers of death, as stated above ([3317]Q[123], AA[4],5). But the sin of fear is not always connected with dangers of death, for a gloss on Ps. 127:1, "Blessed are all they that fear the Lord," says that "it is human fear whereby we dread to suffer carnal dangers, or to lose worldly goods." Again a gloss on Mat. 27:44, "He prayed the third time, saying the selfsame word," says that "evil fear is threefold, fear of death, fear of pain, and fear of contempt." Therefore the sin of fear is not contrary to fortitude.

Objection 2: Further, the chief reason why a man is commended for fortitude is that he exposes himself to the danger of death. Now sometimes a man exposes himself to death through fear of slavery or shame. Thus Augustine relates (De Civ. Dei i) that Cato, in order not to be Caesar's slave, gave himself up to death. Therefore the sin of fear bears a certain likeness to fortitude instead of being opposed thereto.

Objection 3: Further, all despair arises from fear. But despair is opposed not to fortitude but to hope, as stated above (Q[20], A[1]; [3318]FS, Q[40], A[4]). Neither therefore is the sin of fear opposed to fortitude.

On the contrary, The Philosopher (Ethic. ii, 7; iii, 7) states that timidity is opposed to fortitude.

I answer that, As stated above (Q[19], A[3]; [3319]FS, Q[43], A[1]), all fear arises from love; since no one fears save what is contrary to something he loves. Now love is not confined to any particular kind of virtue or vice: but ordinate love is included in every virtue, since every virtuous man loves the good proper to his virtue; while inordinate love is included in every sin, because inordinate love gives use to inordinate desire. Hence in like manner inordinate fear is included in every sin; thus the covetous man fears the loss of money, the intemperate man the loss of pleasure, and so on. But the greatest fear of all is that which has the danger of death for its object, as we find proved in Ethic. iii, 6. Wherefore the inordinateness of this fear is opposed to fortitude which regards dangers of death. For this reason timidity is said to be antonomastically* opposed to fortitude. [*Antonomasia is the figure of speech whereby we substitute the general for the individual term; e.g. The Philosopher for Aristotle: and so timidity, which is inordinate fear of any evil, is employed to denote inordinate fear of the danger of death.]

Reply to Objection 1: The passages quoted refer to inordinate fear in its generic acceptation, which can be opposed to various virtues.

Reply to Objection 2: Human acts are estimated chiefly with reference to the end, as stated above ([3320]FS, Q[1], A[3]; [3321]FS, Q[18], A[6]): and it belongs to a brave man to expose himself to danger of death for the sake of a good. But a man who exposes himself to danger of death in order to escape from slavery or hardships is overcome by fear, which is contrary to fortitude. Hence the Philosopher says (Ethic. iii, 7), that "to die in order to escape poverty, lust, or something disagreeable is an act not of fortitude but of cowardice: for to shun hardships is a mark of effeminacy."

Reply to Objection 3: As stated above ([3322]FS, Q[45], A[2]), fear is the beginning of despair even as hope is the beginning of daring. Wherefore, just as fortitude which employs daring in moderation presupposes hope, so on the other hand despair proceeds from some kind of fear. It does not follow, however, that any kind of despair results from any kind of fear, but that only from fear of the same kind. Now the despair that is opposed to hope is referred to another kind, namely to Divine things; whereas the fear that is opposed to fortitude regards dangers of death. Hence the argument does not prove.

Whether fear is a mortal sin?

Objection 1: It seems that fear is not a mortal sin. For, as stated above ([3323]FS, Q[23], A[1]), fear is in the irascible faculty which is a part of the sensuality. Now there is none but venial sin in the sensuality, as stated above ([3324]FS, Q[74], A[4]). Therefore fear is not a mortal sin.

Objection 2: Further, every mortal sin turns the heart wholly from God. But fear does not this, for a gloss on Judges 7:3, "Whosoever is fearful," etc., says that "a man is fearful when he trembles at the very thought of conflict; yet he is not so wholly terrified at heart, but that he can rally and take courage." Therefore fear is not a mortal sin.

Objection 3: Further, mortal sin is a lapse not only from perfection but also from a precept. But fear does not make one lapse from a precept, but only from perfection; for a gloss on Dt. 20:8, "What man is there that is fearful and fainthearted?" says: "We learn from this that no man can take up the profession of contemplation or spiritual warfare, if he still fears to be despoiled of earthly riches." Therefore fear is not a mortal sin.

On the contrary, For mortal sin alone is the pain of hell due: and yet this is due to the fearful, according to Apoc. 21:8, "But the fearful and unbelieving and the abominable," etc., "shall have their portion in the pool burning with fire and brimstone which is the second death." Therefore fear is a mortal sin.

I answer that, As stated above [3325](A[1]), fear is a sin through being inordinate, that is to say, through shunning what ought not to be shunned according to reason. Now sometimes this inordinateness of fear is confined to the sensitive appetites, without the accession of the rational appetite's consent: and then it cannot be a mortal, but only a venial sin. But sometimes this inordinateness of fear reaches to the rational appetite which is called the will, which deliberately shuns something against the dictate of reason: and this inordinateness of fear is sometimes a mortal, sometimes a venial sin. For if a man through fear of the danger of death or of any other temporal evil is so disposed as to do what is forbidden, or to omit what is commanded by the Divine law, such fear is a mortal sin: otherwise it is a venial sin.

Reply to Objection 1: This argument considers fear as confined to the sensuality.

Reply to Objection 2: This gloss also can be understood as referring to the fear that is confined within the sensuality. Or better still we may reply that a man is terrified with his whole heart when fear banishes his courage beyond remedy. Now even when fear is a mortal sin, it may happen nevertheless that one is not so wilfully terrified that one cannot be persuaded to put fear aside: thus sometimes a man sins mortally by consenting to concupiscence, and is turned aside from accomplishing what he purposed doing.

Reply to Objection 3: This gloss speaks of the fear that turns man aside from a good that is necessary, not for the fulfilment of a precept, but for the perfection of a counsel. Such like fear is not a mortal sin, but is sometimes venial: and sometimes it is not a sin, for instance when one has a reasonable cause for fear.

Whether fear excuses from sin?

Objection 1: It seems that fear does not excuse from sin. For fear is a sin, as stated above [3326](A[1]). But sin does not excuse from sin, rather does it aggravate it. Therefore fear does not excuse from sin.

Objection 2: Further, if any fear excuses from sin, most of all would this be true of the fear of death, to which, as the saying is, a courageous man is subject. Yet this fear, seemingly, is no excuse, because, since death comes, of necessity, to all, it does not seem to be an object of fear. Therefore fear does not excuse from sin.

Objection 3: Further, all fear is of evil, either temporal or spiritual. Now fear of spiritual evil cannot excuse sin, because instead of inducing one to sin, it withdraws one from sin: and fear of temporal evil does not excuse from sin, because according to the Philosopher (Ethic. iii, 6), "one should not fear poverty, nor sickness, nor anything that is not a result of one's own wickedness." Therefore it seems that in no sense does fear excuse from sin.

On the contrary, It is stated in the Decretals (I, Q[1], Cap. Constat.): "A man who has been forcibly and unwillingly ordained by heretics, has an ostensible excuse."

I answer that, As stated above [3327](A[3]), fear is sinful in so far as it runs counter to the order of reason. Now reason judges certain evils to be shunned rather than others. Wherefore it is no sin not to shun what is less to be shunned in order to avoid what reason judges to be more avoided: thus death of the body is more to be avoided than the loss of temporal goods. Hence a man would be excused from sin if through fear of death he were to promise or give something to a robber, and yet he would be guilty of sin were he to give to sinners, rather than to the good to whom he should give in preference. On the other hand, if through fear a man were to avoid evils which according to reason are less to be avoided, and so incur evils which according to reason are more to be avoided, he could not be wholly excused from sin, because such like fear would be inordinate. Now the evils of the soul are more to be feared than the evils of the body. and evils of the body more than evils of external things. Wherefore if one were to incur evils of the soul, namely sins, in order to avoid evils of the body, such as blows or death, or evils of external things, such as loss of money; or if one were to endure evils of the body in order to avoid loss of money, one would not be wholly excused from sin. Yet one's sin would be extenuated somewhat, for what is done through fear is less voluntary, because when fear lays hold of a man he is under a certain necessity of doing a certain thing. Hence the Philosopher (Ethic. iii, 1) says that these things that are done through fear are not simply voluntary, but a mixture of voluntary and involuntary.

Reply to Objection 1: Fear excuses, not in the point of its sinfulness, but in the point of its involuntariness.

Reply to Objection 2: Although death comes, of necessity, to all, yet the shortening of temporal life is an evil and consequently an object of fear.

Reply to Objection 3: According to the opinion of Stoics, who held temporal goods not to be man's goods, it follows in consequence that temporal evils are not man's evils, and that therefore they are nowise to be feared. But according to Augustine (De Lib. Arb. ii) these temporal things are goods of the least account, and this was also the opinion of the Peripatetics. Hence their contraries are indeed to be feared; but not so much that one ought for their sake to renounce that which is good according to virtue.

OF FEARLESSNESS (TWO ARTICLES)

We must now consider the vice of fearlessness: under which head there are two points of inquiry:

(1) Whether it is a sin to be fearless?

(2) Whether it is opposed to fortitude?

Whether fearlessness is a sin?

Objection 1: It seems that fearlessness is not a sin. For that which is reckoned to the praise of a just man is not a sin. Now it is written in praise of the just man (Prov. 28:1): "The just, bold as a lion, shall be without dread." Therefore it is not a sin to be without fear.

Objection 2: Further, nothing is so fearful as death, according to the Philosopher (Ethic. iii, 6). Yet one ought not to fear even death, according to Mat. 10:28, "Fear ye not them that kill the body," etc., nor anything that can be inflicted by man, according to Is. 51:12, "Who art thou, that thou shouldst be afraid of a mortal man?" Therefore it is not a sin to be fearless.

Objection 3: Further, fear is born of love, as stated above ([3328]Q[125], A[2]). Now it belongs to the perfection of virtue to love nothing earthly, since according to Augustine (De Civ. Dei xiv), "the love of God to the abasement of self makes us citizens of the heavenly city." Therefore it is seemingly not a sin to fear nothing earthly.

On the contrary, It is said of the unjust judge (Lk. 18:2) that "he feared not God nor regarded man."

I answer that, Since fear is born of love, we must seemingly judge alike of love and fear. Now it is here a question of that fear whereby one dreads temporal evils, and which results from the love of temporal goods. And every man has it instilled in him by nature to love his own life and whatever is directed thereto; and to do so in due measure, that is, to love these things not as placing his end therein, but as things to be used for the sake of his last end. Hence it is contrary to the natural inclination, and therefore a sin, to fall short of loving them in due measure. Nevertheless, one never lapses entirely from this love: since what is natural cannot be wholly lost: for which reason the Apostle says (Eph. 5:29): "No man ever hated his own flesh." Wherefore even those that slay themselves do so from love of their own flesh, which they desire to free from present stress. Hence it may happen that a man fears death and other temporal evils less than he ought, for the reason that he loves them* less than he ought. [*Viz. the contrary goods. One would expect 'se' instead of 'ea.' We should then read: For the reason that he loves himself less than he ought.] But that he fear none of these things cannot result from an entire lack of love, but only from the fact that he thinks it impossible for him to be afflicted by the evils contrary to the goods he loves. This is sometimes the result of pride of soul presuming on self and despising others, according to the saying of Job 41:24,25: "He [Vulg.: 'who'] was made to fear no one, he beholdeth every high thing": and sometimes it happens through a defect in the reason; thus the Philosopher says (Ethic. iii, 7) that the "Celts, through lack of intelligence, fear nothing." [*"A man would deserve to be called insane and senseless if there were nothing that he feared, not even an earthquake nor a storm at sea, as is said to be the case with the Celts."] It is therefore evident that fearlessness is a vice, whether it result from lack of love, pride of soul, or dullness of understanding: yet the latter is excused from sin if it be invincible.

Reply to Objection 1: The just man is praised for being without fear that withdraws him from good; not that he is altogether fearless, for it is written (Ecclus. 1:28): "He that is without fear cannot be justified."

Reply to Objection 2: Death and whatever else can be inflicted by mortal man are not to be feared so that they make us forsake justice: but they are to be feared as hindering man in acts of virtue, either as regards himself, or as regards the progress he may cause in others. Hence it is written (Prov. 14:16): "A wise man feareth and declineth from evil."

Reply to Objection 3: Temporal goods are to be despised as hindering us from loving and serving God, and on the same score they are not to be feared; wherefore it is written (Ecclus. 34:16): "He that feareth the Lord shall tremble at nothing." But temporal goods are not to be despised, in so far as they are helping us instrumentally to attain those things that pertain to Divine fear and love.

Whether fearlessness is opposed to fortitude?

Objection 1: It seems that fearlessness is not opposed to fortitude. For we judge of habits by their acts. Now no act of fortitude is hindered by a man being fearless: since if fear be removed, one is both brave to endure, and daring to attack. Therefore fearlessness is not opposed to fortitude.

Objection 2: Further, fearlessness is a vice, either through lack of due love, or on account of pride, or by reason of folly. Now lack of due love is opposed to charity, pride is contrary to humility, and folly to prudence or wisdom. Therefore the vice of fearlessness is not opposed to fortitude.

Objection 3: Further, vices are opposed to virtue and extremes to the mean. But one mean has only one extreme on the one side. Since then fortitude has fear opposed to it on the one side and daring on the other, it seems that fearlessness is not opposed thereto.

On the contrary, The Philosopher (Ethic. iii) reckons fearlessness to be opposed to fortitude.

I answer that, As stated above ([3329]Q[123], A[3]), fortitude is concerned about fear and daring. Now every moral virtue observes the rational mean in the matter about which it is concerned. Hence it belongs to fortitude that man should moderate his fear according to reason, namely that he should fear what he ought, and when he ought, and so forth. Now this mode of reason may be corrupted either by excess or by deficiency. Wherefore just as timidity is opposed to fortitude by excess of fear, in so far as a man fears what he ought not, and as he ought not, so too fearlessness is opposed thereto by deficiency of fear, in so far as a man fears not what he ought to fear.

Reply to Objection 1: The act of fortitude is to endure death without fear, and to be aggressive, not anyhow, but according to reason: this the fearless man does not do.

Reply to Objection 2: Fearlessness by its specific nature corrupts the mean of fortitude, wherefore it is opposed to fortitude directly. But in respect of its causes nothing hinders it from being opposed to other virtues.

Reply to Objection 3: The vice of daring is opposed to fortitude by excess of daring, and fearlessness by deficiency of fear. Fortitude imposes the mean on each passion. Hence there is nothing unreasonable in its having different extremes in different respects.

OF DARING [*Excessive daring or foolhardiness] (TWO ARTICLES)

We must now consider daring; and under this head there are two points of inquiry:

(1) Whether daring is a sin?

(2) Whether it is opposed to fortitude?

Whether daring is a sin?

Objection 1: It seems that daring is not a sin. For it is written (Job 39:21) concerning the horse, by which according to Gregory (Moral. xxxi) the godly preacher is denoted, that "he goeth forth boldly to meet armed men [*Vulg.: 'he pranceth boldly, he goeth forth to meet armed men']." But no vice redounds to a man's praise. Therefore it is not a sin to be daring.

Objection 2: Further, according to the Philosopher (Ethic. vi, 9), "one should take counsel in thought, and do quickly what has been counseled." But daring helps this quickness in doing. Therefore daring is not sinful but praiseworthy.

Objection 3: Further, daring is a passion caused by hope, as stated above ([3330]FS, Q[45], A[2]) when we were treating of the passions. But hope is accounted not a sin but a virtue. Neither therefore should daring be accounted a sin.

On the contrary, It is written (Ecclus. 8:18): "Go not on the way with a bold man, lest he burden thee with his evils." Now no man's fellowship is to be avoided save on account of sin. Therefore daring is a sin.

I answer that, Daring, as stated above ([3331]FS, Q[23], A[1]; Q[55]), is a passion. Now a passion is sometimes moderated according to reason, and sometimes it lacks moderation, either by excess or by deficiency, and on this account the passion is sinful. Again, the names of the passions are sometimes employed in the sense of excess, thus we speak of anger meaning not any but excessive anger, in which case it is sinful, and in the same way daring as implying excess is accounted a sin.

Reply to Objection 1: The daring spoken of there is that which is moderated by reason, for in that sense it belongs to the virtue of fortitude.

Reply to Objection 2: It is praiseworthy to act quickly after taking counsel, which is an act of reason. But to wish to act quickly before taking counsel is not praiseworthy but sinful; for this would be to act rashly, which is a vice contrary to prudence, as stated above ([3332]Q[58], A[3]). Wherefore daring which leads one to act quickly is so far praiseworthy as it is directed by reason.

Reply to Objection 3: Some vices are unnamed, and so also are some virtues, as the Philosopher remarks (Ethic. ii, 7; iv, 4,5,6). Hence the names of certain passions have to be applied to certain vices and virtues: and in order to designate vices we employ especially the names of those passions the object of which is an evil, as in the case of hatred, fear, anger and daring. But hope and love have a good for this object, and so we use them rather to designate virtues.

Whether daring is opposed to fortitude?

Objection 1: It seems that daring is not opposed to fortitude. For excess of daring seems to result from presumption of mind. But presumption pertains to pride which is opposed to humility. Therefore daring is opposed to humility rather than to fortitude.

Objection 2: Further, daring does not seem to call for blame, except in so far as it results in harm either to the daring person who puts himself in danger inordinately, or to others whom he attacks with daring, or exposes to danger. But this seemingly pertains to injustice. Therefore daring, as designating a sin, is opposed, not to fortitude but to justice.

Objection 3: Further, fortitude is concerned about fear and daring, as stated above ([3333]Q[123], A[3]). Now since timidity is opposed to fortitude in respect of an excess of fear, there is another vice opposed to timidity in respect of a lack of fear. If then, daring is opposed to fortitude, in the point of excessive daring, there will likewise be a vice opposed to it in the point of deficient daring. But there is no such vice. Therefore neither should daring be accounted a vice in opposition to fortitude.

On the contrary, The Philosopher in both the Second and Third Books of Ethics accounts daring to be opposed to fortitude.

I answer that, As stated above ([3334]Q[126], A[2]), it belongs to a moral virtue to observe the rational mean in the matter about which it is concerned. Wherefore every vice that denotes lack of moderation in the matter of a moral virtue is opposed to that virtue, as immoderate to moderate. Now daring, in so far as it denotes a vice, implies excess of passion, and this excess goes by the name of daring. Wherefore it is evident that it is opposed to the virtue of fortitude which is concerned about fear and daring, as stated above ([3335]Q[122], A[3]).

Reply to Objection 1: Opposition between vice and virtue does not depend chiefly on the cause of the vice but on the vice's very species. Wherefore it is not necessary that daring be opposed to the same virtue as presumption which is its cause.

Reply to Objection 2: Just as the direct opposition of a vice does not depend on its cause, so neither does it depend on its effect. Now the harm done by daring is its effect. Wherefore neither does the opposition of daring depend on this.

Reply to Objection 3: The movement of daring consists in a man taking the offensive against that which is in opposition to him: and nature inclines him to do this except in so far as such inclination is hindered by the fear of receiving harm from that source. Hence the vice which exceeds in daring has no contrary deficiency, save only timidity. Yet daring does not always accompany so great a lack of timidity, for as the Philosopher says (Ethic. iii, 7), "the daring are precipitate and eager to meet danger, yet fail when the danger is present," namely through fear.

OF THE PARTS OF FORTITUDE (ONE ARTICLE)

We must now consider the parts of fortitude; first we shall consider what are the parts of fortitude; and secondly we shall treat of each part.

Whether the parts of fortitude are suitably assigned?

Objection 1: It seems that the parts of fortitude are unsuitably assigned. For Tully (De Invent. Rhet. ii) assigns four parts to fortitude, namely "magnificence," "confidence," "patience," and "perseverance." Now magnificence seems to pertain to liberality; since both are concerned about money, and "a magnificent man must needs be liberal," as the Philosopher observes (Ethic. iv, 2). But liberality is a part of justice, as stated above ([3336]Q[117], A[5]). Therefore magnificence should not be reckoned a part of fortitude.

Objection 2: Further, confidence is apparently the same as hope. But hope does not seem to pertain to fortitude, but is rather a virtue by itself. Therefore confidence should not be reckoned a part of fortitude.

Objection 3: Further, fortitude makes a man behave aright in face of danger. But magnificence and confidence do not essentially imply any relation to danger. Therefore they are not suitably reckoned as parts of fortitude.

Objection 4: Further, according to Tully (De Invent. Rhet. ii) patience denotes endurance of hardships, and he ascribes the same to fortitude. Therefore patience is the same as fortitude and not a part thereof.

Objection 5: Further, that which is a requisite to every virtue should not be reckoned a part of a special virtue. But perseverance is required in every virtue: for it is written (Mat. 24:13): "He that shall persevere to the end he shall be saved." Therefore perseverance should not be accounted a part of fortitude.

Objection 6: Further, Macrobius (De Somn. Scip. i) reckons seven parts of fortitude, namely "magnanimity, confidence, security, magnificence, constancy, forbearance, stability." Andronicus also reckons seven virtues annexed to fortitude, and these are, "courage, strength of will, magnanimity, manliness, perseverance, magnificence." Therefore it seems that Tully's reckoning of the parts of fortitude is incomplete.

Objection 7: Further, Aristotle (Ethic. iii) reckons five parts of fortitude. The first is "civic" fortitude, which produces brave deeds through fear of dishonor or punishment; the second is "military" fortitude, which produces brave deeds as a result of warlike art or experience; the third is the fortitude which produces brave deeds resulting from passion, especially anger; the fourth is the fortitude which makes a man act bravely through being accustomed to overcome; the fifth is the fortitude which makes a man act bravely through being unaccustomed to danger. Now these kinds of fortitude are not comprised under any of the above enumerations. Therefore these enumerations of the parts of fortitude are unfitting.

I answer that, As stated above ([3337]Q[48]), a virtue can have three kinds of parts, subjective, integral, and potential. But fortitude, taken as a special virtue, cannot have subjective parts, since it is not divided into several specifically distinct virtues, for it is about a very special matter.

However, there are quasi-integral and potential parts assigned to it: integral parts, with regard to those things the concurrence of which is requisite for an act of fortitude; and potential parts, because what fortitude practices in face of the greatest hardships, namely dangers of death, certain other virtues practice in the matter of certain minor hardships and these virtues are annexed to fortitude as secondary virtues to the principal virtue. As stated above ([3338]Q[123], AA[3],6), the act of fortitude is twofold, aggression and endurance. Now two things are required for the act of aggression. The first regards preparation of the mind, and consists in one's having a mind ready for aggression. In this respect Tully mentions "confidence," of which he says (De Invent. Rhet. ii) that "with this the mind is much assured and firmly hopeful in great and honorable undertakings." The second regards the accomplishment of the deed, and consists in not failing to accomplish what one has confidently begun. In this respect Tully mentions "magnificence," which he describes as being "the discussion and administration," i.e. accomplishment "of great and lofty undertakings, with a certain broad and noble purpose of mind," so as to combine execution with greatness of purpose. Accordingly if these two be confined to the proper matter of fortitude, namely to dangers of death, they will be quasi-integral parts thereof, because without them there can be no fortitude; whereas if they be referred to other matters involving less hardship, they will be virtues specifically distinct from fortitude, but annexed thereto as secondary virtues to principal: thus "magnificence" is referred by the Philosopher (Ethic. iv) to great expenses, and "magnanimity," which seems to be the same as confidence, to great honors. Again, two things are requisite for the other act of fortitude, viz. endurance. The first is that the mind be not broken by sorrow, and fall away from its greatness, by reason of the stress of threatening evil. In this respect he mentions "patience," which he describes as "the voluntary and prolonged endurance of arduous and difficult things for the sake of virtue or profit." The other is that by the prolonged suffering of hardships man be not wearied so as to lose courage, according to Heb. 12:3, "That you be not wearied, fainting in your minds." In this respect he mentions "perseverance," which accordingly he describes as "the fixed and continued persistence in a well considered purpose." If these two be confined to the proper matter of fortitude, they will be quasi-integral parts thereof; but if they be referred to any kind of hardship they will be virtues distinct from fortitude, yet annexed thereto as secondary to principal.

Reply to Objection 1: Magnificence in the matter of liberality adds a certain greatness: this is connected with the notion of difficulty which is the object of the irascible faculty, that is perfected chiefly by fortitude: and to this virtue, in this respect, it belongs.

Reply to Objection 2: Hope whereby one confides in God is accounted a theological virtue, as stated above (Q[17], A[5]; [3339]FS, Q[62], A[3]). But by confidence which here is accounted a part of fortitude, man hopes in himself, yet under God withal.

Reply to Objection 3: To venture on anything great seems to involve danger, since to fail in such things is very disastrous. Wherefore although magnificence and confidence are referred to the accomplishment of or venturing on any other great things, they have a certain connection with fortitude by reason of the imminent danger.

Reply to Objection 4: Patience endures not only dangers of death, with which fortitude is concerned, without excessive sorrow, but also any other hardships or dangers. In this respect it is accounted a virtue annexed to fortitude: but as referred to dangers of death, it is an integral part thereof.

Reply to Objection 5: Perseverance as denoting persistence in a good deed unto the end, may be a circumstance of every virtue, but it is reckoned a part of fortitude in the sense stated in the body of the Article.

Reply to Objection 6: Macrobius reckons the four aforesaid mentioned by Tully, namely "confidence, magnificence, forbearance," which he puts in the place of patience, and "firmness," which he substitutes for perseverance. And he adds three, two of which, namely "magnanimity" and "security," are comprised by Tully under the head of confidence. But Macrobius is more specific in his enumeration. Because confidence denotes a man's hope for great things: and hope for anything presupposes an appetite stretching forth to great things by desire, and this belongs to magnanimity. For it has been stated above ([3340]FS, Q[40], A[2]) that hope presupposes love and desire of the thing hoped for.

A still better reply is that confidence pertains to the certitude of hope; while magnanimity refers to the magnitude of the thing hoped for. Now hope has no firmness unless its contrary be removed, for sometimes one, for one's own part, would hope for something, but hope is avoided on account of the obstacle of fear, since fear is somewhat contrary to hope, as stated above, ([3341]FS, Q[40], A[4], ad 1). Hence Macrobius adds security, which banishes fear. He adds a third, namely constancy, which may be comprised under magnificence. For in performing deeds of magnificence one needs to have a constant mind. For this reason Tully says that magnificence consists not only in accomplishing great things, but also in discussing them generously in the mind. Constancy may also pertain to perseverance, so that one may be called persevering through not desisting on account of delays, and constant through not desisting on account of any other obstacles.

Those that are mentioned by Andronicus seem to amount to the same as the above. For with Tully and Macrobius he mentions "perseverance" and "magnificence," and with Macrobius, "magnanimity." "Strength of will" is the same as patience or forbearance, for he says that "strength of will is a habit that makes one ready to attempt what ought to be attempted, and to endure what reason says should be endured"—i.e. good courage seems to be the same as assurance, for he defines it as "strength of soul in the accomplishment of its purpose." Manliness is apparently the same as confidence, for he says that "manliness is a habit of self-sufficiency in matters of virtue." Besides magnificence he mentions {andragathia}, i.e. manly goodness which we may render "strenuousness." For magnificence consists not only in being constant in the accomplishment of great deeds, which belongs to constancy, but also in bringing a certain manly prudence and solicitude to that accomplishment, and this belongs to {andragathia}, strenuousness: wherefore he says that {andragathia} is the virtue of a man, whereby he thinks out profitable works.

Accordingly it is evident that all these parts may be reduced to the four principal parts mentioned by Tully.

Reply to Objection 7: The five mentioned by Aristotle fall short of the true notion of virtue, for though they concur in the act of fortitude, they differ as to motive, as stated above ([3342]Q[123], A[1], ad 2); wherefore they are not reckoned parts but modes of fortitude.

OF MAGNANIMITY* (EIGHT ARTICLES)

[*Not in the ordinary restricted sense but as explained by the author]

We must now consider each of the parts of fortitude, including, however, the other parts under those mentioned by Tully, with the exception of confidence, for which we shall substitute magnanimity, of which Aristotle treats. Accordingly we shall consider (1) Magnanimity; (2) Magnificence; (3) Patience; (4) Perseverance. As regards the first we shall treat (1) of magnanimity; (2) of its contrary vices. Under the first head there are eight points of inquiry:

(1) Whether magnanimity is about honors?

(2) Whether magnanimity is only about great honors?

(3) Whether it is a virtue?

(4) Whether it is a special virtue?

(5) Whether it is a part of fortitude?

(6) Of its relation to confidence;

(7) Of its relation to assurance;

(8) Of its relation to goods of fortune.

Whether magnanimity is about honors?

Objection 1: It seems that magnanimity is not about honors. For magnanimity is in the irascible faculty, as its very name shows, since "magnanimity" signifies greatness of mind, and "mind" denotes the irascible part, as appears from De Anima iii, 42, where the Philosopher says that "in the sensitive appetite are desire and mind," i.e. the concupiscible and irascible parts. But honor is a concupiscible good since it is the reward of virtue. Therefore it seems that magnanimity is not about honors.

Objection 2: Further, since magnanimity is a moral virtue, it must needs be about either passions or operations. Now it is not about operations, for then it would be a part of justice: whence it follows that it is about passions. But honor is not a passion. Therefore magnanimity is not about honors.

Objection 3: Further, the nature of magnanimity seems to regard pursuit rather than avoidance, for a man is said to be magnanimous because he tends to great things. But the virtuous are praised not for desiring honors, but for shunning them. Therefore magnanimity is not about honors.

On the contrary, The Philosopher says (Ethic. iv, 3) that "magnanimity is about honor and dishonor."

I answer that, Magnanimity by its very name denotes stretching forth of the mind to great things. Now virtue bears a relationship to two things, first to the matter about which is the field of its activity, secondly to its proper act, which consists in the right use of such matter. And since a virtuous habit is denominated chiefly from its act, a man is said to be magnanimous chiefly because he is minded to do some great act. Now an act may be called great in two ways: in one way proportionately, in another absolutely. An act may be called great proportionately, even if it consist in the use of some small or ordinary thing, if, for instance, one make a very good use of it: but an act is simply and absolutely great when it consists in the best use of the greatest thing.

The things which come into man's use are external things, and among these honor is the greatest simply, both because it is the most akin to virtue, since it is an attestation to a person's virtue, as stated above ([3343]Q[103], AA[1],2); and because it is offered to God and to the best; and again because, in order to obtain honor even as to avoid shame, men set aside all other things. Now a man is said to be magnanimous in respect of things that are great absolutely and simply, just as a man is said to be brave in respect of things that are difficult simply. It follows therefore that magnanimity is about honors.

Reply to Objection 1: Good and evil absolutely considered regard the concupiscible faculty, but in so far as the aspect of difficult is added, they belong to the irascible. Thus it is that magnanimity regards honor, inasmuch, to wit, as honor has the aspect of something great or difficult.

Reply to Objection 2: Although honor is neither a passion nor an operation, yet it is the object of a passion, namely hope, which tends to a difficult good. Wherefore magnanimity is immediately about the passions of hope, and mediately about honor as the object of hope: even so, we have stated ([3344]Q[123], AA[4],5) with regard to fortitude that it is about dangers of death in so far as they are the object of fear and daring.

Reply to Objection 3: Those are worthy of praise who despise riches in such a way as to do nothing unbecoming in order to obtain them, nor have too great a desire for them. If, however, one were to despise honors so as not to care to do what is worthy of honor, this would be deserving of blame. Accordingly magnanimity is about honors in the sense that a man strives to do what is deserving of honor, yet not so as to think much of the honor accorded by man.

Whether magnanimity is essentially about great honors?

Objection 1: It seems that magnanimity is not essentially about great honors. For the proper matter of magnanimity is honor, as stated above [3345](A[1]). But great and little are accidental to honor. Therefore it is not essential to magnanimity to be about great honors.

Objection 2: Further, just as magnanimity is about honor, so is meekness about anger. But it is not essential to meekness to be about either great or little anger. Therefore neither is it essential to magnanimity to be about great honor.

Objection 3: Further, small honor is less aloof from great honor than is dishonor. But magnanimity is well ordered in relation to dishonor, and consequently in relation to small honors also. Therefore it is not only about great honors.

On the contrary, The Philosopher says (Ethic. ii, 7) that magnanimity is about great honors.

I answer that According to the Philosopher (Phys. vii, 17, 18), virtue is a perfection, and by this we are to understand the perfection of a power, and that it regards the extreme limit of that power, as stated in De Coelo i, 116. Now the perfection of a power is not perceived in every operation of that power, but in such operations as are great or difficult: for every power, however imperfect, can extend to ordinary and trifling operations. Hence it is essential to a virtue to be about the difficult and the good, as stated in Ethic. ii, 3.

Now the difficult and the good (which amount to the same) in an act of virtue may be considered from two points of view. First, from the point of view of reason, in so far as it is difficult to find and establish the rational means in some particular matter: and this difficulty is found only in the act of intellectual virtues, and also of justice. The other difficulty is on the part of the matter, which may involve a certain opposition to the moderation of reason, which moderation has to be applied thereto: and this difficulty regards chiefly the other moral virtues, which are about the passions, because the passions resist reason as Dionysius states (Div. Nom. iv, 4).

Now as regards the passions it is to be observed that the greatness of this power of resistance to reason arises chiefly in some cases from the passions themselves, and in others from the things that are the objects of the passions. The passions themselves have no great power of resistance, unless they be violent, because the sensitive appetite, which is the seat of the passions, is naturally subject to reason. Hence the resisting virtues that are about these passions regard only that which is great in such passions: thus fortitude is about very great fear and daring; temperance about the concupiscence of the greatest pleasures, and likewise meekness about the greatest anger. On the other hand, some passions have great power of resistance to reason arising from the external things themselves that are the objects of those passions: such are the love or desire of money or of honor. And for these it is necessary to have a virtue not only regarding that which is greatest in those passions, but also about that which is ordinary or little: because things external, though they be little, are very desirable, as being necessary for human life. Hence with regard to the desire of money there are two virtues, one about ordinary or little sums of money, namely liberality, and another about large sums of money, namely "magnificence."

In like manner there are two virtues about honors, one about ordinary honors. This virtue has no name, but is denominated by its extremes, which are {philotimia}, i.e. love of honor, and {aphilotimia}, i.e. without love of honor: for sometimes a man is commended for loving honor, and sometimes for not caring about it, in so far, to wit, as both these things may be done in moderation. But with regard to great honors there is "magnanimity." Wherefore we must conclude that the proper matter of magnanimity is great honor, and that a magnanimous man tends to such things as are deserving of honor.

Reply to Objection 1: Great and little are accidental to honor considered in itself: but they make a great difference in their relation to reason, the mode of which has to be observed in the use of honor, for it is much more difficult to observe it in great than in little honors.

Reply to Objection 2: In anger and other matters only that which is greatest presents any notable difficulty, and about this alone is there any need of a virtue. It is different with riches and honors which are things existing outside the soul.

Reply to Objection 3: He that makes good use of great things is much more able to make good use of little things. Accordingly the magnanimous man looks upon great honors as a thing of which he is worthy, or even little honors as something he deserves, because, to wit, man cannot sufficiently honor virtue which deserves to be honored by God. Hence he is not uplifted by great honors, because he does not deem them above him; rather does he despise them, and much more such as are ordinary or little. In like manner he is not cast down by dishonor, but despises it, since he recognizes that he does not deserve it.

Whether magnanimity is a virtue?

Objection 1: It seems that magnanimity is not a virtue. For every moral virtue observes the mean. But magnanimity observes not the mean but the greater extreme: because the "magnanimous man deems himself worthy of the greatest things" (Ethic. iv, 3). Therefore magnanimity is not a virtue.

Objection 2: Further, he that has one virtue has them all, as stated above ([3346]FS, Q[65], A[1]). But one may have a virtue without having magnanimity: since the Philosopher says (Ethic. iv, 3) that "whosoever is worthy of little things and deems himself worthy of them, is temperate, but he is not magnanimous." Therefore magnanimity is not a virtue.

Objection 3: Further, "Virtue is a good quality of the mind," as stated above ([3347]FS, Q[55], A[4]). But magnanimity implies certain dispositions of the body: for the Philosopher says (Ethic. iv, 3) of "a magnanimous man that his gait is slow, his voice deep, and his utterance calm." Therefore magnanimity is not a virtue.

Objection 4: Further, no virtue is opposed to another virtue. But magnanimity is opposed to humility, since "the magnanimous deems himself worthy of great things, and despises others," according to Ethic. iv, 3. Therefore magnanimity is not a virtue.

Objection 5: Further, the properties of every virtue are praiseworthy. But magnanimity has certain properties that call for blame. For, in the first place, the magnanimous is unmindful of favors; secondly, he is remiss and slow of action; thirdly, he employs irony [*Cf. Q[113]] towards many; fourthly, he is unable to associate with others; fifthly, because he holds to the barren things rather than to those that are fruitful. Therefore magnanimity is not a virtue.

On the contrary, It is written in praise of certain men (2 Macc. 15:18): "Nicanor hearing of the valor of Judas' companions, and the greatness of courage [animi magnitudinem] with which they fought for their country, was afraid to try the matter by the sword." Now, only deeds of virtue are worthy of praise. Therefore magnanimity which consists in greatness of courage is a virtue.

I answer that, The essence of human virtue consists in safeguarding the good of reason in human affairs, for this is man's proper good. Now among external human things honors take precedence of all others, as stated above [3348](A[1]; [3349]FS, Q[11], A[2], OBJ[3]). Therefore magnanimity, which observes the mode of reason in great honors, is a virtue.

Reply to Objection 1: As the Philosopher again says (Ethic. iv, 3), "the magnanimous in point of quantity goes to extremes," in so far as he tends to what is greatest, "but in the matter of becomingness, he follows the mean," because he tends to the greatest things according to reason, for "he deems himself worthy in accordance with his worth" (Ethic. iv, 3), since his aims do not surpass his deserts.

Reply to Objection 2: The mutual connection of the virtues does not apply to their acts, as though every one were competent to practice the acts of all the virtues. Wherefore the act of magnanimity is not becoming to every virtuous man, but only to great men. on the other hand, as regards the principles of virtue, namely prudence and grace, all virtues are connected together, since their habits reside together in the soul, either in act or by way of a proximate disposition thereto. Thus it is possible for one to whom the act of magnanimity is not competent, to have the habit of magnanimity, whereby he is disposed to practice that act if it were competent to him according to his state.

Reply to Objection 3: The movements of the body are differentiated according to the different apprehensions and emotions of the soul. And so it happens that to magnanimity there accrue certain fixed accidents by way of bodily movements. For quickness of movement results from a man being intent on many things which he is in a hurry to accomplish, whereas the magnanimous is intent only on great things; these are few and require great attention, wherefore they call for slow movement. Likewise shrill and rapid speaking is chiefly competent to those who are quick to quarrel about anything, and this becomes not the magnanimous who are busy only about great things. And just as these dispositions of bodily movements are competent to the magnanimous man according to the mode of his emotions, so too in those who are naturally disposed to magnanimity these conditions are found naturally.

Reply to Objection 4: There is in man something great which he possesses through the gift of God; and something defective which accrues to him through the weakness of nature. Accordingly magnanimity makes a man deem himself worthy of great things in consideration of the gifts he holds from God: thus if his soul is endowed with great virtue, magnanimity makes him tend to perfect works of virtue; and the same is to be said of the use of any other good, such as science or external fortune. On the other hand, humility makes a man think little of himself in consideration of his own deficiency, and magnanimity makes him despise others in so far as they fall away from God's gifts: since he does not think so much of others as to do anything wrong for their sake. Yet humility makes us honor others and esteem them better than ourselves, in so far as we see some of God's gifts in them. Hence it is written of the just man (Ps. 14:4): "In his sight a vile person is contemned [*Douay: 'The malignant is brought to nothing, but he glorifieth,' etc.]," which indicates the contempt of magnanimity, "but he honoreth them that fear the Lord," which points to the reverential bearing of humility. It is therefore evident that magnanimity and humility are not contrary to one another, although they seem to tend in contrary directions, because they proceed according to different considerations.

Reply to Objection 5: These properties in so far as they belong to a magnanimous man call not for blame, but for very great praise. For in the first place, when it is said that the magnanimous is not mindful of those from whom he has received favors, this points to the fact that he takes no pleasure in accepting favors from others unless he repay them with yet greater favor; this belongs to the perfection of gratitude, in the act of which he wishes to excel, even as in the acts of other virtues. Again, in the second place, it is said that he is remiss and slow of action, not that he is lacking in doing what becomes him, but because he does not busy himself with all kinds of works, but only with great works, such as are becoming to him. He is also said, in the third place, to employ irony, not as opposed to truth, and so as either to say of himself vile things that are not true, or deny of himself great things that are true, but because he does not disclose all his greatness, especially to the large number of those who are beneath him, since, as also the Philosopher says (Ethic. iv, 3), "it belongs to a magnanimous man to be great towards persons of dignity and affluence, and unassuming towards the middle class." In the fourth place, it is said that he cannot associate with others: this means that he is not at home with others than his friends: because he altogether shuns flattery and hypocrisy, which belong to littleness of mind. But he associates with all, both great and little, according as he ought, as stated above (ad 1). It is also said, fifthly, that he prefers to have barren things, not indeed any, but good, i.e. virtuous; for in all things he prefers the virtuous to the useful, as being greater: since the useful is sought in order to supply a defect which is inconsistent with magnanimity.

Whether magnanimity is a special virtue?

Objection 1: It seems that magnanimity is not a special virtue. For no special virtue is operative in every virtue. But the Philosopher states (Ethic. iv, 3) that "whatever is great in each virtue belongs to the magnanimous." Therefore magnanimity is not a special virtue.

Objection 2: Further, the acts of different virtues are not ascribed to any special virtue. But the acts of different virtues are ascribed to the magnanimous man. For it is stated in Ethic. iv, 3 that "it belongs to the magnanimous not to avoid reproof" (which is an act of prudence), "nor to act unjustly" (which is an act of justice), "that he is ready to do favors" (which is an act of charity), "that he gives his services readily" (which is an act of liberality), that "he is truthful" (which is an act of truthfulness), and that "he is not given to complaining" (which is an act of patience). Therefore magnanimity is not a special virtue.

Objection 3: Further, every virtue is a special ornament of the soul, according to the saying of Is. 61:10, "He hath clothed me with the garments of salvation," and afterwards he adds, "and as a bride adorned with her jewels." But magnanimity is the ornament of all the virtues, as stated in Ethic. iv. Therefore magnanimity is a general virtue.

On the contrary, The Philosopher (Ethic. ii, 7) distinguishes it from the other virtues.

I answer that, As stated above (Q[123], A[2]), it belongs to a special virtue to establish the mode of reason in a determinate matter. Now magnanimity establishes the mode of reason in a determinate matter, namely honors, as stated above ([3350]AA[1],2): and honor, considered in itself, is a special good, and accordingly magnanimity considered in itself is a special virtue.

Since, however, honor is the reward of every virtue, as stated above ([3351]Q[103], A[1], ad 2), it follows that by reason of its matter it regards all the virtues.

Reply to Objection 1: Magnanimity is not about any kind of honor, but great honor. Now, as honor is due to virtue, so great honor is due to a great deed of virtue. Hence it is that the magnanimous is intent on doing great deeds in every virtue, in so far, to wit, as he tends to what is worthy of great honors.

Reply to Objection 2: Since the magnanimous tends to great things, it follows that he tends chiefly to things that involve a certain excellence, and shuns those that imply defect. Now it savors of excellence that a man is beneficent, generous and grateful. Wherefore he shows himself ready to perform actions of this kind, but not as acts of the other virtues. on the other hand, it is a proof of defect, that a man thinks so much of certain external goods or evils, that for their sake he abandons and gives up justice or any virtue whatever. Again, all concealment of the truth indicates a defect, since it seems to be the outcome of fear. Also that a man be given to complaining denotes a defect, because by so doing the mind seems to give way to external evils. Wherefore these and like things the magnanimous man avoids under a special aspect, inasmuch as they are contrary to his excellence or greatness.

Reply to Objection 3: Every virtue derives from its species a certain luster or adornment which is proper to each virtue: but further adornment results from the very greatness of a virtuous deed, through magnanimity which makes all virtues greater as stated in Ethic. iv, 3.

Whether magnanimity is a part of fortitude?

Objection 1: It seems that magnanimity is not a part of fortitude. For a thing is not a part of itself. But magnanimity appears to be the same as fortitude. For Seneca says (De Quat. Virtut.): "If magnanimity, which is also called fortitude, be in thy soul, thou shalt live in great assurance": and Tully says (De Offic. i): "If a man is brave we expect him to be magnanimous, truth-loving, and far removed from deception." Therefore magnanimity is not a part of fortitude.

Objection 2: Further, the Philosopher (Ethic. iv, 3) says that a magnanimous man is not {philokindynos}, that is, a lover of danger. But it belongs to a brave man to expose himself to danger. Therefore magnanimity has nothing in common with fortitude so as to be called a part thereof.

Objection 3: Further, magnanimity regards the great in things to be hoped for, whereas fortitude regards the great in things to be feared or dared. But good is of more import than evil. Therefore magnanimity is a more important virtue than fortitude. Therefore it is not a part thereof.

On the contrary, Macrobius (De Somn. Scip. i) and Andronicus reckon magnanimity as a part of fortitude.

I answer that, As stated above ([3352]FS, Q[61], A[3]), a principal virtue is one to which it belongs to establish a general mode of virtue in a principal matter. Now one of the general modes of virtue is firmness of mind, because "a firm standing is necessary in every virtue," according to Ethic. ii. And this is chiefly commended in those virtues that tend to something difficult, in which it is most difficult to preserve firmness. Wherefore the more difficult it is to stand firm in some matter of difficulty, the more principal is the virtue which makes the mind firm in that matter.

Now it is more difficult to stand firm in dangers of death, wherein fortitude confirms the mind, than in hoping for or obtaining the greatest goods, wherein the mind is confirmed by magnanimity, for, as man loves his life above all things, so does he fly from dangers of death more than any others. Accordingly it is clear that magnanimity agrees with fortitude in confirming the mind about some difficult matter; but it falls short thereof, in that it confirms the mind about a matter wherein it is easier to stand firm. Hence magnanimity is reckoned a part of fortitude, because it is annexed thereto as secondary to principal.

Reply to Objection 1: As the Philosopher says (Ethic. v, 1,3), "to lack evil is looked upon as a good," wherefore not to be overcome by a grievous evil, such as the danger of death, is looked upon as though it were the obtaining of a great good, the former belonging to fortitude, and the latter to magnanimity: in this sense fortitude and magnanimity may be considered as identical. Since, however, there is a difference as regards the difficulty on the part of either of the aforesaid, it follows that properly speaking magnanimity, according to the Philosopher (Ethic. ii, 7), is a distinct virtue from fortitude.

Reply to Objection 2: A man is said to love danger when he exposes himself to all kinds of dangers, which seems to be the mark of one who thinks "many" the same as "great." This is contrary to the nature of a magnanimous man, for no one seemingly exposes himself to danger for the sake of a thing that he does not deem great. But for things that are truly great, a magnanimous man is most ready to expose himself to danger, since he does something great in the act of fortitude, even as in the acts of the other virtues. Hence the Philosopher says (Ethic. ii, 7) that the magnanimous man is not {mikrokindynos}, i.e. endangering himself for small things, but {megalokindynos}, i.e. endangering himself for great things. And Seneca says (De Quat. Virtut.): "Thou wilt be magnanimous if thou neither seekest dangers like a rash man, nor fearest them like a coward. For nothing makes the soul a coward save the consciousness of a wicked life."

Reply to Objection 3: Evil as such is to be avoided: and that one has to withstand it is accidental; in so far, to wit, as one has to suffer an evil in order to safeguard a good. But good as such is to be desired, and that one avoids it is only accidental, in so far, to wit, as it is deemed to surpass the ability of the one who desires it. Now that which is so essentially is always of more account than that which is so accidentally. Wherefore the difficult in evil things is always more opposed to firmness of mind than the difficult in good things. Hence the virtue of fortitude takes precedence of the virtue of magnanimity. For though good is simply of more import than evil, evil is of more import in this particular respect.

Whether confidence belongs to magnanimity?

Objection 1: It seems that confidence does not belong to magnanimity. For a man may have assurance not only in himself, but also in another, according to 2 Cor. 3:4,5, "Such confidence we have, through Christ towards God, not that we are sufficient to think anything of ourselves, as of ourselves." But this seems inconsistent with the idea of magnanimity. Therefore confidence does not belong to magnanimity.

Objection 2: Further, confidence seems to be opposed to fear, according to Is. 12:2, "I will deal confidently and will not fear." But to be without fear seems more akin to fortitude. Therefore confidence also belongs to fortitude rather than to magnanimity.

Objection 3: Further, reward is not due except to virtue. But a reward is due to confidence, according to Heb. 3:6, where it is said that we are the house of Christ, "if we hold fast the confidence and glory of hope unto the end." Therefore confidence is a virtue distinct from magnanimity: and this is confirmed by the fact that Macrobius enumerates it with magnanimity (In Somn. Scip. i).

On the contrary, Tully (De Suv. Rhet. ii) seems to substitute confidence for magnanimity, as stated above in the preceding Question (ad 6) and in the prologue to this.

I answer that, Confidence takes its name from "fides" [faith]: and it belongs to faith to believe something and in somebody. But confidence belongs to hope, according to Job 11:18, "Thou shalt have confidence, hope being set before thee." Wherefore confidence apparently denotes chiefly that a man derives hope through believing the word of one who promises to help him. Since, however, faith signifies also a strong opinion, and since one may come to have a strong opinion about something, not only on account of another's statement, but also on account of something we observe in another, it follows that confidence may denote the hope of having something, which hope we conceive through observing something either in oneself—for instance, through observing that he is healthy, a man is confident that he will live long. or in another, for instance, through observing that another is friendly to him and powerful, a man is confident that he will receive help from him.

Now it has been stated above (A[1], ad 2) that magnanimity is chiefly about the hope of something difficult. Wherefore, since confidence denotes a certain strength of hope arising from some observation which gives one a strong opinion that one will obtain a certain good, it follows that confidence belongs to magnanimity.

Reply to Objection 1: As the Philosopher says (Ethic. iv, 3), it belongs to the "magnanimous to need nothing," for need is a mark of the deficient. But this is to be understood according to the mode of a man, hence he adds "or scarcely anything." For it surpasses man to need nothing at all. For every man needs, first, the Divine assistance, secondly, even human assistance, since man is naturally a social animal, for he is sufficient by himself to provide for his own life. Accordingly, in so far as he needs others, it belongs to a magnanimous man to have confidence in others, for it is also a point of excellence in a man that he should have at hand those who are able to be of service to him. And in so far as his own ability goes, it belongs to a magnanimous man to be confident in himself.

Reply to Objection 2: As stated above ([3353]FS, Q[23], A[2]; [3354]FS, Q[40], A[4]), when we were treating of the passions, hope is directly opposed to despair, because the latter is about the same object, namely good. But as regards contrariety of objects it is opposed to fear, because the latter's object is evil. Now confidence denotes a certain strength of hope, wherefore it is opposed to fear even as hope is. Since, however, fortitude properly strengthens a man in respect of evil, and magnanimity in respect of the obtaining of good, it follows that confidence belongs more properly to magnanimity than to fortitude. Yet because hope causes daring, which belongs to fortitude, it follows in consequence that confidence pertains to fortitude.

Reply to Objection 3: Confidence, as stated above, denotes a certain mode of hope: for confidence is hope strengthened by a strong opinion. Now the mode applied to an affection may call for commendation of the act, so that it become meritorious, yet it is not this that draws it to a species of virtue, but its matter. Hence, properly speaking, confidence cannot denote a virtue, though it may denote the conditions of a virtue. For this reason it is reckoned among the parts of fortitude, not as an annexed virtue, except as identified with magnanimity by Tully (De Suv. Rhet. ii), but as an integral part, as stated in the preceding Question.

Whether security belongs to magnanimity?

Objection 1: It seems that security does not belong to magnanimity. For security, as stated above (Q[128], ad 6), denotes freedom from the disturbance of fear. But fortitude does this most effectively. Wherefore security is seemingly the same as fortitude. But fortitude does not belong to magnanimity; rather the reverse is the case. Neither therefore does security belong to magnanimity.

Objection 2: Further, Isidore says (Etym. x) that a man "is said to be secure because he is without care." But this seems to be contrary to virtue, which has a care for honorable things, according to 2 Tim. 2:15, "Carefully study to present thyself approved unto God." Therefore security does not belong to magnanimity, which does great things in all the virtues.

Objection 3: Further, virtue is not its own reward. But security is accounted the reward of virtue, according to Job 11:14,18, "If thou wilt put away from thee the iniquity that is in thy hand . . . being buried thou shalt sleep secure." Therefore security does not belong to magnanimity or to any other virtue, as a part thereof.

On the contrary, Tully says (De Offic. i) under the heading: "Magnanimity consists of two things," that "it belongs to magnanimity to give way neither to a troubled mind, nor to man, nor to fortune." But a man's security consists in this. Therefore security belongs to magnanimity.

I answer that, As the Philosopher says (Rhet. ii, 5), "fear makes a man take counsel," because, to wit he takes care to avoid what he fears. Now security takes its name from the removal of this care, of which fear is the cause: wherefore security denotes perfect freedom of the mind from fear, just as confidence denotes strength of hope. Now, as hope directly belongs to magnanimity, so fear directly regards fortitude. Wherefore as confidence belongs immediately to magnanimity, so security belongs immediately to fortitude.

It must be observed, however, that as hope is the cause of daring, so is fear the cause of despair, as stated above when we were treating of the passion ([3355]FS, Q[45], A[2]). Wherefore as confidence belongs indirectly to fortitude, in so far as it makes use of daring, so security belongs indirectly to magnanimity, in so far as it banishes despair.

Reply to Objection 1: Fortitude is chiefly commended, not because it banishes fear, which belongs to security, but because it denotes a firmness of mind in the matter of the passion. Wherefore security is not the same as fortitude, but is a condition thereof.

Reply to Objection 2: Not all security is worthy of praise but only when one puts care aside, as one ought, and in things when one should not fear: in this way it is a condition of fortitude and of magnanimity.

Reply to Objection 3: There is in the virtues a certain likeness to, and participation of, future happiness, as stated above ([3356]FS, Q[5], AA[3],7). Hence nothing hinders a certain security from being a condition of a virtue, although perfect security belongs to virtue's reward.

Whether goods of fortune conduce to magnanimity?

Objection 1: It seems that goods of fortune do not conduce to magnanimity. For according to Seneca (De Ira i: De vita beata xvi): "virtue suffices for itself." Now magnanimity takes every virtue great, as stated above (A[4], ad 3). Therefore goods of fortune do not conduce to magnanimity.

Objection 2: Further, no virtuous man despises what is helpful to him. But the magnanimous man despises whatever pertains to goods of fortune: for Tully says (De Offic. i) under the heading: "Magnanimity consists of two things," that "a great soul is commended for despising external things." Therefore a magnanimous man is not helped by goods of fortune.

Objection 3: Further, Tully adds (De Offic. i) that "it belongs to a great soul so to bear what seems troublesome, as nowise to depart from his natural estate, or from the dignity of a wise man." And Aristotle says (Ethic. iv, 3) that "a magnanimous man does not grieve at misfortune." Now troubles and misfortunes are opposed to goods of fortune, for every one grieves at the loss of what is helpful to him. Therefore external goods of fortune do not conduce to magnanimity.

On the contrary, The Philosopher says (Ethic. iv, 3) that "good fortune seems to conduce to magnanimity."

I answer that, As stated above [3357](A[1]), magnanimity regards two things: honor as its matter, and the accomplishment of something great as its end. Now goods of fortune conduce to both these things. For since honor is conferred on the virtuous, not only by the wise, but also by the multitude who hold these goods of fortune in the highest esteem, the result is that they show greater honor to those who possess goods of fortune. Likewise goods of fortune are useful organs or instruments of virtuous deeds: since we can easily accomplish things by means of riches, power and friends. Hence it is evident that goods of fortune conduce to magnanimity.

Reply to Objection 1: Virtue is said to be sufficient for itself, because it can be without even these external goods; yet it needs them in order to act more expeditiously.

Reply to Objection 2: The magnanimous man despises external goods, inasmuch as he does not think them so great as to be bound to do anything unbecoming for their sake. Yet he does not despise them, but that he esteems them useful for the accomplishment of virtuous deeds.

Reply to Objection 3: If a man does not think much of a thing, he is neither very joyful at obtaining it, nor very grieved at losing it. Wherefore, since the magnanimous man does not think much of external goods, that is goods of fortune, he is neither much uplifted by them if he has them, nor much cast down by their loss.

OF PRESUMPTION (TWO ARTICLES)

We must now consider the vices opposed to magnanimity; and in the first place, those that are opposed thereto by excess. These are three, namely, presumption, ambition, and vainglory. Secondly, we shall consider pusillanimity which is opposed to it by way of deficiency. Under the first head there are two points of inquiry:

(1) Whether presumption is a sin?

(2) Whether it is opposed to magnanimity by excess?

Whether presumption is a sin?

Objection 1: It seems that presumption is not a sin. For the Apostle says: "Forgetting the things that are behind, I stretch forth [Vulg.: 'and stretching forth'] myself to those that are before." But it seems to savor of presumption that one should tend to what is above oneself. Therefore presumption is not a sin.

Objection 2: Further, the Philosopher says (Ethic. i, 7) "we should not listen to those who would persuade us to relish human things because we are men, or mortal things because we are mortal, but we should relish those that make us immortal": and (Metaph. i) "that man should pursue divine things as far as possible." Now divine and immortal things are seemingly far above man. Since then presumption consists essentially in tending to what is above oneself, it seems that presumption is something praiseworthy, rather than a sin.

Objection 3: Further, the Apostle says (2 Cor. 3:5): "Not that we are sufficient to think anything of ourselves, as of ourselves." If then presumption, by which one strives at that for which one is not sufficient, be a sin, it seems that man cannot lawfully even think of anything good: which is absurd. Therefore presumption is not a sin.

On the contrary, It is written (Ecclus. 37:3): "O wicked presumption, whence camest thou?" and a gloss answers: "From a creature's evil will." Now all that comes of the root of an evil will is a sin. Therefore presumption is a sin.

I answer that, Since whatever is according to nature, is ordered by the Divine Reason, which human reason ought to imitate, whatever is done in accordance with human reason in opposition to the order established in general throughout natural things is vicious and sinful. Now it is established throughout all natural things, that every action is commensurate with the power of the agent, nor does any natural agent strive to do what exceeds its ability. Hence it is vicious and sinful, as being contrary to the natural order, that any one should assume to do what is above his power: and this is what is meant by presumption, as its very name shows. Wherefore it is evident that presumption is a sin.

Reply to Objection 1: Nothing hinders that which is above the active power of a natural thing, and yet not above the passive power of that same thing: thus the air is possessed of a passive power by reason of which it can be so changed as to obtain the action and movement of fire, which surpass the active power of air. Thus too it would be sinful and presumptuous for a man while in a state of imperfect virtue to attempt the immediate accomplishment of what belongs to perfect virtue. But it is not presumptuous or sinful for a man to endeavor to advance towards perfect virtue. In this way the Apostle stretched himself forth to the things that were before him, namely continually advancing forward.

Reply to Objection 2: Divine and immortal things surpass man according to the order of nature. Yet man is possessed of a natural power, namely the intellect, whereby he can be united to immortal and Divine things. In this respect the Philosopher says that "man ought to pursue immortal and divine things," not that he should do what it becomes God to do, but that he should be united to Him in intellect and will.

Reply to Objection 3: As the Philosopher says (Ethic. iii, 3), "what we can do by the help of others we can do by ourselves in a sense." Hence since we can think and do good by the help of God, this is not altogether above our ability. Hence it is not presumptuous for a man to attempt the accomplishment of a virtuous deed: but it would be presumptuous if one were to make the attempt without confidence in God's assistance.

Whether presumption is opposed to magnanimity by excess?

Objection 1: It seems that presumption is not opposed to magnanimity by excess. For presumption is accounted a species of the sin against the Holy Ghost, as stated above ([3358]Q[14], A[2];[3359] Q[21], A[1]). But the sin against the Holy Ghost is not opposed to magnanimity, but to charity. Neither therefore is presumption opposed to magnanimity.

Objection 2: Further, it belongs to magnanimity that one should deem oneself worthy of great things. But a man is said to be presumptuous even if he deem himself worthy of small things, if they surpass his ability. Therefore presumption is not directly opposed to magnanimity.

Objection 3: Further, the magnanimous man looks upon external goods as little things. Now according to the Philosopher (Ethic. iv, 3), "on account of external fortune the presumptuous disdain and wrong others, because they deem external goods as something great." Therefore presumption is opposed to magnanimity, not by excess, but only by deficiency.

On the contrary, The Philosopher says (Ethic. ii, 7; iv, 3) that the "vain man," i.e. a vaporer or a wind-bag, which with us denotes a presumptuous man, "is opposed to the magnanimous man by excess."

I answer that, As stated above ([3360]Q[129], A[3], ad 1), magnanimity observes the means, not as regards the quantity of that to which it tends, but in proportion to our own ability: for it does not tend to anything greater than is becoming to us.

Now the presumptuous man, as regards that to which he tends, does not exceed the magnanimous, but sometimes falls far short of him: but he does exceed in proportion to his own ability, whereas the magnanimous man does not exceed his. It is in this way that presumption is opposed to magnanimity by excess.

Reply to Objection 1: It is not every presumption that is accounted a sin against the Holy Ghost, but that by which one contemns the Divine justice through inordinate confidence in the Divine mercy. The latter kind of presumption, by reason of its matter, inasmuch, to wit, as it implies contempt of something Divine, is opposed to charity, or rather to the gift of fear, whereby we revere God. Nevertheless, in so far as this contempt exceeds the proportion to one's own ability, it can be opposed to magnanimity.

Reply to Objection 2: Presumption, like magnanimity, seems to tend to something great. For we are not, as a rule, wont to call a man presumptuous for going beyond his powers in something small. If, however, such a man be called presumptuous, this kind of presumption is not opposed to magnanimity, but to that virtue which is about ordinary honor, as stated above ([3361]Q[129], A[2]).

Reply to Objection 3: No one attempts what is above his ability, except in so far as he deems his ability greater than it is. In this one may err in two ways. First only as regards quantity, as when a man thinks he has greater virtue, or knowledge, or the like, than he has. Secondly, as regards the kind of thing, as when he thinks himself great, and worthy of great things, by reason of something that does not make him so, for instance by reason of riches or goods of fortune. For, as the Philosopher says (Ethic. iv, 3), "those who have these things without virtue, neither justly deem themselves worthy of great things, nor are rightly called magnanimous."

Again, the thing to which a man sometimes tends in excess of his ability, is sometimes in very truth something great, simply as in the case of Peter, whose intent was to suffer for Christ, which has exceeded his power; while sometimes it is something great, not simply, but only in the opinion of fools, such as wearing costly clothes, despising and wronging others. This savors of an excess of magnanimity, not in any truth, but in people's opinion. Hence Seneca says (De Quat. Virtut.) that "when magnanimity exceeds its measure, it makes a man high-handed, proud, haughty restless, and bent on excelling in all things, whether in words or in deeds, without any considerations of virtue." Thus it is evident that the presumptuous man sometimes falls short of the magnanimous in reality, although in appearance he surpasses him.

OF AMBITION (TWO ARTICLES)

We must now consider ambition: and under this head there are two points of inquiry:

(1) Whether it is a sin?

(2) Whether it is opposed to magnanimity by excess?

Whether ambition is a sin?

Objection 1: It seems that ambition is not a sin. For ambition denotes the desire of honor. Now honor is in itself a good thing, and the greatest of external goods: wherefore those who care not for honor are reproved. Therefore ambition is not a sin; rather is it something deserving of praise, in so far as a good is laudably desired.

Objection 2: Further, anyone may, without sin, desire what is due to him as a reward. Now honor is the reward of virtue, as the Philosopher states (Ethic. i, 12; iv, 3; viii, 14). Therefore ambition of honor is not a sin.

Objection 3: Further, that which heartens a man to do good and disheartens him from doing evil, is not a sin. Now honor heartens men to do good and to avoid evil; thus the Philosopher says (Ethic. iii, 8) that "with the bravest men, cowards are held in dishonor, and the brave in honor": and Tully says (De Tusc. Quaest. i) that "honor fosters the arts." Therefore ambition is not a sin.

On the contrary, It is written (1 Cor. 13:5) that "charity is not ambitious, seeketh not her own." Now nothing is contrary to charity, except sin. Therefore ambition is a sin.

I answer that, As stated above ([3362]Q[103], AA[1],2), honor denotes reverence shown to a person in witness of his excellence. Now two things have to be considered with regard to man's honor. The first is that a man has not from himself the thing in which he excels, for this is, as it were, something Divine in him, wherefore on this count honor is due principally, not to him but to God. The second point that calls for observation is that the thing in which man excels is given to him by God, that he may profit others thereby: wherefore a man ought so far to be pleased that others bear witness to his excellence, as this enables him to profit others.

Now the desire of honor may be inordinate in three ways. First, when a man desires recognition of an excellence which he has not: this is to desire more than his share of honor. Secondly, when a man desires honor for himself without referring it to God. Thirdly, when a man's appetite rests in honor itself, without referring it to the profit of others. Since then ambition denotes inordinate desire of honor, it is evident that it is always a sin.

Reply to Objection 1: The desire for good should be regulated according to reason, and if it exceed this rule it will be sinful. In this way it is sinful to desire honor in disaccord with the order of reason. Now those are reproved who care not for honor in accordance with reason's dictate that they should avoid what is contrary to honor.

Reply to Objection 2: Honor is not the reward of virtue, as regards the virtuous man, in this sense that he should seek for it as his reward: since the reward he seeks is happiness, which is the end of virtue. But it is said to be the reward of virtue as regards others, who have nothing greater than honor whereby to reward the virtuous; which honor derives greatness from the very fact that it bears witness to virtue. Hence it is evident that it is not an adequate reward, as stated in Ethic. iv, 3.

Reply to Objection 3: Just as some are heartened to do good and disheartened from doing evil, by the desire of honor, if this be desired in due measure; so, if it be desired inordinately, it may become to man an occasion of doing many evil things, as when a man cares not by what means he obtains honor. Wherefore Sallust says (Catilin.) that "the good as well as the wicked covet honors for themselves, but the one," i.e. the good, "go about it in the right way," whereas "the other," i.e. the wicked, "through lack of the good arts, make use of deceit and falsehood." Yet they who, merely for the sake of honor, either do good or avoid evil, are not virtuous, according to the Philosopher (Ethic. iii, 8), where he says that they who do brave things for the sake of honor are not truly brave.

Whether ambition is opposed to magnanimity by excess?

Objection 1: It seems that ambition is not opposed to magnanimity by excess. For one mean has only one extreme opposed to it on the one side. Now presumption is opposed to magnanimity by excess as stated above ([3363]Q[130], A[2]). Therefore ambition is not opposed to it by excess.

Objection 2: Further, magnanimity is about honors; whereas ambition seems to regard positions of dignity: for it is written (2 Macc. 4:7) that "Jason ambitiously sought the high priesthood." Therefore ambition is not opposed to magnanimity.

Objection 3: Further, ambition seems to regard outward show: for it is written (Acts 25:27) that "Agrippa and Berenice . . . with great pomp [ambitione] . . . had entered into the hall of audience" [*'Praetorium.' The Vulgate has 'auditorium,' but the meaning is the same], and (2 Para. 16:14) that when Asa died they "burned spices and . . . ointments over his body" with very great pomp [ambitione]. But magnanimity is not about outward show. Therefore ambition is not opposed to magnanimity.

On the contrary, Tully says (De Offic. i) that "the more a man exceeds in magnanimity, the more he desires himself alone to dominate others." But this pertains to ambition. Therefore ambition denotes an excess of magnanimity.

I answer that, As stated above [3364](A[1]), ambition signifies inordinate love of honor. Now magnanimity is about honors and makes use of them in a becoming manner. Wherefore it is evident that ambition is opposed to magnanimity as the inordinate to that which is well ordered.

Reply to Objection 1: Magnanimity regards two things. It regards one as its end, in so far as it is some great deed that the magnanimous man attempts in proportion to his ability. In this way presumption is opposed to magnanimity by excess: because the presumptuous man attempts great deeds beyond his ability. The other thing that magnanimity regards is its matter, viz. honor, of which it makes right use: and in this way ambition is opposed to magnanimity by excess. Nor is it impossible for one mean to be exceeded in various respects.

Reply to Objection 2: Honor is due to those who are in a position of dignity, on account of a certain excellence of their estate: and accordingly inordinate desire for positions of dignity pertains to ambition. For if a man were to have an inordinate desire for a position of dignity, not for the sake of honor, but for the sake of a right use of a dignity exceeding his ability, he would not be ambitious but presumptuous.

Reply to Objection 3: The very solemnity of outward worship is a kind of honor, wherefore in such cases honor is wont to be shown. This is signified by the words of James 2:2,3: "If there shall come into your assembly a man having a golden ring, in fine apparel . . . and you . . . shall say to him: Sit thou here well," etc.

Wherefore ambition does not regard outward worship, except in so far as this is a kind of honor.

OF VAINGLORY (FIVE ARTICLES)

We must now consider vainglory: under which head there are five points of inquiry:

(1) Whether desire of glory is a sin?

(2) Whether it is opposed to magnanimity?

(3) Whether it is a mortal sin?

(4) Whether it is a capital vice?

(5) Of its daughters.

Whether the desire of glory is a sin?

Objection 1: It seems that the desire of glory is not a sin. For no one sins in being likened to God: in fact we are commanded (Eph. 5:1): "Be ye . . . followers of God, as most dear children." Now by seeking glory man seems to imitate God, Who seeks glory from men: wherefore it is written (Is. 43:6,7): "Bring My sons from afar, and My daughters from the ends of the earth. And every one that calleth on My name, I have created him for My glory." Therefore the desire for glory is not a sin.

Objection 2: Further, that which incites a mar to do good is apparently not a sin. Now the desire of glory incites men to do good. For Tully says (De Tusc. Quaest. i) that "glory inflames every man to strive his utmost": and in Holy Writ glory is promised for good works, according to Rom. 2:7: "To them, indeed, who according to patience in good work . . . glory and honor" [*Vulg.: 'Who will render to every man according to his works, to them indeed who . . . seek glory and honor and incorruption, eternal life.']. Therefore the desire for glory is not a sin.

Objection 3: Further, Tully says (De Invent. Rhet. ii) that glory is "consistent good report about a person, together with praise": and this comes to the same as what Augustine says (Contra Maximin. iii), viz. that glory is, "as it were, clear knowledge with praise." Now it is no sin to desire praiseworthy renown: indeed, it seems itself to call for praise, according to Ecclus. 41:15, "Take care of a good name," and Rom. 12:17, "Providing good things not only in the sight of God, but also in the sight of all men." Therefore the desire of vainglory is not a sin.

On the contrary, Augustine says (De Civ. Dei v): "He is better advised who acknowledges that even the love of praise is sinful."

I answer that, Glory signifies a certain clarity, wherefore Augustine says (Tract. lxxxii, c, cxiv in Joan.) that to be "glorified is the same as to be clarified." Now clarity and comeliness imply a certain display: wherefore the word glory properly denotes the display of something as regards its seeming comely in the sight of men, whether it be a bodily or a spiritual good. Since, however, that which is clear simply can be seen by many, and by those who are far away, it follows that the word glory properly denotes that somebody's good is known and approved by many, according to the saying of Sallust (Catilin.) [*The quotation is from Livy: Hist., Lib. XXII C, 39]: "I must not boast while I am addressing one man."

But if we take the word glory in a broader sense, it not only consists in the knowledge of many, but also in the knowledge of few, or of one, or of oneself alone, as when one considers one's own good as being worthy of praise. Now it is not a sin to know and approve one's own good: for it is written (1 Cor. 2:12): "Now we have received not the spirit of this world, but the Spirit that is of God that we may know the things that are given us from God." Likewise it is not a sin to be willing to approve one's own good works: for it is written (Mat. 5:16): "Let your light shine before men." Hence the desire for glory does not, of itself, denote a sin: but the desire for empty or vain glory denotes a sin: for it is sinful to desire anything vain, according to Ps. 4:3, "Why do you love vanity, and seek after lying?"

Now glory may be called vain in three ways. First, on the part of the thing for which one seeks glory: as when a man seeks glory for that which is unworthy of glory, for instance when he seeks it for something frail and perishable: secondly, on the part of him from whom he seeks glory, for instance a man whose judgment is uncertain: thirdly, on the part of the man himself who seeks glory, for that he does not refer the desire of his own glory to a due end, such as God's honor, or the spiritual welfare of his neighbor.

Reply to Objection 1: As Augustine says on Jn. 13:13, "You call Me Master and Lord; and you say well" (Tract. lviii in Joan.): "Self-complacency is fraught with danger of one who has to beware of pride. But He Who is above all, however much He may praise Himself, does not uplift Himself. For knowledge of God is our need, not His: nor does any man know Him unless he be taught of Him Who knows." It is therefore evident that God seeks glory, not for His own sake, but for ours. In like manner a man may rightly seek his own glory for the good of others, according to Mat. 5:16, "That they may see your good works, and glorify your Father Who is in heaven."

Reply to Objection 2: That which we receive from God is not vain but true glory: it is this glory that is promised as a reward for good works, and of which it is written (2 Cor. 10:17,18): "He that glorieth let him glory in the Lord, for not he who commendeth himself is approved, but he whom God commendeth." It is true that some are heartened to do works of virtue, through desire for human glory, as also through the desire for other earthly goods. Yet he is not truly virtuous who does virtuous deeds for the sake of human glory, as Augustine proves (De Civ. Dei v).

Reply to Objection 3: It is requisite for man's perfection that he should know himself; but not that he should be known by others, wherefore it is not to be desired in itself. It may, however, be desired as being useful for something, either in order that God may be glorified by men, or that men may become better by reason of the good they know to be in another man, or in order that man, knowing by the testimony of others' praise the good which is in him, may himself strive to persevere therein and to become better. In this sense it is praiseworthy that a man should "take care of his good name," and that he should "provide good things in the sight of God and men": but not that he should take an empty pleasure in human praise.

Whether vainglory is opposed to magnanimity?

Objection 1: It seems that vainglory is not opposed to magnanimity. For, as stated above [3365](A[1]), vainglory consists in glorying in things that are not, which pertains to falsehood; or in earthly and perishable things, which pertains to covetousness; or in the testimony of men, whose judgment is uncertain, which pertains to imprudence. Now these vices are not contrary to magnanimity. Therefore vainglory is not opposed to magnanimity.

Objection 2: Further, vainglory is not, like pusillanimity, opposed to magnanimity by way of deficiency, for this seems inconsistent with vainglory. Nor is it opposed to it by way of excess, for in this way presumption and ambition are opposed to magnanimity, as stated above ([3366]Q[130], A[2];[3367] Q[131], A[2]): and these differ from vainglory. Therefore vainglory is not opposed to magnanimity.

Objection 3: Further, a gloss on Phil. 2:3, "Let nothing be done through contention, neither by vainglory," says: "Some among them were given to dissension and restlessness, contending with one another for the sake of vainglory." But contention [*Cf. Q[38]] is not opposed to magnanimity. Neither therefore is vainglory.

On the contrary, Tully says (De Offic. i) under the heading, "Magnanimity consists in two things: We should beware of the desire for glory, since it enslaves the mind, which a magnanimous man should ever strive to keep untrammeled." Therefore it is opposed to magnanimity.

I answer that, As stated above ([3368]Q[103], A[1], ad 3), glory is an effect of honor and praise: because from the fact that a man is praised, or shown any kind of reverence, he acquires charity in the knowledge of others. And since magnanimity is about honor, as stated above ([3369]Q[129], AA[1],2), it follows that it also is about glory: seeing that as a man uses honor moderately, so too does he use glory in moderation. Wherefore inordinate desire of glory is directly opposed to magnanimity.

Reply to Objection 1: To think so much of little things as to glory in them is itself opposed to magnanimity. Wherefore it is said of the magnanimous man (Ethic. iv) that honor is of little account to him. In like manner he thinks little of other things that are sought for honor's sake, such as power and wealth. Likewise it is inconsistent with magnanimity to glory in things that are not; wherefore it is said of the magnanimous man (Ethic. iv) that he cares more for truth than for opinion. Again it is incompatible with magnanimity for a man to glory in the testimony of human praise, as though he deemed this something great; wherefore it is said of the magnanimous man (Ethic. iv), that he cares not to be praised. And so, when a man looks upon little things as though they were great, nothing hinders this from being contrary to magnanimity, as well as to other virtues.

Reply to Objection 2: He that is desirous of vainglory does in truth fall short of being magnanimous, because he glories in what the magnanimous man thinks little of, as stated in the preceding Reply. But if we consider his estimate, he is opposed to the magnanimous man by way of excess, because the glory which he seeks is something great in his estimation, and he tends thereto in excess of his deserts.

Reply to Objection 3: As stated above ([3370]Q[127], A[2], ad 2), the opposition of vices does not depend on their effects. Nevertheless contention, if done intentionally, is opposed to magnanimity: since no one contends save for what he deems great. Wherefore the Philosopher says (Ethic. iv, 3) that the magnanimous man is not contentious, because nothing is great in his estimation.

Whether vainglory is a mortal sin?

Objection 1: It seems that vainglory is a mortal sin. For nothing precludes the eternal reward except a mortal sin. Now vainglory precludes the eternal reward: for it is written (Mat. 6:1): "Take heed, that you do not give justice before men, to be seen by them: otherwise you shall not have a reward of your Father Who is in heaven." Therefore vainglory is a mortal sin.

Objection 2: Further, whoever appropriates to himself that which is proper to God, sins mortally. Now by desiring vainglory, a man appropriates to himself that which is proper to God. For it is written (Is. 42:8): "I will not give My glory to another," and (1 Tim. 1:17): "To . . . the only God be honor and glory." Therefore vainglory is a mortal sin.

Objection 3: Further, apparently a sin is mortal if it be most dangerous and harmful. Now vainglory is a sin of this kind, because a gloss of Augustine on 1 Thess. 2:4, "God, Who proveth our hearts," says: "Unless a man war against the love of human glory he does not perceive its baneful power, for though it be easy for anyone not to desire praise as long as one does not get it, it is difficult not to take pleasure in it, when it is given." Chrysostom also says (Hom. xix in Matth.) that "vainglory enters secretly, and robs us insensibly of all our inward possessions." Therefore vainglory is a mortal sin.

On the contrary, Chrysostom says [*Hom. xiii in the Opus Imperfectum falsely ascribed to St. John Chrysostom] that "while other vices find their abode in the servants of the devil, vainglory finds a place even in the servants of Christ." Yet in the latter there is no mortal sin. Therefore vainglory is not a mortal sin.

I answer that, As stated above ([3371]Q[24], A[12];[3372] Q[110], A[4];[3373] Q[112], A[2]), a sin is mortal through being contrary to charity. Now the sin of vainglory, considered in itself, does not seem to be contrary to charity as regards the love of one's neighbor: yet as regards the love of God it may be contrary to charity in two ways. In one way, by reason of the matter about which one glories: for instance when one glories in something false that is opposed to the reverence we owe God, according to Ezech. 28:2, "Thy heart is lifted up, and Thou hast said: I am God," and 1 Cor. 4:7, "What hast thou that thou hast not received? And if thou hast received, why dost thou glory, as if thou hadst not received it?" Or again when a man prefers to God the temporal good in which he glories: for this is forbidden (Jer. 9:23,24): "Let not the wise man glory in his wisdom, and let not the strong man glory in his strength, and let not the rich man glory in his riches. But let him that glorieth glory in this, that he understandeth and knoweth Me." Or again when a man prefers the testimony of man to God's; thus it is written in reproval of certain people (Jn. 12:43): "For they loved the glory of men more than the glory of God."

In another way vainglory may be contrary to charity, on the part of the one who glories, in that he refers his intention to glory as his last end: so that he directs even virtuous deeds thereto, and, in order to obtain it, forbears not from doing even that which is against God. In this way it is a mortal sin. Wherefore Augustine says (De Civ. Dei v, 14) that "this vice," namely the love of human praise, "is so hostile to a godly faith, if the heart desires glory more than it fears or loves God, that our Lord said (Jn. 5:44): How can you believe, who receive glory one from another, and the glory which is from God alone, you do not seek?"

If, however, the love of human glory, though it be vain, be not inconsistent with charity, neither as regards the matter gloried in, nor as to the intention of him that seeks glory, it is not a mortal but a venial sin.

Reply to Objection 1: No man, by sinning, merits eternal life: wherefore a virtuous deed loses its power to merit eternal life, if it be done for the sake of vainglory, even though that vainglory be not a mortal sin. On the other hand when a man loses the eternal reward simply through vainglory, and not merely in respect of one act, vainglory is a mortal sin.

Reply to Objection 2: Not every man that is desirous of vainglory, desires the excellence which belongs to God alone. For the glory due to God alone differs from the glory due to a virtuous or rich man.

Reply to Objection 3: Vainglory is stated to be a dangerous sin, not only on account of its gravity, but also because it is a disposition to grave sins, in so far as it renders man presumptuous and too self-confident: and so it gradually disposes a man to lose his inward goods.

Whether vainglory is a capital vice?

Objection 1: It seems that vainglory is not a capital vice. For a vice that always arises from another vice is seemingly not capital. But vainglory always arises from pride. Therefore vainglory is not a capital vice.

Objection 2: Further, honor would seem to take precedence of glory, for this is its effect. Now ambition which is inordinate desire of honor is not a capital vice. Neither therefore is the desire of vainglory.

Objection 3: Further, a capital vice has a certain prominence. But vainglory seems to have no prominence, neither as a sin, because it is not always a mortal sin, nor considered as an appetible good, since human glory is apparently a frail thing, and is something outside man himself. Therefore vainglory is not a capital vice.

On the contrary, Gregory (Moral. xxxi) numbers vainglory among the seven capital vices.

I answer that, The capital vices are enumerated in two ways. For some reckon pride as one of their number: and these do not place vainglory among the capital vices. Gregory, however (Moral. xxxi), reckons pride to be the queen of all the vices, and vainglory, which is the immediate offspring of pride, he reckons to be a capital vice: and not without reason. For pride, as we shall state farther on ([3374]Q[152], AA[1],2), denotes inordinate desire of excellence. But whatever good one may desire, one desires a certain perfection and excellence therefrom: wherefore the end of every vice is directed to the end of pride, so that this vice seems to exercise a kind of causality over the other vices, and ought not to be reckoned among the special sources of vice, known as the capital vices. Now among the goods that are the means whereby man acquires honor, glory seems to be the most conducive to that effect, inasmuch as it denotes the manifestation of a man's goodness: since good is naturally loved and honored by all. Wherefore, just as by the glory which is in God's sight man acquires honor in Divine things, so too by the glory which is in the sight of man he acquires excellence in human things. Hence on account of its close connection with excellence, which men desire above all, it follows that it is most desirable. And since many vices arise from the inordinate desire thereof, it follows that vainglory is a capital vice.

Reply to Objection 1: It is not impossible for a capital vice to arise from pride, since as stated above (in the body of the Article and [3375]FS, Q[84], A[2]) pride is the queen and mother of all the vices.

Reply to Objection 2: Praise and honor, as stated above [3376](A[2]), stand in relation to glory as the causes from which it proceeds, so that glory is compared to them as their end. For the reason why a man loves to be honored and praised is that he thinks thereby to acquire a certain renown in the knowledge of others.

Reply to Objection 3: Vainglory stands prominent under the aspect of desirability, for the reason given above, and this suffices for it to be reckoned a capital vice.

Nor is it always necessary for a capital vice to be a mortal sin; for mortal sin can arise from venial sin, inasmuch as venial sin can dispose man thereto.

Whether the daughters of vainglory are suitably reckoned to be disobedience, boastfulness, hypocrisy, contention, obstinacy, discord, and love of novelties?

Objection 1: It seems that the daughters of vainglory are unsuitably reckoned to be "disobedience, boastfulness, hypocrisy, contention, obstinacy, discord, and eccentricity [*Praesumptio novitatum, literally 'presumption of novelties']." For according to Gregory (Moral. xxiii) boastfulness is numbered among the species of pride. Now pride does not arise from vainglory, rather is it the other way about, as Gregory says (Moral. xxxi). Therefore boastfulness should not be reckoned among the daughters of vainglory.

Objection 2: Further, contention and discord seem to be the outcome chiefly of anger. But anger is a capital vice condivided with vainglory. Therefore it seems that they are not the daughters of vainglory.

Objection 3: Further, Chrysostom says (Hom. xix in Matth.) that vainglory is always evil, but especially in philanthropy, i.e. mercy. And yet this is nothing new, for it is an established custom among men. Therefore eccentricity should not be specially reckoned as a daughter of vainglory.

On the contrary, stands the authority of Gregory (Moral. xxxi), who there assigns the above daughters to vainglory.

I answer that, As stated above (Q[34], A[5]; Q[35], A[4]; [3377]FS, Q[84], AA[3],4), the vices which by their very nature are such as to be directed to the end of a certain capital vice, are called its daughters. Now the end of vainglory is the manifestation of one's own excellence, as stated above ([3378]AA[1],4): and to this end a man may tend in two ways. In one way directly, either by words, and this is boasting, or by deeds, and then if they be true and call for astonishment, it is love of novelties which men are wont to wonder at most; but if they be false, it is hypocrisy. In another way a man strives to make known his excellence by showing that he is not inferior to another, and this in four ways. First, as regards the intellect, and thus we have "obstinacy," by which a man is too much attached to his own opinion, being unwilling to believe one that is better. Secondly, as regards the will, and then we have "discord," whereby a man is unwilling to give up his own will, and agree with others. Thirdly, as regards "speech," and then we have "contention," whereby a man quarrels noisily with another. Fourthly as regards deeds, and this is "disobedience," whereby a man refuses to carry out the command of his superiors.

Reply to Objection 1: As stated above ([3379]Q[112], A[1], ad 2), boasting is reckoned a kind of pride, as regards its interior cause, which is arrogance: but outward boasting, according to Ethic. iv, is directed sometimes to gain, but more often to glory and honor, and thus it is the result of vainglory.

Reply to Objection 2: Anger is not the cause of discord and contention, except in conjunction with vainglory, in that a man thinks it a glorious thing for him not to yield to the will and words of others.

Reply to Objection 3: Vainglory is reproved in connection with almsdeeds on account of the lack of charity apparent in one who prefers vainglory to the good of his neighbor, seeing that he does the latter for the sake of the former. But a man is not reproved for presuming to give alms as though this were something novel.

OF PUSILLANIMITY (TWO ARTICLES)

We must now consider pusillanimity. Under this head there are two points of inquiry:

(1) Whether pusillanimity is a sin?

(2) To what virtue is it opposed?

Whether pusillanimity is a sin?

Objection 1: It seems that pusillanimity is not a sin. For every sin makes a man evil, just as every virtue makes a man good. But a fainthearted man is not evil, as the Philosopher says (Ethic. iv, 3). Therefore pusillanimity is not a sin.

Objection 2: Further, the Philosopher says (Ethic. iv, 3) that "a fainthearted man is especially one who is worthy of great goods, yet does not deem himself worthy of them." Now no one is worthy of great goods except the virtuous, since as the Philosopher again says (Ethic. iv, 3), "none but the virtuous are truly worthy of honor." Therefore the fainthearted are virtuous: and consequently pusillanimity is not a sin.

Objection 3: Further, "Pride is the beginning of all sin" (Ecclus. 10:15). But pusillanimity does not proceed from pride, since the proud man sets himself above what he is, while the fainthearted man withdraws from the things he is worthy of. Therefore pusillanimity is not a sin.

Objection 4: Further, the Philosopher says (Ethic. iv, 3) that "he who deems himself less worthy than he is, is said to be fainthearted." Now sometimes holy men deem themselves less worthy than they are; for instance, Moses and Jeremias, who were worthy of the office God chose them for, which they both humbly declined (Ex. 3:11; Jer. 1:6). Therefore pusillanimity is not a sin.

On the contrary, Nothing in human conduct is to be avoided save sin. Now pusillanimity is to be avoided: for it is written (Col. 3:21): "Fathers, provoke not your children to indignation, lest they be discouraged." Therefore pusillanimity is a sin.

I answer that, Whatever is contrary to a natural inclination is a sin, because it is contrary to a law of nature. Now everything has a natural inclination to accomplish an action that is commensurate with its power: as is evident in all natural things, whether animate or inanimate. Now just as presumption makes a man exceed what is proportionate to his power, by striving to do more than he can, so pusillanimity makes a man fall short of what is proportionate to his power, by refusing to tend to that which is commensurate thereto. Wherefore as presumption is a sin, so is pusillanimity. Hence it is that the servant who buried in the earth the money he had received from his master, and did not trade with it through faint-hearted fear, was punished by his master (Mat. 25; Lk. 19).

Reply to Objection 1: The Philosopher calls those evil who injure their neighbor: and accordingly the fainthearted is said not to be evil, because he injures no one, save accidentally, by omitting to do what might be profitable to others. For Gregory says (Pastoral. i) that if "they who demur to do good to their neighbor in preaching be judged strictly, without doubt their guilt is proportionate to the good they might have done had they been less retiring."

Reply to Objection 2: Nothing hinders a person who has a virtuous habit from sinning venially and without losing the habit, or mortally and with loss of the habit of gratuitous virtue. Hence it is possible for a man, by reason of the virtue which he has, to be worthy of doing certain great things that are worthy of great honor, and yet through not trying to make use of his virtue, he sins sometimes venially, sometimes mortally.

Again it may be replied that the fainthearted is worthy of great things in proportion to his ability for virtue, ability which he derives either from a good natural disposition, or from science, or from external fortune, and if he fails to use those things for virtue, he becomes guilty of pusillanimity.

Reply to Objection 3: Even pusillanimity may in some way be the result of pride: when, to wit, a man clings too much to his own opinion, whereby he thinks himself incompetent for those things for which he is competent. Hence it is written (Prov. 26:16): "The sluggard is wiser in his own conceit than seven men that speak sentences." For nothing hinders him from depreciating himself in some things, and having a high opinion of himself in others. Wherefore Gregory says (Pastoral. i) of Moses that "perchance he would have been proud, had he undertaken the leadership of a numerous people without misgiving: and again he would have been proud, had he refused to obey the command of his Creator."

Reply to Objection 4: Moses and Jeremias were worthy of the office to which they were appointed by God, but their worthiness was of Divine grace: yet they, considering the insufficiency of their own weakness, demurred; though not obstinately lest they should fall into pride.

Whether pusillanimity is opposed to magnanimity?

Objection 1: It seems that pusillanimity is not opposed to magnanimity. For the Philosopher says (Ethic., 3) that "the fainthearted man knows not himself: for he would desire the good things, of which he is worthy, if he knew himself." Now ignorance of self seems opposed to prudence. Therefore pusillanimity is opposed to prudence.

Objection 2: Further our Lord calls the servant wicked and slothful who through pusillanimity refused to make use of the money. Moreover the Philosopher says (Ethic. iv, 3) that the fainthearted seem to be slothful. Now sloth is opposed to solicitude, which is an act of prudence, as stated above ([3380]Q[47], A[9]). Therefore pusillanimity is not opposed to magnanimity.

Objection 3: Further, pusillanimity seems to proceed from inordinate fear: hence it is written (Is. 35:4): "Say to the fainthearted: Take courage and fear not." It also seems to proceed from inordinate anger, according to Col. 3:21, "Fathers, provoke not your children to indignation, lest they be discouraged." Now inordinate fear is opposed to fortitude, and inordinate anger to meekness. Therefore pusillanimity is not opposed to magnanimity.

Objection 4: Further, the vice that is in opposition to a particular virtue is the more grievous according as it is more unlike that virtue. Now pusillanimity is more unlike magnanimity than presumption is. Therefore if pusillanimity is opposed to magnanimity, it follows that it is a more grievous sin than presumption: yet this is contrary to the saying of Ecclus. 37:3, "O wicked presumption, whence camest thou?" Therefore pusillanimity is not opposed to magnanimity.

On the contrary, Pusillanimity and magnanimity differ as greatness and littleness of soul, as their very names denote. Now great and little are opposites. Therefore pusillanimity is opposed to magnanimity.

I answer that, Pusillanimity may be considered in three ways. First, in itself; and thus it is evident that by its very nature it is opposed to magnanimity, from which it differs as great and little differ in connection with the same subject. For just as the magnanimous man tends to great things out of greatness of soul, so the pusillanimous man shrinks from great things out of littleness of soul. Secondly, it may be considered in reference to its cause, which on the part of the intellect is ignorance of one's own qualification, and on the part of the appetite is the fear of failure in what one falsely deems to exceed one's ability. Thirdly, it may be considered in reference to its effect, which is to shrink from the great things of which one is worthy. But, as stated above ([3381]Q[132], A[2], ad 3), opposition between vice and virtue depends rather on their respective species than on their cause or effect. Hence pusillanimity is directly opposed to magnanimity.

Reply to Objection 1: This argument considers pusillanimity as proceeding from a cause in the intellect. Yet it cannot be said properly that it is opposed to prudence, even in respect of its cause: because ignorance of this kind does not proceed from indiscretion but from laziness in considering one's own ability, according to Ethic. iv, 3, or in accomplishing what is within one's power.

Reply to Objection 2: This argument considers pusillanimity from the point of view of its effect.

Reply to Objection 3: This argument considers the point of view of cause. Nor is the fear that causes pusillanimity always a fear of the dangers of death: wherefore it does not follow from this standpoint that pusillanimity is opposed to fortitude. As regards anger, if we consider it under the aspect of its proper movement, whereby a man is roused to take vengeance, it does not cause pusillanimity, which disheartens the soul; on the contrary, it takes it away. If, however, we consider the causes of anger, which are injuries inflicted whereby the soul of the man who suffers them is disheartened, it conduces to pusillanimity.

Reply to Objection 4: According to its proper species pusillanimity is a graver sin than presumption, since thereby a man withdraws from good things, which is a very great evil according to Ethic. iv. Presumption, however, is stated to be "wicked" on account of pride whence it proceeds.

OF MAGNIFICENCE (FOUR ARTICLES)

We must now consider magnificence and the vices opposed to it. With regard to magnificence there are four points of inquiry:

(1) Whether magnificence is a virtue?

(2) Whether it is a special virtue?

(3) What is its matter?

(4) Whether it is a part of fortitude?

Whether magnificence is a virtue?

Objection 1: It seems that magnificence is not a virtue. For whoever has one virtue has all the virtues, as stated above ([3382]FS, Q[65], A[1]). But one may have the other virtues without having magnificence: because the Philosopher says (Ethic. iv, 2) that "not every liberal man is magnificent." Therefore magnificence is not a virtue.

Objection 2: Further, moral virtue observes the mean, according to Ethic. ii, 6. But magnificence does not seemingly observe the mean, for it exceeds liberality in greatness. Now "great" and "little" are opposed to one another as extremes, the mean of which is "equal," as stated in Metaph. x. Hence magnificence observes not the mean, but the extreme. Therefore it is not a virtue.

Objection 3: Further, no virtue is opposed to a natural inclination, but on the contrary perfects it, as stated above ([3383]Q[108], A[2];[3384] Q[117], A[1], OBJ[1]). Now according to the Philosopher (Ethic. iv, 2) the "magnificent man is not lavish towards himself": and this is opposed to the natural inclination one has to look after oneself. Therefore magnificence is not a virtue.

Objection 4: Further, according to the Philosopher (Ethic. vi, 4) "act is right reason about things to be made." Now magnificence is about things to be made, as its very name denotes [*Magnificence= magna facere—i.e. to make great things]. Therefore it is an act rather than a virtue.

On the contrary, Human virtue is a participation of Divine power. But magnificence [virtutis] belongs to Divine power, according to Ps. 47:35: "His magnificence and His power is in the clouds." Therefore magnificence is a virtue.

I answer that, According to De Coelo i, 16, "we speak of virtue in relation to the extreme limit of a thing's power," not as regards the limit of deficiency, but as regards the limit of excess, the very nature of which denotes something great. Wherefore to do something great, whence magnificence takes its name, belongs properly to the very notion of virtue. Hence magnificence denotes a virtue.

Reply to Objection 1: Not every liberal man is magnificent as regards his actions, because he lacks the wherewithal to perform magnificent deeds. Nevertheless every liberal man has the habit of magnificence, either actually or in respect of a proximate disposition thereto, as explained above (Q[129], A[3], ad 2), as also ([3385]FS, Q[65], A[1]) when we were treating of the connection of virtues.

Reply to Objection 2: It is true that magnificence observes the extreme, if we consider the quantity of the thing done: yet it observes the mean, if we consider the rule of reason, which it neither falls short of nor exceeds, as we have also said of magnanimity ([3386]Q[129], A[3], ad 1).

Reply to Objection 3: It belongs to magnificence to do something great. But that which regards a man's person is little in comparison with that which regards Divine things, or even the affairs of the community at large. Wherefore the magnificent man does not intend principally to be lavish towards himself, not that he does not seek his own good, but because to do so is not something great. Yet if anything regarding himself admits of greatness, the magnificent man accomplishes it magnificently: for instance, things that are done once, such as a wedding, or the like; or things that are of a lasting nature; thus it belongs to a magnificent man to provide himself with a suitable dwelling, as stated in Ethic. iv.

Reply to Objection 4: As the Philosopher says (Ethic. vi, 5) "there must needs be a virtue of act," i.e. a moral virtue, whereby the appetite is inclined to make good use of the rule of act: and this is what magnificence does. Hence it is not an act but a virtue.

Whether magnificence is a special virtue?

Objection 1: It seems that magnificence is not a special virtue. For magnificence would seem to consist in doing something great. But it may belong to any virtue to do something great, if the virtue be great: as in the case of one who has a great virtue of temperance, for he does a great work of temperance. Therefore, magnificence is not a special virtue, but denotes a perfect degree of any virtue.

Objection 2: Further, seemingly that which tends to a thing is the same as that which does it. But it belongs to magnanimity to tend to something great, as stated above ([3387]Q[129], AA[1],2). Therefore it belongs to magnanimity likewise to do something great. Therefore magnificence is not a special virtue distinct from magnanimity.

Objection 3: Further, magnificence seems to belong to holiness, for it is written (Ex. 15:11): "Magnificent [Douay: 'glorious'] in holiness," and (Ps. 95:6): "Holiness and magnificence [Douay: 'Majesty'] in His sanctuary." Now holiness is the same as religion, as stated above ([3388]Q[81], A[8]). Therefore magnificence is apparently the same as religion. Therefore it is not a special virtue, distinct from the others.

On the contrary, The Philosopher reckons it with other special virtues (Ethic. ii, 7; iv 2).

I answer that, It belongs to magnificence to do [facere] something great, as its name implies [magnificence= magna facere—i.e. to make great things]. Now "facere" may be taken in two ways, in a strict sense, and in a broad sense. Strictly "facere" means to work something in external matter, for instance to make a house, or something of the kind; in a broad sense "facere" is employed to denote any action, whether it passes into external matter, as to burn or cut, or remain in the agent, as to understand or will.

Accordingly if magnificence be taken to denote the doing of something great, the doing [factio] being understood in the strict sense, it is then a special virtue. For the work done is produced by act: in the use of which it is possible to consider a special aspect of goodness, namely that the work produced [factum] by the act is something great, namely in quantity, value, or dignity, and this is what magnificence does. In this way magnificence is a special virtue.

If, on the other hand, magnificence take its name from doing something great, the doing [facere] being understood in a broad sense, it is not a special virtue.

Reply to Objection 1: It belongs to every perfect virtue to do something great in the genus of that virtue, if "doing" [facere] be taken in the broad sense, but not if it be taken strictly, for this is proper to magnificence.

Reply to Objection 2: It belongs to magnanimity not only to tend to something great, but also to do great works in all the virtues, either by making [faciendo], or by any kind of action, as stated in Ethic. iv, 3: yet so that magnanimity, in this respect, regards the sole aspect of great, while the other virtues which, if they be perfect, do something great, direct their principal intention, not to something great, but to that which is proper to each virtue: and the greatness of the thing done is sometimes consequent upon the greatness of the virtue.

On the other hand, it belongs to magnificence not only to do something great, "doing" [facere] being taken in the strict sense, but also to tend with the mind to the doing of great things. Hence Tully says (De Invent. Rhet. ii) that "magnificence is the discussing and administering of great and lofty undertakings, with a certain broad and noble purpose of mind, discussion" referring to the inward intention, and "administration" to the outward accomplishment. Wherefore just as magnanimity intends something great in every matter, it follows that magnificence does the same in every work that can be produced in external matter [factibili].

Reply to Objection 3: The intention of magnificence is the production of a great work. Now works done by men are directed to an end: and no end of human works is so great as the honor of God: wherefore magnificence does a great work especially in reference to the Divine honor. Wherefore the Philosopher says (Ethic. iv, 2) that "the most commendable expenditure is that which is directed to Divine sacrifices": and this is the chief object of magnificence. For this reason magnificence is connected with holiness, since its chief effect is directed to religion or holiness.

Whether the matter of magnificence is great expenditure?

Objection 1: It seems that the matter of magnificence is not great expenditure. For there are not two virtues about the same matter. But liberality is about expenditure, as stated above ([3389]Q[117], A[2]). Therefore magnificence is not about expenditure.

Objection 2: Further, "every magnificent man is liberal" (Ethic. iv, 2). But liberality is about gifts rather than about expenditure. Therefore magnificence also is not chiefly about expenditure, but about gifts.

Objection 3: Further, it belongs to magnificence to produce an external work. But not even great expenditure is always the means of producing an external work, for instance when one spends much in sending presents. Therefore expenditure is not the proper matter of magnificence.

Objection 4: Further, only the rich are capable of great expenditure. But the poor are able to possess all the virtues, since "the virtues do not necessarily require external fortune, but are sufficient for themselves," as Seneca says (De Ira i: De vita beata xvi). Therefore magnificence is not about great expenditure.

On the contrary, The Philosopher says (Ethic. iv, 2) that "magnificence does not extend, like liberality, to all transactions in money, but only to expensive ones, wherein it exceeds liberality in scale." Therefore it is only about great expenditure.

I answer that, As stated above [3390](A[2]), it belongs to magnificence to intend doing some great work. Now for the doing of a great work, proportionate expenditure is necessary, for great works cannot be produced without great expenditure. Hence it belongs to magnificence to spend much in order that some great work may be accomplished in becoming manner. Wherefore the Philosopher says (Ethic. iv, 2) that "a magnificent man will produce a more magnificent work with equal," i.e. proportionate, "expenditure." Now expenditure is the outlay of a sum of money; and a man may be hindered from making that outlay if he love money too much. Hence the matter of magnificence may be said to be both this expenditure itself, which the magnificent man uses to produce a great work, and also the very money which he employs in going to great expense, and as well as the love of money, which love the magnificent man moderates, lest he be hindered from spending much.

Reply to Objection 1: As stated above ([3391]Q[129], A[2]), those virtues that are about external things experience a certain difficulty arising from the genus itself of the thing about which the virtue is concerned, and another difficulty besides arising from the greatness of that same thing. Hence the need for two virtues, concerned about money and its use; namely, liberality, which regards the use of money in general, and magnificence, which regards that which is great in the use of money.

Reply to Objection 2: The use of money regards the liberal man in one way and the magnificent man in another. For it regards the liberal man, inasmuch as it proceeds from an ordinate affection in respect of money; wherefore all due use of money (such as gifts and expenditure), the obstacles to which are removed by a moderate love of money, belongs to liberality. But the use of money regards the magnificent man in relation to some great work which has to be produced, and this use is impossible without expenditure or outlay.

Reply to Objection 3: The magnificent man also makes gifts of presents, as stated in Ethic. iv, 2, but not under the aspect of gift, but rather under the aspect of expenditure directed to the production of some work, for instance in order to honor someone, or in order to do something which will reflect honor on the whole state: as when he brings to effect what the whole state is striving for.

Reply to Objection 4: The chief act of virtue is the inward choice, and a virtue may have this without outward fortune: so that even a poor man may be magnificent. But goods of fortune are requisite as instruments to the external acts of virtue: and in this way a poor man cannot accomplish the outward act of magnificence in things that are great simply. Perhaps, however, he may be able to do so in things that are great by comparison to some particular work; which, though little in itself, can nevertheless be done magnificently in proportion to its genus: for little and great are relative terms, as the Philosopher says (De Praedic. Cap. Ad aliquid.).

Whether magnificence is a part of fortitude?

Objection 1: It seems that magnificence is not a part of fortitude. For magnificence agrees in matter with liberality, as stated above [3392](A[3]). But liberality is a part, not of fortitude, but of justice. Therefore magnificence is not a part of fortitude.

Objection 2: Further, fortitude is about fear and darings. But magnificence seems to have nothing to do with fear, but only with expenditure, which is a kind of action. Therefore magnificence seems to pertain to justice, which is about actions, rather than to fortitude.

Objection 3: Further, the Philosopher says (Ethic. iv, 2) that "the magnificent man is like the man of science." Now science has more in common with prudence than with fortitude. Therefore magnificence should not be reckoned a part of fortitude.

On the contrary, Tully (De Invent. Rhet. ii) and Macrobius (De Somn. Scip. i) and Andronicus reckon magnificence to be a part of fortitude.

I answer that, Magnificence, in so far as it is a special virtue, cannot be reckoned a subjective part of fortitude, since it does not agree with this virtue in the point of matter: but it is reckoned a part thereof, as being annexed to it as secondary to principal virtue.

In order for a virtue to be annexed to a principal virtue, two things are necessary, as stated above ([3393]Q[80]). The one is that the secondary virtue agree with the principal, and the other is that in some respect it be exceeded thereby. Now magnificence agrees with fortitude in the point that as fortitude tends to something arduous and difficult, so also does magnificence: wherefore seemingly it is seated, like fortitude, in the irascible. Yet magnificence falls short of fortitude, in that the arduous thing to which fortitude tends derives its difficulty from a danger that threatens the person, whereas the arduous thing to which magnificence tends, derives its difficulty from the dispossession of one's property, which is of much less account than danger to one's person. Wherefore magnificence is accounted a part of fortitude.

Reply to Objection 1: Justice regards operations in themselves, as viewed under the aspect of something due: but liberality and magnificence regard sumptuary operations as related to the passions of the soul, albeit in different ways. For liberality regards expenditure in reference to the love and desire of money, which are passions of the concupiscible faculty, and do not hinder the liberal man from giving and spending: so that this virtue is in the concupiscible. On the other hand, magnificence regards expenditure in reference to hope, by attaining to the difficulty, not simply, as magnanimity does, but in a determinate matter, namely expenditure: wherefore magnificence, like magnanimity, is apparently in the irascible part.

Reply to Objection 2: Although magnificence does not agree with fortitude in matter, it agrees with it as the condition of its matter: since it tends to something difficult in the matter of expenditure, even as fortitude tends to something difficult in the matter of fear.

Reply to Objection 3: Magnificence directs the use of art to something great, as stated above and in the preceding Article. Now art is in the reason. Wherefore it belongs to the magnificent man to use his reason by observing proportion of expenditure to the work he has in hand. This is especially necessary on account of the greatness of both those things, since if he did not take careful thought, he would incur the risk of a great loss.

OF MEANNESS* (TWO ARTICLES)

[*"Parvificentia," or doing mean things, just as "magnificentia" is doing great things.]

We must now consider the vices opposed to magnificence: under which head there are two points of inquiry:

(1) Whether meanness is a vice?

(2) Of the vice opposed to it.

Whether meanness is a vice?

Objection 1: It seems that meanness is not a vice. For just as vice moderates great things, so does it moderate little things: wherefore both the liberal and the magnificent do little things. But magnificence is a virtue. Therefore likewise meanness is a virtue rather than a vice.

Objection 2: Further, the Philosopher says (Ethic. iv, 2) that "careful reckoning is mean." But careful reckoning is apparently praiseworthy, since man's good is to be in accordance with reason, as Dionysius states (Div. Nom. iv, 4). Therefore meanness is not a vice.

Objection 3: Further, the Philosopher says (Ethic. iv, 2) that "a mean man is loth to spend money." But this belongs to covetousness or illiberality. Therefore meanness is not a distinct vice from the others.

On the contrary, The Philosopher (Ethic. ii) accounts meanness a special vice opposed to magnificence.

I answer that, As stated above ([3394]FS, Q[1], A[3]; [3395]FS, Q[18], A[6]), moral acts take their species from their end, wherefore in many cases they are denominated from that end. Accordingly a man is said to be mean [parvificus] because he intends to do something little [parvum]. Now according to the Philosopher (De Praedic. Cap. Ad aliquid.) great and little are relative terms: and when we say that a mean man intends to do something little, this must be understood in relation to the kind of work he does. This may be little or great in two ways: in one way as regards the work itself to be done, in another as regards the expense. Accordingly the magnificent man intends principally the greatness of his work, and secondarily he intends the greatness of the expense, which he does not shirk, so that he may produce a great work. Wherefore the Philosopher says (Ethic. iv, 4) that "the magnificent man with equal expenditure will produce a more magnificent result." On the other hand, the mean man intends principally to spend little, wherefore the Philosopher says (Ethic. iv, 2) that "he seeks how he may spend least." As a result of this he intends to produce a little work, that is, he does not shrink from producing a little work, so long as he spends little. Wherefore the Philosopher says that "the mean man after going to great expense forfeits the good" of the magnificent work, "for the trifle" that he is unwilling to spend. Therefore it is evident that the mean man fails to observe the proportion that reason demands between expenditure and work. Now the essence of vice is that it consists in failing to do what is in accordance with reason. Hence it is manifest that meanness is a vice.

Reply to Objection 1: Virtue moderates little things, according to the rule of reason: from which rule the mean man declines, as stated in the Article. For he is called mean, not for moderating little things, but for declining from the rule of reason in moderating great or little things: hence meanness is a vice.

Reply to Objection 2: As the Philosopher says (Rhet. ii, 5), "fear makes us take counsel": wherefore a mean man is careful in his reckonings, because he has an inordinate fear of spending his goods, even in things of the least account. Hence this is not praiseworthy, but sinful and reprehensible, because then a man does not regulate his affections according to reason, but, on the contrary, makes use of his reason in pursuance of his inordinate affections.

Reply to Objection 3: Just as the magnificent man has this in common with the liberal man, that he spends his money readily and with pleasure, so too the mean man in common with the illiberal or covetous man is loth and slow to spend. Yet they differ in this, that illiberality regards ordinary expenditure, while meanness regards great expenditure, which is a more difficult accomplishment: wherefore meanness is less sinful than illiberality. Hence the Philosopher says (Ethic. iv, 2) that "although meanness and its contrary vice are sinful, they do not bring shame on a man, since neither do they harm one's neighbor, nor are they very disgraceful."

Whether there is a vice opposed to meanness?

Objection 1: It seems that there is no vice opposed to meanness. For great is opposed to little. Now, magnificence is not a vice, but a virtue. Therefore no vice is opposed to meanness.

Objection 2: Further, since meanness is a vice by deficiency, as stated above [3396](A[1]), it seems that if any vice is opposed to meanness, it would merely consist in excessive spending. But those who spend much, where they ought to spend little, spend little where they ought to spend much, according to Ethic. iv, 2, and thus they have something of meanness. Therefore there is not a vice opposed to meanness.

Objection 3: Further, moral acts take their species from their end, as stated above [3397](A[1]). Now those who spend excessively, do so in order to make a show of their wealth, as stated in Ethic. iv, 2. But this belongs to vainglory, which is opposed to magnanimity, as stated above (Q[131], A[2]). Therefore no vice is opposed to meanness.

On the contrary, stands the authority of the Philosopher who (Ethic. ii, 8; iv, 2) places magnificence as a mean between two opposite vices.

I answer that, Great is opposed to little. Also little and great are relative terms, as stated above [3398](A[1]). Now just as expenditure may be little in comparison with the work, so may it be great in comparison with the work in that it exceeds the proportion which reason requires to exist between expenditure and work. Hence it is manifest that the vice of meanness, whereby a man intends to spend less than his work is worth, and thus fails to observe due proportion between his expenditure and his work, has a vice opposed to it, whereby a man exceeds this same proportion, by spending more than is proportionate to his work. This vice is called in Greek {banausia}, so called from the Greek {baunos}, because, like the fire in the furnace, it consumes everything. It is also called {apyrokalia}, i.e. lacking good fire, since like fire it consumes all, but not for a good purpose. Hence in Latin it may be called "consumptio" [waste].

Reply to Objection 1: Magnificence is so called from the great work done, but not from the expenditure being in excess of the work: for this belongs to the vice which is opposed to meanness.

Reply to Objection 2: To the one same vice there is opposed the virtue which observes the mean, and a contrary vice. Accordingly, then, the vice of waste is opposed to meanness in that it exceeds in expenditure the value of the work, by spending much where it behooved to spend little. But it is opposed to magnificence on the part of the great work, which the magnificent man intends principally, in so far as when it behooves to spend much, it spends little or nothing.

Reply to Objection 3: Wastefulness is opposed to meanness by the very species of its act, since it exceeds the rule of reason, whereas meanness falls short of it. Yet nothing hinders this from being directed to the end of another vice, such as vainglory or any other.

OF PATIENCE (FIVE ARTICLES)

We must now consider patience. Under this head there are five points of inquiry:

(1) Whether patience is a virtue?

(2) Whether it is the greatest of the virtues?

(3) Whether it can be had without grace?

(4) Whether it is a part of fortitude?

(5) Whether it is the same as longanimity?

Whether patience is a virtue?

Objection 1: It seems that patience is not a virtue. For the virtues are most perfect in heaven, as Augustine says (De Trin. xiv). Yet patience is not there, since no evils have to be borne there, according to Is. 49:10 and Apoc. 7:16, "They shall not hunger nor thirst, neither shall the heat nor the sun strike them." Therefore patience is not a virtue.

Objection 2: Further, no virtue can be found in the wicked, since virtue it is "that makes its possessor good." Yet patience is sometimes found in wicked men; for instance, in the covetous, who bear many evils patiently that they may amass money, according to Eccles. 5:16, "All the days of his life he eateth in darkness, and in many cares, and in misery and in sorrow." Therefore patience is not a virtue.

Objection 3: Further, the fruits differ from the virtues, as stated above ([3399]FS, Q[70], A[1], ad 3). But patience is reckoned among the fruits (Gal. 5:22). Therefore patience is not a virtue.

On the contrary, Augustine says (De Patientia i): "The virtue of the soul that is called patience, is so great a gift of God, that we even preach the patience of Him who bestows it upon us."

I answer that, As stated above ([3400]Q[123], A[1]), the moral virtues are directed to the good, inasmuch as they safeguard the good of reason against the impulse of the passions. Now among the passions sorrow is strong to hinder the good of reason, according to 2 Cor. 7:10, "The sorrow of the world worketh death," and Ecclus. 30:25, "Sadness hath killed many, and there is no profit in it." Hence the necessity for a virtue to safeguard the good of reason against sorrow, lest reason give way to sorrow: and this patience does. Wherefore Augustine says (De Patientia ii): "A man's patience it is whereby he bears evil with an equal mind," i.e. without being disturbed by sorrow, "lest he abandon with an unequal mind the goods whereby he may advance to better things." It is therefore evident that patience is a virtue.

Reply to Objection 1: The moral virtues do not remain in heaven as regards the same act that they have on the way, in relation, namely, to the goods of the present life, which will not remain in heaven: but they will remain in their relation to the end, which will be in heaven. Thus justice will not be in heaven in relation to buying and selling and other matters pertaining to the present life, but it will remain in the point of being subject to God. In like manner the act of patience, in heaven, will not consist in bearing things, but in enjoying the goods to which we had aspired by suffering. Hence Augustine says (De Civ. Dei xiv) that "patience itself will not be in heaven, since there is no need for it except where evils have to be borne: yet that which we shall obtain by patience will be eternal."

Reply to Objection 2: As Augustine says (De Patientia ii; v) "properly speaking those are patient who would rather bear evils without inflicting them, than inflict them without bearing them. As for those who bear evils that they may inflict evil, their patience is neither marvelous nor praiseworthy, for it is no patience at all: we may marvel at their hardness of heart, but we must refuse to call them patient."

Reply to Objection 3: As stated above ([3401]FS, Q[11], A[1]), the very notion of fruit denotes pleasure. And works of virtue afford pleasure in themselves, as stated in Ethic. i, 8. Now the names of the virtues are wont to be applied to their acts. Wherefore patience as a habit is a virtue. but as to the pleasure which its act affords, it is reckoned a fruit, especially in this, that patience safeguards the mind from being overcome by sorrow.

Whether patience is the greatest of the virtues?

Objection 1: It seems that patience is the greatest of the virtues. For in every genus that which is perfect is the greatest. Now "patience hath a perfect work" (James 1:4). Therefore patience is the greatest of the virtues.

Objection 2: Further, all the virtues are directed to the good of the soul. Now this seems to belong chiefly to patience; for it is written (Lk. 21:19): "In your patience you shall possess your souls." Therefore patience is the greatest of the virtues.

Objection 3: Further, seemingly that which is the safeguard and cause of other things is greater than they are. But according to Gregory (Hom. xxxv in Evang.) "patience is the root and safeguard of all the virtues." Therefore patience is the greatest of the virtues.

On the contrary, It is not reckoned among the four virtues which Gregory (Moral. xxii) and Augustine (De Morib. Eccl. xv) call principal.

I answer that, Virtues by their very nature are directed to good. For it is virtue that "makes its possessor good, and renders the latter's work good" (Ethic. ii, 6). Hence it follows that a virtue's superiority and preponderance over other virtues is the greater according as it inclines man to good more effectively and directly. Now those virtues which are effective of good, incline a man more directly to good than those which are a check on the things which lead man away from good: and just as among those that are effective of good, the greater is that which establishes man in a greater good (thus faith, hope, and charity /are greater than prudence and justice); so too among those that are a check on things that withdraw man from good, the greater virtue is the one which is a check on a greater obstacle to good. But dangers of death, about which is fortitude, and pleasures of touch, with which temperance is concerned, withdraw man from good more than any kind of hardship, which is the object of patience. Therefore patience is not the greatest of the virtues, but falls short, not only of the theological virtues, and of prudence and justice which directly establish man in good, but also of fortitude and temperance which withdraw him from greater obstacles to good.

Reply to Objection 1: Patience is said to have a perfect work in bearing hardships: for these give rise first to sorrow, which is moderated by patience; secondly, to anger, which is moderated by meekness; thirdly, to hatred, which charity removes; fourthly, to unjust injury, which justice forbids. Now that which removes the principle is the most perfect.

Yet it does not follow, if patience be more perfect in this respect, that it is more perfect simply.

Reply to Objection 2: Possession denotes undisturbed ownership; wherefore man is said to possess his soul by patience, in so far as it removes by the root the passions that are evoked by hardships and disturb the soul.

Reply to Objection 3: Patience is said to be the root and safeguard of all the virtues, not as though it caused and preserved them directly, but merely because it removes their obstacles.

Whether it is possible to have patience without grace?

Objection 1: It seems that it is possible to have patience without grace. For the more his reason inclines to a thing, the more is it possible for the rational creature to accomplish it. Now it is more reasonable to suffer evil for the sake of good than for the sake of evil. Yet some suffer evil for evil's sake, by their own virtue and without the help of grace; for Augustine says (De Patientia iii) that "men endure many toils and sorrows for the sake of the things they love sinfully." Much more, therefore, is it possible for man, without the help of grace, to bear evil for the sake of good, and this is to be truly patient.

Objection 2: Further, some who are not in a state of grace have more abhorrence for sinful evils than for bodily evils: hence some heathens are related to have endured many hardships rather than betray their country or commit some other misdeed. Now this is to be truly patient. Therefore it seems that it is possible to have patience without the help of grace.

Objection 3: Further, it is quite evident that some go through much trouble and pain in order to regain health of the body. Now the health of the soul is not less desirable than bodily health. Therefore in like manner one may, without the help of grace, endure many evils for the health of the soul, and this is to be truly patient.

On the contrary, It is written (Ps. 61:6): "From Him," i.e. from God, "is my patience."

I answer that, As Augustine says (De Patientia iv), "the strength of desire helps a man to bear toil and pain: and no one willingly undertakes to bear what is painful, save for the sake of that which gives pleasure." The reason of this is because sorrow and pain are of themselves displeasing to the soul, wherefore it would never choose to suffer them for their own sake, but only for the sake of an end. Hence it follows that the good for the sake of which one is willing to endure evils, is more desired and loved than the good the privation of which causes the sorrow that we bear patiently. Now the fact that a man prefers the good of grace to all natural goods, the loss of which may cause sorrow, is to be referred to charity, which loves God above all things. Hence it is evident that patience, as a virtue, is caused by charity, according to 1 Cor. 13:4, "Charity is patient."

But it is manifest that it is impossible to have charity save through grace, according to Rom. 5:5, "The charity of God is poured forth in our hearts by the Holy Ghost Who is given to us." Therefore it is clearly impossible to have patience without the help of grace.

Reply to Objection 1: The inclination of reason would prevail in human nature in the state of integrity. But in corrupt nature the inclination of concupiscence prevails, because it is dominant in man. Hence man is more prone to bear evils for the sake of goods in which the concupiscence delights here and now, than to endure evils for the sake of goods to come, which are desired in accordance with reason: and yet it is this that pertains to true patience.

Reply to Objection 2: The good of a social virtue [*Cf. [3402]FS, Q[61], A[5]] is commensurate with human nature; and consequently the human will can tend thereto without the help of sanctifying grace, yet not without the help of God's grace [*Cf. [3403]FS, Q[109], A[2]]. On the other hand, the good of grace is supernatural, wherefore man cannot tend thereto by a natural virtue. Hence the comparison fails.

Reply to Objection 3: Even the endurance of those evils which a man bears for the sake of his body's health, proceeds from the love a man naturally has for his own flesh. Hence there is no comparison between this endurance and patience which proceeds from a supernatural love.

Whether patience is a part of fortitude?

Objection 1: It seems that patience is not a part of fortitude. For a thing is not part of itself. Now patience is apparently the same as fortitude: because, as stated above ([3404]Q[123], A[6]), the proper act of fortitude is to endure; and this belongs also to patience. For it is stated in the Liber Sententiarum Prosperi [*The quotation is from St. Gregory, Hom. xxxv in Evang.] that "patience consists in enduring evils inflicted by others." Therefore patience is not a part of fortitude.

Objection 2: Further, fortitude is about fear and daring, as stated above ([3405]Q[123], A[3]), and thus it is in the irascible. But patience seems to be about sorrow, and consequently would seem to be in the concupiscible. Therefore patience is not a part of fortitude but of temperance.

Objection 3: Further, the whole cannot be without its part. Therefore if patience is a part of fortitude, there can be no fortitude without patience. Yet sometimes a brave man does not endure evils patiently, but even attacks the person who inflicts the evil. Therefore patience is not a part of fortitude.

On the contrary, Tully (De Invent. Rhet. ii) reckons it a part of fortitude.

I answer that, Patience is a quasi-potential part of fortitude, because it is annexed thereto as secondary to principal virtue. For it belongs to patience "to suffer with an equal mind the evils inflicted by others," as Gregory says in a homily (xxxv in Evang.). Now of those evils that are inflicted by others, foremost and most difficult to endure are those that are connected with the danger of death, and about these evils fortitude is concerned. Hence it is clear that in this matter fortitude has the principal place, and that it lays claim to that which is principal in this matter. Wherefore patience is annexed to fortitude as secondary to principal virtue, for which reason Prosper calls patience brave (Sent. 811).

Reply to Objection 1: It belongs to fortitude to endure, not anything indeed, but that which is most difficult to endure, namely dangers of death: whereas it may pertain to patience to endure any kind of evil.

Reply to Objection 2: The act of fortitude consists not only in holding fast to good against the fear of future dangers, but also in not failing through sorrow or pain occasioned by things present; and it is in the latter respect that patience is akin to fortitude. Yet fortitude is chiefly about fear, which of itself evokes flight which fortitude avoids; while patience is chiefly about sorrow, for a man is said to be patient, not because he does not fly, but because he behaves in a praiseworthy manner by suffering [patiendo] things which hurt him here and now, in such a way as not to be inordinately saddened by them. Hence fortitude is properly in the irascible, while patience is in the concupiscible faculty.

Nor does this hinder patience from being a part of fortitude, because the annexing of virtue to virtue does not regard the subject, but the matter or the form. Nevertheless patience is not to be reckoned a part of temperance, although both are in the concupiscible, because temperance is only about those sorrows that are opposed to pleasures of touch, such as arise through abstinence from pleasures of food and sex: whereas patience is chiefly about sorrows inflicted by other persons. Moreover it belongs to temperance to control these sorrows besides their contrary pleasures: whereas it belongs to patience that a man forsake not the good of virtue on account of such like sorrows, however great they be.

Reply to Objection 3: It may be granted that patience in a certain respect is an integral part of justice, if we consider the fact that a man may patiently endure evils pertaining to dangers of death; and it is from this point of view that the objection argues. Nor is it inconsistent with patience that a man should, when necessary, rise up against the man who inflicts evils on him; for Chrysostom [*Homily v. in the Opus Imperfectum, falsely ascribed to St. John Chrysostom] says on Mat. 4:10, "Begone Satan," that "it is praiseworthy to be patient under our own wrongs, but to endure God's wrongs patiently is most wicked": and Augustine says in a letter to Marcellinus (Ep. cxxxviii) that "the precepts of patience are not opposed to the good of the commonwealth, since in order to ensure that good we fight against our enemies." But in so far as patience regards all kinds of evils, it is annexed to fortitude as secondary to principal virtue.

*Whether patience is the same as longanimity? [*Longsuffering. It is necessary to preserve the Latin word, on account of the comparison with magnanimity.]*

Objection 1: It seems that patience is the same as longanimity. For Augustine says (De Patientia i) that "we speak of patience in God, not as though any evil made Him suffer, but because He awaits the wicked, that they may be converted." Wherefore it is written (Ecclus. 5:4): "The Most High is a patient rewarder." Therefore it seems that patience is the same as longanimity.

Objection 2: Further, the same thing is not contrary to two things. But impatience is contrary to longanimity, whereby one awaits a delay: for one is said to be impatient of delay, as of other evils. Therefore it seems that patience is the same as longanimity.

Objection 3: Further, just as time is a circumstance of wrongs endured, so is place. But no virtue is distinct from patience on the score of place. Therefore in like manner longanimity which takes count of time, in so far as a person waits for a long time, is not distinct from patience.

Objection 4: On the contrary, a gloss [*Origen, Comment. in Ep. ad Rom. ii] on Rom. 2:4, "Or despisest thou the riches of His goodness, and patience, and longsuffering?" says: "It seems that longanimity differs from patience, because those who offend from weakness rather than of set purpose are said to be borne with longanimity: while those who take a deliberate delight in their crimes are said to be borne patiently."

I answer that, Just as by magnanimity a man has a mind to tend to great things, so by longanimity a man has a mind to tend to something a long way off. Wherefore as magnanimity regards hope, which tends to good, rather than daring, fear, or sorrow, which have evil as their object, so also does longanimity. Hence longanimity has more in common with magnanimity than with patience.

Nevertheless it may have something in common with patience, for two reasons. First, because patience, like fortitude, endures certain evils for the sake of good, and if this good is awaited shortly, endurance is easier: whereas if it be delayed a long time, it is more difficult. Secondly, because the very delay of the good we hope for, is of a nature to cause sorrow, according to Prov. 13:12, "Hope that is deferred afflicteth the soul." Hence there may be patience in bearing this trial, as in enduring any other sorrows. Accordingly longanimity and constancy are both comprised under patience, in so far as both the delay of the hoped for good (which regards longanimity) and the toil which man endures in persistently accomplishing a good work (which regards constancy) may be considered under the one aspect of grievous evil.

For this reason Tully (De Invent. Rhet. ii) in defining patience, says that "patience is the voluntary and prolonged endurance of arduous and difficult things for the sake of virtue or profit." By saying "arduous" he refers to constancy in good; when he says "difficult" he refers to the grievousness of evil, which is the proper object of patience; and by adding "continued" or "long lasting," he refers to longanimity, in so far as it has something in common with patience.

This suffices for the Replies to the First and Second Objections.

Reply to Objection 3: That which is a long way off as to place, though distant from us, is not simply distant from things in nature, as that which is a long way off in point of time: hence the comparison fails. Moreover, what is remote as to place offers no difficulty save in the point of time, since what is placed a long way from us is a long time coming to us.

We grant the fourth argument. We must observe, however, that the reason for the difference assigned by this gloss is that it is hard to bear with those who sin through weakness, merely because they persist a long time in evil, wherefore it is said that they are borne with longanimity: whereas the very fact of sinning through pride seems to be unendurable; for which reason those who sin through pride are stated to be borne with patience.

OF PERSEVERANCE (FOUR ARTICLES)

We must now consider perseverance and the vices opposed to it. Under the head of perseverance there are four points of inquiry:

(1) Whether perseverance is a virtue?

(2) Whether it is a part of fortitude?

(3) Of its relation to constancy;

(4) Whether it needs the help of grace?

Whether perseverance is a virtue?

Objection 1: It seems that perseverance is not a virtue. For, according to the Philosopher (Ethic. vii, 7), continency is greater than perseverance. But continency is not a virtue, as stated in Ethic. iv, 9. Therefore perseverance is not a virtue.

Objection 2: Further, "by virtue man lives aright," according to Augustine (De Lib. Arb. ii, 19). Now according to the same authority (De Persever. i), no one can be said to have perseverance while living, unless he persevere until death. Therefore perseverance is not a virtue.

Objection 3: Further, it is requisite of every virtue that one should persist unchangeably in the work of that virtue, as stated in Ethic. ii, 4. But this is what we understand by perseverance: for Tully says (De Invent. Rhet. ii) that "perseverance is the fixed and continued persistence in a well-considered purpose." Therefore perseverance is not a special virtue, but a condition of every virtue.

On the contrary, Andronicus [*Chrysippus: in De Affect.] says that "perseverance is a habit regarding things to which we ought to stand, and those to which we ought not to stand, as well as those that are indifferent." Now a habit that directs us to do something well, or to omit something, is a virtue. Therefore perseverance is a virtue.

I answer that, According to the Philosopher (Ethic. ii, 3), "virtue is about the difficult and the good"; and so where there is a special kind of difficulty or goodness, there is a special virtue. Now a virtuous deed may involve goodness or difficulty on two counts. First, from the act's very species, which is considered in respect of the proper object of that act: secondly, from the length of time, since to persist long in something difficult involves a special difficulty. Hence to persist long in something good until it is accomplished belongs to a special virtue.

Accordingly just as temperance and fortitude are special virtues, for the reason that the one moderates pleasures of touch (which is of itself a difficult thing), while the other moderates fear and daring in connection with dangers of death (which also is something difficult in itself), so perseverance is a special virtue, since it consists in enduring delays in the above or other virtuous deeds, so far as necessity requires.

Reply to Objection 1: The Philosopher is taking perseverance there, as it is found in one who bears those things which are most difficult to endure long. Now it is difficult to endure, not good, but evil. And evils that involve danger of death, for the most part are not endured for a long time, because often they soon pass away: wherefore it is not on this account that perseverance has its chief title to praise. Among other evils foremost are those which are opposed to pleasures of touch, because evils of this kind affect the necessaries of life: such are the lack of food and the like, which at times call for long endurance. Now it is not difficult to endure these things for a long time for one who grieves not much at them, nor delights much in the contrary goods; as in the case of the temperate man, in whom these passions are not violent. But they are most difficult to bear for one who is strongly affected by such things, through lacking the perfect virtue that moderates these passions. Wherefore if perseverance be taken in this sense it is not a perfect virtue, but something imperfect in the genus of virtue. On the other hand, if we take perseverance as denoting long persistence in any kind of difficult good, it is consistent in one who has even perfect virtue: for even if it is less difficult for him to persist, yet he persists in the more perfect good. Wherefore such like perseverance may be a virtue, because virtue derives perfection from the aspect of good rather than from the aspect of difficulty.

Reply to Objection 2: Sometimes a virtue and its act go by the same name: thus Augustine says (Tract. in Joan. lxxix): "Faith is to believe without seeing." Yet it is possible to have a habit of virtue without performing the act: thus a poor man has the habit of magnificence without exercising the act. Sometimes, however, a person who has the habit, begins to perform the act, yet does not accomplish it, for instance a builder begins to build a house, but does not complete it. Accordingly we must reply that the term "perseverance" is sometimes used to denote the habit whereby one chooses to persevere, sometimes for the act of persevering: and sometimes one who has the habit of perseverance chooses to persevere and begins to carry out his choice by persisting for a time, yet completes not the act, through not persisting to the end. Now the end is twofold: one is the end of the work, the other is the end of human life. Properly speaking it belongs to perseverance to persevere to the end of the virtuous work, for instance that a soldier persevere to the end of the fight, and the magnificent man until his work be accomplished. There are, however, some virtues whose acts must endure throughout the whole of life, such as faith, hope, and charity, since they regard the last end of the entire life of man. Wherefore as regards these which are the principal virtues, the act of perseverance is not accomplished until the end of life. It is in this sense that Augustine speaks of perseverance as denoting the consummate act of perseverance.

Reply to Objection 3: Unchangeable persistence may belong to a virtue in two ways. First, on account of the intended end that is proper to that virtue; and thus to persist in good for a long time until the end, belongs to a special virtue called perseverance, which intends this as its special end. Secondly, by reason of the relation of the habit to its subject: and thus unchangeable persistence is consequent upon every virtue, inasmuch as virtue is a "quality difficult to change."

Whether perseverance is a part of fortitude?

Objection 1: It seems that perseverance is not a part of fortitude. For, according to the Philosopher (Ethic. viii, 7), "perseverance is about pains of touch." But these belong to temperance. Therefore perseverance is a part of temperance rather than of fortitude.

Objection 2: Further, every part of a moral virtue is about certain passions which that virtue moderates. Now perseverance does not imply moderation of the passions: since the more violent the passions, the more praiseworthy is it to persevere in accordance with reason. Therefore it seems that perseverance is a part not of a moral virtue, but rather of prudence which perfects the reason.

Objection 3: Further, Augustine says (De Persev. i) that no one can lose perseverance; whereas one can lose the other virtues. Therefore perseverance is greater than all the other virtues. Now a principal virtue is greater than its part. Therefore perseverance is not a part of a virtue, but is itself a principal virtue.

On the contrary, Tully (De Invent. Rhet. ii) reckons perseverance as a part of fortitude.

I answer that, As stated above (Q[123], A[2]; [3406]FS, Q[61], AA[3],4), a principal virtue is one to which is principally ascribed something that lays claim to the praise of virtue, inasmuch as it practices it in connection with its own matter, wherein it is most difficult of accomplishment. In accordance with this it has been stated (Q[123], A[2]) that fortitude is a principal virtue, because it observes firmness in matters wherein it is most difficult to stand firm, namely in dangers of death. Wherefore it follows of necessity that every virtue which has a title to praise for the firm endurance of something difficult must be annexed to fortitude as secondary to principal virtue. Now the endurance of difficulty arising from delay in accomplishing a good work gives perseverance its claim to praise: nor is this so difficult as to endure dangers of death. Therefore perseverance is annexed to fortitude, as secondary to principal virtue.

Reply to Objection 1: The annexing of secondary to principal virtues depends not only on the matter [*Cf.[3407] Q[136], A[4], ad 2], but also on the mode, because in everything form is of more account than matter. Wherefore although, as to matter, perseverance seems to have more in common with temperance than with fortitude, yet, in mode, it has more in common with fortitude, in the point of standing firm against the difficulty arising from length of time.

Reply to Objection 2: The perseverance of which the Philosopher speaks (Ethic. vii, 4,7) does not moderate any passions, but consists merely in a certain firmness of reason and will. But perseverance, considered as a virtue, moderates certain passions, namely fear of weariness or failure on account of the delay. Hence this virtue, like fortitude, is in the irascible.

Reply to Objection 3: Augustine speaks there of perseverance, as denoting, not a virtuous habit, but a virtuous act sustained to the end, according to Mat. 24:13, "He that shall persevere to the end, he shall be saved." Hence it is incompatible with such like perseverance for it to be lost, since it would no longer endure to the end.

Whether constancy pertains to perseverance?

Objection 1: It seems that constancy does not pertain to perseverance. For constancy pertains to patience, as stated above (Q[137], A[5]): and patience differs from perseverance. Therefore constancy does not pertain to perseverance.

Objection 2: Further, "virtue is about the difficult and the good." Now it does not seem difficult to be constant in little works, but only in great deeds, which pertain to magnificence. Therefore constancy pertains to magnificence rather than to perseverance.

Objection 3: Further, if constancy pertained to perseverance, it would seem nowise to differ from it, since both denote a kind of unchangeableness. Yet they differ: for Macrobius (In Somn. Scip. i) condivides constancy with firmness by which he indicates perseverance, as stated above (Q[128] , A[6]). Therefore constancy does not pertain to perseverance.

On the contrary, One is said to be constant because one stands to a thing. Now it belongs to perseverance to stand to certain things, as appears from the definition given by Andronicus. Therefore constancy belongs to perseverance.

I answer that, Perseverance and constancy agree as to end, since it belongs to both to persist firmly in some good: but they differ as to those things which make it difficult to persist in good. Because the virtue of perseverance properly makes man persist firmly in good, against the difficulty that arises from the very continuance of the act: whereas constancy makes him persist firmly in good against difficulties arising from any other external hindrances. Hence perseverance takes precedence of constancy as a part of fortitude, because the difficulty arising from continuance of action is more intrinsic to the act of virtue than that which arises from external obstacles.

Reply to Objection 1: External obstacles to persistence in good are especially those which cause sorrow. Now patience is about sorrow, as stated above ([3408]Q[136], A[1]). Hence constancy agrees with perseverance as to end: while it agrees with patience as to those things which occasion difficulty. Now the end is of most account: wherefore constancy pertains to perseverance rather than to patience.

Reply to Objection 2: It is more difficult to persist in great deeds: yet in little or ordinary deeds, it is difficult to persist for any length of time, if not on account of the greatness of the deed which magnificence considers, yet from its very continuance which perseverance regards. Hence constancy may pertain to both.

Reply to Objection 3: Constancy pertains to perseverance in so far as it has something in common with it: but it is not the same thing in the point of their difference, as stated in the Article.

*Whether perseverance needs the help of grace? [*Cf. FS, Q[109], A[10]]*

Objection 1: It seems that perseverance does not need the help of grace. For perseverance is a virtue, as stated above [3409](A[1]). Now according to Tully (De Invent. Rhet. ii) virtue acts after the manner of nature. Therefore the sole inclination of virtue suffices for perseverance. Therefore this does not need the help of grace.

Objection 2: Further, the gift of Christ's grace is greater than the harm brought upon us by Adam, as appears from Rom. 5:15, seqq. Now "before sin man was so framed that he could persevere by means of what he had received," as Augustine says (De Correp. et Grat. xi). Much more therefore can man, after being repaired by the grace of Christ, persevere without the help of a further grace.

Objection 3: Further, sinful deeds are sometimes more difficult than deeds of virtue: hence it is said in the person of the wicked (Wis. 5:7): "We . . . have walked through hard ways." Now some persevere in sinful deeds without the help of another. Therefore man can also persevere in deeds of virtue without the help of grace.

On the contrary, Augustine says (De Persev. i): "We hold that perseverance is a gift of God, whereby we persevere unto the end, in Christ."

I answer that, As stated above (A[1], ad 2; A[2], ad 3), perseverance has a twofold signification. First, it denotes the habit of perseverance, considered as a virtue. In this way it needs the gift of habitual grace, even as the other infused virtues. Secondly, it may be taken to denote the act of perseverance enduring until death: and in this sense it needs not only habitual grace, but also the gratuitous help of God sustaining man in good until the end of life, as stated above ([3410]FS, Q[109], A[10]), when we were treating of grace. Because, since the free-will is changeable by its very nature, which changeableness is not taken away from it by the habitual grace bestowed in the present life, it is not in the power of the free-will, albeit repaired by grace, to abide unchangeably in good, though it is in its power to choose this: for it is often in our power to choose yet not to accomplish.

Reply to Objection 1: The virtue of perseverance, so far as it is concerned, inclines one to persevere: yet since it is a habit, and a habit is a thing one uses at will, it does not follow that a person who has the habit of virtue uses it unchangeably until death.

Reply to Objection 2: As Augustine says (De Correp. et Grat. xi), "it was given to the first man, not to persevere, but to be able to persevere of his free-will: because then no corruption was in human nature to make perseverance difficult. Now, however, by the grace of Christ, the predestined receive not only the possibility of persevering, but perseverance itself. Wherefore the first man whom no man threatened, of his own free-will rebelling against a threatening God, forfeited so great a happiness and so great a facility of avoiding sin: whereas these, although the world rage against their constancy, have persevered in faith."

Reply to Objection 3: Man is able by himself to fall into sin, but he cannot by himself arise from sin without the help of grace. Hence by falling into sin, so far as he is concerned man makes himself to be persevering in sin, unless he be delivered by God's grace. On the other hand, by doing good he does not make himself to be persevering in good, because he is able, by himself, to sin: wherefore he needs the help of grace for that end.

OF THE VICES OPPOSED TO PERSEVERANCE (TWO ARTICLES)

We must now consider the vices opposed to perseverance; under which head there are two points of inquiry:

(1) Of effeminacy;

(2) Of pertinacity.

Whether effeminacy is opposed to perseverance? [*Mollities, literally 'softness']*

Objection 1: It seems that effeminacy is not opposed to perseverance. For a gloss on 1 Cor. 6:9,10, "Nor adulterers, nor the effeminate, nor liers with mankind," expounds the text thus: "Effeminate—i.e. obscene, given to unnatural vice." But this is opposed to chastity. Therefore effeminacy is not a vice opposed to perseverance.

Objection 2: Further, the Philosopher says (Ethic. vii, 7) that "delicacy is a kind of effeminacy." But to be delicate seems akin to intemperance. Therefore effeminacy is not opposed to perseverance but to temperance.

Objection 3: Further, the Philosopher says (Ethic. vii, 7) that "the man who is fond of amusement is effeminate." Now immoderate fondness of amusement is opposed to {eutrapelia}, which is the virtue about pleasures of play, as stated in Ethic. iv, 8. Therefore effeminacy is not opposed to perseverance.

On the contrary, The Philosopher says (Ethic. vii, 7) that "the persevering man is opposed to the effeminate."

I answer that, As stated above ([3411]Q[137], AA[1],2), perseverance is deserving of praise because thereby a man does not forsake a good on account of long endurance of difficulties and toils: and it is directly opposed to this, seemingly, for a man to be ready to forsake a good on account of difficulties which he cannot endure.

This is what we understand by effeminacy, because a thing is said to be "soft" if it readily yields to the touch. Now a thing is not declared to be soft through yielding to a heavy blow, for walls yield to the battering-ram. Wherefore a man is not said to be effeminate if he yields to heavy blows. Hence the Philosopher says (Ethic. vii, 7) that "it is no wonder, if a person is overcome by strong and overwhelming pleasures or sorrows; but he is to be pardoned if he struggles against them." Now it is evident that fear of danger is more impelling than the desire of pleasure: wherefore Tully says (De Offic. i) under the heading "True magnanimity consists of two things: It is inconsistent for one who is not cast down by fear, to be defeated by lust, or who has proved himself unbeaten by toil, to yield to pleasure." Moreover, pleasure itself is a stronger motive of attraction than sorrow, for the lack of pleasure is a motive of withdrawal, since lack of pleasure is a pure privation. Wherefore, according to the Philosopher (Ethic. vii, 7), properly speaking an effeminate man is one who withdraws from good on account of sorrow caused by lack of pleasure, yielding as it were to a weak motion.

Reply to Objection 1: This effeminacy is caused in two ways. In one way, by custom: for where a man is accustomed to enjoy pleasures, it is more difficult for him to endure the lack of them. In another way, by natural disposition, because, to wit, his mind is less persevering through the frailty of his temperament. This is how women are compared to men, as the Philosopher says (Ethic. vii, 7): wherefore those who are passively sodomitical are said to be effeminate, being womanish themselves, as it were.

Reply to Objection 2: Toil is opposed to bodily pleasure: wherefore it is only toilsome things that are a hindrance to pleasures. Now the delicate are those who cannot endure toils, nor anything that diminishes pleasure. Hence it is written (Dt. 28:56): "The tender and delicate woman, that could not go upon the ground, nor set down her foot for . . . softness [Douay: 'niceness']." Thus delicacy is a kind of effeminacy. But properly speaking effeminacy regards lack of pleasures, while delicacy regards the cause that hinders pleasure, for instance toil or the like.

Reply to Objection 3: In play two things may be considered. In the first place there is the pleasure, and thus inordinate fondness of play is opposed to {eutrapelia}. Secondly, we may consider the relaxation or rest which is opposed to toil. Accordingly just as it belongs to effeminacy to be unable to endure toilsome things, so too it belongs thereto to desire play or any other relaxation inordinately.

Whether pertinacity is opposed to perseverance?

Objection 1: It seems that pertinacity is not opposed to perseverance. For Gregory says (Moral. xxxi) that pertinacity arises from vainglory. But vainglory is not opposed to perseverance but to magnanimity, as stated above ([3412]Q[132], A[2]). Therefore pertinacity is not opposed to perseverance.

Objection 2: Further, if it is opposed to perseverance, this is so either by excess or by deficiency. Now it is not opposed by excess: because the pertinacious also yield to certain pleasure and sorrow, since according to the Philosopher (Ethic. vii, 9) "they rejoice when they prevail, and grieve when their opinions are rejected." And if it be opposed by deficiency, it will be the same as effeminacy, which is clearly false. Therefore pertinacity is nowise opposed to perseverance.

Objection 3: Further, just as the persevering man persists in good against sorrow, so too do the continent and the temperate against pleasures, the brave against fear, and the meek against anger. But pertinacity is over-persistence in something. Therefore pertinacity is not opposed to perseverance more than to other virtues.

On the contrary, Tully says (De Invent. Rhet. ii) that pertinacity is to perseverance as superstition is to religion. But superstition is opposed to religion, as stated above ([3413]Q[92], A[1]). Therefore pertinacity is opposed to perseverance.

I answer that, As Isidore says (Etym. x) "a person is said to be pertinacious who holds on impudently, as being utterly tenacious." "Pervicacious" has the same meaning, for it signifies that a man "perseveres in his purpose until he is victorious: for the ancients called 'vicia' what we call victory." These the Philosopher (Ethic. vii, 9) calls {ischyrognomones}, that is "head-strong," or {idiognomones}, that is "self-opinionated," because they abide by their opinions more than they should; whereas the effeminate man does so less than he ought, and the persevering man, as he ought. Hence it is clear that perseverance is commended for observing the mean, while pertinacity is reproved for exceeding the mean, and effeminacy for falling short of it.

Reply to Objection 1: The reason why a man is too persistent in his own opinion, is that he wishes by this means to make a show of his own excellence: wherefore this is the result of vainglory as its cause. Now it has been stated above ([3414]Q[127], A[2], ad 1;[3415] Q[133], A[2]), that opposition of vices to virtues depends, not on their cause, but on their species.

Reply to Objection 2: The pertinacious man exceeds by persisting inordinately in something against many difficulties: yet he takes a certain pleasure in the end, just as the brave and the persevering man. Since, however, this pleasure is sinful, seeing that he desires it too much, and shuns the contrary pain, he is like the incontinent or effeminate man.

Reply to Objection 3: Although the other virtues persist against the onslaught of the passions, they are not commended for persisting in the same way as perseverance is. As to continence, its claim to praise seems to lie rather in overcoming pleasures. Hence pertinacity is directly opposed to perseverance.

OF THE GIFT OF FORTITUDE (TWO ARTICLES)

We must next consider the gift corresponding to fortitude, and this is the gift of fortitude. Under this head there are two points of inquiry:

(1) Whether fortitude is a gift?

(2) Which among the beatitudes and fruits correspond to it?

Whether fortitude is a gift?

Objection 1: It seems that fortitude is not a gift. For the virtues differ from the gifts: and fortitude is a virtue. Therefore it should not be reckoned a gift.

Objection 2: Further, the acts of the gift remain in heaven, as stated above ([3416]FS, Q[68], A[6]). But the act of fortitude does not remain in heaven: for Gregory says (Moral. i) that "fortitude encourages the fainthearted against hardships, which will be altogether absent from heaven." Therefore fortitude is not a gift.

Objection 3: Further, Augustine says (De Doctr. Christ. ii) that "it is a sign of fortitude to cut oneself adrift from all the deadly pleasures of the passing show." Now noisome pleasures and delights are the concern of temperance rather than of fortitude. Therefore it seems that fortitude is not the gift corresponding to the virtue of fortitude.

On the contrary, Fortitude is reckoned among the other gifts of the Holy Ghost (Is. 11:2).

I answer that, Fortitude denotes a certain firmness of mind, as stated above (Q[123], A[2]; [3417]FS, Q[61], A[3]): and this firmness of mind is required both in doing good and in enduring evil, especially with regard to goods or evils that are difficult. Now man, according to his proper and connatural mode, is able to have this firmness in both these respects, so as not to forsake the good on account of difficulties, whether in accomplishing an arduous work, or in enduring grievous evil. In this sense fortitude denotes a special or general virtue, as stated above (Q[123], A[2]).

Yet furthermore man's mind is moved by the Holy Ghost, in order that he may attain the end of each work begun, and avoid whatever perils may threaten. This surpasses human nature: for sometimes it is not in a man's power to attain the end of his work, or to avoid evils or dangers, since these may happen to overwhelm him in death. But the Holy Ghost works this in man, by bringing him to everlasting life, which is the end of all good deeds, and the release from all perils. A certain confidence of this is infused into the mind by the Holy Ghost Who expels any fear of the contrary. It is in this sense that fortitude is reckoned a gift of the Holy Ghost. For it has been stated above ([3418]FS, Q[68], AA[1],2) that the gifts regard the motion of the mind by the Holy Ghost.

Reply to Objection 1: Fortitude, as a virtue, perfects the mind in the endurance of all perils whatever; but it does not go so far as to give confidence of overcoming all dangers: this belongs to the fortitude that is a gift of the Holy Ghost.

Reply to Objection 2: The gifts have not the same acts in heaven as on the way: for they exercise acts in connection with the enjoyment of the end. Hence the act of fortitude there is to enjoy full security from toil and evil.

Reply to Objection 3: The gift of fortitude regards the virtue of fortitude not only because it consists in enduring dangers, but also inasmuch as it consists in accomplishing any difficult work. Wherefore the gift of fortitude is directed by the gift of counsel, which seems to be concerned chiefly with the greater goods.

Whether the fourth beatitude: "Blessed are they that hunger and thirst after justice," corresponds to the gift of fortitude?

Objection 1: It seems that the fourth beatitude, "Blessed are they that hunger and thirst after justice," does not correspond to the gift of fortitude. For the gift of piety and not the gift of fortitude corresponds to the virtue of justice. Now hungering and thirsting after justice pertain to the act of justice. Therefore this beatitude corresponds to the gift of piety rather than to the gift of fortitude.

Objection 2: Further, hunger and thirst after justice imply a desire for good. Now this belongs properly to charity, to which the gift of wisdom, and not the gift of fortitude, corresponds, as stated above ([3419]Q[45]). Therefore this beatitude corresponds, not to the gift of fortitude, but to the gift of wisdom.

Objection 3: Further, the fruits are consequent upon the beatitudes, since delight is essential to beatitude, according to Ethic. i, 8. Now the fruits, apparently, include none pertaining to fortitude. Therefore neither does any beatitude correspond to it.

On the contrary, Augustine says (De Serm. Dom. in Monte i): "Fortitude becomes the hungry and thirsty: since those who desire to enjoy true goods, and wish to avoid loving earthly and material things, must toil."

I answer that, As stated above ([3420]Q[121], A[2]), Augustine makes the beatitudes correspond to the gifts according to the order in which they are set forth, observing at the same time a certain fittingness between them. Wherefore he ascribes the fourth beatitude, concerning the hunger and thirst for justice, to the fourth gift, namely fortitude.

Yet there is a certain congruity between them, because, as stated (A[1]), fortitude is about difficult things. Now it is very difficult, not merely to do virtuous deeds, which receive the common designation of works of justice, but furthermore to do them with an unsatiable desire, which may be signified by hunger and thirst for justice.

Reply to Objection 1: As Chrysostom says (Hom. xv in Matth.), we may understand here not only particular, but also universal justice, which is related to all virtuous deeds according to Ethic. v, 1, wherein whatever is hard is the object of that fortitude which is a gift.

Reply to Objection 2: Charity is the root of all the virtues and gifts, as stated above (Q[23], A[8], ad 3; [3421]FS, Q[68], A[4], ad 3). Hence whatever pertains to fortitude may also be referred to charity.

Reply to Objection 3: There are two of the fruits which correspond sufficiently to the gift of fortitude: namely, patience, which regards the enduring of evils: and longanimity, which may regard the long delay and accomplishment of goods.

OF THE PRECEPTS OF FORTITUDE (TWO ARTICLES)

We must next consider the precepts of fortitude:

(1) The precepts of fortitude itself;

(2) The precepts of its parts.

Whether the precepts of fortitude are suitably given in the Divine Law?

Objection 1: It seems that the precepts of fortitude are not suitably given in the Divine Law. For the New Law is more perfect than the Old Law. Yet the Old Law contains precepts of fortitude (Dt. 20). Therefore precepts of fortitude should have been given in the New Law also.

Objection 2: Further, affirmative precepts are of greater import than negative precepts, since the affirmative include the negative, but not vice versa. Therefore it is unsuitable for the Divine Law to contain none but negative precepts in prohibition of fear.

Objection 3: Further, fortitude is one of the principal virtues, as stated above (Q[123], A[2]; [3422]FS, Q[61], A[2]). Now the precepts are directed to the virtues as to their end: wherefore they should be proportionate to them. Therefore the precepts of fortitude should have been placed among the precepts of the decalogue, which are the chief precepts of the Law.

On the contrary, stands Holy Writ which contains these precepts.

I answer that, Precepts of law are directed to the end intended by the lawgiver. Wherefore precepts of law must needs be framed in various ways according to the various ends intended by lawgivers, so that even in human affairs there are laws of democracies, others of kingdoms, and others again of tyrannical governments. Now the end of the Divine Law is that man may adhere to God: wherefore the Divine Law contains precepts both of fortitude and of the other virtues, with a view to directing the mind to God. For this reason it is written (Dt. 20:3,4): "Fear ye them not: because the Lord your God is in the midst of you, and will fight for you against your enemies."

As to human laws, they are directed to certain earthly goods, and among them we find precepts of fortitude according to the requirements of those goods.

Reply to Objection 1: The Old Testament contained temporal promises, while the promises of the New Testament are spiritual and eternal, according to Augustine (Contra Faust. iv). Hence in the Old Law there was need for the people to be taught how to fight, even in a bodily contest, in order to obtain an earthly possession. But in the New Testament men were to be taught how to come to the possession of eternal life by fighting spiritually, according to Mat. 11:12, "The kingdom of heaven suffereth violence, and the violent bear it away." Hence Peter commands (1 Pet. 5:8,9): "Your adversary the devil, as a roaring lion, goeth about, seeking whom he may devour: whom resist ye, strong in faith," as also James 4:7: "Resist the devil, and he will fly from you." Since, however, men while tending to spiritual goods may be withdrawn from them by corporal dangers, precepts of fortitude had to be given even in the New Law, that they might bravely endure temporal evils, according to Mat. 10:28, "Fear ye not them that kill the body."

Reply to Objection 2: The law gives general directions in its precepts. But the things that have to be done in cases of danger are not, like the things to be avoided, reducible to some common thing. Hence the precepts of fortitude are negative rather than affirmative.

Reply to Objection 3: As stated above ([3423]Q[122], A[1]), the precepts of the decalogue are placed in the Law, as first principles, which need to be known to all from the outset. Wherefore the precepts of the decalogue had to be chiefly about those acts of justice in which the notion of duty is manifest, and not about acts of fortitude, because it is not so evident that it is a duty for a person not to fear dangers of death.

Whether the precepts of the parts of fortitude are suitably given in the Divine Law?

Objection 1: It seems that the precept of the parts of fortitude are unsuitably given in the Divine Law. For just as patience and perseverance are parts of fortitude, so also are magnificence, magnanimity, and confidence, as stated above ([3424]Q[128]). Now we find precepts of patience in the Divine Law, as also of perseverance. Therefore there should also have been precepts of magnificence and magnanimity.

Objection 2: Further, patience is a very necessary virtue, since it is the guardian of the other virtues, as Gregory says (Hom. in Evang. xxxv). Now the other virtues are commanded absolutely. Therefore patience should not have been commanded merely, as Augustine says (De Serm. Dom. in Monte i), as to the preparedness of the mind.

Objection 3: Further, patience and perseverance are parts of fortitude, as stated above ([3425]Q[128];[3426] Q[136], A[4];[3427] Q[137], A[2]). Now the precepts of fortitude are not affirmative but only negative, as stated above (A[1], ad 2). Therefore the precepts of patience and perseverance should have been negative and not affirmative.

The contrary, however, follows from the way in which they are given by Holy Writ.

I answer that, The Divine Law instructs man perfectly about such things as are necessary for right living. Now in order to live aright man needs not only the principal virtues, but also the secondary and annexed virtues. Wherefore the Divine Law contains precepts not only about the acts of the principal virtues, but also about the acts of the secondary and annexed virtues.

Reply to Objection 1: Magnificence and magnanimity do not belong to the genus of fortitude, except by reason of a certain excellence of greatness which they regard in their respective matters. Now things pertaining to excellence come under the counsels of perfection rather than under precepts of obligation. Wherefore, there was need of counsels, rather than of precepts about magnificence and magnanimity. On the other hand, the hardships and toils of the present life pertain to patience and perseverance, not by reason of any greatness observable in them, but on account of the very nature of those virtues. Hence the need of precepts of patience and perseverance.

Reply to Objection 2: As stated above ([3428]Q[3], A[2]), although affirmative precepts are always binding, they are not binding for always, but according to place and time. Wherefore just as the affirmative precepts about the other virtues are to be understood as to the preparedness of the mind, in the sense that man be prepared to fulfil them when necessary, so too are the precepts of patience to be understood in the same way.

Reply to Objection 3: Fortitude, as distinct from patience and perseverance, is about the greatest dangers wherein one must proceed with caution; nor is it necessary to determine what is to be done in particular. On the other hand, patience and perseverance are about minor hardships and toils, wherefore there is less danger in determining, especially in general, what is to be done in such cases.

OF TEMPERANCE (EIGHT ARTICLES)

In the next place we must consider temperance: (1) Temperance itself; (2) its parts; (3) its precepts. With regard to temperance we must consider (1) temperance itself; (2) the contrary vices.

Under the first head there are eight points of inquiry:

(1) Whether temperance is a virtue?

(2) Whether it is a special virtue?

(3) Whether it is only about desires and pleasures?

(4) Whether it is only about pleasures of touch?

(5) Whether it is about pleasures of taste, as such, or only as a kind of touch?

(6) What is the rule of temperance?

(7) Whether it is a cardinal, or principal, virtue?

(8) Whether it is the greatest of virtues ?

Whether temperance is a virtue?

Objection 1: It seems that temperance is not a virtue. For no virtue goes against the inclination of nature, since "there is in us a natural aptitude for virtue," as stated in Ethic. ii, 1. Now temperance withdraws us from pleasures to which nature inclines, according to Ethic. ii, 3,8. Therefore temperance is not a virtue.

Objection 2: Further, virtues are connected with one another, as stated above ([3429]FS, Q[65], A[1]). But some people have temperance without having the other virtues: for we find many who are temperate, and yet covetous or timid. Therefore temperance is not a virtue.

Objection 3: Further, to every virtue there is a corresponding gift, as appears from what we have said above ([3430]FS, Q[68], A[4]). But seemingly no gift corresponds to temperance, since all the gifts have been already ascribed to the other virtues (QQ[8],9,19,45,52, 71,139). Therefore temperance is not a virtue.

On the contrary, Augustine says (Music. vi, 15): "Temperance is the name of a virtue."

I answer that, As stated above ([3431]FS, Q[55], A[3]), it is essential to virtue to incline man to good. Now the good of man is to be in accordance with reason, as Dionysius states (Div. Nom. iv). Hence human virtue is that which inclines man to something in accordance with reason. Now temperance evidently inclines man to this, since its very name implies moderation or temperateness, which reason causes. Therefore temperance is a virtue.

Reply to Objection 1: Nature inclines everything to whatever is becoming to it. Wherefore man naturally desires pleasures that are becoming to him. Since, however, man as such is a rational being, it follows that those pleasures are becoming to man which are in accordance with reason. From such pleasures temperance does not withdraw him, but from those which are contrary to reason. Wherefore it is clear that temperance is not contrary to the inclination of human nature, but is in accord with it. It is, however, contrary to the inclination of the animal nature that is not subject to reason.

Reply to Objection 2: The temperance which fulfils the conditions of perfect virtue is not without prudence, while this is lacking to all who are in sin. Hence those who lack other virtues, through being subject to the opposite vices, have not the temperance which is a virtue, though they do acts of temperance from a certain natural disposition, in so far as certain imperfect virtues are either natural to man, as stated above ([3432]FS, Q[63], A[1]), or acquired by habituation, which virtues, through lack of prudence, are not perfected by reason, as stated above ([3433]FS, Q[65], A[1]).

Reply to Objection 3: Temperance also has a corresponding gift, namely, fear, whereby man is withheld from the pleasures of the flesh, according to Ps. 118:120: "Pierce Thou my flesh with Thy fear." The gift of fear has for its principal object God, Whom it avoids offending, and in this respect it corresponds to the virtue of hope, as stated above ([3434]Q[19], A[9], ad 1). But it may have for its secondary object whatever a man shuns in order to avoid offending God. Now man stands in the greatest need of the fear of God in order to shun those things which are most seductive, and these are the matter of temperance: wherefore the gift of fear corresponds to temperance also.

Whether temperance is a special virtue?

Objection 1: It would seem that temperance is not a special virtue. For Augustine says (De Morib. Eccl. xv) that "it belongs to temperance to preserve one's integrity and freedom from corruption for God's sake." But this is common to every virtue. Therefore temperance is not a special virtue.

Objection 2: Further, Ambrose says (De Offic. i, 42) that "what we observe and seek most in temperance is tranquillity of soul." But this is common to every virtue. Therefore temperance is not a special virtue.

Objection 3: Further, Tully says (De Offic. i, 27) that "we cannot separate the beautiful from the virtuous," and that "whatever is just is beautiful." Now the beautiful is considered as proper to temperance, according to the same authority (Tully, De Offic. i, 27). Therefore temperance is not a special virtue.

On the contrary, The Philosopher (Ethic. ii, 7; iii, 10) reckons it a special virtue.

I answer that, It is customary in human speech to employ a common term in a restricted sense in order to designate the principal things to which that common term is applicable: thus the word "city" is used antonomastically* to designate Rome. [*Antonomasia is the figure of speech whereby we substitute the general for the individual term; e.g. The Philosopher for Aristotle]. Accordingly the word "temperance" has a twofold acceptation. First, in accordance with its common signification: and thus temperance is not a special but a general virtue, because the word "temperance" signifies a certain temperateness or moderation, which reason appoints to human operations and passions: and this is common to every moral virtue. Yet there is a logical difference between temperance and fortitude, even if we take them both as general virtues: since temperance withdraws man from things which seduce the appetite from obeying reason, while fortitude incites him to endure or withstand those things on account of which he forsakes the good of reason.

On the other hand, if we take temperance antonomastically, as withholding the appetite from those things which are most seductive to man, it is a special virtue, for thus it has, like fortitude, a special matter.

Reply to Objection 1: Man's appetite is corrupted chiefly by those things which seduce him into forsaking the rule of reason and Divine law. Wherefore integrity, which Augustine ascribes to temperance, can, like the latter, be taken in two ways: first, in a general sense, and secondly in a sense of excellence.

Reply to Objection 2: The things about which temperance is concerned have a most disturbing effect on the soul, for the reason that they are natural to man, as we shall state further on ([3435]AA[4],5). Hence tranquillity of soul is ascribed to temperance by way of excellence, although it is a common property of all the virtues.

Reply to Objection 3: Although beauty is becoming to every virtue, it is ascribed to temperance, by way of excellence, for two reasons. First, in respect of the generic notion of temperance, which consists in a certain moderate and fitting proportion, and this is what we understand by beauty, as attested by Dionysius (Div. Nom. iv). Secondly, because the things from which temperance withholds us, hold the lowest place in man, and are becoming to him by reason of his animal nature, as we shall state further on ([3436]AA[4],5; Q[142], A[4]), wherefore it is natural that such things should defile him. In consequence beauty is a foremost attribute of temperance which above all hinders man from being defiled. In like manner honesty [*Honesty must be taken here in its broad sense as synonymous with moral goodness, from the point of view of decorum] is a special attribute of temperance: for Isidore says (Etym. x): "An honest man is one who has no defilement, for honesty means an honorable state." This is most applicable to temperance, which withstands the vices that bring most dishonor on man, as we shall state further on (Q[142], A[4]).

Whether temperance is only about desires and pleasures?

Objection 1: It would seem that temperance is not only about desires and pleasures. For Tully says (De Invent. Rhet. ii, 54) that "temperance is reason's firm and moderate mastery of lust and other wanton emotions of the mind." Now all the passions of the soul are called emotions of the mind. Therefore it seems that temperance is not only about desires and pleasures.

Objection 2: Further, "Virtue is about the difficult and the good" [*Ethic. ii, 3]. Now it seems more difficult to temper fear, especially with regard to dangers of death, than to moderate desires and pleasures, which are despised on account of deadly pains and dangers, according to Augustine (QQ[83], qu. 36). Therefore it seems that the virtue of temperance is not chiefly about desires and pleasures.

Objection 3: Further, according to Ambrose (De Offic. i, 43) "the grace of moderation belongs to temperance": and Tully says (De Offic. ii, 27) that "it is the concern of temperance to calm all disturbances of the mind and to enforce moderation." Now moderation is needed, not only in desires and pleasures, but also in external acts and whatever pertains to the exterior. Therefore temperance is not only about desires and pleasures.

On the contrary, Isidore says (Etym.) [*The words quoted do not occur in the work referred to; Cf. his De Summo Bono xxxvii, xlii, and De Different. ii, 39]: that "it is temperance whereby lust and desire are kept under control."

I answer that, As stated above (Q[123], A[12]; Q[136], A[1]), it belongs to moral virtue to safeguard the good of reason against the passions that rebel against reason. Now the movement of the soul's passions is twofold, as stated above ([3437]FS, Q[23], A[2]), when we were treating of the passions: the one, whereby the sensitive appetite pursues sensible and bodily goods, the other whereby it flies from sensible and bodily evils.

The first of these movements of the sensitive appetite rebels against reason chiefly by lack of moderation. Because sensible and bodily goods, considered in their species, are not in opposition to reason, but are subject to it as instruments which reason employs in order to attain its proper end: and that they are opposed to reason is owing to the fact that the sensitive appetite fails to tend towards them in accord with the mode of reason. Hence it belongs properly to moral virtue to moderate those passions which denote a pursuit of the good.

On the other hand, the movement of the sensitive appetite in flying from sensible evil is mostly in opposition to reason, not through being immoderate, but chiefly in respect of its flight: because, when a man flies from sensible and bodily evils, which sometimes accompany the good of reason, the result is that he flies from the good of reason. Hence it belongs to moral virtue to make man while flying from evil to remain firm in the good of reason.

Accordingly, just as the virtue of fortitude, which by its very nature bestows firmness, is chiefly concerned with the passion, viz. fear, which regards flight from bodily evils, and consequently with daring, which attacks the objects of fear in the hope of attaining some good, so, too, temperance, which denotes a kind of moderation, is chiefly concerned with those passions that tend towards sensible goods, viz. desire and pleasure, and consequently with the sorrows that arise from the absence of those pleasures. For just as daring presupposes objects of fear, so too such like sorrow arises from the absence of the aforesaid pleasures.

Reply to Objection 1: As stated above ([3438]FS, Q[23], AA[1],2; [3439]FS, Q[25], A[1]), when we were treating of the passions, those passions which pertain to avoidance of evil, presuppose the passions pertaining to the pursuit of good; and the passions of the irascible presuppose the passions of the concupiscible. Hence, while temperance directly moderates the passions of the concupiscible which tend towards good, as a consequence, it moderates all the other passions, inasmuch as moderation of the passions that precede results in moderation of the passions that follow: since he that is not immoderate in desire is moderate in hope, and grieves moderately for the absence of the things he desires.

Reply to Objection 2: Desire denotes an impulse of the appetite towards the object of pleasure and this impulse needs control, which belongs to temperance. on the other hand fear denotes a withdrawal of the mind from certain evils, against which man needs firmness of mind, which fortitude bestows. Hence temperance is properly about desires, and fortitude about fears.

Reply to Objection 3: External acts proceed from the internal passions of the soul: wherefore their moderation depends on the moderation of the internal passions.

Whether temperance is only about desires and pleasures of touch?

Objection 1: It would seem that temperance is not only about desires and pleasures of touch. For Augustine says (De Morib. Eccl. xix) that "the function of temperance is to control and quell the desires which draw us to the things which withdraw us from the laws of God and from the fruit of His goodness"; and a little further on he adds that "it is the duty of temperance to spurn all bodily allurements and popular praise." Now we are withdrawn from God's laws not only by the desire for pleasures of touch, but also by the desire for pleasures of the other senses, for these, too, belong to the bodily allurements, and again by the desire for riches or for worldly glory: wherefore it is written (1 Tim. 6:10). "Desire [*'Cupiditas,' which is the Douay version following the Greek {philargyria} renders 'desire of money'] is the root of all evils." Therefore temperance is not only about desires of pleasures of touch.

Objection 2: Further, the Philosopher says (Ethic. iv, 3) that "one who is worthy of small things and deems himself worthy of them is temperate, but he is not magnificent." Now honors, whether small or great, of which he is speaking there, are an object of pleasure, not of touch, but in the soul's apprehension. Therefore temperance is not only about desires for pleasures of touch.

Objection 3: Further, things that are of the same genus would seem to pertain to the matter of a particular virtue under one same aspect. Now all pleasures of sense are apparently of the same genus. Therefore they all equally belong to the matter of temperance.

Objection 4: Further, spiritual pleasures are greater than the pleasures of the body, as stated above ([3440]FS, Q[31], A[5]) in the treatise on the passions. Now sometimes men forsake God's laws and the state of virtue through desire for spiritual pleasures, for instance, through curiosity in matters of knowledge: wherefore the devil promised man knowledge, saying (Gn. 3:5): "Ye shall be as Gods, knowing good and evil." Therefore temperance is not only about pleasures of touch.

Objection 5: Further, if pleasures of touch were the proper matter of temperance, it would follow that temperance is about all pleasures of touch. But it is not about all, for instance, about those which occur in games. Therefore pleasures of touch are not the proper matter of temperance.

On the contrary, The Philosopher says (Ethic. iii, 10) that "temperance is properly about desires of pleasures of touch."

I answer that, As stated above [3441](A[3]), temperance is about desires and pleasures in the same way as fortitude is about fear and daring. Now fortitude is about fear and daring with respect to the greatest evils whereby nature itself is dissolved; and such are dangers of death. Wherefore in like manner temperance must needs be about desires for the greatest pleasures. And since pleasure results from a natural operation, it is so much the greater according as it results from a more natural operation. Now to animals the most natural operations are those which preserve the nature of the individual by means of meat and drink, and the nature of the species by the union of the sexes. Hence temperance is properly about pleasures of meat and drink and sexual pleasures. Now these pleasures result from the sense of touch. Wherefore it follows that temperance is about pleasures of touch.

Reply to Objection 1: In the passage quoted Augustine apparently takes temperance, not as a special virtue having a determinate matter, but as concerned with the moderation of reason, in any matter whatever: and this is a general condition of every virtue. However, we may also reply that if a man can control the greatest pleasures, much more can he control lesser ones. Wherefore it belongs chiefly and properly to temperance to moderate desires and pleasures of touch, and secondarily other pleasures.

Reply to Objection 2: The Philosopher takes temperance as denoting moderation in external things, when, to wit, a man tends to that which is proportionate to him, but not as denoting moderation in the soul's emotions, which pertains to the virtue of temperance.

Reply to Objection 3: The pleasures of the other senses play a different part in man and in other animals. For in other animals pleasures do not result from the other senses save in relation to sensibles of touch: thus the lion is pleased to see the stag, or to hear its voice, in relation to his food. On the other hand man derives pleasure from the other senses, not only for this reason, but also on account of the becomingness of the sensible object. Wherefore temperance is about the pleasures of the other senses, in relation to pleasures of touch, not principally but consequently: while in so far as the sensible objects of the other senses are pleasant on account of their becomingness, as when a man is pleased at a well-harmonized sound, this pleasure has nothing to do with the preservation of nature. Hence these passions are not of such importance that temperance can be referred to them antonomastically.

Reply to Objection 4: Although spiritual pleasures are by their nature greater than bodily pleasures, they are not so perceptible to the senses, and consequently they do not so strongly affect the sensitive appetite, against whose impulse the good of reason is safeguarded by moral virtue. We may also reply that spiritual pleasures, strictly speaking, are in accordance with reason, wherefore they need no control, save accidentally, in so far as one spiritual pleasure is a hindrance to another greater and more binding.

Reply to Objection 5: Not all pleasures of touch regard the preservation of nature, and consequently it does not follow that temperance is about all pleasures of touch.

Whether temperance is about the pleasures proper to the taste?

Objection 1: It would seem that temperance is about pleasures proper to the taste. For pleasures of the taste result from food and drink, which are more necessary to man's life than sexual pleasures, which regard the touch. But according to what has been said [3442](A[4]), temperance is about pleasures in things that are necessary to human life. Therefore temperance is about pleasures proper to the taste rather than about those proper to the touch.

Objection 2: Further, temperance is about the passions rather than about things themselves. Now, according to De Anima ii, 3, "the touch is the sense of food," as regards the very substance of the food, whereas "savor" which is the proper object of the taste, is "the pleasing quality of the food." Therefore temperance is about the taste rather than about the touch.

Objection 3: Further, according to Ethic. vii, 4,7: "temperance and intemperance are about the same things, and so are continence and incontinence, perseverance, and effeminacy," to which delicacy pertains. Now delicacy seems to regard the delight taken in savors which are the object of the taste. Therefore temperance is about pleasures proper to the taste.

On the contrary, The Philosopher says (Ethic. iii, 10) that "seemingly temperance and intemperance have little if anything to do with the taste."

I answer that, As stated above [3443](A[4]), temperance is about the greatest pleasures, which chiefly regard the preservation of human life either in the species or in the individual. In these matters certain things are to be considered as principal and others as secondary. The principal thing is the use itself of the necessary means, of the woman who is necessary for the preservation of the species, or of food and drink which are necessary for the preservation of the individual: while the very use of these necessary things has a certain essential pleasure annexed thereto.

In regard to either use we consider as secondary whatever makes the use more pleasurable, such as beauty and adornment in woman, and a pleasing savor and likewise odor in food. Hence temperance is chiefly about the pleasure of touch, that results essentially from the use of these necessary things, which use is in all cases attained by the touch. Secondarily, however, temperance and intemperance are about pleasures of the taste, smell, or sight, inasmuch as the sensible objects of these senses conduce to the pleasurable use of the necessary things that have relation to the touch. But since the taste is more akin to the touch than the other senses are, it follows that temperance is more about the taste than about the other senses.

Reply to Objection 1: The use of food and the pleasure that essentially results therefrom pertain to the touch. Hence the Philosopher says (De Anima ii, 3) that "touch is the sense of food, for food is hot or cold, wet or dry." To the taste belongs the discernment of savors, which make the food pleasant to eat, in so far as they are signs of its being suitable for nourishment.

Reply to Objection 2: The pleasure resulting from savor is additional, so to speak, whereas the pleasure of touch results essentially from the use of food and drink.

Reply to Objection 3: Delicacy regards principally the substance of the food, but secondarily it regards its delicious savor and the way in which it is served.

Whether the rule of temperance depends on the need of the present life?

Objection 1: It would seem that the rule of temperance does not depend on the needs of the present life. For higher things are not regulated according to lower. Now, as temperance is a virtue of the soul, it is above the needs of the body. Therefore the rule of temperance does not depend on the needs of the body.

Objection 2: Further, whoever exceeds a rule sins. Therefore if the needs of the body were the rule of temperance, it would be a sin against temperance to indulge in any other pleasure than those required by nature, which is content with very little. But this would seem unreasonable.

Objection 3: Further, no one sins in observing a rule. Therefore if the need of the body were the rule of temperance, there would be no sin in using any pleasure for the needs of the body, for instance, for the sake of health. But this is apparently false. Therefore the need of the body is not the rule of temperance.

On the contrary, Augustine says (De Morib. Eccl. xxi): "In both Testaments the temperate man finds confirmation of the rule forbidding him to love the things of this life, or to deem any of them desirable for its own sake, and commanding him to avail himself of those things with the moderation of a user not the attachment of a lover, in so far as they are requisite for the needs of this life and of his station."

I answer that, As stated above [3444](A[1]; Q[109], A[2]; Q[123], A[12]), the good of moral virtue consists chiefly in the order of reason: because "man's good is to be in accord with reason," as Dionysius asserts (Div. Nom. iv). Now the principal order of reason is that by which it directs certain things towards their end, and the good of reason consists chiefly in this order; since good has the aspect of end, and the end is the rule of whatever is directed to the end. Now all the pleasurable objects that are at man's disposal, are directed to some necessity of this life as to their end. Wherefore temperance takes the need of this life, as the rule of the pleasurable objects of which it makes use, and uses them only for as much as the need of this life requires.

Reply to Objection 1: As stated above, the need of this life is regarded as a rule in so far as it is an end. Now it must be observed that sometimes the end of the worker differs from the end of the work, thus it is clear that the end of building is a house, whereas sometimes the end of the builder is profit. Accordingly the end and rule of temperance itself is happiness; while the end and rule of the thing it makes use of is the need of human life, to which whatever is useful for life is subordinate.

Reply to Objection 2: The need of human life may be taken in two ways. First, it may be taken in the sense in which we apply the term "necessary" to that without which a thing cannot be at all; thus food is necessary to an animal. Secondly, it may be taken for something without which a thing cannot be becomingly. Now temperance regards not only the former of these needs, but also the latter. Wherefore the Philosopher says (Ethic. iii, 11) that "the temperate man desires pleasant things for the sake of health, or for the sake of a sound condition of body." Other things that are not necessary for this purpose may be divided into two classes. For some are a hindrance to health and a sound condition of body; and these temperance makes not use of whatever, for this would be a sin against temperance. But others are not a hindrance to those things, and these temperance uses moderately, according to the demands of place and time, and in keeping with those among whom one dwells. Hence the Philosopher (Ethic. iii, 11) says that the "temperate man also desires other pleasant things," those namely that are not necessary for health or a sound condition of body, "so long as they are not prejudicial to these things."

Reply to Objection 3: As stated (ad 2), temperance regards need according to the requirements of life, and this depends not only on the requirements of the body, but also on the requirements of external things, such as riches and station, and more still on the requirements of good conduct. Hence the Philosopher adds (Ethic. iii, 11) that "the temperate man makes use of pleasant things provided that not only they be not prejudicial to health and a sound bodily condition, but also that they be not inconsistent with good," i.e. good conduct, nor "beyond his substance," i.e. his means. And Augustine says (De Morib. Eccl. xxi) that the "temperate man considers the need" not only "of this life" but also "of his station."

Whether temperance is a cardinal virtue?

Objection 1: It would seem that temperance is not a cardinal virtue. For the good of moral virtue depends on reason. But temperance is about those things that are furthest removed from reason, namely about pleasures common to us and the lower animals, as stated in Ethic. iii, 10. Therefore temperance, seemingly, is not a principal virtue.

Objection 2: Further, the greater the impetus the more difficult is it to control. Now anger, which is controlled by meekness, seems to be more impetuous than desire, which is controlled by temperance. For it is written (Prov. 27:4): "Anger hath no mercy, nor fury when it breaketh forth; and who can bear the violence [impetum] of one provoked?" Therefore meekness is a principal virtue rather than temperance.

Objection 3: Further, hope as a movement of the soul takes precedence of desire and concupiscence, as stated above ([3445]FS, Q[25], A[4]). But humility controls the presumption of immoderate hope. Therefore, seemingly, humility is a principal virtue rather than temperance which controls concupiscence.

On the contrary, Gregory reckons temperance among the principal virtues (Moral. ii, 49).

I answer that, As stated above (Q[123], A[11]; Q[61], A[3]), a principal or cardinal virtue is so called because it has a foremost claim to praise on account of one of those things that are requisite for the notion of virtue in general. Now moderation, which is requisite in every virtue, deserves praise principally in pleasures of touch, with which temperance is concerned, both because these pleasures are most natural to us, so that it is more difficult to abstain from them, and to control the desire for them, and because their objects are more necessary to the present life, as stated above [3446](A[4]). For this reason temperance is reckoned a principal or cardinal virtue.

Reply to Objection 1: The longer the range of its operation, the greater is the agent's power [virtus] shown to be: wherefore the very fact that the reason is able to moderate desires and pleasures that are furthest removed from it, proves the greatness of reason's power. This is how temperance comes to be a principal virtue.

Reply to Objection 2: The impetuousness of anger is caused by an accident, for instance, a painful hurt; wherefore it soon passes, although its impetus be great. On the other hand, the impetuousness of the desire for pleasures of touch proceeds from a natural cause, wherefore it is more lasting and more general, and consequently its control regards a more principal virtue.

Reply to Objection 3: The object of hope is higher than the object of desire, wherefore hope is accounted the principal passion in the irascible. But the objects of desires and pleasures of touch move the appetite with greater force, since they are more natural. Therefore temperance, which appoints the mean in such things, is a principal virtue.

Whether temperance is the greatest of the virtues?

Objection 1: It would seem that temperance is the greatest of the virtues. For Ambrose says (De Offic. i, 43) that "what we observe and seek most in temperance is the safeguarding of what is honorable, and the regard for what is beautiful." Now virtue deserves praise for being honorable and beautiful. Therefore temperance is the greatest of the virtues.

Objection 2: Further, the more difficult the deed the greater the virtue. Now it is more difficult to control desires and pleasures of touch than to regulate external actions, the former pertaining to temperance and the latter to justice. Therefore temperance is a greater virtue than justice.

Objection 3: Further, seemingly the more general a thing is, the more necessary and the better it is. Now fortitude is about dangers of death which occur less frequently than pleasures of touch, for these occur every day; so that temperance is in more general use than fortitude. Therefore temperance is a more excellent virtue than fortitude.

On the contrary, The Philosopher says (Rhet. i, 9) that the "greatest virtues are those which are most profitable to others, for which reason we give the greatest honor to the brave and the just."

I answer that, As the Philosopher declares (Ethic. i, 2) "the good of the many is more of the godlike than the good of the individual," wherefore the more a virtue regards the good of the many, the better it is. Now justice and fortitude regard the good of the many more than temperance does, since justice regards the relations between one man and another, while fortitude regards dangers of battle which are endured for the common weal: whereas temperance moderates only the desires and pleasures which affect man himself. Hence it is evident that justice and fortitude are more excellent virtues than temperance: while prudence and the theological virtues are more excellent still.

Reply to Objection 1: Honor and beauty are especially ascribed to temperance, not on account of the excellence of the good proper to temperance, but on account of the disgrace of the contrary evil from which it withdraws us, by moderating the pleasures common to us and the lower animals.

Reply to Objection 2: Since virtue is about the difficult and the good, the excellence of a virtue is considered more under the aspect of good, wherein justice excels, than under the aspect of difficult, wherein temperance excels.

Reply to Objection 3: That which is general because it regards the many conduces more to the excellence of goodness than that which is general because it occurs frequently: fortitude excels in the former way, temperance in the latter. Hence fortitude is greater simply, although in some respects temperance may be described as greater not only than fortitude but also than justice.

OF THE VICES OPPOSED TO TEMPERANCE (FOUR ARTICLES)

We must now consider the vices opposed to temperance. Under this head there are four points of inquiry:

(1) Whether insensibility is a sin?

(2) Whether intemperance is a childish sin?

(3) Of the comparison between intemperance and timidity;

(4) Whether intemperance is the most disgraceful of vices?

Whether insensibility is a vice?

Objection 1: It would seem that insensibility is not a vice. For those are called insensible who are deficient with regard to pleasures of touch. Now seemingly it is praiseworthy and virtuous to be altogether deficient in such matters: for it is written (Dan. 10:2,3): "In those days Daniel mourned the days of three weeks, I ate no desirable bread, and neither flesh nor wine entered my mouth, neither was I anointed with ointment." Therefore insensibility is not a sin.

Objection 2: Further, "man's good is to be in accord with reason," according to Dionysius (Div. Nom. iv). Now abstinence from all pleasures of touch is most conducive to man's progress in the good of reason: for it is written (Dan. 1:17) that "to the children" who took pulse for their food (Dan. 1:12), "God gave knowledge, and understanding in every book and wisdom." Therefore insensibility, which rejects these pleasures altogether, is not sinful.

Objection 3: Further, that which is a very effective means of avoiding sin would seem not to be sinful. Now the most effective remedy in avoiding sin is to shun pleasures, and this pertains to insensibility. For the Philosopher says (Ethic. ii, 9) that "if we deny ourselves pleasures we are less liable to sin." Therefore there is nothing vicious in insensibility.

On the contrary, Nothing save vice is opposed to virtue. Now insensibility is opposed to the virtue of temperance according to the Philosopher (Ethic. ii, 7; iii, 11). Therefore insensibility is a vice.

I answer that, Whatever is contrary to the natural order is vicious. Now nature has introduced pleasure into the operations that are necessary for man's life. Wherefore the natural order requires that man should make use of these pleasures, in so far as they are necessary for man's well-being, as regards the preservation either of the individual or of the species. Accordingly, if anyone were to reject pleasure to the extent of omitting things that are necessary for nature's preservation, he would sin, as acting counter to the order of nature. And this pertains to the vice of insensibility.

It must, however, be observed that it is sometimes praiseworthy, and even necessary for the sake of an end, to abstain from such pleasures as result from these operations. Thus, for the sake of the body's health, certain persons refrain from pleasures of meat, drink, and sex; as also for the fulfilment of certain engagements: thus athletes and soldiers have to deny themselves many pleasures, in order to fulfil their respective duties. In like manner penitents, in order to recover health of soul, have recourse to abstinence from pleasures, as a kind of diet, and those who are desirous of giving themselves up to contemplation and Divine things need much to refrain from carnal things. Nor do any of these things pertain to the vice of insensibility, because they are in accord with right reason.

Reply to Objection 1: Daniel abstained thus from pleasures, not through any horror of pleasure as though it were evil in itself, but for some praiseworthy end, in order, namely, to adapt himself to the heights of contemplation by abstaining from pleasures of the body. Hence the text goes on to tell of the revelation that he received immediately afterwards.

Reply to Objection 2: Since man cannot use his reason without his sensitive powers. which need a bodily organ. as stated in the [3447]FP, Q[84], AA[7],8, man needs to sustain his body in order that he may use his reason. Now the body is sustained by means of operations that afford pleasure: wherefore the good of reason cannot be in a man if he abstain from all pleasures. Yet this need for using pleasures of the body will be greater or less, according as man needs more or less the powers of his body in accomplishing the act of reason. Wherefore it is commendable for those who undertake the duty of giving themselves to contemplation, and of imparting to others a spiritual good, by a kind of spiritual procreation, as it were, to abstain from many pleasures, but not for those who are in duty bound to bodily occupations and carnal procreation.

Reply to Objection 3: In order to avoid sin, pleasure must be shunned, not altogether, but so that it is not sought more than necessity requires.

Whether intemperance is a childish sin?

Objection 1: It would seem that intemperance is not a childish sin. For Jerome in commenting on Mat. 18:3, "Unless you be converted, and become as little children," says that "a child persists not in anger, is unmindful of injuries, takes no pleasure in seeing a beautiful woman," all of which is contrary to intemperance. Therefore intemperance is not a childish sin.

Objection 2: Further, children have none but natural desires. Now "in respect of natural desires few sin by intemperance," according to the Philosopher (Ethic. iii, 11). Therefore intemperance is not a childish sin.

Objection 3: Further, children should be fostered and nourished: whereas concupiscence and pleasure, about which intemperance is concerned, are always to be thwarted and uprooted, according to Col. 3:5, "Mortify . . . your members upon the earth, which are . . . concupiscence" [*Vulg.: 'your members which are upon the earth, fornication . . . concupiscence'], etc. Therefore intemperance is not a childish sin.

On the contrary, The Philosopher says (Ethic. iii, 12) that "we apply the term intemperance* to childish faults." [*{Akolasia} which Aristotle refers to {kolazo} to punish, so that its original sense would be 'impunity' or 'unrestraint.']

I answer that, A thing is said to be childish for two reasons. First, because it is becoming to children, and the Philosopher does not mean that the sin of intemperance is childish in this sense. Secondly. by way of likeness, and it is in this sense that sins of intemperance are said to be childish. For the sin of intemperance is one of unchecked concupiscence, which is likened to a child in three ways. First, as rewards that which they both desire, for like a child concupiscence desires something disgraceful. This is because in human affairs a thing is beautiful according as it harmonizes with reason. Wherefore Tully says (De Offic. i, 27) under the heading "Comeliness is twofold," that "the beautiful is that which is in keeping with man's excellence in so far as his nature differs from other animals." Now a child does not attend to the order of reason; and in like manner "concupiscence does not listen to reason," according to Ethic. vii, 6. Secondly, they are alike as to the result. For a child, if left to his own will, becomes more self-willed: hence it is written (Ecclus. 30:8): "A horse not broken becometh stubborn, and a child left to himself will become headstrong." So, too, concupiscence, if indulged, gathers strength: wherefore Augustine says (Confess. viii, 5): "Lust served became a custom, and custom not resisted became necessity." Thirdly, as to the remedy which is applied to both. For a child is corrected by being restrained; hence it is written (Prov. 23:13,14): "Withhold not correction from a child . . . Thou shalt beat him with a rod, and deliver his soul from Hell." In like manner by resisting concupiscence we moderate it according to the demands of virtue. Augustine indicates this when he says (Music. vi, 11) that if the mind be lifted up to spiritual things, and remain fixed "thereon, the impulse of custom," i.e. carnal concupiscence, "is broken, and being suppressed is gradually weakened: for it was stronger when we followed it, and though not wholly destroyed, it is certainly less strong when we curb it." Hence the Philosopher says (Ethic. iii, 12) that "as a child ought to live according to the direction of his tutor, so ought the concupiscible to accord with reason."

Reply to Objection 1: This argument takes the term "childish" as denoting what is observed in children. It is not in this sense that the sin of intemperance is said to be childish, but by way of likeness, as stated above.

Reply to Objection 2: A desire may be said to be natural in two ways. First, with regard to its genus, and thus temperance and intemperance are about natural desires, since they are about desires of food and sex, which are directed to the preservation of nature. Secondly, a desire may be called natural with regard to the species of the thing that nature requires for its own preservation; and in this way it does not happen often that one sins in the matter of natural desires, for nature requires only that which supplies its need, and there is no sin in desiring this, save only where it is desired in excess as to quantity. This is the only way in which sin can occur with regard to natural desires, according to the Philosopher (Ethic. iii, 11).

There are other things in respect of which sins frequently occur, and these are certain incentives to desire devised by human curiosity [*Cf. Q[167]], such as the nice [curiosa] preparation of food, or the adornment of women. And though children do not affect these things much, yet intemperance is called a childish sin for the reason given above.

Reply to Objection 3: That which regards nature should be nourished and fostered in children, but that which pertains to the lack of reason in them should not be fostered, but corrected, as stated above.

Whether cowardice is a greater vice than intemperance? [*Cf. Q[125]]*

Objection 1: It would seem that cowardice is a greater vice than intemperance. For a vice deserves reproach through being opposed to the good of virtue. Now cowardice is opposed to fortitude, which is a more excellent virtue than temperance, as stated above [3448](A[2]; Q[141], A[8]). Therefore cowardice is a greater vice than intemperance.

Objection 2: Further, the greater the difficulty to be surmounted, the less is a man to be reproached for failure, wherefore the Philosopher says (Ethic. vii, 7) that "it is no wonder, in fact it is pardonable, if a man is mastered by strong and overwhelming pleasures or pains." Now seemingly it is more difficult to control pleasures than other passions; hence it is stated in Ethic. ii, 3, that "it is more difficult to contend against pleasure than against anger, which would seem to be stronger than fear." Therefore intemperance, which is overcome by pleasure, is a less grievous sin than cowardice, which is overcome by fear.

Objection 3: Further, it is essential to sin that it be voluntary. Now cowardice is more voluntary than intemperance, since no man desires to be intemperate, whereas some desire to avoid dangers of death, which pertains to cowardice. Therefore cowardice is a more grievous sin than intemperance.

On the contrary, The Philosopher says (Ethic. iii, 12) that "intemperance seems more akin to voluntary action than cowardice." Therefore it is more sinful.

I answer that, one may be compared with another in two ways. First, with regard to the matter or object; secondly, on the part of the man who sins: and in both ways intemperance is a more grievous sin than cowardice.

First, as regards the matter. For cowardice shuns dangers of death, to avoid which the principal motive is the necessity of preserving life. On the other hand, intemperance is about pleasures, the desire of which is not so necessary for the preservation of life, because, as stated above (A[2], ad 2), intemperance is more about certain annexed pleasures or desires than about natural desires or pleasures. Now the more necessary the motive of sin the less grievous the sin. Wherefore intemperance is a more grievous vice than cowardice, on the part of the object or motive matter.

In like manner again, on the part of the man who sins, and this for three reasons. First, because the more sound-minded a man is, the more grievous his sin, wherefore sins are not imputed to those who are demented. Now grave fear and sorrow, especially in dangers of death, stun the human mind, but not so pleasure which is the motive of intemperance. Secondly, because the more voluntary a sin the graver it is. Now intemperance has more of the voluntary in it than cowardice has, and this for two reasons. The first is because actions done through fear have their origin in the compulsion of an external agent, so that they are not simply voluntary but mixed, as stated in Ethic. iii, 1, whereas actions done for the sake of pleasure are simply voluntary. The second reason is because the actions of an intemperate man are more voluntary individually and less voluntary generically. For no one would wish to be intemperate, yet man is enticed by individual pleasures which make of him an intemperate man. Hence the most effective remedy against intemperance is not to dwell on the consideration of singulars. It is the other way about in matters relating to cowardice: because the particular action that imposes itself on a man is less voluntary, for instance to cast aside his shield, and the like, whereas the general purpose is more voluntary, for instance to save himself by flight. Now that which is more voluntary in the particular circumstances in which the act takes place, is simply more voluntary. Wherefore intemperance, being simply more voluntary than cowardice, is a greater vice. Thirdly, because it is easier to find a remedy for intemperance than for cowardice, since pleasures of food and sex, which are the matter of intemperance, are of everyday occurrence, and it is possible for man without danger by frequent practice in their regard to become temperate; whereas dangers of death are of rare occurrence, and it is more dangerous for man to encounter them frequently in order to cease being a coward.

Reply to Objection 1: The excellence of fortitude in comparison with temperance may be considered from two standpoints. First, with regard to the end, which has the aspect of good: because fortitude is directed to the common good more than temperance is. And from this point of view cowardice has a certain precedence over intemperance, since by cowardice some people forsake the defense of the common good. Secondly, with regard to the difficulty, because it is more difficult to endure dangers of death than to refrain from any pleasures whatever: and from this point of view there is no need for cowardice to take precedence of intemperance. For just as it is a greater strength that does not succumb to a stronger force, so on the other hand to be overcome by a stronger force is proof of a lesser vice, and to succumb to a weaker force, is the proof of a greater vice.

Reply to Objection 2: Love of self-preservation, for the sake of which one shuns perils of death, is much more connatural than any pleasures whatever of food and sex which are directed to the preservation of life. Hence it is more difficult to overcome the fear of dangers of death, than the desire of pleasure in matters of food and sex: although the latter is more difficult to resist than anger, sorrow, and fear, occasioned by certain other evils.

Reply to Objection 3: The voluntary, in cowardice, depends rather on a general than on a particular consideration: wherefore in such cases we have the voluntary not simply but in a restricted sense.

Whether intemperance is the most disgraceful of sins?

Objection 1: It would seem that intemperance is not the most disgraceful of sins. As honor is due to virtue so is disgrace due to sin. Now some sins are more grievous than intemperance: for instance murder, blasphemy, and the like. Therefore intemperance is not the most disgraceful of sins.

Objection 2: Further, those sins which are the more common are seemingly less disgraceful, since men are less ashamed of them. Now sins of intemperance are most common, because they are about things connected with the common use of human life, and in which many happen to sin. Therefore sins of intemperance do not seem to be most disgraceful.

Objection 3: Further, the Philosopher says (Ethic. vii, 6) temperance and intemperance are about human desires and pleasures. Now certain desires and pleasures are more shameful than human desires and pleasures; such are brutal pleasures and those caused by disease as the Philosopher states (Ethic. vii, 5). Therefore intemperance is not the most disgraceful of sins.

On the contrary, The Philosopher says (Ethic. iii, 10) that "intemperance is justly more deserving of reproach than other vices."

I answer that, Disgrace is seemingly opposed to honor and glory. Now honor is due to excellence, as stated above ([3449]Q[103], A[1]), and glory denotes clarity ([3450]Q[103], A[1], ad 3). Accordingly intemperance is most disgraceful for two reasons. First, because it is most repugnant to human excellence, since it is about pleasures common to us and the lower animals, as stated above ([3451]Q[141], AA[2],3). Wherefore it is written (Ps. 48:21): "Man, when he was in honor, did not understand: he hath been compared to senseless beasts, and made like to them." Secondly, because it is most repugnant to man's clarity or beauty; inasmuch as the pleasures which are the matter of intemperance dim the light of reason from which all the clarity and beauty of virtue arises: wherefore these pleasures are described as being most slavish.

Reply to Objection 1: As Gregory says [*Moral. xxxiii. 12], "the sins of the flesh," which are comprised under the head of intemperance, although less culpable, are more disgraceful. The reason is that culpability is measured by inordinateness in respect of the end, while disgrace regards shamefulness, which depends chiefly on the unbecomingness of the sin in respect of the sinner.

Reply to Objection 2: The commonness of a sin diminishes the shamefulness and disgrace of a sin in the opinion of men, but not as regards the nature of the vices themselves.

Reply to Objection 3: When we say that intemperance is most disgraceful, we mean in comparison with human vices, those, namely, that are connected with human passions which to a certain extent are in conformity with human nature. But those vices which exceed the mode of human nature are still more disgraceful. Nevertheless such vices are apparently reducible to the genus of intemperance, by way of excess: for instance, if a man delight in eating human flesh, or in committing the unnatural vice.

OF THE PARTS OF TEMPERANCE, IN GENERAL (ONE ARTICLE)

We must now consider the parts of temperance: we shall consider these same parts (1) in general; (2) each of them in particular.

Whether the parts of temperance are rightly assigned?

Objection 1: It would seem that Tully (De Invent. Rhet. ii, 54) unbecomingly assigns the parts of temperance, when he asserts them to be "continence, mildness, and modesty." For continence is reckoned to be distinct from virtue (Ethic. vii, 1): whereas temperance is comprised under virtue. Therefore continence is not a part of temperance.

Objection 2: Further, mildness seemingly softens hatred or anger. But temperance is not about these things, but about pleasures of touch, as stated above ([3452]Q[141], A[4]). Therefore mildness is not a part of temperance.

Objection 3: Further, modesty concerns external action, wherefore the Apostle says (Phil. 4:5): "Let your modesty be known to all men." Now external actions are the matter of justice, as stated above ([3453]Q[58], A[8]). Therefore modesty is a part of justice rather than of temperance.

Objection 4: Further, Macrobius (In Somn. Scip. i, 8) reckons many more parts of temperance: for he says that "temperance results in modesty, shamefacedness, abstinence, chastity, honesty, moderation, lowliness, sobriety, purity." Andronicus also says [*De Affectibus] that "the companions of temperance are gravity, continence, humility, simplicity, refinement, method, contentment." [*'Per-se-sufficientiam' which could be rendered 'self-sufficiency,' but for the fact that this is taken in a bad sense. See[3454] Q[169], A[1].] Therefore it seems that Tully insufficiently reckoned the parts of temperance.

I answer that, As stated above (QQ[48],128), a cardinal virtue may have three kinds of parts, namely integral, subjective, and potential. The integral parts of a virtue are the conditions the concurrence of which are necessary for virtue: and in this respect there are two integral parts of temperance, "shamefacedness," whereby one recoils from the disgrace that is contrary to temperance, and "honesty," whereby one loves the beauty of temperance. For, as stated above ([3455]Q[141], A[2], ad 3), temperance more than any other virtue lays claim to a certain comeliness, and the vices of intemperance excel others in disgrace.

The subjective parts of a virtue are its species: and the species of a virtue have to be differentiated according to the difference of matter or object. Now temperance is about pleasures of touch, which are of two kinds. For some are directed to nourishment: and in these as regards meat, there is "abstinence," and as regards drink properly there is "sobriety." Other pleasures are directed to the power of procreation, and in these as regards the principal pleasure of the act itself of procreation, there is "chastity," and as to the pleasures incidental to the act, resulting, for instance, from kissing, touching, or fondling, we have "purity."

The potential parts of a principal virtue are called secondary virtues: for while the principal virtue observes the mode in some principal matter, these observe the mode in some other matter wherein moderation is not so difficult. Now it belongs to temperance to moderate pleasures of touch, which are most difficult to moderate. Wherefore any virtue that is effective of moderation in some matter or other, and restrains the appetite in its impulse towards something, may be reckoned a part of temperance, as a virtue annexed thereto.

This happens in three ways: first, in the inward movements of the soul; secondly, in the outward movements and actions of the body; thirdly, in outward things. Now besides the movement of concupiscence, which temperance moderates and restrains, we find in the soul three movements towards a particular object. In the first place there is the movement of the will when stirred by the impulse of passion: and this movement is restrained by "continence," the effect of which is that, although a man suffer immoderate concupiscences, his will does not succumb to them. Another inward movement towards something is the movement of hope, and of the resultant daring, and this is moderated or restrained by "humility." The third movement is that of anger, which tends towards revenge, and this is restrained by "meekness" or "mildness."

With regard to bodily movements and actions, moderation and restraint is the effect of "modesty," which, according to Andronicus, has three parts. The first of these enables one to discern what to do and what not to do, and to observe the right order, and to persevere in what we do: this he assigns to "method." The second is that a man observe decorum in what he does, and this he ascribes to "refinement." The third has to do with the conversation or any other intercourse between a man and his friends, and this is called "gravity."

With regard to external things, a twofold moderation has to be observed. First, we must not desire too many, and to this Macrobius assigns "lowliness," and Andronicus "contentment"; secondly, we must not be too nice in our requirements, and to this Macrobius ascribes "moderation," Andronicus "simplicity."

Reply to Objection 1: It is true that continence differs from virtue, just as imperfect differs from perfect, as we shall state further on ([3456]Q[165], A[1]); and in this sense it is condivided with virtue. Yet it has something in common with temperance both as to matter, since it is about pleasures of touch, and as to mode, since it is a kind of restraint. Hence it is suitably assigned as a part of temperance.

Reply to Objection 2: Mildness or meekness is reckoned a part of temperance not because of a likeness of matter, but because they agree as to the mode of restraint and moderation as stated above.

Reply to Objection 3: In the matter of external action justice considers what is due to another. Modesty does not consider this, but only a certain moderation. Hence it is reckoned a part not of justice but of temperance.

Reply to Objection 4: Under modesty Tully includes whatever pertains to the moderation of bodily movements and external things, as well as the moderation of hope which we reckoned as pertaining to humility.

OF SHAMEFACEDNESS (FOUR ARTICLES)

We must now consider the parts of temperance in particular: and in the first place the integral parts, which are shamefacedness and honesty. With regard to shamefacedness there are four points of inquiry:

(1) Whether shamefacedness is a virtue?

(2) What is its object?

(3) Who are the cause of a man being ashamed?

(4) What kind of people are ashamed?

Whether shamefacedness is a virtue?

Objection 1: It seems that shamefacedness is a virtue. For it is proper to a virtue "to observe the mean as fixed by reason": this is clear from the definition of virtue given in Ethic. ii, 6. Now shamefacedness observes the mean in this way, as the Philosopher observes (Ethic. ii, 7). Therefore shamefacedness is a virtue.

Objection 2: Further, whatever is praiseworthy is either a virtue or something connected with virtue. Now shamefacedness is praiseworthy. But it is not part of a virtue. For it is not a part of prudence, since it is not in the reason but in the appetite; nor is it a part of justice. since shamefacedness implies a certain passion, whereas justice is not about the passions; nor again is it a part of fortitude, because it belongs to fortitude to be persistent and aggressive, while it belongs to shamefacedness to recoil from something; nor lastly is it a part of temperance, since the latter is about desires, whereas shamefacedness is a kind of fear according as the Philosopher states (Ethic. iv, 9) and Damascene (De Fide Orth. ii, 15). Hence it follows that shamefacedness is a virtue.

Objection 3: Further, the honest and the virtuous are convertible according to Tully (De Offic. i, 27). Now shamefacedness is a part of honesty: for Ambrose says

(De Offic. i, 43) that "shamefacedness is the companion and familiar of the restful mind, averse to wantonness, a stranger to any kind of excess, the friend of sobriety and the support of what is honest, a seeker after the beautiful." Therefore shamefacedness is a virtue.

Objection 4: Further, every vice is opposed to a virtue. Now certain vices are opposed to shamefacedness, namely shamelessness and inordinate prudery. Therefore shamefacedness is a virtue.

Objection 5: Further, "like acts beget like habits," according to Ethic. ii, 1. Now shamefacedness implies a praiseworthy act; wherefore from many such acts a habit results. But a habit of praiseworthy deeds is a virtue, according to the Philosopher (Ethic. i, 12). Therefore shamefacedness is a virtue.

On the contrary, The Philosopher says (Ethic. ii, 7; iv, 9) that shamefacedness is not a virtue.

I answer that, Virtue is taken in two ways, in a strict sense and in a broad sense. Taken strictly virtue is a perfection, as stated in Phys. vii, 17,18. Wherefore anything that is inconsistent with perfection, though it be good, falls short of the notion of virtue. Now shamefacedness is inconsistent with perfection, because it is the fear of something base, namely of that which is disgraceful. Hence Damascene says (De Fide Orth. ii, 15) that "shamefacedness is fear of a base action." Now just as hope is about a possible and difficult good, so is fear about a possible and arduous evil, as stated above ([3457]FS, Q[40], A[1]; [3458]FS, Q[41], A[2]; [3459]FS, Q[42], A[3]), when we were treating of the passions. But one who is perfect as to a virtuous habit, does not apprehend that which would be disgraceful and base to do, as being possible and arduous, that is to say difficult for him to avoid; nor does he actually do anything base, so as to be in fear of disgrace. Therefore shamefacedness, properly speaking, is not a virtue, since it falls short of the perfection of virtue.

Taken, however, in a broad sense virtue denotes whatever is good and praiseworthy in human acts or passions; and in this way /shamefacedness is sometimes called a virtue, since it is a praiseworthy passion.

Reply to Objection 1: Observing the mean is not sufficient for the notion of virtue, although it is one of the conditions included in virtue's definition: but it is requisite, in addition to this, that it be "an elective habit," that is to say, operating from choice. Now shamefacedness denotes, not a habit but a passion, nor does its movement result from choice, but from an impulse of passion. Hence it falls short of the notion of virtue.

Reply to Objection 2: As stated above, shamefacedness is fear of baseness and disgrace. Now it has been stated ([3460]Q[142], A[4]) that the vice of intemperance is most base and disgraceful. Wherefore shamefacedness pertains more to temperance than to any other virtue, by reason of its motive cause, which is a base action though not according to the species of the passion, namely fear. Nevertheless in so far as the vices opposed to other virtues are base and disgraceful, shamefacedness may also pertain to other virtues.

Reply to Objection 3: Shamefacedness fosters honesty, by removing that which is contrary thereto, but not so as to attain to the perfection of honesty.

Reply to Objection 4: Every defect causes a vice, but not every good is sufficient for the notion of virtue. Consequently it does not follow that whatever is directly opposed to vice is a virtue, although every vice is opposed to a virtue, as regards its origin. Hence shamelessness, in so far as it results from excessive love of disgraceful things, is opposed to temperance.

Reply to Objection 5: Being frequently ashamed causes the habit of an acquired virtue whereby one avoids disgraceful things which are the object of shamefacedness, without continuing to be ashamed in their regard: although as a consequence of this acquired virtue, a man would be more ashamed, if confronted with the matter of shamefacedness.

Whether shamefacedness is about a disgraceful action?

Objection 1: It would seem that shamefacedness is not about a disgraceful action. For the Philosopher says (Ethic. iv, 9) that "shamefacedness is fear of disgrace." Now sometimes those who do nothing wrong suffer ignominy, according to Ps. 67:8, "For thy sake I have borne reproach, shame hath covered my face." Therefore shamefacedness is not properly about a disgraceful action.

Objection 2: Further, nothing apparently is disgraceful but what is sinful. Yet man is ashamed of things that are not sins, for instance when he performs a menial occupation. Therefore it seems that shamefacedness is not properly about a disgraceful action.

Objection 3: Further, virtuous deeds are not disgraceful but most beautiful according to Ethic. i, 8. Yet sometimes people are ashamed to do virtuous deeds, according to Lk. 9:26, "He that shall be ashamed of Me and My words, of him the Son of man shall be ashamed," etc. Therefore shamefacedness is not about a disgraceful action.

Objection 4: Further, if shamefacedness were properly about a disgraceful action, it would follow that the more disgraceful the action the more ashamed would one be. Yet sometimes a man is more ashamed of lesser sins, while he glories in those which are most grievous, according to Ps. 51:3, "Why dost thou glory in malice?" Therefore shamefacedness is not properly about a disgraceful action.

On the contrary, Damascene (De Fide Orth. ii, 15) and Gregory of Nyssa [*Nemesius, (De Nat. Hom. xx)] say that "shamefacedness is fear of doing a disgraceful deed or of a disgraceful deed done."

I answer that, As stated above ([3461]FS, Q[41], A[2]; [3462]FS, Q[42], A[3]), when we were treating of the passions, fear is properly about an arduous evil, one, namely, that is difficult to avoid. Now disgrace is twofold. There is the disgrace inherent to vice, which consists in the deformity of a voluntary act: and this, properly speaking, has not the character of an arduous evil. For that which depends on the will alone does not appear to be arduous and above man's ability: wherefore it is not apprehended as fearful, and for this reason the Philosopher says (Rhet. ii, 5) that such evils are not a matter of fear.

The other kind of disgrace is penal so to speak, and it consists in the reproach that attaches to a person, just as the clarity of glory consists in a person being honored. And since this reproach has the character of an arduous evil, just as honor has the character of an arduous good, shamefacedness, which is fear of disgrace, regards first and foremost reproach or ignominy. And since reproach is properly due to vice, as honor is due to virtue, it follows that shamefacedness regards also the disgrace inherent to vice. Hence the Philosopher says (Rhet. ii, 5) that "a man is less ashamed of those defects which are not the result of any fault of his own."

Now shamefacedness regards fault in two ways. In one way a man refrains from vicious acts through fear of reproach: in another way a man while doing a disgraceful deed avoids the public eye through fear of reproach. In the former case, according to Gregory of Nyssa (Nemesius, De Nat. Hom. xx), we speak of a person "blushing," in the latter we say that he is "ashamed." Hence he says that "the man who is ashamed acts in secret, but he who blushes fears to be disgraced."

Reply to Objection 1: Shamefacedness properly regards disgrace as due to sin which is a voluntary defect. Hence the Philosopher says (Rhet. ii, 6) that "a man is more ashamed of those things of which he is the cause." Now the virtuous man despises the disgrace to which he is subject on account of virtue, because he does not deserve it; as the Philosopher says of the magnanimous (Ethic. iv, 3). Thus we find it said of the apostles (Acts 5:41) that "they (the apostles) went from the presence of the council, rejoicing that they were accounted worthy to suffer reproach for the name of Jesus." It is owing to imperfection of virtue that a man is sometimes ashamed of the reproaches which he suffers on account of virtue, since the more virtuous a man is, the more he despises external things, whether good or evil. Wherefore it is written (Is. 51:7): "Fear ye not the reproach of men."

Reply to Objection 2: As stated above ([3463]Q[63], A[3]), though honor is not really due save to virtue alone, yet it regards a certain excellence: and the same applies to reproach, for though it is properly due to sin alone, yet, at least in man's opinion, it regards any kind of defect. Hence a man is ashamed of poverty, disrepute, servitude, and the like.

Reply to Objection 3: Shamefacedness does not regard virtuous deeds as such. Yet it happens accidentally that a man is ashamed of them either because he looks upon them as vicious according to human opinion, or because he is afraid of being marked as presumptuous or hypocritical for doing virtuous deeds.

Reply to Objection 4: Sometimes more grievous sins are less shameful, either because they are less disgraceful, as spiritual sins in comparison with sins of the flesh, or because they connote a certain abundance of some temporal good; thus a man is more ashamed of cowardice than of daring, of theft than of robbery, on account of a semblance of power. The same applies to other sins.

Whether man is more shamefaced of those who are more closely connected with him?

Objection 1: It would seem that man is not more shamefaced of those who are more closely connected with him. For it is stated in Rhet. ii, 6 that "men are more shamefaced of those from whom they desire approbation." Now men desire this especially from people of the better sort who are sometimes not connected with them. Therefore man is not more shamefaced of those who are more closely connected with him.

Objection 2: Further, seemingly those are more closely connected who perform like deeds. Now man is not made ashamed of his sin by those whom he knows to be guilty of the same sin, because according to Rhet. ii, 6, "a man does not forbid his neighbor what he does himself." Therefore he is not more shamefaced of those who are most closely connected with him.

Objection 3: Further, the Philosopher says (Rhet. ii, 6) that "men take more shame from those who retail their information to many, such as jokers and fable-tellers." But those who are more closely connected with a man do not retail his vices. Therefore one should not take shame chiefly from them.

Objection 4: Further, the Philosopher says (Rhet. ii, 6) that "men are most liable to be made ashamed by those among whom they have done nothing amiss; by those of whom they ask something for the first time; by those whose friends they wish to become." Now these are less closely connected with us. Therefore man is not made most ashamed by those who are more closely united to him.

On the contrary, It is stated in Rhet. ii, 6 that "man is made most ashamed by those who are to be continually with him."

I answer that, Since reproach is opposed to honor, just as honor denotes attestation to someone's excellence, especially the excellence which is according to virtue, so too reproach, the fear of which is shamefacedness, denotes attestation to a person's defect, especially that which results from sin. Hence the more weighty a person's attestation is considered to be, the more does he make another person ashamed. Now a person's attestation may be considered as being more weighty, either because he is certain of the truth or because of its effect. Certitude of the truth attaches to a person's attestations for two reasons. First on account of the rectitude of his judgement, as in the case of wise and virtuous men, by whom man is more desirous of being honored and by whom he is brought to a greater sense of shame. Hence children and the lower animals inspire no one with shame, by reason of their lack of judgment. Secondly, on account of his knowledge of the matter attested, because "everyone judges well of what is known to him" [*Ethic. i, 3]. In this way we are more liable to be made ashamed by persons connected with us, since they are better acquainted with our deeds: whereas strangers and persons entirely unknown to us, who are ignorant of what we do, inspire us with no shame at all.

An attestation receives weight from its effect by reason of some advantage or harm resulting therefrom; wherefore men are more desirous of being honored by those who can be of use to them, and are more liable to be made ashamed by those who are able to do them some harm. And for this reason again, in a certain respect, persons connected with us make us more ashamed, since we are to be continually in their society, as though this entailed a continual harm to us: whereas the harm that comes from strangers and passersby ceases almost at once.

Reply to Objection 1: People of the better sort make us ashamed for the same reason as those who are more closely connected with us; because just as the attestation of the better men carries more weight since they have a more universal knowledge of things, and in their judgments hold fast to the truth: so, too, the attestation of those among whom we live is more cogent since they know more about our concerns in detail.

Reply to Objection 2: We fear not the attestation of those who are connected with us in the likeness of sin, because we do not think that they look upon our defect as disgraceful.

Reply to Objection 3: Tale-bearers make us ashamed on account of the harm they do by making many think ill of us.

Reply to Objection 4: Even those among whom we have done no wrong, make us more ashamed, on account of the harm that would follow, because, to wit, we should forfeit the good opinion they had of us: and again because when contraries are put in juxtaposition their opposition seems greater, so that when a man notices something disgraceful in one whom he esteemed good, he apprehends it as being the more disgraceful. The reason why we are made more ashamed by those of whom we ask something for the first time, or whose friends we wish to be, is that we fear to suffer some injury, by being disappointed in our request, or by failing to become their friends.

Whether even virtuous men can be ashamed?

Objection 1: It would seem that even virtuous men can be ashamed. For contraries have contrary effects. Now those who excel in wickedness are not ashamed, according to Jer. 3:3, "Thou hadst a harlot's forehead, thou wouldst not blush." Therefore those who are virtuous are more inclined to be ashamed.

Objection 2: Further, the Philosopher says (Rhet. ii, 6) that "men are ashamed not only of vice, but also of the signs of evil": and this happens also in the virtuous. Therefore virtuous men can be ashamed.

Objection 3: Further, shamefacedness is "fear of disgrace" [*Ethic. iv, 9]. Now virtuous people may happen to be ignominious, for instance if they are slandered, or if they suffer reproach undeservedly. Therefore a virtuous man can be ashamed.

Objection 4: Further, shamefacedness is a part of temperance, as stated above ([3464]Q[143]). Now a part is not separated from its whole. Since then temperance is in a virtuous man, it means that shamefacedness is also.

On the contrary, The Philosopher says (Ethic. iv, 9) that a "virtuous man is not shamefaced."

I answer that, As stated above ([3465]AA[1],2) shamefacedness is fear of some disgrace. Now it may happen in two ways that an evil is not feared: first, because it is not reckoned an evil; secondly because one reckons it impossible with regard to oneself, or as not difficult to avoid.

Accordingly shame may be lacking in a person in two ways. First, because the things that should make him ashamed are not deemed by him to be disgraceful; and in this way those who are steeped in sin are without shame, for instead of disapproving of their sins, they boast of them. Secondly, because they apprehend disgrace as impossible to themselves, or as easy to avoid. In this way the old and the virtuous are not shamefaced. Yet they are so disposed, that if there were anything disgraceful in them they would be ashamed of it. Wherefore the Philosopher says (Ethic. iv, 9) that "shame is in the virtuous hypothetically."

Reply to Objection 1: Lack of shame occurs in the best and in the worst men through different causes, as stated in the Article. In the average men it is found, in so far as they have a certain love of good, and yet are not altogether free from evil.

Reply to Objection 2: It belongs to the virtuous man to avoid not only vice, but also whatever has the semblance of vice, according to 1 Thess. 5:22, "From all appearance of evil refrain yourselves." The Philosopher, too, says (Ethic. iv, 9) that the virtuous man should avoid "not only what is really evil, but also those things that are regarded as evil."

Reply to Objection 3: As stated above (A[1], ad 1) the virtuous man despises ignominy and reproach, as being things he does not deserve, wherefore he is not much ashamed of them. Nevertheless, to a certain extent, shame, like the other passions, may forestall reason.

Reply to Objection 4: Shamefacedness is a part of temperance, not as though it entered into its essence, but as a disposition to it: wherefore Ambrose says (De Offic. i, 43) that "shamefacedness lays the first foundation of temperance," by inspiring man with the horror of whatever is disgraceful.

OF HONESTY* (FOUR ARTICLES)

[*Honesty must be taken here in its broad sense as synonymous with moral goodness, from the point of view of decorum.]

We must now consider honesty, under which head there are four points of inquiry:

(1) The relation between the honest and the virtuous;

(2) Its relation with the beautiful [*As honesty here denotes moral goodness, so beauty stands for moral beauty];

(3) Its relation with the useful and the pleasant;

(4) Whether honesty is a part of temperance?

Whether honesty is the same as virtue?

Objection 1: It would seem that honesty is not the same as virtue. For Tully says (De Invent. Rhet. ii, 53) that "the honest is what is desired for its own sake." Now virtue is desired, not for its own sake, but for the sake of happiness, for the Philosopher says (Ethic. i, 9) that "happiness is the reward and the end of virtue." Therefore honesty is not the same as virtue.

Objection 2: Further, according to Isidore (Etym. x) "honesty means an honorable state." Now honor is due to many things besides virtue, since "it is praise that is the proper due of virtue" (Ethic. i, 12). Therefore honesty is not the same as virtue.

Objection 3: Further, the "principal part of virtue is the interior choice," as the Philosopher says (Ethic. viii, 13). But honesty seems to pertain rather to exterior conduct, according to 1 Cor. 14:40, "Let all things be done decently [honeste] and according to order" among you. Therefore honesty is not the same as virtue.

Objection 4: Further, honesty apparently consists in external wealth. According to Ecclus. 11:14, "good things and evil, life and death [poverty and riches] are from God" [*The words in brackets are omitted in the Leonine edition. For riches the Vulgate has 'honestas']. But virtue does not consist in external wealth. Therefore honesty is not the same as virtue.

On the contrary, Tully (De Offic. i, 5; Rhet. ii, 53) divides honesty into the four principal virtues, into which virtue is also divided. Therefore honesty is the same as virtue.

I answer that, As Isidore says (Etym. x) "honesty means an honorable state," wherefore a thing may be said to be honest through being worthy of honor. Now honor, as stated above ([3466]Q[144], A[2], ad 2), is due to excellence: and the excellence of a man is gauged chiefly according to his virtue, as stated in Phys. vii, 17. Therefore, properly speaking, honesty refers to the same thing as virtue.

Reply to Objection 1: According to the Philosopher (Ethic. i, 7), of those things that are desired for their own sake, some are desired for their own sake alone, and never for the sake of something else, such as happiness which is the last end; while some are desired, not only for their own sake, inasmuch as they have an aspect of goodness in themselves, even if no further good accrued to us through them, but also for the sake of something else, inasmuch as they are conducive to some more perfect good. It is thus that the virtues are desirable for their own sake: wherefore Tully says (De Invent. Rhet. ii, 52) that "some things allure us by their own force, and attract us by their own worth, such as virtue, truth, knowledge." And this suffices to give a thing the character of honest.

Reply to Objection 2: Some of the things which are honored besides virtue are more excellent than virtue, namely God and happiness, and such like things are not so well known to us by experience as virtue which we practice day by day. Hence virtue has a greater claim to the name of honesty. Other things which are beneath virtue are honored, in so far as they are a help to the practice of virtue, such as rank, power, and riches [*Ethic. i, 8]. For as the Philosopher says (Ethic. iv, 3) that these things "are honored by some people, but in truth it is only the good man who is worthy of honor." Now a man is good in respect of virtue. Wherefore praise is due to virtue in so far as the latter is desirable for the sake of something else, while honor is due to virtue for its own sake: and it is thus that virtue has the character of honesty.

Reply to Objection 3: As we have stated honest denotes that to which honor is due. Now honor is an attestation to someone's excellence, as stated above ([3467]Q[103], AA[1],2). But one attests only to what one knows; and the internal choice is not made known save by external actions. Wherefore external conduct has the character of honesty, in so far as it reflects internal rectitude. For this reason honesty consists radically in the internal choice, but its expression lies in the external conduct.

Reply to Objection 4: It is because the excellence of wealth is commonly regarded as making a man deserving of honor, that sometimes the name of honesty is given to external prosperity.

Whether the honest is the same as the beautiful?

Objection 1: It would seem that the honest is not the same as the beautiful. For the aspect of honest is derived from the appetite, since the honest is "what is desirable for its own sake" [*Cicero, De Invent. Rhet. ii, 53]. But the beautiful regards rather the faculty of vision to which it is pleasing. Therefore the beautiful is not the same as the honest.

Objection 2: Further, beauty requires a certain clarity, which is characteristic of glory: whereas the honest regards honor. Since then honor and glory differ, as stated above ([3468]Q[103], A[1], ad 3), it seems also that the honest and the beautiful differ.

Objection 3: Further, honesty is the same as virtue, as stated above [3469](A[1]). But a certain beauty is contrary to virtue, wherefore it is written (Ezech. 16:15): "Trusting in thy beauty thou playest the harlot because of thy renown." Therefore the honest is not the same as the beautiful.

On the contrary, The Apostle says (1 Cor. 12:23,24): "Those that are our uncomely [inhonesta] parts, have more abundant comeliness [honestatem], but our comely [honesta] parts have no need." Now by uncomely parts he means the baser members, and by comely parts the beautiful members. Therefore the honest and the beautiful are apparently the same.

I answer that, As may be gathered from the words of Dionysius (Div. Nom. iv), beauty or comeliness results from the concurrence of clarity and due proportion. For he states that God is said to be beautiful, as being "the cause of the harmony and clarity of the universe." Hence the beauty of the body consists in a man having his bodily limbs well proportioned, together with a certain clarity of color. In like manner spiritual beauty consists in a man's conduct or actions being well proportioned in respect of the spiritual clarity of reason. Now this is what is meant by honesty, which we have stated [3470](A[1]) to be the same as virtue; and it is virtue that moderates according to reason all that is connected with man. Wherefore "honesty is the same as spiritual beauty." Hence Augustine says (QQ[83], qu. 30): "By honesty I mean intelligible beauty, which we properly designate as spiritual," and further on he adds that "many things are beautiful to the eye, which it would be hardly proper to call honest."

Reply to Objection 1: The object that moves the appetite is an apprehended good. Now if a thing is perceived to be beautiful as soon as it is apprehended, it is taken to be something becoming and good. Hence Dionysius says (Div. Nom. iv) that "the beautiful and the good are beloved by all." Wherefore the honest, inasmuch as it implies spiritual beauty, is an object of desire, and for this reason Tully says (De Offic. i, 5): "Thou perceivest the form and the features, so to speak, of honesty; and were it to be seen with the eye, would, as Plato declares, arouse a wondrous love of wisdom."

Reply to Objection 2: As stated above ([3471]Q[103], A[1], ad 3), glory is the effect of honor: because through being honored or praised, a person acquires clarity in the eyes of others. Wherefore, just as the same thing makes a man honorable and glorious, so is the same thing honest and beautiful.

Reply to Objection 3: This argument applies to the beauty of the body: although it might be replied that to be proud of one's honesty is to play the harlot because of one's spiritual beauty, according to Ezech. 28:17, "Thy heart was lifted up with thy beauty, thou hast lost thy wisdom in thy beauty."

Whether the honest differs from the useful and the pleasant?

Objection 1: It would seem that the honest does not differ from the useful and the pleasant. For the honest is "what is desirable for its own sake" [*Cicero, De Invent. Rhet. ii, 53]. Now pleasure is desired for its own sake, for "it seems ridiculous to ask a man why he wishes to be pleased," as the Philosopher remarks (Ethic. x, 2). Therefore the honest does not differ from the pleasant.

Objection 2: Further, riches are comprised under the head of useful good: for Tully says (De Invent. Rhet. ii, 52): "There is a thing that attracts the desire not by any force of its own, nor by its very nature, but on account of its fruitfulness and utility": and "that is money." Now riches come under the head of honesty, for it is written (Ecclus. 11:14): "Poverty and riches [honestas] are from God," and (Ecclus. 13:2): "He shall take a burden upon him that hath fellowship with one more honorable," i.e. richer, "than himself." Therefore the honest differs not from the useful.

Objection 3: Further, Tully proves (De Offic. ii, 3) that nothing can be useful unless it be honest: and Ambrose makes the same statement (De Offic. ii, 6). Therefore the useful differs not from the honest.

On the contrary, Augustine says (Q[83], qu. 30): "The honest is that which is desirable for its own sake: the useful implies reference to something else."

I answer that, The honest concurs in the same subject with the useful and the pleasant, but it differs from them in aspect. For, as stated above [3472](A[2]), a thing is said to be honest, in so far as it has a certain beauty through being regulated by reason. Now whatever is regulated in accordance with reason is naturally becoming to man. Again, it is natural for a thing to take pleasure in that which is becoming to it. Wherefore an honest thing is naturally pleasing to man: and the Philosopher proves this with regard to acts of virtue (Ethic. i, 8). Yet not all that is pleasing is honest, since a thing may be becoming according to the senses, but not according to reason. A pleasing thing of this kind is beside man's reason which perfects his nature. Even virtue itself, which is essentially honest, is referred to something else as its end namely happiness. Accordingly the honest the useful, and the pleasant concur in the one subject.

Nevertheless they differ in aspect. For a thing is said to be honest as having a certain excellence deserving of honor on account of its spiritual beauty: while it is said to be pleasing, as bringing rest to desire, and useful, as referred to something else. The pleasant, however, extends to more things than the useful and the honest: since whatever is useful and honest is pleasing in some respect, whereas the converse does not hold (Ethic. ii, 3).

Reply to Objection 1: A thing is said to be honest, if it is desired for its own sake by the rational appetite. which tends to that which is in accordance with reason: while a thing is said to be pleasant if it is desired for its own sake by the sensitive appetite.

Reply to Objection 2: Riches are denominated honesty according of the opinion of the many who honor wealth: or because they are intended to be the instruments of virtuous deeds, as stated above (A[1], ad 2).

Reply to Objection 3: Tully and Ambrose mean to say that nothing incompatible with honesty can be simply and truly useful, since it follows that it is contrary to man's last end, which is a good in accordance with reason; although it may perhaps be useful in some respect, with regard to a particular end. But they do not mean to say that every useful thing as such may be classed among those that are honest.

Whether honesty should be reckoned a part of temperance?

Objection 1: It would seem that honesty should not be reckoned a part of temperance. For it is not possible for a thing to be part and whole in respect of one same thing. Now "temperance is a part of honesty," according to Tully (De Invent. Rhet. ii, 53). Therefore honesty is not a part of temperance.

Objection 2: Further, it is stated (3 Esdra 3:21) that "wine . . . makes all thoughts honest." But the use of wine, especially in excess, in which sense the passage quoted should seemingly be taken, pertains to intemperance rather than to temperance. Therefore honesty is not a part of temperance.

Objection 3: Further, the honest is that which is deserving of honor. Now "it is the just and the brave who receive most honor," according to the Philosopher (Rhet. i, 9). Therefore honesty pertains, not to temperance, but rather to justice and fortitude: wherefore Eleazar said as related in 2 Macc. 6:28: "I suffer an honorable [honesta] death, for the most venerable and most holy laws."

On the contrary, Macrobius [*In Somn. Scip. i] reckons honesty a part of temperance, and Ambrose (De Offic. i, 43) ascribes honesty as pertaining especially to temperance.

I answer that, As stated above [3473](A[2]), honesty is a kind of spiritual beauty. Now the disgraceful is opposed to the beautiful: and opposites are most manifest of one another. Wherefore seemingly honesty belongs especially to temperance, since the latter repels that which is most disgraceful and unbecoming to man, namely animal lusts. Hence by its very name temperance is most significative of the good of reason to which it belongs to moderate and temper evil desires. Accordingly honesty, as being ascribed for a special reason to temperance, is reckoned as a part thereof, not as a subjective part, nor as an annexed virtue, but as an integral part or condition attaching thereto.

Reply to Objection 1: Temperance is accounted a subjective part of honesty taken in a wide sense: it is not thus that the latter is reckoned a part of temperance.

Reply to Objection 2: When a man is intoxicated, "the wine makes his thoughts honest" according to his own reckoning because he deems himself great and deserving of honor [*Cf.[3474] Q[148], A[6]].

Reply to Objection 3: Greater honor is due to justice and fortitude than to temperance, because they excel in the point of a greater good: yet greater honor is due to temperance, because the vices which it holds in check are the most deserving of reproach, as stated above. Thus honesty is more to be ascribed to temperance according to the rule given by the Apostle (1 Cor. 12:23) when he says that "our uncomely parts have more abundant comeliness," which, namely, destroys whatever is uncomely.

OF ABSTINENCE (TWO ARTICLES)

We must now consider the subjective parts of temperance: first, those which are about pleasures of food; secondly, those which are about pleasures of sex. The first consideration will include abstinence, which is about meat and drink, and sobriety, which is specifically about drink.

With regard to abstinence three points have to be considered: (1) Abstinence itself; (2) its act which is fasting; (3) its opposite vice which is gluttony. Under the first head there are two points of inquiry:

(1) Whether abstinence is a virtue?

(2) Whether it is a special virtue?

Whether abstinence is a virtue?

Objection 1: It seems that abstinence is not a virtue. For the Apostle says (1 Cor. 4:20): "The kingdom of God is not in speech but in power [virtute]." Now the kingdom of God does not consist in abstinence, for the Apostle says (Rom. 14:17): "The kingdom of God is not meat and drink," where a gloss [*Cf. St. Augustine, QQ. Evang. ii, qu. 11] observes that "justice consists neither in abstaining nor in eating." Therefore abstinence is not a virtue.

Objection 2: Further, Augustine says (Confess. x, 11) addressing himself to God: "This hast Thou taught me, that I should set myself to take food as physic." Now it belongs not to virtue, but to the medical art to regulate medicine. Therefore, in like manner, to regulate one's food, which belongs to abstinence, is an act not of virtue but of art.

Objection 3: Further, every virtue "observes the mean," as stated in Ethic. ii, 6,7. But abstinence seemingly inclines not to the mean but to deficiency, since it denotes retrenchment. Therefore abstinence is not a virtue.

Objection 4: Further, no virtue excludes another virtue. But abstinence excludes patience: for Gregory says (Pastor. iii, 19) that "impatience not unfrequently dislodges the abstainer's mind from its peaceful seclusion." Likewise he says (Pastor. iii, 19) that "sometimes the sin of pride pierces the thoughts of the abstainer," so that abstinence excludes humility. Therefore abstinence is not a virtue.

On the contrary, It is written (2 Pet. 1:5,6): "Join with your faith virtue, and with virtue knowledge, and with knowledge abstinence"; where abstinence is numbered among other virtues. Therefore abstinence is a virtue.

I answer that, Abstinence by its very name denotes retrenchment of food. Hence the term abstinence may be taken in two ways. First, as denoting retrenchment of food absolutely, and in this way it signifies neither a virtue nor a virtuous act, but something indifferent. Secondly, it may be taken as regulated by reason, and then it signifies either a virtuous habit or a virtuous act. This is the meaning of Peter's words quoted above, where he says that we ought "to join abstinence with knowledge," namely that in abstaining from food a man should act with due regard for those among whom he lives, for his own person, and for the requirements of health.

Reply to Objection 1: The use of and abstinence from food, considered in themselves, do not pertain to the kingdom of God, since the Apostle says (1 Cor. 8:8): "Meat doth not commend us to God. For neither, if we eat not [*Vulg.: 'Neither if we eat . . . nor if we eat not'], shall we have the less, nor if we eat, shall we have the more," i.e. spiritually. Nevertheless they both belong to the kingdom of God, in so far as they are done reasonably through faith and love of God.

Reply to Objection 2: The regulation of food, in the point of quantity and quality, belongs to the art of medicine as regards the health of the body: but in the point of internal affections with regard to the good of reason, it belongs to abstinence. Hence Augustine says (QQ. Evang. ii, qu. 11): "It makes no difference whatever to virtue what or how much food a man takes, so long as he does it with due regard for the people among whom he lives, for his own person, and for the requirements of his health: but it matters how readily and uncomplainingly he does without food when bound by duty or necessity to abstain."

Reply to Objection 3: It belongs to temperance to bridle the pleasures which are too alluring to the soul, just as it belongs to fortitude to strengthen the soul against fears that deter it from the good of reason. Wherefore, just as fortitude is commended on account of a certain excess, from which all the parts of fortitude take their name, so temperance is commended for a kind of deficiency, from which all its parts are denominated. Hence abstinence, since it is a part of temperance, is named from deficiency, and yet it observes the mean, in so far as it is in accord with right reason.

Reply to Objection 4: Those vices result from abstinence in so far as it is not in accord with right reason. For right reason makes one abstain as one ought, i.e. with gladness of heart, and for the due end, i.e. for God's glory and not one's own.

Whether abstinence is a special virtue?

Objection 1: It would seem that abstinence is not a special virtue. For every virtue is praiseworthy by itself. But abstinence is not praiseworthy by itself; for Gregory says (Pastor. iii, 19) that "the virtue of abstinence is praised only on account of the other virtues." Therefore abstinence is not a special virtue.

Objection 2: Further, Augustine [*Fulgentius] says (De Fide ad Pet. xlii) that "the saints abstain from meat and drink, not that any creature of God is evil, but merely in order to chastise the body." Now this belongs to chastity, as its very name denotes. Therefore abstinence is not a special virtue distinct from chastity.

Objection 3: Further, as man should be content with moderate meat, so should he be satisfied with moderate clothes, according to 1 Tim. 6:8, "Having food, and wherewith to be covered, with these we should be [Vulg.: 'are'] content." Now there is no special virtue in being content with moderate clothes. Neither, therefore, is there in abstinence which moderates food.

On the contrary, Macrobius [*In Somn. Scip. i, 8] reckons abstinence as a special part of temperance.

I answer that, As stated above ([3475]Q[136], A[1];[3476] Q[141], A[3]) moral virtue maintains the good of reason against the onslaught of the passions: hence whenever we find a special motive why a passion departs from the good of reason, there is need of a special virtue. Now pleasures of the table are of a nature to withdraw man from the good of reason, both because they are so great, and because food is necessary to man who needs it for the maintenance of life, which he desires above all other things. Therefore abstinence is a special virtue.

Reply to Objection 1: Virtues are of necessity connected together, as stated above ([3477]FS, Q[65], A[1]). Wherefore one virtue receives help and commendation from another, as justice from fortitude. Accordingly in this way the virtue of abstinence receives commendation on account of the other virtues.

Reply to Objection 2: The body is chastised by means of abstinence, not only against the allurements of lust, but also against those of gluttony: since by abstaining a man gains strength for overcoming the onslaughts of gluttony, which increase in force the more he yields to them. Yet abstinence is not prevented from being a special virtue through being a help to chastity, since one virtue helps another.

Reply to Objection 3: The use of clothing was devised by art, whereas the use of food is from nature. Hence it is more necessary to have a special virtue for the moderation of food than for the moderation of clothing.

OF FASTING (EIGHT ARTICLES)

We must now consider fasting: under which head there are eight points of inquiry:

(1) Whether fasting is an act of virtue?

(2) Of what virtue is it the act?

(3) Whether it is a matter of precept?

(4) Whether anyone is excused from fulfilling this precept?

(5) The time of fasting;

(6) Whether it is requisite for fasting to eat but once?

(7) The hour of eating for those who fast;

(8) The meats from which it is necessary to abstain.

Whether fasting is an act of virtue?

Objection 1: It would seem that fasting is not an act of virtue. For every act of virtue is acceptable to God. But fasting is not always acceptable to God, according to Is. 58:3, "Why have we fasted and Thou hast not regarded?" Therefore fasting is not an act of virtue.

Objection 2: Further, no act of virtue forsakes the mean of virtue. Now fasting forsakes the mean of virtue, which in the virtue of abstinence takes account of the necessity of supplying the needs of nature, whereas by fasting something is retrenched therefrom: else those who do not fast would not have the virtue of abstinence. Therefore fasting is not an act of virtue.

Objection 3: Further, that which is competent to all, both good and evil, is not an act of virtue. Now such is fasting, since every one is fasting before eating. Therefore fasting is not an act of virtue.

On the contrary, It is reckoned together with other virtuous acts (2 Cor. 6:5,6) where the Apostle says: "In fasting, in knowledge, in chastity, etc. [Vulg.: 'in chastity, in knowledge']."

I answer that, An act is virtuous through being directed by reason to some virtuous [honestum] [*Cf.[3478] Q[145], A[1]] good. Now this is consistent with fasting, because fasting is practiced for a threefold purpose. First, in order to bridle the lusts of the flesh, wherefore the Apostle says (2 Cor. 6:5,6): "In fasting, in chastity," since fasting is the guardian of chastity. For, according to Jerome [*Contra Jov. ii.] "Venus is cold when Ceres and Bacchus are not there," that is to say, lust is cooled by abstinence in meat and drink. Secondly, we have recourse to fasting in order that the mind may arise more freely to the contemplation of heavenly things: hence it is related (Dan. 10) of Daniel that he received a revelation from God after fasting for three weeks. Thirdly, in order to satisfy for sins: wherefore it is written (Joel 2:12): "Be converted to Me with all your heart, in fasting and in weeping and in mourning." The same is declared by Augustine in a sermon (De orat. et Jejun. [*Serm. lxxii (ccxxx, de Tempore)]): "Fasting cleanses the soul, raises the mind, subjects one's flesh to the spirit, renders the heart contrite and humble, scatters the clouds of concupiscence, quenches the fire of lust, kindles the true light of chastity."

Reply to Objection 1: An act that is virtuous generically may be rendered vicious by its connection with certain circumstances. Hence the text goes on to say: "Behold in the day of your fast your own will is founded," and a little further on (Is. 58:4): "You fast for debates and strife and strike with the fist wickedly." These words are expounded by Gregory (Pastor. iii, 19) as follows: "The will indicates joy and the fist anger. In vain then is the flesh restrained if the mind allowed to drift to inordinate movements be wrecked by vice." And Augustine says (in the same sermon) that "fasting loves not many words, deems wealth superfluous, scorns pride, commends humility, helps man to perceive what is frail and paltry."

Reply to Objection 2: The mean of virtue is measured not according to quantity but according to right reason, as stated in Ethic. ii, 6. Now reason judges it expedient, on account of some special motive, for a man to take less food than would be becoming to him under ordinary circumstances, for instance in order to avoid sickness, or in order to perform certain bodily works with greater ease: and much more does reason direct this to the avoidance of spiritual evils and the pursuit of spiritual goods. Yet reason does not retrench so much from one's food as to refuse nature its necessary support: thus Jerome says:* "It matters not whether thou art a long or a short time in destroying thyself, since to afflict the body immoderately, whether by excessive lack of nourishment, or by eating or sleeping too little, is to offer a sacrifice of stolen goods." [*The quotation is from the Corpus of Canon Law (Cap. Non mediocriter, De Consecrationibus, dist. 5). Gratian there ascribes the quotation to St. Jerome, but it is not to be found in the saint's works.] In like manner right reason does not retrench so much from a man's food as to render him incapable of fulfilling his duty. Hence Jerome says (in the same reference) "Rational man forfeits his dignity, if he sets fasting before chastity, or night-watchings before the well-being of his senses."

Reply to Objection 3: The fasting of nature, in respect of which a man is said to be fasting until he partakes of food, consists in a pure negation, wherefore it cannot be reckoned a virtuous act. Such is only the fasting of one who abstains in some measure from food for a reasonable purpose. Hence the former is called natural fasting [jejunium jejunii] [*Literally the 'fast of fasting']: while the latter is called the faster's fast, because he fasts for a purpose.

Whether fasting is an act of abstinence?

Objection 1: It would seem that fasting is not an act of abstinence. For Jerome [*The quotation is from the Ordinary Gloss, where the reference is lacking] commenting on Mat. 17:20, "This kind of devil" says: "To fast is to abstain not only from food but also from all manner of lusts." Now this belongs to every virtue. Therefore fasting is not exclusively an act of abstinence.

Objection 2: Further, Gregory says in a Lenten Homily (xvi in Evang.) that "the Lenten fast is a tithe of the whole year." Now paying tithes is an act of religion, as stated above ([3479]Q[87], A[1]). Therefore fasting is an act of religion and not of abstinence.

Objection 3: Further, abstinence is a part of temperance, as stated above (QQ[143],146, A[1], ad 3). Now temperance is condivided with fortitude, to which it belongs to endure hardships, and this seems very applicable to fasting. Therefore fasting is not an act of abstinence.

On the contrary, Isidore says (Etym. vi, 19) that "fasting is frugality of fare and abstinence from food."

I answer that, Habit and act have the same matter. Wherefore every virtuous act about some particular matter belongs to the virtue that appoints the mean in that matter. Now fasting is concerned with food, wherein the mean is appointed by abstinence. Wherefore it is evident that fasting is an act of abstinence.

Reply to Objection 1: Properly speaking fasting consists in abstaining from food, but speaking metaphorically it denotes abstinence from anything harmful, and such especially is sin.

We may also reply that even properly speaking fasting is abstinence from all manner of lust, since, as stated above (A[1], ad 1), an act ceases to be virtuous by the conjunction of any vice.

Reply to Objection 2: Nothing prevents the act of one virtue belonging to another virtue, in so far as it is directed to the end of that virtue, as explained above ([3480]Q[32], A[1], ad 2;[3481] Q[85], A[3]). Accordingly there is no reason why fasting should not be an act of religion, or of chastity, or of any other virtue.

Reply to Objection 3: It belongs to fortitude as a special virtue, to endure, not any kind of hardship, but only those connected with the danger of death. To endure hardships resulting from privation of pleasure of touch, belongs to temperance and its parts: and such are the hardships of fasting.

Whether fasting is a matter of precept?

Objection 1: It would seem that fasting is not a matter of precept. For precepts are not given about works of supererogation which are a matter of counsel. Now fasting is a work of supererogation: else it would have to be equally observed at all places and times. Therefore fasting is not a matter of precept.

Objection 2: Further, whoever infringes a precept commits a mortal sin. Therefore if fasting were a matter of precept, all who do not fast would sin mortally, and a widespreading snare would be laid for men.

Objection 3: Further, Augustine says (De Vera Relig. 17) that "the Wisdom of God having taken human nature, and called us to a state of freedom, instituted a few most salutary sacraments whereby the community of the Christian people, that is, of the free multitude, should be bound together in subjection to one God." Now the liberty of the Christian people seems to be hindered by a great number of observances no less than by a great number of sacraments. For Augustine says (Ad inquis. Januar., Ep. lv) that "whereas God in His mercy wished our religion to be distinguished by its freedom and the evidence and small number of its solemn sacraments, some people render it oppressive with slavish burdens." Therefore it seems that the Church should not have made fasting a matter of precept.

On the contrary, Jerome (Ad Lucin., Ep. lxxi) speaking of fasting says: "Let each province keep to its own practice, and look upon the commands of the elders as though they were laws of the apostles." Therefore fasting is a matter of precept.

I answer that, Just as it belongs to the secular authority to make legal precepts which apply the natural law to matters of common weal in temporal affairs, so it belongs to ecclesiastical superiors to prescribe by statute those things that concern the common weal of the faithful in spiritual goods.

Now it has been stated above [3482](A[1]) that fasting is useful as atoning for and preventing sin, and as raising the mind to spiritual things. And everyone is bound by the natural dictate of reason to practice fasting as far as it is necessary for these purposes. Wherefore fasting in general is a matter of precept of the natural law, while the fixing of the time and manner of fasting as becoming and profitable to the Christian people, is a matter of precept of positive law established by ecclesiastical authority: the latter is the Church fast, the former is the fast prescribed by nature.

Reply to Objection 1: Fasting considered in itself denotes something not eligible but penal: yet it becomes eligible in so far as it is useful to some end. Wherefore considered absolutely it is not binding under precept, but it is binding under precept to each one that stands in need of such a remedy. And since men, for the most part, need this remedy, both because "in many things we all offend" (James 3:2), and because "the flesh lusteth against the spirit" (Gal. 5:17), it was fitting that the Church should appoint certain fasts to be kept by all in common. In doing this the Church does not make a precept of a matter of supererogation, but particularizes in detail that which is of general obligation.

Reply to Objection 2: Those commandments which are given under the form of a general precept, do not bind all persons in the same way, but subject to the requirements of the end intended by the lawgiver. It will be a mortal sin to disobey a commandment through contempt of the lawgiver's authority, or to disobey it in such a way as to frustrate the end intended by him: but it is not a mortal sin if one fails to keep a commandment, when there is a reasonable motive, and especially if the lawgiver would not insist on its observance if he were present. Hence it is that not all, who do not keep the fasts of the Church, sin mortally.

Reply to Objection 3: Augustine is speaking there of those things "that are neither contained in the authorities of Holy Scripture, nor found among the ordinances of bishops in council, nor sanctioned by the custom of the universal Church." On the other hand, the fasts that are of obligation are appointed by the councils of bishops and are sanctioned by the custom of the universal Church. Nor are they opposed to the freedom of the faithful, rather are they of use in hindering the slavery of sin, which is opposed to spiritual freedom, of which it is written (Gal. 5:13): "You, brethren, have been called unto liberty; only make not liberty an occasion to the flesh."

Whether all are bound to keep the fasts of the Church?

Objection 1: It would seem that all are bound to keep the fasts of the Church. For the commandments of the Church are binding even as the commandments of God, according to Lk. 10:16, "He that heareth you heareth Me." Now all are bound to keep the commandments of God. Therefore in like manner all are bound to keep the fasts appointed by the Church.

Objection 2: Further, children especially are seemingly not exempt from fasting, on account of their age: for it is written (Joel 2:15): "Sanctify a fast," and further on (Joel 2:16): "Gather together the little ones, and them that suck the breasts." Much more therefore are all others bound to keen the fasts.

Objection 3: Further, spiritual things should be preferred to temporal, and necessary things to those that are not necessary. Now bodily works are directed to temporal gain; and pilgrimages, though directed to spiritual things, are not a matter of necessity. Therefore, since fasting is directed to a spiritual gain, and is made a necessary thing by the commandment of the Church, it seems that the fasts of the Church ought not to be omitted on account of a pilgrimage, or bodily works.

Objection 4: Further, it is better to do a thing willingly than through necessity, as stated in 2 Cor. 9:7. Now the poor are wont to fast through necessity, owing to lack of food. Much more therefore ought they to fast willingly.

On the contrary, It seems that no righteous man is bound to fast. For the commandments of the Church are not binding in opposition to Christ's teaching. But our Lord said (Lk. 5:34) that "the children of the bridegroom cannot fast whilst the bridegroom is with them [*Vulg.: 'Can you make the children of the bridegroom fast, whilst the bridegroom is with them?']." Now He is with all the righteous by dwelling in them in a special manner [*Cf. [3483]FP, Q[8], A[3]], wherefore our Lord said (Mat. 28:20): "Behold I am with you . . . even to the consummation of the world." Therefore the righteous are not bound by the commandment of the Church to fast.

I answer that, As stated above ([3484]FS, Q[90], A[2]; [3485]FS, Q[98], AA[2],6), general precepts are framed according to the requirements of the many.

Wherefore in making such precepts the lawgiver considers what happens generally and for the most part, and he does not intend the precept to be binding on a person in whom for some special reason there is something incompatible with observance of the precept. Yet discretion must be brought to bear on the point. For if the reason be evident, it is lawful for a man to use his own judgment in omitting to fulfil the precept, especially if custom be in his favor, or if it be difficult for him to have recourse to superior authority. on the other hand, if the reason be doubtful, one should have recourse to the superior who has power to grant a dispensation in such cases. And this must be done in the fasts appointed by the Church, to which all are bound in general, unless there be some special obstacle to this observance.

Reply to Objection 1: The commandments of God are precepts of the natural law, which are, of themselves, necessary for salvation. But the commandments of the Church are about matters which are necessary for salvation, not of themselves, but only through the ordinance of the Church. Hence there may be certain obstacles on account of which certain persons are not bound to keep the fasts in question.

Reply to Objection 2: In children there is a most evident reason for not fasting, both on account of their natural weakness, owing to which they need to take food frequently, and not much at a time, and because they need much nourishment owing to the demands of growth, which results from the residuum of nourishment. Wherefore as long as the stage of growth lasts, which as a rule lasts until they have completed the third period of seven years, they are not bound to keep the Church fasts: and yet it is fitting that even during that time they should exercise themselves in fasting, more or less, in accordance with their age. Nevertheless when some great calamity threatens, even children are commanded to fast, in sign of more severe penance, according to Jonah 3:7, "Let neither men nor beasts . . . taste anything . . . nor drink water."

Reply to Objection 3: Apparently a distinction should be made with regard to pilgrims and working people. For if the pilgrimage or laborious work can be conveniently deferred or lessened without detriment to the bodily health and such external conditions as are necessary for the upkeep of bodily or spiritual life, there is no reason for omitting the fasts of the Church. But if one be under the necessity of starting on the pilgrimage at once, and of making long stages, or of doing much work, either for one's bodily livelihood, or for some need of the spiritual life, and it be impossible at the same time to keep the fasts of the Church, one is not bound to fast: because in ordering fasts the Church would not seem to have intended to prevent other pious and more necessary undertakings. Nevertheless, in such cases one ought seemingly, to seek the superior's dispensation; except perhaps when the above course is recognized by custom, since when superiors are silent they would seem to consent.

Reply to Objection 4: Those poor who can provide themselves with sufficient for one meal are not excused, on account of poverty, from keeping the fasts of the Church. On the other hand, those would seem to be exempt who beg their food piecemeal, since they are unable at any one time to have a sufficiency of food.

Reply to Objection 5: This saying of our Lord may be expounded in three ways. First, according to Chrysostom (Hom. xxx in Matth.), who says that "the disciples, who are called children of the bridegroom, were as yet of a weakly disposition, wherefore they are compared to an old garment." Hence while Christ was with them in body they were to be fostered with kindness rather than drilled with the harshness of fasting. According to this interpretation, it is fitting that dispensations should be granted to the imperfect and to beginners, rather than to the elders and the perfect, according to a gloss on Ps. 130:2, "As a child that is weaned is towards his mother." Secondly, we may say with Jerome [*Bede, Comment. in Luc. v] that our Lord is speaking here of the fasts of the observances of the Old Law. Wherefore our Lord means to say that the apostles were not to be held back by the old observances, since they were to be filled with the newness of grace. Thirdly, according to Augustine (De Consensu Evang. ii, 27), who states that fasting is of two kinds. one pertains to those who are humbled by disquietude, and this is not befitting perfect men, for they are called "children of the bridegroom"; hence when we read in Luke: "The children of the bridegroom cannot fast [*Hom. xiii, in Matth.]," we read in Mat. 9:15: "The children of the bridegroom cannot mourn [*Vulg.: 'Can the children of the bridegroom mourn?']." The other pertains to the mind that rejoices in adhering to spiritual things: and this fasting is befitting the perfect.

Whether the times for the Church fast are fittingly ascribed?

Objection 1: It would seem that the times for the Church fast are unfittingly appointed. For we read (Mat. 4) that Christ began to fast immediately after being baptized. Now we ought to imitate Christ, according to 1 Cor. 4:16, "Be ye followers of me, as I also am of Christ." Therefore we ought to fast immediately after the Epiphany when Christ's baptism is celebrated.

Objection 2: Further, it is unlawful in the New Law to observe the ceremonies of the Old Law. Now it belongs to the solemnities of the Old Law to fast in certain particular months: for it is written (Zech. 8:19): "The fast of the fourth month and the fast of the fifth, and the fast of the seventh, and the fast of the tenth shall be to the house of Judah, joy and gladness and great solemnities." Therefore the fast of certain months, which are called Ember days, are unfittingly kept in the Church.

Objection 3: Further, according to Augustine (De Consensu Evang. ii, 27), just as there is a fast "of sorrow," so is there a fast "of joy." Now it is most becoming that the faithful should rejoice spiritually in Christ's Resurrection. Therefore during the five weeks which the Church solemnizes on account of Christ's Resurrection, and on Sundays which commemorate the Resurrection, fasts ought to be appointed.

On the contrary, stands the general custom of the Church.

I answer that, As stated above ([3486]AA[1],3), fasting is directed to two things, the deletion of sin, and the raising of the mind to heavenly things. Wherefore fasting ought to be appointed specially for those times, when it behooves man to be cleansed from sin, and the minds of the faithful to be raised to God by devotion: and these things are particularly requisite before the feast of Easter, when sins are loosed by baptism, which is solemnly conferred on Easter-eve, on which day our Lord's burial is commemorated, because "we are buried together with Christ by baptism unto death" (Rom. 6:4). Moreover at the Easter festival the mind of man ought to be devoutly raised to the glory of eternity, which Christ restored by rising from the dead, and so the Church ordered a fast to be observed immediately before the Paschal feast; and for the same reason, on the eve of the chief festivals, because it is then that one ought to make ready to keep the coming feast devoutly. Again it is the custom in the Church for Holy orders to be conferred every quarter of the year (in sign whereof our Lord fed four thousand men with seven loaves, which signify the New Testament year as Jerome says [*Comment. in Marc. viii]): and then both the ordainer, and the candidates for ordination, and even the whole people, for whose good they are ordained, need to fast in order to make themselves ready for the ordination. Hence it is related (Lk. 6:12) that before choosing His disciples our Lord "went out into a mountain to pray": and Ambrose [*Exposit. in Luc.] commenting on these words says: "What shouldst thou do, when thou desirest to undertake some pious work, since Christ prayed before sending His apostles?"

With regard to the forty day's fast, according to Gregory (Hom. xvi in Evang.) there are three reasons for the number. First, "because the power of the Decalogue is accomplished in the four books of the Holy Gospels: since forty is the product of ten multiplied by four." Or "because we are composed of four elements in this mortal body through whose lusts we transgress the Lord's commandments which are delivered to us in the Decalogue. Wherefore it is fitting we should punish that same body forty times. or, because, just as under the Law it was commanded that tithes should be paid of things, so we strive to pay God a tithe of days, for since a year is composed of three hundred and sixty-six days, by punishing ourselves for thirty-six days" (namely, the fasting days during the six weeks of Lent) "we pay God a tithe of our year." According to Augustine (De Doctr. Christ. ii, 16) a fourth reason may be added. For the Creator is the "Trinity," Father, Son, and Holy Ghost: while the number "three" refers to the invisible creature, since we are commanded to love God, with our whole heart, with our whole soul, and with our whole mind: and the number "four" refers to the visible creature, by reason of heat, cold, wet and dry. Thus the number "ten" [*Ten is the sum of three, three, and four] signifies all things, and if this be multiplied by four which refers to the body whereby we make use of things, we have the number forty.

Each fast of the Ember days is composed of three days, on account of the number of months in each season: or on account of the number of Holy orders which are conferred at these times.

Reply to Objection 1: Christ needed not baptism for His own sake, but in order to commend baptism to us. Wherefore it was competent for Him to fast, not before, but after His baptism, in order to invite us to fast before our baptism.

Reply to Objection 2: The Church keeps the Ember fasts, neither at the very same time as the Jews, nor for the same reasons. For they fasted in July, which is the fourth month from April (which they count as the first), because it was then that Moses coming down from Mount Sinai broke the tables of the Law (Ex. 32), and that, according to Jer. 39:2, "the walls of the city were first broken through." In the fifth month, which we call August, they fasted because they were commanded not to go up on to the mountain, when the people had rebelled on account of the spies (Num. 14): also in this month the temple of Jerusalem was burnt down by Nabuchodonosor (Jer. 52) and afterwards by Titus. In the seventh month which we call October, Godolias was slain, and the remnants of the people were dispersed (Jer. 51). In the tenth month, which we call January, the people who were with Ezechiel in captivity heard of the destruction of the temple (Ezech. 4).

Reply to Objection 3: The "fasting of joy" proceeds from the instigation of the Holy Ghost Who is the Spirit of liberty, wherefore this fasting should not be a matter of precept. Accordingly the fasts appointed by the commandment of the Church are rather "fasts of sorrow" which are inconsistent with days of joy. For this reason fasting is not ordered by the Church during the whole of the Paschal season, nor on Sundays: and if anyone were to fast at these times in contradiction to the custom of Christian people, which as Augustine declares (Ep. xxxvi) "is to be considered as law," or even through some erroneous opinion (thus the Manichees fast, because they deem such fasting to be of obligation)—he would not be free from sin. Nevertheless fasting considered in itself is commendable at all times; thus Jerome wrote (Ad Lucin., Ep. lxxi): "Would that we might fast always."

Whether it is requisite for fasting that one eat but once?

Objection 1: It would seem that it is not requisite for fasting that one eat but once. For, as stated above [3487](A[2]), fasting is an act of the virtue of abstinence, which observes due quantity of food not less than the number of meals. Now the quantity of food is not limited for those who fast. Therefore neither should the number of meals be limited.

Objection 2: Further, Just as man is nourished by meat, so is he by drink: wherefore drink breaks the fast, and for this reason we cannot receive the Eucharist after drinking. Now we are not forbidden to drink at various hours of the day. Therefore those who fast should not be forbidden to eat several times.

Objection 3: Further, digestives are a kind of food: and yet many take them on fasting days after eating. Therefore it is not essential to fasting to take only one meal.

On the contrary, stands the common custom of the Christian people.

I answer that, Fasting is instituted by the Church in order to bridle concupiscence, yet so as to safeguard nature. Now only one meal is seemingly sufficient for this purpose, since thereby man is able to satisfy nature; and yet he withdraws something from concupiscence by minimizing the number of meals. Therefore it is appointed by the Church, in her moderation, that those who fast should take one meal in the day.

Reply to Objection 1: It was not possible to fix the same quantity of food for all, on account of the various bodily temperaments, the result being that one person needs more, and another less food: whereas, for the most part, all are able to satisfy nature by only one meal.

Reply to Objection 2: Fasting is of two kinds [*Cf. A[1], ad 3]. One is the natural fast, which is requisite for receiving the Eucharist. This is broken by any kind of drink, even of water, after which it is not lawful to receive the Eucharist. The fast of the Church is another kind and is called the "fasting of the faster," and this is not broken save by such things as the Church intended to forbid in instituting the fast. Now the Church does not intend to command abstinence from drink, for this is taken more for bodily refreshment, and digestion of the food consumed, although it nourishes somewhat. It is, however, possible to sin and lose the merit of fasting, by partaking of too much drink: as also by eating immoderately at one meal.

Reply to Objection 3: Although digestives nourish somewhat they are not taken chiefly for nourishment, but for digestion. Hence one does not break one's fast by taking them or any other medicines, unless one were to take digestives, with a fraudulent intention, in great quantity and by way of food.

Whether the ninth hour is suitably fixed for the faster's meal?

Objection 1: It would seem that the ninth hour is not suitably fixed for the faster's meal. For the state of the New Law is more perfect than the state of the Old Law. Now in the Old Testament they fasted until evening, for it is written (Lev. 23:32): "It is a sabbath . . . you shall afflict your souls," and then the text continues: "From evening until evening you shall celebrate your sabbaths." Much more therefore under the New Testament should the fast be ordered until the evening.

Objection 2: Further, the fast ordered by the Church is binding on all. But all are not able to know exactly the ninth hour. Therefore it seems that the fixing of the ninth hour should not form part of the commandment to fast.

Objection 3: Further, fasting is an act of the virtue of abstinence, as stated above [3488](A[2]). Now the mean of moral virtue does not apply in the same way to all, since what is much for one is little for another, as stated in Ethic. ii, 6. Therefore the ninth hour should not be fixed for those who fast.

On the contrary, The Council of Chalons [*The quotation is from the Capitularies (Cap. 39) of Theodulf, bishop of Orleans (760–821) and is said to be found in the Corpus Juris, Cap. Solent, dist. 1, De Consecratione] says: "During Lent those are by no means to be credited with fasting who eat before the celebration of the office of Vespers," which in the Lenten season is said after the ninth hour. Therefore we ought to fast until the ninth hour.

I answer that, As stated above ([3489]AA[1],3,5), fasting is directed to the deletion and prevention of sin. Hence it ought to add something to the common custom, yet so as not to be a heavy burden to nature. Now the right and common custom is for men to eat about the sixth hour: both because digestion is seemingly finished (the natural heat being withdrawn inwardly at night-time on account of the surrounding cold of the night), and the humor spread about through the limbs (to which result the heat of the day conduces until the sun has reached its zenith), and again because it is then chiefly that the nature of the human body needs assistance against the external heat that is in the air, lest the humors be parched within.

Hence, in order that those who fast may feel some pain in satisfaction for their sins, the ninth hour is suitably fixed for their meal.

Moreover, this hour agrees with the mystery of Christ's Passion, which was brought to a close at the ninth hour, when "bowing His head, He gave up the ghost" (Jn. 19:30): because those who fast by punishing their flesh, are conformed to the Passion of Christ, according to Gal. 5:24, "They that are Christ's, have crucified their flesh with the vices and concupiscences."

Reply to Objection 1: The state of the Old Testament is compared to the night, while the state of the New Testament is compared to the day, according to Rom. 13:12, "The night is passed and the day is at hand." Therefore in the Old Testament they fasted until night, but not in the New Testament.

Reply to Objection 2: Fasting requires a fixed hour based, not on a strict calculation, but on a rough estimate: for it suffices that it be about the ninth hour, and this is easy for anyone to ascertain.

Reply to Objection 3: A little more or a little less cannot do much harm. Now it is not a long space of time from the sixth hour at which men for the most part are wont to eat, until the ninth hour, which is fixed for those who fast. Wherefore the fixing of such a time cannot do much harm to anyone, whatever his circumstances may be. If however this were to prove a heavy burden to a man on account of sickness, age, or some similar reason, he should be dispensed from fasting, or be allowed to forestall the hour by a little.

Whether it is fitting that those who fast should be bidden to abstain from flesh meat, eggs, and milk foods?

Objection 1: It would seem unfitting that those who fast should be bidden to abstain from flesh meat, eggs, and milk foods. For it has been stated above [3490](A[6]) that fasting was instituted as a curb on the concupiscence of the flesh. Now concupiscence is kindled by drinking wine more than by eating flesh; according to Prov. 20:1, "Wine is a luxurious thing," and Eph. 5:18, "Be not drunk with wine, wherein is luxury." Since then those who fast are not forbidden to drink wine, it seems that they should not be forbidden to eat flesh meat.

Objection 2: Further, some fish are as delectable to eat as the flesh of certain animals. Now "concupiscence is desire of the delectable," as stated above ([3491]FS, Q[30], A[1]). Therefore since fasting which was instituted in order to bridle concupiscence does not exclude the eating of fish, neither should it exclude the eating of flesh meat.

Objection 3: Further, on certain fasting days people make use of eggs and cheese. Therefore one can likewise make use of them during the Lenten fast.

On the contrary, stands the common custom of the faithful.

I answer that, As stated above [3492](A[6]), fasting was instituted by the Church in order to bridle the concupiscences of the flesh, which regard pleasures of touch in connection with food and sex. Wherefore the Church forbade those who fast to partake of those foods which both afford most pleasure to the palate, and besides are a very great incentive to lust. Such are the flesh of animals that take their rest on the earth, and of those that breathe the air and their products, such as milk from those that walk on the earth, and eggs from birds. For, since such like animals are more like man in body, they afford greater pleasure as food, and greater nourishment to the human body, so that from their consumption there results a greater surplus available for seminal matter, which when abundant becomes a great incentive to lust. Hence the Church has bidden those who fast to abstain especially from these foods.

Reply to Objection 1: Three things concur in the act of procreation, namely, heat, spirit [*Cf. P. I., Q. 118, A[1], ad 3], and humor. Wine and other things that heat the body conduce especially to heat: flatulent foods seemingly cooperate in the production of the vital spirit: but it is chiefly the use of flesh meat which is most productive of nourishment, that conduces to the production of humor. Now the alteration occasioned by heat, and the increase in vital spirits are of short duration, whereas the substance of the humor remains a long time. Hence those who fast are forbidden the use of flesh meat rather than of wine or vegetables which are flatulent foods.

Reply to Objection 2: In the institution of fasting, the Church takes account of the more common occurrences. Now, generally speaking, eating flesh meat affords more pleasure than eating fish, although this is not always the case. Hence the Church forbade those who fast to eat flesh meat, rather than to eat fish.

Reply to Objection 3: Eggs and milk foods are forbidden to those who fast, for as much as they originate from animals that provide us with flesh: wherefore the prohibition of flesh meat takes precedence of the prohibition of eggs and milk foods. Again the Lenten fast is the most solemn of all, both because it is kept in imitation of Christ, and because it disposes us to celebrate devoutly the mysteries of our redemption. For this reason the eating of flesh meat is forbidden in every fast, while the Lenten fast lays a general prohibition even on eggs and milk foods. As to the use of the latter things in other fasts the custom varies among different people, and each person is bound to conform to that custom which is in vogue with those among whom he is dwelling. Hence Jerome says [*Augustine, De Lib. Arb. iii, 18; cf. De Nat. et Grat. lxvii]: "Let each province keep to its own practice, and look upon the commands of the elders as though they were the laws of the apostles."

OF GLUTTONY (SIX ARTICLES)

We must now consider gluttony. Under this head there are six points of inquiry:

(1) Whether gluttony is a sin?

(2) Whether it is a mortal sin?

(3) Whether it is the greatest of sins?

(4) Its species;

(5) Whether it is a capital sin?

(6) Its daughters.

Whether gluttony is a sin?

Objection 1: It would seem that gluttony is not a sin. For our Lord said (Mat. 15:11): "Not that which goeth into the mouth defileth a man." Now gluttony regards food which goes into a man. Therefore, since every sin defiles a man, it seems that gluttony is not a sin.

Objection 2: Further, "No man sins in what he cannot avoid" [*Ep. lxxi, ad Lucin.]. Now gluttony is immoderation in food; and man cannot avoid this, for Gregory says (Moral. xxx, 18): "Since in eating pleasure and necessity go together, we fail to discern between the call of necessity and the seduction of pleasure," and Augustine says (Confess. x, 31): "Who is it, Lord, that does not eat a little more than necessary?" Therefore gluttony is not a sin.

Objection 3: Further, in every kind of sin the first movement is a sin. But the first movement in taking food is not a sin, else hunger and thirst would be sinful. Therefore gluttony is not a sin.

On the contrary, Gregory says (Moral. xxx, 18) that "unless we first tame the enemy dwelling within us, namely our gluttonous appetite, we have not even stood up to engage in the spiritual combat." But man's inward enemy is sin. Therefore gluttony is a sin.

I answer that, Gluttony denotes, not any desire of eating and drinking, but an inordinate desire. Now desire is said to be inordinate through leaving the order of reason, wherein the good of moral virtue consists: and a thing is said to be a sin through being contrary to virtue. Wherefore it is evident that gluttony is a sin.

Reply to Objection 1: That which goes into man by way of food, by reason of its substance and nature, does not defile a man spiritually. But the Jews, against whom our Lord is speaking, and the Manichees deemed certain foods to make a man unclean, not on account of their signification, but by reason of their nature [*Cf. [3493]FS, Q[102], A[6], ad 1]. It is the inordinate desire of food that defiles a man spiritually.

Reply to Objection 2: As stated above, the vice of gluttony does not regard the substance of food, but in the desire thereof not being regulated by reason. Wherefore if a man exceed in quantity of food, not from desire of food, but through deeming it necessary to him, this pertains, not to gluttony, but to some kind of inexperience. It is a case of gluttony only when a man knowingly exceeds the measure in eating, from a desire for the pleasures of the palate.

Reply to Objection 3: The appetite is twofold. There is the natural appetite, which belongs to the powers of the vegetal soul. In these powers virtue and vice are impossible, since they cannot be subject to reason; wherefore the appetitive power is differentiated from the powers of secretion, digestion, and excretion, and to it hunger and thirst are to be referred. Besides this there is another, the sensitive appetite, and it is in the concupiscence of this appetite that the vice of gluttony consists. Hence the first movement of gluttony denotes inordinateness in the sensitive appetite, and this is not without sin.

Whether gluttony is a mortal sin?

Objection 1: It would seem that gluttony is not a mortal sin. For every mortal sin is contrary to a precept of the Decalogue: and this, apparently, does not apply to gluttony. Therefore gluttony is not a mortal sin.

Objection 2: Further, every mortal sin is contrary to charity, as stated above ([3494]Q[132], A[3]). But gluttony is not opposed to charity, neither as regards the love of God, nor as regards the love of one's neighbor. Therefore gluttony is never a mortal sin.

Objection 3: Further, Augustine says in a sermon on Purgatory [*Cf. Append. to St. Augustine's works: Serm. civ (xli, de sanctis)]: "Whenever a man takes more meat and drink than is necessary, he should know that this is one of the lesser sins." But this pertains to gluttony. Therefore gluttony is accounted among the lesser, that is to say venial, sins.

Objection 4: On the contrary, Gregory says (Moral. xxx, 18): "As long as the vice of gluttony has a hold on a man, all that he has done valiantly is forfeited by him: and as long as the belly is unrestrained, all virtue comes to naught." But virtue is not done away save by mortal sin. Therefore gluttony is a mortal sin.

I answer that, As stated above [3495](A[1]), the vice of gluttony properly consists in inordinate concupiscence. Now the order of reason in regulating the concupiscence may be considered from two points of view. First, with regard to things directed to the end, inasmuch as they may be incommensurate and consequently improportionate to the end; secondly, with regard to the end itself, inasmuch as concupiscence turns man away from his due end. Accordingly, if the inordinate concupiscence in gluttony be found to turn man away from the last end, gluttony will be a mortal sin. This is the case when he adheres to the pleasure of gluttony as his end, for the sake of which he contemns God, being ready to disobey God's commandments, in order to obtain those pleasures. On the other hand, if the inordinate concupiscence in the vice of gluttony be found to affect only such things as are directed to the end, for instance when a man has too great a desire for the pleasures of the palate, yet would not for their sake do anything contrary to God's law, it is a venial sin.

Reply to Objection 1: The vice of gluttony becomes a mortal sin by turning man away from his last end: and accordingly, by a kind of reduction, it is opposed to the precept of hallowing the sabbath, which commands us to rest in our last end. For mortal sins are not all directly opposed to the precepts of the Decalogue, but only those which contain injustice: because the precepts of the Decalogue pertain specially to justice and its parts, as stated above ([3496]Q[122], A[1]).

Reply to Objection 2: In so far as it turns man away from his last end, gluttony is opposed to the love of God, who is to be loved, as our last end, above all things: and only in this respect is gluttony a mortal sin.

Reply to Objection 3: This saying of Augustine refers to gluttony as denoting inordinate concupiscence merely in regard of things directed to the end.

Reply to Objection 4: Gluttony is said to bring virtue to naught, not so much on its own account, as on account of the vices which arise from it. For Gregory says (Pastor. iii, 19): "When the belly is distended by gluttony, the virtues of the soul are destroyed by lust."

Whether gluttony is the greatest of sins?

Objection 1: It would seem that gluttony is the greatest of sins. For the grievousness of a sin is measured by the grievousness of the punishment. Now the sin of gluttony is most grievously punished, for Chrysostom says [*Hom. xiii in Matth.]: "Gluttony turned Adam out of Paradise, gluttony it was that drew down the deluge at the time of Noah." According to Ezech. 16:49, "This was the iniquity of Sodom, thy sister . . . fulness of bread," etc. Therefore the sin of gluttony is the greatest of all.

Objection 2: Further, in every genus the cause is the most powerful. Now gluttony is apparently the cause of other sins, for a gloss on Ps. 135:10, "Who smote Egypt with their first-born," says: "Lust, concupiscence, pride are the first-born of gluttony." Therefore gluttony is the greatest of sins.

Objection 3: Further, man should love himself in the first place after God, as stated above ([3497]Q[25], A[4]). Now man, by the vice of gluttony, inflicts an injury on himself: for it is written (Ecclus. 37:34): "By surfeiting many have perished." Therefore gluttony is the greatest of sins, at least excepting those that are against God.

On the contrary, The sins of the flesh, among which gluttony is reckoned, are less culpable according to Gregory (Moral. xxxiii).

I answer that, The gravity of a sin may be measured in three ways. First and foremost it depends on the matter in which the sin is committed: and in this way sins committed in connection with Divine things are the greatest. From this point of view gluttony is not the greatest sin, for it is about matters connected with the nourishment of the body. Secondly, the gravity of a sin depends on the person who sins, and from this point of view the sin of gluttony is diminished rather than aggravated, both on account of the necessity of taking food, and on account of the difficulty of proper discretion and moderation in such matters. Thirdly, from the point of view of the result that follows, and in this way gluttony has a certain gravity, inasmuch as certain sins are occasioned thereby.

Reply to Objection 1: These punishments are to be referred to the vices that resulted from gluttony, or to the root from which gluttony sprang, rather than to gluttony itself. For the first man was expelled from Paradise on account of pride, from which he went on to an act of gluttony: while the deluge and the punishment of the people of Sodom were inflicted for sins occasioned by gluttony.

Reply to Objection 2: This objection argues from the standpoint of the sins that result from gluttony. Nor is a cause necessarily more powerful, unless it be a direct cause: and gluttony is not the direct cause but the accidental cause, as it were, and the occasion of other vices.

Reply to Objection 3: The glutton intends, not the harm to his body, but the pleasure of eating: and if injury results to his body, this is accidental. Hence this does not directly affect the gravity of gluttony, the guilt of which is nevertheless aggravated, if a man incur some bodily injury through taking too much food.

Whether the species of gluttony are fittingly distinguished?

Objection 1: It seems that the species of gluttony are unfittingly distinguished by Gregory who says (Moral. xxx, 18): "The vice of gluttony tempts us in five ways. Sometimes it forestalls the hour of need; sometimes it seeks costly meats; sometimes it requires the food to be daintily cooked; sometimes it exceeds the measure of refreshment by taking too much; sometimes we sin by the very heat of an immoderate appetite"—which are contained in the following verse: "Hastily, sumptuously, too much, greedily, daintily."

For the above are distinguished according to diversity of circumstance. Now circumstances, being the accidents of an act, do not differentiate its species. Therefore the species of gluttony are not distinguished according to the aforesaid.

Objection 2: Further, as time is a circumstance, so is place. If then gluttony admits of one species in respect of time, it seems that there should likewise be others in respect of place and other circumstances.

Objection 3: Further, just as temperance observes due circumstances, so do the other moral virtues. Now the species of the vices opposed to the other moral virtues are not distinguished according to various circumstances. Neither, therefore, are the species of gluttony distinguished thus.

On the contrary, stands the authority of Gregory quoted above.

I answer that, As stated above [3498](A[1]), gluttony denotes inordinate concupiscence in eating. Now two things are to be considered in eating, namely the food we eat, and the eating thereof. Accordingly, the inordinate concupiscence may be considered in two ways. First, with regard to the food consumed: and thus, as regards the substance or species of food a man seeks "sumptuous"—i.e. costly food; as regards its quality, he seeks food prepared too nicely—i.e. "daintily"; and as regards quantity, he exceeds by eating "too much."

Secondly, the inordinate concupiscence is considered as to the consumption of food: either because one forestalls the proper time for eating, which is to eat "hastily," or one fails to observe the due manner of eating, by eating "greedily."

Isidore [*De Summo Bon. ii, 42] comprises the first and second under one heading, when he says that the glutton exceeds in "what" he eats, or in "how much," "how" or "when he eats."

Reply to Objection 1: The corruption of various circumstances causes the various species of gluttony, on account of the various motives, by reason of which the species of moral things are differentiated. For in him that seeks sumptuous food, concupiscence is aroused by the very species of the food; in him that forestalls the time concupiscence is disordered through impatience of delay, and so forth.

Reply to Objection 2: Place and other circumstances include no special motive connected with eating, that can cause a different species of gluttony.

Reply to Objection 3: In all other vices, whenever different circumstances correspond to different motives, the difference of circumstances argues a specific difference of vice: but this does not apply to all circumstances, as stated above ([3499]FS, Q[72], A[9]).

Whether gluttony is a capital vice?

Objection 1: It would seem that gluttony is not a capital vice. For capital vices denote those whence, under the aspect of final cause, other vices originate. Now food, which is the matter of gluttony, has not the aspect of end, since it is sought, not for its own sake, but for the body's nourishment. Therefore gluttony is not a capital vice.

Objection 2: Further, a capital vice would seem to have a certain pre-eminence in sinfulness. But this does not apply to gluttony, which, in respect of its genus, is apparently the least of sins, seeing that it is most akin to what is in respect of its genus, is apparently the least gluttony is not a capital vice.

Objection 3: Further, sin results from a man forsaking the food of virtue on account of something useful to the present life, or pleasing to the senses. Now as regards goods having the aspect of utility, there is but one capital vice, namely covetousness. Therefore, seemingly, there would be but one capital vice in respect of pleasures: and this is lust, which is a greater vice than gluttony, and is about greater pleasures. Therefore gluttony is not a capital vice.

On the contrary, Gregory (Moral. xxxi, 45) reckons gluttony among the capital vices.

I answer that, As stated above ([3500]FS, Q[84], A[3]), a capital vice denotes one from which, considered as final cause, i.e. as having a most desirable end, other vices originate: wherefore through desiring that end men are incited to sin in many ways. Now an end is rendered most desirable through having one of the conditions of happiness which is desirable by its very nature: and pleasure is essential to happiness, according to Ethic. i, 8; x, 3,7,8. Therefore the vice of gluttony, being about pleasures of touch which stand foremost among other pleasures, is fittingly reckoned among the capital vices.

Reply to Objection 1: It is true that food itself is directed to something as its end: but since that end, namely the sustaining of life, is most desirable and whereas life cannot be sustained without food, it follows that food too is most desirable: indeed, nearly all the toil of man's life is directed thereto, according to Eccles. 6:7, "All the labor of man is for his mouth." Yet gluttony seems to be about pleasures of food rather than about food itself; wherefore, as Augustine says (De Vera Relig. liii), "with such food as is good for the worthless body, men desire to be fed," wherein namely the pleasure consists, "rather than to be filled: since the whole end of that desire is this—not to thirst and not to hunger."

Reply to Objection 2: In sin the end is ascertained with respect to the conversion, while the gravity of sin is determined with regard to the aversion. Wherefore it does not follow that the capital sin which has the most desirable end surpasses the others in gravity.

Reply to Objection 3: That which gives pleasure is desirable in itself: and consequently corresponding to its diversity there are two capital vices, namely gluttony and lust. On the other hand, that which is useful is desirable, not in itself, but as directed to something else: wherefore seemingly in all useful things there is one aspect of desirability. Hence there is but one capital vice, in respect of such things.

Whether six daughters are fittingly assigned to gluttony?

Objection 1: It would seem that six daughters are unfittingly assigned to gluttony, to wit, "unseemly joy, scurrility, uncleanness, loquaciousness, and dullness of mind as regards the understanding." For unseemly joy results from every sin, according to Prov. 2:14, "Who are glad when they have done evil, and rejoice in most wicked things." Likewise dullness of mind is associated with every sin, according to Prov. 14:22, "They err that work evil." Therefore they are unfittingly reckoned to be daughters of gluttony.

Objection 2: Further, the uncleanness which is particularly the result of gluttony would seem to be connected with vomiting, according to Is. 28:8, "All tables were full of vomit and filth." But this seems to be not a sin but a punishment; or even a useful thing that is a matter of counsel, according to Ecclus. 31:25, "If thou hast been forced to eat much, arise, go out, and vomit; and it shall refresh thee." Therefore it should not be reckoned among the daughters of gluttony.

Objection 3: Further, Isidore (QQ. in Deut. xvi) reckons scurrility as a daughter of lust. Therefore it should not be reckoned among the daughters of gluttony.

On the contrary, Gregory (Moral. xxxi, 45) assigns these daughters to gluttony.

I answer that, As stated above ([3501]AA[1],2,3), gluttony consists properly in an immoderate pleasure in eating and drinking. Wherefore those vices are reckoned among the daughters of gluttony, which are the results of eating and drinking immoderately. These may be accounted for either on the part of the soul or on the part of the body. on the part of the soul these results are of four kinds. First, as regards the reason, whose keenness is dulled by immoderate meat and drink, and in this respect we reckon as a daughter of gluttony, "dullness of sense in the understanding," on account of the fumes of food disturbing the brain. Even so, on the other hand, abstinence conduces to the penetrating power of wisdom, according to Eccles. 2:3, "I thought in my heart to withdraw my flesh from wine, that I might turn my mind in wisdom." Secondly, as regards the. appetite, which is disordered in many ways by immoderation in eating and drinking, as though reason were fast asleep at the helm, and in this respect "unseemly joy" is reckoned, because all the other inordinate passions are directed to joy or sorrow, as stated in Ethic. ii, 5. To this we must refer the saying of 3 Esdra 3:20, that "wine . . . gives every one a confident and joyful mind." Thirdly, as regards inordinate words, and thus we have "loquaciousness," because as Gregory says (Pastor. iii, 19), "unless gluttons were carried away by immoderate speech, that rich man who is stated to have feasted sumptuously every day would not have been so tortured in his tongue." Fourthly, as regards inordinate action, and in this way we have "scurrility," i.e. a kind of levity resulting from lack of reason, which is unable not only to bridle the speech, but also to restrain outward behavior. Hence a gloss on Eph. 5:4, "Or foolish talking or scurrility," says that "fools call this geniality—i.e. jocularity, because it is wont to raise a laugh." Both of these, however, may be referred to the words which may happen to be sinful, either by reason of excess which belongs to "loquaciousness," or by reason of unbecomingness, which belongs to "scurrility."

On the part of the body, mention is made of "uncleanness," which may refer either to the inordinate emission of any kind of superfluities, or especially to the emission of the semen. Hence a gloss on Eph. 5:3, "But fornication and all uncleanness," says: "That is, any kind of incontinence that has reference to lust."

Reply to Objection 1: Joy in the act or end of sin results from every sin, especially the sin that proceeds from habit, but the random riotous joy which is described as "unseemly" arises chiefly from immoderate partaking of meat or drink. In like manner, we reply that dullness of sense as regards matters of choice is common to all sin, whereas dullness of sense in speculative matters arises chiefly from gluttony, for the reason given above.

Reply to Objection 2: Although it does one good to vomit after eating too much, yet it is sinful to expose oneself to its necessity by immoderate meat or drink. However, it is no sin to procure vomiting as a remedy for sickness if the physician prescribes it.

Reply to Objection 3: Scurrility proceeds from the act of gluttony, and not from the lustful act, but from the lustful will: wherefore it may be referred to either vice.

OF SOBRIETY (FOUR ARTICLES)

We must now consider sobriety and the contrary vice, namely drunkenness. As regards sobriety there are four points of inquiry:

(1) What is the matter of sobriety?

(2) Whether it is a special virtue?

(3) Whether the use of wine is lawful?

(4) To whom especially is sobriety becoming?

Whether drink is the matter of sobriety?

Objection 1: It would seem that drink is not the matter proper to sobriety. For it is written (Rom. 12:3): "Not to be more wise than it behooveth to be wise, but to be wise unto sobriety." Therefore sobriety is also about wisdom, and not only about drink.

Objection 2: Further, concerning the wisdom of God, it is written (Wis. 8:7) that "she teacheth sobriety [Douay: 'temperance'], and prudence, and justice, and fortitude," where sobriety stands for temperance. Now temperance is not only about drink, but also about meat and sexual matters. Therefore sobriety is not only about drink.

Objection 3: Further, sobriety would seem to take its name from "measure" [*'Bria,' a measure, a cup; Cf. Facciolati and Forcellini's Lexicon]. Now we ought to be guided by the measure in all things appertaining to us: for it is written (Titus 2:12): "We should live soberly and justly and godly," where a gloss remarks: "Soberly, in ourselves"; and (1 Tim. 2:9): "Women . . . in decent apparel, adorning themselves with modesty and sobriety." Consequently it would seem that sobriety regards not only the interior man, but also things appertaining to external apparel. Therefore drink is not the matter proper to sobriety.

On the contrary, It is written (Ecclus. 31:32): "Wine taken with sobriety is equal life to men; if thou drink it moderately, thou shalt be sober."

I answer that, When a virtue is denominated from some condition common to the virtues, the matter specially belonging to it is that in which it is most difficult and most commendable to satisfy that condition of virtue: thus fortitude is about dangers of death, and temperance about pleasures of touch. Now sobriety takes its name from "measure," for a man is said to be sober because he observes the "bria," i.e. the measure. Wherefore sobriety lays a special claim to that matter wherein /the observance of the measure is most deserving of praise. Such matter is the drinking of intoxicants, because the measured use thereof is most profitable, while immoderate excess therein is most harmful, since it hinders the use of reason even more than excessive eating. Hence it is written (Ecclus. 31:37,38): "Sober drinking is health to soul and body; wine drunken with excess raiseth quarrels, and wrath and many ruins." For this reason sobriety is especially concerned with drink, not any kind of drink, but that which by reason of its volatility is liable to disturb the brain, such as wine and all intoxicants. Nevertheless, sobriety may be employed in a general sense so as to apply to any matter, as stated above ([3502]Q[123], A[2];[3503] Q[141], A[2]) with regard to fortitude and temperance.

Reply to Objection 1: Just as the material wine intoxicates a man as to his body, so too, speaking figuratively, the consideration of wisdom is said to be an inebriating draught, because it allures the mind by its delight, according to Ps. 22:5, "My chalice which inebriateth me, how goodly is it!" Hence sobriety is applied by a kind of metaphor in speaking of the contemplation of wisdom.

Reply to Objection 2: All the things that belong properly to temperance are necessary to the present life, and their excess is harmful. Wherefore it behooves one to apply a measure in all such things. This is the business of sobriety: and for this reason sobriety is used to designate temperance. Yet slight excess is more harmful in drink than in other things, wherefore sobriety is especially concerned with drink.

Reply to Objection 3: Although a measure is needful in all things, sobriety is not properly employed in connection with all things, but only in those wherein there is most need for a measure.

Whether sobriety is by itself a special virtue?

Objection 1: It would seem that sobriety is not by itself a special virtue. For abstinence is concerned with both meat and drink. Now there is no special virtue about meat. Therefore neither is sobriety, which is about drink, a special virtue.

Objection 2: Further, abstinence and gluttony are about pleasures of touch as sensitive to food. Now meat and drink combine together to make food, since an animal needs a combination of wet and dry nourishment. Therefore sobriety, which is about drink, is not a. special virtue.

Objection 3: Further, just as in things pertaining to nourishment, drink is distinguished from meat, so are there various kinds of meats and of drinks. Therefore if sobriety is by itself a special virtue, seemingly there will be a special virtue corresponding to each different kind of meat or drink, which is unreasonable. Therefore it would seem that sobriety is not a special virtue.

On the contrary, Macrobius [*In Somno Scip. i, 8] reckons sobriety to be a special part of temperance.

I answer that, As stated above ([3504]Q[146], A[2]), it belongs to moral virtue to safeguard the good of reason against those things which may hinder it. Hence wherever we find a special hindrance to reason, there must needs be a special virtue to remove it. Now intoxicating drink is a special kind of hindrance to the use of reason, inasmuch as it disturbs the brain by its fumes. Wherefore in order to remove this hindrance to reason a special virtue, which is sobriety, is requisite.

Reply to Objection 1: Meat and drink are alike capable of hindering the good of reason, by embroiling the reason with immoderate pleasure: and in this respect abstinence is about both meat and drink alike. But intoxicating drink is a special kind of hindrance, as stated above, wherefore it requires a special virtue.

Reply to Objection 2: The virtue of abstinence is about meat and drink, considered, not as food but as a hindrance to reason. Hence it does not follow that special kinds of virtue correspond to different kinds of food.

Reply to Objection 3: In all intoxicating drinks there is one kind of hindrance to the use of reason: so that the difference of drinks bears an accidental relation to virtue. Hence this difference does not call for a difference of virtue. The same applies to the difference of meats.

Whether the use of wine is altogether unlawful?

Objection 1: It would seem that the use of wine is altogether unlawful. For without wisdom, a man cannot be in the state of salvation: since it is written (Wis. 7:28): "God loveth none but him that dwelleth with wisdom," and further on (Wis. 9:19): "By wisdom they were healed, whosoever have pleased Thee, O Lord, from the beginning." Now the use of wine is a hindrance to wisdom, for it is written (Eccles. 2:3): "I thought in my heart to withdraw my flesh from wine, that I might turn my mind to wisdom." Therefore wine-drinking is altogether unlawful.

Objection 2: Further, the Apostle says (Rom. 14:21): "It is good not to eat flesh, and not to drink wine, nor anything whereby thy brother is offended or scandalized, or made weak." Now it is sinful to forsake the good of virtue, as likewise to scandalize one's brethren. Therefore it is unlawful to make use of wine.

Objection 3: Further, Jerome says [*Contra Jovin. i] that "after the deluge wine and flesh were sanctioned: but Christ came in the last of the ages and brought back the end into line with the beginning." Therefore it seems unlawful to use wine under the Christian law.

On the contrary, The Apostle says (1 Tim. 5:23): "Do not still drink water, but use a little wine for thy stomach's sake, and thy frequent infirmities"; and it is written (Ecclus. 31:36): "Wine drunken with moderation is the joy of the soul and the heart."

I answer that, No meat or drink, considered in itself, is unlawful, according to Mat. 15:11, "Not that which goeth into the mouth defileth a man." Wherefore it is not unlawful to drink wine as such. Yet it may become unlawful accidentally. This is sometimes owing to a circumstance on the part of the drinker, either because he is easily the worse for taking wine, or because he is bound by a vow not to drink wine: sometimes it results from the mode of drinking, because to wit he exceeds the measure in drinking: and sometimes it is on account of others who would be scandalized thereby.

Reply to Objection 1: A man may have wisdom in two ways. First, in a general way, according as it is sufficient for salvation: and in this way it is required, in order to have wisdom, not that a man abstain altogether from wine, but that he abstain from its immoderate use. Secondly, a man may have wisdom in some degree of perfection: and in this way, in order to receive wisdom perfectly, it is requisite for certain persons that they abstain altogether from wine, and this depends on circumstances of certain persons and places.

Reply to Objection 2: The Apostle does not declare simply that it is good to abstain from wine, but that it is good in the case where this would give scandal to certain people.

Reply to Objection 3: Christ withdraws us from some things as being altogether unlawful, and from others as being obstacles to perfection. It is in the latter way that he withdraws some from the use of wine, that they may aim at perfection, even as from riches and the like.

Whether sobriety is more requisite in persons of greater standing?

Objection 1: It would seem that sobriety is more requisite in persons of greater standing. For old age gives a man a certain standing; wherefore honor and reverence are due to the old, according to Lev. 19:32, "Rise up before the hoary head, and honor the person of the aged man." Now the Apostle declares that old men especially should be exhorted to sobriety, according to Titus 2:2, "That the aged man be sober." Therefore sobriety is most requisite in persons of standing.

Objection 2: Further, a bishop has the highest degree in the Church: and the Apostle commands him to be sober, according to 1 Tim. 3:2, "It behooveth . . . a bishop to be blameless, the husband of one wife, sober, prudent," etc. Therefore sobriety is chiefly required in persons of high standing.

Objection 3: Further, sobriety denotes abstinence from wine. Now wine is forbidden to kings, who hold the highest place in human affairs: while it is allowed to those who are in a state of affliction, according to Prov. 31:4, "Give not wine to kings," and further on (Prov. 31:6), "Give strong drink to them that are sad, and wine to them that are grieved in mind." Therefore sobriety is more requisite in persons of standing.

On the contrary, The Apostle says (1 Tim. 3:11): "The women in like manner, chaste . . . sober," etc., and (Titus 2:6) "Young men in like manner exhort that they be sober."

I answer that, Virtue includes relationship to two things, to the contrary vices which it removes, and to the end to which it leads. Accordingly a particular virtue is more requisite in certain persons for two reasons. First, because they are more prone to the concupiscences which need to be restrained by virtue, and to the vices which are removed by virtue. In this respect, sobriety is most requisite in the young and in women, because concupiscence of pleasure thrives in the young on account of the heat of youth, while in women there is not sufficient strength of mind to resist concupiscence. Hence, according to Valerius Maximus [*Dict. Fact. Memor. ii, 1] among the ancient Romans women drank no wine. Secondly, sobriety is more requisite in certain persons, as being more necessary for the operations proper to them. Now immoderate use of wine is a notable obstacle to the use of reason: wherefore sobriety is specially prescribed to the old, in whom reason should be vigorous in instructing others: to bishops and all ministers of the

Church, who should fulfil their spiritual duties with a devout mind; and to kings, who should rule their subjects with wisdom.

This suffices for the Replies to the Objections.

OF DRUNKENNESS (FOUR ARTICLES)

We must now consider drunkenness. Under this head there are four points of inquiry:

(1) Whether drunkenness is a sin?

(2) Whether it is a mortal sin?

(3) Whether it is the most grievous sin?

(4) Whether it excuses from sin?

Whether drunkenness is a sin?

Objection 1: It would seem that drunkenness is not a sin. For every sin has a corresponding contrary sin, thus timidity is opposed to daring, and presumption to pusillanimity. But no sin is opposed to drunkenness. Therefore drunkenness is not a sin.

Objection 2: Further, every sin is voluntary [*Augustine, De Vera Relig. xiv]. But no man wishes to be drunk, since no man wishes to be deprived of the use of reason. Therefore drunkenness is not a sin.

Objection 3: Further, whoever causes another to sin, sins himself. Therefore, if drunkenness were a sin, it would follow that it is a sin to ask a man to drink that which makes him drunk, which would seem very hard.

Objection 4: Further, every sin calls for correction. But correction is not applied to drunkards: for Gregory [*Cf. Canon Denique, dist. 4 where Gratian refers to a letter of St. Gregory to St. Augustine of Canterbury] says that "we must forbear with their ways, lest they become worse if they be compelled to give up the habit." Therefore drunkenness is not a sin.

On the contrary, The Apostle says (Rom. 13:13): "Not in rioting and drunkenness."

I answer that, Drunkenness may be understood in two ways. First, it may signify the defect itself of a man resulting from his drinking much wine, the consequence being that he loses the use of reason. In this sense drunkenness denotes not a sin, but a penal defect resulting from a fault. Secondly, drunkenness may denote the act by which a man incurs this defect. This act may cause drunkenness in two ways. In one way, through the wine being too strong, without the drinker being cognizant of this: and in this way too, drunkenness may occur without sin, especially if it is not through his negligence, and thus we believe that Noah was made drunk as related in Gn. 9. In another way drunkenness may result from inordinate concupiscence and use of wine: in this way it is accounted a sin, and is comprised under gluttony as a species under its genus. For gluttony is divided into "surfeiting [Douay:,'rioting'] and drunkenness," which are forbidden by the Apostle (Rom. 13:13).

Reply to Objection 1: As the Philosopher says (Ethic. iii, 11), insensibility which is opposed to temperance "is not very common," so that like its species which are opposed to the species of intemperance it has no name. Hence the vice opposed to drunkenness is unnamed; and yet if a man were knowingly to abstain from wine to the extent of molesting nature grievously, he would not be free from sin.

Reply to Objection 2: This objection regards the resulting defect which is involuntary: whereas immoderate use of wine is voluntary, and it is in this that the sin consists.

Reply to Objection 3: Even as he that is drunk is excused if he knows not the strength of the wine, so too is he that invites another to drink excused from sin, if he be unaware that the drinker is the kind of person to be made drunk by the drink offered. But if ignorance be lacking neither is excused from sin.

Reply to Objection 4: Sometimes the correction of a sinner is to be foregone, as stated above ([3505]Q[33], A[6]). Hence Augustine says in a letter (Ad Aurel. Episc. Ep. xxii), "Meseems, such things are cured not by bitterness, severity, harshness, but by teaching rather than commanding, by advice rather than threats. Such is the course to be followed with the majority of sinners: few are they whose sins should be treated with severity."

Whether drunkenness is a mortal sin?

Objection 1: It would seem that drunkenness is not a mortal sin. For Augustine says in a sermon on Purgatory [*Serm. civ in the Appendix to St. Augustine's works] that "drunkenness if indulged in assiduously, is a mortal sin." Now assiduity denotes a circumstance which does not change the species of a sin; so that it cannot aggravate a sin infinitely, and make a mortal sin of a venial sin, as shown above ([3506]FS, Q[88], A[5]). Therefore if drunkenness /is not a mortal sin for some other reason, neither is it for this.

Objection 2: Further, Augustine says [*Serm. civ in the Appendix to St. Augustine's works]: "Whenever a man takes more meat and drink than is necessary, he should know that this is one of the lesser sins." Now the lesser sins are called venial. Therefore drunkenness, which is caused by immoderate drink, is a venial sin.

Objection 3: Further, no mortal sin should be committed on the score of medicine. Now some drink too much at the advice of the physician, that they may be purged by vomiting; and from this excessive drink drunkenness ensues. Therefore drunkenness is not a mortal sin.

On the contrary, We read in the Canons of the apostles (Can. xli, xlii): "A bishop, priest or deacon who is given to drunkenness or gambling, or incites others thereto, must either cease or be deposed; a subdeacon, reader or precentor who does these things must either give them up or be excommunicated; the same applies to the laity." Now such punishments are not inflicted save for mortal sins. Therefore drunkenness is a mortal sin.

I answer that, The sin of drunkenness, as stated in the foregoing Article, consists in the immoderate use and concupiscence of wine. Now this may happen to a man in three ways. First, so that he knows not the drink to be immoderate and intoxicating: and then drunkenness may be without sin, as stated above [3507](A[1]). Secondly, so that he perceives the drink to be immoderate, but without knowing it to be intoxicating, and then drunkenness may involve a venial sin. Thirdly, it may happen that a man is well aware that the drink is immoderate and intoxicating, and yet he would rather be drunk than abstain from drink. Such a man is a drunkard properly speaking, because morals take their species not from things that occur accidentally and beside the intention, but from that which is directly intended. In this way drunkenness is a mortal sin, because then a man willingly and knowingly deprives himself of the use of reason, whereby he performs virtuous deeds and avoids sin, and thus he sins mortally by running the risk of falling into sin. For Ambrose says (De Patriarch. [*De Abraham i.]): "We learn that we should shun drunkenness, which prevents us from avoiding grievous sins. For the things we avoid when sober, we unknowingly commit through drunkenness." Therefore drunkenness, properly speaking, is a mortal sin.

Reply to Objection 1: Assiduity makes drunkenness a mortal sin, not on account of the mere repetition of the act, but because it is impossible for a man to become drunk assiduously, without exposing himself to drunkenness knowingly and willingly, since he has many times experienced the strength of wine and his own liability to drunkenness.

Reply to Objection 2: To take more meat or drink than is necessary belongs to the vice of gluttony, which is not always a mortal sin: but knowingly to take too much drink to the point of being drunk, is a mortal sin. Hence Augustine says (Confess. x, 31): "Drunkenness is far from me: Thou wilt have mercy, that it come not near me. But full feeding sometimes hath crept upon Thy servant."

Reply to Objection 3: As stated above ([3508]Q[141], A[6]), meat and drink should be moderate in accordance with the demands of the body's health. Wherefore, just as it happens sometimes that the meat and drink which are moderate for a healthy man are immoderate for a sick man, so too it may happen conversely, that what is excessive for a healthy man is moderate for one that is ailing. In this way when a man eats or drinks much at the physician's advice in order to provoke vomiting, he is not to be deemed to have taken excessive meat or drink. There is, however, no need for intoxicating drink in order to procure vomiting, since this is caused by drinking lukewarm water: wherefore this is no sufficient cause for excusing a man from drunkenness.

Whether drunkenness is the gravest of sins?

Objection 1: It would seem that drunkenness is the gravest of sins. For Chrysostom says (Hom. lviii in Matth.) that "nothing gains the devil's favor so much as drunkenness and lust, the mother of all the vices." And it is written in the Decretals (Dist. xxxv, can. Ante omnia): "Drunkenness, more than anything else, is to be avoided by the clergy, for it foments and fosters all the vices."

Objection 2: Further, from the very fact that a thing excludes the good of reason, it is a sin. Now this is especially the effect of drunkenness. Therefore drunkenness is the greatest of sins.

Objection 3: Further, the gravity of a sin is shown by the gravity of its punishment. Now seemingly drunkenness is punished most severely; for Ambrose says

[*De Elia et de Jejunio v] that "there would be no slavery, were there no drunkards." Therefore drunkenness is the greatest of sins.

On the contrary, According to Gregory (Moral. xxxiii, 12), spiritual vices are greater than carnal vices. Now drunkenness is one of the carnal vices. Therefore it is not the greatest of sins.

I answer that, A thing is said to be evil because it removes a good. Wherefore the greater the good removed by an evil, the graver the evil. Now it is evident that a Divine good is greater than a human good. Wherefore the sins that are directly against God are graver than the sin of drunkenness, which is directly opposed to the good of human reason.

Reply to Objection 1: Man is most prone to sins of intemperance, because such like concupiscences and pleasures are connatural to us, and for this reason these sins are said to find greatest favor with the devil, not for being graver than other sins, but because they occur more frequently among men.

Reply to Objection 2: The good of reason is hindered in two ways: in one way by that which is contrary to reason, in another by that which takes away the use of reason. Now that which is contrary to reason has more the character of an evil, than that which takes away the use of reason for a time, since the use of reason, which is taken away by drunkenness, may be either good or evil, whereas the goods of virtue, which are taken away by things that are contrary to reason, are always good.

Reply to Objection 3: Drunkenness was the occasional cause of slavery, in so far as Cham brought the curse of slavery on to his descendants, for having laughed at his father when the latter was made drunk. But slavery was not the direct punishment of drunkenness.

Whether drunkenness excuses from sin?

Objection 1: It would seem that drunkenness does not excuse from sin. For the Philosopher says (Ethic. iii, 5) that "the drunkard deserves double punishment." Therefore drunkenness aggravates a sin instead of excusing from it.

Objection 2: Further, one sin does not excuse another, but increases it. Now drunkenness is a sin. Therefore it is not an excuse for sin.

Objection 3: Further, the Philosopher says (Ethic. vii, 3) that just as man's reason is tied by drunkenness, so is it by concupiscence. But concupiscence is not an excuse for sin: neither therefore is drunkenness.

On the contrary, According to Augustine (Contra Faust. xxii, 43), Lot was to be excused from incest on account of drunkenness.

I answer that, Two things are to be observed in drunkenness, as stated above [3509](A[1]), namely the resulting defect and the preceding act. on the part of the resulting defect whereby the use of reason is fettered, drunkenness may be an excuse for sin, in so far as it causes an act to be involuntary through ignorance. But on the part of the preceding act, a distinction would seem necessary; because, if the drunkenness that results from that act be without sin, the subsequent sin is entirely excused from fault, as perhaps in the case of Lot. If, however, the preceding act was sinful, the person is not altogether excused from the subsequent sin, because the latter is rendered voluntary through the voluntariness of the preceding act, inasmuch as it was through doing something unlawful that he fell into the subsequent sin. Nevertheless, the resulting sin is diminished, even as the character of voluntariness is diminished. Wherefore Augustine says (Contra Faust. xxii, 44) that "Lot's guilt is to be measured, not by the incest, but by his drunkenness."

Reply to Objection 1: The Philosopher does not say that the drunkard deserves more severe punishment, but that he deserves double punishment for his twofold sin. Or we may reply that he is speaking in view of the law of a certain Pittacus, who, as stated in Polit. ii, 9, ordered "those guilty of assault while drunk to be more severely punished than if they had been sober, because they do wrong in more ways than one." In this, as Aristotle observes (Polit. ii, 9), "he seems to have considered the advantage," namely of the prevention of wrong, "rather than the leniency which one should have for drunkards," seeing that they are not in possession of their faculties.

Reply to Objection 2: Drunkenness may be an excuse for sin, not in the point of its being itself a sin, but in the point of the defect that results from it, as stated above.

Reply to Objection 3: Concupiscence does not altogether fetter the reason, as drunkenness does, unless perchance it be so vehement as to make a man insane. Yet the passion of concupiscence diminishes sin, because it is less grievous to sin through weakness than through malice.

OF CHASTITY (FOUR ARTICLES)

We must next consider chastity: (1) The virtue itself of chastity: (2) virginity, which is a part of chastity: (3) lust, which is the contrary vice. Under the first head there are four points of inquiry:

(1) Whether chastity is a virtue?

(2) Whether it is a general virtue?

(3) Whether it is a virtue distinct from abstinence?

(4) Of its relation to purity.

Whether chastity is a virtue?

Objection 1: It would seem that chastity is not a virtue. For here we are treating of virtues of the soul. But chastity, seemingly, belongs to the body: for a person is said to be chaste because he behaves in a certain way as regards the use of certain parts of the body. Therefore chastity is not a virtue.

Objection 2: Further, virtue is "a voluntary habit," as stated in Ethic. ii, 6. But chastity, apparently, is not voluntary, since it can be taken away by force from a woman to whom violence is done. Therefore it seems that chastity is not a virtue.

Objection 3: Further, there is no virtue in unbelievers. Yet some unbelievers are chaste. Therefore chastity is not a virtue.

Objection 4: Further, the fruits are distinct from the virtues. But chastity is reckoned among the fruits (Gal. 5:23). Therefore chastity is not a virtue.

On the contrary, Augustine says (De Decem Chord. [*Serm. ix de Tempore]): "Whereas thou shouldst excel thy wife in virtue, since chastity is a virtue, thou yieldest to the first onslaught of lust, while thou wishest thy wife to be victorious."

I answer that, Chastity takes its name from the fact that reason "chastises" concupiscence, which, like a child, needs curbing, as the Philosopher states (Ethic. iii, 12). Now the essence of human virtue consists in being something moderated by reason, as shown above ([3510]FS, Q[64], A[1]). Therefore it is evident that chastity is a virtue.

Reply to Objection 1: Chastity does indeed reside in the soul as its subject, though its matter is in the body. For it belongs to chastity that a man make moderate use of bodily members in accordance with the judgment of his reason and the choice of his will.

Reply to Objection 2: As Augustine says (De Civ. Dei i, 18), "so long as her mind holds to its purpose, whereby she has merited to be holy even in body, not even the violence of another's lust can deprive her body of its holiness, which is safeguarded by her persevering continency." He also says (De Civ. Dei i, 18) that "in the mind there is a virtue which is the companion of fortitude, whereby it is resolved to suffer any evil whatsoever rather than consent to evil."

Reply to Objection 3: As Augustine says (Contra Julian. iv, 3), "it is impossible to have any true virtue unless one be truly just; nor is it possible to be just unless one live by faith." Whence he argues that in unbelievers there is neither true chastity, nor any other virtue, because, to wit, they are not referred to the due end, and as he adds (Contra Julian. iv, 3) "virtues are distinguished from vices not by their functions," i.e. their acts, "but by their ends."

Reply to Objection 4: Chastity is a virtue in so far as it works in accordance with reason, but in so far as it delights in its act, it is reckoned among the fruits.

Whether chastity is a general virtue?

Objection 1: It would seem that chastity is a general virtue. For Augustine says (De Mendacio xx) that "chastity of the mind is the well-ordered movement of the mind that does not prefer the lesser to the greater things." But this belongs to every virtue. Therefore chastity is a general virtue.

Objection 2: Further, "Chastity" takes its name from "chastisement" [*Cf. A[1]]. Now every movement of the appetitive part should be chastised by reason. Since, then, every moral virtue curbs some movement of the appetite, it seems that every moral virtue is chastity.

Objection 3: Further, chastity is opposed to fornication. But fornication seems to belong to every kind of sin: for it is written (Ps. 72:27): "Thou shalt destroy

[Vulg.: 'hast destroyed'] all them that go awhoring from [Douay: 'are disloyal to'] Thee." Therefore chastity is a general virtue.

On the contrary, Macrobius [*In Somn. Scip. i, 8] reckons it to be a part of temperance.

I answer that, The word "chastity" is employed in two ways. First, properly; and thus it is a special virtue having a special matter, namely the concupiscences relating to venereal pleasures. Secondly, the word "chastity" is employed metaphorically: for just as a mingling of bodies conduces to venereal pleasure which is the proper matter of chastity and of lust its contrary vice, so too the spiritual union of the mind with certain things conduces to a pleasure which is the matter of a spiritual chastity metaphorically speaking, as well as of a spiritual fornication likewise metaphorically so called. For if the human mind delight in the spiritual union with that to which it behooves it to be united, namely God, and refrains from delighting in union with other things against the requirements of the order established by God, this may be called a spiritual chastity, according to 2 Cor. 11:2, "I have espoused you to one husband, that I may present you as a chaste virgin to Christ." If, on the other hand, the mind be united to any other things whatsoever, against the prescription of the Divine order, it will be called spiritual fornication, according to Jer. 3:1, "But thou hast prostituted thyself to many lovers." Taking chastity in this sense, it is a general virtue, because every virtue withdraws the human mind from delighting in a union with unlawful things. Nevertheless, the essence of this chastity consists principally in charity and the other theological virtues, whereby the human mind is united to God.

Reply to Objection 1: This argument takes chastity in the metaphorical sense.

Reply to Objection 2: As stated above [3511](A[1]; Q[142], A[2]), the concupiscence of that which gives pleasure is especially likened to a child, because the desire of pleasure is connatural to us, especially of pleasures of touch which are directed to the maintenance of nature. Hence it is that if the concupiscence of such pleasures be fostered by consenting to it, it will wax very strong, as in the case of a child left to his own will. Wherefore the concupiscence of these pleasures stands in very great need of being chastised: and consequently chastity is applied antonomastically to such like concupiscences, even as fortitude is about those matters wherein we stand in the greatest need of strength of mind.

Reply to Objection 3: This argument considers spiritual fornication metaphorically so called, which is opposed to spiritual chastity, as stated.

Whether chastity is a distinct virtue from abstinence?

Objection 1: It would seem that chastity is not a distinct virtue from abstinence. Because where the matter is generically the same, one virtue suffices. Now it would seem that things pertaining to the same sense are of one genus. Therefore, since pleasures of the palate which are the matter of abstinence, and venereal pleasures which are the matter of chastity, pertain to the touch, it seems that chastity is not a distinct virtue from abstinence.

Objection 2: Further, the Philosopher (Ethic. iii, 12) likens all vices of intemperance to childish sins, which need chastising. Now "chastity" takes its name from "chastisement" of the contrary vices. Since then certain vices are bridled by abstinence, it seems that abstinence is chastity.

Objection 3: Further, the pleasures of the other senses are the concern of temperance in so far as they refer to pleasures of touch; which are the matter of temperance. Now pleasures of the palate, which are the matter of abstinence, are directed to venereal pleasures, which are the matter of chastity: wherefore Jerome says [*Ep. cxlvii ad Amand. Cf. Gratian, Dist. xliv.], commenting on Titus 1:7, "Not given to wine, no striker," etc.: "The belly and the organs of generation are neighbors, that the neighborhood of the organs may indicate their complicity in vice." Therefore abstinence and chastity are not distinct virtues.

On the contrary, The Apostle (2 Cor. 6:5,6) reckons "chastity" together with "fastings" which pertain to abstinence.

I answer that, As stated above ([3512]Q[141], A[4]), temperance is properly about the concupiscences of the pleasures of touch: so that where there are different kinds of pleasure, there are different virtues comprised under temperance. Now pleasures are proportionate to the actions whose perfections they are, as stated in Ethic. ix, 4,5: and it is evident that actions connected with the use of food whereby the nature of the individual is maintained differ generically from actions connected with the use of matters venereal, whereby the nature of the species is preserved. Therefore chastity, which is about venereal pleasures, is a distinct virtue from abstinence, which is about pleasures of the palate.

Reply to Objection 1: Temperance is chiefly about pleasures of touch, not as regards the sense's judgment concerning the objects of touch. which judgment is of uniform character concerning all such objects, but as regards the use itself of those objects, as stated in Ethic. iii, 10. Now the uses of meats, drinks, and venereal matters differ in character. Wherefore there must needs be different virtues, though they regard the one sense.

Reply to Objection 2: Venereal pleasures are more impetuous, and are more oppressive on the reason than the pleasures of the palate: and therefore they are in greater need of chastisement and restraint, since if one consent to them this increases the force of concupiscence and weakens the strength of the mind. Hence Augustine says (Soliloq. i, 10): "I consider that nothing so casts down the manly mind from its heights as the fondling of women, and those bodily contacts which belong to the married state."

Reply to Objection 3: The pleasures of the other senses do not pertain to the maintenance of man's nature, except in so far as they are directed to pleasures of touch. Wherefore in the matter of such pleasures there is no other virtue comprised under temperance. But the pleasures of the palate, though directed somewhat to venereal pleasures, are essentially directed to the preservation of man's life: wherefore by their very nature they have a special virtue, although this virtue which is called abstinence directs its act to chastity as its end.

Whether purity belongs especially to chastity?

Objection 1: It would seem that purity does not belong especially to chastity. For Augustine says (De Civ. Dei i, 18) that "purity is a virtue of the soul." Therefore it is not something belonging to chastity, but is of itself a virtue distinct from chastity.

Objection 2: Further, "pudicitia" [purity] is derived from "pudor," which is equivalent to shame. Now shame, according to Damascene [*De Fide Orth. ii, 15], is about a disgraceful act, and this is common to all sinful acts. Therefore purity belongs no more to chastity than to the other virtues.

Objection 3: Further, the Philosopher says (Ethic. iii, 12) that "every kind of intemperance is most deserving of reproach." Now it would seem to belong to purity to avoid all that is deserving of reproach. Therefore purity belongs to all the parts of temperance, and not especially to chastity.

On the contrary, Augustine says (De Perseverantia xx): "We must give praise to purity, that he who has ears to hear, may put to none but a lawful use the organs intended for procreation." Now the use of these organs is the proper matter of chastity. Therefore purity belongs properly to chastity.

I answer that, As stated above (OBJ[2]), "pudicitia" [purity] takes its name from "pudor," which signifies shame. Hence purity must needs be properly about the things of which man is most ashamed. Now men are most ashamed of venereal acts, as Augustine remarks (De Civ. Dei xiv, 18), so much so that even the conjugal act, which is adorned by the honesty [*Cf. Q[145]] of marriage, is not devoid of shame: and this because the movement of the organs of generation is not subject to the command of reason, as are the movements of the other external members. Now man is ashamed not only of this sexual union but also of all the signs thereof, as the Philosopher observes (Rhet. ii, 6). Consequently purity regards venereal matters properly, and especially the signs thereof, such as impure looks, kisses, and touches. And since the latter are more wont to be observed, purity regards rather these external signs, while chastity regards rather sexual union. Therefore purity is directed to chastity, not as a virtue distinct therefrom, but as expressing a circumstance of chastity. Nevertheless the one is sometimes used to designate the other.

Reply to Objection 1: Augustine is here speaking of purity as designating chastity.

Reply to Objection 2: Although every vice has a certain disgrace, the vices of intemperance are especially disgraceful, as stated above ([3513]Q[142], A[4]).

Reply to Objection 3: Among the vices of intemperance, venereal sins are most deserving of reproach, both on account of the insubordination of the genital organs, and because by these sins especially, the reason is absorbed.

OF VIRGINITY (FIVE ARTICLES)

We must now consider virginity: and under this head there are five points of inquiry:

(1) In what does virginity consist?

(2) Whether it is lawful?

(3) Whether it is a virtue?

(4) Of its excellence in comparison with marriage;

(5) Of its excellence in comparison with the other virtues.

Whether virginity consists in integrity of the flesh?

Objection 1: It would seem that virginity does not consist in integrity of the flesh. For Augustine says (De Nup. et Concup.) [*The quotation is from De Sancta Virgin. xiii] that "virginity is the continual meditation on incorruption in a corruptible flesh." But meditation does not concern the flesh. Therefore virginity is not situated in the flesh.

Objection 2: Further, virginity denotes a kind of purity. Now Augustine says (De Civ. Dei i, 18) that "purity dwells in the soul." Therefore virginity is not incorruption of the flesh.

Objection 3: Further, the integrity of the flesh would seem to consist in the seal of virginal purity. Yet sometimes the seal is broken without loss of virginity. For Augustine says (De Civ. Dei i, 18) that "those organs may be injured through being wounded by mischance. Physicians, too, sometimes do for the sake of health that which makes one shudder to see: and a midwife has been known to destroy by touch the proof of virginity that she sought." And he adds: "Nobody, I think, would be so foolish as to deem this maiden to have forfeited even bodily sanctity, though she lost the integrity of that organ." Therefore virginity does not consist in incorruption of the flesh.

Objection 4: Further, corruption of the flesh consists chiefly in resolution of the semen: and this may take place without copulation, whether one be asleep or awake. Yet seemingly virginity is not lost without copulation: for Augustine says (De Virgin. xiii) that "virginal integrity and holy continency that refrains from all sexual intercourse is the portion of angels." Therefore virginity does not consist in incorruption of the flesh.

On the contrary, Augustine says (De Virgin. viii) that "virginity is continence whereby integrity of the flesh is vowed, consecrated and observed in honor of the Creator of both soul and flesh."

I answer that, Virginity takes its name apparently from "viror" [freshness], and just as a thing is described as fresh and retaining its freshness, so long as it is not parched by excessive heat, so too, virginity denotes that the person possessed thereof is unseared by the heat of concupiscence which is experienced in achieving the greatest bodily pleasure which is that of sexual intercourse. Hence, Ambrose says (De Virgin. i, 5) that "virginal chastity is integrity free of pollution."

Now venereal pleasures offer three points for consideration. The first is on the part of the body, viz. the violation of the seal of virginity. The second is the link between that which concerns the soul and that which concerns the body, and this is the resolution of the semen, causing sensible pleasure. The third is entirely on the part of the soul, namely the purpose of attaining this pleasure. Of these three the first is accidental to the moral act, which as such must be considered in reference to the soul. The second stands in the relation of matter to the moral act, since the sensible passions are the matters of moral acts. But the third stands in the position of form and complement, because the essence of morality is perfected in that which concerns the reason. Since then virginity consists in freedom from the aforesaid corruption, it follows that the integrity of the bodily organ is accidental to virginity; while freedom from pleasure in resolution of the semen is related thereto materially; and the purpose of perpetually abstaining from this pleasure is the formal and completive element in virginity.

Reply to Objection 1: This definition of Augustine's expresses directly that which is formal in virginity. For "meditation" denotes reason's purpose; and the addition "perpetual" does not imply that a virgin must always retain this meditation actually, but that she should bear in mind the purpose of always persevering therein. The material element is expressed indirectly by the words "on incorruption in a corruptible body." This is added to show the difficulty of virginity: for if the flesh were incorruptible, it would not be difficult to maintain a perpetual meditation on incorruption.

Reply to Objection 2: It is true that purity, as to its essence, is in the soul; but as to its matter, it is in the body: and it is the same with virginity. Wherefore Augustine says (De Virgin. viii) that "although virginity resides in the flesh," and for this reason is a bodily quality, "yet it is a spiritual thing, which a holy continency fosters and preserves."

Reply to Objection 3: As stated above, the integrity of a bodily organ is accidental to virginity, in so far as a person, through purposely abstaining from venereal pleasure, retains the integrity of a bodily organ. Hence if the organ lose its integrity by chance in some other way, this is no more prejudicial to virginity than being deprived of a hand or foot.

Reply to Objection 4: Pleasure resulting from resolution of semen may arise in two ways. If this be the result of the mind's purpose, it destroys virginity, whether copulation takes place or not. Augustine, however, mentions copulation, because such like resolution is the ordinary and natural result thereof. In another way this may happen beside the purpose of the mind, either during sleep, or through violence and without the mind's consent, although the flesh derives pleasure from it, or again through weakness of nature, as in the case of those who are subject to a flow of semen. In such cases virginity is not forfeit, because such like pollution is not the result of impurity which excludes virginity.

Whether virginity is unlawful?

Objection 1: It would seem that virginity is unlawful. For whatever is contrary to a precept of the natural law is unlawful. Now just as the words of Gn. 2:16, "Of every tree" that is in "paradise, thou shalt eat," indicate a precept of the natural law, in reference to the preservation of the individual, so also the words of Gn. 1:28, "Increase and multiply, and fill the earth," express a precept of the natural law, in reference to the preservation of the species. Therefore just as it would be a sin to abstain from all food, as this would be to act counter to the good of the individual, so too it is a sin to abstain altogether from the act of procreation, for this is to act against the good of the species.

Objection 2: Further, whatever declines from the mean of virtue is apparently sinful. Now virginity declines from the mean of virtue, since it abstains from all venereal pleasures: for the Philosopher says (Ethic. ii, 2), that "he who revels in every pleasure, and abstains from not even one, is intemperate: but he who refrains from all is loutish and insensible." Therefore virginity is something sinful.

Objection 3: Further, punishment is not due save for a vice. Now in olden times those were punished who led a celibate life, as Valerius Maximus asserts [*Dict. Fact. Mem. ii, 9]. Hence according to Augustine (De Vera Relig. iii) Plato "is said to have sacrificed to nature, in order that he might atone for his perpetual continency as though it were a sin." Therefore virginity is a sin.

On the contrary, No sin is a matter of direct counsel. But virginity is a matter of direct counsel: for it is written (1 Cor. 7:25): "Concerning virgins I have no commandment of the Lord: but I give counsel." Therefore virginity is not an unlawful thing.

I answer that, In human acts, those are sinful which are against right reason. Now right reason requires that things directed to an end should be used in a measure proportionate to that end. Again, man's good is threefold as stated in Ethic. i, 8; one consisting in external things, for instance riches; another, consisting in bodily goods; the third, consisting in the goods of the soul among which the goods of the contemplative life take precedence of the goods of the active life, as the Philosopher shows (Ethic. x, 7), and as our Lord declared (Lk. 10:42), "Mary hath chosen the better part." Of these goods those that are external are directed to those which belong to the body, and those which belong to the body are directed to those which belong to the soul; and furthermore those which belong to the active life are directed to those which belong to the life of contemplation. Accordingly, right reason dictates that one use external goods in a measure proportionate to the body, and in like manner as regards the rest. Wherefore if a man refrain from possessing certain things (which otherwise it were good for him to possess), for the sake of his body's good, or of the contemplation of truth, this is not sinful, but in accord /with right reason. In like manner if a man abstain from bodily pleasures, in order more freely to give himself to the contemplation of truth, this is in accordance with the rectitude of reason. Now holy virginity refrains from all venereal pleasure in order more freely to have leisure for Divine contemplation: for the Apostle says (1 Cor. 7:34): "The unmarried woman and the virgin thinketh on the things of the Lord: that she may be holy in both body and in spirit. But she that is married thinketh on the things of the world, how she may please her husband." Therefore it follows that virginity instead of being sinful is worthy of praise.

Reply to Objection 1: A precept implies a duty, as stated above ([3514]Q[122], A[1]). Now there are two kinds of duty. There is the duty that has to be fulfilled by one person; and a duty of this kind cannot be set aside without sin. The other duty has to be fulfilled by the multitude, and the fulfilment of this kind of duty is not binding on each one of the multitude. For the multitude has many obligations which cannot be discharged by the individual; but are fulfilled by one person doing this, and another doing that. Accordingly the precept of natural law which binds man to eat must needs be fulfilled by each individual, otherwise the individual cannot be sustained. On the other hand, the precept of procreation regards the whole multitude of men, which needs not only to multiply in body, but also to advance spiritually. Wherefore sufficient provision is made for the human multitude, if some betake themselves to carnal procreation, while others abstaining from this betake themselves to the contemplation of Divine things, for the beauty and welfare of the whole human race. Thus too in an army, some take sentry duty, others are standard-bearers, and others fight with the sword: yet all these things are necessary for the multitude, although they cannot be done by one person.

Reply to Objection 2: The person who, beside the dictate of right reason, abstains from all pleasures through aversion, as it were, for pleasure as such, is insensible as a country lout. But a virgin does not refrain from every pleasure, but only from that which is venereal: and abstains therefrom according to right reason, as stated above. Now the mean of virtue is fixed with reference, not to quantity but to right reason, as stated in Ethic. ii, 6: wherefore it is said of the magnanimous (Ethic. iv, 3) that "in point of quantity he goes to the extreme, but in point of becomingness he follows the mean."

Reply to Objection 3: Laws are framed according to what occurs more frequently. Now it seldom happened in olden times that anyone refrained from all venereal pleasure through love of the contemplation of truth: as Plato alone is related to have done. Hence it was not through thinking this a sin, that he offered sacrifice, but "because he yielded to the false opinion of his fellow countrymen," as Augustine remarks (De Vera Relig. iii).

Whether virginity is a virtue?

Objection 1: It would seem that virginity is not a virtue. For "no virtue is in us by nature," as the Philosopher says (Ethic. ii, 1). Now virginity is in us by nature, since all are virgins when born. Therefore virginity is not a virtue.

Objection 2: Further, whoever has one virtue has all virtues, as stated above ([3515]FS, Q[65], A[1]). Yet some have other virtues without having virginity: else, since none can go to the heavenly kingdom without virtue, no one could go there without virginity, which would involve the condemnation of marriage. Therefore virginity is not a virtue.

Objection 3: Further, every virtue is recovered by penance. But virginity is not recovered by penance: wherefore Jerome says [*Ep. xxii ad Eustoch.]: "Other things God can do, but He cannot restore the virgin after her downfall." Therefore seemingly virginity is not a virtue.

Objection 4: Further, no virtue is lost without sin. Yet virginity is lost without sin, namely by marriage. Therefore virginity is not a virtue.

Objection 5: Further, virginity is condivided with widowhood and conjugal purity. But neither of these is a virtue. Therefore virginity is not a virtue.

On the contrary, Ambrose says (De Virgin. i, 3): "Love of virginity moves us to say something about virginity, lest by passing it over we should seem to cast a slight on what is a virtue of high degree."

I answer that, As stated above [3516](A[1]), the formal and completive element in virginity is the purpose of abstaining from venereal pleasure, which purpose is rendered praiseworthy by its end, in so far, to wit, as this is done in order to have leisure for Divine things: while the material element in virginity is integrity of the flesh free of all experience of venereal pleasure. Now it is manifest that where a good action has a special matter through having a special excellence, there is a special kind of virtue: for example, magnificence which is about great expenditure is for this reason a special virtue distinct from liberality, which is about all uses of money in general. Now to keep oneself free from the experience of venereal pleasure has an excellence of its own deserving of greater praise than keeping oneself free from inordinate venereal pleasure. Wherefore virginity is a special virtue being related to chastity as magnificence to liberality.

Reply to Objection 1: Men have from their birth that which is material in virginity, namely integrity of the flesh and freedom from venereal experience. But they have not that which is formal in virginity, namely the purpose of safeguarding this integrity for God's sake, which purpose gives virginity its character of virtue. Hence Augustine says (De Virgin. xi): "Nor do we praise virgins for being virgins, but, because their virginity is consecrated to God by holy continency."

Reply to Objection 2: Virtues are connected together by reason of that which is formal in them, namely charity, or by reason of prudence, as stated above ([3517]Q[129], A[3], ad 2), but not by reason of that which is material in them. For nothing hinders a virtuous man from providing the matter of one virtue, and not the matter of another virtue: thus a poor man has the matter of temperance, but not that of magnificence. It is in this way that one who has the other virtues lacks the matter of virginity, namely the aforesaid integrity of the flesh: nevertheless he can have that which is formal in virginity, his mind being so prepared that he has the purpose of safeguarding this same integrity of the flesh, should it be fitting for him to do so: even as a poor man may be so prepared in mind as to have the purpose of being magnificent in his expenditure, were he in a position to do so: or again as a prosperous man is so prepared in mind as to purpose bearing misfortune with equanimity: without which preparedness of the mind no man can be virtuous.

Reply to Objection 3: Virtue can be recovered by penance as regards that which is formal in virtue, but not as to that which is material therein. For if a magnificent man has squandered all his wealth he does not recover his riches by repenting of his sin. In like manner a person who has lost virginity by sin, recovers by repenting, not the matter of virginity but the purpose of virginity.

As regards the matter of virginity there is that which can be miraculously restored by God, namely the integrity of the organ, which we hold to be accidental to virginity: while there is something else which cannot be restored even by miracle, to wit, that one who has experienced venereal lust should cease to have had that experience. For God cannot make that which is done not to have been done, as stated in the [3518]FP, Q[25] , A[4].

Reply to Objection 4: Virginity as a virtue denotes the purpose, confirmed by vow, of observing perpetual integrity. For Augustine says (De Virgin. viii) that "by virginity, integrity of the flesh is vowed, consecrated and observed in honor of the Creator of both soul and flesh." Hence virginity, as a virtue, is never lost without sin.

Reply to Objection 5: Conjugal chastity is deserving of praise merely because it abstains from unlawful pleasures: hence no excellence attaches to it above that of chastity in general. Widowhood, however, adds something to chastity in general; but it does not attain to that which is perfect in this matter, namely to entire freedom from venereal pleasure; virginity alone achieves this. Wherefore virginity alone is accounted a virtue above chastity, even as magnificence is reckoned above liberality.

Whether virginity is more excellent than marriage?

Objection 1: It would seem that virginity is not more excellent than marriage. For Augustine says (De Bono Conjug. xxi): "Continence was equally meritorious in John who remained unmarried and Abraham who begot children." Now a greater virtue has greater merit. Therefore virginity is not a greater virtue than conjugal chastity.

Objection 2: Further, the praise accorded a virtuous man depends on his virtue. If, then, virginity were preferable to conjugal continence, it would seem to follow that every virgin is to be praised more than any married woman. But this is untrue. Therefore virginity is not preferable to marriage.

Objection 3: Further, the common good takes precedence of the private good, according to the Philosopher (Ethic. i, 2). Now marriage is directed to the common good: for Augustine says (De Bono Conjug. xvi): "What food is to a man's wellbeing, such is sexual intercourse to the welfare of the human race." On the other hand, virginity is ordered to the individual good, namely in order to avoid what the Apostle calls the "tribulation of the flesh," to which married people are subject (1 Cor. 7:28). Therefore virginity is not greater than conjugal continence.

On the contrary, Augustine says (De Virgin. xix): "Both solid reason and the authority of Holy Writ show that neither is marriage sinful, nor is it to be equaled to the good of virginal continence or even to that of widowhood."

I answer that, According to Jerome (Contra Jovin. i) the error of Jovinian consisted in holding virginity not to be preferable to marriage. This error is refuted above all by the example of Christ Who both chose a virgin for His mother, and remained Himself a virgin, and by the teaching of the Apostle who (1 Cor. 7) counsels virginity as the greater good. It is also refuted by reason, both because a Divine good takes precedence of a human good, and because the good of the soul is preferable to the good of the body, and again because the good of the contemplative life is better than that of the active life. Now virginity is directed to the good of the soul in respect of the contemplative life, which consists in thinking "on the things of God" [Vulg.: 'the Lord'], whereas marriage is directed to the good of the body, namely the bodily increase of the human race, and belongs to the active life, since the man and woman who embrace the married life have to think "on the things of the world," as the Apostle says (1 Cor. 7:34). Without doubt therefore virginity is preferable to conjugal continence.

Reply to Objection 1: Merit is measured not only by the kind of action, but still more by the mind of the agent. Now Abraham had a mind so disposed, that he was prepared to observe virginity, if it were in keeping with the times for him to do so. Wherefore in him conjugal continence was equally meritorious with the virginal continence of John, as regards the essential reward, but not as regards the accidental reward. Hence Augustine says (De Bono Conjug. xxi) that both "the celibacy of John and the marriage of Abraham fought Christ's battle in keeping with the difference of the times: but John was continent even in deed, whereas Abraham was continent only in habit."

Reply to Objection 2: Though virginity is better than conjugal continence, a married person may be better than a virgin for two reasons. First, on the part of chastity itself; if to wit, the married person is more prepared in mind to observe virginity, if it should be expedient, than the one who is actually a virgin. Hence Augustine (De Bono Conjug. xxii) charges the virgin to say: "I am no better than

Abraham, although the chastity of celibacy is better than the chastity of marriage." Further on he gives the reason for this: "For what I do now, he would have done better, if it were fitting for him to do it then; and what they did I would even do now if it behooved me now to do it." Secondly, because perhaps the person who is not a virgin has some more excellent virtue. Wherefore Augustine says (De Virgin. xliv): "Whence does a virgin know the things that belong to the Lord, however solicitous she be about them, if perchance on account of some mental fault she be not yet ripe for martyrdom, whereas this woman to whom she delighted in preferring herself is already able to drink the chalice of the Lord?"

Reply to Objection 3: The common good takes precedence of the private good, if it be of the same genus: but it may be that the private good is better generically. It is thus that the virginity that is consecrated to God is preferable to carnal fruitfulness. Hence Augustine says (De Virgin. ix): "It must be confessed that the fruitfulness of the flesh, even of those women who in these times seek naught else from marriage but children in order to make them servants of Christ, cannot compensate for lost virginity."

Whether virginity is the greatest of virtues?

Objection 1: It would seem that virginity is the greatest of virtues. For Cyprian says (De Virgin. [*De Habitu Virg.]): "We address ourselves now to the virgins. Sublime is their glory, but no less exalted is their vocation. They are a flower of the Church's sowing, the pride and ornament of spiritual grace, the most honored portion of Christ's flock."

Objection 2: Further, a greater reward is due to the greater virtue. Now the greatest reward is due to virginity, namely the hundredfold fruit, according to a gloss on Mat. 13:23. Therefore virginity is the greatest of the virtues.

Objection 3: Further, the more a virtue conforms us to Christ, the greater it is. Now virginity above all conforms us to Christ; for it is declared in the Apocalypse 14:4 that virgins "follow the Lamb whithersoever He goeth," and (Apoc. 14:3) that they sing "a new canticle," which "no" other "man" could say. Therefore virginity is the greatest of the virtues.

On the contrary, Augustine says (De Virgin. xlvi): "No one, methinks, would dare prefer virginity to martyrdom," and (De Virgin. xlv): "The authority of the Church informs the faithful in no uncertain manner, so that they know in what place the martyrs and the holy virgins who have departed this life are commemorated in the Sacrament of the Altar." By this we are given to understand that martyrdom, and also the monastic state, are preferable to virginity.

I answer that, A thing may excel all others in two ways. First, in some particular genus: and thus virginity is most excellent, namely in the genus of chastity, since it surpasses the chastity both of widowhood and of marriage. And because comeliness is ascribed to chastity antonomastically, it follows that surpassing beauty is ascribed to chastity. Wherefore Ambrose says (De Virgin. i, 7): "Can anyone esteem any beauty greater than a virgin's, since she is beloved of her King, approved by her Judge, dedicated to her Lord, consecrated to her God?" Secondly, a thing may be most excellent simply, and in this way virginity is not the most excellent of the virtues. Because the end always excels that which is directed to the end; and the more effectively a thing is directed to the end, the better it is. Now the end which renders virginity praiseworthy is that one may have leisure for Divine things, as stated above [3519](A[4]). Wherefore the theological virtues as well as the virtue of religion, the acts of which consist in being occupied about Divine things, are preferable to virginity. Moreover, martyrs work more mightily in order to cleave to God—since for this end they hold their own life in contempt; and those who dwell in monasteries—since for this end they give up their own will and all that they may possess—than virgins who renounce venereal pleasure for that same purpose. Therefore virginity is not simply the greatest of virtues.

Reply to Objection 1: Virgins are "the more honored portion of Christ's flock," and "their glory more sublime" in comparison with widows and married women.

Reply to Objection 2: The hundredfold fruit is ascribed to virginity, according to Jerome [*Ep. cxxiii ad Ageruch.], on account of its superiority to widowhood, to which the sixtyfold fruit is ascribed, and to marriage, to which is ascribed the thirtyfold fruit. But according to Augustine (De QQ. Evang. i, 9), "the hundredfold fruit is given to martyrs, the sixtyfold to virgins, and the thirtyfold to married persons." Wherefore it does not follow that virginity is simply the greatest of virtues, but only in comparison with other degrees of chastity.

Reply to Objection 3: Virgins "follow the Lamb whithersoever He goeth," because they imitate Christ, by integrity not only of the mind but also of the flesh, as Augustine says (De Virgin. xxvii). Wherefore they follow the Lamb in more ways, but this does not imply that they follow more closely, because other virtues make us cleave to God more closely by imitation of the mind. The "new hymn" which virgins alone sing, is their joy at having preserved integrity of the flesh.

OF LUST (FIVE ARTICLES)

We must next consider the vice of lust which is opposed to chastity: (1) Lust in general; (2) its species. Under the first head there are five points of inquiry:

(1) What is the matter of lust?

(2) Whether all copulation is unlawful?

(3) Whether lust is a mortal sin?

(4) Whether lust is a capital vice?

(5) Concerning its daughters.

Whether the matter of lust is only venereal desires and pleasures?

Objection 1: It would seem that the matter of lust is not only venereal desires and pleasures. For Augustine says (Confess. ii, 6) that "lust affects to be called surfeit and abundance." But surfeit regards meat and drink, while abundance refers to riches. Therefore lust is not properly about venereal desires and pleasures.

Objection 2: Further, it is written (Prov. 20:1): "Wine is a lustful [Douay: 'luxurious'] thing." Now wine is connected with pleasure of meat and drink. Therefore these would seem to be the matter of lust.

Objection 3: Further, lust is defined "as the desire of wanton pleasure" [*Alexander of Hales, Summ. Theol. ii, cxvli]. But wanton pleasure regards not only venereal matters but also many others. Therefore lust is not only about venereal desires and pleasures.

On the contrary, To the lustful it is said (De Vera Relig. iii [*Written by St. Augustine]): "He that soweth in the flesh, of the flesh shall reap corruption." Now the sowing of the flesh refers to venereal pleasures. Therefore these belong to lust.

I answer that, As Isidore says (Etym. x), "a lustful man is one who is debauched with pleasures." Now venereal pleasures above all debauch a man's mind. Therefore lust is especially concerned with such like pleasures.

Reply to Objection 1: Even as temperance chiefly and properly applies to pleasures of touch, yet consequently and by a kind of likeness is referred to other matters, so too, lust applies chiefly to venereal pleasures, which more than anything else work the greatest havoc in a man's mind, yet secondarily it applies to any other matters pertaining to excess. Hence a gloss on Gal. 5:19 says "lust is any kind of surfeit."

Reply to Objection 2: Wine is said to be a lustful thing, either in the sense in which surfeit in any matter is ascribed to lust, or because the use of too much wine affords an incentive to venereal pleasure.

Reply to Objection 3: Although wanton pleasure applies to other matters, the name of lust has a special application to venereal pleasures, to which also wantonness is specially applicable, as Augustine remarks (De Civ. xiv, 15,16).

Whether no venereal act can be without sin?

Objection 1: It would seem that no venereal act can be without sin. For nothing but sin would seem to hinder virtue. Now every venereal act is a great hindrance to virtue. For Augustine says (Soliloq. i, 10): "I consider that nothing so casts down the manly mind from its height as the fondling of a woman, and those bodily contacts." Therefore, seemingly, no venereal act is without sin.

Objection 2: Further, any excess that makes one forsake the good of reason is sinful, because virtue is corrupted by "excess" and "deficiency" as stated in Ethic. ii, 2. Now in every venereal act there is excess of pleasure, since it so absorbs the mind, that "it is incompatible with the act of understanding," as the Philosopher observes (Ethic. vii, 11); and as Jerome [*Origen, Hom. vi in Num.; Cf. Jerome, Ep. cxxiii ad Ageruch.] states, rendered the hearts of the prophets, for the moment, insensible to the spirit of prophecy. Therefore no venereal act can be without sin.

Objection 3: Further, the cause is more powerful than its effect. Now original sin is transmitted to children by concupiscence, without which no venereal act is possible, as Augustine declares (De Nup. et Concup. i, 24). Therefore no venereal act can be without sin.

On the contrary, Augustine says (De Bono Conjug. xxv): "This is a sufficient answer to heretics, if only they will understand that no sin is committed in that which is against neither nature, nor morals, nor a commandment": and he refers to the act of sexual intercourse between the patriarchs of old and their several wives. Therefore not every venereal act is a sin.

I answer that, A sin, in human acts, is that which is against the order of reason. Now the order of reason consists in its ordering everything to its end in a fitting manner. Wherefore it is no sin if one, by the dictate of reason, makes use of certain things in a fitting manner and order for the end to which they are adapted, provided this end be something truly good. Now just as the preservation of the bodily nature of one individual is a true good, so, too, is the preservation of the nature of the human species a very great good. And just as the use of food is directed to the preservation of life in the individual, so is the use of venereal acts directed to the preservation of the whole human race. Hence Augustine says (De Bono Conjug. xvi): "What food is to a man's well being, such is sexual intercourse to the welfare of the whole human race." Wherefore just as the use of food can be without sin, if it be taken in due manner and order, as required for the welfare of the body, so also the use of venereal acts can be without sin, provided they be performed in due manner and order, in keeping with the end of human procreation.

Reply to Objection 1: A thing may be a hindrance to virtue in two ways. First, as regards the ordinary degree of virtue, and as to this nothing but sin is an obstacle to virtue. Secondly, as regards the perfect degree of virtue, and as to this virtue may be hindered by that which is not a sin, but a lesser good. In this way sexual intercourse casts down the mind not from virtue, but from the height, i.e. the perfection of virtue. Hence Augustine says (De Bono Conjug. viii): "Just as that was good which Martha did when busy about serving holy men, yet better still that which Mary did in hearing the word of God: so, too, we praise the good of Susanna's conjugal chastity, yet we prefer the good of the widow Anna, and much more that of the Virgin Mary."

Reply to Objection 2: As stated above (Q[152], A[2], ad 2; [3520]FS, Q[64], A[2]), the mean of virtue depends not on quantity but on conformity with right reason: and consequently the exceeding pleasure attaching to a venereal act directed according to reason, is not opposed to the mean of virtue. Moreover, virtue is not concerned with the amount of pleasure experienced by the external sense, as this depends on the disposition of the body; what matters is how much the interior appetite is affected by that pleasure. Nor does it follow that the act in question is contrary to virtue, from the fact that the free act of reason in considering spiritual things is incompatible with the aforesaid pleasure. For it is not contrary to virtue, if the act of reason be sometimes interrupted for something that is done in accordance with reason, else it would be against virtue for a person to set himself to sleep. That venereal concupiscence and pleasure are not subject to the command and moderation of reason, is due to the punishment of the first sin, inasmuch as the reason, for rebelling against God, deserved that its body should rebel against it, as Augustine says (De Civ. Dei xiii, 13).

Reply to Objection 3: As Augustine says (De Civ. Dei xiii, 13), "the child, shackled with original sin, is born of fleshly concupiscence (which is not imputed as sin to the regenerate) as of a daughter of sin." Hence it does not follow that the act in question is a sin, but that it contains something penal resulting from the first sin.

Whether the lust that is about venereal acts can be a sin?

Objection 1: It would seem that lust about venereal acts cannot be a sin. For the venereal act consists in the emission of semen which is the surplus from food, according to the Philosopher (De Gener. Anim. i, 18). But there is no sin attaching to the emission of other superfluities. Therefore neither can there be any sin in venereal acts.

Objection 2: Further, everyone can lawfully make what use he pleases of what is his. But in the venereal act a man uses only what is his own, except perhaps in adultery or rape. Therefore there can be no sin in venereal acts, and consequently lust is no sin.

Objection 3: Further, every sin has an opposite vice. But, seemingly, no vice is opposed to lust. Therefore lust is not a sin.

On the contrary, The cause is more powerful than its effect. Now wine is forbidden on account of lust, according to the saying of the Apostle (Eph. 5:18), "Be not drunk with wine wherein is lust [Douay: 'luxury']." Therefore lust is forbidden.

Further, it is numbered among the works of the flesh: Gal. 5:19 [Douay: 'luxury'].

I answer that, The more necessary a thing is, the more it behooves one to observe the order of reason in its regard; wherefore the more sinful it becomes if the order of reason be forsaken. Now the use of venereal acts, as stated in the foregoing Article, is most necessary for the common good, namely the preservation of the human race. Wherefore there is the greatest necessity for observing the order of reason in this matter: so that if anything be done in this connection against the dictate of reason's ordering, it will be a sin. Now lust consists essentially in exceeding the order and mode of reason in the matter of venereal acts. Wherefore without any doubt lust is a sin.

Reply to Objection 1: As the Philosopher says in the same book (De Gener. Anim. i, 18), "the semen is a surplus that is needed." For it is said to be superfluous, because it is the residue from the action of the nutritive power, yet it is needed for the work of the generative power. But the other superfluities of the human body are such as not to be needed, so that it matters not how they are emitted, provided one observe the decencies of social life. It is different with the emission of semen, which should be accomplished in a manner befitting the end for which it is needed.

Reply to Objection 2: As the Apostle says (1 Cor. 6:20) in speaking against lust, "You are bought with a great price: glorify and bear God in your body." Wherefore by inordinately using the body through lust a man wrongs God Who is the Supreme Lord of our body. Hence Augustine says (De Decem. Chord. 10 [*Serm. ix (xcvi de Temp.)]): "God Who thus governs His servants for their good, not for His, made this order and commandment, lest unlawful pleasures should destroy His temple which thou hast begun to be."

Reply to Objection 3: The opposite of lust is not found in many, since men are more inclined to pleasure. Yet the contrary vice is comprised under insensibility, and occurs in one who has such a dislike for sexual intercourse as not to pay the marriage debt.

Whether lust is a capital vice?

Objection 1: It seems that lust is not a capital vice. For lust is apparently the same as "uncleanness," according to a gloss on Eph. 5:3 (Cf. 2 Cor. 12:21). But uncleanness is a daughter of gluttony, according to Gregory (Moral. xxxi, 45). Therefore lust is not a capital vice.

Objection 2: Further, Isidore says (De Summo Bono ii, 39) that "as pride of mind leads to the depravity of lust, so does humility of mind safeguard the chastity of the flesh." Now it is seemingly contrary to the nature of a capital vice to arise from another vice. Therefore lust is not a capital vice.

Objection 3: Further, lust is caused by despair, according to Eph. 4:19, "Who despairing, have given themselves up to lasciviousness." But despair is not a capital vice; indeed, it is accounted a daughter of sloth, as stated above ([3521]Q[35], A[4], ad 2). Much less, therefore, is lust a capital vice.

On the contrary, Gregory (Moral. xxxi, 45) places lust among the capital vices.

I answer that, As stated above (Q[148], A[5]; [3522]FS, Q[84], AA[3],4), a capital vice is one that has a very desirable end, so that through desire for that end, a man proceeds to commit many sins, all of which are said to arise from that vice as from a principal vice. Now the end of lust is venereal pleasure, which is very great.

Wherefore this pleasure is very desirable as regards the sensitive appetite, both on account of the intensity of the pleasure, and because such like concupiscence is connatural to man. Therefore it is evident that lust is a capital vice.

Reply to Objection 1: As stated above ([3523]Q[148], A[6]), according to some, the uncleanness which is reckoned a daughter of gluttony is a certain uncleanness of the body, and thus the objection is not to the point. If, however, it denote the uncleanness of lust, we must reply that it is caused by gluttony materially—in so far as gluttony provides the bodily matter of lust—and not under the aspect of final cause, in which respect chiefly the capital vices are said to be the cause of others.

Reply to Objection 2: As stated above ([3524]Q[132], A[4], ad 1), when we were treating of vainglory, pride is accounted the common mother of all sins, so that even the capital vices originate therefrom.

Reply to Objection 3: Certain persons refrain from lustful pleasures chiefly through hope of the glory to come, which hope is removed by despair, so that the latter is a cause of lust, as removing an obstacle thereto, not as its direct cause; whereas this is seemingly necessary for a capital vice.

Whether the daughters of lust are fittingly described?

Objection 1: It would seem that the daughters of lust are unfittingly reckoned to be "blindness of mind, thoughtlessness, inconstancy, rashness, self-love, hatred of God, love of this world and abhorrence or despair of a future world." For mental blindness, thoughtlessness and rashness pertain to imprudence, which is to be found in every sin, even as prudence is in every virtue. Therefore they should not be reckoned especially as daughters of lust.

Objection 2: Further, constancy is reckoned a part of fortitude, as stated above (Q[128], ad 6;[3525] Q[137], A[3]). But lust is contrary, not to fortitude but to temperance. Therefore inconstancy is not a daughter of lust.

Objection 3: Further, "Self-love extending to the contempt of God" is the origin of every sin, as Augustine says (De Civ. Dei xiv, 28). Therefore it should not be accounted a daughter of lust.

Objection 4: Further, Isidore [*QQ. in Deut., qu. xvi] mentions four, namely, "obscene," "scurrilous," "wanton" and "foolish talking." There the aforesaid enumeration would seem to be superfluous.

On the contrary, stands the authority of Gregory (Moral. xxxi, 45).

I answer that, When the lower powers are strongly moved towards their objects, the result is that the higher powers are hindered and disordered in their acts. Now the effect of the vice of lust is that the lower appetite, namely the concupiscible, is most vehemently intent on its object, to wit, the object of pleasure, on account of the vehemence of the pleasure. Consequently the higher powers, namely the reason and the will, are most grievously disordered by lust.

Now the reason has four acts in matters of action. First there is simple understanding, which apprehends some end as good, and this act is hindered by lust, according to Dan. 13:56, "Beauty hath deceived thee, and lust hath perverted thy heart." In this respect we have "blindness of mind." The second act is counsel about what is to be done for the sake of the end: and this is also hindered by the concupiscence of lust. Hence Terence says (Eunuch., act 1, sc. 1), speaking of lecherous love: "This thing admits of neither counsel nor moderation, thou canst not control it by counseling." In this respect there is "rashness," which denotes absence of counsel, as stated above ([3526]Q[53], A[3]). The third act is judgment about the things to be done, and this again is hindered by lust. For it is said of the lustful old men (Dan. 13:9): "They perverted their own mind . . . that they might not . . . remember just judgments." In this respect there is "thoughtlessness." The fourth act is the reason's command about the thing to be done, and this also is impeded by lust, in so far as through being carried away by concupiscence, a man is hindered from doing what his reason ordered to be done. [To this "inconstancy" must be referred.] [*The sentence in brackets is omitted in the Leonine edition.] Hence Terence says (Eunuch., act 1, sc. 1) of a man who declared that he would leave his mistress: "One little false tear will undo those words."

On the part of the will there results a twofold inordinate act. One is the desire for the end, to which we refer "self-love," which regards the pleasure which a man desires inordinately, while on the other hand there is "hatred of God," by reason of His forbidding the desired pleasure. The other act is the desire for the things directed to the end. With regard to this there is "love of this world," whose pleasures a man desires to enjoy, while on the other hand there is "despair of a future world," because through being held back by carnal pleasures he cares not to obtain spiritual pleasures, since they are distasteful to him.

Reply to Objection 1: According to the Philosopher (Ethic. vi, 5), intemperance is the chief corruptive of prudence: wherefore the vices opposed to prudence arise chiefly from lust, which is the principal species of intemperance.

Reply to Objection 2: The constancy which is a part of fortitude regards hardships and objects of fear; but constancy in refraining from pleasures pertains to continence which is a part of temperance, as stated above ([3527]Q[143]). Hence the inconstancy which is opposed thereto is to be reckoned a daughter of lust. Nevertheless even the first named inconstancy arises from lust, inasmuch as the latter enfeebles a man's heart and renders it effeminate, according to Osee 4:11, "Fornication and wine and drunkenness take away the heart [Douay: 'understanding']." Vegetius, too, says (De Re Milit. iii) that "the less a man knows of the pleasures of life, the less he fears death." Nor is there any need, as we have repeatedly stated, for the daughters of a capital vice to agree with it in matter (cf.[3528] Q[35], A[4], ad 2;[3529] Q[118], A[8], ad 1;[3530] Q[148], A[6]).

Reply to Objection 3: Self-love in respect of any goods that a man desires for himself is the common origin of all sins; but in the special point of desiring carnal pleasures for oneself, it is reckoned a daughter of lust.

Reply to Objection 4: The sins mentioned by Isidore are inordinate external acts, pertaining in the main to speech; wherein there is a fourfold inordinateness. First, on account of the matter, and to this we refer "obscene words": for since "out of the abundance of the heart the mouth speaketh" (Mat. 12:34), the lustful man, whose heart is full of lewd concupiscences, readily breaks out into lewd words. Secondly, on account of the cause: for, since lust causes thoughtlessness and rashness, the result is that it makes a man speak without weighing or giving a thought to his words. which are described as "scurrilous." Thirdly, on account of the end: for since the lustful man seeks pleasure, he directs his speech thereto, and so gives utterance to "wanton words." Fourthly, on account of the sentiments expressed by his words, for through causing blindness of mind, lust perverts a man's sentiments, and so he gives way "to foolish talking," for instance, by expressing a preference for the pleasures he desires to anything else.

OF THE PARTS OF LUST (TWELVE ARTICLES)

We must now consider the parts of lust, under which head there are twelve points of inquiry:

(1) Into what parts is lust divided?

(2) Whether simple fornication is a mortal sin?

(3) Whether it is the greatest of sins?

(4) Whether there is mortal sin in touches, kisses and such like seduction?

(5) Whether nocturnal pollution is a mortal sin?

(6) Of seduction;

(7) Of rape;

(8) Of adultery;

(9) Of incest;

(10) Of sacrilege;

(11) Of the sin against nature;

(12) Of the order of gravity in the aforesaid sins.

Whether six species are fittingly assigned to lust?

Objection 1: It would seem that six species are unfittingly assigned to lust, namely, "simple fornication, adultery, incest, seduction, rape, and the unnatural vice." For diversity of matter does not diversify the species. Now the aforesaid division is made with regard to diversity of matter, according as the woman with whom a man has intercourse is married or a virgin, or of some other condition. Therefore it seems that the species of lust are diversified in this way.

Objection 2: Further, seemingly the species of one vice are not differentiated by things that belong to another vice. Now adultery does not differ from simple fornication, save in the point of a man having intercourse with one who is another's, so that he commits an injustice. Therefore it seems that adultery should not be reckoned a species of lust.

Objection 3: Further, just as a man may happen to have intercourse with a woman who is bound to another man by marriage, so may it happen that a man has intercourse with a woman who is bound to God by vow. Therefore sacrilege should be reckoned a species of lust, even as adultery is.

Objection 4: Further, a married man sins not only if he be with another woman, but also if he use his own wife inordinately. But the latter sin is comprised under lust. Therefore it should be reckoned among the species thereof.

Objection 5: Further, the Apostle says (2 Cor. 12:21): "Lest again, when I come, God humble me among you, and I mourn many of them /that sinned before, and have not done penance for the uncleanness and fornication and lasciviousness that they have committed." Therefore it seems that also uncleanness and lasciviousness should be reckoned species of lust, as well as fornication.

Objection 6: Further, the thing divided is not to be reckoned among its parts. But lust is reckoned together with the aforesaid: for it is written (Gal. 5:19): "The works of the flesh are manifest, which are fornication, uncleanness, immodesty, lust [Douay: 'luxury']." Therefore it seems that fornication is unfittingly reckoned a species of lust.

On the contrary, The aforesaid division is given in the Decretals 36, qu. i [*Append. Grat. ad can. Lex illa].

I answer that As stated above ([3531]Q[153], A[3]), the sin of lust consists in seeking venereal pleasure not in accordance with right reason. This may happen in two ways. First, in respect of the matter wherein this pleasure is sought; secondly, when, whereas there is due matter, other due circumstances are not observed. And since a circumstance, as such, does not specify a moral act, whose species is derived from its object which is also its matter, it follows that the species of lust must be assigned with respect to its matter or object.

Now this same matter may be discordant with right reason in two ways. First, because it is inconsistent with the end of the venereal act. In this way, as hindering the begetting of children, there is the "vice against nature," which attaches to every venereal act from which generation cannot follow; and, as hindering the due upbringing and advancement of the child when born, there is "simple fornication," which is the union of an unmarried man with an unmarried woman. Secondly, the matter wherein the venereal act is consummated may be discordant with right reason in relation to other persons; and this in two ways. First, with regard to the woman, with whom a man has connection, by reason of due honor not being paid to her; and thus there is "incest," which consists in the misuse of a woman who is related by consanguinity or affinity. Secondly, with regard to the person under whose authority the woman is placed: and if she be under the authority of a husband, it is "adultery," if under the authority of her father, it is "seduction," in the absence of violence, and "rape" if violence be employed.

These species are differentiated on the part of the woman rather than of the man, because in the venereal act the woman is passive and is by way of matter, whereas the man is by way of agent; and it has been stated above (OBJ[1]) that the aforesaid species are assigned with regard to a difference of matter.

Reply to Objection 1: The aforesaid diversity of matter is connected with a formal difference of object, which difference results from different modes of opposition to right reason, as stated above.

Reply to Objection 2: As stated above ([3532]FS, Q[18], A[7]), nothing hinders the deformities of different vices concurring in the one act, and in this way adultery is comprised under lust and injustice. Nor is this deformity of injustice altogether accidental to lust: since the lust that obeys concupiscence so far as to lead to injustice, is thereby shown to be more grievous.

Reply to Objection 3: Since a woman, by vowing continence, contracts a spiritual marriage with God, the sacrilege that is committed in the violation of such a woman is a spiritual adultery. In like manner, the other kinds of sacrilege pertaining to lustful matter are reduced to other species of lust.

Reply to Objection 4: The sin of a husband with his wife is not connected with undue matter, but with other circumstances, which do not constitute the species of a moral act, as stated above ([3533]FS, Q[18], A[2]).

Reply to Objection 5: As a gloss says on this passage, "uncleanness" stands for lust against nature, while "lasciviousness" is a man's abuse of boys, wherefore it would appear to pertain to seduction. We may also reply that "lasciviousness" relates to certain acts circumstantial to the venereal act, for instance kisses, touches, and so forth.

Reply to Objection 6: According to a gloss on this passage "lust" there signifies any kind of excess.

Whether simple fornication is a mortal sin?

Objection 1: It would seem that simple fornication is not a mortal sin. For things that come under the same head would seem to be on a par with one another. Now fornication comes under the same head as things that are not mortal sins: for it is written (Acts 15:29): "That you abstain from things sacrificed to idols, and from blood, and from things strangled, and from fornication." But there is not mortal sin in these observances, according to 1 Tim. 4:4, "Nothing is rejected that is received with thanksgiving." Therefore fornication is not a mortal sin.

Objection 2: Further, no mortal sin is the matter of a Divine precept. But the Lord commanded (Osee 1:2): "Go take thee a wife of fornications, and have of her children of fornications." Therefore fornication is not a mortal sin.

Objection 3: Further, no mortal sin is mentioned in Holy Writ without disapprobation. Yet simple fornication is mentioned without disapprobation by Holy Writ in connection with the patriarchs. Thus we read (Gn. 16:4) that Abraham went in to his handmaid Agar; and further on (Gn. 30:5, 9) that Jacob went in to Bala and Zelpha the handmaids of his wives; and again (Gn. 38:18) that Juda was with Thamar whom he thought to be a harlot. Therefore simple fornication is not a mortal sin.

Objection 4: Further, every mortal sin is contrary to charity. But simple fornication is not contrary to charity, neither as regards the love of God, since it is not a sin directly against. God, nor as regards the love of our neighbor, since thereby no one is injured. Therefore simple fornication is not a mortal sin.

Objection 5: Further, every mortal sin leads to eternal perdition. But simple fornication has not this result: because a gloss of Ambrose [*The quotation is from the Gloss of Peter Lombard, who refers it to St. Ambrose: whereas it is from Hilary the deacon] on 1 Tim. 4:8, "Godliness is profitable to all things," says: "The whole of Christian teaching is summed up in mercy and godliness: if a man conforms to this, even though he gives way to the inconstancy of the flesh, doubtless he will be punished, but he will not perish." Therefore simple fornication is not a mortal sin.

Objection 6: Further, Augustine says (De Bono Conjug. xvi) that "what food is to the well-being of the body, such is sexual intercourse to the welfare of the human race." But inordinate use of food is not always a mortal sin. Therefore neither is all inordinate sexual intercourse; and this would seem to apply especially to simple fornication, which is the least grievous of the aforesaid species.

On the contrary, It is written (Tob. 4:13): "Take heed to keep thyself . . . from all fornication, and beside thy wife never endure to know a crime." Now crime denotes a mortal sin. Therefore fornication and all intercourse with other than one's wife is a mortal sin.

Further, nothing but mortal sin debars a man from God's kingdom. But fornication debars him, as shown by the words of the Apostle (Gal. 5:21), who after mentioning fornication and certain other vices, adds: "They who do such things shall not obtain the kingdom of God." Therefore simple fornication is a mortal sin.

Further, it is written in the Decretals (XXII, qu. i, can. Praedicandum): "They should know that the same penance is to be enjoined for perjury as for adultery, fornication, and wilful murder and other criminal offenses." Therefore simple fornication is a criminal or mortal sin.

I answer that, Without any doubt we must hold simple fornication to be a mortal sin, notwithstanding that a gloss [*St. Augustine, QQ. in Deut., qu. 37] on Dt. 23:17, says: "This is a prohibition against going with whores, whose vileness is venial." For instead of "venial" it should be "venal," since such is the wanton's trade. In order to make this evident, we must take note that every sin committed directly against human life is a mortal sin. Now simple fornication implies an inordinateness that tends to injure the life of the offspring to be born of this union. For we find in all animals where the upbringing of the offspring needs care of both male and female, that these come together not indeterminately, but the male with a certain female, whether one or several; such is the case with all birds: while, on the other hand, among those animals, where the female alone suffices for the offspring's upbringing, the union is indeterminate, as in the case of dogs and like animals. Now it is evident that the upbringing of a human child requires not only the mother's care for his nourishment, but much more the care of his father as guide and guardian, and under whom he progresses in goods both internal and external. Hence human nature rebels against an indeterminate union of the sexes and demands that a man should be united to a determinate woman and should abide with her a long time or even for a whole lifetime. Hence it is that in the human race the male has a natural solicitude for the certainty of offspring, because on him devolves the upbringing of the child: and this certainly would cease if the union of sexes were indeterminate.

This union with a certain definite woman is called matrimony; which for the above reason is said to belong to the natural law. Since, however, the union of the sexes is directed to the common good of the whole human race, and common goods depend on the law for their determination, as stated above ([3534]FS, Q[90], A[2]), it follows that this union of man and woman, which is called matrimony, is determined by some law. What this determination is for us will be stated in the Third Part of this work (XP, Q[50], seqq.), where we shall treat of the sacrament of matrimony. Wherefore, since fornication is an indeterminate union of the sexes, as something incompatible with matrimony, it is opposed to the good of the child's upbringing, and consequently it is a mortal sin.

Nor does it matter if a man having knowledge of a woman by fornication, make sufficient provision for the upbringing of the child: because a matter that comes under the determination of the law is judged according to what happens in general, and not according to what may happen in a particular case.

Reply to Objection 1: Fornication is reckoned in conjunction with these things, not as being on a par with them in sinfulness, but because the matters mentioned there were equally liable to cause dispute between Jews and Gentiles, and thus prevent them from agreeing unanimously. For among the Gentiles, fornication was not deemed unlawful, on account of the corruption of natural reason: whereas the Jews, taught by the Divine law, considered it to be unlawful. The other things mentioned were loathsome to the Jews through custom introduced by the law into their daily life. Hence the Apostles forbade these things to the Gentiles, not as though they were unlawful in themselves, but because they were loathsome to the Jews, as stated above ([3535]FS, Q[103], A[4], ad 3).

Reply to Objection 2: Fornication is said to be a sin, because it is contrary to right reason. Now man's reason is right, in so far as it is ruled by the Divine Will, the first and supreme rule. Wherefore that which a man does by God's will and in obedience to His command, is not contrary to right reason, though it may seem contrary to the general order of reason: even so, that which is done miraculously by the Divine power is not contrary to nature, though it be contrary to the usual course of nature. Therefore just as Abraham did not sin in being willing to slay his innocent son, because he obeyed God, although considered in itself it was contrary to right human reason in general, so, too, Osee sinned not in committing fornication by God's command. Nor should such a copulation be strictly called fornication, though it be so called in reference to the general course of things. Hence Augustine says (Confess. iii, 8): "When God commands a thing to be done against the customs or agreement of any people, though it were never done by them heretofore, it is to be done"; and afterwards he adds: "For as among the powers of human society, the greater authority is obeyed in preference to the lesser, so must God in preference to all."

Reply to Objection 3: Abraham and Jacob went in to their handmaidens with no purpose of fornication, as we shall show further on when we treat of matrimony ([3536]XP, Q[65], A[5], ad 2). As to Juda there is no need to excuse him, for he also caused Joseph to be sold.

Reply to Objection 4: Simple fornication is contrary to the love of our neighbor, because it is opposed to the good of the child to be born, as we have shown, since it is an act of generation accomplished in a manner disadvantageous to the future child.

Reply to Objection 5: A person, who, while given to works of piety, yields to the inconstancy of the flesh, is freed from eternal loss, in so far as these works dispose him to receive the grace to repent, and because by such works he makes satisfaction for his past inconstancy; but not so as to be freed by pious works, if he persist in carnal inconstancy impenitent until death.

Reply to Objection 6: One copulation may result in the begetting of a man, wherefore inordinate copulation, which hinders the good of the future child, is a mortal sin as to the very genus of the act, and not only as to the inordinateness of concupiscence. On the other hand, one meal does not hinder the good of a man's whole life, wherefore the act of gluttony is not a mortal sin by reason of its genus. It would, however, be a mortal sin, if a man were knowingly to partake of a food which would alter the whole condition of his life, as was the case with Adam.

Nor is it true that fornication is the least of the sins comprised under lust, for the marriage act that is done out of sensuous pleasure is a lesser sin.

Whether fornication is the most grievous of sins?

Objection 1: It would seem that fornication is the most grievous of sins. For seemingly a sin is the more grievous according as it proceeds from a greater sensuous pleasure. Now the greatest sensuous pleasure is in fornication, for a gloss on 1 Cor. 7:9 says that the "flame of sensuous pleasure is most fierce in lust." Therefore it seems that fornication is the gravest of sins.

Objection 2: Further, a sin is the more grievous that is committed against a person more closely united to the sinner: thus he sins more grievously who strikes his father than one who strikes a stranger. Now according to 1 Cor. 6:18, "He that committeth fornication sinneth against his own body," which is most intimately connected with a man. Therefore it seems that fornication is the most grievous of sins.

Objection 3: Further, the greater a good is, the graver would seem to be the sin committed against it. Now the sin of fornication is seemingly opposed to the good of the whole human race, as appears from what was said in the foregoing Article. It is also against Christ, according to 1 Cor. 6:15, "Shall I . . . take the members of Christ, and make them the members of a harlot?" Therefore fornication is the most grievous of sins.

On the contrary, Gregory says (Moral. xxxiii, 12) that the sins of the flesh are less grievous than spiritual sins.

I answer that, The gravity of a sin may be measured in two ways, first with regard to the sin in itself, secondly with regard to some accident. The gravity of a sin is measured with regard to the sin itself, by reason of its species, which is determined according to the good to which that sin is opposed. Now fornication is contrary to the good of the child to be born. Wherefore it is a graver sin, as to its species, than those sins which are contrary to external goods, such as theft and the like; while it is less grievous than those which are directly against God, and sins that are injurious to the life of one already born, such as murder.

Reply to Objection 1: The sensual pleasure that aggravates a sin is that which is in the inclination of the will. But the sensual pleasure that is in the sensitive appetite, lessens sin, because a sin is the less grievous according as it is committed under the impulse of a greater passion. It is in this way that the greatest sensual pleasure is in fornication. Hence Augustine says (De Agone Christiano [*Serm. ccxciii; ccl de Temp.; see Appendix to St. Augustine's works]) that of all a Christian's conflicts, the most difficult combats are those of chastity; wherein the fight is a daily one, but victory rare: and Isidore declares (De Summo Bono ii, 39) that "mankind is subjected to the devil by carnal lust more than by anything else," because, to wit, the vehemence of this passion is more difficult to overcome.

Reply to Objection 2: The fornicator is said to sin against his own body, not merely because the pleasure of fornication is consummated in the flesh, which is also the case in gluttony, but also because he acts against the good of his own body by an undue resolution and defilement thereof, and an undue association with another. Nor does it follow from this that fornication is the most grievous sin, because in man reason is of greater value than the body, wherefore if there be a sin more opposed to reason, it will be more grievous.

Reply to Objection 3: The sin of fornication is contrary to the good of the human race, in so far as it is prejudicial to the individual begetting of the one man that may be born. Now one who is already an actual member of the human species attains to the perfection of the species more than one who is a man potentially, and from this point of view murder is a more grievous sin than fornication and every kind of lust, through being more opposed to the good of the human species. Again, a Divine good is greater than the good of the human race: and therefore those sins also that are against God are more grievous. Moreover, fornication is a sin against God, not directly as though the fornicator intended to offend God, but consequently, in the same way as all mortal sins. And just as the members of our body are Christ's members, so too, our spirit is one with Christ, according to 1 Cor. 6:17, "He who is joined to the Lord is one spirit." Wherefore also spiritual sins are more against Christ than fornication is.

Whether there can be mortal sin in touches and kisses?

Objection 1: It would seem that there is no mortal sin in touches and kisses. For the Apostle says (Eph. 5:3): "Fornication and all uncleanness, or covetousness, let it not so much as be named among you, as becometh saints," then he adds: "Or obscenity" (which a gloss refers to "kissing and fondling"), "or foolish talking" (as "soft speeches"), "or scurrility" (which "fools call geniality—i.e. jocularity"), and afterwards he continues (Eph. 5:5): "For know ye this and understand that no fornicator, or unclean, or covetous person (which is the serving of idols), hath inheritance in the kingdom of Christ and of God," thus making no further mention of obscenity, as neither of foolish talking or scurrility. Therefore these are not mortal sins.

Objection 2: Further, fornication is stated to be a mortal sin as being prejudicial to the good of the future child's begetting and upbringing. But these are not affected by kisses and touches or blandishments. Therefore there is no mortal sin in these.

Objection 3: Further, things that are mortal sins in themselves can never be good actions. Yet kisses, touches, and the like can be done sometimes without sin. Therefore they are not mortal sins in themselves.

On the contrary, A lustful look is less than a touch, a caress or a kiss. But according to Mat. 5:28, "Whosoever shall look on a woman to lust after her hath already committed adultery with her in his heart." Much more therefore are lustful kisses and other like things mortal sins.

Further, Cyprian says (Ad Pompon, de Virgin., Ep. lxii), "By their very intercourse, their blandishments, their converse, their embraces, those who are associated in a sleep that knows neither honor nor shame, acknowledge their disgrace and crime." Therefore by doing these things a man is guilty of a crime, that is, of mortal sin.

I answer that, A thing is said to be a mortal works. /sin in two ways. First, by reason of its species, and in this way a kiss, caress, or touch does not, of its very nature, imply a mortal sin, for it is possible to do such things without lustful pleasure, either as being the custom of one's country, or on account of some obligation or reasonable cause. Secondly, a thing is said to be a mortal sin by reason of its cause: thus he who gives an alms, in order to lead someone into heresy, sins mortally on account of his corrupt intention. Now it has been stated above ([3537]FS, Q[74], A[8]), that it is a mortal sin not only to consent to the act, but also to the delectation of a mortal sin. Wherefore since fornication is a mortal sin, and much more so the other kinds of lust, it follows that in such like sins not only consent to the act but also consent to the pleasure is a mortal sin. Consequently, when these kisses and caresses are done for this delectation, it follows that they are mortal sins, and only in this way are they said to be lustful. Therefore in so far as they are lustful, they are mortal sins.

Reply to Objection 1: The Apostle makes no further mention of these three because they are not sinful except as directed to those that he had mentioned before.

Reply to Objection 2: Although kisses and touches do not by their very nature hinder the good of the human offspring, they proceed from lust, which is the source of this hindrance: and on this account they are mortally sinful.

Reply to Objection 3: This argument proves that such things are not mortal sins in their species.

Whether nocturnal pollution is a mortal sin?

Objection 1: It would seem that nocturnal pollution is a sin. For the same things are the matter of merit and demerit. Now a man may merit while he sleeps, as was the case with Solomon, who while asleep obtained the gift of wisdom from the Lord (3 Kings 3:2, Par. 1). Therefore a man may demerit while asleep; and thus nocturnal pollution would seem to be a sin.

Objection 2: Further, whoever has the use of reason can sin. Now a man has the use of reason while asleep, since in our sleep we frequently discuss matters, choose this rather than that, consenting to one thing, or dissenting to another. Therefore one may sin while asleep, so that nocturnal pollution is not prevented by sleep from being a sin, seeing that it is a sin according to its genus.

Objection 3: Further, it is useless to reprove and instruct one who cannot act according to or against reason. Now man, while asleep, is instructed and reproved by God, according to Job 33:15,16, "By a dream in a vision by night, when deep sleep is wont to lay hold of men [*Vulg.: 'When deep sleep falleth upon men.' St. Thomas is apparently quoting from memory, as the passage is given correctly above[3538], Q[95], A[6], OBJ[1]] . . . Then He openeth the ears of men, and teaching instructeth them in what they are to learn." Therefore a man, while asleep, can act according to or against his reason, and this is to do good or sinful actions, and thus it seems that nocturnal pollution is a sin.

On the contrary, Augustine says (Gen. ad lit. xii, 15): "When the same image that comes into the mind of a speaker presents itself to the mind of the sleeper, so that the latter is unable to distinguish the imaginary from the real union of bodies, the flesh is at once moved, with the result that usually follows such motions; and yet there is as little sin in this as there is in speaking and therefore thinking about such things while one is awake."

I answer that, Nocturnal pollution may be considered in two ways. First, in itself; and thus it has not the character of a sin. For every sin depends on the judgment of reason, since even the first movement of the sensuality has nothing sinful in it, except in so far as it can be suppressed by reason; wherefore in the absence of reason's judgment, there is no sin in it. Now during sleep reason has not a free judgment. For there is no one who while sleeping does not regard some of the images formed by his imagination as though they were real, as stated above in the [3539]FP, Q[84], A[8], ad 2. Wherefore what a man does while he sleeps and is deprived of reason's judgment, is not imputed to him as a sin, as neither are the actions of a maniac or an imbecile.

Secondly, nocturnal pollution may be considered with reference to its cause. This may be threefold. One is a bodily cause. For when there is excess of seminal humor in the body, or when the humor is disintegrated either through overheating of the body or some other disturbance, the sleeper dreams things that are connected with the discharge of this excessive or disintegrated humor: the same thing happens when nature is cumbered with other superfluities, so that phantasms relating to the discharge of those superfluities are formed in the imagination. Accordingly if this excess of humor be due to a sinful cause (for instance excessive eating or drinking), nocturnal pollution has the character of sin from its cause: whereas if the excess or disintegration of these superfluities be not due to a sinful cause, nocturnal pollution is not sinful, neither in itself nor in its cause.

A second cause of nocturnal pollution is on the part of the soul and the inner man: for instance when it happens to the sleeper on account of some previous thought.

For the thought which preceded while he was awake, is sometimes purely speculative, for instance when one thinks about the sins of the flesh for the purpose of discussion; while sometimes it is accompanied by a certain emotion either of concupiscence or of abhorrence. Now nocturnal pollution is more apt to arise from thinking about carnal sins with concupiscence for such pleasures, because this leaves its trace and inclination in the soul, so that the sleeper is more easily led in his imagination to consent to acts productive of pollution. In this sense the Philosopher says (Ethic. i, 13) that "in so far as certain movements in some degree pass" from the waking state to the state of sleep, "the dreams of good men are better than those of any other people": and Augustine says (Gen. ad lit. xii, 15) that "even during sleep, the soul may have conspicuous merit on account of its good disposition." Thus it is evident that nocturnal pollution may be sinful on the part of its cause. on the other hand, it may happen that nocturnal pollution ensues after thoughts about carnal acts, though they were speculative, or accompanied by abhorrence, and then it is not sinful, neither in itself nor in its cause.

The third cause is spiritual and external; for instance when by the work of a devil the sleeper's phantasms are disturbed so as to induce the aforesaid result. Sometimes this is associated with a previous sin, namely the neglect to guard against the wiles of the devil. Hence the words of the hymn at even: "Our enemy repress, that so our bodies no uncleanness know" [*Translation W. K. Blount].

On the other hand, this may occur without any fault on man's part, and through the wickedness of the devil alone. Thus we read in the Collationes Patrum (Coll. xxii, 6) of a man who was ever wont to suffer from nocturnal pollution on festivals, and that the devil brought this about in order to prevent him from receiving Holy Communion. Hence it is manifest that nocturnal pollution is never a sin, but is sometimes the result of a previous sin.

Reply to Objection 1: Solomon did not merit to receive wisdom from God while he was asleep. He received it in token of his previous desire. It is for this reason that his petition is stated to have been pleasing to God (3 Kings 3:10), as Augustine observes (Gen. ad lit. xii, 15).

Reply to Objection 2: The use of reason is more or less hindered in sleep, according as the inner sensitive powers are more or less overcome by sleep, on account of the violence or attenuation of the evaporations. Nevertheless it is always hindered somewhat, so as to be unable to elicit a judgment altogether free, as stated in the [3540]FP, Q[84], A[8], ad 2. Therefore what it does then is not imputed to it as a sin.

Reply to Objection 3: Reason's apprehension is not hindered during sleep to the same extent as its judgment, for this is accomplished by reason turning to sensible objects, which are the first principles of human thought. Hence nothing hinders man's reason during sleep from apprehending anew something arising out of the traces left by his previous thoughts and phantasms presented to him, or again through Divine revelation, or the interference of a good or bad angel.

Whether seduction should be reckoned a species of lust?

Objection 1: It would seem that seduction should not be reckoned a species of lust. For seduction denotes the unlawful violation of a virgin, according to the Decretals (XXXVI, qu. 1) [*Append. Grat. ad can. Lex illa]. But this may occur between an unmarried man and an unmarried woman, which pertains to fornication. Therefore seduction should not be reckoned a species of lust, distinct from fornication.

Objection 2: Further, Ambrose says (De Patriarch. [*De Abraham i, 4]): "Let no man be deluded by human laws: all seduction is adultery." Now a species is not contained under another that is differentiated in opposition to it. Therefore since adultery is a species of lust, it seems that seduction should not be reckoned a species of lust.

Objection 3: Further, to do a person an injury would seem to pertain to injustice rather than to lust. Now the seducer does an injury to another, namely the violated maiden's father, who "can take the injury as personal to himself" [*Gratian, ad can. Lex illa], and sue the seducer for damages. Therefore seduction should not be reckoned a species of lust.

On the contrary, Seduction consists properly in the venereal act whereby a virgin is violated. Therefore, since lust is properly about venereal actions, it would seem that seduction is a species of lust.

I answer that, When the matter of a vice has a special deformity, we must reckon it to be a determinate species of that vice. Now lust is a sin concerned with venereal matter, as stated above ([3541]Q[153], A[1]). And a special deformity attaches to the violation of a virgin who is under her father's care: both on the part of the maid, who through being violated without any previous compact of marriage is both hindered from contracting a lawful marriage and is put on the road to a wanton life from which she was withheld lest she should lose the seal of virginity: and on the part of the father, who is her guardian, according to Ecclus. 42:11, "Keep a sure watch over a shameless daughter, lest at any time she make thee become a laughing-stock to thy enemies." Therefore it is evident that seduction which denotes the unlawful violation of a virgin, while still under the guardianship of her parents, is a determinate species of lust.

Reply to Objection 1: Although a virgin is free from the bond of marriage, she is not free from her father's power. Moreover, the seal of virginity is a special obstacle to the intercourse of fornication, in that it should be removed by marriage only. Hence seduction is not simple fornication, since the latter is intercourse with harlots, women, namely, who are no longer virgins, as a gloss observes on 2 Cor. 12:, "And have not done penance for the uncleanness and fornication," etc.

Reply to Objection 2: Ambrose here takes seduction in another sense, as applicable in a general way to any sin of lust. Wherefore seduction, in the words quoted, signifies the intercourse between a married man and any woman other than his wife. This is clear from his adding: "Nor is it lawful for the husband to do what the wife may not." In this sense, too, we are to understand the words of Num. 5:13: "If [Vulg.: 'But'] the adultery is secret, and cannot be provided by witnesses, because she was not found in adultery [stupro]."

Reply to Objection 3: Nothing prevents a sin from having a greater deformity through being united to another sin. Now the sin of lust obtains a greater deformity from the sin of injustice, because the concupiscence would seem to be more inordinate, seeing that it refrains not from the pleasurable object so that it may avoid an injustice. In fact a twofold injustice attaches to it. One is on the part of the virgin, who, though not violated by force, is nevertheless seduced, and thus the seducer is bound to compensation. Hence it is written (Ex. 22:16,17): "If a man seduce a virgin not yet espoused, and lie with her, he shall endow her and have her to wife. If the maid's father will not give her to him, he shall give money according to the dowry, which virgins are wont to receive." The other injury is done to the maid's father: wherefore the seducer is bound by the Law to a penalty in his regard. For it is written (Dt. 22:28,29): "If a man find a damsel that is a virgin, who is not espoused, and taking her, lie with her, and the matter come to judgment: he that lay with her shall give to the father of the maid fifty sicles of silver, and shall have her to wife, and because he hath humbled her, he may not put her away all the days of his life": and this, lest he should prove to have married her in mockery, as Augustine observes. [*QQ. in Dt., qu. xxxiv.]

Whether rape is a species of lust, distinct from seduction?

Objection 1: It would seem that rape is not a species of lust, distinct from seduction. For Isidore says (Etym. v, 26) that "seduction [stuprum], or rape, properly speaking, is unlawful intercourse, and takes its name from its causing corruption:

wherefore he that is guilty of rape is a seducer." Therefore it seems that rape should not be reckoned a species of lust distinct from seduction.

Objection 2: Further, rape, apparently, implies violence. For it is stated in the Decretals (XXXVI, qu. 1 [*Append. Grat. ad can. Lex illa]) that "rape is committed when a maid is taken away by force from her father's house that after being violated she may be taken to wife." But the employment of force is accidental to lust, for this essentially regards the pleasure of intercourse. Therefore it seems that rape should not be reckoned a determinate species of lust.

Objection 3: Further, the sin of lust is curbed by marriage: for it is written (1 Cor. 7:2): "For fear of fornication, let every man have his own wife." Now rape is an obstacle to subsequent marriage, for it was enacted in the council of Meaux: "We decree that those who are guilty of rape, or of abducting or seducing women, should not have those women in marriage, although they should have subsequently married them with the consent of their parents." Therefore rape is not a determinate species of lust distinct from seduction.

Objection 4: Further, a man may have knowledge of his newly married wife without committing a sin of lust. Yet he may commit rape if he take her away by force from her parents' house, and have carnal knowledge of her. Therefore rape should not be reckoned a determinate species of lust.

On the contrary, Rape is unlawful sexual intercourse, as Isidore states (Etym. v, 26). But this pertains to the sin of lust. Therefore rape is a species of lust.

I answer that, Rape, in the sense in which we speak of it now, is a species of lust: and sometimes it coincides with seduction; sometimes there is rape without seduction, and sometimes seduction without rape.

They coincide when a man employs force in order unlawfully to violate a virgin. This force is employed sometimes both towards the virgin and towards her father; and sometimes towards the father and not to the virgin, for instance if she allows herself to be taken away by force from her father's house. Again, the force employed in rape differs in another way, because sometimes a maid is taken away by force from her parents' house, and is forcibly violated: while sometimes, though taken away by force, she is not forcibly violated, but of her own consent, whether by act of fornication or by the act of marriage: for the conditions of rape remain no matter how force is employed. There is rape without seduction if a man abduct a widow or one who is not a virgin. Hence Pope Symmachus says [*Ep. v ad Caesarium; Cf. can. Raptores xxxvi, qu. 2], "We abhor abductors whether of widows or of virgins on account of the heinousness of their crime."

There is seduction without rape when a man, without employing force, violates a virgin unlawfully.

Reply to Objection 1: Since rape frequently coincides with seduction, the one is sometimes used to signify the other.

Reply to Objection 2: The employment of force would seem to arise from the greatness of concupiscence, the result being that a man does not fear to endanger himself by offering violence.

Reply to Objection 3: The rape of a maiden who is promised in marriage is to be judged differently from that of one who is not so promised. For one who is promised in marriage must be restored to her betrothed, who has a right to her in virtue of their betrothal: whereas one that is not promised to another must first of all be restored to her father's care, and then the abductor may lawfully marry her with her parents' consent. Otherwise the marriage is unlawful, since whosoever steals a thing he is bound to restore it. Nevertheless rape does not dissolve a marriage already contracted, although it is an impediment to its being contracted. As to the decree of the council in question, it was made in abhorrence of this crime, and has been abrogated. Wherefore Jerome [*The quotation is from Can. Tria. xxxvi, qu. 2] declares the contrary: "Three kinds of lawful marriage," says he, "are mentioned in Holy Writ. The first is that of a chaste maiden given away lawfully in her maidenhood to a man. The second is when a man finds a maiden in the city, and by force has carnal knowledge of her. If the father be willing, the man shall endow her according to the father's estimate, and shall pay the price of her purity [*Cf. Dt. 22:23–29]. The third is, when the maiden is taken away from such a man, and is given to another at the father's will."

We may also take this decree to refer to those who are promised to others in marriage, especially if the betrothal be expressed by words in the present tense.

Reply to Objection 4: The man who is just married has, in virtue of the betrothal, a certain right in her: wherefore, although he sins by using violence, he is not guilty of the crime of rape. Hence Pope Gelasius says [*Can. Lex illa, xxvii, qu. 2; xxxvi, qu. 1]: "This law of bygone rulers stated that rape was committed when a maiden, with regard to whose marriage nothing had so far been decided, was taken away by force."

Whether adultery is determinate species of lust, distinct from the other species?

Objection 1: It would seem that adultery is not a determinate species of lust, distinct from the other species. For adultery takes its name from a man having intercourse "with a woman who is not his own [ad alteram]," according to a gloss [*St. Augustine: Serm. li, 13 de Divers. lxiii] on Ex. 20:14. Now a woman who is not one's own may be of various conditions, namely either a virgin, or under her father's care, or a harlot, or of any other description. Therefore it seems that adultery is not a species of lust distinct from the others.

Objection 2: Further, Jerome says [*Contra Jovin. i]: "It matters not for what reason a man behaves as one demented. Hence Sixtus the Pythagorean says in his Maxims: He that is insatiable of his wife is an adulterer," and in like manner one who is over enamored of any woman. Now every kind of lust includes a too ardent love. Therefore adultery is in every kind of lust: and consequently it should not be reckoned a species of lust.

Objection 3: Further, where there is the same kind of deformity, there would seem to be the same species of sin. Now, apparently, there is the same kind of deformity in seduction and adultery: since in either case a woman is violated who is under another person's authority. Therefore adultery is not a determinate species of lust, distinct from the others.

On the contrary, Pope Leo [*St. Augustine, De Bono Conjug. iv; Cf. Append. Grat. ad can. Ille autem. xxxii, qu. 5] says that "adultery is sexual intercourse with another man or woman in contravention of the marriage compact, whether through the impulse of one's own lust, or with the consent of the other party." Now this implies a special deformity of lust. Therefore adultery is a determinate species of lust.

I answer that, Adultery, as its name implies, "is access to another's marriage-bed [ad alienum torum]" [*Cf. Append. Gratian, ad can. Ille autem. xxxii, qu. 1]. By so doing a man is guilty of a twofold offense against chastity and the good of human procreation. First, by accession to a woman who is not joined to him in marriage, which is contrary to the good of the upbringing of his own children. Secondly, by accession to a woman who is united to another in marriage, and thus he hinders the good of another's children. The same applies to the married woman who is corrupted by adultery. Wherefore it is written (Ecclus. 23:32,33): "Every woman . . . that leaveth her husband . . . shall be guilty of sin. For first she hath been unfaithful to the law of the Most High" (since there it is commanded: "Thou shalt not commit adultery"); "and secondly, she hath offended against her husband," by making it uncertain that the children are his: "thirdly, she hath fornicated in adultery, and hath gotten children of another man," which is contrary to the good of her offspring. The first of these, however, is common to all mortal sins, while the two others belong especially to the deformity of adultery. Hence it is manifest that adultery is a determinate species of lust, through having a special deformity in venereal acts.

Reply to Objection 1: If a married man has intercourse with another woman, his sin may be denominated either with regard to him, and thus it is always adultery, since his action is contrary to the fidelity of marriage, or with regard to the woman with whom he has intercourse; and thus sometimes it is adultery, as when a married man has intercourse with another's wife; and sometimes it has the character of seduction, or of some other sin, according to various conditions affecting the woman with whom he has intercourse: and it has been stated above [3542](A[1]) that the species of lust correspond to the various conditions of women.

Reply to Objection 2: Matrimony is specially ordained for the good of human offspring, as stated above [3543](A[2]). But adultery is specially opposed to matrimony, in the point of breaking the marriage faith which is due between husband and wife. And since the man who is too ardent a lover of his wife acts counter to the good of marriage if he use her indecently, although he be not unfaithful, he may in a sense be called an adulterer; and even more so than he that is too ardent a lover of another woman.

Reply to Objection 3: The wife is under her husband's authority, as united to him in marriage: whereas the maid is under her father's authority, as one who is to be married by that authority. Hence the sin of adultery is contrary to the good of marriage in one way, and the sin of seduction in another; wherefore they are reckoned to differ specifically. Of other matters concerning adultery we shall speak in the Third Part [*[3544]XP, Q[59], A[3] ; XP, QQ[60],62], when we treat of matrimony.

Whether incest is a determinate species of lust?

Objection 1: It would seem that incest is not a determinate species of lust. For incest [*'Incestus' is equivalent to 'in-castus = 'unchaste'] takes its name from being a privation of chastity. But all kinds of lust are opposed to chastity. Therefore it seems that incest is not a species of lust, but is lust itself in general.

Objection 2: Further, it is stated in the Decretals (XXXVI, qu. 1 [*Cf. Append. Grat. ad can. Lex illa]) that "incest is intercourse between a man and a woman related by consanguinity or affinity." Now affinity differs from consanguinity. Therefore it is not one but several species of lust.

Objection 3: Further, that which does not, of itself, imply a deformity, does not constitute a determinate species of vice. But intercourse between those who are related by consanguinity or affinity does not, of itself, contain any deformity, else it would never have been lawful. Therefore incest is not a determinate species of lust.

On the contrary, The species of lust are distinguished according to the various conditions of women with whom a man has unlawful intercourse. Now incest implies a special condition on the part of the woman, because it is unlawful intercourse with a woman related by consanguinity or affinity as stated (OBJ[2]). Therefore incest is a determinate species of lust.

I answer that, As stated above ([3545]AA[1],6) wherever we find something incompatible with the right use of venereal actions, there must needs be a determinate species of lust. Now sexual intercourse with women related by consanguinity or affinity is unbecoming to venereal union on three counts. First, because man naturally owes a certain respect to his parents and therefore to his other blood relations, who are descended in near degree from the same parents: so much so indeed that among the ancients, as Valerius Maximus relates [*Dict. Fact. Memor. ii, 1], it was not deemed right for a son to bathe with his father, lest they should see one another naked. Now from what has been said (Q[142], A[4]: Q[151], A[4]), it is evident that in venereal acts there is a certain shamefulness inconsistent with respect, wherefore men are ashamed of them. Wherefore it is unseemly that such persons should be united in venereal intercourse. This reason seems to be indicated (Lev. 18:7) where we read: "She is thy mother, thou shalt not uncover her nakedness," and the same is expressed further on with regard to others.

The second reason is because blood relations must needs live in close touch with one another. Wherefore if they were not debarred from venereal union, opportunities of venereal intercourse would be very frequent and thus men's minds would be enervated by lust. Hence in the Old Law [*Lev. 18] the prohibition was apparently directed specially to those persons who must needs live together.

The third reason is, because this would hinder a man from having many friends: since through a man taking a stranger to wife, all his wife's relations are united to him by a special kind of friendship, as though they were of the same blood as himself. Wherefore Augustine says (De Civ. Dei xv, 16): "The demands of charity are most perfectly satisfied by men uniting together in the bonds that the various ties of friendship require, so that they may live together in a useful and becoming amity; nor should one man have many relationships in one, but each should have one."

Aristotle adds another reason (2 Polit. ii): for since it is natural that a man should have a liking for a woman of his kindred, if to this be added the love that has its origin in venereal intercourse, his love would be too ardent and would become a very great incentive to lust: and this is contrary to chastity. Hence it is evident that incest is a determinate species of lust.

Reply to Objection 1: Unlawful intercourse between persons related to one another would be most prejudicial to chastity, both on account of the opportunities it affords, and because of the excessive ardor of love, as stated in the Article. Wherefore the unlawful intercourse between such persons is called "incest" antonomastically.

Reply to Objection 2: Persons are related by affinity through one who is related by consanguinity: and therefore since the one depends on the other, consanguinity and affinity entail the same kind of unbecomingness.

Reply to Objection 3: There is something essentially unbecoming and contrary to natural reason in sexual intercourse between persons related by blood, for instance between parents and children who are directly and immediately related to one another, since children naturally owe their parents honor. Hence the Philosopher instances a horse (De Animal. ix, 47) which covered its own mother by mistake and threw itself over a precipice as though horrified at what it had done, because some animals even have a natural respect for those that have begotten them. There is not the same essential unbecomingness attaching to other persons who are related to one another not directly but through their parents: and, as to this, becomingness or unbecomingness varies according to custom, and human or Divine law: because, as stated above [3546](A[2]), sexual intercourse, being directed to the common good, is subject to law. Wherefore, as Augustine says (De Civ. Dei xv, 16), whereas the union of brothers and sisters goes back to olden times, it became all the more worthy of condemnation when religion forbade it.

Whether sacrilege can be a species of lust?

Objection 1: It would seem that sacrilege cannot be a species of lust. For the same species is not contained under different genera that are not subalternated to one another. Now sacrilege is a species of irreligion, as stated above ([3547]Q[99], A[2]). Therefore sacrilege cannot be reckoned a species of lust.

Objection 2: Further, the Decretals (XXXVI, qu. 1 [*Append. Grat. ad can. Lex illa]), do not place sacrilege among other sins which are reckoned species of lust. Therefore it would seem not to be a species of lust.

Objection 3: Further, something derogatory to a sacred thing may be done by the other kinds of vice, as well as by lust. But sacrilege is not reckoned a species of gluttony, or of any other similar vice. Therefore neither should it be reckoned a species of lust.

On the contrary, Augustine says (De Civ. Dei xv, 16) that "if it is wicked, through covetousness, to go beyond one's earthly bounds, how much more wicked is it through venereal lust to transgress the bounds of morals!" Now to go beyond one's earthly bounds in sacred matters is a sin of sacrilege. Therefore it is likewise a sin of sacrilege to overthrow the bounds of morals through venereal desire in sacred matters. But venereal desire pertains to lust. Therefore sacrilege is a species of lust.

I answer that, As stated above ([3548]FS, Q[18], AA[6],7), the act of a virtue or vice, that is directed to the end of another virtue or vice, assumes the latter's species: thus, theft committed for the sake of adultery, passes into the species of adultery. Now it is evident that as Augustine states (De Virgin. 8), the observance of chastity, by being directed to the worship of God, becomes an act of religion, as in the case of those who vow and keep chastity. Wherefore it is manifest that lust also, by violating something pertaining to the worship of God, belongs to the species of sacrilege: and in this way sacrilege may be accounted a species of lust.

Reply to Objection 1: Lust, by being directed to another vice as its end, becomes a species of that vice: and so a species of lust may be also a species of irreligion, as of a higher genus.

Reply to Objection 2: The enumeration referred to, includes those sins which are species of lust by their very nature: whereas sacrilege is a species of lust in so far as it is directed to another vice as its end, and may coincide with the various species of lust. For unlawful intercourse between persons mutually united by spiritual relationship, is a sacrilege after the manner of incest. Intercourse with a virgin consecrated to God, inasmuch as she is the spouse of Christ, is sacrilege resembling adultery. If the maiden be under her father's authority, it will be spiritual seduction; and if force be employed it will be spiritual rape, which kind of rape even the civil law punishes more severely than others. Thus the Emperor Justinian says [*Cod. i, iii de Episc. et Cler. 5]: "If any man dare, I will not say to rape, but even to tempt a consecrated virgin with a view to marriage, he shall be liable to capital punishment."

Reply to Objection 3: Sacrilege is committed on a consecrated thing. Now a consecrated thing is either a consecrated person, who is desired for sexual intercourse, and thus it is a kind of lust, or it is desired for possession, and thus it is a kind of injustice. Sacrilege may also come under the head of anger, for instance, if through anger an injury be done to a consecrated person. Again, one may commit a sacrilege by partaking gluttonously of sacred food. Nevertheless, sacrilege is ascribed more specially to lust which is opposed to chastity for the observance of which certain persons are specially consecrated.

Whether the unnatural vice is a species of lust?

Objection 1: It would seem that the unnatural vice is not a species of lust. For no mention of the vice against nature is made in the enumeration given above (A[1], OBJ[1]). Therefore it is not a species of lust.

Objection 2: Further, lust is contrary to virtue; and so it is comprised under vice. But the unnatural vice is comprised not under vice, but under bestiality, according to the Philosopher (Ethic. vii, 5). Therefore the unnatural vice is not a species of lust.

Objection 3: Further, lust regards acts directed to human generation, as stated above ([3549]Q[153], A[2]): Whereas the unnatural vice concerns acts from which generation cannot follow. Therefore the unnatural vice is not a species of lust.

On the contrary, It is reckoned together with the other species of lust (2 Cor. 12:21) where we read: "And have not done penance for the uncleanness, and fornication, and lasciviousness," where a gloss says: "Lasciviousness, i.e., unnatural lust."

I answer that, As stated above ([3550]AA[6],9) wherever there occurs a special kind of deformity whereby the venereal act is rendered unbecoming, there is a determinate species of lust. This may occur in two ways: First, through being contrary to right reason, and this is common to all lustful vices; secondly, because, in addition, it is contrary to the natural order of the venereal act as becoming to the human race: and this is called "the unnatural vice." This may happen in several ways. First, by procuring pollution, without any copulation, for the sake of venereal pleasure: this pertains to the sin of "uncleanness" which some call "effeminacy." Secondly, by copulation with a thing of undue species, and this is called "bestiality." Thirdly, by copulation with an undue sex, male with male, or female with female, as the Apostle states (Rom. 1:27): and this is called the "vice of sodomy." Fourthly, by not observing the natural manner of copulation, either as to undue means, or as to other monstrous and bestial manners of copulation.

Reply to Objection 1: There we enumerated the species of lust that are not contrary to human nature: wherefore the unnatural vice was omitted.

Reply to Objection 2: Bestiality differs from vice, for the latter is opposed to human virtue by a certain excess in the same matter as the virtue, and therefore is reducible to the same genus.

Reply to Objection 3: The lustful man intends not human generation but venereal pleasures. It is possible to have this without those acts from which human generation follows: and it is that which is sought in the unnatural vice.

Whether the unnatural vice is the greatest sin among the species of lust?

Objection 1: It would seem that the unnatural vice is not the greatest sin among the species of lust. For the more a sin is contrary to charity the graver it is. Now adultery, seduction and rape which are injurious to our neighbor are seemingly more contrary to the love of our neighbor, than unnatural sins, by which no other person is injured. Therefore the unnatural sin is not the greatest among the species of lust.

Objection 2: Further, sins committed against God would seem to be the most grievous. Now sacrilege is committed directly against God, since it is injurious to the Divine worship. Therefore sacrilege is a graver sin than the unnatural vice.

Objection 3: Further, seemingly, a sin is all the more grievous according as we owe a greater love to the person against whom that sin is committed. Now the order of charity requires that a man love more those persons who are united to him—and such are those whom he defiles by incest—than persons who are not connected with him, and whom in certain cases he defiles by the unnatural vice. Therefore incest is a graver sin than the unnatural vice.

Objection 4: Further, if the unnatural vice is most grievous, the more it is against nature the graver it would seem to be. Now the sin of uncleanness or effeminacy would seem to be most contrary to nature, since it would seem especially in accord with nature that agent and patient should be distinct from one another. Hence it would follow that uncleanness is the gravest of unnatural vices. But this is not true. Therefore unnatural vices are not the most grievous among sins of lust.

On the contrary, Augustine says (De adult. conjug. [*The quotation is from Cap. Adulterii xxxii, qu. 7. Cf. Augustine, De Bono Conjugali, viii.]) that "of all these," namely the sins belonging to lust, "that which is against nature is the worst."

I answer that, In every genus, worst of all is the corruption of the principle on which the rest depend. Now the principles of reason are those things that are according to nature, because reason presupposes things as determined by nature, before disposing of other things according as it is fitting. This may be observed both in speculative and in practical matters. Wherefore just as in speculative matters the most grievous and shameful error is that which is about things the knowledge of which is naturally bestowed on man, so in matters of action it is most grave and shameful to act against things as determined by nature. Therefore, since by the unnatural vices man transgresses that which has been determined by nature with regard to the use of venereal actions, it follows that in this matter this sin is gravest of all. After it comes incest, which, as stated above [3551](A[9]), is contrary to the natural respect which we owe persons related to us.

With regard to the other species of lust they imply a transgression merely of that which is determined by right reason, on the presupposition, however, of natural principles. Now it is more against reason to make use of the venereal act not only with prejudice to the future offspring, but also so as to injure another person besides. Wherefore simple fornication, which is committed without injustice to another person, is the least grave among the species of lust. Then, it is a greater injustice to have intercourse with a woman who is subject to another's authority as regards the act of generation, than as regards merely her guardianship. Wherefore adultery is more grievous than seduction. And both of these are aggravated by the use of violence. Hence rape of a virgin is graver than seduction, and rape of a wife than adultery. And all these are aggravated by coming under the head of sacrilege, as stated above (A[10], ad 2).

Reply to Objection 1: Just as the ordering of right reason proceeds from man, so the order of nature is from God Himself: wherefore in sins contrary to nature, whereby the very order of nature is violated, an injury is done to God, the Author of nature. Hence Augustine says (Confess. iii, 8): "Those foul offenses that are against nature should be everywhere and at all times detested and punished, such as were those of the people of Sodom, which should all nations commit, they should all stand guilty of the same crime, by the law of God which hath not so made men that they should so abuse one another. For even that very intercourse which should be between God and us is violated, when that same nature, of which He is the Author, is polluted by the perversity of lust."

Reply to Objection 2: Vices against nature are also against God, as stated above (ad 1), and are so much more grievous than the depravity of sacrilege, as the order impressed on human nature is prior to and more firm than any subsequently established order.

Reply to Objection 3: The nature of the species is more intimately united to each individual, than any other individual is. Wherefore sins against the specific nature are more grievous.

Reply to Objection 4: Gravity of a sin depends more on the abuse of a thing than on the omission of the right use. Wherefore among sins against nature, the lowest place belongs to the sin of uncleanness, which consists in the mere omission of copulation with another. While the most grievous is the sin of bestiality, because use of the due species is not observed. Hence a gloss on Gn. 37:2, "He accused his brethren of a most wicked crime," says that "they copulated with cattle." After this comes the sin of sodomy, because use of the right sex is not observed. Lastly comes the sin of not observing the right manner of copulation, which is more grievous if the abuse regards the "vas" than if it affects the manner of copulation in respect of other circumstances.

OF CONTINENCE (FOUR ARTICLES)

We must next consider the potential parts of temperance: (1) continence; (2) clemency; (3) modesty. Under the first head we must consider continence and incontinence. With regard to continence there are four points of inquiry:

(1) Whether continence is a virtue?

(2) What is its matter?

(3) What is its subject?

(4) Of its comparison with temperance.

Whether continence is a virtue?

Objection 1: It would seem that continence is not a virtue. For species and genus are not co-ordinate members of the same division. But continence is co-ordinated with virtue, according to the Philosopher (Ethic. vii, 1,9). Therefore continence is not a virtue.

Objection 2: Further, no one sins by using a virtue, since, according to Augustine (De Lib. Arb. ii, 18,19), "a virtue is a thing that no one makes ill use of." Yet one may sin by containing oneself: for instance, if one desire to do a good, and contain oneself from doing it. Therefore continence is not a virtue.

Objection 3: Further, no virtue withdraws man from that which is lawful, but only from unlawful things: for a gloss on Gal. 5:23, "Faith, modesty," etc., says that by continence a man refrains even from things that are lawful. Therefore continence is not a virtue.

On the contrary, Every praiseworthy habit would seem to be a virtue. Now such is continence, for Andronicus says [*De Affectibus] that "continence is a habit unconquered by pleasure." Therefore continence is a virtue.

I answer that, The word "continence" is taken by various people in two ways. For some understand continence to denote abstention from all venereal pleasure: thus the Apostle joins continence to chastity (Gal. 5:23). In this sense perfect continence is virginity in the first place, and widowhood in the second. Wherefore the same applies to continence understood thus, as to virginity which we have stated above ([3552]Q[152], A[3]) to be a virtue. Others, however, understand continence as signifying that whereby a man resists evil desires, which in him are vehement. In this sense the Philosopher takes continence (Ethic. vii, 7), and thus also it is used in the Conferences of the Fathers (Collat. xii, 10,11). In this way continence has something of the nature of a virtue, in so far, to wit, as the reason stands firm in opposition to the passions, lest it be led astray by them: yet it does not attain to the perfect nature of a moral virtue, by which even the sensitive appetite is subject to reason so that vehement passions contrary to reason do not arise in the sensitive appetite. Hence the Philosopher says (Ethic. iv, 9) that "continence is not a virtue but a mixture," inasmuch as it has something of virtue, and somewhat falls short of virtue.

If, however, we take virtue in a broad sense, for any principle of commendable actions, we may say that continence is a virtue.

Reply to Objection 1: The Philosopher includes continence in the same division with virtue in so far as the former falls short of virtue.

Reply to Objection 2: Properly speaking, man is that which is according to reason. Wherefore from the very fact that a man holds [tenet se] to that which is in accord with reason, he is said to contain himself. Now whatever pertains to perversion of reason is not according to reason. Hence he alone is truly said to be continent who stands to that which is in accord with right reason, and not to that which is in accord with perverse reason. Now evil desires are opposed to right reason, even as good desires are opposed to perverse reason. Wherefore he is properly and truly continent who holds to right reason, by abstaining from evil desires, and not he who holds to perverse reason, by abstaining from good desires: indeed, the latter should rather be said to be obstinate in evil.

Reply to Objection 3: The gloss quoted takes continence in the first sense, as denoting a perfect virtue, which refrains not merely from unlawful goods, but also from certain lawful things that are lesser goods, in order to give its whole attention to the more perfect goods.

Whether desires for pleasures of touch are the matter of continence?

Objection 1: It would seem that desires for pleasures of touch are not the matter of continence. For Ambrose says (De Offic. i, 46): "General decorum by its consistent form and the perfection of what is virtuous is restrained* in its every action." [*"Continentem" according to St. Thomas' reading; St. Ambrose wrote "concinentem = harmonious"].

Objection 2: Further, continence takes its name from a man standing for the good of right reason, as stated above (A[1], ad 2). Now other passions lead men astray from right reason with greater vehemence than the desire for pleasures of touch: for instance, the fear of mortal dangers, which stupefies a man, and anger which makes him behave like a madman, as Seneca remarks [*De Ira i, 1]. Therefore continence does not properly regard the desires for pleasures of touch.

Objection 3: Further, Tully says (De Invent. Rhet. ii, 54): "It is continence that restrains cupidity with the guiding hand of counsel." Now cupidity is generally used to denote the desire for riches rather than the desire for pleasures of touch, according to 1 Tim. 6:10, "Cupidity [Douay: 'The desire of money'] ({philargyria}), is the root of all evils." Therefore continence is not properly about the desires for pleasures of touch

Objection 4: Further, there are pleasures of touch not only in venereal matters but also in eating. But continence is wont to be applied only to the use of venereal matters. Therefore the desire for pleasures of touch is not its proper matter.

Objection 5: Further, among pleasures of touch some are not human but bestial, both as regards food—for instance, the pleasure of eating human flesh; and as regards venereal matters—for instance the abuse of animals or boys. But continence is not about such like things, as stated in Ethic. vii, 5. Therefore desires for pleasures of touch are not the proper matter of continence.

On the contrary, The Philosopher says (Ethic. vii, 4) that "continence and incontinence are about the same things as temperance and intemperance." Now temperance and intemperance are about the desires for pleasures of touch, as stated above ([3553]Q[141], A[4]). Therefore continence and incontinence are also about that same matter.

I answer that, Continence denotes, by its very name, a certain curbing, in so far as a man contains himself from following his passions. Hence continence is properly said in reference to those passions which urge a man towards the pursuit of something, wherein it is praiseworthy that reason should withhold man from pursuing: whereas it is not properly about those passions, such as fear and the like, which denote some kind of withdrawal: since in these it is praiseworthy to remain firm in pursuing what reason dictates, as stated above (Q[123], AA[3],4). Now it is to be observed that natural inclinations are the principles of all supervening inclinations, as stated above ([3554]FP, Q[60], A[2]). Wherefore the more they follow the inclination of nature, the more strongly do the passions urge to the pursuance of an object. Now nature inclines chiefly to those things that are necessary to it, whether for the maintenance of the individual, such as food, or for the maintenance of the species, such as venereal acts, the pleasures of which pertain to the touch. Therefore continence and incontinence refer properly to desires for pleasures of touch.

Reply to Objection 1: Just as temperance may be used in a general sense in connection with any matter; but is properly applied to that matter wherein it is best for man to be curbed: so, too, continence properly speaking regards that matter wherein it is best and most difficult to contain oneself, namely desires for pleasures of touch, and yet in a general sense and relatively may be applied to any other matter: and in this sense Ambrose speaks of continence.

Reply to Objection 2: Properly speaking we do not speak of continence in relation to fear, but rather of firmness of mind which fortitude implies. As to anger, it is true that it begets an impulse to the pursuit of something, but this impulse follows an apprehension of the soul—in so far as a man apprehends that someone has injured him—rather than an inclination of nature. Wherefore a man may be said to be continent of anger, relatively but not simply.

Reply to Objection 3: External goods, such as honors, riches and the like, as the Philosopher says (Ethic. vii, 4), seem to be objects of choice in themselves indeed, but not as being necessary for the maintenance of nature. Wherefore in reference to such things we speak of a person as being continent or incontinent, not simply, but relatively, by adding that they are continent or incontinent in regard to wealth, or honor and so forth. Hence Tully either understood continence in a general sense, as including relative continence, or understood cupidity in a restricted sense as denoting desire for pleasures of touch.

Reply to Objection 4: Venereal pleasures are more vehement than pleasures of the palate: wherefore we are wont to speak of continence and incontinence in reference to venereal matters rather than in reference to food; although according to the Philosopher they are applicable to both.

Reply to Objection 5: Continence is a good of the human reason: wherefore it regards those passions which can be connatural to man. Hence the Philosopher says (Ethic. vii, 5) that "if a man were to lay hold of a child with desire of eating him or of satisfying an unnatural passion whether he follow up his desire or not, he is said to be continent [*See A[4]], not absolutely, but relatively."

Whether the subject of continence is the concupiscible power?

Objection 1: It would seem that the subject of continence is the concupiscible power. For the subject of a virtue should be proportionate to the virtue's matter. Now the matter of continence, as stated [3555](A[2]), is desires for the pleasures of touch, which pertain to the concupiscible power. Therefore continence is in the concupiscible power.

Objection 2: Further, "Opposites are referred to one same thing" [*Categ. viii]. But incontinence is in the concupiscible, whose passions overcome reason, for Andronicus says [*De Affectibus] that "incontinence is the evil inclination of the concupiscible, by following which it chooses wicked pleasures in disobedience to reason." Therefore continence is likewise in the concupiscible.

Objection 3: Further, the subject of a human virtue is either the reason, or the appetitive power, which is divided into the will, the concupiscible and the irascible. Now continence is not in the reason, for then it would be an intellectual virtue; nor is it in the will, since continence is about the passions which are not in the will; nor again is it in the irascible, because it is not properly about the passions of the irascible, as stated above (A[2], ad 2). Therefore it follows that it is in the concupiscible.

On the contrary, Every virtue residing in a certain power removes the evil act of that power. But continence does not remove the evil act of the concupiscible: since "the continent man has evil desires," according to the Philosopher (Ethic. vii, 9). Therefore continence is not in the concupiscible power.

I answer that, Every virtue while residing in a subject, makes that subject have a different disposition from that which it has while subjected to the opposite vice. Now the concupiscible has the same disposition in one who is continent and in one who is incontinent, since in both of them it breaks out into vehement evil desires. Wherefore it is manifest that continence is not in the concupiscible as its subject. Again the reason has the same disposition in both, since both the continent and the incontinent have right reason, and each of them, while undisturbed by passion, purposes not to follow his unlawful desires. Now the primary difference between them is to be found in their choice: since the continent man, though subject to vehement desires, chooses not to follow them, because of his reason; whereas the incontinent man chooses to follow them, although his reason forbids.

Hence continence must needs reside in that power of the soul, whose act it is to choose; and that is the will, as stated above ([3556]FS, Q[13], A[1]).

Reply to Objection 1: Continence has for its matter the desires for pleasures of touch, not as moderating them (this belongs to temperance which is in the concupiscible), but its business with them is to resist them. For this reason it must be in another power, since resistance is of one thing against another.

Reply to Objection 2: The will stands between reason and the concupiscible, and may be moved by either. In the continent man it is moved by the reason, in the incontinent man it is moved by the concupiscible. Hence continence may be ascribed to the reason as to its first mover, and incontinence to the concupiscible power: though both belong immediately to the will as their proper subject.

Reply to Objection 3: Although the passions are not in the will as their subject, yet it is in the power of the will to resist them: thus it is that the will of the continent man resists desires.

Whether continence is better than temperance?

Objection 1: It would seem that continence is better than temperance. For it is written (Ecclus. 26:20): "No price is worthy of a continent soul." Therefore no virtue can be equalled to continence.

Objection 2: Further, the greater the reward a virtue merits, the greater the virtue. Now continence apparently merits the greater reward; for it is written (2 Tim. 2:5): "He . . . is not crowned, except he strive lawfully," and the continent man, since he is subject to vehement evil desires, strives more than the temperate man, in whom these things are not vehement. Therefore continence is a greater virtue than temperance.

Objection 3: Further, the will is a more excellent power than the concupiscible. But continence is in the will, whereas temperance is in the concupiscible, as stated above [3557](A[3]). Therefore continence is a greater virtue than temperance.

On the contrary, Tully (De Invent. Rhet. ii, 54) and Andronicus [*De Affectibus] reckon continence to be annexed to temperance, as to a principal virtue.

I answer that, As stated above [3558](A[1]), continence has a twofold signification. In one way it denotes cessation from all venereal pleasures; and if continence be taken in this sense, it is greater than temperance considered absolutely, as may be gathered from what we said above (Q[152], A[5]) concerning the preeminence of virginity over chastity considered absolutely. In another way continence may be taken as denoting the resistance of the reason to evil desires when they are vehement in a man: and in this sense temperance is far greater than continence, because the good of a virtue derives its praise from that which is in accord with reason. Now the good of reason flourishes more in the temperate man than in the continent man, because in the former even the sensitive appetite is obedient to reason, being tamed by reason so to speak, whereas in the continent man the sensitive appetite strongly resists reason by its evil desires. Hence continence is compared to temperance, as the imperfect to the perfect.

Reply to Objection 1: The passage quoted may be understood in two ways. First in reference to the sense in which continence denotes abstinence from all things venereal: and thus it means that "no price is worthy of a continent soul," in the genus of chastity the fruitfulness of the flesh is the purpose of marriage is equalled to the continence of virginity or of widowhood, as stated above ([3559]Q[152], AA[4],5). Secondly it may be understood in reference to the general sense in which continence denotes any abstinence from things unlawful: and thus it means that "no price is worthy of a continent soul," because its value is not measured with gold or silver, which are appreciable according to weight.

Reply to Objection 2: The strength or weakness of concupiscence may proceed from two causes. For sometimes it is owing to a bodily cause: because some people by their natural temperament are more prone to concupiscence than others; and again opportunities for pleasure which inflame the concupiscence are nearer to hand for some people than for others. Such like weakness of concupiscence diminishes merit, whereas strength of concupiscence increases it. on the other hand, weakness or strength of concupiscence arises from a praiseworthy spiritual cause, for instance the vehemence of charity, or the strength of reason, as in the case of a temperate man. In this way weakness of concupiscence, by reason of its cause, increases merit, whereas strength of concupiscence diminishes it.

Reply to Objection 3: The will is more akin to the reason than the concupiscible power is. Wherefore the good of reason—on account of which virtue is praised by the very fact that it reaches not only to the will but also to the concupiscible power, as happens in the temperate man—is shown to be greater than if it reach only to the will, as in the case of one who is continent.

OF INCONTINENCE (FOUR ARTICLES)

We must now consider incontinence: and under this head there are four points of inquiry:

(1) Whether incontinence pertains to the soul or to the body?

(2) Whether incontinence is a sin?

(3) The comparison between incontinence and intemperance;

(4) Which is the worse, incontinence in anger, or incontinence in desire?

Whether incontinence pertains to the soul or to the body?

Objection 1: It would seem that incontinence pertains not to the soul but to the body. For sexual diversity comes not from the soul but from the body. Now sexual diversity causes diversity of incontinence: for the Philosopher says (Ethic. vii, 5) that women are not described either as continent or as incontinent. Therefore incontinence pertains not to the soul but to the body.

Objection 2: Further, that which pertains to the soul does not result from the temperament of the body. But incontinence results from the bodily temperament: for the Philosopher says (Ethic. vii, 7) that "it is especially people of a quick or choleric and atrabilious temper whose incontinence is one of unbridled desire." Therefore incontinence regards the body.

Objection 3: Further, victory concerns the victor rather than the vanquished. Now a man is said to be incontinent, because "the flesh lusteth against the spirit," and overcomes it. Therefore incontinence pertains to the flesh rather than to the soul.

On the contrary, Man differs from beast chiefly as regards the soul. Now they differ in respect of continence and incontinence, for we ascribe neither continence nor incontinence to the beasts, as the Philosopher states (Ethic. vii, 3). Therefore incontinence is chiefly on the part of the soul.

I answer that, Things are ascribed to their direct causes rather than to those which merely occasion them. Now that which is on the part of the body is merely an occasional cause of incontinence; since it is owing to a bodily disposition that vehement passions can arise in the sensitive appetite which is a power of the organic body. Yet these passions, however vehement they be, are not the sufficient cause of incontinence, but are merely the occasion thereof, since, so long as the use of reason remains, man is always able to resist his passions. If, however, the passions gain such strength as to take away the use of reason altogether—as in the case of those who become insane through the vehemence of their passions—the essential conditions of continence or incontinence cease, because such people do not retain the judgment of reason, which the continent man follows and the incontinent forsakes. From this it follows that the direct cause of incontinence is on the part of the soul, which fails to resist a passion by the reason. This happens in two ways, according to the Philosopher (Ethic. vii, 7): first, when the soul yields to the passions, before the reason has given its counsel; and this is called "unbridled incontinence" or "impetuosity": secondly, when a man does not stand to what has been counselled, through holding weakly to reason's judgment; wherefore this kind of incontinence is called "weakness." Hence it is manifest that incontinence pertains chiefly to the soul.

Reply to Objection 1: The human soul is the form of the body, and has certain powers which make use of bodily organs. The operations of these organs conduce somewhat to those operations of the soul which are accomplished without bodily instruments, namely to the acts of the intellect and of the will, in so far as the intellect receives from the senses, and the will is urged by passions of the sensitive appetite. Accordingly, since woman, as regards the body, has a weak temperament, the result is that for the most part, whatever she holds to, she holds to it weakly; although in /rare cases the opposite occurs, according to Prov. 31:10, "Who shall find a valiant woman?" And since small and weak things "are accounted as though they were not" [*Aristotle, Phys. ii, 5] the Philosopher speaks of women as though they had not the firm judgment of reason, although the contrary happens in some women. Hence he states that "we do not describe women as being continent, because they are vacillating" through being unstable of reason, and "are easily led" so that they follow their passions readily.

Reply to Objection 2: It is owing to the impulse of passion that a man at once follows his passion before his reason counsels him. Now the impulse of passion may arise either from its quickness, as in bilious persons [*Cf. [3560]FS, Q[46], A[5]], or from its vehemence, as in the melancholic, who on account of their earthy temperament are most vehemently aroused. Even so, on the other hand, a man fails to stand to that which is counselled, because he holds to it in weakly fashion by reason of the softness of his temperament, as we have stated with regard to woman (ad 1). This is also the case with phlegmatic temperaments, for the same reason as in women. And these results are due to the fact that the bodily temperament is an occasional but not a sufficient cause of incontinence, as stated above.

Reply to Objection 3: In the incontinent man concupiscence of the flesh overcomes the spirit, not necessarily, but through a certain negligence of the spirit in not resisting strongly.

Whether incontinence is a sin?

Objection 1: It would seem that incontinence is not a sin. For as Augustine says (De Lib. Arb. iii, 18): "No man sins in what he cannot avoid." Now no man can by himself avoid incontinence, according to Wis. 8:21, "I know [Vulg.: 'knew'] that I could not . . . be continent, except God gave it." Therefore incontinence is not a sin.

Objection 2: Further, apparently every sin originates in the reason. But the judgment of reason is overcome in the incontinent man. Therefore incontinence is not a sin.

Objection 3: Further, no one sins in loving God vehemently. Now a man becomes incontinent through the vehemence of divine love: for Dionysius says (Div. Nom. iv) that "Paul, through incontinence of divine love, exclaimed: I live, now not I" (Gal. 2:20). Therefore incontinence is not a sin.

On the contrary, It is numbered together with other sins (2 Tim. 3:3) where it is written: "Slanderers, incontinent, unmerciful," etc. Therefore incontinence is a sin.

I answer that, Incontinence about a matter may be considered in two ways. First it may be considered properly and simply: and thus incontinence is about concupiscences of pleasures of touch, even as intemperance is, as we have said in reference to continence ([3561]Q[155], A[2]). In this way incontinence is a sin for two reasons: first, because the incontinent man goes astray from that which is in accord with reason; secondly, because he plunges into shameful pleasures. Hence the Philosopher says (Ethic. vii, 4) that "incontinence is censurable not only because it is wrong"—that is, by straying from reason—"but also because it is wicked"—that is, by following evil desires. Secondly, incontinence about a matter is considered, properly—inasmuch as it is a straying from reason—but not simply; for instance when a man does not observe the mode of reason in his desire for honor, riches, and so forth, which seem to be good in themselves. About such things there is incontinence, not simply but relatively, even as we have said above in reference to continence ([3562]Q[155], A[2], ad 3). In this way incontinence is a sin, not from the fact that one gives way to wicked desires, but because one fails to observe the mode of reason even in the desire for things that are of themselves desirable.

Thirdly, incontinence is said to be about a matter, not properly, but metaphorically. for instance about the desires for things of which one cannot make an evil use, such as the desire for virtue. A man may be said to be incontinent in these matters metaphorically, because just as the incontinent man is entirely led by his evil desire, even so is a man entirely led by his good desire which is in accord with reason. Such like incontinence is no sin, but pertains to the perfection of virtue.

Reply to Objection 1: Man can avoid sin and do good, yet not without God's help, according to Jn. 15:5: "Without Me you can do nothing." Wherefore the fact that man needs God's help in order to be continent, does not show incontinence to be no sin, for, as stated in Ethic. iii, 3, "what we can do by means of a friend we do, in a way, ourselves."

Reply to Objection 2: The judgment of reason is overcome in the incontinent man, not necessarily, for then he would commit no sin, but through a certain negligence on account of his not standing firm in resisting the passion by holding to the judgment formed by his reason.

Reply to Objection 3: This argument takes incontinence metaphorically and not properly.

Whether the incontinent man sins more gravely than the intemperate?

Objection 1: It would seem that the incontinent man sins more gravely than the intemperate. For, seemingly, the more a man acts against his conscience, the more gravely he sins, according to Lk. 12:47, "That servant who knew the will of his lord . . . and did not . . . shall be beaten with many stripes." Now the incontinent man would seem to act against his conscience more than the intemperate because, according to Ethic. vii, 3, the incontinent man, though knowing how wicked are the things he desires, nevertheless acts through passion, whereas the intemperate man judges what he desires to be good. Therefore the incontinent man sins more gravely than the intemperate.

Objection 2: Further, apparently, the graver a sin is, the more incurable it is: wherefore the sins against the Holy Ghost, being most grave, are declared to be unpardonable. Now the sin of incontinence would appear to be more incurable than the sin of intemperance. For a person's sin is cured by admonishment and correction, which seemingly are no good to the incontinent man, since he knows he is doing wrong, and does wrong notwithstanding: whereas it seems to the intemperate man that he is doing well, so that it were good for him to be admonished. Therefore it would appear that the incontinent man sins more gravely than the intemperate.

Objection 3: Further, the more eagerly man sins, the more grievous his sin. Now the incontinent sins more eagerly than the intemperate, since the incontinent man has vehement passions and desires, which the intemperate man does not always have. Therefore the incontinent man sins more gravely than the intemperate.

On the contrary, Impenitence aggravates every sin: wherefore Augustine says (De Verb. Dom. serm. xi, 12,13) that "impenitence is a sin against the Holy Ghost." Now according to the Philosopher (Ethic. vii, 8) "the intemperate man is not inclined to be penitent, for he holds on to his choice: but every incontinent man is inclined to repentance." Therefore the intemperate man sins more gravely than the incontinent.

I answer that, According to Augustine [*De Duab. Anim. x, xi] sin is chiefly an act of the will, because "by the will we sin and live aright" [*Retract. i, 9]. Consequently where there is a greater inclination of the will to sin, there is a graver sin. Now in the intemperate man, the will is inclined to sin in virtue of its own choice, which proceeds from a habit acquired through custom: whereas in the incontinent man, the will is inclined to sin through a passion. And since passion soon passes, whereas a habit is "a disposition difficult to remove," the result is that the incontinent man repents at once, as soon as the passion has passed; but not so the intemperate man; in fact he rejoices in having sinned, because the sinful act has become connatural to him by reason of his habit. Wherefore in reference to such persons it is written (Prov. 2:14) that "they are glad when they have done evil, and rejoice in most wicked things." Hence it follows that "the intemperate man is much worse than the incontinent," as also the Philosopher declares (Ethic. vii, 7).

Reply to Objection 1: Ignorance in the intellect sometimes precedes the inclination of the appetite and causes it, and then the greater the ignorance, the more does it diminish or entirely excuse the sin, in so far as it renders it involuntary. On the other hand, ignorance in the reason sometimes follows the inclination of the appetite, and then such like ignorance, the greater it is, the graver the sin, because the inclination of the appetite is shown thereby to be greater. Now in both the incontinent and the intemperate man, ignorance arises from the appetite being inclined to something, either by passion, as in the incontinent, or by habit, as in the intemperate. Nevertheless greater ignorance results thus in the intemperate than in the incontinent. In one respect as regards duration, since in the incontinent man this ignorance lasts only while the passion endures, just as an attack of intermittent fever lasts as long as the humor is disturbed: whereas the ignorance of the intemperate man endures without ceasing, on account of the endurance of the habit, wherefore it is likened to phthisis or any chronic disease, as the Philosopher says (Ethic. vii, 8). In another respect the ignorance of the intemperate man is greater as regards the thing ignored. For the ignorance of the incontinent man regards some particular detail of choice (in so far as he deems that he must choose this particular thing now): whereas the intemperate man's ignorance is about the end itself, inasmuch as he judges this thing good, in order that he may follow his desires without being curbed. Hence the Philosopher says (Ethic. vii, 7,8) that "the incontinent man is better than the intemperate, because he retains the best principle [*{To beltiston, e arche}, 'the best thing, i.e. the principle']," to wit, the right estimate of the end.

Reply to Objection 2: Mere knowledge does not suffice to cure the incontinent man, for he needs the inward assistance of grace which quenches concupiscence, besides the application of the external remedy of admonishment and correction, which induce him to begin to resist his desires, so that concupiscence is weakened, as stated above ([3563]Q[142], A[2]). By these same means the intemperate man can be cured. But his curing is more difficult, for two reasons. The first is on the part of reason, which is corrupt as regards the estimate of the last end, which holds the same position as the principle in demonstrations. Now it is more difficult to bring back to the truth one who errs as to the principle; and it is the same in practical matters with one who errs in regard to the end. The other reason is on the part of the inclination of the appetite: for in the intemperate man this proceeds from a habit, which is difficult to remove, whereas the inclination of the incontinent man proceeds from a passion, which is more easily suppressed.

Reply to Objection 3: The eagerness of the will, which increases a sin, is greater in the intemperate man than in the incontinent, as explained above. But the eagerness of concupiscence in the sensitive appetite is sometimes greater in the incontinent man, because he does not sin except through vehement concupiscence, whereas the intemperate man sins even through slight concupiscence and sometimes forestalls it. Hence the Philosopher says (Ethic. vii, 7) that we blame more the intemperate man, "because he pursues pleasure without desiring it or with calm," i.e. slight desire. "For what would he have done if he had desired it with passion?"

Whether the incontinent in anger is worse than the incontinent in desire?

Objection 1: It would seem that the incontinent in anger is worse than the incontinent in desire. For the more difficult it is to resist the passion, the less grievous, apparently is incontinence: wherefore the Philosopher says (Ethic. vii, 7): "It is not wonderful, indeed it is pardonable if a person is overcome by strong and overwhelming pleasures or pains." Now, "as Heraclitus says, it is more difficult to resist desire than anger" [*Ethic. ii. 3]. Therefore incontinence of desire is less grievous than incontinence of anger.

Objection 2: Further, one is altogether excused from sin if the passion be so vehement as to deprive one of the judgment of reason, as in the case of one who becomes demented through passion. Now he that is incontinent in anger retains more of the judgment of reason, than one who is incontinent in desire: since "anger listens to reason somewhat, but desire does not" as the Philosopher states (Ethic. vii, 6). Therefore the incontinent in anger is worse than the incontinent in desire.

Objection 3: Further, the more dangerous a sin the more grievous it is. Now incontinence of anger would seem to be more dangerous, since it leads a man to a greater sin, namely murder, for this is a more grievous sin than adultery, to which incontinence of desire leads. Therefore incontinence of anger is graver than incontinence of desire.

On the contrary, The Philosopher says (Ethic. vii, 6) that "incontinence of anger is less disgraceful than incontinence of desire."

I answer that, The sin of incontinence may be considered in two ways. First, on the part of the passion which occasions the downfall of reason. In this way incontinence of desire is worse than incontinence of anger, because the movement of desire is more inordinate than the movement of anger. There are four reasons for this, and the Philosopher indicates them, Ethic. vii, 6: First, because the movement of anger partakes somewhat of reason, since the angry man tends to avenge the injury done to him, and reason dictates this in a certain degree. Yet he does not tend thereto perfectly, because he does not intend the due mode of vengeance. on the other hand, the movement of desire is altogether in accord with sense and nowise in accord with reason. Secondly, because the movement of anger results more from the bodily temperament owing to the quickness of the movement of the bile which tends to anger. Hence one who by bodily temperament is disposed to anger is more readily angry than one who is disposed to concupiscence is liable to be concupiscent: wherefore also it happens more often that the children of those who are disposed to anger are themselves disposed to anger, than that the children of those who are disposed to concupiscence are also disposed to concupiscence. Now that which results from the natural disposition of the body is deemed more deserving of pardon. Thirdly, because anger seeks to work openly, whereas concupiscence is fain to disguise itself and creeps in by stealth. Fourthly, because he who is subject to concupiscence works with pleasure, whereas the angry man works as though forced by a certain previous displeasure.

Secondly, the sin of incontinence may be considered with regard to the evil into which one falls through forsaking reason; and thus incontinence of anger is, for the most part, more grievous, because it leads to things that are harmful to one's neighbor.

Reply to Objection 1: It is more difficult to resist pleasure perseveringly than anger, because concupiscence is enduring. But for the moment it is more difficult to resist anger, on account of its impetuousness.

Reply to Objection 2: Concupiscence is stated to be without reason, not as though it destroyed altogether the judgment of reason, but because nowise does it follow the judgment of reason: and for this reason it is more disgraceful.

Reply to Objection 3: This argument considers incontinence with regard to its result.

OF CLEMENCY AND MEEKNESS (FOUR ARTICLES)

We must next consider clemency and meekness, and the contrary vices. Concerning the virtues themselves there are four points of inquiry:

(1) Whether clemency and meekness are altogether identical?

(2) Whether each of them is a virtue?

(3) Whether each is a part of temperance?

(4) Of their comparison with the other virtues.

Whether clemency and meekness are absolutely the same?

Objection 1: It would seem that clemency and meekness are absolutely the same. For meekness moderates anger, according to the Philosopher (Ethic. iv, 5). Now anger is "desire of vengeance" [*Aristotle, Rhet. ii, 2]. Since, then, clemency "is leniency of a superior in inflicting punishment on an inferior," as Seneca states (De Clementia ii, 3), and vengeance is taken by means of punishment, it would seem that clemency and meekness are the same.

Objection 2: Further, Tully says (De Invent. Rhet. ii, 54) that "clemency is a virtue whereby the mind is restrained by kindness when unreasonably provoked to hatred of a person," so that apparently clemency moderates hatred. Now, according to Augustine [*Ep. ccxi], hatred is caused by anger; and this is the matter of meekness and clemency. Therefore seemingly clemency and meekness are absolutely the same.

Objection 3: Further, the same vice is not opposed to different virtues. But the same vice, namely cruelty, is opposed to meekness and clemency. Therefore it seems that meekness and clemency are absolutely the same.

On the contrary, According to the aforesaid definition of Seneca (OBJ[1]) "clemency is leniency of a superior towards an inferior": whereas meekness is not merely of superior to inferior, but of each to everyone. Therefore meekness and clemency are not absolutely the same.

I answer that, As stated in Ethic. ii, 3, a moral virtue is "about passions and actions." Now internal passions are principles of external actions, and are likewise obstacles thereto. Wherefore virtues that moderate passions, to a certain extent, concur towards the same effect as virtues that moderate actions, although they differ specifically. Thus it belongs properly to justice to restrain man from theft, whereunto he is inclined by immoderate love or desire of money, which is restrained by liberality; so that liberality concurs with justice towards the effect, which is abstention from theft. This applies to the case in point; because through the passion of anger a man is provoked to inflict a too severe punishment, while it belongs directly to clemency to mitigate punishment, and this might be prevented by excessive anger.

Consequently meekness, in so far as it restrains the onslaught of anger, concurs with clemency towards the same effect; yet they differ from one another, inasmuch as clemency moderates external punishment, while meekness properly mitigates the passion of anger.

Reply to Objection 1: Meekness regards properly the desire itself of vengeance; whereas clemency regards the punishment itself which is applied externally for the purpose of vengeance.

Reply to Objection 2: Man's affections incline to the moderation of things that are unpleasant to him in themselves. Now it results from one man loving another that he takes no pleasure in the latter's punishment in itself, but only as directed to something else, for instance justice, or the correction of the person punished. Hence love makes one quick to mitigate punishment—and this pertains to clemency—while hatred is an obstacle to such mitigation. For this reason Tully says that "the mind provoked to hatred" that is to punish too severely, "is restrained by clemency," from inflicting too severe a punishment, so that clemency directly moderates not hatred but punishment.

Reply to Objection 3: The vice of anger, which denotes excess in the passion of anger, is properly opposed to meekness, which is directly concerned with the passion of anger; while cruelty denotes excess in punishing. Wherefore Seneca says (De Clementia ii, 4) that "those are called cruel who have reason for punishing, but lack moderation in punishing." Those who delight in a man's punishment for its own sake may be called savage or brutal, as though lacking the human feeling that leads one man to love another.

Whether both clemency and meekness are virtues?

Objection 1: It would seem that neither clemency nor meekness is a virtue. For no virtue is opposed to another virtue. Yet both of these are apparently opposed to severity, which is a virtue. Therefore neither clemency nor meekness is a virtue.

Objection 2: Further, "Virtue is destroyed by excess and defect" [*Ethic. ii, 2]. But both clemency and meekness consist in a certain decrease; for clemency decreases punishment, and meekness decreases anger. Therefore neither clemency nor meekness is a virtue.

Objection 3: Further, meekness or mildness is included (Mat. 5:4) among the beatitudes, and (Gal. 5:23) among the fruits. Now the virtues differ from the beatitudes and fruits. Therefore they are not comprised under virtue.

On the contrary, Seneca says (De Clementia ii, 5): "Every good man is conspicuous for his clemency and meekness." Now it is virtue properly that belongs to a good man, since "virtue it is that makes its possessor good, and renders his works good also" (Ethic. ii, 6). Therefore clemency and meekness are virtues.

I answer that, The nature of moral virtue consists in the subjection of appetite to reason, as the Philosopher declares (Ethic. i, 13). Now this is verified both in clemency and in meekness. For clemency, in mitigating punishment, "is guided by reason," according to Seneca (De Clementia ii, 5), and meekness, likewise, moderates anger according to right reason, as stated in Ethic. iv, 5. Wherefore it is manifest that both clemency and meekness are virtues.

Reply to Objection 1: Meekness is not directly opposed to severity; for meekness is about anger. On the other hand, severity regards the external infliction of punishment, so that accordingly it would seem rather to be opposed to clemency, which also regards external punishing, as stated above [3564](A[1]). Yet they are not really opposed to one another, since they are both according to right reason. For severity is inflexible in the infliction of punishment when right reason requires it; while clemency mitigates punishment also according to right reason, when and where this is requisite. Wherefore they are not opposed to one another as they are not about the same thing.

Reply to Objection 2: According to the Philosopher (Ethic. iv, 5), "the habit that observes the mean in anger is unnamed; so that the virtue is denominated from the diminution of anger, and is designated by the name of meekness." For the virtue is more akin to diminution than to excess, because it is more natural to man to desire vengeance for injuries done to him, than to be lacking in that desire, since "scarcely anyone belittles an injury done to himself," as Sallust observes [*Cf. Q[120]]. As to clemency, it mitigates punishment, not in respect of that which is according to right reason, but as regards that which is according to common law, which is the object of legal justice: yet on account of some particular consideration, it mitigates the punishment, deciding, as it were, that a man is not to be punished any further. Hence Seneca says (De Clementia ii, 1): "Clemency grants this, in the first place, that those whom she sets free are declared immune from all further punishment; and remission of punishment due amounts to a pardon." Wherefore it is clear that clemency is related to severity as equity [the Greek 'epieikeia' [*Cf. Q[120]]] to legal justice, whereof severity is a part, as regards the infliction of punishment in accordance with the law. Yet clemency differs from equity, as we shall state further on (A[3], ad 1).

Reply to Objection 3: The beatitudes are acts of virtue: while the fruits are delights in virtuous acts. Wherefore nothing hinders meekness being reckoned both virtue, and beatitude and fruit.

Whether the aforesaid virtues are parts of temperance?

Objection 1: It would seem that the aforesaid virtues are not parts of temperance. For clemency mitigates punishment, as stated above [3565](A[2]). But the Philosopher (Ethic. v, 10) ascribes this to equity, which pertains to justice, as stated above (Q[120], A[2]). Therefore seemingly clemency is not a part of temperance.

Objection 2: Further, temperance is concerned with concupiscences; whereas meekness and clemency regard, not concupiscences, but anger and vengeance. Therefore they should not be reckoned parts of temperance.

Objection 3: Further, Seneca says (De Clementia ii, 4): "A man may be said to be of unsound mind when he takes pleasure in cruelty." Now this is opposed to clemency and meekness. Since then an unsound mind is opposed to prudence, it seems that clemency and meekness are parts of prudence rather than of temperance.

On the contrary, Seneca says (De Clementia ii, 3) that "clemency is temperance of the soul in exercising the power of taking revenge." Tully also (De Invent. Rhet. ii, 54) reckons clemency a part of temperance.

I answer that, Parts are assigned to the principal virtues, in so far as they imitate them in some secondary matter as to the mode whence the virtue derives its praise and likewise its name. Thus the mode and name of justice consist in a certain "equality," those of fortitude in a certain "strength of mind," those of temperance in a certain "restraint," inasmuch as it restrains the most vehement concupiscences of the pleasures of touch. Now clemency and meekness likewise consist in a certain restraint, since clemency mitigates punishment, while meekness represses anger, as stated above ([3566]AA[1],2). Therefore both clemency and meekness are annexed to temperance as principal virtue, and accordingly are reckoned to be parts thereof.

Reply to Objection 1: Two points must be considered in the mitigation of punishment. one is that punishment should be mitigated in accordance with the lawgiver's intention, although not according to the letter of the law; and in this respect it pertains to equity. The other point is a certain moderation of a man's inward disposition, so that he does not exercise his power of inflicting punishment. This belongs properly to clemency, wherefore Seneca says (De Clementia ii, 3) that "it is temperance of the soul in exercising the power of taking revenge." This moderation of soul comes from a certain sweetness of disposition, whereby a man recoils from anything that may be painful to another. Wherefore Seneca says (De Clementia ii, 3) that "clemency is a certain smoothness of the soul"; for, on the other hand, there would seem to be a certain roughness of soul in one who fears not to pain others.

Reply to Objection 2: The annexation of secondary to principal virtues depends on the mode of virtue, which is, so to speak, a kind of form of the virtue, rather than on the matter. Now meekness and clemency agree with temperance in mode, as stated above, though they agree not in matter.

Reply to Objection 3: "Unsoundness" is corruption of "soundness." Now just as soundness of body is corrupted by the body lapsing from the condition due to the human species, so unsoundness of mind is due to the mind lapsing from the disposition due to the human species. This occurs both in respect of the reason, as when a man loses the use of reason, and in respect of the appetitive power, as when a man loses that humane feeling whereby "every man is naturally friendly towards all other men" (Ethic. viii, 1). The unsoundness of mind that excludes the use of reason is opposed to prudence. But that a man who takes pleasure in the punishment of others is said to be of unsound mind, is because he seems on this account to be devoid of the humane feeling which gives rise to clemency.

Whether clemency and meekness are the greatest virtues?

Objection 1: It would seem that clemency and meekness are the greatest virtues. For virtue is deserving of praise chiefly because it directs man to happiness that consists in the knowledge of God. Now meekness above all directs man to the knowledge of God: for it is written (James 1:21): "With meekness receive the ingrafted word," and (Ecclus. 5:13): "Be meek to hear the word" of God. Again, Dionysius says (Ep. viii ad Demophil.) that "Moses was deemed worthy of the Divine apparition on account of his great meekness." Therefore meekness is the greatest of virtues.

Objection 2: Further, seemingly a virtue is all the greater according as it is more acceptable to God and men. Now meekness would appear to be most acceptable to God. For it is written (Ecclus. 1:34,35): "That which is agreeable" to God is "faith and meekness"; wherefore Christ expressly invites us to be meek like unto Himself (Mat. 11:29), where He says: "Learn of Me, because I am meek and humble of heart"; and Hilary declares [*Comment. in Matth. iv, 3] that "Christ dwells in us by our meekness of soul." Again, it is most acceptable to men; wherefore it is written (Ecclus. 3:19): "My son, do thy works in meekness, and thou shalt be beloved above the glory of men": for which reason it is also declared (Prov. 20:28) that the King's "throne is strengthened by clemency." Therefore meekness and clemency are the greatest of virtues.

Objection 3: Further, Augustine says (De Serm. Dom. in Monte i, 2) that "the meek are they who yield to reproaches, and resist not evil, but overcome evil by good." Now this seems to pertain to mercy or piety which would seem to be the greatest of virtues: because a gloss of Ambrose [*Hilary the deacon] on 1 Tim. 4:8, "Piety [Douay: 'Godliness'] is profitable to all things," observes that "piety is the sum total of the Christian religion." Therefore meekness and clemency are the greatest virtues.

On the contrary, They are not reckoned as principal virtues, but are annexed to another, as to a principal, virtue.

I answer that, Nothing prevents certain virtues from being greatest, not indeed simply, nor in every respect, but in a particular genus. It is impossible for clemency or meekness to be absolutely the greatest virtues, since they owe their praise to the fact that they withdraw a man from evil, by mitigating anger or punishment. Now it is more perfect to obtain good than to lack evil. Wherefore those virtues like faith, hope, charity, and likewise prudence and justice, which direct one to good simply, are absolutely greater virtues than clemency and meekness.

Yet nothing prevents clemency and meekness from having a certain restricted excellence among the virtues which resist evil inclinations. For anger, which is mitigated by meekness, is, on account of its impetuousness, a very great obstacle to man's free judgment of truth: wherefore meekness above all makes a man self-possessed. Hence it is written (Ecclus. 10:31): "My son, keep thy soul in meekness." Yet the concupiscences of the pleasures of touch are more shameful, and harass more incessantly, for which reason temperance is more rightly reckoned as a principal virtue. as stated above ([3567]Q[141], A[7], ad 2). As to clemency, inasmuch as it mitigates punishment, it would seem to approach nearest to charity, the greatest of the virtues, since thereby we do good towards our neighbor, and hinder his evil.

Reply to Objection 1: Meekness disposes man to the knowledge of God, by removing an obstacle; and this in two ways. First, because it makes man self-possessed by mitigating his anger, as stated above; secondly, because it pertains to meekness that a man does not contradict the words of truth, which many do through being disturbed by anger. Wherefore Augustine says (De Doctr. Christ. ii, 7): "To be meek is not to contradict Holy Writ, whether we understand it, if it condemn our evil ways, or understand it not, as though we might know better and have a clearer insight of the truth."

Reply to Objection 2: Meekness and clemency make us acceptable to God and men, in so far as they concur with charity, the greatest of the virtues, towards the same effect, namely the mitigation of our neighbor's evils.

Reply to Objection 3: Mercy and piety agree indeed with meekness and clemency by concurring towards the same effect, namely the mitigation of our neighbor's evils. Nevertheless they differ as to motive. For piety relieves a neighbor's evil through reverence for a superior, for instance God or one's parents: mercy relieves a neighbor's evil, because this evil is displeasing to one, in so far as one looks upon it as affecting oneself, as stated above ([3568]Q[30], A[2]): and this results from friendship which makes friends rejoice and grieve for the same things: meekness does this, by removing anger that urges to vengeance, and clemency does this through leniency of soul, in so far as it judges equitable that a person be no further punished.

OF ANGER (EIGHT ARTICLES)

We must next consider the contrary vices: (1) Anger that is opposed to meekness; (2) Cruelty that is opposed to clemency. Concerning anger there are eight points of inquiry:

(1) Whether it is lawful to be angry?

(2) Whether anger is a sin?

(3) Whether it is a mortal sin?

(4) Whether it is the most grievous of sins?

(5) Of its species;

(6) Whether anger is a capital vice?

(7) Of its daughters;

(8) Whether it has a contrary vice?

Whether it is lawful to be angry?

Objection 1: It would seem that it cannot be lawful to be angry. For Jerome in his exposition on Mat. 5:22, "Whosoever is angry with his brother," etc. says: "Some codices add 'without cause.' However, in the genuine codices the sentence is unqualified, and anger is forbidden altogether." Therefore it is nowise lawful to be angry.

Objection 2: Further, according to Dionysius (Div. Nom. iv) "The soul's evil is to be without reason." Now anger is always without reason: for the Philosopher says (Ethic. vii, 6) that "anger does not listen perfectly to reason"; and Gregory says (Moral. v, 45) that "when anger sunders the tranquil surface of the soul, it mangles and rends it by its riot"; and Cassian says (De Inst. Caenob. viii, 6): "From whatever cause it arises, the angry passion boils over and blinds the eye of the mind." Therefore it is always evil to be angry.

Objection 3: Further, anger is "desire for vengeance" [*Aristotle, Rhet. ii, 2] according to a gloss on Lev. 19:17, "Thou shalt not hate thy brother in thy heart." Now it would seem unlawful to desire vengeance, since this should be left to God, according to Dt. 32:35, "Revenge is Mine." Therefore it would seem that to be angry is always an evil.

Objection 4: Further, all that makes us depart from likeness to God is evil. Now anger always makes us depart from likeness to God, since God judges with tranquillity according to Wis. 12:18. Therefore to be angry is always an evil.

On the contrary, Chrysostom [*Hom. xi in the Opus Imperfectum, falsely ascribed to St. John Chrysostom] says: "He that is angry without cause, shall be in danger; but he that is angry with cause, shall not be in danger: for without anger, teaching will be useless, judgments unstable, crimes unchecked." Therefore to be angry is not always an evil.

I answer that, Properly speaking anger is a passion of the sensitive appetite, and gives its name to the irascible power, as stated above ([3569]FS, Q[46], A[1]) when we were treating of the passions. Now with regard to the passions of the soul, it is to be observed that evil may be found in them in two ways. First by reason of the passion's very species, which is derived from the passion's object. Thus envy, in respect of its species, denotes an evil, since it is displeasure at another's good, and such displeasure is in itself contrary to reason: wherefore, as the Philosopher remarks (Ethic. ii, 6), "the very mention of envy denotes something evil." Now this does not apply to anger, which is the desire for revenge, since revenge may be desired both well and ill. Secondly, evil is found in a passion in respect of the passion's quantity, that is in respect of its excess or deficiency; and thus evil may be found in anger, when, to wit, one is angry, more or less than right reason demands. But if one is angry in accordance with right reason, one's anger is deserving of praise.

Reply to Objection 1: The Stoics designated anger and all the other passions as emotions opposed to the order of reason; and accordingly they deemed anger and all other passions to be evil, as stated above ([3570]FS, Q[24], A[2]) when we were treating of the passions. It is in this sense that Jerome considers anger; for he speaks of the anger whereby one is angry with one's neighbor, with the intent of doing him a wrong.—But, according to the Peripatetics, to whose opinion Augustine inclines (De Civ. Dei ix, 4), anger and the other passions of the soul are movements of the sensitive appetite, whether they be moderated or not, according to reason: and in this sense anger is not always evil.

Reply to Objection 2: Anger may stand in a twofold relation to reason. First, antecedently; in this way it withdraws reason from its rectitude, and has therefore the character of evil. Secondly, consequently, inasmuch as the movement of the sensitive appetite is directed against vice and in accordance with reason, this anger is good, and is called "zealous anger." Wherefore Gregory says (Moral. v, 45): "We must beware lest, when we use anger as an instrument of virtue, it overrule the mind, and go before it as its mistress, instead of following in reason's train, ever ready, as its handmaid, to obey." This latter anger, although it hinder somewhat the judgment of reason in the execution of the act, does not destroy the rectitude of reason. Hence Gregory says (Moral. v, 45) that "zealous anger troubles the eye of reason, whereas sinful anger blinds it." Nor is it incompatible with virtue that the deliberation of reason be interrupted in the execution of what reason has deliberated: since art also would be hindered in its act, if it were to deliberate about what has to be done, while having to act.

Reply to Objection 3: It is unlawful to desire vengeance considered as evil to the man who is to be punished, but it is praiseworthy to desire vengeance as a corrective of vice and for the good of justice; and to this the sensitive appetite can tend, in so far as it is moved thereto by the reason: and when revenge is taken in accordance with the order of judgment, it is God's work, since he who has power to punish "is God's minister," as stated in Rom. 13:4.

Reply to Objection 4: We can and ought to be like to God in the desire for good; but we cannot be altogether likened to Him in the mode of our desire, since in God there is no sensitive appetite, as in us, the movement of which has to obey reason. Wherefore Gregory says (Moral. v, 45) that "anger is more firmly erect in withstanding vice, when it bows to the command of reason."

Whether anger is a sin?

Objection 1: It would seem that anger is not a sin. For we demerit by sinning. But "we do not demerit by the passions, even as neither do we incur blame thereby," as stated in Ethic. ii, 5. Consequently no passion is a sin. Now anger is a passion as stated above ([3571]FS, Q[46], A[1]) in the treatise on the passions. Therefore anger is not a sin.

Objection 2: Further, in every sin there is conversion to some mutable good. But in anger there is conversion not to a mutable good, but to a person's evil. Therefore anger is not a sin.

Objection 3: Further, "No man sins in what he cannot avoid," as Augustine asserts [*De Lib. Arb. iii, 18]. But man cannot avoid anger, for a gloss on Ps. 4:5, "Be ye angry and sin not," says: "The movement of anger is not in our power." Again, the Philosopher asserts (Ethic. vii, 6) that "the angry man acts with displeasure." Now displeasure is contrary to the will. Therefore anger is not a sin.

Objection 4: Further, sin is contrary to nature, according to Damascene [*De Fide Orth. ii, 4,30]. But it is not contrary to man's nature to be angry, and it is the natural act of a power, namely the irascible; wherefore Jerome says in a letter [*Ep. xii ad Anton. Monach.] that "to be angry is the property of man." Therefore it is not a sin to be angry.

On the contrary, The Apostle says (Eph. 4:31): "Let all indignation and anger [*Vulg.: 'Anger and indignation'] . . . be put away from you."

I answer that, Anger, as stated above [3572](A[1]), is properly the name of a passion. A passion of the sensitive appetite is good in so far as it is regulated by reason, whereas it is evil if it set the order of reason aside. Now the order of reason, in regard to anger, may be considered in relation to two things. First, in relation to the appetible object to which anger tends, and that is revenge. Wherefore if one desire revenge to be taken in accordance with the order of reason, the desire of anger is praiseworthy, and is called "zealous anger" [*Cf. Greg., Moral. v, 45]. On the other hand, if one desire the taking of vengeance in any way whatever contrary to the order of reason, for instance if he desire the punishment of one who has not deserved it, or beyond his deserts, or again contrary to the order prescribed by law, or not for the due end, namely the maintaining of justice and the correction of defaults, then the desire of anger will be sinful, and this is called sinful anger.

Secondly, the order of reason in regard to anger may be considered in relation to the mode of being angry, namely that the movement of anger should not be immoderately fierce, neither internally nor externally; and if this condition be disregarded, anger will not lack sin, even though just vengeance be desired.

Reply to Objection 1: Since passion may be either regulated or not regulated by reason, it follows that a passion considered absolutely does not include the notion of merit or demerit, of praise or blame. But as regulated by reason, it may be something meritorious and deserving of praise; while on the other hand, as not regulated by reason, it may be demeritorious and blameworthy. Wherefore the Philosopher says (Ethic. ii, 5) that "it is he who is angry in a certain way, that is praised or blamed."

Reply to Objection 2: The angry man desires the evil of another, not for its own sake but for the sake of revenge, towards which his appetite turns as to a mutable good.

Reply to Objection 3: Man is master of his actions through the judgment of his reason, wherefore as to the movements that forestall that judgment, it is not in man's power to prevent them as a whole, i.e. so that none of them arise, although his reason is able to check each one, if it arise. Accordingly it is stated that the movement of anger is not in man's power, to the extent namely that no such movement arise. Yet since this movement is somewhat in his power, it is not entirely sinless if it be inordinate. The statement of the Philosopher that "the angry man acts with displeasure," means that he is displeased, not with his being angry, but with the injury which he deems done to himself: and through this displeasure he is moved to seek vengeance.

Reply to Objection 4: The irascible power in man is naturally subject to his reason, wherefore its act is natural to man, in so far as it is in accord with reason, and in so far as it is against reason, it is contrary to man's nature.

Whether all anger is a mortal sin?

Objection 1: It would seem that all anger is a mortal sin. For it is written (Job 5:2): "Anger killeth the foolish man [*Vulg.: 'Anger indeed killeth the foolish']," and he speaks of the spiritual killing, whence mortal sin takes its name. Therefore all anger is a mortal sin.

Objection 2: Further, nothing save mortal sin is deserving of eternal condemnation. Now anger deserves eternal condemnation; for our Lord said (Mat. 5:22): "Whosoever is angry with his brother shall be in danger of the judgment": and a gloss on this passage says that "the three things mentioned there, namely judgment, council, and hell-fire, signify in a pointed manner different abodes in the state of eternal damnation corresponding to various sins." Therefore anger is a mortal sin.

Objection 3: Further, whatsoever is contrary to charity is a mortal sin. Now anger is of itself contrary to charity, as Jerome declares in his commentary on Mat. 5:22, "Whosoever is angry with his brother," etc. where he says that this is contrary to the love of your neighbor. Therefore anger is a mortal sin.

On the contrary, A gloss on Ps. 4:5, "Be ye angry and sin not," says: "Anger is venial if it does not proceed to action."

I answer that, The movement of anger may be inordinate and sinful in two ways, as stated above [3573](A[2]). First, on the part of the appetible object, as when one desires unjust revenge; and thus anger is a mortal sin in the point of its genus, because it is contrary to charity and justice. Nevertheless such like anger may happen to be a venial sin by reason of the imperfection of the act. This imperfection is considered either in relation to the subject desirous of vengeance, as when the movement of anger forestalls the judgment of his reason; or in relation to the desired object, as when one desires to be avenged in a trifling matter, which should be deemed of no account, so that even if one proceeded to action, it would not be a mortal sin, for instance by pulling a child slightly by the hair, or by some other like action. Secondly, the movement of anger may be inordinate in the mode of being angry, for instance, if one be too fiercely angry inwardly, or if one exceed in the outward signs of anger. In this way anger is not a mortal sin in the point of its genus; yet it may happen to be a mortal sin, for instance if through the fierceness of his anger a man fall away from the love of God and his neighbor.

Reply to Objection 1: It does not follow from the passage quoted that all anger is a mortal sin, but that the foolish are killed spiritually by anger, because, through not checking the movement of anger by their reason, they fall into mortal sins, for instance by blaspheming God or by doing injury to their neighbor.

Reply to Objection 2: Our Lord said this of anger, by way of addition to the words of the Law: "Whosoever shall kill shall be in danger of the judgment" (Mat. 5:21). Consequently our Lord is speaking here of the movement of anger wherein a man desires the killing or any grave injury of his neighbor: and should the consent of reason be given to this desire, without doubt it will be a mortal sin.

Reply to Objection 3: In the case where anger is contrary to charity, it is a mortal sin, but it is not always so, as appears from what we have said.

Whether anger is the most grievous sin?

Objection 1: It would seem that anger is the most grievous sin. For Chrysostom says [*Hom. xlviii in Joan.] that "nothing is more repulsive than the look of an angry man, and nothing uglier than a ruthless* face, and most of all than a cruel soul." [*'Severo.' The correct text is 'Si vero.' The translation would then run thus . . . 'and nothing uglier.' And if his 'face is ugly, how much uglier is his soul!']. Therefore anger is the most grievous sin.

Objection 2: Further, the more hurtful a sin is, the worse it would seem to be; since, according to Augustine (Enchiridion xii), "a thing is said to be evil because it hurts." Now anger is most hurtful, because it deprives man of his reason, whereby he is master of himself; for Chrysostom says (Hom. xlviii in Joan.) that "anger differs in no way from madness; it is a demon while it lasts, indeed more troublesome than one harassed by a demon." Therefore anger is the most grievous sin.

Objection 3: Further, inward movements are judged according to their outward effects. Now the effect of anger is murder, which is a most grievous sin. Therefore anger is a most grievous sin.

On the contrary, Anger is compared to hatred as the mote to the beam; for Augustine says in his Rule (Ep. ccxi): "Lest anger grow into hatred and a mote become a beam." Therefore anger is not the most grievous sin.

I answer that, As stated above ([3574]AA[1],2), the inordinateness of anger is considered in a twofold respect, namely with regard to an undue object, and with regard to an undue mode of being angry. As to the appetible object which it desires, anger would seem to be the least of sins, for anger desires the evil of punishment for some person, under the aspect of a good that is vengeance. Hence on the part of the evil which it desires the sin of anger agrees with those sins which desire the evil of our neighbor, such as envy and hatred; but while hatred desires absolutely another's evil as such, and the envious man desires another's evil through desire of his own glory, the angry man desires another's evil under the aspect of just revenge. Wherefore it is evident that hatred is more grievous than envy, and envy than anger: since it is worse to desire evil as an evil, than as a good; and to desire evil as an external good such as honor or glory, than under the aspect of the rectitude of justice. On the part of the good, under the aspect of which the angry man desires an evil, anger concurs with the sin of concupiscence that tends to a good. In this respect again, absolutely speaking. the sin of anger is apparently less grievous than that of concupiscence, according as the good of justice, which the angry man desires, is better than the pleasurable or useful good which is desired by the subject of concupiscence. Wherefore the Philosopher says (Ethic. vii, 4) that "the incontinent in desire is more disgraceful than the incontinent in anger."

On the other hand, as to the inordinateness which regards the mode of being angry, anger would seem to have a certain pre-eminence on account of the strength and quickness of its movement, according to Prov. 27:4, "Anger hath no mercy, nor fury when it breaketh forth: and who can bear the violence of one provoked?" Hence Gregory says (Moral. v, 45): "The heart goaded by the pricks of anger is convulsed, the body trembles, the tongue entangles itself, the face is inflamed, the eyes are enraged and fail utterly to recognize those whom we know: the tongue makes sounds indeed, but there is no sense in its utterance."

Reply to Objection 1: Chrysostom is alluding to the repulsiveness of the outward gestures which result from the impetuousness of anger.

Reply to Objection 2: This argument considers the inordinate movement of anger, that results from its impetuousness, as stated above.

Reply to Objection 3: Murder results from hatred and envy no less than from anger: yet anger is less grievous, inasmuch as it considers the aspect of justice, as stated above.

Whether the Philosopher suitably assigns the species of anger?

Objection 1: It would seem that the species of anger are unsuitably assigned by the Philosopher (Ethic. iv, 5) where he says that some angry persons are "choleric," some "sullen," and some "ill-tempered" or "stern." According to him, a person is said to be "sullen" whose anger "is appeased with difficulty and endures a long time." But this apparently pertains to the circumstance of time. Therefore it seems that anger can be differentiated specifically in respect also of the other circumstances.

Objection 2: Further, he says (Ethic. iv, 5) that "ill-tempered" or "stern" persons "are those whose anger is not appeased without revenge, or punishment." Now this also pertains to the unquenchableness of anger. Therefore seemingly the ill-tempered is the same as bitterness.

Objection 3: Further, our Lord mentions three degrees of anger, when He says (Mat. 5:22): "Whosoever is angry with his brother, shall be in danger of the judgment: and whosoever shall say to his brother, Raca, shall be in danger of the council, and whosoever shall say" to his brother, "Thou fool." But these degrees are not referable to the aforesaid species. Therefore it seems that the above division of anger is not fitting.

On the contrary, Gregory of Nyssa [*Nemesius, De Nat. Hom. xxi] says "there are three species of irascibility," namely, "the anger which is called wrath [*'Fellea,' i.e. like gall. But in [3575]FS, Q[46], A[8], St. Thomas quoting the same authority has {Cholos} which we render 'wrath']," and "ill-will" which is a disease of the mind, and "rancour." Now these three seem to coincide with the three aforesaid. For "wrath" he describes as "having beginning and movement," and the Philosopher (Ethic. iv, 5) ascribes this to "choleric" persons: "ill-will" he describes as "an anger that endures and grows old," and this the Philosopher ascribes to "sullenness"; while he describes "rancour" as "reckoning the time for vengeance," which tallies with the Philosopher's description of the "ill-tempered." The same division is given by Damascene (De Fide Orth. ii, 16). Therefore the aforesaid division assigned by the Philosopher is not unfitting.

I answer that, The aforesaid distinction may be referred either to the passion, or to the sin itself of anger. We have already stated when treating of the passions ([3576]FS, Q[46], A[8]) how it is to be applied to the passion of anger. And it would seem that this is chiefly what Gregory of Nyssa and Damascene had in view. Here, however, we have to take the distinction of these species in its application to the sin of anger, and as set down by the Philosopher.

For the inordinateness of anger may be considered in relation to two things. First, in relation to the origin of anger, and this regards "choleric" persons, who are angry too quickly and for any slight cause. Secondly, in relation to the duration of anger, for that anger endures too long; and this may happen in two ways. In one way, because the cause of anger, to wit, the inflicted injury, remains too long in a man's memory, the result being that it gives rise to a lasting displeasure, wherefore he is "grievous" and "sullen" to himself. In another way, it happens on the part of vengeance, which a man seeks with a stubborn desire: this applies to "ill-tempered" or "stern" people, who do not put aside their anger until they have inflicted punishment.

Reply to Objection 1: It is not time, but a man's propensity to anger, or his pertinacity in anger, that is the chief point of consideration in the aforesaid species.

Reply to Objection 2: Both "sullen" and "ill-tempered" people have a long-lasting anger, but for different reasons. For a "sullen" person has an abiding anger on account of an abiding displeasure, which he holds locked in his breast; and as he does not break forth into the outward signs of anger, others cannot reason him out of it, nor does he of his own accord lay aside his anger, except his displeasure wear away with time and thus his anger cease. On the other hand, the anger of "ill-tempered" persons is long-lasting on account of their intense desire for revenge, so that it does not wear out with time, and can be quelled only by revenge.

Reply to Objection 3: The degrees of anger mentioned by our Lord do not refer to the different species of anger, but correspond to the course of the human act [*Cf. [3577]FS, Q[46], A[8], OBJ[3]]. For the first degree is an inward conception, and in reference to this He says: "Whosoever is angry with his brother." The second degree is when the anger is manifested by outward signs, even before it breaks out into effect; and in reference to this He says: "Whosoever shall say to his brother, Raca!" which is an angry exclamation. The third degree is when the sin conceived inwardly breaks out into effect. Now the effect of anger is another's hurt under the aspect of revenge; and the least of hurts is that which is done by a mere word;

wherefore in reference to this He says: "Whosoever shall say to his brother Thou fool!" Consequently it is clear that the second adds to the first, and the third to both the others; so that, if the first is a mortal sin, in the case referred to by our Lord, as stated above (A[3], ad 2), much more so are the others. Wherefore some kind of condemnation is assigned as corresponding to each one of them. In the first case "judgment" is assigned, and this is the least severe, for as Augustine says [*Serm. Dom. in Monte i, 9], "where judgment is to be delivered, there is an opportunity for defense": in the second case "council" is assigned, "whereby the judges deliberate together on the punishment to be inflicted": to the third case is assigned "hell-fire," i.e. "decisive condemnation."

Whether anger should be reckoned among the capital vices?

Objection 1: It would seem that anger should not be reckoned among the capital sins. For anger is born of sorrow which is a capital vice known by the name of sloth. Therefore anger should not be reckoned a capital vice.

Objection 2: Further, hatred is a graver sin than anger. Therefore it should be reckoned a capital vice rather than anger.

Objection 3: Further, a gloss on Prov. 29:22, "An angry [Douay: 'passionate'] man provoketh quarrels," says: "Anger is the door to all vices: if it be closed, peace is ensured within to all the virtues; if it be opened, the soul is armed for every crime." Now no capital vice is the origin of all sins, but only of certain definite ones. Therefore anger should not be reckoned among the capital vices.

On the contrary, Gregory (Moral. xxxi, 45) places anger among the capital vices.

I answer that, As stated above ([3578]FS, Q[84], A[3],4), a capital vice is defined as one from which many vices arise. Now there are two reasons for which many vices can arise from anger. The first is on the part of its object which has much of the aspect of desirability, in so far as revenge is desired under the aspect of just or honest*, which is attractive by its excellence, as stated above [3579](A[4]). [*Honesty must be taken here in its broad sense as synonymous with moral goodness, from the point of view of decorum; Cf. Q[145], A[1]]. The second is on the part of its impetuosity, whereby it precipitates the mind into all kinds of inordinate action. Therefore it is evident that anger is a capital vice.

Reply to Objection 1: The sorrow whence anger arises is not, for the most part, the vice of sloth, but the passion of sorrow, which results from an injury inflicted.

Reply to Objection 2: As stated above (Q[118], A[7]; Q[148], A[5]; Q[153], A[4]; [3580]FS, Q[84], A[4]), it belongs to the notion of a capital vice to have a most desirable end, so that many sins are committed through the desire thereof. Now anger, which desires evil under the aspect of good, has a more desirable end than hatred has, since the latter desires evil under the aspect of evil: wherefore anger is more a capital vice than hatred is.

Reply to Objection 3: Anger is stated to be the door to the vices accidentally, that is by removing obstacles, to wit by hindering the judgment of reason, whereby man is withdrawn from evil. It is, however, directly the cause of certain special sins, which are called its daughters.

Whether six daughters are fittingly assigned to anger?

Objection 1: It would seem that six daughters are unfittingly assigned to anger, namely "quarreling, swelling of the mind, contumely, clamor, indignation and blasphemy." For blasphemy is reckoned by Isidore [*QQ. in Deut., qu. xvi] to be a daughter of pride. Therefore it should not be accounted a daughter of anger.

Objection 2: Further, hatred is born of anger, as Augustine says in his rule (Ep. ccxi). Therefore it should be placed among the daughters of anger.

Objection 3: Further, "a swollen mind" would seem to be the same as pride. Now pride is not the daughter of a vice, but "the mother of all vices," as Gregory states (Moral. xxxi, 45). Therefore swelling of the mind should not be reckoned among the daughters of anger.

On the contrary, Gregory (Moral. xxxi, 45) assigns these daughters to anger.

I answer that, Anger may be considered in three ways. First, as consisting in thought, and thus two vices arise from anger. one is on the part of the person with whom a man is angry, and whom he deems unworthy [indignum] of acting thus towards him, and this is called "indignation." The other vice is on the part of the man himself, in so far as he devises various means of vengeance, and with such like thoughts fills his mind, according to Job 15:2, "Will a wise man . . . fill his stomach with burning heat?" And thus we have "swelling of the mind."

Secondly, anger may be considered, as expressed in words: and thus a twofold disorder arises from anger. One is when a man manifests his anger in his manner of speech, as stated above (A[5], ad 3) of the man who says to his brother, "Raca": and this refers to "clamor," which denotes disorderly and confused speech. The other disorder is when a man breaks out into injurious words, and if these be against God, it is "blasphemy," if against one's neighbor, it is "contumely."

Thirdly, anger may be considered as proceeding to deeds; and thus anger gives rise to "quarrels," by which we are to understand all manner of injuries inflicted on one's neighbor through anger.

Reply to Objection 1: The blasphemy into which a man breaks out deliberately proceeds from pride, whereby a man lifts himself up against God: since, according to Ecclus. 10:14, "the beginning of the pride of man is to fall off from God," i.e. to fall away from reverence for Him is the first part of pride [*Cf.[3581] Q[162], A[7], ad 2]; and this gives rise to blasphemy. But the blasphemy into which a man breaks out through a disturbance of the mind, proceeds from anger.

Reply to Objection 2: Although hatred sometimes arises from anger, it has a previous cause, from which it arises more directly, namely displeasure, even as, on the other hand, love is born of pleasure. Now through displeasure, a man is moved sometimes to anger, sometimes to hatred. Wherefore it was fitting to reckon that hatred arises from sloth rather than from anger.

Reply to Objection 3: Swelling of the mind is not taken here as identical with pride, but for a certain effort or daring attempt to take vengeance; and daring is a vice opposed to fortitude.

Whether there is a vice opposed to anger resulting from lack of anger?

Objection 1: It would seem that there. is not a vice opposed to anger, resulting from lack of anger. For no vice makes us like to God. Now by being entirely without anger, a man becomes like to God, Who judges "with tranquillity" (Wis. 12:18). Therefore seemingly it is not a vice to be altogether without anger.

Objection 2: Further, it is not a vice to lack what is altogether useless. But the movement of anger is useful for no purpose, as Seneca proves in the book he wrote on anger (De Ira i, 9, seqq.). Therefore it seems that lack of anger is not a vice.

Objection 3: Further, according to Dionysius (Div. Nom. iv), "man's evil is to be without reason." Now the judgment of reason remains unimpaired, if all movement of anger be done away. Therefore no lack of anger amounts to a vice.

On the contrary, Chrysostom [*Hom. xi in Matth. in the Opus Imperfectum, falsely ascribed to St. John Chrysostom] says: "He who is not angry, whereas he has cause to be, sins. For unreasonable patience is the hotbed of many vices, it fosters negligence, and incites not only the wicked but even the good to do wrong."

I answer that, Anger may be understood in two ways. In one way, as a simple movement of the will, whereby one inflicts punishment, not through passion, but in virtue of a judgment of the reason: and thus without doubt lack of anger is a sin. This is the sense in which anger is taken in the saying of Chrysostom, for he says (Hom. xi in Matth., in the Opus Imperfectum, falsely ascribed to St. John Chrysostom): "Anger, when it has a cause, is not anger but judgment. For anger, properly speaking, denotes a movement of passion": and when a man is angry with reason, his anger is no longer from passion: wherefore he is said to judge, not to be angry. In another way anger is taken for a movement of the sensitive appetite, which is with passion resulting from a bodily transmutation. This movement is a necessary sequel, in man, to the movement of his will, since the lower appetite necessarily follows the movement of the higher appetite, unless there be an obstacle. Hence the movement of anger in the sensitive appetite cannot be lacking altogether, unless the movement of the will be altogether lacking or weak. Consequently lack of the passion of anger is also a vice, even as the lack of movement in the will directed to punishment by the judgment of reason.

Reply to Objection 1: He that is entirely without anger when he ought to be angry, imitates God as to lack of passion, but not as to God's punishing by judgment.

Reply to Objection 2: The passion of anger, like all other movements of the sensitive appetite, is useful, as being conducive to the more prompt execution [*Cf. [3582]FS, Q[24], A[3]] of reason's dictate: else, the sensitive appetite in man would be to no purpose, whereas "nature does nothing without purpose" [*Aristotle, De Coelo i, 4].

Reply to Objection 3: When a man acts inordinately, the judgment of his reason is cause not only of the simple movement of the will but also of the passion in the sensitive appetite, as stated above. Wherefore just as the removal of the effect is a sign that the cause is removed, so the lack of anger is a sign that the judgment of reason is lacking.

OF CRUELTY (TWO ARTICLES)

We must now consider cruelty, under which head there are two points of inquiry:

(1) Whether cruelty is opposed to clemency?

(2) Of its comparison with savagery or brutality.

Whether cruelty is opposed to clemency?

Objection 1: It would seem that cruelty is not opposed to clemency. For Seneca says (De Clementia ii, 4) that "those are said to be cruel who exceed in punishing," which is contrary to justice. Now clemency is reckoned a part, not of justice but of temperance. Therefore apparently cruelty is not opposed to clemency.

Objection 2: Further, it is written (Jer. 6:23): "They are cruel, and will have no mercy"; so that cruelty would seem opposed to mercy. Now mercy is not the same as clemency, as stated above ([3583]Q[157], A[4], ad 3). Therefore cruelty is not opposed to clemency.

Objection 3: Further, clemency is concerned with the infliction of punishment, as stated above ([3584]Q[157], A[1]): whereas cruelty applies to the withdrawal of beneficence, according to Prov. 11:17, "But he that is cruel casteth off even his own kindred." Therefore cruelty is not opposed to clemency.

On the contrary, Seneca says (De Clementia ii, 4) that "the opposite of clemency is cruelty, which is nothing else but hardness of heart in exacting punishment."

I answer that, Cruelty apparently takes its name from "cruditas" [rawness]. Now just as things when cooked and prepared are wont to have an agreeable and sweet savor, so when raw they have a disagreeable and bitter taste. Now it has been stated above ([3585]Q[157], A[3], ad 1; A[4], ad 3) that clemency denotes a certain smoothness or sweetness of soul, whereby one is inclined to mitigate punishment. Hence cruelty is directly opposed to clemency.

Reply to Objection 1: Just as it belongs to equity to mitigate punishment according to reason, while the sweetness of soul which inclines one to this belongs to clemency: so too, excess in punishing, as regards the external action, belongs to injustice; but as regards the hardness of heart, which makes one ready to increase punishment, belongs to cruelty.

Reply to Objection 2: Mercy and clemency concur in this, that both shun and recoil from another's unhappiness, but in different ways. For it belongs to mercy [*Cf.[3586] Q[30], A[1]] to relieve another's unhappiness by a beneficent action, while it belongs to clemency to mitigate another's unhappiness by the cessation of punishment. And since cruelty denotes excess in exacting punishment, it is more directly opposed to clemency than to mercy; yet on account of the mutual likeness of these virtues, cruelty is sometimes taken for mercilessness.

Reply to Objection 3: Cruelty is there taken for mercilessness, which is lack of beneficence. We may also reply that withdrawal of beneficence is in itself a punishment.

Whether cruelty differs from savagery or brutality?

Objection 1: It would seem that cruelty differs not from savagery or brutality. For seemingly one vice is opposed in one way to one virtue. Now both savagery and cruelty are opposed to clemency by way of excess. Therefore it would seem that savagery and cruelty are the same.

Objection 2: Further, Isidore says (Etym. x) that "severity is as it were savagery with verity, because it holds to justice without attending to piety": so that savagery would seem to exclude that mitigation of punishment in delivering judgment which is demanded by piety. Now this has been stated to belong to cruelty (A[1], ad 1). Therefore cruelty is the same as savagery.

Objection 3: Further, just as there is a vice opposed to a virtue by way of excess, so is there a vice opposed to it by way of deficiency, which latter is opposed both to the virtue which is the mean, and to the vice which is in excess. Now the same vice pertaining to deficiency is opposed to both cruelty and savagery, namely remission or laxity. For Gregory says (Moral. xx, 5): "Let there be love, but not that which enervates, let there be severity, but without fury, let there be zeal without unseemly savagery, let there be piety without undue clemency." Therefore savagery is the same as cruelty.

On the contrary, Seneca says (De Clementia ii, 4) that "a man who is angry without being hurt, or with one who has not offended him, is not said to be cruel, but to be brutal or savage."

I answer that, "Savagery" and "brutality" take their names from a likeness to wild beasts which are also described as savage. For animals of this kind attack man that they may feed on his body, and not for some motive of justice the consideration of which belongs to reason alone. Wherefore, properly speaking, brutality or savagery applies to those who in inflicting punishment have not in view a default of the person punished, but merely the pleasure they derive from a man's torture. Consequently it is evident that it is comprised under bestiality: for such like pleasure is not human but bestial, and resulting as it does either from evil custom, or from a corrupt nature, as do other bestial emotions. On the other hand, cruelty not only regards the default of the person punished, but exceeds in the mode of punishing: wherefore cruelty differs from savagery or brutality, as human wickedness differs from bestiality, as stated in Ethic. vii, 5.

Reply to Objection 1: Clemency is a human virtue; wherefore directly opposed to it is cruelty which is a form of human wickedness. But savagery or brutality is comprised under bestiality, wherefore it is directly opposed not to clemency, but to a more excellent virtue, which the Philosopher (Ethic. vii, 5) calls "heroic" or "god-like," which according to us, would seem to pertain to the gifts of the Holy Ghost. Consequently we may say that savagery is directly opposed to the gift of piety.

Reply to Objection 2: A severe man is not said to be simply savage, because this implies a vice; but he is said to be "savage as regards the truth," on account of some likeness to savagery which is not inclined to mitigate punishment.

Reply to Objection 3: Remission of punishment is not a vice, except it disregard the order of justice, which requires a man to be punished on account of his offense, and which cruelty exceeds. On the other hand, cruelty disregards this order altogether. Wherefore remission of punishment is opposed to cruelty, but not to savagery.

OF MODESTY (TWO ARTICLES)

We must now consider modesty: and (1) Modesty in general; (2) Each of its species. Under the first head there are two points of inquiry:

(1) Whether modesty is a part of temperance?

(2) What is the matter of modesty?

Whether modesty is a part of temperance?

Objection 1: It would seem that modesty is not a part of temperance. For modesty is denominated from mode. Now mode is requisite in every virtue: since virtue is directed to good; and "good," according to Augustine (De Nat. Boni 3), "consists in mode, species, and order." Therefore modesty is a general virtue, and consequently should not be reckoned a part of temperance.

Objection 2: Further, temperance would seem to be deserving of praise chiefly on account of its moderation. Now this gives modesty its name. Therefore modesty is the same as temperance, and not one of its parts.

Objection 3: Further, modesty would seem to regard the correction of our neighbor, according to 2 Tim. 2:24,25, "The servant of the Lord must not wrangle, but be mild towards all men . . . with modesty admonishing them that resist the truth." Now admonishing wrong-doers is an act of justice or of charity, as stated above ([3587]Q[33], A[1]). Therefore seemingly modesty is a part of justice rather than of temperance.

On the contrary, Tully (De Invent. Rhet. ii, 54) reckons modesty as a part of temperance.

I answer that, As stated above ([3588]Q[141], A[4];[3589] Q[157], A[3]), temperance brings moderation into those things wherein it is most difficult to be moderate, namely the concupiscences of pleasures of touch. Now whenever there is a special virtue about some matter of very great moment, there must needs be another virtue about matters of lesser import: because the life of man requires to be regulated by the virtues with regard to everything: thus it was stated above ([3590]Q[134], A[3], ad 1), that while magnificence is about great expenditure, there is need in addition for liberality, which is concerned with ordinary expenditure. Hence there is need for a virtue to moderate other lesser matters where moderation is not so difficult. This virtue is called modesty, and is annexed to temperance as its principal.

Reply to Objection 1: When a name is common to many it is sometimes appropriated to those of the lowest rank; thus the common name of angel is appropriated to the lowest order of angels. In the same way, mode which is observed by all virtues in common, is specially appropriated to the virtue which prescribes the mode in the slightest things.

Reply to Objection 2: Some things need tempering on account of their strength, thus we temper strong wine. But moderation is necessary in all things: wherefore temperance is more concerned with strong passions, and modesty about weaker passions.

Reply to Objection 3: Modesty is to be taken there for the general moderation which is necessary in all virtues.

Whether modesty is only about outward actions?

Objection 1: It would seem that modesty is only about outward actions. For the inward movements of the passions cannot be known to other persons. Yet the Apostle enjoins (Phil. 4:5): "Let your modesty be known to all men." Therefore modesty is only about outward actions.

Objection 2: Further, the virtues that are about the passions are distinguished from justice which is about operations. Now modesty is seemingly one virtue. Therefore, if it be about outward works, it will not be concerned with inward passions.

Objection 3: Further, no one same virtue is both about things pertaining to the appetite—which is proper to the moral virtues—and about things pertaining to knowledge—which is proper to the intellectual virtues—and again about things pertaining to the irascible and concupiscible faculties. Therefore, if modesty be one virtue, it cannot be about all these things.

On the contrary, In all these things it is necessary to observe the "mode" whence modesty takes its name. Therefore modesty is about all of them.

I answer that, As stated above [3591](A[1]), modesty differs from temperance, in that temperance moderates those matters where restraint is most difficult, while modesty moderates those that present less difficulty. Authorities seem to have had various opinions about modesty. For wherever they found a special kind of good or a special difficulty of moderation, they withdrew it from the province of modesty, which they confined to lesser matters. Now it is clear to all that the restraint of pleasures of touch presents a special difficulty: wherefore all distinguished temperance from modesty.

In addition to this, moreover, Tully (De Invent. Rhet. ii, 54) considered that there was a special kind of good in the moderation of punishment; wherefore he severed clemency also from modesty, and held modesty to be about the remaining ordinary matters that require moderation. These seemingly are of four kinds. one is the movement of the mind towards some excellence, and this is moderated by "humility." The second is the desire of things pertaining to knowledge, and this is moderated by "studiousness" which is opposed to curiosity. The third regards bodily movements and actions, which require to be done becomingly and honestly [*Cf.[3592] Q[145], A[1]], whether we act seriously or in play. The fourth regards outward show, for instance in dress and the like.

To some of these matters, however, other authorities appointed certain special virtues: thus Andronicus [*De Affectibus] mentions "meekness, simplicity, humility," and other kindred virtues, of which we have spoken above (Q[143]); while Aristotle (Ethic. ii, 7) assigned {eutrapelia} to pleasures in games, as stated above ([3593]FS, Q[60], A[5]). All these are comprised under modesty as understood by Tully; and in this way modesty regards not only outward but also inward actions.

Reply to Objection 1: The Apostle speaks of modesty as regarding externals. Nevertheless the moderation of the inner man may be shown by certain outward signs.

Reply to Objection 2: Various virtues assigned by various authorities are comprised under modesty. Wherefore nothing prevents modesty from regarding matters which require different virtues. Yet there is not so great a difference between the various parts of modesty, as there is between justice, which is about operations, and temperance, which is about passions, because in actions and passions that present no great difficulty on the part of the matter, but only on the part of moderation, there is but one virtue, one namely for each kind of moderation.

Wherefore the Reply to the Third Objection also is clear.

OF HUMILITY (SIX ARTICLES)

We must consider next the species of modesty: (1) Humility, and pride which is opposed to it; (2) Studiousness, and its opposite, Curiosity; (3) Modesty as affecting words or deeds; (4) Modesty as affecting outward attire.

Concerning humility there are six points of inquiry:

(1) Whether humility is a virtue?

(2) Whether it resides in the appetite, or in the judgment of reason?

(3) Whether by humility one ought to subject oneself to all men?

(4) Whether it is a part of modesty or temperance?

(5) Of its comparison with the other virtues;

(6) Of the degrees of humility.

Whether humility is a virtue?

Objection 1: It would seem that humility is not a virtue. For virtue conveys the notion of a penal evil, according to Ps. 104:18, "They humbled his feet in fetters." Therefore humility is not a virtue.

Objection 2: Further, virtue and vice are mutually opposed. Now humility seemingly denotes a vice, for it is written (Ecclus. 19:23): "There is one that humbleth himself wickedly." Therefore humility is not a virtue.

Objection 3: Further, no virtue is opposed to another virtue. But humility is apparently opposed to the virtue of magnanimity, which aims at great things, whereas humility shuns them. Therefore it would seem that humility is not a virtue.

Objection 4: Further, virtue is "the disposition of that which is perfect" (Phys. vii, text. 17). But humility seemingly belongs to the imperfect: wherefore it becomes not God to be humble, since He can be subject to none. Therefore it seems that humility is not a virtue.

Objection 5: Further, every moral virtue is about actions and passions, according to Ethic. ii, 3. But humility is not reckoned by the Philosopher among the virtues that are about passions, nor is it comprised under justice which is about actions. Therefore it would seem not to be a virtue.

On the contrary, Origen commenting on Lk. 1:48, "He hath regarded the humility of His handmaid," says (Hom. viii in Luc.): "One of the virtues, humility, is particularly commended in Holy Writ; for our Saviour said: 'Learn of Me, because I am meek, and humble of heart.'"

I answer that, As stated above ([3594]FS, Q[23], A[2]) when we were treating of the passions, the difficult good has something attractive to the appetite, namely the aspect of good, and likewise something repulsive to the appetite, namely the difficulty of obtaining it. In respect of the former there arises the movement of hope, and in respect of the latter, the movement of despair. Now it has been stated above ([3595]FS, Q[61], A[2]) that for those appetitive movements which are a kind of impulse towards an object, there is need of a moderating and restraining moral virtue, while for those which are a kind of recoil, there is need, on the part of the appetite, of a moral virtue to strengthen it and urge it on. Wherefore a twofold virtue is necessary with regard to the difficult good: one, to temper and restrain the mind, lest it tend to high things immoderately; and this belongs to the virtue of humility: and another to strengthen the mind against despair, and urge it on to the pursuit of great things according to right reason; and this is magnanimity. Therefore it is evident that humility is a virtue.

Reply to Objection 1: As Isidore observes (Etym. x), "a humble man is so called because he is, as it were, 'humo acclinis'" [*Literally, 'bent to the ground'], i.e. inclined to the lowest place. This may happen in two ways. First, through an extrinsic principle, for instance when one is cast down by another, and thus humility is a punishment. Secondly, through an intrinsic principle: and this may be done sometimes well, for instance when a man, considering his own failings, assumes the lowest place according to his mode: thus Abraham said to the Lord (Gn. 18:27), "I will speak to my Lord, whereas I am dust and ashes." In this way humility is a virtue. Sometimes, however, this may be ill-done, for instance when man, "not understanding his honor, compares himself to senseless beasts, and becomes like to them" (Ps. 48:13).

Reply to Objection 2: As stated (ad 1), humility, in so far as it is a virtue, conveys the notion of a praiseworthy self-abasement to the lowest place. Now this is sometimes done merely as to outward signs and pretense: wherefore this is "false humility," of which Augustine says in a letter (Ep. cxlix) that it is "grievous pride," since to wit, it would seem to aim at excellence of glory. Sometimes, however, this is done by an inward movement of the soul, and in this way, properly speaking, humility is reckoned a virtue, because virtue does not consist externals, but chiefly in the inward choice of the mind, as the Philosopher states (Ethic. ii, 5).

Reply to Objection 3: Humility restrains the appetite from aiming at great things against right reason: while magnanimity urges the mind to great things in accord with right reason. Hence it is clear that magnanimity is not opposed to humility: indeed they concur in this, that each is according to right reason.

Reply to Objection 4: A thing is said to be perfect in two ways. First absolutely; such a thing contains no defect, neither in its nature nor in respect of anything else, and thus God alone is perfect. To Him humility is fitting, not as regards His Divine nature, but only as regards His assumed nature. Secondly, a thing may be said to be perfect in a restricted sense, for instance in respect of its nature or state or time. Thus a virtuous man is perfect: although in comparison with God his perfection is found wanting, according to the word of Is. 40:17, "All nations are before Him as if they had no being at all." In this way humility may be competent to every man.

Reply to Objection 5: The Philosopher intended to treat of virtues as directed to civic life, wherein the subjection of one man to another is defined according to the ordinance of the law, and consequently is a matter of legal justice. But humility, considered as a special virtue, regards chiefly the subjection of man to God, for Whose sake he humbles himself by subjecting himself to others.

Whether humility has to do with the appetite?

Objection 1: It would seem that humility concerns, not the appetite but the judgment of reason. Because humility is opposed to pride. Now pride concerns things pertaining to knowledge: for Gregory says (Moral. xxxiv, 22) that "pride, when it extends outwardly to the body, is first of all shown in the eyes": wherefore it is written (Ps. 130:1), "Lord, my heart is not exalted, nor are my eyes lofty." Now eyes are the chief aids to knowledge. Therefore it would seem that humility is chiefly concerned with knowledge, whereby one thinks little of oneself.

Objection 2: Further, Augustine says (De Virginit. xxxi) that "almost the whole of Christian teaching is humility." Consequently nothing contained in Christian teaching is incompatible with humility. Now Christian teaching admonishes us to seek the better things, according to 1 Cor. 12:31, "Be zealous for the better gifts." Therefore it belongs to humility to restrain not the desire of difficult things but the estimate thereof.

Objection 3: Further, it belongs to the same virtue both to restrain excessive movement, and to strengthen the soul against excessive withdrawal: thus fortitude both curbs daring and fortifies the soul against fear. Now it is magnanimity that strengthens the soul against the difficulties that occur in the pursuit of great things. Therefore if humility were to curb the desire of great things, it would follow that humility is not a distinct virtue from magnanimity, which is evidently false. Therefore humility is concerned, not with the desire but with the estimate of great things.

Objection 4: Further, Andronicus [*De Affectibus] assigns humility to outward show; for he says that humility is "the habit of avoiding excessive expenditure and parade." Therefore it is not concerned with the movement of the appetite.

On the contrary, Augustine says (De Poenit. [*Serm. cccli]) that "the humble man is one who chooses to be an abject in the house of the Lord, rather than to dwell in the tents of sinners." But choice concerns the appetite. Therefore humility has to do with the appetite rather than with the estimative power.

I answer that, As stated above [3596](A[1]), it belongs properly to humility, that a man restrain himself from being borne towards that which is above him. For this purpose he must know his disproportion to that which surpasses his capacity. Hence knowledge of one's own deficiency belongs to humility, as a rule guiding the appetite. Nevertheless humility is essentially in the appetite itself; and consequently it must be said that humility, properly speaking, moderates the movement of the appetite.

Reply to Objection 1: Lofty eyes are a sign of pride, inasmuch as it excludes respect and fear: for fearing and respectful persons are especially wont to lower the eyes, as though not daring to compare themselves with others. But it does not follow from this that humility is essentially concerned with knowledge.

Reply to Objection 2: It is contrary to humility to aim at greater things through confiding in one's own powers: but to aim at greater things through confidence in God's help, is not contrary to humility; especially since the more one subjects oneself to God, the more is one exalted in God's sight. Hence Augustine says (De Virginit. xxxi): "It is one thing to raise oneself to God, and another to raise oneself up against God. He that abases himself before Him, him He raiseth up; he that raises himself up against Him, him He casteth down."

Reply to Objection 3: In fortitude there is the same reason for restraining daring and for strengthening the soul against fear: since the reason in both cases is that man should set the good of reason before dangers of death. But the reason for restraining presumptuous hope which pertains to humility is not the same as the reason for strengthening the soul against despair. Because the reason for strengthening the soul against despair is the acquisition of one's proper good lest man, by despair, render himself unworthy of a good which was competent to him; while the chief reason for suppressing presumptuous hope is based on divine reverence, which shows that man ought not to ascribe to himself more than is competent to him according to the position in which God has placed him. Wherefore humility would seem to denote in the first place man's subjection to God; and for this reason Augustine (De Serm. Dom. in Monte i, 4) ascribes humility, which he understands by poverty of spirit, to the gift of fear whereby man reveres God. Hence it follows that the relation of fortitude to daring differs from that of humility to hope. Because fortitude uses daring more than it suppresses it: so that excess of daring is more like fortitude than lack of daring is. On the other hand, humility suppresses hope or confidence in self more than it uses it; wherefore excessive self-confidence is more opposed to humility than lack of confidence is.

Reply to Objection 4: Excess in outward expenditure and parade is wont to be done with a view of boasting, which is suppressed by humility. Accordingly humility has to do, in a secondary way, with externals, as signs of the inward movement of the appetite.

Whether one ought, by humility, to subject oneself to all men?

Objection 1: It would seem that one ought not, by humility, to subject oneself to all men. For, as stated above (A[2], ad 3), humility consists chiefly in man's subjection to God. Now one ought not to offer to a man that which is due to God, as is the case with all acts of religious worship. Therefore, by humility, one ought not to subject oneself to man.

Objection 2: Further, Augustine says (De Nat. et Gratia xxxiv): "Humility should take the part of truth, not of falsehood." Now some men are of the highest rank, who cannot, without falsehood, subject themselves to their inferiors. Therefore one ought not, by humility, to subject oneself to all men.

Objection 3: Further no one ought to do that which conduces to the detriment of another's spiritual welfare. But if a man subject himself to another by humility, this is detrimental to the person to whom he subjects himself; for the latter might wax proud, or despise the other. Hence Augustine says in his Rule (Ep. ccxi): "Lest through excessive humility the superior lose his authority." Therefore a man ought not, by humility, to subject himself to all.

On the contrary, It is written (Phil. 2:3): "In humility, let each esteem others better than themselves."

I answer that, We may consider two things in man, namely that which is God's, and that which is man's. Whatever pertains to defect is man's: but whatever pertains to man's welfare and perfection is God's, according to the saying of Osee 13:9, "Destruction is thy own, O Israel; thy help is only in Me." Now humility, as stated above (A[1], ad 5; A[2], ad 3), properly regards the reverence whereby man is subject to God. Wherefore every man, in respect of that which is his own, ought to subject himself to every neighbor, in respect of that which the latter has of God's: but humility does not require a man to subject what he has of God's to that which may seem to be God's in another. For those who have a share of God's gifts know that they have them, according to 1 Cor. 2:12: "That we may know the things that are given us from God." Wherefore without prejudice to humility they may set the gifts they have received from God above those that others appear to have received from Him; thus the Apostle says (Eph. 3:5): "(The mystery of Christ) was not known to the sons of men as it is now revealed to His holy apostles." In like manner. humility does not require a man to subject that which he has of his own to that which his neighbor has of man's: otherwise each one would have to esteem himself a greater sinner than anyone else: whereas the Apostle says without prejudice to humility (Gal. 2:15): "We by nature are Jews, and not of the Gentiles, sinners." Nevertheless a man may esteem his neighbor to have some good which he lacks himself, or himself to have some evil which another has not: by reason of which, he may subject himself to him with humility.

Reply to Objection 1: We must not only revere God in Himself, but also that which is His in each one, although not with the same measure of reverence as we revere God. Wherefore we should subject ourselves with humility to all our neighbors for God's sake, according to 1 Pet. 2:13, "Be ye subject . . . to every human creature for God's sake"; but to God alone do we owe the worship of latria.

Reply to Objection 2: If we set what our neighbor has of God's above that which we have of our own, we cannot incur falsehood. Wherefore a gloss [*St. Augustine, QQ. lxxxiii, qu. 71] on Phil. 2:3, "Esteem others better than themselves," says: "We must not esteem by pretending to esteem; but we should in truth think it possible for another person to have something that is hidden to us and whereby he is better than we are, although our own good whereby we are apparently better than he, be not hidden."

Reply to Objection 3: Humility, like other virtues, resides chiefly inwardly in the soul. Consequently a man, by an inward act of the soul, may subject himself to another, without giving the other man an occasion of detriment to his spiritual welfare. This is what Augustine means in his Rule (Ep. ccxi): "With fear, the superior should prostrate himself at your feet in the sight of God." On the other hand, due moderation must be observed in the outward acts of humility even as of other virtues, lest they conduce to the detriment of others. If, however, a man does as he ought, and others take therefrom an occasion of sin, this is not imputed to the man who acts with humility; since he does not give scandal, although others take it.

Whether humility is a part of modesty or temperance?

Objection 1: It would seem that humility is not a part of modesty or temperance. For humility regards chiefly the reverence whereby one is subject to God, as stated above [3597](A[3]). Now it belongs to a theological virtue to have God for its object. Therefore humility should be reckoned a theological virtue rather than a part of temperance or modesty.

Objection 2: Further, temperance is in the concupiscible, whereas humility would seem to be in the irascible, just as pride which is opposed to it, and whose object is something difficult. Therefore apparently humility is not a part of temperance or modesty.

Objection 3: Further, humility and magnanimity are about the same object, as stated above (A[1], ad 3). But magnanimity is reckoned a part, not of temperance but of fortitude, as stated above ([3598]Q[129], A[5]). Therefore it would seem that humility is not a part of temperance or modesty.

On the contrary, Origen says (Hom. viii super Luc.): "If thou wilt hear the name of this virtue, and what it was called by the philosophers, know that humility which God regards is the same as what they called {metriotes}, i.e. measure or moderation." Now this evidently pertains to modesty or temperance. Therefore humility is a part of modesty or temperance.

I answer that, As stated above ([3599]Q[137], A[2], ad 1;[3600] Q[157], A[3], ad 2), in assigning parts to a virtue we consider chiefly the likeness that results from the mode of the virtue. Now the mode of temperance, whence it chiefly derives its praise, is the restraint or suppression of the impetuosity of a passion. Hence whatever virtues restrain or suppress, and the actions which moderate the impetuosity of the emotions, are reckoned parts of temperance. Now just as meekness suppresses the movement of anger, so does humility suppress the movement of hope, which is the movement of a spirit aiming at great things. Wherefore, like meekness, humility is accounted a part of temperance. For this reason the Philosopher (Ethic. iv, 3) says that a man who aims at small things in proportion to his mode is not magnanimous but "temperate," and such a man we may call humble. Moreover, for the reason given above ([3601]Q[160], A[2]), among the various parts of temperance, the one under which humility is comprised is modesty as understood by Tully (De Invent. Rhet. ii, 54), inasmuch as humility is nothing else than a moderation of spirit: wherefore it is written (1 Pet. 3:4): "In the incorruptibility of a quiet and meek spirit."

Reply to Objection 1: The theological virtues, whose object is our last end, which is the first principle in matters of appetite, are the causes of all the other virtues. Hence the fact that humility is caused by reverence for God does not prevent it from being a part of modesty or temperance.

Reply to Objection 2: Parts are assigned to a principal virtue by reason of a sameness, not of subject or matter, but of formal mode, as stated above ([3602]Q[137], A[2], ad 1;[3603] Q[157], A[3], ad 2). Consequently, although humility is in the irascible as its subject, it is assigned as a part of modesty or temperance by reason of its mode.

Reply to Objection 3: Although humility and magnanimity agree as to matter, they differ as to mode, by reason of which magnanimity is reckoned a part of fortitude, and humility a part of temperance.

Whether humility is the greatest of the virtues?

Objection 1: It would seem that humility is the greatest of the virtues. For Chrysostom, expounding the story of the Pharisee and the publican (Lk. 18), says [*Eclog. hom. vii de Humil. Animi.] that "if humility is such a fleet runner even when hampered by sin that it overtakes the justice that is the companion of pride, whither will it not reach if you couple it with justice? It will stand among the angels by the judgment seat of God." Hence it is clear that humility is set above justice. Now justice is either the most exalted of all the virtues, or includes all virtues, according to the Philosopher (Ethic. v, 1). Therefore humility is the greatest of the virtues.

Objection 2: Further, Augustine says (De Verb. Dom., Serm. [*S. 10, C[1]]): "Are you thinking of raising the great fabric of spirituality? Attend first of all to the foundation of humility." Now this would seem to imply that humility is the foundation of all virtue. Therefore apparently it is greater than the other virtues.

Objection 3: Further, the greater virtue deserves the greater reward. Now the greatest reward is due to humility, since "he that humbleth himself shall be exalted" (Lk. 14:11). Therefore humility is the greatest of virtues.

Objection 4: Further, according to Augustine (De Vera Relig. 16), "Christ's whole life on earth was a lesson in moral conduct through the human nature which He assumed." Now He especially proposed His humility for our example, saying (Mat. 11:29): "Learn of Me, because I am meek and humble of heart." Moreover, Gregory says (Pastor. iii, 1) that the "lesson proposed to us in the mystery of our redemption is the humility of God." Therefore humility would seem to be the greatest of virtues.

On the contrary, Charity is set above all the virtues, according to Col. 3:14, "Above all . . . things have charity." Therefore humility is not the greatest of virtues.

I answer that, The good of human virtue pertains to the order of reason: which order is considered chiefly in reference to the end: wherefore the theological virtues are the greatest because they have the last end for their object. Secondarily, however, it is considered in reference to the ordering of the means to the end. This ordinance, as to its essence, is in the reason itself from which it issues, but by participation it is in the appetite ordered by the reason; and this ordinance is the effect of justice, especially of legal justice. Now humility makes a man a good subject to ordinance of all kinds and in all matters; while every other virtue has this effect in some special matter. Therefore after the theological virtues, after the intellectual virtues which regard the reason itself, and after justice, especially legal justice, humility stands before all others.

Reply to Objection 1: Humility is not set before justice, but before that justice which is coupled with pride, and is no longer a virtue; even so, on the other hand, sin is pardoned through humility: for it is said of the publican (Lk. 18:14) that through the merit of his humility "he went down into his house justified." Hence Chrysostom says [*De incompr. Nat. Dei, Hom. v]: "Bring me a pair of two-horse chariots: in the one harness pride with justice, in the other sin with humility: and you will see that sin outrunning justice wins not by its own strength, but by that of humility: while you will see the other pair beaten, not by the weakness of justice, but by the weight and size of pride."

Reply to Objection 2: Just as the orderly assembly of virtues is, by reason of a certain likeness, compared to a building, so again that which is the first step in the acquisition of virtue is likened to the foundation, which is first laid before the rest of the building. Now the virtues are in truth infused by God. Wherefore the first step in the acquisition of virtue may be understood in two ways. First by way of removing obstacles: and thus humility holds the first place, inasmuch as it expels pride, which "God resisteth," and makes man submissive and ever open to receive the influx of Divine grace. Hence it is written (James 4:6): "God resisteth the proud, and giveth grace to the humble." In this sense humility is said to be the foundation of the spiritual edifice. Secondly, a thing is first among virtues directly, because it is the first step towards God. Now the first step towards God is by faith, according to Heb. 11:6, "He that cometh to God must believe." In this sense faith is the foundation in a more excellent way than humility.

Reply to Objection 3: To him that despises earthly things, heavenly things are promised: thus heavenly treasures are promised to those who despise earthly riches, according to Mat. 6:19,20, "Lay not up to yourselves treasures on earth . . . but lay up to yourselves treasures in heaven." Likewise heavenly consolations are promised to those who despise worldly joys, according to Mat. 4:5, "Blessed are they that mourn, for they shall be comforted." In the same way spiritual uplifting is promised to humility, not that humility alone merits it, but because it is proper to it to despise earthly uplifting. Wherefore Augustine says (De Poenit. [*Serm. cccli]): "Think not that he who humbles himself remains for ever abased, for it is written: 'He shall be exalted.' And do not imagine that his exaltation in men's eyes is effected by bodily uplifting."

Reply to Objection 4: The reason why Christ chiefly proposed humility to us, was because it especially removes the obstacle to man's spiritual welfare consisting in man's aiming at heavenly and spiritual things, in which he is hindered by striving to become great in earthly things. Hence our Lord, in order to remove an obstacle to our spiritual welfare, showed by giving an example of humility, that outward exaltation is to be despised. Thus humility is, as it were, a disposition to man's untrammeled access to spiritual and divine goods. Accordingly as perfection is greater than disposition, so charity, and other virtues whereby man approaches God directly, are greater than humility.

Whether twelve degrees of humility are fittingly distinguished in the Rule of the Blessed Benedict?

Objection 1: It would seem that the twelve degrees of humility that are set down in the Rule of the Blessed Benedict [*St. Thomas gives these degrees in the reverse order to that followed by St. Benedict] are unfittingly distinguished. The first is to be "humble not only in heart, but also to show it in one's very person, one's eyes fixed on the ground"; the second is "to speak few and sensible words, and not to be loud of voice"; the third is "not to be easily moved, and disposed to laughter";

the fourth is "to maintain silence until one is asked"; the fifth is "to do nothing but to what one is exhorted by the common rule of the monastery"; the sixth is "to believe and acknowledge oneself viler than all"; the seventh is "to think oneself worthless and unprofitable for all purposes"; the eighth is "to confess one's sin"; the ninth is "to embrace patience by obeying under difficult and contrary circumstances"; the tenth is "to subject oneself to a superior"; the eleventh is "not to delight in fulfilling one's own desires"; the twelfth is "to fear God and to be always mindful of everything that God has commanded." For among these there are some things pertaining to the other virtues, such as obedience and patience. Again there are some that seem to involve a false opinion—and this is inconsistent with any virtue—namely to declare oneself more despicable than all men, and to confess and believe oneself to be in all ways worthless and unprofitable. Therefore these are unfittingly placed among the degrees of humility.

Objection 2: Further, humility proceeds from within to externals, as do other virtues. Therefore in the aforesaid degrees, those which concern outward actions are unfittingly placed before those which pertain to inward actions.

Objection 3: Further, Anselm (De Simil. ci, seqq.) gives seven degrees of humility, the first of which is "to acknowledge oneself contemptible"; the second, "to grieve for this"; the third, "to confess it"; the fourth, "to convince others of this, that is to wish them to believe it"; the fifth, "to bear patiently that this be said of us"; the sixth, "to suffer oneself to be treated with contempt"; the seventh, "to love being thus treated." Therefore the aforesaid degrees would seem to be too numerous.

Objection 4: Further, a gloss on Mat. 3:15 says: "Perfect humility has three degrees. The first is to subject ourselves to those who are above us, and not to set ourselves above our equals: this is sufficient. The second is to submit to our equals, and not to set ourselves before our inferiors; this is called abundant humility. The third degree is to subject ourselves to inferiors, and in this is perfect righteousness." Therefore the aforesaid degrees would seem to be too numerous.

Objection 5: Further, Augustine says (De Virginit. xxxi): "The measure of humility is apportioned to each one according to his rank. It is imperiled by pride, for the greater a man is the more liable is he to be entrapped." Now the measure of a man's greatness cannot be fixed according to a definite number of degrees. Therefore it would seem that it is not possible to assign the aforesaid degrees to humility.

I answer that, As stated above [3604](A[2]) humility has essentially to do with the appetite, in so far as a man restrains the impetuosity of his soul, from tending inordinately to great things: yet its rule is in the cognitive faculty, in that we should not deem ourselves to be above what we are. Also, the principle and origin of both these things is the reverence we bear to God. Now the inward disposition of humility leads to certain outward signs in words, deeds, and gestures, which manifest that which is hidden within, as happens also with the other virtues. For "a man is known by his look, and a wise man, when thou meetest him, by his countenance" (Ecclus. 19:26). Wherefore the aforesaid degrees of humility include something regarding the root of humility, namely the twelfth degree, "that a man fear God and bear all His commandments in mind."

Again, they include certain things with regard to the appetite, lest one aim inordinately at one's own excellence. This is done in three ways. First, by not following one's own will, and this pertains to the eleventh degree; secondly, by regulating it according to one's superior judgment, and this applies to the tenth degree; thirdly, by not being deterred from this on account of the difficulties and hardships that come in our way, and this belongs to the ninth degree.

Certain things also are included referring to the estimate a man forms in acknowledging his own deficiency, and this in three ways. First by acknowledging and avowing his own shortcomings; this belongs to the eighth degree: secondly, by deeming oneself incapable of great things, and this pertains to the seventh degree: thirdly, that in this respect one should put others before oneself, and this belongs to the sixth degree.

Again, some things are included that refer to outward signs. One of these regards deeds, namely that in one's work one should not depart from the ordinary way; this applies to the fifth degree. Two others have reference to words, namely that one should not be in a hurry to speak, which pertains to the fourth degree, and that one be not immoderate in speech, which refers to the second. The others have to do with outward gestures, for instance in restraining haughty looks, which regards the first, and in outwardly checking laughter and other signs of senseless mirth, and this belongs to the third degree.

Reply to Objection 1: It is possible, without falsehood, to deem and avow oneself the most despicable of men, as regards the hidden faults which we acknowledge in ourselves, and the hidden gifts of God which others have. Hence Augustine says (De Virginit. lii): "Bethink you that some persons are in some hidden way better than you, although outwardly you are better than they." Again, without falsehood one may avow and believe oneself in all ways unprofitable and useless in respect of one's own capability, so as to refer all one's sufficiency to God, according to 2 Cor. 3:5, "Not that we are sufficient to think anything of ourselves as of ourselves: but our sufficiency is from God." And there is nothing unbecoming in ascribing to humility those things that pertain to other virtues, since, just as one vice arises from another, so, by a natural sequence, the act of one virtue proceeds from the act of another.

Reply to Objection 2: Man arrives at humility in two ways. First and chiefly by a gift of grace, and in this way the inner man precedes the outward man. The other way is by human effort, whereby he first of all restrains the outward man, and afterwards succeeds in plucking out the inward root. It is according to this order that the degrees of humility are here enumerated.

Reply to Objection 3: All the degrees mentioned by Anselm are reducible to knowledge, avowal, and desire of one's own abasement. For the first degree belongs to the knowledge of one's own deficiency; but since it would be wrong for one to love one's own failings, this is excluded by the second degree. The third and fourth degrees regard the avowal of one's own deficiency; namely that not merely one simply assert one's failing, but that one convince another of it. The other three degrees have to do with the appetite, which seeks, not outward excellence, but outward abasement, or bears it with equanimity, whether it consist of words or deeds. For as Gregory says (Regist. ii, 10, Ep. 36), "there is nothing great in being humble towards those who treat us with regard, for even worldly people do this: but we should especially be humble towards those who make us suffer," and this belongs to the fifth and sixth degrees: or the appetite may even go so far as lovingly to embrace external abasement, and this pertains to the seventh degree; so that all these degrees are comprised under the sixth and seventh mentioned above.

Reply to Objection 4: These degrees refer, not to the thing itself, namely the nature of humility, but to the degrees among men, who are either of higher or lower or of equal degree.

Reply to Objection 5: This argument also considers the degrees of humility not according to the nature of the thing, in respect of which the aforesaid degrees are assigned, but according to the various conditions of men.

OF PRIDE (EIGHT ARTICLES)

We must next consider pride, and (1) pride in general; (2) the first man's sin, which we hold to have been pride. Under the first head there are eight points of inquiry:

(1) Whether pride is a sin?

(2) Whether it is a special vice?

(3) Wherein does it reside as in its subject?

(4) Of its species;

(5) Whether it is a mortal sin?

(6) Whether it is the most grievous of all sins?

(7) Of its relation to other sins;

(8) Whether it should be reckoned a capital vice?

Whether pride is a sin?

Objection 1: It would seem that pride is not a sin. For no sin is the object of God's promise. For God's promises refer to what He will do; and He is not the author of sin. Now pride is numbered among the Divine promises: for it is written (Is. 60:15): "I will make thee to be an everlasting pride [Douay: 'glory'], a joy unto generation and generation." Therefore pride is not a sin.

Objection 2: Further, it is not a sin to wish to be like unto God: for every creature has a natural desire for this; and especially does this become the rational creature which is made to God's image and likeness. Now it is said in Prosper's Lib. Sent. 294, that "pride is love of one's own excellence, whereby one is likened to God who is supremely excellent." Hence Augustine says (Confess. ii, 6): "Pride imitates exaltedness; whereas Thou alone art God exalted over all." Therefore pride is not a sin.

Objection 3: Further, a sin is opposed not only to a virtue but also to a contrary vice, as the Philosopher states (Ethic. ii, 8). But no vice is found to be opposed to pride. Therefore pride is not a sin.

On the contrary, It is written (Tob. 4:14): "Never suffer pride to reign in thy mind or in thy words."

I answer that, Pride [superbia] is so called because a man thereby aims higher [supra] than he is; wherefore Isidore says (Etym. x): "A man is said to be proud, because he wishes to appear above (super) what he really is"; for he who wishes to overstep beyond what he is, is proud. Now right reason requires that every man's will should tend to that which is proportionate to him. Therefore it is evident that pride denotes something opposed to right reason, and this shows it to have the character of sin, because according to Dionysius (Div. Nom. iv, 4), "the soul's evil is to be opposed to reason." Therefore it is evident that pride is a sin.

Reply to Objection 1: Pride [superbia] may be understood in two ways. First, as overpassing [supergreditur] the rule of reason, and in this sense we say that it is a sin. Secondly, it may simply denominate "super-abundance"; in which sense any super-abundant thing may be called pride: and it is thus that God promises pride as significant of super-abundant good. Hence a gloss of Jerome on the same passage (Is. 61:6) says that "there is a good and an evil pride"; or "a sinful pride which God resists, and a pride that denotes the glory which He bestows."

It may also be replied that pride there signifies abundance of those things in which men may take pride.

Reply to Objection 2: Reason has the direction of those things for which man has a natural appetite; so that if the appetite wander from the rule of reason, whether by excess or by default, it will be sinful, as is the case with the appetite for food which man desires naturally. Now pride is the appetite for excellence in excess of right reason. Wherefore Augustine says (De Civ. Dei xiv, 13) that pride is the "desire for inordinate exaltation": and hence it is that, as he asserts (De Civ. Dei xiv, 13; xix, 12), "pride imitates God inordinately: for it hath equality of fellowship under Him, and wishes to usurp Hi. dominion over our fellow-creatures."

Reply to Objection 3: Pride is directly opposed to the virtue of humility, which, in a way, is concerned about the same matter as magnanimity, as stated above ([3605]Q[161], A[1], ad 3). Hence the vice opposed to pride by default is akin to the vice of pusillanimity, which is opposed by default to magnanimity. For just as it belongs to magnanimity to urge the mind to great things against despair, so it belongs to humility to withdraw the mind from the inordinate desire of great things against presumption. Now pusillanimity, if we take it for a deficiency in pursuing great things, is properly opposed to magnanimity by default; but if we take it for the mind's attachment to things beneath what is becoming to a man, it is opposed to humility by default; since each proceeds from a smallness of mind. In the same way, on the other hand, pride may be opposed by excess, both to magnanimity and humility, from different points of view: to humility, inasmuch as it scorns subjection, to magnanimity, inasmuch as it tends to great things inordinately. Since, however, pride implies a certain elation, it is more directly opposed to humility, even as pusillanimity, which denotes littleness of soul in tending towards great things, is more directly opposed to magnanimity.

Whether pride is a special sin?

Objection 1: It would seem that pride is not a special sin. For Augustine says (De Nat. et Grat. xxix) that "you will find no sin that is not labelled pride"; and Prosper says (De Vita Contempl. iii, 2) that "without pride no sin is, or was, or ever will be possible." Therefore pride is a general sin.

Objection 2: Further, a gloss on Job 33:17, "That He may withdraw man from wickedness [*Vulg.: 'From the things that he is doing, and may deliver him from pride']," says that "a man prides himself when he transgresses His commandments by sin." Now according to Ambrose [*De Parad. viii], "every sin is a transgression of the Divine law, and a disobedience of the heavenly commandments." Therefore every sin is pride.

Objection 3: Further, every special sin is opposed to a special virtue. But pride is opposed to all the virtues, for Gregory says (Moral. xxxiv, 23): "Pride is by no means content with the destruction of one virtue; it raises itself up against all the powers of the soul, and like an all-pervading and poisonous disease corrupts the whole body"; and Isidore says (Etym. [*De Summo Bono ii, 38]) that it is "the downfall of all virtues." Therefore pride is not a special sin.

Objection 4: Further, every special sin has a special matter. Now pride has a general matter, for Gregory says (Moral. xxxiv, 23) that "one man is proud of his gold, another of his eloquence: one is elated by mean and earthly things, another by sublime and heavenly virtues." Therefore pride is not a special but a general sin.

On the contrary, Augustine says (De Nat. et Grat. xxix): "If he look into the question carefully, he will find that, according to God's law, pride is a very different sin from other vices." Now the genus is not different from its species. Therefore pride is not a general but a special sin.

I answer that, The sin of pride may be considered in two ways. First with regard to its proper species, which it has under the aspect of its proper object. In this way pride is a special sin, because it has a special object: for it is inordinate desire of one's own excellence, as stated (A[1], ad 2). Secondly, it may be considered as having a certain influence towards other sins. In this way it has somewhat of a generic character, inasmuch as all sins may arise from pride, in two ways. First directly, through other sins being directed to the end of pride which is one's own excellence, to which may be directed anything that is inordinately desired. Secondly, indirectly and accidentally as it were, that is by removing an obstacle, since pride makes a man despise the Divine law which hinders him from sinning, according to Jer. 2:20, "Thou hast broken My yoke, thou hast burst My bands, and thou saidst: I will not serve."

It must, however, be observed that this generic character of pride admits of the possibility of all vices arising from pride sometimes, but it does not imply that all vices originate from pride always. For though one may break the commandments of the Law by any kind of sin, through contempt which pertains to pride, yet one does not always break the Divine commandments through contempt, but sometimes through ignorance. and sometimes through weakness: and for this reason Augustine says (De Nat. et Grat. xxix) that "many things are done amiss which are not done through pride."

Reply to Objection 1: These words are introduced by Augustine into his book De Nat. et Grat., not as being his own, but as those of someone with whom he is arguing. Hence he subsequently disproves the assertion, and shows that not all sins are committed through pride. We might, however, reply that these authorities must be understood as referring to the outward effect of pride, namely the breaking of the commandments, which applies to every sin, and not to the inward act of pride, namely contempt of the commandment. For sin is committed, not always through contempt, but sometimes through ignorance, sometimes through weakness, as stated above.

Reply to Objection 2: A man may sometimes commit a sin effectively, but not affectively; thus he who, in ignorance, slays his father, is a parricide effectively, but not affectively, since he did not intend it. Accordingly he who breaks God's commandment is said to pride himself against God, effectively always, but not always affectively.

Reply to Objection 3: A sin may destroy a virtue in two ways. In one way by direct contrariety to a virtue, and thus pride does not corrupt every virtue, but only humility; even as every special sin destroys the special virtue opposed to it, by acting counter thereto. In another way a sin destroys a virtue, by making ill use of that virtue: and thus pride destroys every virtue, in so far as it finds an occasion of pride in every virtue, just as in everything else pertaining to excellence. Hence it does not follow that it is a general sin.

Reply to Objection 4: Pride regards a special aspect in its object, which aspect may be found in various matters: for it is inordinate love of one's excellence, and excellence may be found in various things.

Whether the subject of pride is the irascible faculty?

Objection 1: It would seem that the subject of pride is not the irascible faculty. For Gregory says (Moral. xxiii, 17): "A swollen mind is an obstacle to truth, for the swelling shuts out the light." Now the knowledge of truth pertains, not to the irascible but to the rational faculty. Therefore pride is not in the irascible.

Objection 2: Further, Gregory says (Moral. xxiv, 8) that "the proud observe other people's conduct not so as to set themselves beneath them with humility, but so as to set themselves above them with pride": wherefore it would seem that pride originates in undue observation. Now observation pertains not to the irascible but to the rational faculty.

Objection 3: Further. pride seeks pre-eminence not only in sensible things, but also in spiritual and intelligible things: while it consists essentially in the contempt of God, according to Ecclus. 10:14, "The beginning of the pride of man is to fall off from God." Now the irascible, since it is a part of the sensitive appetite, cannot extend to God and things intelligible. Therefore pride cannot be in the irascible.

Objection 4: Further, as stated in Prosper's Liber Sententiarum, sent. 294, "Pride is love of one's own excellence." But love is not in the irascible, but in the concupiscible. Therefore pride is not in the irascible.

On the contrary, Gregory (Moral. ii, 49) opposes pride to the gift of fear. Now fear belongs to the irascible. Therefore pride is in the irascible.

I answer that, The subject of any virtue or vice is to be ascertained from its proper object: for the object of a habit or act cannot be other than the object of the power, which is the subject of both. Now the proper object of pride is something difficult, for pride is the desire of one's own excellence, as stated above

([3606]AA[1],2). Wherefore pride must needs pertain in some way to the irascible faculty. Now the irascible may be taken in two ways. First in a strict sense, and thus it is a part of the sensitive appetite, even as anger, strictly speaking, is a passion of the sensitive appetite. Secondly, the irascible may be taken in a broader sense, so as to belong also to the intellective appetite, to which also anger is sometimes ascribed. It is thus that we attribute anger to God and the angels, not as a passion, but as denoting the sentence of justice pronouncing judgment. Nevertheless the irascible understood in this broad sense is not distinct from the concupiscible power, as stated above in the [3607]FP, Q[59], A[4]; FS, Q[82], A[5], ad 1 and 2.

Consequently if the difficult thing which is the object of pride, were merely some sensible object, whereto the sensitive appetite might tend, pride would have to be in the irascible which is part of the sensitive appetite. But since the difficult thing which pride has in view is common both to sensible and to spiritual things, we must needs say that the subject of pride is the irascible not only strictly so called, as a part of the sensitive appetite, but also in its wider acceptation, as applicable to the intellective appetite. Wherefore pride is ascribed also to the demons.

Reply to Objection 1: Knowledge of truth is twofold. One is purely speculative, and pride hinders this indirectly by removing its cause. For the proud man subjects not his intellect to God, that he may receive the knowledge of truth from Him, according to Mat. 11:25, "Thou hast hid these things from the wise and the prudent," i.e. from the proud, who are wise and prudent in their own eyes, "and hast revealed them to little ones," i.e. to the humble.

Nor does he deign to learn anything from man, whereas it is written (Ecclus. 6:34): "If thou wilt incline thy ear, thou shalt receive instruction." The other knowledge of truth is affective, and this is directly hindered by pride, because the proud, through delighting in their own excellence, disdain the excellence of truth; thus Gregory says (Moral. xxiii, 17) that "the proud, although certain hidden truths be conveyed to their understanding, cannot realize their sweetness: and if they know of them they cannot relish them." Hence it is written (Prov. 11:2): "Where humility is there also is wisdom."

Reply to Objection 2: As stated above ([3608]Q[161], AA[2], 6), humility observes the rule of right reason whereby a man has true self-esteem. Now pride does not observe this rule of right reason, for he esteems himself greater than he is: and this is the outcome of an inordinate desire for his own excellence, since a man is ready to believe what he desires very much, the result being that his appetite is borne towards things higher than what become him. Consequently whatsoever things lead a man to inordinate self-esteem lead him to pride: and one of those is the observing of other people's failings, just as, on the other hand, in the words of Gregory (Moral. xxiii, 17), "holy men, by a like observation of other people's virtues, set others above themselves." Accordingly the conclusion is not that pride is in the rational faculty, but that one of its causes is in the reason.

Reply to Objection 3: Pride is in the irascible, not only as a part of the sensitive appetite, but also as having a more general signification, as stated above.

Reply to Objection 4: According to Augustine (De Civ. Dei xiv, 7,9), "love precedes all other emotions of the soul, and is their cause," wherefore it may be employed to denote any of the other emotions. It is in this sense that pride is said to be "love of one's own excellence," inasmuch as love makes a man presume inordinately on his superiority over others, and this belongs properly to pride.

Whether the four species of pride are fittingly assigned by Gregory?

Objection 1: It seems that the four species of pride are unfittingly assigned by Gregory, who says (Moral. xxiii, 6): "There are four marks by which every kind of pride of the arrogant betrays itself; either when they think that their good is from themselves, or if they believe it to be from above, yet they think that it is due to their own merits; or when they boast of having what they have not, or despise others and wish to appear the exclusive possessors of what they have." For pride is a vice distinct from unbelief, just as humility is a distinct virtue from faith. Now it pertains to unbelief, if a man deem that he has not received his good from God, or that he has the good of grace through his own merits. Therefore this should not be reckoned a species of pride.

Objection 2: Further, the same thing should not be reckoned a species of different genera. Now boasting is reckoned a species of lying, as stated above ([3609]Q[110], A[2];[3610] Q[112]). Therefore it should not be accounted a species of pride.

Objection 3: Further, some other things apparently pertain to pride, which are not mentioned here. For Jerome [*Reference unknown] says that "nothing is so indicative of pride as to show oneself ungrateful": and Augustine says (De Civ. Dei xiv, 14) that "it belongs to pride to excuse oneself of a sin one has committed." Again, presumption whereby one aims at having what is above one, would seem to have much to do with pride. Therefore the aforesaid division does not sufficiently account for the different species of pride.

Objection 4: Further, we find other divisions of pride. For Anselm [*Eadmer, De Similit. xxii, seqq.] divides the uplifting of pride, saying that there is "pride of will, pride of speech, end pride of deed." Bernard [*De Grad. Humil. et Superb. x, seqq.] also reckons twelve degrees of pride, namely "curiosity, frivolity of mind, senseless mirth, boasting, singularity, arrogance, presumption, defense of one's sins, deceitful confession, rebelliousness, license, sinful habit." Now these apparently are not comprised under the species mentioned by Gregory. Therefore the latter would seem to be assigned unfittingly.

On the contrary, The authority of Gregory suffices.

I answer that, As stated above ([3611]AA[1],2,3), pride denotes immoderate desire of one's own excellence, a desire, to wit, that is not in accord with right reason. Now it must be observed that all excellence results from a good possessed. Such a good may be considered in three ways. First, in itself. For it is evident that the greater the good that one has, the greater the excellence that one derives from it. Hence when a man ascribes to himself a good greater than what he has, it follows that his appetite tends to his own excellence in a measure exceeding his competency: and thus we have the third species of pride, namely "boasting of having what one has not."

Secondly, it may be considered with regard to its cause, in so far as to have a thing of oneself is more excellent than to have it of another. Hence when a man esteems the good he has received of another as though he had it of himself, the result is that his appetite is borne towards his own excellence immoderately. Now one is cause of one's own good in two ways, efficiently and meritoriously: and thus we have the first two species of pride, namely "when a man thinks he has from himself that which he has from God," or "when he believes that which he has received from above to be due to his own merits."

Thirdly, it may be considered with regard to the manner of having it, in so far as a man obtains greater excellence through possessing some good more excellently than other men; the result again being that his appetite is borne inordinately towards his own excellence: and thus we have the fourth species of pride, which is "when a man despises others and wishes to be singularly conspicuous."

Reply to Objection 1: A true judgment may be destroyed in two ways. First, universally: and thus in matters of faith, a true judgment is destroyed by unbelief. Secondly, in some particular matter of choice, and unbelief does not do this. Thus a man who commits fornication, judges that for the time being it is good for him to commit fornication; yet he is not an unbeliever, as he would be, were he to say that universally fornication is good. It is thus in the question in point: for it pertains to unbelief to assert universally that there is a good which is not from God, or that grace is given to men for their merits, whereas, properly speaking, it belongs to pride and not to unbelief, through inordinate desire of one's own excellence, to boast of one's goods as though one had them of oneself, or of one's own merits.

Reply to Objection 2: Boasting is reckoned a species of lying, as regards the outward act whereby a man falsely ascribes to himself what he has not: but as regards the inward arrogance of the heart it is reckoned by Gregory to be a species of pride.

Reply to Objection 3: The ungrateful man ascribes to himself what he has from another: wherefore the first two species of pride pertain to ingratitude. To excuse oneself of a sin one has committed, belongs to the third species, since by so doing a man ascribes to himself the good of innocence which he has not. To aim presumptuously at what is above one, would seem to belong chiefly to the fourth species, which consists in wishing to be preferred to others.

Reply to Objection 4: The three mentioned by Anselm correspond to the progress of any particular sin: for it begins by being conceived in thought, then is uttered in word, and thirdly is accomplished in deed.

The twelve degrees mentioned by Bernard are reckoned by way of opposition to the twelve degrees of humility, of which we have spoken above ([3612]Q[161], A[6]). For the first degree of humility is to "be humble in heart, and to show it in one's very person, one's eyes fixed on the ground": and to this is opposed "curiosity," which consists in looking around in all directions curiously and inordinately. The second degree of humility is "to speak few and sensible words, and not to be loud of voice": to this is opposed "frivolity of mind," by which a man is proud of speech. The third degree of humility is "not to be easily moved and disposed to laughter," to which is opposed "senseless mirth." The fourth degree of humility is "to maintain silence until one is asked," to which is opposed "boasting." The fifth degree of humility is "to do nothing but to what one is exhorted by the common rule of the monastery," to which is opposed "singularity," whereby a man wishes to seem more holy than others. The sixth degree of humility is "to believe and acknowledge oneself viler than all," to which is opposed "arrogance," whereby a man sets himself above others. The seventh degree of humility is "to think oneself worthless and unprofitable for all purposes," to which is opposed "presumption," whereby a man thinks himself capable of things that are above him. The eighth degree of humility is "to confess one's sins," to which is opposed "defense of one's sins." The ninth degree is "to embrace patience by obeying under difficult and contrary circumstances," to which is opposed "deceitful confession," whereby a man being unwilling to be punished for his sins confesses them deceitfully. The tenth degree of humility is "obedience," to which is opposed "rebelliousness." The eleventh degree of humility is "not to delight in fulfilling one's own desires"; to this is opposed "license," whereby a man delights in doing freely whatever he will. The last degree of humility is "fear of God": to this is opposed "the habit of sinning," which implies contempt of God.

In these twelve degrees not only are the species of pride indicated, but also certain things that precede and follow them, as we have stated above with regard to humility ([3613]Q[161], A[6]).

Whether pride is a mortal sin?

Objection 1: It would seem that pride is not a mortal sin. For a gloss on Ps. 7:4, "O Lord my God, if I have done this thing," says: "Namely, the universal sin which is pride." Therefore if pride were a mortal sin, so would every sin be.

Objection 2: Further, every mortal sin is contrary to charity. But pride is apparently not contrary to charity, neither as to the love of God, nor as to the love of one's neighbor, because the excellence which, by pride, one desires inordinately, is not always opposed to God's honor, or our neighbor's good. Therefore pride is not a mortal sin.

Objection 3: Further, every mortal sin is opposed to virtue. But pride is not opposed to virtue; on the contrary, it arises therefrom, for as Gregory says (Moral. xxxiv, 23), "sometimes a man is elated by sublime and heavenly virtues." Therefore pride is not a mortal sin.

On the contrary, Gregory says (Moral. xxxiv, 23) that "pride is a most evident sign of the reprobate, and contrariwise, humility of the elect." But men do not become reprobate on account of venial sins. Therefore pride is not a venial but a mortal sin.

I answer that, Pride is opposed to humility. Now humility properly regards the subjection of man to God, as stated above ([3614]Q[161], A[1], ad 5). Hence pride properly regards lack of this subjection, in so far as a man raises himself above that which is appointed to him according to the Divine rule or measure, against the saying of the Apostle (2 Cor. 10:13), "But we will not glory beyond our measure; but according to the measure of the rule which God hath measured to us." Wherefore it is written (Ecclus. 10:14): "The beginning of the pride of man is to fall off from God" because, to wit, the root of pride is found to consist in man not being, in some way, subject to God and His rule. Now it is evident that not to be subject to God is of its very nature a mortal sin, for this consists in turning away from God: and consequently pride is, of its genus, a mortal sin. Nevertheless just as in other sins which are mortal by their genus (for instance fornication and adultery) there are certain motions that are venial by reason of their imperfection (through forestalling the judgment of reason, and being without its consent), so too in the matter of pride it happens that certain motions of pride are venial sins, when reason does not consent to them.

Reply to Objection 1: As stated above [3615](A[2]) pride is a general sin, not by its essence but by a kind of influence, in so far as all sins may have their origin in pride. Hence it does not follow that all sins are mortal, but only such as arise from perfect pride, which we have stated to be a mortal sin.

Reply to Objection 2: Pride is always contrary to the love of God, inasmuch as the proud man does not subject himself to the Divine rule as he ought. Sometimes it is also contrary to the love of our neighbor; when, namely, a man sets himself inordinately above his neighbor: and this again is a transgression of the Divine rule, which has established order among men, so that one ought to be subject to another.

Reply to Objection 3: Pride arises from virtue, not as from its direct cause, but as from an accidental cause, in so far as a man makes a virtue an occasion for pride. And nothing prevents one contrary from being the accidental cause of another, as stated in Phys. viii, 1. Hence some are even proud of their humility.

Whether pride is the most grievous of sins?

Objection 1: It would seem that pride is not the most grievous of sins. For the more difficult a sin is to avoid, the less grievous it would seem to be. Now pride is most difficult to avoid; for Augustine says in his Rule (Ep. ccxi), "Other sins find their vent in the accomplishment of evil deeds, whereas pride lies in wait for good deeds to destroy them." Therefore pride is not the most grievous of sins.

Objection 2: Further, "The greater evil is opposed to the greater good," as the Philosopher asserts (Ethic. viii, 10). Now humility to which pride is opposed is not the greatest of virtues, as stated above (Q[61], A[5]). Therefore the vices that are opposed to greater virtues, such as unbelief, despair, hatred of God, murder, and so forth, are more grievous sins than pride.

Objection 3: Further, the greater evil is not punished by a lesser evil. But pride is sometimes punished by other sins according to Rom. 1:28, where it is stated that on account of their pride of heart, men of science were delivered "to a reprobate sense, to do those things which are not convenient." Therefore pride is not the most grievous of sins.

On the contrary, A gloss on Ps. 118:51, "The proud did iniquitously," says: "The greatest sin in man is pride."

I answer that, Two things are to be observed in sin, conversion to a mutable good, and this is the material part of sin; and aversion from the immutable good, and this gives sin its formal aspect and complement. Now on the part of the conversion, there is no reason for pride being the greatest of sins, because uplifting which pride covets inordinately, is not essentially most incompatible with the good of virtue. But on the part of the aversion, pride has extreme gravity, because in other sins man turns away from God, either through ignorance or through weakness, or through desire for any other good whatever; whereas pride denotes aversion from God simply through being unwilling to be subject to God and His rule. Hence Boethius [*Cf. Cassian, de Caenob. Inst. xii, 7] says that "while all vices flee from God, pride alone withstands God"; for which reason it is specially stated (James 4:6) that "God resisteth the proud." Wherefore aversion from God and His commandments, which is a consequence as it were in other sins, belongs to pride by its very nature, for its act is the contempt of God. And since that which belongs to a thing by its nature is always of greater weight than that which belongs to it through something else, it follows that pride is the most grievous of sins by its genus, because it exceeds in aversion which is the formal complement of sin.

Reply to Objection 1: A sin is difficult to avoid in two ways. First, on account of the violence of its onslaught; thus anger is violent in its onslaught on account of its impetuosity; and "still more difficult is it to resist concupiscence, on account of its connaturality," as stated in Ethic. ii, 3,9. A difficulty of this kind in avoiding sin diminishes the gravity of the sin; because a man sins the more grievously, according as he yields to a less impetuous temptation, as Augustine says (De Civ. Dei xiv, 12,15).

Secondly, it is difficult to avoid a sin, on account of its being hidden. In this way it is difficult to avoid pride, since it takes occasion even from good deeds, as stated (A[5], ad 3). Hence Augustine says pointedly that it "lies in wait for good deeds"; and it is written (Ps. 141:4): "In the way wherein I walked, the proud [*Cf. Ps. 139:6, 'The proud have hidden a net for me.'] [Vulg.: 'they'] have hidden a snare for me." Hence no very great gravity attaches to the movement of pride while creeping in secretly, and before it is discovered by the judgment of reason: but once discovered by reason, it is easily avoided, both by considering one's own infirmity, according to Ecclus. 10:9, "Why is earth and ashes proud?" and by considering God's greatness, according to Job 15:13, "Why doth thy spirit swell against God?" as well as by considering the imperfection of the goods on which man prides himself, according to Is. 40:6, "All flesh is grass, and all the glory thereof as the flower of the field"; and farther on (Is. 64:6), "all our justices" are become "like the rag of a menstruous woman."

Reply to Objection 2: Opposition between a vice and a virtue is inferred from the object, which is considered on the part of conversion. In this way pride has no claim to be the greatest of sins, as neither has humility to be the greatest of virtues. But it is the greatest on the part of aversion, since it brings greatness upon other sins. For unbelief, by the very fact of its arising out of proud contempt, is rendered more grievous than if it be the outcome of ignorance or weakness. The same applies to despair and the like.

Reply to Objection 3: Just as in syllogisms that lead to an impossible conclusion one is sometimes convinced by being faced with a more evident absurdity, so too, in order to overcome their pride, God punishes certain men by allowing them to fall into sins of the flesh, which though they be less grievous are more evidently shameful. Hence Isidore says (De Summo Bono ii, 38) that "pride is the worst of all vices; whether because it is appropriate to those who are of highest and foremost rank, or because it originates from just and virtuous deeds, so that its guilt is less perceptible. on the other hand, carnal lust is apparent to all, because from the outset it is of a shameful nature: and yet, under God's dispensation, it is less grievous than pride. For he who is in the clutches of pride and feels it not, falls into the lusts of the flesh, that being thus humbled he may rise from his abasement."

From this indeed the gravity of pride is made manifest. For just as a wise physician, in order to cure a worse disease, allows the patient to contract one that is less dangerous, so the sin of pride is shown to be more grievous by the very fact that, as a remedy, God allows men to fall into other sins.

Whether pride is the first sin of all?

Objection 1: It would seem that pride is not the first sin of all. For the first is maintained in all that follows. Now pride does not accompany all sins, nor is it the origin of all: for Augustine says (De Nat. et Grat. xx) that many things are done "amiss which are not done with pride." Therefore pride is not the first sin of all.

Objection 2: Further, it is written (Ecclus. 10:14) that the "beginning of . . . pride is to fall off from God." Therefore falling away from God precedes pride.

Objection 3: Further, the order of sins would seem to be according to the order of virtues. Now, not humility but faith is the first of all virtues. Therefore pride is not the first sin of all.

Objection 4: Further, it is written (2 Tim. 3:13): "Evil men and seducers shall grow worse and worse"; so that apparently man's beginning of wickedness is not the greatest of sins. But pride is the greatest of sins as stated in the foregoing Article. Therefore pride is not the first sin.

Objection 5: Further, resemblance and pretense come after the reality. Now the Philosopher says (Ethic. iii, 7) that "pride apes fortitude and daring." Therefore the vice of daring precedes the vice of pride.

On the contrary, It is written (Ecclus. 10:15): "Pride is the beginning of all sin."

I answer that, The first thing in every genus is that which is essential. Now it has been stated above [3616](A[6]) that aversion from God, which is the formal complement of sin, belongs to pride essentially, and to other sins, consequently. Hence it is that pride fulfils the conditions of a first thing, and is "the beginning of all sins," as stated above ([3617]FS, Q[84], A[2]), when we were treating of the causes of sin on the part of the aversion which is the chief part of sin.

Reply to Objection 1: Pride is said to be "the beginning of all sin," not as though every sin originated from pride, but because any kind of sin is naturally liable to arise from pride.

Reply to Objection 2: To fall off from God is said to be the beginning of pride, not as though it were a distinct sin from pride, but as being the first part of pride. For it has been said above [3618](A[5]) that pride regards chiefly subjection to God which it scorns, and in consequence it scorns to be subject to a creature for God's sake.

Reply to Objection 3: There is no need for the order of virtues to be the same as that of vices. For vice is corruptive of virtue. Now that which is first to be generated is the last to be corrupted. Wherefore as faith is the first of virtues, so unbelief is the last of sins, to which sometimes man is led by other sins. Hence a gloss on Ps. 136:7, "Rase it, rase it, even to the foundation thereof," says that "by heaping vice upon vice a man will lapse into unbelief," and the Apostle says (1 Tim. 1:19) that "some rejecting a good conscience have made shipwreck concerning the faith."

Reply to Objection 4: Pride is said to be the most grievous of sins because that which gives sin its gravity is essential to pride. Hence pride is the cause of gravity in other sins. Accordingly previous to pride there may be certain less grievous sins that are committed through ignorance or weakness. But among the grievous sins the first is pride, as the cause whereby other sins are rendered more grievous. And as that which is the first in causing sins is the last in the withdrawal from sin, a gloss on Ps. 18:13, "I shall be cleansed from the greatest sin," says: "Namely from the sin of pride, which is the last in those who return to God, and the first in those who withdraw from God."

Reply to Objection 5: The Philosopher associates pride with feigned fortitude, not that it consists precisely in this, but because man thinks he is more likely to be uplifted before men, if he seem to be daring or brave.

Whether pride should be reckoned a capital vice?

Objection 1: It would seem that pride should be reckoned a capital vice, since Isidore [*Comment. in Deut. xvi] and Cassian [*De Inst. Caenob. v, 1: Collat. v, 2] number pride among the capital vices.

Objection 2: Further, pride is apparently the same as vainglory, since both covet excellence. Now vainglory is reckoned a capital vice. Therefore pride also should be reckoned a capital vice.

Objection 3: Further, Augustine says (De Virginit. xxxi) that "pride begets envy, nor is it ever without this companion." Now envy is reckoned a capital vice, as stated above ([3619]Q[36], A[4]). Much more therefore is pride a capital vice.

On the contrary, Gregory (Moral. xxxi, 45) does not include pride among the capital vices.

I answer that, As stated above ([3620]AA[2],5, ad 1) pride may be considered in two ways; first in itself, as being a special sin; secondly, as having a general influence towards all sins. Now the capital vices are said to be certain special sins from which many kinds of sin arise. Wherefore some, considering pride in the light of a special sin, numbered it together with the other capital vices. But Gregory, taking into consideration its general influence towards all vices, as explained above (A[2], OBJ[3]), did not place it among the capital vices, but held it to be the "queen and mother of all the vices." Hence he says (Moral. xxxi, 45): "Pride, the queen of vices, when it has vanquished and captured the heart, forthwith delivers it into the hands of its lieutenants the seven principal vices, that they may despoil it and produce vices of all kinds."

This suffices for the Reply to the First Objection.

Reply to Objection 2: Pride is not the same as vainglory, but is the cause thereof: for pride covets excellence inordinately: while vainglory covets the outward show of excellence.

Reply to Objection 3: The fact that envy, which is a capital vice, arises from pride, does not prove that pride is a capital vice, but that it is still more principal than the capital vices themselves.

OF THE FIRST MAN'S SIN (FOUR ARTICLES)

We must now consider the first man's sin which was pride: and (1) his sin; (2) its punishment; (3) the temptation whereby he was led to sin.

Under the first head there are four points of inquiry:

(1) Whether pride was the first man's first sin?

(2) What the first man coveted by sinning?

(3) Whether his sin was more grievous than all other sins?

(4) Which sinned more grievously, the man or the woman?

Whether pride was the first man's first sin?

Objection 1: It would seem that pride was not the first man's first sin. For the Apostle says (Rom. 5:19) that "by the disobedience of one man many were made sinners." Now the first man's first sin is the one by which all men were made sinners in the point of original sin. Therefore disobedience, and not pride, was the first man's first sin.

Objection 2: Further, Ambrose says, commenting on Lk. 4:3, "And the devil said to Him," that the devil in tempting Christ observed the same order as in overcoming the first man. Now Christ was first tempted to gluttony, as appears from Mat. 4:3, where it was said to Him: "If thou be the Son of God, command that these stones be made bread." Therefore the first man's first sin was not pride but gluttony.

Objection 3: Further, man sinned at the devil's suggestion. Now the devil in tempting man promised him knowledge (Gn. 3:5). Therefore inordinateness in man was through the desire of knowledge, which pertains to curiosity. Therefore curiosity, and not pride, was the first sin.

Objection 4: Further, a gloss [*St. Augustine, Gen. ad lit. xi] on 1 Tim. 2:14, "The woman being seduced was in the transgression," says: "The Apostle rightly calls this seduction, for they were persuaded to accept a falsehood as being true; namely that God had forbidden them to touch that tree, because He knew that if they touched it, they would be like gods, as though He who made them men, begrudged them the godhead . . ." Now it pertains to unbelief to believe such a thing. Therefore man's first sin was unbelief and not pride.

On the contrary, It is written (Ecclus. 10:15): "Pride is the beginning of all sin." Now man's first sin is the beginning of all sin, according to Rom. 5:12, "By one man sin entered into this world." Therefore man's first sin was pride.

I answer that, Many movements may concur towards one sin, and the character of sin attaches to that one in which inordinateness is first found. And it is evident that inordinateness is in the inward movement of the soul before being in the outward act of the body; since, as Augustine says (De Civ. Dei i, 18), the sanctity of the body is not forfeited so long as the sanctity of the soul remains. Also, among the inward movements, the appetite is moved towards the end before being moved towards that which is desired for the sake of the end; and consequently man's first sin was where it was possible for his appetite to be directed to an inordinate end. Now man was so appointed in the state of innocence, that there was no rebellion of the flesh against the spirit. Wherefore it was not possible for the first inordinateness in the human appetite to result from his coveting a sensible good, to which the concupiscence of the flesh tends against the order of reason. It remains therefore that the first inordinateness of the human appetite resulted from his coveting inordinately some spiritual good. Now he would not have coveted it inordinately, by desiring it according to his measure as established by the Divine rule. Hence it follows that man's first sin consisted in his coveting some spiritual good above his measure: and this pertains to pride. Therefore it is evident that man's first sin was pride.

Reply to Objection 1: Man's disobedience to the Divine command was not willed by man for his own sake, for this could not happen unless one presuppose inordinateness in his will. It remains therefore that he willed it for the sake of something else. Now the first thing he coveted inordinately was his own excellence; and consequently his disobedience was the result of his pride. This agrees with the statement of Augustine, who says (Ad Oros [*Dial. QQ. lxv, qu. 4]) that "man puffed up with pride obeyed the serpent's prompting, and scorned God's commands."

Reply to Objection 2: Gluttony also had a place in the sin of our first parents. For it is written (Gn. 3:6): "The woman saw that the tree was good to eat, and fair to the eyes, and delightful to behold, and she took of the fruit thereof, and did eat." Yet the very goodness and beauty of the fruit was not their first motive for sinning, but the persuasive words of the serpent, who said (Gn. 3:5): "Your eyes shall be opened and you shall be as Gods": and it was by coveting this that the woman fell into pride. Hence the sin of gluttony resulted from the sin of pride.

Reply to Objection 3: The desire for knowledge resulted in our first parents from their inordinate desire for excellence. Hence the serpent began by saying: "You shall be as Gods," and added: "Knowing good and evil."

Reply to Objection 4: According to Augustine (Gen. ad lit. xi, 30), "the woman had not believed the serpent's statement that they were debarred by God from a good and useful thing, were her mind not already filled with the love of her own power, and a certain proud self-presumption." This does not mean that pride preceded the promptings of the serpent, but that as soon as the serpent had spoken his words of persuasion, her mind was puffed up, the result being that she believed the demon to have spoken truly.

Whether the first man's pride consisted in his coveting God's likeness?

Objection 1: It would seem that the first man's pride did not consist in his coveting the Divine likeness. For no one sins by coveting that which is competent to him according to his nature. Now God's likeness is competent to man according to his nature: for it is written (Gn. 1:26): "Let us make man to our image and likeness." Therefore he did not sin by coveting God's likeness.

Objection 2: Further, it would seem that man coveted God's likeness in order that he might obtain knowledge of good and evil: for this was the serpent's suggestion: "You shall be as Gods knowing good and evil." Now the desire of knowledge is natural to man, according to the saying of the Philosopher at the beginning of his Metaphysics i, 1: "All men naturally desire knowledge." Therefore he did not sin by coveting God's likeness.

Objection 3: Further, no wise man chooses the impossible. Now the first man was endowed with wisdom, according to Ecclus. 17:5, "He filled them with the knowledge of understanding." Since then every sin consists in a deliberate act of the appetite, namely choice, it would seem that the first man did not sin by coveting something impossible. But it is impossible for man to be like God, according to the saying of Ex. 15:11, "Who is like to Thee among the strong, O Lord?" Therefore the first man did not sin by coveting God's likeness.

On the contrary, Augustine commenting on Ps. 68:5 [*Enarr. in Ps. 68], "Then did I restore [Douay: 'pay'] that which I took not away," says: "Adam and Eve wished to rob the Godhead and they lost happiness."

I answer that, likeness is twofold. One is a likeness of absolute equality [*Cf. [3621]FP, Q[93], A[1]]: and such a likeness to God our first parents did not covet, since such a likeness to God is not conceivable to the mind, especially of a wise man.

The other is a likeness of imitation, such as is possible for a creature in reference to God, in so far as the creature participates somewhat of God's likeness according to its measure. For Dionysius says (Div. Nom. ix): "The same things are like and unlike to God; like, according as they imitate Him, as far as He can be imitated; unlike, according as an effect falls short of its cause." Now every good existing in a creature is a participated likeness of the first good.

Wherefore from the very fact that man coveted a spiritual good above his measure, as stated in the foregoing Article, it follows that he coveted God's likeness inordinately.

It must, however, be observed that the proper object of the appetite is a thing not possessed. Now spiritual good, in so far as the rational creature participates in the Divine likeness, may be considered in reference to three things. First, as to natural being: and this likeness was imprinted from the very outset of their creation, both on man—of whom it is written (Gn. 1:26) that God made man "to His image and likeness"—and on the angel, of whom it is written (Ezech. 28:12): "Thou wast the seal of resemblance." Secondly, as to knowledge: and this likeness was bestowed on the angel at his creation, wherefore immediately after the words just quoted, "Thou wast the seal of resemblance," we read: "Full of wisdom." But the first man, at his creation, had not yet received this likeness actually but only in potentiality. Thirdly, as to the power of operation: and neither angel nor man received this likeness actually at the very outset of his creation, because to each there remained something to be done whereby to obtain happiness.

Accordingly, while both (namely the devil and the first man) coveted God's likeness inordinately, neither of them sinned by coveting a likeness of nature. But the first man sinned chiefly by coveting God's likeness as regards "knowledge of good and evil," according to the serpent's instigation, namely that by his own natural power he might decide what was good, and what was evil for him to do; or again that he should of himself foreknow what good and what evil would befall him. Secondarily he sinned by coveting God's likeness as regards his own power of operation, namely that by his own natural power he might act so as to obtain happiness. Hence Augustine says (Gen. ad lit. xi, 30) that "the woman's mind was filled with love of her own power." On the other hand, the devil sinned by coveting God's likeness, as regards power. Wherefore Augustine says (De Vera Relig. 13) that "he wished to enjoy his own power rather than God's." Nevertheless both coveted somewhat to be equal to God, in so far as each wished to rely on himself in contempt of the order of the Divine rule.

Reply to Objection 1: This argument considers the likeness of nature: and man did not sin by coveting this, as stated.

Reply to Objection 2: It is not a sin to covet God's likeness as to knowledge, absolutely; but to covet this likeness inordinately, that is, above one's measure, this is a sin. Hence Augustine commenting on Ps. 70:18, "O God, who is like Thee?" says: "He who desires to be of himself, even as God is of no one, wishes wickedly to be like God. Thus did the devil, who was unwilling to be subject to Him, and man who refused to be, as a servant, bound by His command."

Reply to Objection 3: This argument considers the likeness of equality.

Whether the sin of our first parents was more grievous than other sins?

Objection 1: It would seem that the sin of our first parents was more grievous than other sins. For Augustine says (De Civ. Dei xiv, 15): "Great was the wickedness in sinning, when it was so easy to avoid sin." Now it was very easy for our first parents to avoid sin, because they had nothing within them urging them to sin. Therefore the sin of our first parents was more grievous than other sins.

Objection 2: Further, punishment is proportionate to guilt. Now the sin of our first parents was most severely punished, since by it "death entered into this world," as the Apostle says (Rom. 5:12). Therefore that sin was more grievous than other sins.

Objection 3: Further, the first in every genus is seemingly the greatest (Metaph. ii, 4 [*Ed. Diel. i, 1]). Now the sin of our first parents was the first among sins of men. Therefore it was the greatest.

On the contrary, Origen says [*Peri Archon i, 3]: "I think that a man who stands on the highest step of perfection cannot fail or fall suddenly: this can happen only by degrees and little by little." Now our first parents were established on the highest and perfect grade. Therefore their first sin was not the greatest of all sins.

I answer that, There is a twofold gravity to be observed in sin. one results from the very species of the sin: thus we say that adultery is a graver sin than simple fornication. The other gravity of sin results from some circumstance of place, person, or time. The former gravity is more essential to sin and is of greater moment: hence a sin is said to be grave in respect of this gravity rather than of the other. Accordingly we must say that the first man's sin was not graver than all other sins of men, as regards the species of the sin. For though pride, of its genus, has a certain preeminence over other sins, yet the pride whereby one denies or blasphemes God is greater than the pride whereby one covets God's likeness inordinately, such as the pride of our first parents, as stated [3622](A[2]).

But if we consider the circumstances of the persons who sinned, that sin was most grave on account of the perfection of their state. We must accordingly conclude that this sin was most grievous relatively but not simply.

Reply to Objection 1: This argument considers the gravity of sin as resulting from the person of the sinner.

Reply to Objection 2: The severity of the punishment awarded to that first sin corresponds to the magnitude of the sin, not as regards its species but as regards its being the first sin: because it destroyed the innocence of our original state, and by robbing it of innocence brought disorder upon the whole human nature.

Reply to Objection 3: Where things are directly subordinate, the first must needs be the greatest. Such is not the order among sins, for one follows from another accidentally. And thus it does not follow that the first sin is the greatest.

Whether Adam's sin was more grievous than Eve's?

Objection 1: It would seem that Adam's sin was more grievous than Eve's. For it is written (1 Tim. 2:14): "Adam was not seduced, but the woman being seduced was in the transgression": and so it would seem that the woman sinned through ignorance, but the man through assured knowledge. Now the latter is the graver sin, according to Lk. 12:47,48, "That servant who knew the will of his lord . . . and did not according to his will, shall be beaten with many stripes: but he that knew not, and did things worthy of stripes, shall be beaten with few stripes." Therefore Adam's sin was more grievous than Eve's.

Objection 2: Further, Augustine says (De Decem Chordis 3 [*Serm. ix; xcvi de Temp.]): "If the man is the head, he should live better, and give an example of good deeds to his wife, that she may imitate him." Now he who ought to do better, sins more grievously, if he commit a sin. Therefore Adam sinned more grievously than Eve.

Objection 3: Further, the sin against the Holy Ghost would seem to be the most grievous. Now Adam, apparently, sinned against the Holy Ghost, because while sinning he relied on God's mercy [*Cf.[3623] Q[21], A[2], OBJ[3]. St. Thomas is evidently alluding to the words of Peter Lombard quoted there], and this pertains to the sin of presumption. Therefore it seems that Adam sinned more grievously than Eve.

On the contrary, Punishment corresponds to guilt. Now the woman was more grievously punished than the man, as appears from Gn. 3. Therefore she sinned more grievously than the man.

I answer that, As stated [3624](A[3]), the gravity of a sin depends on the species rather than on a circumstance of that sin. Accordingly we must assert that, if we consider the condition attaching to these persons, the man's sin is the more grievous, because he was more perfect than the woman.

As regards the genus itself of the sin, the sin of each is considered to be equal, for each sinned by pride. Hence Augustine says (Gen. ad lit. xi, 35): "Eve in excusing herself betrays disparity of sex, though parity of pride."

But as regards the species of pride, the woman sinned more grievously, for three reasons. First, because she was more puffed up than the man. For the woman believed in the serpent's persuasive words, namely that God had forbidden them to eat of the tree, lest they should become like to Him; so that in wishing to attain to God's likeness by eating of the forbidden fruit, her pride rose to the height of desiring to obtain something against God's will. On the other hand, the man did not believe this to be true; wherefore he did not wish to attain to God's likeness against God's will: but his pride consisted in wishing to attain thereto by his own power. Secondly, the woman not only herself sinned, but suggested sin to the man; wherefore she sinned against both God and her neighbor. Thirdly, the man's sin was diminished by the fact that, as Augustine says (Gen. ad lit. xi, 42), "he consented to the sin out of a certain friendly good-will, on account of which a man sometimes will offend God rather than make an enemy of his friend. That he ought not to have done so is shown by the just issue of the Divine sentence."

It is therefore evident that the woman's sin was more grievous than the man's.

Reply to Objection 1: The woman was deceived because she was first of all puffed up with pride. Wherefore her ignorance did not excuse, but aggravated her sin, in so far as it was the cause of her being puffed up with still greater pride.

Reply to Objection 2: This argument considers the circumstance of personal condition, on account of which the man's sin was more grievous than the woman's.

Reply to Objection 3: The man's reliance on God's mercy did not reach to contempt of God's justice, wherein consists the sin against the Holy Ghost, but as Augustine says (Gen. ad lit. xi [*De Civ. Dei xiv, 11]), it was due to the fact that, "having had no experience of God's severity, he thought the sin to be venial," i.e. easily forgiven [*Cf. [3625]FS, Q[89], A[3], ad 1].

OF THE PUNISHMENTS OF THE FIRST MAN'S SIN (TWO ARTICLES)

We must now consider the punishments of the first sin; and under this head there are two points of inquiry: (1) Death, which is the common punishment; (2) the other particular punishments mentioned in Genesis.

Whether death is the punishment of our first parents' sin?

Objection 1: It would seem that death is not the punishment of our first parents' sin. For that which is natural to man cannot be called a punishment of sin, because sin does not perfect nature but vitiates it. Now death is natural to man: and this is evident both from the fact that his body is composed of contraries, and because "mortal" is included in the definition of man. Therefore death is not a punishment of our first parents' sin.

Objection 2: Further, death and other bodily defects are similarly found in man as well as in other animals, according to Eccles. 3:19, "The death of man and of beasts is one, and the condition of them both equal." But in dumb animals death is not a punishment of sin. Therefore neither is it so in men.

Objection 3: Further, the sin of our first parents was the sin of particular individuals: whereas death affects the entire human nature. Therefore it would seem that it is not a punishment of our first parents' sin.

Objection 4: Further, all are equally descended from our first parents. Therefore if death were the punishment of our first parents' sin, it would follow that all men would suffer death in equal measure. But this is clearly untrue, since some die sooner, and some more painfully, than others. Therefore death is not the punishment of the first sin.

Objection 5: Further, the evil of punishment is from God, as stated above ([3626]FP, Q[48], A[6]; [3627]FP, Q[49], A[2]). But death, apparently, is not from God: for it is written (Wis. 1:13): "God made not death." Therefore death is not the punishment of the first sin.

Objection 6: Further, seemingly, punishments are not meritorious, since merit is comprised under good, and punishment under evil. Now death is sometimes meritorious, as in the case of a martyr's death. Therefore it would seem that death is not a punishment.

Objection 7: Further, punishment would seem to be painful. But death apparently cannot be painful, since man does not feel it when he is dead, and he cannot feel it when he is not dying. Therefore death is not a punishment of sin.

Objection 8: Further, if death were a punishment of sin, it would have followed sin immediately. But this is not true, for our first parents lived a long time after their sin (Gn. 5:5). Therefore, seemingly, death is not a punishment of sin.

On the contrary, The Apostle says (Rom. 5:12): "By one man sin entered into this world, and by sin death."

I answer that, If any one, on account of his fault, be deprived of a favor bestowed on him the privation of that favor is a punishment of that fault. Now as we stated in the [3628]FP, Q[95], A[1]; [3629]FP, Q[97], A[1], God bestowed this favor on man, in his primitive state, that as long as his mind was subject to God, the lower powers of his soul would be subject to his rational mind, and his body to his soul. But inasmuch as through sin man's mind withdrew from subjection to God, the result was that neither were his lower powers wholly subject to his reason, whence there followed so great a rebellion of the carnal appetite against the reason: nor was the body wholly subject to the soul; whence arose death and other bodily defects. For life and soundness of body depend on the body being subject to the soul, as the perfectible is subject to its perfection. Consequently, on the other hand, death, sickness, and all defects of the body are due to the lack of the body's subjection to the soul.

It is therefore evident that as the rebellion of the carnal appetite against the spirit is a punishment of our first parents' sin, so also are death and all defects of the body.

Reply to Objection 1: A thing is said to be natural if it proceeds from the principles of nature. Now the essential principles of nature are form and matter. The form of man is his rational soul, which is, of itself, immortal: wherefore death is not natural to man on the part of his form. The matter of man is a body such as is composed of contraries, of which corruptibility is a necessary consequence, and in this respect death is natural to man. Now this condition attached to the nature of the human body results from a natural necessity, since it was necessary for the human body to be the organ of touch, and consequently a mean between objects of touch: and this was impossible, were it not composed of contraries, as the Philosopher states (De Anima ii, 11). On the other hand, this condition is not attached to the adaptability of matter to form because, if it were possible, since the form is incorruptible, its matter should rather be incorruptible. In the same way a saw needs to be of iron, this being suitable to its form and action, so that its hardness may make it fit for cutting. But that it be liable to rust is a necessary result of such a matter and is not according to the agent's choice; for, if the craftsman were able, of the iron he would make a saw that would not rust. Now God Who is the author of man is all-powerful, wherefore when He first made man, He conferred on him the favor of being exempt from the necessity resulting from such a matter: which favor, however, was withdrawn through the sin of our first parents. Accordingly death is both natural on account of a condition attaching to matter, and penal on account of the loss of the Divine favor preserving man from death [*Cf. [3630]FS, Q[85], A[6]].

Reply to Objection 2: This likeness of man to other animals regards a condition attaching to matter, namely the body being composed of contraries. But it does not regard the form, for man's soul is immortal, whereas the souls of dumb animals are mortal.

Reply to Objection 3: Our first parents were made by God not only as particular individuals, but also as principles of the whole human nature to be transmitted by them to their posterity, together with the Divine favor preserving them from death. Hence through their sin the entire human nature, being deprived of that favor in their posterity, incurred death.

Reply to Objection 4: A twofold defect arises from sin. One is by way of a punishment appointed by a judge: and such a defect should be equal in those to whom the sin pertains equally. The other defect is that which results accidentally from this punishment; for instance, that one who has been deprived of his sight for a sin he has committed, should fall down in the road. Such a defect is not proportionate to the sin, nor does a human judge take it into account, since he cannot foresee chance happenings. Accordingly, the punishment appointed for the first sin and proportionately corresponding thereto, was the withdrawal of the Divine favor whereby the rectitude and integrity of human nature was maintained. But the defects resulting from this withdrawal are death and other penalties of the present life. Wherefore these punishments need not be equal in those to whom the first sin equally appertains. Nevertheless, since God foreknows all future events, Divine providence has so disposed that these penalties are apportioned in different ways to various people. This is not on account of any merits or demerits previous to this life, as Origen held [*Peri Archon ii, 9]: for this is contrary to the words of Rom.

9:11, "When they . . . had not done any good or evil"; and also contrary to statements made in the [3631]FP, Q[90], A[4]; [3632]FP, Q[118], A[3], namely that the soul is not created before the body: but either in punishment of their parents' sins, inasmuch as the child is something belonging to the father, wherefore parents are often punished in their children; or again it is for a remedy intended for the spiritual welfare of the person who suffers these penalties, to wit that he may thus be turned away from his sins, or lest he take pride in his virtues, and that he may be crowned for his patience.

Reply to Objection 5: Death may be considered in two ways. First, as an evil of human nature, and thus it is not of God, but is a defect befalling man through his fault. Secondly, as having an aspect of good, namely as being a just punishment, and thus it is from God. Wherefore Augustine says (Retract. i, 21) that God is not the author of death, except in so far as it is a punishment.

Reply to Objection 6: As Augustine says (De Civ. Dei xiii, 5), "just as the wicked abuse not only evil but also good things, so do the righteous make good use not only of good but also of evil things. Hence it is that both evil men make evil use of the law, though the law is good, while good men die well, although death is an evil." Wherefore inasmuch as holy men make good use of death, their death is to them meritorious.

Reply to Objection 7: Death may be considered in two ways. First, as the privation of life, and thus death cannot be felt, since it is the privation of sense and life. In this way it involves not pain of sense but pain of loss. Secondly, it may be considered as denoting the corruption which ends in the aforesaid privation. Now we may speak of corruption even as of generation in two ways: in one way as being the term of alteration, and thus in the first instant in which life departs, death is said to be present. In this way also death has no pain of sense. In another way corruption may be taken as including the previous alteration: thus a person is said to die, when he is in motion towards death; just as a thing is said to be engendered, while in motion towards the state of having been engendered: and thus death may be painful.

Reply to Objection 8: According to Augustine (Gen. ad lit. [*De Pecc. Mer. et Rem. i, 16. Cf. Gen. ad lit. ii. 32]), "although our first parents lived thereafter many years, they began to die on the day when they heard the death-decree, condemning them to decline to old age."

Whether the particular punishments of our first parents are suitably appointed in Scripture?

Objection 1: It would seem that the particular punishments of our first parents are unsuitably appointed in Scripture. For that which would have occurred even without sin should not be described as a punishment for sin. Now seemingly there would have been "pain in child-bearing," even had there been no sin: for the disposition of the female sex is such that offspring cannot be born without pain to the bearer. Likewise the "subjection of woman to man" results from the perfection of the male, and the imperfection of the female sex. Again it belongs to the nature of the earth "to bring forth thorns and thistles," and this would have occurred even had there been no sin. Therefore these are unsuitable punishments of the first sin.

Objection 2: Further, that which pertains to a person's dignity does not, seemingly, pertain to his punishment. But the "multiplying of conceptions" pertains to a woman's dignity. Therefore it should not be described as the woman's punishment.

Objection 3: Further, the punishment of our first parents' sin is transmitted to all, as we have stated with regard to death [3633](A[1]). But all "women's conceptions" are not "multiplied," nor does "every man eat bread in the sweat of his face." Therefore these are not suitable punishments of the first sin.

Objection 4: Further, the place of paradise was made for man. Now nothing in the order of things should be without purpose. Therefore it would seem that the exclusion of man from paradise was not a suitable punishment of man.

Objection 5: Further, this place of the earthly paradise is said to be naturally inaccessible. Therefore it was useless to put other obstacles in the way lest man should return thither, to wit the cherubim, and the "flaming sword turning every way."

Objection 6: Further, immediately after his sin man was subject to the necessity of dying, so that he could not be restored to immortality by the beneficial tree of life. Therefore it was useless to forbid him to eat of the tree of life, as instanced by the words of Gn. 3:22: "See, lest perhaps he . . . take . . . of the tree of life . . . and live for ever."

Objection 7: Further, to mock the unhappy seems inconsistent with mercy and clemency, which are most of all ascribed to God in Scripture, according to Ps. 144:9, "His tender mercies are over all His works." Therefore God is unbecomingly described as mocking our first parents, already reduced through sin to unhappy straits, in the words of Gn. 3:22, "Behold Adam is become as one of Us, knowing good and evil."

Objection 8: Further, clothes are necessary to man, like food, according to 1 Tim. 6:8, "Having food, and wherewith to be covered, with these we are content." Therefore just as food was appointed to our first parents before their sin, so also should clothing have been ascribed to them. Therefore after their sin it was unsuitable to say that God made for them garments of skin.

Objection 9: Further, the punishment inflicted for a sin should outweigh in evil the gain realized through the sin: else the punishment would not deter one from sinning. Now through sin our first parents gained in this, that their eyes were opened, according to Gn. 3:7. But this outweighs in good all the penal evils which are stated to have resulted from sin. Therefore the punishments resulting from our first parents' sin are unsuitably described.

On the contrary, These punishments were appointed by God, Who does all things, "in number, weight, and measure [*Vulg.: 'Thou hast ordered all things in measure, and number, and weight.']" (Wis. 11:21).

I answer that, As stated in the foregoing Article, on account of their sin, our first parents were deprived of the Divine favor, whereby the integrity of human nature was maintained in them, and by the withdrawal of this favor human nature incurred penal defects. Hence they were punished in two ways. In the first place by being deprived of that which was befitting the state of integrity, namely the place of the earthly paradise: and this is indicated (Gn. 3:23) where it is stated that "God sent him out of the paradise of pleasure." And since he was unable, of himself, to return to that state of original innocence, it was fitting that obstacles should be placed against his recovering those things that were befitting his original state, namely food (lest he should take of the tree of life) and place; for "God placed before . . . paradise . . . Cherubim, and a flaming sword." Secondly, they were punished by having appointed to them things befitting a nature bereft of the aforesaid favor: and this as regards both the body and the soul. With regard to the body, to which pertains the distinction of sex, one punishment was appointed to the woman and another to the man. To the woman punishment was appointed in respect of two things on account of which she is united to the man; and these are the begetting of children, and community of works pertaining to family life. As regards the begetting of children, she was punished in two ways: first in the weariness to which she is subject while carrying the child after conception, and this is indicated in the words (Gn. 3:16), "I will multiply thy sorrows, and thy conceptions"; secondly, in the pain which she suffers in giving birth, and this is indicated by the words (Gn. 3:16), "In sorrow shalt thou bring forth." As regards family life she was punished by being subjected to her husband's authority, and this is conveyed in the words (Gn. 3:16), "Thou shalt be under thy husband's power."

Now, just as it belongs to the woman to be subject to her husband in matters relating to the family life, so it belongs to the husband to provide the necessaries of that life. In this respect he was punished in three ways. First, by the barrenness of the earth, in the words (Gn. 3:17), "Cursed is the earth in thy work." Secondly, by the cares of his toil, without which he does not win the fruits of the earth; hence the words (Gn. 3:17), "With labor and toil shalt thou eat thereof all the days of thy life." Thirdly, by the obstacles encountered by the tillers of the soil, wherefore it is written (Gn. 3:18), "Thorns and thistles shall it bring forth to thee."

Likewise a triple punishment is ascribed to them on the part of the soul. First, by reason of the confusion they experienced at the rebellion of the flesh against the spirit; hence it is written (Gn. 3:7): "The eyes of them both were opened; and . . . they perceived themselves to be naked." Secondly, by the reproach for their sin, indicated by the words (Gn. 3:22), "Behold Adam is become as one of Us." Thirdly, by the reminder of their coming death, when it was said to him (Gn. 3:19): "Dust thou art and into dust thou shalt return." To this also pertains that God made them garments of skin, as a sign of their mortality.

Reply to Objection 1: In the state of innocence child-bearing would have been painless: for Augustine says (De Civ. Dei xiv, 26): "Just as, in giving birth, the mother would then be relieved not by groans of pain, but by the instigations of maturity, so in bearing and conceiving the union of both sexes would be one not of lustful desire but of deliberate action" [*Cf. [3634]FP, Q[98], A[2]].

The subjection of the woman to her husband is to be understood as inflicted in punishment of the woman, not as to his headship (since even before sin the man was the "head" and governor "of the woman"), but as to her having now to obey her husband's will even against her own.

If man had not sinned, the earth would have brought forth thorns and thistles to be the food of animals, but not to punish man, because their growth would bring no labor or punishment for the tiller of the soil, as Augustine says (Gen. ad lit. iii, 18). Alcuin [*Interrog. et Resp. in Gen. lxxix], however, holds that, before sin, the earth brought forth no thorns and thistles, whatever: but the former opinion is the better.

Reply to Objection 2: The multiplying of her conceptions was appointed as a punishment to the woman, not on account of the begetting of children, for this would have been the same even before sin, but on account of the numerous sufferings to which the woman is subject, through carrying her offspring after conception. Hence it is expressly stated: "I will multiply thy sorrows, and thy conceptions."

Reply to Objection 3: These punishments affect all somewhat. For any woman who conceives must needs suffer sorrows and bring forth her child with pain: except the Blessed Virgin, who "conceived without corruption, and bore without pain" [*St. Bernard, Serm. in Dom. inf. oct. Assum. B. V. M.], because her conceiving was not according to the law of nature, transmitted from our first parents. And if a woman neither conceives nor bears, she suffers from the defect of barrenness, which outweighs the aforesaid punishments. Likewise whoever tills the soil must needs eat his bread in the sweat of his brow: while those who do not themselves work on the land, are busied with other labors, for "man is born to labor" (Job 5:7): and thus they eat the bread for which others have labored in the sweat of their brow.

Reply to Objection 4: Although the place of the earthly paradise avails not man for his use, it avails him for a lesson; because he knows himself deprived of that place on account of sin, and because by the things that have a bodily existence in that paradise, he is instructed in things pertaining to the heavenly paradise, the way to which is prepared for man by Christ.

Reply to Objection 5: Apart from the mysteries of the spiritual interpretation, this place would seem to be inaccessible, chiefly on account of the extreme heat in the middle zone by reason of the nighness of the sun. This is denoted by the "flaming sword," which is described as "turning every way," as being appropriate to the circular movement that causes this heat. And since the movements of corporal creatures are set in order through the ministry of the angels, according to Augustine (De Trin. iii, 4), it was fitting that, besides the sword turning every way, there should be cherubim "to keep the way of the tree of life." Hence Augustine says (Gen. ad lit. xi, 40): "It is to be believed that even in the visible paradise this was done by heavenly powers indeed, so that there was a fiery guard set there by the ministry of angels."

Reply to Objection 6: After sin, if man had ate of the tree of life, he would not thereby have recovered immortality, but by means of that beneficial food he might have prolonged his life. Hence in the words "And live for ever," "for ever" signifies "for a long time." For it was not expedient for man to remain longer in the unhappiness of this life.

Reply to Objection 7: According to Augustine (Gen. ad lit. xi, 39), "these words of God are not so much a mockery of our first parents as a deterrent to others, for whose benefit these things are written, lest they be proud likewise, because Adam not only failed to become that which he coveted to be, but did not keep that to which he was made."

Reply to Objection 8: Clothing is necessary to man in his present state of unhappiness for two reasons. First, to supply a deficiency in respect of external harm caused by, for instance, extreme heat or cold. Secondly, to hide his ignominy and to cover the shame of those members wherein the rebellion of the flesh against the spirit is most manifest. Now these two motives do not apply to the primitive state. because then man's body could not be hurt by any outward thing, as stated in the [3635]FP, Q[97], A[2], nor was there in man's body anything shameful that would bring confusion on him. Hence it is written (Gn. 2:23): "And they were both naked, to wit Adam and his wife, and were not ashamed." The same cannot be said of food, which is necessary to entertain the natural heat, and to sustain the body.

Reply to Objection 9: As Augustine says (Gen. ad lit. xi, 31), "We must not imagine that our first parents were created with their eyes closed, especially since it is stated that the woman saw that the tree was fair, and good to eat. Accordingly the eyes of both were opened so that they saw and thought on things which had not occurred to their minds before, this was a mutual concupiscence such as they had not hitherto."

OF OUR FIRST PARENTS' TEMPTATION (TWO ARTICLES)

We must now consider our first parents' temptation, concerning which there are two points of inquiry:

(1) Whether it was fitting for man to be tempted by the devil?

(2) Of the manner and order of that temptation.

Whether it was fitting for man to be tempted by the devil?

Objection 1: It would seem that it was not fitting for man to be tempted by the devil. For the same final punishment is appointed to the angels' sin and to man's, according to Mat. 25:41, "Go [Vulg.: 'Depart from Me'] you cursed into everlasting fire, which was prepared for the devil and his angels." Now the angels' first sin did not follow a temptation from without. Therefore neither should man's first sin have resulted from an outward temptation.

Objection 2: Further, God, Who foreknows the future, knew that through the demon's temptation man would fall into sin, and thus He knew full well that it was not expedient for man to be tempted. Therefore it would seem unfitting for God to allow him to be tempted.

Objection 3: Further, it seems to savor of punishment that anyone should have an assailant, just as on the other hand the cessation of an assault is akin to a reward. Now punishment should not precede fault. Therefore it was unfitting for man to be tempted before he sinned.

On the contrary, It is written (Ecclus. 34:11): "He that hath not been tempted [Douay: 'tried'], what manner of things doth he know?"

I answer that, God's wisdom "orders all things sweetly" (Wis. 8:1), inasmuch as His providence appoints to each one that which is befitting it according to its nature. For as Dionysius says (Div. Nom. iv), "it belongs to providence not to destroy, but to maintain, nature." Now it is a condition attaching to human nature that one creature can be helped or impeded by another. Wherefore it was fitting that God should both allow man in the state of innocence to be tempted by evil angels, and should cause him to be helped by good angels. And by a special favor of grace, it was granted him that no creature outside himself could harm him against his own will, whereby he was able even to resist the temptation of the demon.

Reply to Objection 1: Above the human nature there is another that admits of the possibility of the evil of fault: but there is not above the angelic nature. Now only one that is already become evil through sin can tempt by leading another into evil. Hence it was fitting that by an evil angel man should be tempted to sin, even as according to the order of nature he is moved forward to perfection by means of a good angel. An angel could be perfected in good by something above him, namely by God, but he could not thus be led into sin, because according to James 1:13, "God is not a tempter of evils."

Reply to Objection 2: Just as God knew that man, through being tempted, would fall into sin, so too He knew that man was able, by his free will, to resist the tempter. Now the condition attaching to man's nature required that he should be left to his own will, according to Ecclus. 15:14, "God left" man "in the hand of his own counsel." Hence Augustine says (Gen. ad lit. xi, 4): "It seems to me that man would have had no prospect of any special praise, if he were able to lead a good life simply because there was none to persuade him to lead an evil life; since both by nature he had the power, and in his power he had the will, not to consent to the persuader."

Reply to Objection 3: An assault is penal if it be difficult to resist it: but, in the state of innocence, man was able, without any difficulty, to resist temptation. Consequently the tempter's assault was not a punishment to man.

Whether the manner and order of the first temptation was fitting?

Objection 1: It would seem that the manner and order of the first temptation was not fitting. For just as in the order of nature the angel was above man, so was the man above the woman. Now sin came upon man through an angel: therefore in like manner it should have come upon the woman through the man; in other words the woman should have been tempted by the man, and not the other way about.

Objection 2: Further, the temptation of our first parents was by suggestion. Now the devil is able to make suggestions to man without making use of an outward sensible creature. Since then our first parents were endowed with a spiritual mind, and adhered less to sensible than to intelligible things, it would have been more fitting for man to be tempted with a merely spiritual, instead of an outward, temptation.

Objection 3: Further, one cannot fittingly suggest an evil except through some apparent good. But many other animals have a greater appearance of good than the serpent has. Therefore man was unfittingly tempted by the devil through a serpent.

Objection 4: Further, the serpent is an irrational animal. Now wisdom, speech, and punishment are not befitting an irrational animal. Therefore the serpent is unfittingly described (Gn. 3:1) as "more subtle than any of the beasts of the earth," or as "the most prudent of all beasts" according to another version [*The Septuagint]: and likewise is unfittingly stated to have spoken to the woman, and to have been punished by God.

On the contrary, That which is first in any genus should be proportionate to all that follow it in that genus. Now in every kind of sin we find the same order as in the first temptation. For, according to Augustine (De Trin. xii, 12), it begins with the concupiscence of sin in the sensuality, signified by the serpent; extends to the lower reason, by pleasure, signified by the woman; and reaches to the higher reason by consent in the sin, signified by the man. Therefore the order of the first temptation was fitting.

I answer that, Man is composed of a twofold nature, intellective and sensitive. Hence the devil, in tempting man, made use of a twofold incentive to sin: one on the part of the intellect, by promising the Divine likeness through the acquisition of knowledge which man naturally desires to have; the other on the part of sense. This he did by having recourse to those sensible things, which are most akin to man, partly by tempting the man through the woman who was akin to him in the same species; partly by tempting the woman through the serpent, who was akin to them in the same genus; partly by suggesting to them to eat of the forbidden fruit, which was akin to them in the proximate genus.

Reply to Objection 1: In the act of tempting the devil was by way of principal agent; whereas the woman was employed as an instrument of temptation in bringing about the downfall of the man, both because the woman was weaker than the man, and consequently more liable to be deceived, and because, on account of her union with man, the devil was able to deceive the man especially through her. Now there is no parity between principal agent and instrument, because the principal agent must exceed in power, which is not requisite in the instrumental agent.

Reply to Objection 2: A suggestion whereby the devil suggests something to man spiritually, shows the devil to have more power against man than outward suggestion has, since by an inward suggestion, at least, man's imagination is changed by the devil [*Cf. [3636]FP, Q[91], A[3]]; whereas by an outward suggestion, a change is wrought merely on an outward creature. Now the devil had a minimum of power against man before sin, wherefore he was unable to tempt him by inward suggestion, but only by outward suggestion.

Reply to Objection 3: According to Augustine (Gen. ad lit. xi, 3), "we are not to suppose that the devil chose the serpent as his means of temptation; but as he was possessed of the lust of deceit, he could only do so by the animal he was allowed to use for that purpose."

Reply to Objection 4: According to Augustine (Gen. ad lit. xi, 29), "the serpent is described as most prudent or subtle, on account of the cunning of the devil, who wrought his wiles in it: thus, we speak of a prudent or cunning tongue, because it is the instrument of a prudent or cunning man in advising something prudently or cunningly. Nor indeed (Gen. ad lit. xi, 28) did the serpent understand the sounds which were conveyed through it to the woman; nor again are we to believe that its soul was changed into a rational nature, since not even men, who are rational by nature, know what they say when a demon speaks in them. Accordingly (Gen. ad lit. xi, 29) the serpent spoke to man, even as the ass on which Balaam sat spoke to him, except that the former was the work of a devil, whereas the latter was the work of an angel. Hence (Gen. ad lit. xi, 36) the serpent was not asked why it had done this, because it had not done this in its own nature, but the devil in it, who was already condemned to everlasting fire on account of his sin: and the words addressed to the serpent were directed to him who wrought through the serpent."

Moreover, as again Augustine says (Super Gen. contra Manich. ii, 17,18), "his, that is, the devil's, punishment mentioned here is that for which we must be on our guard against him, not that which is reserved till the last judgment. For when it was said to him: 'Thou art cursed among all cattle and beasts of the earth,' the cattle are set above him, not in power, but in the preservation of their nature, since the cattle lost no heavenly bliss, seeing that they never had it, but they continue to live in the nature which they received." It is also said to him: "'Upon thy breast and belly shalt thou creep,'" according to another version [*The Septuagint] "Here the breast signifies pride, because it is there that the impulse of the soul dominates, while the belly denotes carnal desire, because this part of the body is softest to the touch: and on these he creeps to those whom he wishes to deceive." The words,

"'Earth shalt thou eat all the days of thy life' may be understood in two ways. Either 'Those shall belong to thee, whom thou shalt deceive by earthly lust,' namely sinners who are signified under the name of earth, or a third kind of temptation, namely curiosity, is signified by these words: for to eat earth is to look into things deep and dark." The putting of enmities between him and the woman "means that we cannot be tempted by the devil, except through that part of the soul which bears or reflects the likeness of a woman. The seed of the devil is the temptation to evil, the seed of the woman is the fruit of good works, whereby the temptation to evil is resisted. Wherefore the serpent lies in wait for the woman's heel, that if at any time she fall away towards what is unlawful, pleasure may seize hold of her: and she watches his head that she may shut him out at the very outset of the evil temptation."

OF STUDIOUSNESS (TWO ARTICLES)

We must next consider studiousness and its opposite, curiosity. Concerning studiousness there are two points of inquiry:

(1) What is the matter of studiousness?

(2) Whether it is a part of temperance?

Whether the proper matter of studiousness is knowledge?

Objection 1: It would seem that knowledge is not the proper matter of studiousness. For a person is said to be studious because he applies study to certain things. Now a man ought to apply study to every matter, in order to do aright what has to be done. Therefore seemingly knowledge is not the special matter of studiousness.

Objection 2: Further, studiousness is opposed to curiosity. Now curiosity, which is derived from "cura" [care], may also refer to elegance of apparel and other such things, which regard the body; wherefore the Apostle says (Rom. 13:14): "Make not provision [curam] for the flesh in its concupiscences."

Objection 3: Further it is written (Jer. 6:13): "From the least of them even to the greatest, all study [Douay: 'are given to'] covetousness." Now covetousness is not properly about knowledge, but rather about the possession of wealth, as stated above ([3637]Q[118], A[2]). Therefore studiousness, which is derived from "study," is not properly about knowledge.

On the contrary, It is written (Prov. 27:11): "Study wisdom, my son, and make my heart joyful, that thou mayest give an answer to him that reproacheth." Now study, which is commended as a virtue, is the same as that to which the Law urges. Therefore studiousness is properly about "knowledge."

I answer that, Properly speaking, study denotes keen application of the mind to something. Now the mind is not applied to a thing except by knowing that thing.

Wherefore the mind's application to knowledge precedes its application to those things to which man is directed by his knowledge. Hence study regards knowledge in the first place, and as a result it regards any other things the working of which requires to be directed by knowledge. Now the virtues lay claim to that matter about which they are first and foremost; thus fortitude is concerned about dangers of death, and temperance about pleasures of touch. Therefore studiousness is properly ascribed to knowledge.

Reply to Objection 1: Nothing can be done aright as regards other matters, except in so far as is previously directed by the knowing reason. Hence studiousness, to whatever matter it be applied, has a prior regard for knowledge.

Reply to Objection 2: Man's mind is drawn, on account of his affections, towards the things for which he has an affection, according to Mat. 6:21, "Where thy treasure is, there is thy heart also." And since man has special affection for those things which foster the flesh, it follows that man's thoughts are concerned about things that foster his flesh, so that man seeks to know how he may best sustain his body. Accordingly curiosity is accounted to be about things pertaining to the body by reason of things pertaining to knowledge.

Reply to Objection 3: Covetousness craves the acquisition of gain, and for this it is very necessary to be skilled in earthly things. Accordingly studiousness is ascribed to things pertaining to covetousness.

Whether studiousness is a part of temperance?

Objection 1: It would seem that studiousness is not a part of temperance. For a man is said to be studious by reason of his studiousness. Now all virtuous persons without exception are called studious according to the Philosopher, who frequently employs the term "studious" ({spoudaios}) in this sense (Ethic. ix, 4,8,9). [*In the same sense Aristotle says in Ethic. iii, 2, that "every vicious person is ignorant of what he ought to do."] Therefore studiousness is a general virtue, and not a part of temperance.

Objection 2: Further, studiousness, as stated [3638](A[1]), pertains to knowledge. But knowledge has no connection with the moral virtues which are in the appetitive part of the soul, and pertains rather to the intellectual virtues which are in the cognitive part: wherefore solicitude is an act of prudence as stated above (Q[47], A[9]). Therefore studiousness is not a part of temperance.

Objection 3: Further, a virtue that is ascribed as part of a principal virtue resembles the latter as to mode. Now studiousness does not resemble temperance as to mode, because temperance takes its name from being a kind of restraint, wherefore it is more opposed to the vice that is in excess: whereas studiousness is denominated from being the application of the mind to something, so that it would seem to be opposed to the vice that is in default, namely, neglect of study, rather than to the vice which is in excess, namely curiosity. wherefore, on account of its resemblance to the latter, Isidore says (Etym. x) that "a studious man is one who is curious to study." Therefore studiousness is not a part of temperance.

On the contrary, Augustine says (De Morib. Eccl. 21): "We are forbidden to be curious: and this is a great gift that temperance bestows." Now curiosity is prevented by moderate studiousness. Therefore studiousness is a part of temperance.

I answer that, As stated above ([3639]Q[141], AA[3],4,5), it belongs to temperance to moderate the movement of the appetite, lest it tend excessively to that which is desired naturally. Now just as in respect of his corporeal nature man naturally desires the pleasures of food and sex, so, in respect of his soul, he naturally desires to know something; thus the Philosopher observes at the beginning of his Metaphysics i, 1: "All men have a natural desire for knowledge."

The moderation of this desire pertains to the virtue of studiousness; wherefore it follows that studiousness is a potential part of temperance, as a subordinate virtue annexed to a principal virtue. Moreover, it is comprised under modesty for the reason given above ([3640]Q[160], A[2]).

Reply to Objection 1: Prudence is the complement of all the moral virtues, as stated in Ethic. vi, 13. Consequently, in so far as the knowledge of prudence pertains to all the virtues, the term "studiousness," which properly regards knowledge, is applied to all the virtues.

Reply to Objection 2: The act of a cognitive power is commanded by the appetitive power, which moves all the powers, as stated above ([3641]FS, Q[9], A[1]). Wherefore knowledge regards a twofold good. One is connected with the act of knowledge itself; and this good pertains to the intellectual virtues, and consists in man having a true estimate about each thing. The other good pertains to the act of the appetitive power, and consists in man's appetite being directed aright in applying the cognitive power in this or that way to this or that thing. And this belongs to the virtue of seriousness. Wherefore it is reckoned among the moral virtues.

Reply to Objection 3: As the Philosopher says (Ethic. ii, 93) in order to be virtuous we must avoid those things to which we are most naturally inclined. Hence it is that, since nature inclines us. chiefly to fear dangers of death, and to seek pleasures of the flesh, fortitude is chiefly commended for a certain steadfast perseverance against such dangers, and temperance for a certain restraint from pleasures of the flesh. But as regards knowledge, man has contrary inclinations. For on the part of the soul, he is inclined to desire knowledge of things; and so it behooves him to exercise a praiseworthy restraint on this desire, lest he seek knowledge immoderately: whereas on the part of his bodily nature, man is inclined to avoid the trouble of seeking knowledge. Accordingly, as regards the first inclination studiousness is a kind of restraint, and it is in this sense that it is reckoned a part of temperance. But as to the second inclination, this virtue derives its praise from a certain keenness of interest in seeking knowledge of things; and from this it takes its name. The former is more essential to this virtue than the latter: since the desire to know directly regards knowledge, to which studiousness is directed, whereas the trouble of learning is an obstacle to knowledge, wherefore it is regarded by this virtue indirectly, as by that which removes an obstacle.

OF CURIOSITY (TWO ARTICLES)

We must next consider curiosity, under which head there are two points of inquiry:

(1) Whether the vice of curiosity can regard intellective knowledge?

(2) Whether it is about sensitive knowledge?

Whether curiosity can be about intellective knowledge?

Objection 1: It would seem that curiosity cannot be about intellective knowledge. Because, according to the Philosopher (Ethic. ii, 6), there can be no mean and extremes in things which are essentially good. Now intellective knowledge is essentially good: because man's perfection would seem to consist in his intellect being reduced from potentiality to act, and this is done by the knowledge of truth. For Dionysius says (Div. Nom. iv) that "the good of the human soul is to be in accordance with reason," whose perfection consists in knowing the truth. Therefore the vice of curiosity cannot be about intellective knowledge.

Objection 2: Further, that which makes man like to God, and which he receives from God, cannot be an evil. Now all abundance of knowledge is from God, according to Ecclus. 1:1, "All wisdom is from the Lord God," and Wis. 7:17, "He hath given me the true knowledge of things that are, to know the disposition of the whole world, and the virtues of the elements," etc. Again, by knowing the truth man is likened to God, since "all things are naked and open to His eyes" (Heb. 4:13), and "the Lord is a God of all knowledge" (1 Kings 2:3). Therefore however abundant knowledge of truth may be, it is not evil but good. Now the desire of good is not sinful. Therefore the vice of curiosity cannot be about the intellective knowledge of truth.

Objection 3: Further, if the vice of curiosity can be about any kind of intellective knowledge, it would be chiefly about the philosophical sciences. But, seemingly, there is no sin in being intent on them: for Jerome says (Super Daniel 1:8): "Those who refused to partake of the king's meat and wine, lest they should be defiled, if they had considered the wisdom and teaching of the Babylonians to be sinful, would never have consented to learn that which was unlawful": and Augustine says (De Doctr. Christ. ii, 40) that "if the philosophers made any true statements, we must claim them for our own use, as from unjust possessors." Therefore curiosity about intellective knowledge cannot be sinful.

On the contrary, Jerome [*Comment. in Ep. ad Ephes. iv, 17] says: "Is it not evident that a man who day and night wrestles with the dialectic art, the student of natural science whose gaze pierces the heavens, walks in vanity of understanding and darkness of mind?" Now vanity of understanding and darkness of mind are sinful. Therefore curiosity about intellective sciences may be sinful.

I answer that, As stated above ([3642]Q[166], A[2], ad 2) studiousness is directly, not about knowledge itself, but about the desire and study in the pursuit of knowledge. Now we must judge differently of the knowledge itself of truth, and of the desire and study in the pursuit of the knowledge of truth. For the knowledge of truth, strictly speaking, is good, but it may be evil accidentally, by reason of some result, either because one takes pride in knowing the truth, according to 1 Cor. 8:1, "Knowledge puffeth up," or because one uses the knowledge of truth in order to sin.

On the other hand, the desire or study in pursuing the knowledge of truth may be right or wrong. First, when one tends by his study to the knowledge of truth as having evil accidentally annexed to it, for instance those who study to know the truth that they may take pride in their knowledge. Hence Augustine says (De Morib. Eccl. 21): "Some there are who forsaking virtue, and ignorant of what God is, and of the majesty of that nature which ever remains the same, imagine they are doing something great, if with surpassing curiosity and keenness they explore the whole mass of this body which we call the world. So great a pride is thus begotten, that one would think they dwelt in the very heavens about which they argue." In like manner, those who study to learn something in order to sin are engaged in a sinful study, according to the saying of Jer. 9:5, "They have taught their tongue to speak lies, they have labored to commit iniquity."

Secondly, there may be sin by reason of the appetite or study directed to the learning of truth being itself inordinate; and this in four ways. First, when a man is withdrawn by a less profitable study from a study that is an obligation incumbent on him; hence Jerome says [*Epist. xxi ad Damas]: "We see priests forsaking the gospels and the prophets, reading stage-plays, and singing the love songs of pastoral idylls." Secondly, when a man studies to learn of one, by whom it is unlawful to be taught, as in the case of those who seek to know the future through the demons. This is superstitious curiosity, of which Augustine says (De Vera Relig. 4): "Maybe, the philosophers were debarred from the faith by their sinful curiosity in seeking knowledge from the demons."

Thirdly, when a man desires to know the truth about creatures, without referring his knowledge to its due end, namely, the knowledge of God. Hence Augustine says (De Vera Relig. 29) that "in studying creatures, we must not be moved by empty and perishable curiosity; but we should ever mount towards immortal and abiding things."

Fourthly, when a man studies to know the truth above the capacity of his own intelligence, since by so doing men easily fall into error: wherefore it is written (Ecclus. 3:22): "Seek not the things that are too high for thee, and search not into things above thy ability . . . and in many of His works be not curious," and further on (Ecclus. 3:26), "For . . . the suspicion of them hath deceived many, and hath detained their minds in vanity."

Reply to Objection 1: Man's good consists in the knowledge of truth; yet man's sovereign good consists, not in the knowledge of any truth, but in the perfect knowledge of the sovereign truth, as the Philosopher states (Ethic. x, 7,8). Hence there may be sin in the knowledge of certain truths, in so far as the desire of such knowledge is not directed in due manner to the knowledge of the sovereign truth, wherein supreme happiness consists.

Reply to Objection 2: Although this argument shows that the knowledge of truth is good in itself, this does not prevent a man from misusing the knowledge of truth for an evil purpose, or from desiring the knowledge of truth inordinately, since even the desire for good should be regulated in due manner.

Reply to Objection 3: The study of philosophy is in itself lawful and commendable, on account of the truth which the philosophers acquired through God revealing it to them, as stated in Rom. 1:19. Since, however, certain philosophers misuse the truth in order to assail the faith, the Apostle says (Col. 2:8): "Beware lest any man cheat you by philosophy and vain deceit, according to the tradition of men . . . and not according to Christ": and Dionysius says (Ep. vii ad Polycarp.) of certain philosophers that "they make an unholy use of divine things against that which is divine, and by divine wisdom strive to destroy the worship of God."

Whether the vice of curiosity is about sensitive knowledge?

Objection 1: It would seem that the vice of curiosity is not about sensitive knowledge. For just as some things are known by the sense of sight, so too are some things known by the senses of touch and taste. Now the vice concerned about objects of touch and taste is not curiosity but lust or gluttony. Therefore seemingly neither is the vice of curiosity about things known by the sight.

Objection 2: Further, curiosity would seem to refer to watching games; wherefore Augustine says (Confess. vi, 8) that when "a fall occurred in the fight, a mighty cry of the whole people struck him strongly, and overcome by curiosity Alypius opened his eyes." But it does not seem to be sinful to watch games, because it gives pleasure on account of the representation, wherein man takes a natural delight, as the Philosopher states (Poet. vi). Therefore the vice of curiosity is not about the knowledge of sensible objects.

Objection 3: Further, it would seem to pertain to curiosity to inquire into our neighbor's actions, as Bede observes [*Comment. in 1 Jn. 2:16]. Now, seemingly, it is not a sin to inquire into the actions of others, because according to Ecclus. 17:12, God "gave to every one of them commandment concerning his neighbor." Therefore the vice of curiosity does not regard the knowledge of such like particular sensible objects.

On the contrary, Augustine says (De Vera Relig. 38) that "concupiscence of the eyes makes men curious." Now according to Bede (Comment. in 1 Jn. 2:16) "concupiscence of the eyes refers not only to the learning of magic arts, but also to sight-seeing, and to the discovery and dispraise of our neighbor's faults," and all these are particular objects of sense. Therefore since concupiscence of the eves is a sin, even as concupiscence of the flesh and pride of life, which are members of the same division (1 Jn. 2:16), it seems that the vice of curiosity is about the knowledge of sensible things.

I answer that, The knowledge of sensible things is directed to two things. For in the first place, both in man and in other animals, it is directed to the upkeep of the body, because by knowledge of this kind, man and other animals avoid what is harmful to them, and seek those things that are necessary for the body's sustenance. In the second place, it is directed in a manner special to man, to intellective knowledge, whether speculative or practical. Accordingly to employ study for the purpose of knowing sensible things may be sinful in two ways. First, when the sensitive knowledge is not directed to something useful, but turns man away from some useful consideration. Hence Augustine says (Confess. x, 35), "I go no more to see a dog coursing a hare in the circus; but in the open country, if I happen to be passing, that coursing haply will distract me from some weighty thought, and draw me after it . . . and unless Thou, having made me see my weakness, didst speedily admonish me, I become foolishly dull." Secondly, when the knowledge of sensible things is directed to something harmful, as looking on a woman is directed to lust: even so the busy inquiry into other people's actions is directed to detraction. on the other hand, if one be ordinately intent on the knowledge of sensible things by reason of the necessity of sustaining nature, or for the sake of the study of intelligible truth, this studiousness about the knowledge of sensible things is virtuous.

Reply to Objection 1: Lust and gluttony are about pleasures arising from the use of objects of touch, whereas curiosity is about pleasures arising from the knowledge acquired through all the senses. According to Augustine (Confess. x, 35) "it is called concupiscence of the eyes" because "the sight is the sense chiefly used for obtaining knowledge, so that all sensible things are said to be seen," and as he says further on: "By this it may more evidently be discerned wherein pleasure and wherein curiosity is the object of the senses; for pleasure seeketh objects beautiful, melodious, fragrant, savory, soft; but curiosity, for trial's sake, seeketh even the contraries of these, not for the sake of suffering annoyance, but out of the lust of experiment and knowledge."

Reply to Objection 2: Sight-seeing becomes sinful, when it renders a man prone to the vices of lust and cruelty on account of things he sees represented. Hence Chrysostom says [*Hom. vi in Matth.] that such sights make men adulterers and shameless.

Reply to Objection 3: One may watch other people's actions or inquire into them, with a good intent, either for one's own good—that is in order to be encouraged to better deeds by the deeds of our neighbor—or for our neighbor's good—that is in order to correct him, if he do anything wrong, according to the rule of charity and the duty of one's position. This is praiseworthy, according to Heb. 10:24, "Consider one another to provoke unto charity and to good works." But to observe our neighbor's faults with the intention of looking down upon them, or of detracting them, or even with no further purpose than that of disturbing them, is sinful: hence it is written (Prov. 24:15), "Lie not in wait, nor seek after wickedness in the house of the just, nor spoil his rest."

OF MODESTY AS CONSISTING IN THE OUTWARD MOVEMENTS OF THE BODY (FOUR ARTICLES)

We must next consider modesty as consisting in the outward movements of the body, and under this head there are four points of inquiry:

(1) Whether there can be virtue and vice in the outward movements of the body that are done seriously?

(2) Whether there can be a virtue about playful actions?

(3) Of the sin consisting in excess of play;

(4) Of the sin consisting in lack of play.

Whether any virtue regards the outward movements of the body?

Objection 1: It would seem that no virtue regards the outward movements of the body. For every virtue pertains to the spiritual beauty of the soul, according to Ps. 44:14, "All the glory of the king's daughter is within," and a gloss adds, "namely, in the conscience." Now the movements of the body are not within, but without. Therefore there can be no virtue about them.

Objection 2: Further, "Virtues are not in us by nature," as the Philosopher states (Ethic. ii, 1). But outward bodily movements are in man by nature, since it is by nature that some are quick, and some slow of movement, and the same applies to other differences of outward movements. Therefore there is no virtue about movements of this kind.

Objection 3: Further, every moral virtue is either about actions directed to another person, as justice, or about passions, as temperance and fortitude. Now outward bodily movements are not directed to another person, nor are they passions. Therefore no virtue is connected with them.

Objection 4: Further, study should be applied to all works of virtue, as stated above ([3643]Q[166], A[1], OBJ[1]; A[2], ad 1). Now it is censurable to apply study to the ordering of one's outward movements: for Ambrose says (De Offic. i, 18): "A becoming gait is one that reflects the carriage of authority, has the tread of gravity, and the foot-print of tranquillity: yet so that there be neither study nor affectation, but natural and artless movement." Therefore seemingly there is no virtue about the style of outward movements.

On the contrary, The beauty of honesty [*Cf.[3644] Q[145], A[1]] pertains to virtue. Now the style of outward movements pertains to the beauty of honesty. For Ambrose says (De Offic. i, 18): "The sound of the voice and the gesture of the body are distasteful to me, whether they be unduly soft and nerveless, or coarse and boorish. Let nature be our model; her reflection is gracefulness of conduct and beauty of honesty." Therefore there is a virtue about the style of outward movement.

I answer that, Moral virtue consists in the things pertaining to man being directed by his reason. Now it is manifest that the outward movements of man are dirigible by reason, since the outward members are set in motion at the command of reason. Hence it is evident that there is a moral virtue concerned with the direction of these movements.

Now the direction of these movements may be considered from a twofold standpoint. First, in respect of fittingness to the person; secondly, in respect of fittingness to externals, whether persons, business, or place. Hence Ambrose says (De Offic. i, 18): "Beauty of conduct consists in becoming behavior towards others, according to their sex and person," and this regards the first. As to the second, he adds: "This is the best way to order our behavior, this is the polish becoming to every action."

Hence Andronicus [*De Affectibus] ascribes two things to these outward movements: namely "taste" [ornatus] which regards what is becoming to the person, wherefore he says that it is the knowledge of what is becoming in movement and behavior; and "methodicalness" [bona ordinatio] which regards what is becoming to the business in hand, and to one's surroundings, wherefore he calls it "the practical knowledge of separation," i.e. of the distinction of "acts."

Reply to Objection 1: Outward movements are signs of the inward disposition, according to Ecclus. 19:27, "The attire of the body, and the laughter of the teeth, and the gait of the man, show what he is"; and Ambrose says (De Offic. i, 18) that "the habit of mind is seen in the gesture of the body," and that "the body's movement is an index of the soul."

Reply to Objection 2: Although it is from natural disposition that a man is inclined to this or that style of outward movement, nevertheless what is lacking to nature can be supplied by the efforts of reason. Hence Ambrose says (De Offic. i, 18): "Let nature guide the movement: and if nature fail in any respect, surely effort will supply the defect."

Reply to Objection 3: As stated (ad 1) outward movements are indications of the inward disposition, and this regards chiefly the passions of the soul. Wherefore Ambrose says (De Offic. i, 18) that "from these things," i.e. the outward movements, "the man that lies hidden in our hearts is esteemed to be either frivolous, or boastful, or impure, or on the other hand sedate, steady, pure, and free from blemish." It is moreover from our outward movements that other men form their judgment about us, according to Ecclus. 19:26, "A man is known by his look, and a wise man, when thou meetest him, is known by his countenance." Hence moderation of outward movements is directed somewhat to other persons, according to the saying of Augustine in his Rule (Ep. ccxi), "In all your movements, let nothing be done to offend the eye of another, but only that which is becoming to the holiness of your state." Wherefore the moderation of outward movements may be reduced to two virtues, which the Philosopher mentions in Ethic. iv, 6,7. For, in so far as by outward movements we are directed to other persons, the moderation of our outward movements belongs to "friendliness or affability" [*Cf.[3645] Q[114], A[1]]. This regards pleasure or pain which may arise from words or deeds in reference to others with whom a man comes in contact. And, in so far as outward movements are signs of our inward disposition, their moderation belongs to the virtue of truthfulness [*Cf. Q[9]], whereby a man, by word and deed, shows himself to be such as he is inwardly.

Reply to Objection 4: It is censurable to study the style of one's outward movements, by having recourse to pretense in them, so that they do not agree with one's inward disposition. Nevertheless it behooves one to study them, so that if they be in any way inordinate, this may be corrected. Hence Ambrose says (De Offic. i, 18): "Let them be without artifice, but not without correction."

Whether there can be a virtue about games?

Objection 1: It would seem that there cannot be a virtue about games. For Ambrose says (De Offic. i, 23): "Our Lord said: 'Woe to you who laugh, for you shall weep.' Wherefore I consider that all, and not only excessive, games should be avoided." Now that which can be done virtuously is not to be avoided altogether. Therefore there cannot be a virtue about games.

Objection 2: Further, "Virtue is that which God forms in us, without us," as stated above ([3646]FS, Q[55], A[4]). Now Chrysostom says [*Hom. vi in Matth.]: "It is not God, but the devil, that is the author of fun. Listen to what happened to those who played: 'The people sat down to eat and drink, and they rose up to play.'" Therefore there can be no virtue about games.

Objection 3: Further, the Philosopher says (Ethic. x, 6) that "playful actions are not directed to something else." But it is a requisite of virtue that the agent in choosing should "direct his action to something else," as the Philosopher states (Ethic. ii, 4). Therefore there can be no virtue about games.

On the contrary, Augustine says (Music. ii, 15): "I pray thee, spare thyself at times: for it becomes a wise man sometimes to relax the high pressure of his attention to work." Now this relaxation of the mind from work consists in playful words or deeds. Therefore it becomes a wise and virtuous man to have recourse to such things at times. Moreover the Philosopher [*Ethic. ii, 7; iv, 8] assigns to games the virtue of {eutrapelia}, which we may call "pleasantness."

I answer that, Just as man needs bodily rest for the body's refreshment, because he cannot always be at work, since his power is finite and equal to a certain fixed amount of labor, so too is it with his soul, whose power is also finite and equal to a fixed amount of work. Consequently when he goes beyond his measure in a certain work, he is oppressed and becomes weary, and all the more since when the soul works, the body is at work likewise, in so far as the intellective soul employs forces that operate through bodily organs. Now sensible goods are connatural to man, and therefore, when the soul arises above sensibles, through being intent on the operations of reason, there results in consequence a certain weariness of soul, whether the operations with which it is occupied be those of the practical or of the speculative reason. Yet this weariness is greater if the soul be occupied with the work of contemplation, since thereby it is raised higher above sensible things; although perhaps certain outward works of the practical reason entail a greater bodily labor. In either case, however, one man is more soul-wearied than another, according as he is more intensely occupied with works of reason. Now just as weariness of the body is dispelled by resting the body, so weariness of the soul must needs be remedied by resting the soul: and the soul's rest is pleasure, as stated above ([3647]FS, Q[25], A[2]; [3648]FS, Q[31], A[1], ad 2). Consequently, the remedy for weariness of soul must needs consist in the application of some pleasure, by slackening the tension of the reason's study. Thus in the Conferences of the Fathers xxiv, 21, it is related of Blessed John the Evangelist, that when some people were scandalized on finding him playing together with his disciples, he is said to have told one of them who carried a bow to shoot an arrow. And when the latter had done this several times, he asked him whether he could do it indefinitely, and the man answered that if he continued doing it, the bow would break. Whence the Blessed John drew the inference that in like manner man's mind would break if its tension were never relaxed.

Now such like words or deeds wherein nothing further is sought than the soul's delight, are called playful or humorous. Hence it is necessary at times to make use of them, in order to give rest, as it were, to the soul. This is in agreement with the statement of the Philosopher (Ethic. iv, 8) that "in the intercourse of this life there is a kind of rest that is associated with games": and consequently it is sometimes necessary to make use of such things.

Nevertheless it would seem that in this matter there are three points which require especial caution. The first and chief is that the pleasure in question should not be sought in indecent or injurious deeds or words. Wherefore Tully says (De Offic. i, 29) that "one kind of joke is discourteous, insolent, scandalous, obscene." Another thing to be observed is that one lose not the balance of one's mind altogether. Hence Ambrose says (De Offic. i, 20): "We should beware lest, when we seek relaxation of mind, we destroy all that harmony which is the concord of good works": and Tully says (De Offic. i, 29), that, "just as we do not allow children to enjoy absolute freedom in their games, but only that which is consistent with good behavior, so our very fun should reflect something of an upright mind." Thirdly, we must be careful, as in all other human actions, to conform ourselves to persons, time, and place, and take due account of other circumstances, so that our fun "befit the hour and the man," as Tully says (De Offic. i, 29).

Now these things are directed according to the rule of reason: and a habit that operates according to reason is virtue. Therefore there can be a virtue about games. The Philosopher gives it the name of wittiness ({eutrapelia}), and a man is said to be pleasant through having a happy turn* of mind, whereby he gives his words and deeds a cheerful turn: and inasmuch as this virtue restrains a man from immoderate fun, it is comprised under modesty. [*{Eutrapelia} is derived from {trepein} = 'to turn'].

Reply to Objection 1: As stated above, fun should fit with business and persons; wherefore Tully says (De Invent. Rhet. i, 17) that "when the audience is weary, it will be useful for the speaker to try something novel or amusing, provided that joking be not incompatible with the gravity of the subject." Now the sacred doctrine is concerned with things of the greatest moment, according to Prov. 8:6, "Hear, for I will speak of great things." Wherefore Ambrose does not altogether exclude fun from human speech, but from the sacred doctrine; hence he begins by saying: "Although jokes are at times fitting and pleasant, nevertheless they are incompatible with the ecclesiastical rule; since how can we have recourse to things which are not to be found in Holy Writ?"

Reply to Objection 2: This saying of Chrysostom refers to the inordinate use of fun, especially by those who make the pleasure of games their end; of whom it is written (Wis. 15:12): "They have accounted our life a pastime." Against these Tully says (De Offic. i, 29): "We are so begotten by nature that we appear to be made not for play and fun, but rather for hardships, and for occupations of greater gravity and moment."

Reply to Objection 3: Playful actions themselves considered in their species are not directed to an end: but the pleasure derived from such actions is directed to the recreation and rest of the soul, and accordingly if this be done with moderation, it is lawful to make use of fun. Hence Tully says (De Offic. i, 29): "It is indeed lawful to make use of play and fun, but in the same way as we have recourse to sleep and other kinds of rest, then only when we have done our duty by grave and serious matters."

Whether there can be sin in the excess of play?

Objection 1: It would seem that there cannot be sin in the excess of play. For that which is an excuse for sin is not held to be sinful. Now play is sometimes an excuse for sin, for many things would be grave sins if they were done seriously, whereas if they be done in fun, are either no sin or but slightly sinful. Therefore it seems that there is no sin in excessive play.

Objection 2: Further, all other vices are reducible to the seven capital vices, as Gregory states (Moral. xxxi, 17). But excess of play does not seem reducible to any of the capital vices. Therefore it would seem not to be a sin.

Objection 3: Further, comedians especially would seem to exceed in play, since they direct their whole life to playing. Therefore if excess of play were a sin, all actors would be in a state of sin; moreover all those who employ them, as well as those who make them any payment, would sin as accomplices of their sin. But this would seem untrue; for it is related in the Lives of the Fathers (ii. 16; viii. 63) that is was revealed to the Blessed Paphnutius that a certain jester would be with him in the life to come.

On the contrary, A gloss on Prov. 14:13, "Laughter shall be mingled with sorrow and mourning taketh hold of the end of joy," remarks: "A mourning that will last for ever." Now there is inordinate laughter and inordinate joy in excessive play.

Therefore there is mortal sin therein, since mortal sin alone is deserving of everlasting mourning.

I answer that, In all things dirigible according to reason, the excessive is that which goes beyond, and the deficient is that which falls short of the rule of reason. Now it has been stated [3649](A[2]) that playful or jesting words or deeds are dirigible according to reason. Wherefore excessive play is that which goes beyond the rule of reason: and this happens in two ways. First, on account of the very species of the acts employed for the purpose of fun, and this kind of jesting, according to Tully (De Offic. i, 29), is stated to be "discourteous, insolent, scandalous, and obscene," when to wit a man, for the purpose of jesting, employs indecent words or deeds, or such as are injurious to his neighbor, these being of themselves mortal sins. And thus it is evident that excessive play is a mortal sin.

Secondly, there may be excess in play, through lack of due circumstances: for instance when people make use of fun at undue times or places, or out of keeping with the matter in hand, or persons. This may be sometimes a mortal sin on account of the strong attachment to play, when a man prefers the pleasure he derives therefrom to the love of God, so as to be willing to disobey a commandment of God or of the Church rather than forego, such like amusements. Sometimes, however, it is a venial sin, for instance where a man is not so attached to amusement as to be willing for its sake to do anything in disobedience to God.

Reply to Objection 1: Certain things are sinful on account of the intention alone, because they are done in order to injure someone. Such an intention is excluded by their being done in fun, the intention of which is to please, not to injure: in these cases fun excuses from sin, or diminishes it. Other things, however, are sins according to their species, such as murder, fornication, and the like: and fun is no excuse for these; in fact they make fun scandalous and obscene.

Reply to Objection 2: Excessive play pertains to senseless mirth, which Gregory (Moral. xxxi, 17) calls a daughter of gluttony. Wherefore it is written (Ex. 32:6): "The people sat down to eat and drink, and they rose up to play."

Reply to Objection 3: As stated [3650](A[2]), play is necessary for the intercourse of human life. Now whatever is useful to human intercourse may have a lawful employment ascribed to it. Wherefore the occupation of play-actors, the object of which is to cheer the heart of man, is not unlawful in itself; nor are they in a state of sin provided that their playing be moderated, namely that they use no unlawful words or deeds in order to amuse, and that they do not introduce play into undue matters and seasons. And although in human affairs, they have no other occupation in reference to other men, nevertheless in reference to themselves, and to

God, they perform other actions both serious and virtuous, such as prayer and the moderation of their own passions and operations, while sometimes they give alms to the poor. Wherefore those who maintain them in moderation do not sin but act justly, by rewarding them for their services. on the other hand, if a man spends too much on such persons, or maintains those comedians who practice unlawful mirth, he sins as encouraging them in their sin. Hence Augustine says (Tract. c. in Joan.) that "to give one's property to comedians is a great sin, not a virtue"; unless by chance some play-actor were in extreme need, in which case one would have to assist him, for Ambrose says (De Offic. [*Quoted in Canon Pasce, dist. 86]): "Feed him that dies of hunger; for whenever thou canst save a man by feeding him, if thou hast not fed him, thou hast slain him."

Whether there is a sin in lack of mirth?

Objection 1: It would seem that there is no sin in lack of mirth. For no sin is prescribed to a penitent. But Augustine speaking of a penitent says (De Vera et Falsa Poenit. 15) [*Spurious]: "Let him refrain from games and the sights of the world, if he wishes to obtain the grace of a full pardon." Therefore there is no sin in lack of mirth.

Objection 2: Further, no sin is included in the praise given to holy men. But some persons are praised for having refrained from mirth; for it is written (Jer. 15:17): "I sat not in the assembly of jesters," and (Tobias 3:17): "Never have I joined myself with them that play; neither have I made myself partaker with them that walk in lightness." Therefore there can be no sin in the lack of mirth.

Objection 3: Further, Andronicus counts austerity to be one of the virtues, and he describes it as a habit whereby a man neither gives nor receives the pleasures of conversation. Now this pertains to the lack of mirth. Therefore the lack of mirth is virtuous rather than sinful.

On the contrary, The Philosopher (Ethic. ii, 7; iv, 8) reckons the lack of mirth to be a vice.

I answer that, In human affairs whatever is against reason is a sin. Now it is against reason for a man to be burdensome to others, by offering no pleasure to others, and by hindering their enjoyment. Wherefore Seneca [*Martin of Braga, Formula Vitae Honestae: cap. De Continentia] says (De Quat. Virt., cap. De Continentia): "Let your conduct be guided by wisdom so that no one will think you rude, or despise you as a cad." Now a man who is without mirth, not only is lacking in playful speech, but is also burdensome to others, since he is deaf to the moderate mirth of others. Consequently they are vicious, and are said to be boorish or rude, as the Philosopher states (Ethic. iv, 8).

Since, however, mirth is useful for the sake of the rest and pleasures it affords; and since, in human life, pleasure and rest are not in quest for their own sake, but for the sake of operation, as stated in Ethic. x, 6, it follows that "lack of mirth is less sinful than excess thereof." Hence the Philosopher says (Ethic. ix, 10): "We should make few friends for the sake of pleasure, since but little sweetness suffices to season life, just as little salt suffices for our meat."

Reply to Objection 1: Mirth is forbidden the penitent because he is called upon to mourn for his sins. Nor does this imply a vice in default, because this very diminishment of mirth in them is in accordance with reason.

Reply to Objection 2: Jeremias speaks there in accordance with the times, the state of which required that man should mourn; wherefore he adds: "I sat alone, because Thou hast filled me with threats." The words of Tobias 3 refer to excessive mirth; and this is evident from his adding: "Neither have I made myself partaker with them that walk in lightness."

Reply to Objection 3: Austerity, as a virtue, does not exclude all pleasures, but only such as are excessive and inordinate; wherefore it would seem to pertain to affability, which the Philosopher (Ethic. iv, 6) calls "friendliness," or {eutrapelia}, otherwise wittiness. Nevertheless he names and defines it thus in respect of its agreement with temperance, to which it belongs to restrain pleasure.

OF MODESTY IN THE OUTWARD APPAREL (TWO ARTICLES)

We must now consider modesty as connected with the outward apparel, and under this head there are two points of inquiry:

(1) Whether there can be virtue and vice in connection with outward apparel?

(2) Whether women sin mortally by excessive adornment?

Whether there can be virtue and vice in connection with outward apparel?

Objection 1: It would seem that there cannot be virtue and vice in connection with outward apparel. For outward adornment does not belong to us by nature, wherefore it varies according to different times and places. Hence Augustine says (De Doctr. Christ. iii, 12) that "among the ancient Romans it was scandalous for one to wear a cloak with sleeves and reaching to the ankles, whereas now it is scandalous for anyone hailing from a reputable place to be without them." Now according to the Philosopher (Ethic. ii, 1) there is in us a natural aptitude for the virtues. Therefore there is no virtue or vice about such things.

Objection 2: Further, if there were virtue and vice in connection with outward attire, excess in this matter would be sinful. Now excess in outward attire is not apparently sinful, since even the ministers of the altar use most precious vestments in the sacred ministry. Likewise it would seem not to be sinful to be lacking in this, for it is said in praise of certain people (Heb. 11:37): "They wandered about in sheepskins and in goatskins." Therefore it seems that there cannot be virtue and vice in this matter.

Objection 3: Further, every virtue is either theological, or moral, or intellectual. Now an intellectual virtue is not conversant with matter of this kind, since it is a perfection regarding the knowledge of truth. Nor is there a theological virtue connected therewith, since that has God for its object; nor are any of the moral virtues enumerated by the Philosopher (Ethic. ii, 7), connected with it. Therefore it seems that there cannot be virtue and vice in connection with this kind of attire.

On the contrary, Honesty [*Cf. Q[145]] pertains to virtue. Now a certain honesty is observed in the outward apparel; for Ambrose says (De Offic. i, 19): "The body should be bedecked naturally and without affectation, with simplicity, with negligence rather than nicety, not with costly and dazzling apparel, but with ordinary clothes, so that nothing be lacking to honesty and necessity, yet nothing be added to increase its beauty." Therefore there can be virtue and vice in the outward attire.

I answer that, It is not in the outward things themselves which man uses, that there is vice, but on the part of man who uses them immoderately. This lack of moderation occurs in two ways. First, in comparison with the customs of those among whom one lives; wherefore Augustine says (Confess. iii, 8): "Those offenses which are contrary to the customs of men, are to be avoided according to the customs generally prevailing, so that a thing agreed upon and confirmed by custom or law of any city or nation may not be violated at the lawless pleasure of any, whether citizen or foreigner. For any part, which harmonizeth not with its whole, is offensive." Secondly, the lack of moderation in the use of these things may arise from the inordinate attachment of the user, the result being that a man sometimes takes too much pleasure in using them, either in accordance with the custom of those among whom he dwells or contrary to such custom. Hence Augustine says (De Doctr. Christ. iii, 12): "We must avoid excessive pleasure in the use of things, for it leads not only wickedly to abuse the customs of those among whom we dwell, but frequently to exceed their bounds, so that, whereas it lay hidden, while under the restraint of established morality, it displays its deformity in a most lawless outbreak."

In point of excess, this inordinate attachment occurs in three ways. First when a man seeks glory from excessive attention to dress; in so far as dress and such like things are a kind of ornament. Hence Gregory says (Hom. xl in Ev.): "There are some who think that attention to finery and costly dress is no sin. Surely, if this were no fault, the word of God would not say so expressly that the rich man who was tortured in hell had been clothed in purple and fine linen. No one, forsooth, seeks costly apparel" (such, namely, as exceeds his estate) "save for vainglory." Secondly, when a man seeks sensuous pleasure from excessive attention to dress, in so far as dress is directed to the body's comfort. Thirdly, when a man is too solicitous [*Cf.[3651] Q[55], A[6]] in his attention to outward apparel.

Accordingly Andronicus [*De Affectibus] reckons three virtues in connection with outward attire; namely "humility," which excludes the seeking of glory, wherefore he says that humility is "the habit of avoiding excessive expenditure and parade";

"contentment" [*Cf. Q[143], OBJ[4]], which excludes the seeking of sensuous pleasure, wherefore he says that "contentedness is the habit that makes a man satisfied with what is suitable, and enables him to determine what is becoming in his manner of life" (according to the saying of the Apostle, 1 Tim. 6:8): "Having food and wherewith to be covered, with these let us be content;"—and "simplicity," which excludes excessive solicitude about such things, wherefore he says that "simplicity is a habit that makes a man contented with what he has."

In the point of deficiency there may be inordinate attachment in two ways. First, through a man's neglect to give the requisite study or trouble to the use of outward apparel. Wherefore the Philosopher says (Ethic. vii, 7) that "it is a mark of effeminacy to let one's cloak trail on the ground to avoid the trouble of lifting it up." Secondly, by seeking glory from the very lack of attention to outward attire. Hence Augustine says (De Serm. Dom. in Monte ii, 12) that "not only the glare and pomp of outward things, but even dirt and the weeds of mourning may be a subject of ostentation, all the more dangerous as being a decoy under the guise of God's service"; and the Philosopher says (Ethic. iv, 7) that "both excess and inordinate defect are a subject of ostentation."

Reply to Objection 1: Although outward attire does not come from nature, it belongs to natural reason to moderate it; so that we are naturally inclined to be the recipients of the virtue that moderates outward raiment.

Reply to Objection 2: Those who are placed in a position of dignity, or again the ministers of the altar, are attired in more costly apparel than others, not for the sake of their own glory, but to indicate the excellence of their office or of the Divine worship: wherefore this is not sinful in them. Hence Augustine says (De Doctr. Christ. iii, 12): "Whoever uses outward things in such a way as to exceed the bounds observed by the good people among whom he dwells, either signifies something by so doing, or is guilty of sin, inasmuch as he uses these things for sensual pleasure or ostentation."

Likewise there may be sin on the part of deficiency: although it is not always a sin to wear coarser clothes than other people. For, if this be done through ostentation or pride, in order to set oneself above others, it is a sin of superstition; whereas, if this be done to tame the flesh, or to humble the spirit, it belongs to the virtue of temperance. Hence Augustine says (De Doctr. Christ. iii, 12): "Whoever uses transitory things with greater restraint than is customary with those among whom he dwells, is either temperate or superstitious." Especially, however, is the use of coarse raiment befitting to those who by word and example urge others to repentance, as did the prophets of whom the Apostle is speaking in the passage quoted.

Wherefore a gloss on Mat. 3:4, says: "He who preaches penance, wears the garb of penance."

Reply to Objection 3: This outward apparel is an indication of man's estate; wherefore excess, deficiency, and mean therein, are referable to the virtue of truthfulness, which the Philosopher (Ethic. ii, 7) assigns to deeds and words, which are indications of something connected with man's estate.

Whether the adornment of women is devoid of mortal sin?

Objection 1: It would seem that the adornment of women is not devoid of mortal sin. For whatever is contrary to a precept of the Divine law is a mortal sin. Now the adornment of women is contrary to a precept of the Divine law; for it is written (1 Pet. 3:3): "Whose," namely women's, "adorning, let it not be the outward plaiting of the hair, or the wearing of gold, or the putting on of apparel." Wherefore a gloss of Cyprian says: "Those who are clothed in silk and purple cannot sincerely put on Christ: those who are bedecked with gold and pearls and trinkets have forfeited the adornments of mind and body." Now this is not done without a mortal sin. Therefore the adornment of women cannot be devoid of mortal sin.

Objection 2: Further, Cyprian says (De Habit. Virg.): "I hold that not only virgins and widows, but also wives and all women without exception, should be admonished that nowise should they deface God's work and fabric, the clay that He has fashioned, with the aid of yellow pigments, black powders or rouge, or by applying any dye that alters the natural features." And afterwards he adds: "They lay hands on God, when they strive to reform what He has formed. This is an assault on the Divine handiwork, a distortion of the truth. Thou shalt not be able to see God, having no longer the eyes that God made, but those the devil has unmade; with him shalt thou burn on whose account thou art bedecked." But this is not due except to mortal sin. Therefore the adornment of women is not devoid of mortal sin.

Objection 3: Further, just as it is unbecoming for a woman to wear man's clothes, so is it unbecoming for her to adorn herself inordinately. Now the former is a sin, for it is written (Dt. 22:5): "A woman shall not be clothed with man's apparel, neither shall a man use woman's apparel." Therefore it seems that also the excessive adornment of women is a mortal sin.

Objection 4: On the contrary, If this were true it would seem that the makers of these means of adornment sin mortally.

I answer that, As regards the adornment of women, we must bear in mind the general statements made above [3652](A[1]) concerning outward apparel, and also something special, namely that a woman's apparel may incite men to lust, according to Prov. 7:10, "Behold a woman meeteth him in harlot's attire, prepared to deceive souls."

Nevertheless a woman may use means to please her husband, lest through despising her he fall into adultery. Hence it is written (1 Cor. 7:34) that the woman "that is married thinketh on the things of the world, how she may please her husband." Wherefore if a married woman adorn herself in order to please her husband she can do this without sin.

But those women who have no husband nor wish to have one, or who are in a state of life inconsistent with marriage, cannot without sin desire to give lustful pleasure to those men who see them, because this is to incite them to sin. And if indeed they adorn themselves with this intention of provoking others to lust, they sin mortally; whereas if they do so from frivolity, or from vanity for the sake of ostentation, it is not always mortal, but sometimes venial. And the same applies to men in this respect. Hence Augustine says (Ep. ccxlv ad Possid.): "I do not wish you to be hasty in forbidding the wearing of gold or costly attire except in the case of those who being neither married nor wishful to marry, should think how they may please God: whereas the others think on the things of the world, either husbands how they may please their wives, or wives how they may please their husbands, except that it is unbecoming for women though married to uncover their hair, since the Apostle commands them to cover the head." Yet in this case some might be excused from sin, when they do this not through vanity but on account of some contrary custom: although such a custom is not to be commended.

Reply to Objection 1: As a gloss says on this passage, "The wives of those who were in distress despised their husbands, and decked themselves that they might please other men": and the Apostle forbids this. Cyprian is speaking in the same sense; yet he does not forbid married women to adorn themselves in order to please their husbands, lest the latter be afforded an occasion of sin with other women. Hence the Apostle says (1 Tim. 2:9): "Women . . . in ornate [Douay: 'decent'] apparel, adorning themselves with modesty and sobriety, not with plaited hair, or gold, or pearls, or costly attire": whence we are given to understand that women are not forbidden to adorn themselves soberly and moderately but to do so excessively, shamelessly, and immodestly.

Reply to Objection 2: Cyprian is speaking of women painting themselves: this is a kind of falsification, which cannot be devoid of sin. Wherefore Augustine says (Ep.

ccxlv ad Possid.): "To dye oneself with paints in order to have a rosier or a paler complexion is a lying counterfeit. I doubt whether even their husbands are willing to be deceived by it, by whom alone" (i.e. the husbands) "are they to be permitted, but not ordered, to adorn themselves." However, such painting does not always involve a mortal sin, but only when it is done for the sake of sensuous pleasure or in contempt of God, and it is to like cases that Cyprian refers.

It must, however, be observed that it is one thing to counterfeit a beauty one has not, and another to hide a disfigurement arising from some cause such as sickness or the like. For this is lawful, since according to the Apostle (1 Cor. 12:23), "such as we think to be the less honorable members of the body, about these we put more abundant honor."

Reply to Objection 3: As stated in the foregoing Article, outward apparel should be consistent with the estate of the person, according to the general custom. Hence it is in itself sinful for a woman to wear man's clothes, or vice versa; especially since this may be a cause of sensuous pleasure; and it is expressly forbidden in the Law (Dt. 22) because the Gentiles used to practice this change of attire for the purpose of idolatrous superstition. Nevertheless this may be done sometimes without sin on account of some necessity, either in order to hide oneself from enemies, or through lack of other clothes, or for some similar motive.

Reply to Objection 4: In the case of an art directed to the production of goods which men cannot use without sin, it follows that the workmen sin in making such things, as directly affording others an occasion of sin; for instance, if a man were to make idols or anything pertaining to idolatrous worship. But in the case of an art the products of which may be employed by man either for a good or for an evil use, such as swords, arrows, and the like, the practice of such an art is not sinful. These alone should be called arts; wherefore Chrysostom says [*Hom. xlix super Matth.]: "The name of art should be applied to those only which contribute towards and produce necessaries and mainstays of life." In the case of an art that produces things which for the most part some people put to an evil use, although such arts are not unlawful in themselves, nevertheless, according to the teaching of Plato, they should be extirpated from the State by the governing authority. Accordingly, since women may lawfully adorn themselves, whether to maintain the fitness of their estate, or even by adding something thereto, in order to please their husbands, it follows that those who make such means of adornment do not sin in the practice of their art, except perhaps by inventing means that are superfluous and fantastic. Hence Chrysostom says (Super Matth.) that "even the shoemakers' and clothiers' arts stand in need of restraint, for they have lent their art to lust, by abusing its needs, and debasing art by art."

OF THE PRECEPTS OF TEMPERANCE (TWO ARTICLES)

We must next consider the precepts of temperance:

(1) The precepts of temperance itself;

(2) The precepts of its parts.

Whether the precepts of temperance are suitably given in the Divine law?

Objection 1: It would seem that the precepts of temperance are unsuitably given in the Divine law. Because fortitude is a greater virtue than temperance, as stated above (Q[123], A[12]; Q[141], A[8]; [3653]FS, Q[66], A[4]). Now there is no precept of fortitude among the precepts of the decalogue, which are the most important among the precepts of the Law. Therefore it was unfitting to include among the precepts of the decalogue the prohibition of adultery, which is contrary to temperance, as stated above (Q[154], AA[1],8).

Objection 2: Further, temperance is not only about venereal matters, but also about pleasures of meat and drink. Now the precepts of the decalogue include no prohibition of a vice pertaining to pleasures of meat and drink, or to any other species of lust. Neither, therefore, should they include a precept prohibiting adultery, which pertains to venereal pleasure.

Objection 3: Further, in the lawgiver's intention inducement to virtue precedes the prohibition of vice, since vices are forbidden in order that obstacles to virtue may be removed. Now the precepts of the decalogue are the most important in the Divine law. Therefore the precepts of the decalogue should have included an affirmative precept directly prescribing the virtue of temperance, rather than a negative precept forbidding adultery which is directly opposed thereto.

On the contrary, stands the authority of Scripture in the decalogue (Ex. 20:14, 17).

I answer that, As the Apostle says (1 Tim. 1:5), "the end of the commandment is charity," which is enjoined upon us in the two precepts concerning the love of God and of our neighbor. Wherefore the decalogue contains those precepts which tend more directly to the love of God and of our neighbor. Now among the vices opposed to temperance, adultery would seem most of all opposed to the love of our neighbor, since thereby a man lays hold of another's property for his own use, by abusing his neighbor's wife. Wherefore the precepts of the decalogue include a special prohibition of adultery, not only as committed in deed, but also as desired in thought.

Reply to Objection 1: Among the species of vices opposed to fortitude there is not one that is so directly opposed to the love of our neighbor as adultery, which is a species of lust that is opposed to temperance. And yet the vice of daring, which is opposed to fortitude, is wont to be sometimes the cause of murder, which is forbidden by one of the precepts of the decalogue: for it is written (Ecclus. 8:18): "Go not on the way with a bold man lest he burden thee with his evils."

Reply to Objection 2: Gluttony is not directly opposed to the love of our neighbor, as adultery is. Nor indeed is any other species of lust, for a father is not so wronged by the seduction of the virgin over whom he has no connubial right, as is the husband by the adultery of his wife, for he, not the wife herself, has power over her body [*1 Cor. 7:4].

Reply to Objection 3: As stated above ([3654]Q[122], AA[1],4) the precepts of the decalogue are universal principles of the Divine law; hence they need to be common precepts. Now it was not possible to give any common affirmative precepts of temperance, because the practice of temperance varies according to different times, as Augustine remarks (De Bono Conjug. xv, 7), and according to different human laws and customs.

Whether the precepts of the virtues annexed to temperance are suitably given in the Divine law?

Objection 1: It would seem that the precepts of the virtues annexed to temperance are unsuitably given in the Divine law. For the precepts of the Decalogue, as stated above (A[1], ad 3), are certain universal principles of the whole Divine law. Now "pride is the beginning of all sin," according to Ecclus. 10:15. Therefore among the precepts of the Decalogue there should have been one forbidding pride.

Objection 2: Further, a place before all should have been given in the decalogue to those precepts by which men are especially induced to fulfil the Law, because these would seem to be the most important. Now since humility subjects man to God, it would seem most of all to dispose man to the fulfilment of the Divine law; wherefore obedience is accounted one of the degrees of humility, as stated above ([3655]Q[161], A[6]); and the same apparently applies to meekness, the effect of which is that a man does not contradict the Divine Scriptures, as Augustine observes (De Doctr. Christ. ii, 7). Therefore it seems that the Decalogue should have contained precepts of humility and meekness.

Objection 3: Further, it was stated in the foregoing Article that adultery is forbidden in the decalogue, because it is contrary to the love of our neighbor. But inordinateness of outward movements, which is contrary to modesty, is opposed to neighborly love: wherefore Augustine says in his Rule (Ep. ccxii): "In all your movements let nothing be done to offend the eye of any person whatever." Therefore it seems that this kind of inordinateness should also have been forbidden by a precept of the Decalogue.

On the contrary, suffices the authority of Scripture.

I answer that, The virtues annexed to temperance may be considered in two ways: first, in themselves; secondly, in their effects. Considered in themselves they have no direct connection with the love of God or of our neighbor; rather do they regard a certain moderation of things pertaining to man himself. But considered in their effects, they may regard the love of God or of our neighbor: and in this respect the decalogue contains precepts that relate to the prohibition of the effects of the vices opposed to the parts of temperance. Thus the effect of anger, which is opposed to meekness, is sometimes that a man goes on to commit murder (and this is forbidden in the Decalogue), and sometimes that he refuses due honor to his parents, which may also be the result of pride, which leads many to transgress the precepts of the first table.

Reply to Objection 1: Pride is the beginning of sin, but it lies hidden in the heart; and its inordinateness is not perceived by all in common. Hence there was no place for its prohibition among the precepts of the Decalogue, which are like first self-evident principles.

Reply to Objection 2: Those precepts which are essentially an inducement to the observance of the Law presuppose the Law to be already given, wherefore they cannot be first precepts of the Law so as to have a place in the Decalogue.

Reply to Objection 3: Inordinate outward movement is not injurious to one's neighbor, if we consider the species of the act, as are murder, adultery, and theft, which are forbidden in the decalogue; but only as being signs of an inward inordinateness, as stated above ([3656]Q[168], A[1], ad 1,3).

TREATISE ON GRATUITOUS GRACES (QQ[171]-182)

OF PROPHECY (SIX ARTICLES)

After treating individually of all the virtues and vices that pertain to men of all conditions and estates, we must now consider those things which pertain especially to certain men. Now there is a triple difference between men as regards things connected with the soul's habits and acts. First, in reference to the various gratuitous graces, according to 1 Cor. 12:4, 7: "There are diversities of graces . . . and to one . . . by the Spirit is given the word of wisdom, to another the word of knowledge," etc. Another difference arises from the diversities of life, namely the active and the contemplative life, which correspond to diverse purposes of operation, wherefore it is stated (1 Cor. 12:4, 7) that "there are diversities of operations." For the purpose of operation in Martha, who "was busy about much serving," which pertains to the active life, differed from the purpose of operation in Mary, "who sitting . . . at the Lord's feet, heard His word" (Lk. 10:39,40), which pertains to the contemplative life. A third difference corresponds to the various duties and states of life, as expressed in Eph. 4:11, "And He gave some apostles; and some prophets; and other some evangelists; and other some pastors and doctors": and this pertains to diversity of ministries, of which it is written (1 Cor. 12:5): "There are diversities of ministries."

With regard to gratuitous graces, which are the first object to be considered, it must be observed that some of them pertain to knowledge, some to speech, and some to operation. Now all things pertaining to knowledge may be comprised under "prophecy," since prophetic revelation extends not only to future events relating to man, but also to things relating to God, both as to those which are to be believed by all and are matters of "faith," and as to yet higher mysteries, which concern the perfect and belong to "wisdom." Again, prophetic revelation is about things pertaining to spiritual substances, by whom we are urged to good or evil; this pertains to the "discernment of spirits." Moreover it extends to the direction of human acts, and this pertains to "knowledge," as we shall explain further on ([3657]Q[177]). Accordingly we must first of all consider prophecy, and rapture which is a degree of prophecy.

Prophecy admits of four heads of consideration: (1) its essence; (2) its cause; (3) the mode of prophetic knowledge; (4) the division of prophecy.

Under the first head there are six points of inquiry:

(1) Whether prophecy pertains to knowledge?

(2) Whether it is a habit?

(3) Whether it is only about future contingencies?

(4) Whether a prophet knows all possible matters of prophecy?

(5) Whether a prophet distinguishes that which he perceives by the gift of God, from that which he perceives by his own spirit?

(6) Whether anything false can be the matter of prophecy?

Whether prophecy pertains to knowledge?

Objection 1: It would seem that prophecy does not pertain to knowledge. For it is written (Ecclus. 48:14) that after death the body of Eliseus prophesied, and further on (Ecclus. 49:18) it is said of Joseph that "his bones were visited, and after death they prophesied." Now no knowledge remains in the body or in the bones after death. Therefore prophecy does not pertain to knowledge.

Objection 2: Further, it is written (1 Cor. 14:3): "He that prophesieth, speaketh to men unto edification." Now speech is not knowledge itself, but its effect. Therefore it would seem that prophecy does not pertain to knowledge.

Objection 3: Further, every cognitive perfection excludes folly and madness. Yet both of these are consistent with prophecy; for it is written (Osee 9:7): "Know ye, O Israel, that the prophet was foolish and mad [*Vulg.: 'the spiritual man was mad']." Therefore prophecy is not a cognitive perfection.

Objection 4: Further, just as revelation regards the intellect, so inspiration regards, apparently, the affections, since it denotes a kind of motion. Now prophecy is described as "inspiration" or "revelation," according to Cassiodorus [*Prolog. super Psalt. i]. Therefore it would seem that prophecy does not pertain to the intellect more than to the affections.

On the contrary, It is written (1 Kings 9:9): "For he that is now called a prophet, in time past was called a seer." Now sight pertains to knowledge. Therefore prophecy pertains to knowledge.

I answer that, Prophecy first and chiefly consists in knowledge, because, to wit, prophets know things that are far [procul] removed from man's knowledge. Wherefore they may be said to take their name from {phanos}, "apparition," because things appear to them from afar. Wherefore, as Isidore states (Etym. vii, 8), "in the Old Testament, they were called Seers, because they saw what others saw not, and surveyed things hidden in mystery." Hence among heathen nations they were known as "vates, on account of their power of mind [vi mentis]," [*The Latin 'vates' is from the Greek {phates}, and may be rendered 'soothsayer'] (Etym. viii, 7).

Since, however, it is written (1 Cor. 12:7): "The manifestation of the Spirit is given to every man unto profit," and further on (1 Cor. 14:12): "Seek to abound unto the edification of the Church," it follows that prophecy consists secondarily in speech, in so far as the prophets declare for the instruction of others, the things they know through being taught of God, according to the saying of Is. 21:10, "That which I have heard of the Lord of hosts, the God of Israel, I have declared unto you." Accordingly, as Isidore says (Etym. viii, 7), "prophets" may be described as "proefatores [foretellers], because they tell from afar [porro fantur]," that is, speak from a distance, "and foretell the truth about things to come."

Now those things above human ken which are revealed by God cannot be confirmed by human reason, which they surpass as regards the operation of the Divine power, according to Mk. 16:20, "They . . . preached everywhere, the Lord working withal and confirming the word with signs that followed." Hence, thirdly, prophecy is concerned with the working of miracles, as a kind of confirmation of the prophetic utterances. Wherefore it is written (Dt. 34:10,11): "There arose no more a prophet in Israel like unto Moses, whom the Lord knew face to face, in all the signs and wonders."

Reply to Objection 1: These passages speak of prophecy in reference to the third point just mentioned, which regards the proof of prophecy.

Reply to Objection 2: The Apostle is speaking there of the prophetic utterances.

Reply to Objection 3: Those prophets who are described as foolish and mad are not true but false prophets, of whom it is said (Jer. 3:16): "Hearken not to the words of the prophets that prophesy to you, and deceive you; they speak a vision of their own heart, and not out of the mouth of the Lord," and (Ezech. 13:3): "Woe to the foolish prophets, that follow their own spirit, and see nothing."

Reply to Objection 4: It is requisite to prophecy that the intention of the mind be raised to the perception of Divine things: wherefore it is written (Ezech. 2:1): "Son of man, stand upon thy feet, and I will speak to thee." This raising of the intention is brought about by the motion of the Holy Ghost, wherefore the text goes on to say: "And the Spirit entered into me . . . and He set me upon my feet." After the mind's intention has been raised to heavenly things, it perceives the things of God; hence the text continues: "And I heard Him speaking to me." Accordingly inspiration is requisite for prophecy, as regards the raising of the mind, according to Job 32:8, "The inspiration of the Almighty giveth understanding": while revelation is necessary, as regards the very perception of Divine things, whereby prophecy is completed; by its means the veil of darkness and ignorance is removed, according to Job 12:22, "He discovereth great things out of darkness."

Whether prophecy is a habit?

Objection 1: It would seem that prophecy is a habit. For according to Ethic. ii, 5, "there are three things in the soul, power, passion, and habit." Now prophecy is not a power, for then it would be in all men, since the powers of the soul are common to them. Again it is not a passion, since the passions belong to the appetitive faculty, as stated above ([3658]FS, Q[22] , A[2]); whereas prophecy pertains principally to knowledge, as stated in the foregoing Article. Therefore prophecy is a habit.

Objection 2: Further, every perfection of the soul, which is not always in act, is a habit. Now prophecy is a perfection of the soul; and it is not always in act, else a prophet could not be described as asleep. Therefore seemingly prophecy is a habit.

Objection 3: Further, prophecy is reckoned among the gratuitous graces. Now grace is something in the soul, after the manner of a habit, as stated above ([3659]FS, Q[110], A[2]). Therefore prophecy is a habit.

On the contrary, A habit is something "whereby we act when we will," as the Commentator [*Averroes or Ibn Roshd, 1120–1198] says (De Anima iii). But a man cannot make use of prophecy when he will, as appears in the case of Eliseus (4 Kings 3:15), "who on Josaphat inquiring of him concerning the future, and the spirit of prophecy failing him, caused a minstrel to be brought to him, that the spirit of prophecy might come down upon him through the praise of psalmody, and fill his mind with things to come," as Gregory observes (Hom. i super Ezech.). Therefore prophecy is not a habit.

I answer that, As the Apostle says (Eph. 5:13), "all that is made manifest is light," because, to wit, just as the manifestation of the material sight takes place through material light, so too the manifestation of intellectual sight takes place through intellectual light. Accordingly manifestation must be proportionate to the light by means of which it takes place, even as an effect is proportionate to its cause. Since then prophecy pertains to a knowledge that surpasses natural reason, as stated above [3660](A[1]), it follows that prophecy requires an intellectual light surpassing the light of natural reason. Hence the saying of Micah 7:8: "When I sit in darkness, the Lord is my light." Now light may be in a subject in two ways: first, by way of an abiding form, as material light is in the sun, and in fire; secondly, by way of a passion, or passing impression, as light is in the air. Now the prophetic light is not in the prophet's intellect by way of an abiding form, else a prophet would always be able to prophesy, which is clearly false. For Gregory says (Hom. i super Ezech.): "Sometimes the spirit of prophecy is lacking to the prophet, nor is it always within the call of his mind, yet so that in its absence he knows that its presence is due to a gift." Hence Eliseus said of the Sunamite woman (4 Kings 4:27): "Her soul is in anguish, and the Lord hath hid it from me, and hath not told me." The reason for this is that the intellectual light that is in a subject by way of an abiding and complete form, perfects the intellect chiefly to the effect of knowing the principle of the things manifested by that light; thus by the light of the active intellect the intellect knows chiefly the first principles of all things known naturally. Now the principle of things pertaining to supernatural knowledge, which are manifested by prophecy, is God Himself, Whom the prophets do not see in His essence, although He is seen by the blessed in heaven, in whom this light is by way of an abiding and complete form, according to Ps. 35:10, "In Thy light we shall see light."

It follows therefore that the prophetic light is in the prophet's soul by way of a passion or transitory impression. This is indicated Ex. 33:22: "When my glory shall pass, I will set thee in a hole of the rock," etc., and 3 Kings 19:11: "Go forth and stand upon the mount before the Lord; and behold the Lord passeth," etc. Hence it is that even as the air is ever in need of a fresh enlightening, so too the prophet's mind is always in need of a fresh revelation; thus a disciple who has not yet acquired the principles of an art needs to have every detail explained to him. Wherefore it is written (Is. 1:4): "In the morning He wakeneth my ear, so that I may hear Him as a master." This is also indicated by the very manner in which prophecies are uttered: thus it is stated that "the Lord spake to such and such a prophet," or that "the word of the Lord," or "the hand of the Lord was made upon him."

But a habit is an abiding form. Wherefore it is evident that, properly speaking, prophecy is not a habit.

Reply to Objection 1: This division of the Philosopher's does not comprise absolutely all that is in the soul, but only such as can be principles of moral actions, which are done sometimes from passion, sometimes from habit, sometimes from mere power, as in the case of those who perform an action from the judgment of their reason before having the habit of that action.

However, prophecy may be reduced to a passion, provided we understand passion to denote any kind of receiving, in which sense the Philosopher says (De Anima iii, 4) that "to understand is, in a way, to be passive." For just as, in natural knowledge, the possible intellect is passive to the light of the active intellect, so too in prophetic knowledge the human intellect is passive to the enlightening of the Divine light.

Reply to Objection 2: Just as in corporeal things, when a passion ceases, there remains a certain aptitude to a repetition of the passion—thus wood once ignited is more easily ignited again, so too in the prophet's intellect, after the actual enlightenment has ceased, there remains an aptitude to be enlightened anew—thus when the mind has once been aroused to devotion, it is more easily recalled to its former devotion. Hence Augustine says (De orando Deum. Ep. cxxx, 9) that our prayers need to be frequent, "lest devotion be extinguished as soon as it is kindled."

We might, however, reply that a person is called a prophet, even while his prophetic enlightenment ceases to be actual, on account of his being deputed by God, according to Jer. 1:5, "And I made thee a prophet unto the nations."

Reply to Objection 3: Every gift of grace raises man to something above human nature, and this may happen in two ways. First, as to the substance of the act—for instance, the working of miracles, and the knowledge of the uncertain and hidden things of Divine wisdom—and for such acts man is not granted a habitual gift of grace. Secondly, a thing is above human nature as to the mode but not the substance of the act—for instance to love God and to know Him in the mirror of His creatures—and for this a habitual gift of grace is bestowed.

Whether prophecy is only about future contingencies?

Objection 1: It would seem that prophecy is only about future contingencies. For Cassiodorus says [*Prol. super Psalt. i] that "prophecy is a Divine inspiration or revelation, announcing the issue of things with unchangeable truth." Now issues pertain to future contingencies. Therefore the prophetic revelation is about future contingencies alone.

Objection 2: Further, according to 1 Cor. 12, the grace of prophecy is differentiated from wisdom and faith, which are about Divine things; and from the discernment of spirits, which is about created spirits; and from knowledge, which is about human things. Now habits and acts are differentiated by their objects, as stated above ([3661]FS, Q[54], A[2]). Therefore it seems that the object of prophecy is not connected with any of the above. Therefore it follows that it is about future contingencies alone.

Objection 3: Further, difference of object causes difference of species, as stated above ([3662]FS, Q[54], A[2]). Therefore, if one prophecy is about future contingencies, and another about other things, it would seem to follow that these are different species of prophecy.

On the contrary, Gregory says (Hom. i super Ezech.) that some prophecies are "about the future, for instance (Is. 7:14), 'Behold a virgin shall conceive, and bear a son'"; some are "about the past, as (Gn. 1:1), 'In the beginning God created heaven and earth'"; some are "about the present," as (1 Cor. 14:24,25), "If all prophesy, and there come in one that believeth not . . . the secrets of his heart are made manifest." Therefore prophecy is not about future contingencies alone.

I answer that, A manifestation made by means of a certain light can extend to all those things that are subject to that light: thus the body's sight extends to all colors, and the soul's natural knowledge extends to whatever is subject to the light of the active intellect. Now prophetic knowledge comes through a Divine light, whereby it is possible to know all things both Divine and human, both spiritual and corporeal; and consequently the prophetic revelation extends to them all. Thus by the ministry of spirits a prophetic revelation concerning the perfections of God and the angels was made to Is. 6:1, where it is written, "I saw the Lord sitting upon a throne high and elevated." Moreover his prophecy contains matters referring to natural bodies, according to the words of Is. 40:12, "Who hath measured the waters in the hollow of His hand," etc. It also contains matters relating to human conduct, according to Is. 58:1, "Deal thy bread to the hungry," etc.; and besides this it contains things pertaining to future events, according to Is. 47:9, "Two things shall come upon thee suddenly in one day, barrenness and widowhood."

Since, however, prophecy is about things remote from our knowledge, it must be observed that the more remote things are from our knowledge the more pertinent they are to prophecy. Of such things there are three degrees. One degree comprises things remote from the knowledge, either sensitive or intellective, of some particular man, but not from the knowledge of all men; thus a particular man knows by sense things present to him locally, which another man does not know by human sense, since they are removed from him. Thus Eliseus knew prophetically what his disciple Giezi had done in his absence (4 Kings 5:26), and in like manner the secret thoughts of one man are manifested prophetically to another, according to 1

Cor. 14:25; and again in this way what one man knows by demonstration may be revealed to another prophetically.

The second degree comprises those things which surpass the knowledge of all men without exception, not that they are in themselves unknowable, but on account of a defect in human knowledge; such as the mystery of the Trinity, which was revealed by the Seraphim saying: "Holy, Holy, Holy," etc. (Is. 6:3).

The last degree comprises things remote from the knowledge of all men, through being in themselves unknowable; such are future contingencies, the truth of which is indeterminate. And since that which is predicated universally and by its very nature, takes precedence of that which is predicated in a limited and relative sense, it follows that revelation of future events belongs most properly to prophecy, and from this prophecy apparently takes its name. Hence Gregory says (Hom. i super Ezech.): "And since a prophet is so called because he foretells the future, his name loses its significance when he speaks of the past or present."

Reply to Objection 1: Prophecy is there defined according to its proper signification; and it is in this sense that it is differentiated from the other gratuitous graces.

Reply to Objection 2: This is evident from what has just been said. We might also reply that all those things that are the matter of prophecy have the common aspect of being unknowable to man except by Divine revelation; whereas those that are the matter of "wisdom," "knowledge," and the "interpretation of speeches," can be known by man through natural reason, but are manifested in a higher way through the enlightening of the Divine light. As to "faith," although it is about things invisible to man, it is not concerned with the knowledge of the things believed, but with a man's certitude of assent to things known by others.

Reply to Objection 3: The formal element in prophetic knowledge is the Divine light, which being one, gives unity of species to prophecy, although the things prophetically manifested by the Divine light are diverse.

Whether by the Divine revelation a prophet knows all that can be known prophetically?

Objection 1: It would seem that by the Divine revelation a prophet knows all that can be known prophetically. For it is written (Amos 3:7): "The Lord God doth nothing without revealing His secret to His servants the prophets." Now whatever is revealed prophetically is something done by God. Therefore there is not one of them but what is revealed to the prophet.

Objection 2: Further, "God's works are perfect" (Dt. 32:4). Now prophecy is a "Divine revelation," as stated above [3663](A[3]). Therefore it is perfect; and this would not be so unless all possible matters of prophecy were revealed prophetically, since "the perfect is that which lacks nothing" (Phys. iii, 6). Therefore all possible matters of prophecy are revealed to the prophet.

Objection 3: Further, the Divine light which causes prophecy is more powerful than the right of natural reason which is the cause of human science. Now a man who has acquired a science knows whatever pertains to that science; thus a grammarian knows all matters of grammar. Therefore it would seem that a prophet knows all matters of prophecy.

On the contrary, Gregory says (Hom. i super Ezech.) that "sometimes the spirit of prophecy indicates the present to the prophet's mind and nowise the future; and sometimes it points not to the present but to the future." Therefore the prophet does not know all matters of prophecy.

I answer that, Things which differ from one another need not exist simultaneously, save by reason of some one thing in which they are connected and on which they depend: thus it has been stated above ([3664]FS, Q[65], AA[1],2) that all the virtues must needs exist simultaneously on account of prudence and charity. Now all the things that are known through some principle are connected in that principle and depend thereon. Hence he who knows a principle perfectly, as regards all to which its virtue extends, knows at the same time all that can be known through that principle; whereas if the common principle is unknown, or known only in a general way, it does not follow that one knows all those things at the same time, but each of them has to be manifested by itself, so that consequently some of them may be known, and some not.

Now the principle of those things that are prophetically manifested by the Divine light is the first truth, which the prophets do not see in itself. Wherefore there is no need for their knowing all possible matters of prophecy; but each one knows some of them according to the special revelation of this or that matter.

Reply to Objection 1: The Lord reveals to the prophets all things that are necessary for the instruction of the faithful; yet not all to every one, but some to one, and some to another.

Reply to Objection 2: Prophecy is by way of being something imperfect in the genus of Divine revelation: hence it is written (1 Cor. 13:8) that "prophecies shall be made void," and that "we prophesy in part," i.e. imperfectly. The Divine revelation will be brought to its perfection in heaven; wherefore the same text continues (1 Cor. 113:10): "When that which is perfect is come, that which is in part shall be done away." Consequently it does not follow that nothing is lacking to prophetic revelation, but that it lacks none of those things to which prophecy is directed.

Reply to Objection 3: He who has a science knows the principles of that science, whence whatever is pertinent to that science depends; wherefore to have the habit of a science perfectly, is to know whatever is pertinent to that science. But God Who is the principle of prophetic knowledge is not known in Himself through prophecy; wherefore the comparison fails.

Whether the prophet always distinguishes what he says by his own spirit from what he says by the prophetic spirit?

Objection 1: It would seem that the prophet always distinguishes what he says by his own spirit from what he says by the prophetic spirit. For Augustine states (Confess. vi, 13) that his mother said "she could, through a certain feeling, which in words she could not express, discern betwixt Divine revelations, and the dreams of her own soul." Now prophecy is a Divine revelation, as stated above [3665](A[3]). Therefore the prophet always distinguishes what he says by the spirit of prophecy, from what he says by his own spirit.

Objection 2: Further, God commands nothing impossible, as Jerome [*Pelagius. Ep. xvi, among the supposititious works of St. Jerome] says. Now the prophets were commanded (Jer. 23:28): "The prophet that hath a dream, let him tell a dream; and he that hath My word, let him speak My word with truth." Therefore the prophet can distinguish what he has through the spirit of prophecy from what he sees otherwise.

Objection 3: Further, the certitude resulting from a Divine light is greater than that which results from the light of natural reason. Now he that has science, by the light of natural reason knows for certain that he has it. Therefore he that has prophecy by a Divine light is much more certain that he has it.

On the contrary, Gregory says (Hom. i super Ezech.): "It must be observed that sometimes the holy prophets, when consulted, utter certain things by their own spirit, through being much accustomed to prophesying, and think they are speaking by the prophetic spirit."

I answer that, The prophet's mind is instructed by God in two ways: in one way by an express revelation, in another way by a most mysterious instinct to "which the human mind is subjected without knowing it," as Augustine says (Gen. ad lit. ii, 17). Accordingly the prophet has the greatest certitude about those things which he knows by an express revelation, and he has it for certain that they are revealed to him by God; wherefore it is written (Jer. 26:15): "In truth the Lord sent me to you, to speak all these words in your hearing." Else, were he not certain about this, the faith which relies on the utterances of the prophet would not be certain. A sign of the prophet's certitude may be gathered from the fact that Abraham being admonished in a prophetic vision, prepared to sacrifice his only-begotten son, which he nowise would have done had he not been most certain of the Divine revelation.

On the other hand, his position with regard to the things he knows by instinct is sometimes such that he is unable to distinguish fully whether his thoughts are conceived of Divine instinct or of his own spirit. And those things which we know by Divine instinct are not all manifested with prophetic certitude, for this instinct is something imperfect in the genus of prophecy. It is thus that we are to understand the saying of Gregory. Lest, however, this should lead to error, "they are very soon set aright by the Holy Ghost [*For instance, cf. 2 Kings 7:3 seqq.], and from Him they hear the truth, so that they reproach themselves for having said what was untrue," as Gregory adds (Hom. i super Ezech.).

The arguments set down in the first place consider the revelation that is made by the prophetic spirit; wherefore the answer to all the objections is clear.

Whether things known or declared prophetically can be false?

Objection 1: It would seem that things known or declared prophetically can be false. For prophecy is about future contingencies, as stated above (A[3]). Now future contingencies may possibly not happen; else they would happen of necessity. Therefore the matter of prophecy can be false.

Objection 2: Further, Isaias prophesied to Ezechias saying (Is. 38:1): "Take order with thy house, for thou shalt surely die, and shalt not live," and yet fifteen years were added to his life (4 Kings 20:6). Again the Lord said (Jer. 18:7,8): "I will suddenly speak against a nation and against a kingdom, to root out and to pull down and to destroy it. If that nation against which I have spoken shall repent of their evil, I also will repent of the evil that I have thought to do them." This is instanced in the example of the Ninevites, according to Jn. 3:10: "The Lord [Vulg.: 'God'] had mercy with regard to the evil which He had said that He would do to them, and He did it not." Therefore the matter of prophecy can be false.

Objection 3: Further, in a conditional proposition, whenever the antecedent is absolutely necessary, the consequent is absolutely necessary, because the consequent of a conditional proposition stands in the same relation to the antecedent, as the conclusion to the premises in a syllogism, and a syllogism whose premises are necessary always leads to a necessary conclusion, as we find proved in I Poster. 6. But if the matter of a prophecy cannot be false, the following conditional proposition must needs be true: "If a thing has been prophesied, it will be." Now the antecedent of this conditional proposition is absolutely necessary, since it is about the past. Therefore the consequent is also necessary absolutely; yet this is unfitting, for then prophecy would not be about contingencies. Therefore it is untrue that the matter of prophecy cannot be false.

On the contrary, Cassiodorus says [*Prol. in Psalt. i] that "prophecy is a Divine inspiration or revelation, announcing the issue of things with invariable truth." Now the truth of prophecy would not be invariable, if its matter could be false. Therefore nothing false can come under prophecy.

I answer that, As may be gathered from what has been said ([3666]AA[1],3,5), prophecy is a kind of knowledge impressed under the form of teaching on the prophet's intellect, by Divine revelation. Now the truth of knowledge is the same in disciple and teacher since the knowledge of the disciple is a likeness of the knowledge of the teacher, even as in natural things the form of the thing generated is a likeness of the form of the generator. Jerome speaks in this sense when he says [*Comment. in Daniel ii, 10] that "prophecy is the seal of the Divine foreknowledge." Consequently the same truth must needs be in prophetic knowledge and utterances, as in the Divine knowledge, under which nothing false can possibly come, as stated in the [3667]FP, Q[16], A[8]. Therefore nothing false can come under prophecy.

Reply to Objection 1: As stated in the [3668]FP, Q[14], A[13] the certitude of the Divine foreknowledge does not exclude the contingency of future singular events, because that knowledge regards the future as present and already determinate to one thing. Wherefore prophecy also, which is an "impressed likeness" or "seal of the Divine foreknowledge," does not by its unchangeable truth exclude the contingency of future things.

Reply to Objection 2: The Divine foreknowledge regards future things in two ways. First, as they are in themselves, in so far, to wit, as it sees them in their presentiality: secondly, as in their causes, inasmuch as it sees the order of causes in relation to their effects. And though future contingencies, considered as in themselves, are determinate to one thing, yet, considered as in their causes, they are not so determined but that they can happen otherwise. Again, though this twofold knowledge is always united in the Divine intellect, it is not always united in the prophetic revelation, because an imprint made by an active cause is not always on a par with the virtue of that cause. Hence sometimes the prophetic revelation is an imprinted likeness of the Divine foreknowledge, in so far as the latter regards future contingencies in themselves: and such things happen in the same way as foretold, for example this saying of Is. 7:14: "Behold a virgin shall conceive." Sometimes, however, the prophetic revelation is an imprinted likeness of the Divine foreknowledge as knowing the order of causes to effects; and then at times the event is otherwise than foretold. Yet the prophecy does not cover a falsehood, for the meaning of the prophecy is that inferior causes, whether they be natural causes or human acts, are so disposed as to lead to such a result. In this way we are to understand the saying of Is. 38:1: "Thou shalt die, and not live"; in other words, "The disposition of thy body has a tendency to death": and the saying of Jonah 3:4, "Yet forty days, and Nineveh shall be destroyed," that is to say, "Its merits demand that it should be destroyed." God is said "to repent," metaphorically, inasmuch as He bears Himself after the manner of one who repents, by "changing His sentence, although He changes not His counsel" [*Cf. [3669]FP, Q[19], A[7], ad 2].

Reply to Objection 3: Since the same truth of prophecy is the same as the truth of Divine foreknowledge, as stated above, the conditional proposition: "If this was prophesied, it will be," is true in the same way as the proposition: "If this was foreknown, it will be": for in both cases it is impossible for the antecedent not to be. Hence the consequent is necessary, considered, not as something future in our regard, but as being present to the Divine foreknowledge, as stated in the [3670]FP, Q[14], A[13], ad 2.

OF THE CAUSE OF PROPHECY (SIX ARTICLES)

We must now consider the cause of prophecy. Under this head there are six points of inquiry:

(1) Whether prophecy is natural?

(2) Whether it is from God by means of the angels?

(3) Whether a natural disposition is requisite for prophecy?

(4) Whether a good life is requisite?

(5) Whether any prophecy is from the demons?

(6) Whether prophets of the demons ever tell what is true?

Whether prophecy can be natural?

Objection 1: It would seem that prophecy can be natural. For Gregory says (Dial. iv, 26) that "sometimes the mere strength of the soul is sufficiently cunning to foresee certain things": and Augustine says (Gen. ad lit. xii, 13) that the human soul, according as it is withdrawn from the sense of the body, is able to foresee the future [*Cf. [3671]FP, Q[86], A[4], ad 2]. Now this pertains to prophecy. Therefore the soul can acquire prophecy naturally.

Objection 2: Further, the human soul's knowledge is more alert while one wakes than while one sleeps. Now some, during sleep, naturally foresee the future, as the Philosopher asserts (De Somn. et Vigil. [*De Divinat. per Somn. ii, which is annexed to the work quoted]). Much more therefore can a man naturally foreknow the future.

Objection 3: Further, man, by his nature, is more perfect than dumb animals. Yet some dumb animals have foreknowledge of future things that concern them. Thus ants foreknow the coming rains, which is evident from their gathering grain into their nest before the rain commences; and in like manner fish foreknow a coming storm, as may be gathered from their movements in avoiding places exposed to storm. Much more therefore can men foreknow the future that concerns themselves, and of such things is prophecy. Therefore prophecy comes from nature.

Objection 4: Further, it is written (Prov. 29:18): "When prophecy shall fail, the people shall be scattered abroad"; wherefore it is evident that prophecy is necessary for the stability of the human race. Now "nature does not fail in necessaries" [*Aristotle, de Anima iii, 9]. Therefore it seems that prophecy is from nature.

On the contrary, It is written (2 Pet. 1:21): "For prophecy came not by the will of man at any time, but the holy men of God spoke, inspired by the Holy Ghost." Therefore prophecy comes not from nature, but through the gift of the Holy Ghost.

I answer that, As stated above (Q[171], A[6], ad 2) prophetic foreknowledge may regard future things in two ways: in one way, as they are in themselves; in another way, as they are in their causes. Now, to foreknow future things, as they are in themselves, is proper to the Divine intellect, to Whose eternity all things are present, as stated in the [3672]FP, Q[14], A[13]. Wherefore such like foreknowledge of the future cannot come from nature, but from Divine revelation alone. On the other hand, future things can be foreknown in their causes with a natural knowledge even by man: thus a physician foreknows future health or death in certain causes, through previous experimental knowledge of the order of those causes to such effects. Such like knowledge of the future may be understood to be in a man by nature in two ways. In one way that the soul, from that which it holds, is able to foreknow the future, and thus Augustine says (Gen. ad lit. xii, 13): "Some have deemed the human soul to contain a certain power of divination." This seems to be in accord with the opinion of Plato [*Phaed. xxvii; Civit. vi], who held that our souls have knowledge of all things by participating in the ideas; but that this knowledge is obscured in them by union with the body; yet in some more, in others less, according to a difference in bodily purity. According to this it might be said that men, whose souls are not much obscured through union with the body, are able to foreknow such like future things by their own knowledge. Against this opinion Augustine says (Gen. ad lit. xii, 13): "How is it that the soul cannot always have this power of divination, since it always wishes to have it?"

Since, however, it seems truer, according to the opinion of Aristotle, that the soul acquires knowledge from sensibles, as stated in the [3673]FP, Q[84], A[6], it is better to have recourse to another explanation, and to hold that men have no such foreknowledge of the future, but that they can acquire it by means of experience, wherein they are helped by their natural disposition, which depends on the perfection of a man's imaginative power, and the clarity of his understanding.

Nevertheless this latter foreknowledge of the future differs in two ways from the former, which comes through Divine revelation. First, because the former can be about any events whatever, and this infallibly; whereas the latter foreknowledge, which can be had naturally, is about certain effects, to which human experience may extend. Secondly, because the former prophecy is "according to the unchangeable truth" [*[3674]Q[171], A[3], OBJ[1]], while the latter is not, and can cover a falsehood. Now the former foreknowledge, and not the latter, properly belongs to prophecy, because, as stated above ([3675]Q[171], A[3]), prophetic knowledge is of things which naturally surpass human knowledge. Consequently we must say that prophecy strictly so called cannot be from nature, but only from Divine revelation.

Reply to Objection 1: When the soul is withdrawn from corporeal things, it becomes more adapted to receive the influence of spiritual substances [*Cf. FP, Q[88], A[4], ad 2], and also is more inclined to receive the subtle motions which take place in the human imagination through the impression of natural causes, whereas it is hindered from receiving them while occupied with sensible things. Hence Gregory says (Dial. iv, 26) that "the soul, at the approach of death, foresees certain future things, by reason of the subtlety of its nature," inasmuch as it is receptive even of slight impressions. Or again, it knows future things by a revelation of the angels; but not by its own power, because according to Augustine (Gen. ad lit. xii, 13), "if this were so, it would be able to foreknow the future whenever it willed," which is clearly false.

Objection 2: Knowledge of the future by means of dreams, comes either from the revelation of spiritual substances, or from a corporeal cause, as stated above ([3676]Q[95], A[6]), when we were treating of divination. Now both these causes are more applicable to a person while asleep than while awake, because, while awake, the soul is occupied with external sensibles, so that it is less receptive of the subtle impressions either of spiritual substances, or even of natural causes; although as regards the perfection of judgment, the reason is more alert in waking than in sleeping.

Reply to Objection 3: Even dumb animals have no foreknowledge of future events, except as these are foreknown in their causes, whereby their imagination is moved more than man's, because man's imagination, especially in waking, is more disposed according to reason than according to the impression of natural causes. Yet reason effects much more amply in man, that which the impression of natural causes effects in dumb animals; and Divine grace by inspiring the prophecy assists man still more.

Reply to Objection 4: The prophetic light extends even to the direction of human acts; and in this way prophecy is requisite for the government of a people, especially in relation to Divine worship; since for this nature is not sufficient, and grace is necessary.

Whether prophetic revelation comes through the angels?

Objection 1: It would seem that prophetic revelation does not come through the angels. For it is written (Wis. 7:27) that Divine wisdom "conveyeth herself into holy souls," and "maketh the friends of God, and the prophets." Now wisdom makes the friends of God immediately. Therefore it also makes the prophets immediately, and not through the medium of the angels.

Objection 2: Further, prophecy is reckoned among the gratuitous graces. But the gratuitous graces are from the Holy Ghost, according to 1 Cor. 12:4, "There are diversities of graces, but the same Spirit." Therefore the prophetic revelation is not made by means of an angel.

Objection 3: Further, Cassiodorus [*Prol. in Psalt. i] says that prophecy is a "Divine revelation": whereas if it were conveyed by the angels, it would be called an angelic revelation. Therefore prophecy is not bestowed by means of the angels.

On the contrary, Dionysius says (Coel. Hier. iv): "Our glorious fathers received Divine visions by means of the heavenly powers"; and he is speaking there of prophetic visions. Therefore prophetic revelation is conveyed by means of the angels.

I answer that, As the Apostle says (Rom. 13:1), "Things that are of God are well ordered [*Vulg.: 'Those that are, are ordained of God.']." Now the Divine ordering, according to Dionysius [*Coel. Hier. iv; Eccl. Hier. v], is such that the lowest things are directed by middle things. Now the angels hold a middle position between God and men, in that they have a greater share in the perfection of the Divine goodness than men have. Wherefore the Divine enlightenments and revelations are conveyed from God to men by the angels. Now prophetic knowledge is bestowed by Divine enlightenment and revelation. Therefore it is evident that it is conveyed by the angels.

Reply to Objection 1: Charity which makes man a friend of God, is a perfection of the will, in which God alone can form an impression; whereas prophecy is a perfection of the intellect, in which an angel also can form an impression, as stated in the [3677]FP, Q[111], A[1], wherefore the comparison fails between the two.

Reply to Objection 2: The gratuitous graces are ascribed to the Holy Ghost as their first principle: yet He works grace of this kind in men by means of the angels.

Reply to Objection 3: The work of the instrument is ascribed to the principal agent by whose power the instrument acts. And since a minister is like an instrument, prophetic revelation, which is conveyed by the ministry of the angels, is said to be Divine.

Whether a natural disposition is requisite for prophecy?

Objection 1: It would seem that a natural disposition is requisite for prophecy. For prophecy is received by the prophet according to the disposition of the recipient, since a gloss of Jerome on Amos 1:2, "The Lord will roar from Sion," says: "Anyone who wishes to make a comparison naturally turns to those things of which he has experience, and among which his life is spent. For example, sailors compare their enemies to the winds, and their losses to a shipwreck. In like manner Amos, who was a shepherd, likens the fear of God to that which is inspired by the lion's roar." Now that which is received by a thing according to the mode of the recipient requires a natural disposition. Therefore prophecy requires a natural disposition.

Objection 2: Further, the considerations of prophecy are more lofty than those of acquired science. Now natural indisposition hinders the considerations of acquired science, since many are prevented by natural indisposition from succeeding to grasp the speculations of science. Much more therefore is a natural disposition requisite for the contemplation of prophecy.

Objection 3: Further, natural indisposition is a much greater obstacle than an accidental impediment. Now the considerations of prophecy are hindered by an accidental occurrence. For Jerome says in his commentary on Matthew [*The quotation is from Origen, Hom. vi in Num.] that "at the time of the marriage act, the presence of the Holy Ghost will not be vouchsafed, even though it be a prophet that fulfils the duty of procreation." Much more therefore does a natural indisposition hinder prophecy; and thus it would seem that a good natural disposition is requisite for prophecy.

On the contrary, Gregory says in a homily for Pentecost (xxx in Ev.): "He," namely the Holy Ghost, "fills the boy harpist and makes him a Psalmist; He fills the herdsman plucking wild figs, and makes him a prophet." Therefore prophecy requires no previous disposition, but depends on the will alone of the Holy Ghost, of Whom it is written (1 Cor. 12:2): "All these things, one and the same Spirit worketh, dividing to every one according as He will."

I answer that, As stated above [3678](A[1]), prophecy in its true and exact sense comes from Divine inspiration; while that which comes from a natural cause is not called prophecy except in a relative sense. Now we must observe that as God Who is the universal efficient cause requires neither previous matter nor previous disposition of matter in His corporeal effects, for He is able at the same instant to bring into being matter and disposition and form, so neither does He require a previous disposition in His spiritual effects, but is able to produce both the spiritual effect and at the same time the fitting disposition as requisite according to the order of nature. More than this, He is able at the same time, by creation, to produce the subject, so as to dispose a soul for prophecy and give it the prophetic grace, at the very instant of its creation.

Reply to Objection 1: It matters not to prophecy by what comparisons the thing prophesied is expressed; and so the Divine operation makes no change in a prophet in this respect. Yet if there be anything in him incompatible with prophecy, it is removed by the Divine power.

Reply to Objection 2: The considerations of science proceed from a natural cause, and nature cannot work without a previous disposition in matter. This cannot be said of God Who is the cause of prophecy.

Reply to Objection 3: A natural indisposition, if not removed, might be an obstacle to prophetic revelation, for instance if a man were altogether deprived of the natural senses. In the same way a man might be hindered from the act of prophesying by some very strong passion, whether of anger, or of concupiscence as in coition, or by any other passion. But such a natural indisposition as this is removed by the Divine power, which is the cause of prophecy.

Whether a good life is requisite for prophecy?

Objection 1: It would seem that a good life is requisite for prophecy. For it is written (Wis. 7:27) that the wisdom of God "through nations conveyeth herself into holy souls," and "maketh the friends of God, and prophets." Now there can be no holiness without a good life and sanctifying grace. Therefore prophecy cannot be without a good life and sanctifying grace.

Objection 2: Further, secrets are not revealed save to a friend, according to Jn. 15:15, "But I have called you friends, because all things whatsoever I have heard of

My Father, I have made known to you." Now God reveals His secrets to the prophets (Amos 3:7). Therefore it would seem that the prophets are the friends of God; which is impossible without charity. Therefore seemingly prophecy cannot be without charity; and charity is impossible without sanctifying grace.

Objection 3: Further, it is written (Mat. 7:15): "Beware of false prophets, who come to you in the clothing of sheep, but inwardly they are ravening wolves." Now all who are without grace are likened inwardly to a ravening wolf, and consequently all such are false prophets. Therefore no man is a true prophet except he be good by grace.

Objection 4: Further, the Philosopher says (De Somn. et Vigil. [*Cf. De Divinat. per Somn. i, which is annexed to the work quoted]) that "if interpretation of dreams is from God, it is unfitting for it to be bestowed on any but the best." Now it is evident that the gift of prophecy is from God. Therefore the gift of prophecy is vouchsafed only to the best men.

On the contrary, To those who had said, "Lord, have we not prophesied in Thy name?" this reply is made: "I never knew you" (Mat. 7:22,23). Now "the Lord knoweth who are His" (2 Tim. 2:19). Therefore prophecy can be in those who are not God's by grace.

I answer that, A good life may be considered from two points of view. First, with regard to its inward root, which is sanctifying grace. Secondly, with regard to the inward passions of the soul and the outward actions. Now sanctifying grace is given chiefly in order that man's soul may be united to God by charity. Wherefore Augustine says (De Trin. xv, 18): "A man is not transferred from the left side to the right, unless he receive the Holy Ghost, by Whom he is made a lover of God and of his neighbor." Hence whatever can be without charity can be without sanctifying grace, and consequently without goodness of life. Now prophecy can be without charity; and this is clear on two counts. First, on account of their respective acts: for prophecy pertains to the intellect, whose act precedes the act of the will, which power is perfected by charity. For this reason the Apostle (1 Cor. 13) reckons prophecy with other things pertinent to the intellect, that can be had without charity. Secondly, on account of their respective ends. For prophecy like other gratuitous graces is given for the good of the Church, according to 1 Cor. 12:7, "The manifestation of the Spirit is given to every man unto profit"; and is not directly intended to unite man's affections to God, which is the purpose of charity. Therefore prophecy can be without a good life, as regards the first root of this goodness.

If, however, we consider a good life, with regard to the passions of the soul, and external actions, from this point of view an evil life is an obstacle to prophecy. For prophecy requires the mind to be raised very high in order to contemplate spiritual things, and this is hindered by strong passions, and the inordinate pursuit of external things. Hence we read of the sons of the prophets (4 Kings 4:38) that they "dwelt together with [Vulg.: 'before']" Eliseus, leading a solitary life, as it were, lest worldly employment should be a hindrance to the gift of prophecy.

Reply to Objection 1: Sometimes the gift of prophecy is given to a man both for the good of others, and in order to enlighten his own mind; and such are those whom Divine wisdom, "conveying itself" by sanctifying grace to their minds, "maketh the friends of God, and prophets." Others, however, receive the gift of prophecy merely for the good of others. Hence Jerome commenting on Mat. 7:22, says: "Sometimes prophesying, the working of miracles, and the casting out of demons are accorded not to the merit of those who do these things, but either to the invoking the name of Christ, or to the condemnation of those who invoke, and for the good of those who see and hear."

Reply to Objection 2: Gregory [*Hom. xxvii in Ev.] expounding this passage [*Jn. 15:15] says: "Since we love the lofty things of heaven as soon as we hear them, we know them as soon as we love them, for to love is to know. Accordingly He had made all things known to them, because having renounced earthly desires they were kindled by the torches of perfect love." In this way the Divine secrets are not always revealed to prophets.

Reply to Objection 3: Not all wicked men are ravening wolves, but only those whose purpose is to injure others. For Chrysostom says [*Opus Imperf. in Matth., Hom. xix, among the works of St. John Chrysostom, and falsely ascribed to him] that "Catholic teachers, though they be sinners, are called slaves of the flesh, but never ravening wolves, because they do not purpose the destruction of Christians." And since prophecy is directed to the good of others, it is manifest that such are false prophets, because they are not sent for this purpose by God.

Reply to Objection 4: God's gifts are not always bestowed on those who are simply the best, but sometimes are vouchsafed to those who are best as regards the receiving of this or that gift. Accordingly God grants the gift of prophecy to those whom He judges best to give it to.

Whether any prophecy comes from the demons?

Objection 1: It would seem that no prophecy comes from the demons. For prophecy is "a Divine revelation," according to Cassiodorus [*Prol. in Psalt. i]. But that which is done by a demon is not Divine. Therefore no prophecy can be from a demon.

Objection 2: Further, some kind of enlightenment is requisite for prophetic knowledge, as stated above (Q[171], AA[2],3). Now the demons do not enlighten the human intellect, as stated above in the FP, Q[119], A[3]. Therefore no prophecy can come from the demons.

Objection 3: Further, a sign is worthless if it betokens contraries. Now prophecy is a sign in confirmation of faith; wherefore a gloss on Rom. 12:6, "Either prophecy to be used according to the rule of faith," says: "Observe that in reckoning the graces, he begins with prophecy, which is the first proof of the reasonableness of our faith; since believers, after receiving the Spirit, prophesied." Therefore prophecy cannot be bestowed by the demons.

On the contrary, It is written (3 Kings 18:19): "Gather unto me all Israel unto mount Carmel, and the prophets of Baal four hundred and fifty, and the prophets of the grove four hundred, who eat at Jezebel's table." Now these were worshippers of demons. Therefore it would seem that there is also a prophecy from the demons.

I answer that, As stated above ([3679]Q[171], A[1]), prophecy denotes knowledge far removed from human knowledge. Now it is evident that an intellect of a higher order can know some things that are far removed from the knowledge of an inferior intellect. Again, above the human intellect there is not only the Divine intellect, but also the intellects of good and bad angels according to the order of nature. Hence the demons, even by their natural knowledge, know certain things remote from men's knowledge, which they can reveal to men: although those things which God alone knows are remote simply and most of all.

Accordingly prophecy, properly and simply, is conveyed by Divine revelations alone; yet the revelation which is made by the demons may be called prophecy in a restricted sense. Wherefore those men to whom something is revealed by the demons are styled in the Scriptures as prophets, not simply, but with an addition, for instance as "false prophets," or "prophets of idols." Hence Augustine says (Gen. ad lit. xii, 19): "When the evil spirit lays hold of a man for such purposes as these," namely visions, "he makes him either devilish, or possessed, or a false prophet."

Reply to Objection 1: Cassiodorus is here defining prophecy in its proper and simple acceptation.

Reply to Objection 2: The demons reveal what they know to men, not by enlightening the intellect, but by an imaginary vision, or even by audible speech; and in this way this prophecy differs from true prophecy.

Reply to Objection 3: The prophecy of the demons can be distinguished from Divine prophecy by certain, and even outward, signs. Hence Chrysostom says [*Opus Imperf. in Matth., Hom. xix, falsely ascribed to St. John Chrysostom] that "some prophesy by the spirit of the devil, such as diviners, but they may be discerned by the fact that the devil sometimes utters what is false, the Holy Ghost never." Wherefore it is written (Dt. 18:21,22): "If in silent thought thou answer: How shall I know the word that the Lord hath spoken? Thou shalt have this sign: Whatsoever that same prophet foretelleth in the name of the Lord, and it come not to pass, that thing the Lord hath not spoken."

Whether the prophets of the demons ever foretell the truth?

Objection 1: It would seem that the prophets of the demons never foretell the truth. For Ambrose [*Hilary the Deacon (Ambrosiaster) on 1 Cor. 12:3] says that "Every truth, by whomsoever spoken, is from the Holy Ghost." Now the prophets of the demons do not speak from the Holy Ghost, because "there is no concord between Christ and Belial [*'What concord hath Christ with Belial?']" (2 Cor. 6:15). Therefore it would seem that they never foretell the truth.

Objection 2: Further, just as true prophets are inspired by the Spirit of truth, so the prophets of the demons are inspired by the spirit of untruth, according to 3 Kings 22:22, "I will go forth, and be a lying spirit in the mouth of all his prophets." Now the prophets inspired by the Holy Ghost never speak false, as stated above (Q[111], A[6]). Therefore the prophets of the demons never speak truth.

Objection 3: Further, it is said of the devil (Jn. 8:44) that "when he speaketh a lie, he speaketh of his own, for the devil is a liar, and the father thereof," i.e. of lying. Now by inspiring his prophets, the devil speaks only of his own, for he is not appointed God's minister to declare the truth, since "light hath no fellowship with darkness [*Vulg.: 'What fellowship hath light with darkness?']" (2 Cor. 6:14). Therefore the prophets of the demons never foretell the truth.

On the contrary, A gloss on Num. 22:14, says that "Balaam was a diviner, for he sometimes foreknew the future by help of the demons and the magic art." Now he foretold many true things, for instance that which is to be found in Num. 24:17: "A star shall rise out of Jacob, and a scepter shall spring up from Israel." Therefore even the prophets of the demons foretell the truth.

I answer that, As the good is in relation to things, so is the true in relation to knowledge. Now in things it is impossible to find one that is wholly devoid of good. Wherefore it is also impossible for any knowledge to be wholly false, without some mixture of truth. Hence Bede says [*Comment. in Luc. xvii, 12; Cf. Augustine, QQ. Evang. ii, 40] that "no teaching is so false that it never mingles truth with falsehood." Hence the teaching of the demons, with which they instruct their prophets, contains some truths whereby it is rendered acceptable. For the intellect is led astray to falsehood by the semblance of truth, even as the will is seduced to evil by the semblance of goodness. Wherefore Chrysostom says [*Opus Imperf. in Matth., Hom. xix, falsely ascribed to St. John Chrysostom]: "The devil is allowed sometimes to speak true things, in order that his unwonted truthfulness may gain credit for his lie."

Reply to Objection 1: The prophets of the demons do not always speak from the demons' revelation, but sometimes by Divine inspiration. This was evidently the case with Balaam, of whom we read that the Lord spoke to him (Num. 22:12), though he was a prophet of the demons, because God makes use even of the wicked for the profit of the good. Hence He foretells certain truths even by the demons' prophets, both that the truth may be rendered more credible, since even its foes bear witness to it, and also in order that men, by believing such men, may be more easily led on to truth. Wherefore also the Sibyls foretold many true things about Christ.

Yet even when the demons' prophets are instructed by the demons, they foretell the truth, sometimes by virtue of their own nature, the author of which is the Holy Ghost, and sometimes by revelation of the good spirits, as Augustine declares (Gen. ad lit. xii, 19): so that even then this truth which the demons proclaim is from the Holy Ghost.

Reply to Objection 2: A true prophet is always inspired by the Spirit of truth, in Whom there is no falsehood, wherefore He never says what is not true; whereas a false prophet is not always instructed by the spirit of untruth, but sometimes even by the Spirit of truth. Even the very spirit of untruth sometimes declares true things, sometimes false, as stated above.

Reply to Objection 3: Those things are called the demons' own, which they have of themselves, namely lies and sins; while they have, not of themselves but of God, those things which belong to them by nature: and it is by virtue of their own nature that they sometimes foretell the truth, as stated above (ad 1). Moreover God makes use of them to make known the truth which is to be accomplished through them, by revealing Divine mysteries to them through the angels, as already stated (Gen. ad lit. xii, 19; [3680]FP, Q[109], A[4], ad 1).

OF THE MANNER IN WHICH PROPHETIC KNOWLEDGE IS CONVEYED (FOUR ARTICLES)

We must now consider the manner in which prophetic knowledge is conveyed, and under this head there are four points of inquiry:

(1) Whether the prophets see God's very essence?

(2) Whether the prophetic revelation is effected by the infusion of certain species, or by the infusion of Divine light alone?

(3) Whether prophetic revelation is always accompanied by abstraction from the sense?

(4) Whether prophecy is always accompanied by knowledge of the things prophesied?

Whether the prophets see the very essence of God?

Objection 1: It would seem that the prophets see the very essence of God, for a gloss on Is. 38:1, "Take order with thy house, for thou shalt die and not live," says: "Prophets can read in the book of God's foreknowledge in which all things are written." Now God's foreknowledge is His very essence. Therefore prophets see God's very essence.

Objection 2: Further, Augustine says (De Trin. ix, 7) that "in that eternal truth from which all temporal things are made, we see with the mind's eye the type both of our being and of our actions." Now, of all men, prophets have the highest knowledge of Divine things. Therefore they, especially, see the Divine essence.

Objection 3: Further, future contingencies are foreknown by the prophets "with unchangeable truth." Now future contingencies exist thus in God alone. Therefore the prophets see God Himself.

On the contrary, The vision of the Divine essence is not made void in heaven; whereas "prophecy is made void" (1 Cor. 13:8). Therefore prophecy is not conveyed by a vision of the Divine essence.

I answer that, Prophecy denotes Divine knowledge as existing afar off. Wherefore it is said of the prophets (Heb. 11:13) that "they were beholding . . . afar off." But those who are in heaven and in the state of bliss see, not as from afar off, but rather, as it were, from near at hand, according to Ps. 139:14, "The upright shall dwell with Thy countenance." Hence it is evident that prophetic knowledge differs from the perfect knowledge, which we shall have in heaven, so that it is distinguished therefrom as the imperfect from the perfect, and when the latter comes the former is made void, as appears from the words of the Apostle (1 Cor. 13:10).

Some, however, wishing to discriminate between prophetic knowledge and the knowledge of the blessed, have maintained that the prophets see the very essence of God (which they call the "mirror of eternity") [*Cf. De Veritate, xii, 6; Sent. II, D, XI, part 2, art. 2, ad 4], not, however, in the way in which it is the object of the blessed, but as containing the types [*Cf. FP, Q[15]] of future events. But this is altogether impossible. For God is the object of bliss in His very essence, according to the saying of Augustine (Confess. v, 4): "Happy whoso knoweth Thee, though he know not these," i.e. creatures. Now it is not possible to see the types of creatures in the very essence of God without seeing It, both because the Divine essence is Itself the type of all things that are made—the ideal type adding nothing to the Divine essence save only a relationship to the creature—and because knowledge of a thing in itself—and such is the knowledge of God as the object of heavenly bliss—precedes knowledge of that thing in its relation to something else—and such is the knowledge of God as containing the types of things. Consequently it is impossible for prophets to see God as containing the types of creatures, and yet not as the object of bliss. Therefore we must conclude that the prophetic vision is not the vision of the very essence of God, and that the prophets do not see in the Divine essence Itself the things they do see, but that they see them in certain images, according as they are enlightened by the Divine light.

Wherefore Dionysius (Coel. Hier. iv), in speaking of prophetic visions, says that "the wise theologian calls that vision divine which is effected by images of things lacking a bodily form through the seer being rapt in divine things." And these images illumined by the Divine light have more of the nature of a mirror than the Divine essence: since in a mirror images are formed from other things, and this cannot be said of God. Yet the prophet's mind thus enlightened may be called a mirror, in so far as a likeness of the truth of the Divine foreknowledge is formed therein, for which reason it is called the "mirror of eternity," as representing God's foreknowledge, for God in His eternity sees all things as present before Him, as stated above ([3681]Q[172], A[1]).

Reply to Objection 1: The prophets are said to read the book of God's foreknowledge, inasmuch as the truth is reflected from God's foreknowledge on the prophet's mind.

Reply to Objection 2: Man is said to see in the First Truth the type of his existence, in so far as the image of the First Truth shines forth on man's mind, so that he is able to know himself.

Reply to Objection 3: From the very fact that future contingencies are in God according to unalterable truth, it follows that God can impress a like knowledge on the prophet's mind without the prophet seeing God in His essence.

Whether, in prophetic revelation, new species of things are impressed on the prophet's mind, or merely a new light?

Objection 1: It would seem that in prophetic revelation no new species of things are impressed on the prophet's mind, but only a new light. For a gloss of Jerome on Amos 1:2 says that "prophets draw comparisons from things with which they are conversant." But if prophetic vision were effected by means of species newly impressed, the prophet's previous experience of things would be inoperative. Therefore no new species are impressed on the prophet's soul, but only the prophetic light.

Objection 2: Further, according to Augustine (Gen. ad lit. xii, 9), "it is not imaginative but intellective vision that makes the prophet"; wherefore it is declared (Dan. 10:1) that "there is need of understanding in a vision." Now intellective vision, as stated in the same book (Gen. ad lit. xii, 6) is not effected by means of images, but by the very truth of things. Therefore it would seem that prophetic revelation is not effected by impressing species on the soul.

Objection 3: Further, by the gift of prophecy the Holy Ghost endows man with something that surpasses the faculty of nature. Now man can by his natural faculties form all kinds of species of things. Therefore it would seem that in prophetic revelation no new species of things are impressed, but merely an intellectual light.

On the contrary, It is written (Osee 12:10): "I have multiplied" their "visions, and I have used similitudes, by the ministry of the prophets." Now multiplicity of visions results, not from a diversity of intellectual light, which is common to every prophetic vision, but from a diversity of species, whence similitudes also result.

Therefore it seems that in prophetic revelation new species of things are impressed, and not merely an intellectual light.

I answer that, As Augustine says (Gen. ad lit. xii, 9), "prophetic knowledge pertains most of all to the intellect." Now two things have to be considered in connection with the knowledge possessed by the human mind, namely the acceptance or representation of things, and the judgment of the things represented. Now things are represented to the human mind under the form of species: and according to the order of nature, they must be represented first to the senses, secondly to the imagination, thirdly to the passive intellect, and these are changed by the species derived from the phantasms, which change results from the enlightening action of the active intellect. Now in the imagination there are the forms of sensible things not only as received from the senses, but also transformed in various ways, either on account of some bodily transformation (as in the case of people who are asleep or out of their senses), or through the coordination of the phantasms, at the command of reason, for the purpose of understanding something. For just as the various arrangements of the letters of the alphabet convey various ideas to the understanding, so the various coordinations of the phantasms produce various intelligible species of the intellect.

As to the judgment formed by the human mind, it depends on the power of the intellectual light.

Now the gift of prophecy confers on the human mind something which surpasses the natural faculty in both these respects, namely as to the judgment which depends on the inflow of intellectual light, and as to the acceptance or representation of things, which is effected by means of certain species. Human teaching may be likened to prophetic revelation in the second of these respects, but not in the first. For a man represents certain things to his disciple by signs of speech, but he cannot enlighten him inwardly as God does.

But it is the first of these two that holds the chief place in prophecy, since judgment is the complement of knowledge. Wherefore if certain things are divinely represented to any man by means of imaginary likenesses, as happened to Pharaoh (Gn. 41:1–7) and to Nabuchodonosor (Dan. 4:1–2), or even by bodily likenesses, as happened to Balthasar (Dan. 5:5), such a man is not to be considered a prophet, unless his mind be enlightened for the purpose of judgment; and such an apparition is something imperfect in the genus of prophecy. Wherefore some [*Rabbi Moyses, Doct. Perplex. II, xxxvi] have called this "prophetic ecstasy," and such is divination by dreams. And yet a man will be a prophet, if his intellect be enlightened merely for the purpose of judging of things seen in imagination by others, as in the case of Joseph who interpreted Pharaoh's dream. But, as Augustine says

(Gen. ad lit. xii, 9), "especially is he a prophet who excels in both respects, so," to wit, "as to see in spirit likenesses significant of things corporeal, and understand them by the quickness of his intellect."

Now sensible forms are divinely presented to the prophet's mind, sometimes externally by means of the senses—thus Daniel saw the writing on the wall (Dan. 5:25)—sometimes by means of imaginary forms, either of exclusively Divine origin and not received through the senses (for instance, if images of colors were imprinted on the imagination of one blind from birth), or divinely coordinated from those derived from the senses—thus Jeremiah saw the "boiling caldron . . . from the face of the north" (Jer. 1:13)—or by the direct impression of intelligible species on the mind, as in the case of those who receive infused scientific knowledge or wisdom, such as Solomon or the apostles.

But intellectual light is divinely imprinted on the human mind—sometimes for the purpose of judging of things seen by others, as in the case of Joseph, quoted above, and of the apostles whose understanding our Lord opened "that they might understand the scriptures" (Lk. 24:45); and to this pertains the "interpretation of speeches"—sometimes for the purpose of judging according to Divine truth, of the things which a man apprehends in the ordinary course of nature—sometimes for the purpose of discerning truthfully and efficaciously what is to be done, according to Is. 63:14, "The Spirit of the Lord was their leader."

Hence it is evident that prophetic revelation is conveyed sometimes by the mere infusion of light, sometimes by imprinting species anew, or by a new coordination of species.

Reply to Objection 1: As stated above, sometimes in prophetic revelation imaginary species previously derived from the senses are divinely coordinated so as to accord with the truth to be revealed, and then previous experience is operative in the production of the images, but not when they are impressed on the mind wholly from without.

Reply to Objection 2: Intellectual vision is not effected by means of bodily and individual images, but by an intelligible image. Hence Augustine says (De Trin. ix, 11) that "the soul possesses a certain likeness of the species known to it." Sometimes this intelligible image is, in prophetic revelation, imprinted immediately by God, sometimes it results from pictures in the imagination, by the aid of the prophetic light, since a deeper truth is gathered from these pictures in the imagination by means of the enlightenment of the higher light.

Reply to Objection 3: It is true that man is able by his natural powers to form all kinds of pictures in the imagination, by simply considering these pictures, but not so that they be directed to the representation of intelligible truths that surpass his intellect, since for this purpose he needs the assistance of a supernatural light.

Whether the prophetic vision is always accompanied by abstraction from the senses?

Objection 1: It would seem that the prophetic vision is always accompanied by abstraction from the senses. For it is written (Num. 12:6): "If there be among you a prophet of the Lord, I will appear to him in a vision, or I will speak to him in a dream." Now a gloss says at the beginning of the Psalter, "a vision that takes place by dreams and apparitions consists of things which seem to be said or done." But when things seem to be said or done, which are neither said nor done, there is abstraction from the senses. Therefore prophecy is always accompanied by abstraction from the senses.

Objection 2: Further, when one power is very intent on its own operation, other powers are drawn away from theirs; thus men who are very intent on hearing something fail to see what takes place before them. Now in the prophetic vision the intellect is very much uplifted, and intent on its act. Therefore it seems that the prophetic vision is always accompanied by abstraction from the senses.

Objection 3: Further, the same thing cannot, at the same time, tend in opposite directions. Now in the prophetic vision the mind tends to the acceptance of things from above, and consequently it cannot at the same time tend to sensible objects. Therefore it would seem necessary for prophetic revelation to be always accompanied by abstraction from the senses.

Objection 4: On the contrary, It is written (1 Cor. 14:32): "The spirits of the prophets are subject to the prophets." Now this were impossible if the prophet were not in possession of his faculties, but abstracted from his senses. Therefore it would seem that prophetic vision is not accompanied by abstraction from the senses.

I answer that, As stated in the foregoing Article, the prophetic revelation takes place in four ways: namely, by the infusion of an intelligible light, by the infusion of intelligible species, by impression or coordination of pictures in the imagination, and by the outward presentation of sensible images. Now it is evident that there is no abstraction from the senses, when something is presented to the prophet's mind by means of sensible species—whether these be divinely formed for this special purpose, as the bush shown to Moses (Ex. 3:2), and the writing shown to Daniel (Dan. 5:)—or whether they be produced by other causes; yet so that they are ordained by Divine providence to be prophetically significant of something, as, for instance, the Church was signified by the ark of Noah.

Again, abstraction from the external senses is not rendered necessary when the prophet's mind is enlightened by an intellectual light, or impressed with intelligible species, since in us the perfect judgment of the intellect is effected by its turning to sensible objects, which are the first principles of our knowledge, as stated in the [3682]FP, Q[84], A[6].

When, however, prophetic revelation is conveyed by images in the imagination, abstraction from the senses is necessary lest the things thus seen in imagination be taken for objects of external sensation. Yet this abstraction from the senses is sometimes complete, so that a man perceives nothing with his senses; and sometimes it is incomplete, so that he perceives something with his senses, yet does not fully discern the things he perceives outwardly from those he sees in imagination. Hence Augustine says (Gen. ad lit. xii, 12): "Those images of bodies which are formed in the soul are seen just as bodily things themselves are seen by the body, so that we see with our eyes one who is present, and at the same time we see with the soul one who is absent, as though we saw him with our eyes."

Yet this abstraction from the senses takes place in the prophets without subverting the order of nature, as is the case with those who are possessed or out of their senses; but is due to some well-ordered cause. This cause may be natural—for instance, sleep—or spiritual—for instance, the intenseness of the prophets' contemplation; thus we read of Peter (Acts 10:9) that while he was praying in the supper-room [*Vulg.: 'the house-top' or 'upper-chamber'] "he fell into an ecstasy"—or he may be carried away by the Divine power, according to the saying of Ezechiel 1:3: "The hand of the Lord was upon him."

Reply to Objection 1: The passage quoted refers to prophets in whom imaginary pictures were formed or coordinated, either while asleep, which is denoted by the word "dream," or while awake, which is signified by the word "vision."

Reply to Objection 2: When the mind is intent, in its act, upon distant things which are far removed from the senses, the intensity of its application leads to abstraction from the senses; but when it is intent, in its act, upon the coordination of or judgment concerning objects of sense, there is no need for abstraction from the senses.

Reply to Objection 3: The movement of the prophetic mind results not from its own power, but from a power acting on it from above. Hence there is no abstraction from the senses when the prophet's mind is led to judge or coordinate matters relating to objects of sense, but only when the mind is raised to the contemplation of certain more lofty things.

Reply to Objection 4: The spirit of the prophets is said to be subject to the prophets as regards the prophetic utterances to which the Apostle refers in the words quoted; because, to wit, the prophets in declaring what they have seen speak their own mind, and are not thrown off their mental balance, like persons who are possessed, as Priscilla and Montanus maintained. But as regards the prophetic revelation itself, it would be more correct to say that the prophets are subject to the. spirit of prophecy, i.e. to the prophetic gift.

Whether prophets always know the things which they prophesy?

Objection 1: It would seem that the prophets always know the things which they prophesy. For, as Augustine says (Gen. ad lit. xii, 9), "those to whom signs were shown in spirit by means of the likenesses of bodily things, had not the gift of prophecy, unless the mind was brought into action, so that those signs were also understood by them." Now what is understood cannot be unknown. Therefore the prophet is not ignorant of what he prophesies.

Objection 2: Further, the light of prophecy surpasses the light of natural reason. Now one who possesses a science by his natural light, is not ignorant of his scientific acquirements. Therefore he who utters things by the prophetic light cannot ignore them.

Objection 3: Further, prophecy is directed for man's enlightenment; wherefore it is written (2 Pet. 1:19): "We have the more firm prophetical word, whereunto you do well to attend, as to a light that shineth in a dark place." Now nothing can enlighten others unless it be lightsome in itself. Therefore it would seem that the prophet is first enlightened so as to know what he declares to others.

On the contrary, It is written (Jn. 11:51): "And this he" (Caiphas) "spoke, not of himself, but being the High Priest of that year, he prophesied that Jesus should die for the nation," etc. Now Caiphas knew this not. Therefore not every prophet knows what he prophesies.

I answer that, In prophetic revelation the prophet's mind is moved by the Holy Ghost, as an instrument that is deficient in regard to the principal agent. Now the prophet's mind is moved not only to apprehend something, but also to speak or to do something; sometimes indeed to all these three together, sometimes to two, sometimes to one only, and in each case there may be a defect in the prophet's knowledge. For when the prophet's mind is moved to think or apprehend a thing, sometimes he is led merely to apprehend that thing, and sometimes he is further led to know that it is divinely revealed to him.

Again, sometimes the prophet's mind is moved to speak something, so that he understands what the Holy Ghost means by the words he utters; like David who said (2 Kings 23:2): "The Spirit of the Lord hath spoken by me"; while, on the other hand, sometimes the person whose mind is moved to utter certain words knows not what the Holy Ghost means by them, as was the case with Caiphas (Jn. 11:51).

Again, when the Holy Ghost moves a man's mind to do something, sometimes the latter understands the meaning of it, like Jeremias who hid his loin-cloth in the Euphrates (Jer. 13:1–11); while sometimes he does not understand it—thus the soldiers, who divided Christ's garments, understood not the meaning of what they did.

Accordingly, when a man knows that he is being moved by the Holy Ghost to think something, or signify something by word or deed, this belongs properly to prophecy; whereas when he is moved, without his knowing it, this is not perfect prophecy, but a prophetic instinct. Nevertheless it must be observed that since the prophet's mind is a defective instrument, as stated above, even true prophets know not all that the Holy Ghost means by the things they see, or speak, or even do.

And this suffices for the Replies to the Objections, since the arguments given at the beginning refer to true prophets whose minds are perfectly enlightened from above.

OF THE DIVISION OF PROPHECY (SIX ARTICLES)

We must now consider the division of prophecy, and under this head there are six points of inquiry:

(1) The division of prophecy into its species;

(2) Whether the more excellent prophecy is that which is without imaginative vision?

(3) The various degrees of prophecy;

(4) Whether Moses was the greatest of the prophets?

(5) Whether a comprehensor can be a prophet?

(6) Whether prophecy advanced in perfection as time went on?

Whether prophecy is fittingly divided into the prophecy of divine predestination, of foreknowledge, and of denunciation?

Objection 1: It would seem that prophecy is unfittingly divided according to a gloss on Mat. 1:23, "Behold a virgin shall be with child," where it is stated that "one kind of prophecy proceeds from the Divine predestination, and must in all respects be accomplished so that its fulfillment is independent of our will, for instance the one in question. Another prophecy proceeds from God's foreknowledge: and into this our will enters. And another prophecy is called denunciation, which is significative of God's disapproval." For that which results from every prophecy should not be reckoned a part of prophecy. Now all prophecy is according to the Divine foreknowledge, since the prophets "read in the book of foreknowledge," as a gloss says on Is. 38:1. Therefore it would seem that prophecy according to foreknowledge should not be reckoned a species of prophecy.

Objection 2: Further, just as something is foretold in denunciation, so is something foretold in promise, and both of these are subject to alteration. For it is written (Jer. 18:7,8): "I will suddenly speak against a nation and against a kingdom, to root out, and to pull down, and to destroy it. If that nation against which I have spoken shall repent of their evil, I also will repent"—and this pertains to the prophecy of denunciation, and afterwards the text continues in reference to the prophecy of promise (Jer. 18:9,10): "I will suddenly speak of a nation and of a kingdom, to build up and plant it. If it shall do evil in My sight . . . I will repent of the good that I have spoken to do unto it." Therefore as there is reckoned to be a prophecy of denunciation, so should there be a prophecy of promise.

Objection 3: Further, Isidore says (Etym. vii, 8): "There are seven kinds of prophecy. The first is an ecstasy, which is the transport of the mind: thus Peter saw a vessel descending from heaven with all manner of beasts therein. The second kind is a vision, as we read in Isaias, who says (Is. 6:1): 'I saw the Lord sitting,' etc. The third kind is a dream: thus Jacob in a dream, saw a ladder. The fourth kind is from the midst of a cloud: thus God spake to Moses. The fifth kind is a voice from heaven, as that which called to Abraham saying (Gn. 22:11): 'Lay not thy hand upon the boy.' The sixth kind is taking up a parable, as in the example of Balaam (Num. 23:7; 24:15). The seventh kind is the fullness of the Holy Ghost, as in the case of nearly all the prophets." Further, he mentions three kinds of vision; "one by the eyes of the body, another by the soul's imagination, a third by the eyes of the mind." Now these are not included in the aforesaid division. Therefore it is insufficient.

On the contrary, stands the authority of Jerome to whom the gloss above quoted is ascribed.

I answer that, The species of moral habits and acts are distinguished according to their objects. Now the object of prophecy is something known by God and surpassing the faculty of man. Wherefore, according to the difference of such things, prophecy is divided into various species, as assigned above. Now it has been stated above (Q[71], A[6], ad 2) that the future is contained in the Divine knowledge in two ways. First, as in its cause: and thus we have the prophecy of "denunciation," which is not always fulfilled. but it foretells the relation of cause to effect, which is sometimes hindered by some other occurrence supervening. Secondly, God foreknows certain things in themselves—either as to be accomplished by Himself, and of such things is the prophecy of "predestination," since, according to Damascene (De Fide Orth. ii, 30), "God predestines things which are not in our power"—or as to be accomplished through man's free-will, and of such is the prophecy of "foreknowledge." This may regard either good or evil, which does not apply to the prophecy of predestination, since the latter regards good alone. And since predestination is comprised under foreknowledge, the gloss in the beginning of the Psalter assigns only two species to prophecy, namely of "foreknowledge," and of "denunciation."

Reply to Objection 1: Foreknowledge, properly speaking, denotes precognition of future events in themselves, and in this sense it is reckoned a species of prophecy. But in so far as it is used in connection with future events, whether as in themselves, or as in their causes, it is common to every species of prophecy.

Reply to Objection 2: The prophecy of promise is included in the prophecy of denunciation, because the aspect of truth is the same in both. But it is denominated in preference from denunciation, because God is more inclined to remit punishment than to withdraw promised blessings.

Reply to Objection 3: Isidore divides prophecy according to the manner of prophesying. Now we may distinguish the manner of prophesying—either according to man's cognitive powers, which are sense, imagination, and intellect, and then we have the three kinds of vision mentioned both by him and by Augustine (Gen. ad lit. xii, 6,7)—or according to the different ways in which the prophetic current is received. Thus as regards the enlightening of the intellect there is the "fullness of the Holy Ghost" which he mentions in the seventh place. As to the imprinting of pictures on the imagination he mentions three, namely "dreams," to which he gives the third place; "vision," which occurs to the prophet while awake and regards any kind of ordinary object, and this he puts in the second place; and "ecstasy," which results from the mind being uplifted to certain lofty things, and to this he assigns the first place. As regards sensible signs he reckons three kinds of prophecy, because a sensible sign is—either a corporeal thing offered externally to the sight, such as "a cloud," which he mentions in the fourth place—or a "voice" sounding from without and conveyed to man's hearing—this he puts in the fifth place—or a voice proceeding from a man, conveying something under a similitude, and this pertains to the "parable" to which he assigns the sixth place.

Whether the prophecy which is accompanied by intellective and imaginative vision is more excellent than that which is accompanied by intellective vision alone?

Objection 1: It would seem that the prophecy which has intellective and imaginative vision is more excellent than that which is accompanied by intellective vision alone. For Augustine says (Gen. ad lit. xii, 9): "He is less a prophet, who sees in spirit nothing but the signs representative of things, by means of the images of things corporeal: he is more a prophet, who is merely endowed with the understanding of these signs; but most of all is he a prophet, who excels in both ways," and this refers to the prophet who has intellective together with imaginative vision. Therefore this kind of prophecy is more excellent.

Objection 2: Further, the greater a thing's power is, the greater the distance to which it extends. Now the prophetic light pertains chiefly to the mind, as stated above ([3683]Q[173], A[2]). Therefore apparently the prophecy that extends to the imagination is greater than that which is confined to the intellect.

Objection 3: Further, Jerome (Prol. in Lib. Reg.) distinguishes the "prophets" from the "sacred writers." Now all those whom he calls prophets (such as Isaias, Jeremias, and the like) had intellective together with imaginative vision: but not those whom he calls sacred writers, as writing by the inspiration of the Holy Ghost (such as Job, David, Solomon, and the like). Therefore it would seem more proper to call prophets those who had intellective together with imaginative vision, than those who had intellective vision alone.

Objection 4: Further, Dionysius says (Coel. Hier. i) that "it is impossible for the Divine ray to shine on us, except as screened round about by the many-colored sacred veils." Now the prophetic revelation is conveyed by the infusion of the divine ray. Therefore it seems that it cannot be without the veils of phantasms.

On the contrary, A gloss says at the beginning of the Psalter that "the most excellent manner of prophecy is when a man prophesies by the mere inspiration of the Holy Ghost, apart from any outward assistance of deed, word, vision, or dream."

I answer that, The excellence of the means is measured chiefly by the end. Now the end of prophecy is the manifestation of a truth that surpasses the faculty of man. Wherefore the more effective this manifestation is, the more excellent the prophecy. But it is evident that the manifestation of divine truth by means of the bare contemplation of the truth itself, is more effective than that which is conveyed under the similitude of corporeal things, for it approaches nearer to the heavenly vision whereby the truth is seen in God's essence. Hence it follows that the prophecy whereby a supernatural truth is seen by intellectual vision, is more excellent than that in which a supernatural truth is manifested by means of the similitudes of corporeal things in the vision of the imagination.

Moreover the prophet's mind is shown thereby to be more lofty: even as in human teaching the hearer, who is able to grasp the bare intelligible truth the master propounds, is shown to have a better understanding than one who needs to be taken by the hand and helped by means of examples taken from objects of sense. Hence it is said in commendation of David's prophecy (2 Kings 23:3): "The strong one of Israel spoke to me," and further on (2 Kings 23:4): "As the light of the morning, when the sun riseth, shineth in the morning without clouds."

Reply to Objection 1: When a particular supernatural truth has to be revealed by means of corporeal images, he that has both, namely the intellectual light and the imaginary vision, is more a prophet than he that has only one, because his prophecy is more perfect; and it is in this sense that Augustine speaks as quoted above. Nevertheless the prophecy in which the bare intelligible truth is revealed is greater than all.

Reply to Objection 2: The same judgment does not apply to things that are sought for their own sake, as to things sought for the sake of something else. For in things sought for their own sake, the agent's power is the more effective according as it extends to more numerous and more remote objects; even so a physician is thought more of, if he is able to heal more people, and those who are further removed from health. on the other hand, in things sought only for the sake of something else, that agent would seem to have greater power, who is able to achieve his purpose with fewer means and those nearest to hand: thus more praise is awarded the physician who is able to heal a sick person by means of fewer and more gentle remedies. Now, in the prophetic knowledge, imaginary vision is required, not for its own sake, but on account of the manifestation of the intelligible truth. Wherefore prophecy is all the more excellent according as it needs it less.

Reply to Objection 3: The fact that a particular predicate is applicable to one thing and less properly to another, does not prevent this latter from being simply better than the former: thus the knowledge of the blessed is more excellent than the knowledge of the wayfarer, although faith is more properly predicated of the latter knowledge, because faith implies an imperfection of knowledge. In like manner prophecy implies a certain obscurity, and remoteness from the intelligible truth; wherefore the name of prophet is more properly applied to those who see by imaginary vision. And yet the more excellent prophecy is that which is conveyed by intellectual vision, provided the same truth be revealed in either case. If, however, the intellectual light be divinely infused in a person, not that he may know some supernatural things, but that he may be able to judge, with the certitude of divine truth, of things that can be known by human reason, such intellectual prophecy is beneath that which is conveyed by an imaginary vision leading to a supernatural truth. It was this kind of prophecy that all those had who are included in the ranks of the prophets, who moreover were called prophets for the special reason that they exercised the prophetic calling officially. Hence they spoke as God's representatives, saying to the people: "Thus saith the Lord": but not so the authors of the "sacred writings," several of whom treated more frequently of things that can be known by human reason, not in God's name, but in their own, yet with the assistance of the Divine light withal.

Reply to Objection 4: In the present life the enlightenment by the divine ray is not altogether without any veil of phantasms, because according to his present state of life it is unnatural to man not to understand without a phantasm. Sometimes, however, it is sufficient to have phantasms abstracted in the usual way from the senses without any imaginary vision divinely vouchsafed, and thus prophetic vision is said to be without imaginary vision.

Whether the degrees of prophecy can be distinguished according to the imaginary vision?

Objection 1: It would seem that the degrees of prophecy cannot be distinguished according to the imaginary vision. For the degrees of a thing bear relation to something that is on its own account, not on account of something else. Now, in prophecy, intellectual vision is sought on its own account, and imaginary vision on account of something else, as stated above (A[2], ad 2). Therefore it would seem that the degrees of prophecy are distinguished not according to imaginary, but only according to intellectual, vision.

Objection 2: Further, seemingly for one prophet there is one degree of prophecy. Now one prophet receives revelation through various imaginary visions. Therefore a difference of imaginary visions does not entail a difference of prophecy.

Objection 3: Further, according to a gloss [*Cassiodorus, super Prolog. Hieron. in Psalt.], prophecy consists of words, deeds, dreams, and visions. Therefore the degrees of prophecy should not be distinguished according to imaginary vision, to which vision and dreams pertain, rather than according to words and deeds.

On the contrary, The medium differentiates the degrees of knowledge: thus science based on direct [*"Propter quid"] proofs is more excellent than science based on indirect [*"Quia"] premises or than opinion, because it comes through a more excellent medium. Now imaginary vision is a kind of medium in prophetic knowledge. Therefore the degrees of prophecy should be distinguished according to imaginary vision.

I answer that, As stated above ([3684]Q[173], A[2]), the prophecy wherein, by the intelligible light, a supernatural truth is revealed through an imaginary vision, holds the mean between the prophecy wherein a supernatural truth is revealed without imaginary vision, and that wherein through the intelligible light and without an imaginary vision, man is directed to know or do things pertaining to human conduct. Now knowledge is more proper to prophecy than is action; wherefore the lowest degree of prophecy is when a man, by an inward instinct, is moved to perform some outward action. Thus it is related of Samson (Judges

15:14) that "the Spirit of the Lord came strongly upon him, and as the flax [*'Lina.' St. Thomas apparently read 'ligna' ('wood')] is wont to be consumed at the approach of fire, so the bands with which he was bound were broken and loosed." The second degree of prophecy is when a man is enlightened by an inward light so as to know certain things, which, however, do not go beyond the bounds of natural knowledge: thus it is related of Solomon (3 Kings 4:32,33) that "he spoke . . . parables . . . and he treated about trees from the cedar that is in Libanus unto the hyssop that cometh out of the wall, and he discoursed of beasts and of fowls, and of creeping things and of fishes": and all of this came from divine inspiration, for it was stated previously (3 Kings 4:29): "God gave to Solomon wisdom and understanding exceeding much."

Nevertheless these two degrees are beneath prophecy properly so called, because they do not attain to supernatural truth. The prophecy wherein supernatural truth is manifested through imaginary vision is differentiated first according to the difference between dreams which occur during sleep, and vision which occurs while one is awake. The latter belongs to a higher degree of prophecy, since the prophetic light that draws the soul away to supernatural things while it is awake and occupied with sensible things would seem to be stronger than that which finds a man's soul asleep and withdrawn from objects of sense. Secondly the degrees of this prophecy are differentiated according to the expressiveness of the imaginary signs whereby the intelligible truth is conveyed. And since words are the most expressive signs of intelligible truth, it would seem to be a higher degree of prophecy when the prophet, whether awake or asleep, hears words expressive of an intelligible truth, than when he sees things significative of truth, for instance "the seven full ears of corn" signified "seven years of plenty" (Gn. 41:22, 26). In such like signs prophecy would seem to be the more excellent, according as the signs are more expressive, for instance when Jeremias saw the burning of the city under the figure of a boiling cauldron (Jer. 1:13). Thirdly, it is evidently a still higher degree of prophecy when a prophet not only sees signs of words or deeds, but also, either awake or asleep, sees someone speaking or showing something to him, since this proves the prophet's mind to have approached nearer to the cause of the revelation. Fourthly, the height of a degree of prophecy may be measured according to the appearance of the person seen: for it is a higher degree of prophecy, if he who speaks or shows something to the waking or sleeping prophet be seen by him under the form of an angel, than if he be seen by him under the form of man: and higher still is it, if he be seen by the prophet whether asleep or awake, under the appearance of God, according to Is. 6:1, "I saw the Lord sitting."

But above all these degrees there is a third kind of prophecy, wherein an intelligible and supernatural truth is shown without any imaginary vision. However, this goes beyond the bounds of prophecy properly so called, as stated above (A[2], ad

3); and consequently the degrees of prophecy are properly distinguished according to imaginary vision.

Reply to Objection 1: We are unable to know how to distinguish the intellectual light, except by means of imaginary or sensible signs. Hence the difference in the intellectual light is gathered from the difference in the things presented to the imagination.

Reply to Objection 2: As stated above ([3685]Q[171], A[2]), prophecy is by way, not of an abiding habit, but of a transitory passion; wherefore there is nothing inconsistent if one and the same prophet, at different times, receive various degrees of prophetic revelation.

Reply to Objection 3: The words and deeds mentioned there do not pertain to the prophetic revelation, but to the announcement, which is made according to the disposition of those to whom that which is revealed to the prophet is announced; and this is done sometimes by words, sometimes by deeds. Now this announcement, and the working of miracles, are something consequent upon prophecy, as stated above ([3686]Q[171], A[1]).

Whether Moses was the greatest of the prophets?

Objection 1: It would seem that Moses was not the greatest of the prophets. For a gloss at the beginning of the Psalter says that "David is called the prophet by way of excellence." Therefore Moses was not the greatest of all.

Objection 2: Further, greater miracles were wrought by Josue, who made the sun and moon to stand still (Josh. 10:12–14), and by Isaias, who made the sun to turn back (Is. 38:8), than by Moses, who divided the Red Sea (Ex. 14:21). In like manner greater miracles were wrought by Elias, of whom it is written (Ecclus. 48:4,5): "Who can glory like to thee? Who raisedst up a dead man from below." Therefore Moses was not the greatest of the prophets.

Objection 3: Further, it is written (Mat. 11:11) that "there hath not risen, among them that are born of women, a greater than John the Baptist." Therefore Moses was not greater than all the prophets.

On the contrary, It is written (Dt. 34:10): "There arose no more a prophet in Israel like unto Moses."

I answer that, Although in some respect one or other of the prophets was greater than Moses, yet Moses was simply the greatest of all. For, as stated above [3687](A[3]; Q[171], A[1]), in prophecy we may consider not only the knowledge, whether by intellectual or by imaginary vision, but also the announcement and the confirmation by miracles. Accordingly Moses was greater than the other prophets. First, as regards the intellectual vision, since he saw God's very essence, even as Paul in his rapture did, according to Augustine (Gen. ad lit. xii, 27). Hence it is written (Num. 12:8) that he saw God "plainly and not by riddles." Secondly, as regards the imaginary vision, which he had at his call, as it were, for not only did he hear words, but also saw one speaking to him under the form of God, and this not only while asleep, but even when he was awake. Hence it is written (Ex. 33:11) that "the Lord spoke to Moses face to face, as a man is wont to speak to his friend." Thirdly, as regards the working of miracles which he wrought on a whole nation of unbelievers. Wherefore it is written (Dt. 34:10,11): "There arose no more a prophet in Israel like unto Moses, whom the Lord knew face to face: in all the signs and wonders, which He sent by him, to do in the land of Egypt to Pharaoh, and to all his servants, and to his whole land."

Reply to Objection 1: The prophecy of David approaches near to the vision of Moses, as regards the intellectual vision, because both received a revelation of intelligible and supernatural truth, without any imaginary vision. Yet the vision of Moses was more excellent as regards the knowledge of the Godhead; while David more fully knew and expressed the mysteries of Christ's incarnation.

Reply to Objection 2: These signs of the prophets mentioned were greater as to the substance of the thing done; yet the miracles of Moses were greater as regards the way in which they were done, since they were wrought on a whole people.

Reply to Objection 3: John belongs to the New Testament, whose ministers take precedence even of Moses, since they are spectators of a fuller revelation, as stated in 2 Cor. 3.

Whether there is a degree of prophecy in the blessed?

Objection 1: It would seem that there is a degree of prophecy in the blessed. For, as stated above [3688](A[4]), Moses saw the Divine essence, and yet he is called a prophet. Therefore in like manner the blessed can be called prophets.

Objection 2: Further, prophecy is a "divine revelation." Now divine revelations are made even to the blessed angels. Therefore even blessed angels can be prophets.

Objection 3: Further, Christ was a comprehensor from the moment of His conception; and yet He calls Himself a prophet (Mat. 13:57), when He says: "A prophet is not without honor, save in his own country." Therefore even comprehensors and the blessed can be called prophets.

Objection 4: Further, it is written of Samuel (Ecclus. 46:23): "He lifted up his voice from the earth in prophecy to blot out the wickedness of the nation." Therefore other saints can likewise be called prophets after they have died.

On the contrary, The prophetic word is compared (2 Pet. 1:19) to a "light that shineth in a dark place." Now there is no darkness in the blessed. Therefore they cannot be called prophets.

I answer that, Prophecy denotes vision of some supernatural truth as being far remote from us. This happens in two ways. First, on the part of the knowledge itself, because, to wit, the supernatural truth is not known in itself, but in some of its effects; and this truth will be more remote if it be known by means of images of corporeal things, than if it be known in its intelligible effects; and such most of all is the prophetic vision, which is conveyed by images and likenesses of corporeal things. Secondly, vision is remote on the part of the seer, because, to wit, he has not yet attained completely to his ultimate perfection, according to 2 Cor. 5:6, "While we are in the body, we are absent from the Lord."

Now in neither of these ways are the blessed remote; wherefore they cannot be called prophets.

Reply to Objection 1: This vision of Moses was interrupted after the manner of a passion, and was not permanent like the beatific vision, wherefore he was as yet a seer from afar. For this reason his vision did not entirely lose the character of prophecy.

Reply to Objection 2: The divine revelation is made to the angels, not as being far distant, but as already wholly united to God; wherefore their revelation has not the character of prophecy.

Reply to Objection 3: Christ was at the same time comprehensor and wayfarer [*Cf. TP, QQ[9], seqq.]. Consequently the notion of prophecy is not applicable to Him as a comprehensor, but only as a wayfarer.

Reply to Objection 4: Samuel had not yet attained to the state of blessedness. Wherefore although by God's will the soul itself of Samuel foretold to Saul the issue of the war as revealed to him by God, this pertains to the nature of prophecy. It is not the same with the saints who are now in heaven. Nor does it make any difference that this is stated to have been brought about by the demons' art, because although the demons are unable to evoke the soul of a saint, or to force it to do any particular thing, this can be done by the power of God, so that when the demon is consulted, God Himself declares the truth by His messenger: even as He gave a true answer by Elias to the King's messengers who were sent to consult the god of Accaron (4 Kings 1).

It might also be replied [*The Book of Ecclesiasticus was not as yet declared by the Church to be Canonical Scripture; Cf. [3689]FP, Q[89], A[8], ad 2] that it was not the soul of Samuel, but a demon impersonating him; and that the wise man calls him Samuel, and describes his prediction as prophetic, in accordance with the thoughts of Saul and the bystanders who were of this opinion.

Whether the degrees of prophecy change as time goes on?

Objection 1: It would seem that the degrees of prophecy change as time goes on. For prophecy is directed to the knowledge of Divine things, as stated above [3690](A[2]). Now according to Gregory (Hom. in Ezech.), "knowledge of God went on increasing as time went on." Therefore degrees of prophecy should be distinguished according to the process of time.

Objection 2: Further, prophetic revelation is conveyed by God speaking to man; while the prophets declared both in words and in writing the things revealed to them. Now it is written (1 Kings 3:1) that before the time of Samuel "the word of the Lord was precious," i.e. rare; and yet afterwards it was delivered to many. In like manner the books of the prophets do not appear to have been written before the time of Isaias, to whom it was said (Is. 8:1): "Take thee a great book and write in it with a man's pen," after which many prophets wrote their prophecies. Therefore it would seem that in course of time the degree of prophecy made progress.

Objection 3: Further, our Lord said (Mat. 11:13): "The prophets and the law prophesied until John"; and afterwards the gift of prophecy was in Christ's disciples in a much more excellent manner than in the prophets of old, according to Eph. 3:5, "In other generations" the mystery of Christ "was not known to the sons of men, as it is now revealed to His holy apostles and prophets in the Spirit." Therefore it would seem that in course of time the degree of prophecy advanced.

On the contrary, As stated above [3691](A[4]), Moses was the greatest of the prophets, and yet he preceded the other prophets. Therefore prophecy did not advance in degree as time went on.

I answer that, As stated above [3692](A[2]), prophecy is directed to the knowledge of Divine truth, by the contemplation of which we are not only instructed in faith, but also guided in our actions, according to Ps. 42:3, "Send forth Thy light and Thy truth: they have conducted me." Now our faith consists chiefly in two things: first, in the true knowledge of God, according to Heb. 11:6, "He that cometh to

God must believe that He is"; secondly, in the mystery of Christ's incarnation, according to Jn. 14:1, "You believe in God, believe also in Me." Accordingly, if we speak of prophecy as directed to the Godhead as its end, it progressed according to three divisions of time, namely before the law, under the law, and under grace. For before the law, Abraham and the other patriarchs were prophetically taught things pertinent to faith in the Godhead. Hence they are called prophets, according to Ps. 104:15, "Do no evil to My prophets," which words are said especially on behalf of Abraham and Isaac. Under the Law prophetic revelation of things pertinent to faith in the Godhead was made in a yet more excellent way than hitherto, because then not only certain special persons or families but the whole people had to be instructed in these matters. Hence the Lord said to Moses (Ex. 6:2,3): "I am the Lord that appeared to Abraham, to Isaac, and to Jacob, by the name of God almighty, and My name Adonai I did not show to them"; because previously the patriarchs had been taught to believe in a general way in God, one and Almighty, while Moses was more fully instructed in the simplicity of the Divine essence, when it was said to him (Ex. 3:14): "I am Who am"; and this name is signified by Jews in the word "Adonai" on account of their veneration for that unspeakable name. Afterwards in the time of grace the mystery of the Trinity was revealed by the Son of God Himself, according to Mat. 28:19: "Going . . . teach ye all nations, baptizing them in the name of the Father, and of the Son, and of the Holy Ghost."

In each state, however, the most excellent revelation was that which was given first. Now the first revelation, before the Law, was given to Abraham, for it was at that time that men began to stray from faith in one God by turning aside to idolatry, whereas hitherto no such revelation was necessary while all persevered in the worship of one God. A less excellent revelation was made to Isaac, being founded on that which was made to Abraham. Wherefore it was said to him (Gn. 26:24): "I am the God of Abraham thy father," and in like manner to Jacob (Gn. 28:13): "I am the God of Abraham thy father, and the God of Isaac." Again in the state of the Law the first revelation which was given to Moses was more excellent, and on this revelation all the other revelations to the prophets were founded. And so, too, in the time of grace the entire faith of the Church is founded on the revelation vouchsafed to the apostles, concerning the faith in one God and three Persons, according to Mat. 16:18, "On this rock," i.e. of thy confession, "I will build My Church."

As to the faith in Christ's incarnation, it is evident that the nearer men were to Christ, whether before or after Him, the more fully, for the most part, were they instructed on this point, and after Him more fully than before, as the Apostle declares (Eph. 3:5).

As regards the guidance of human acts, the prophetic revelation varied not according to the course of time, but according as circumstances required, because as it is written (Prov. 29:18), "When prophecy shall fail, the people shall be scattered abroad." Wherefore at all times men were divinely instructed about what they were to do, according as it was expedient for the spiritual welfare of the elect.

Reply to Objection 1: The saying of Gregory is to be referred to the time before Christ's incarnation, as regards the knowledge of this mystery.

Reply to Objection 2: As Augustine says (De Civ. Dei xviii, 27), "just as in the early days of the Assyrian kingdom promises were made most explicitly to Abraham, so at the outset of the western Babylon," which is Rome, "and under its sway Christ was to come, in Whom were to be fulfilled the promises made through the prophetic oracles testifying in word and writing to that great event to come," the promises, namely, which were made to Abraham. "For while prophets were scarcely ever lacking to the people of Israel from the time that they began to have kings, it was exclusively for their benefit, not for that of the nations. But when those prophetic writings were being set up with greater publicity, which at some future time were to benefit the nations, it was fitting to begin when this city," Rome to wit, "was being built, which was to govern the nations."

The reason why it behooved that nation to have a number of prophets especially at the time of the kings, was that then it was not over-ridden by other nations, but had its own king; wherefore it behooved the people, as enjoying liberty, to have prophets to teach them what to do.

Reply to Objection 3: The prophets who foretold the coming of Christ could not continue further than John, who with his finger pointed to Christ actually present. Nevertheless as Jerome says on this passage, "This does not mean that there were no more prophets after John. For we read in the Acts of the apostles that Agabus and the four maidens, daughters of Philip, prophesied." John, too, wrote a prophetic book about the end of the Church; and at all times there have not been lacking persons having the spirit of prophecy, not indeed for the declaration of any new doctrine of faith, but for the direction of human acts. Thus Augustine says (De Civ. Dei v, 26) that "the emperor Theodosius sent to John who dwelt in the Egyptian desert, and whom he knew by his ever-increasing fame to be endowed with the prophetic spirit: and from him he received a message assuring him of victory."

OF RAPTURE (SIX ARTICLES)

We must now consider rapture. Under this head there are six points of inquiry:

(1) Whether the soul of man is carried away to things divine?

(2) Whether rapture pertains to the cognitive or to the appetitive power?

(3) Whether Paul when in rapture saw the essence of God?

(4) Whether he was withdrawn from his senses?

(5) Whether, when in that state, his soul was wholly separated from his body?

(6) What did he know, and what did he not know about this matter?

Whether the soul of man is carried away to things divine?

Objection 1: It would seem that the soul of man is not carried away to things divine. For some define rapture as "an uplifting by the power of a higher nature, from that which is according to nature to that which is above nature" [*Reference unknown; Cf. De Veritate xiii, 1]. Now it is in accordance with man's nature that he be uplifted to things divine; for Augustine says at the beginning of his Confessions: "Thou madest us, Lord, for Thyself, and our heart is restless, till it rest in Thee." Therefore man's soul is not carried away to things divine.

Objection 2: Further, Dionysius says (Div. Nom. viii) that "God's justice is seen in this that He treats all things according to their mode and dignity." But it is not in accordance with man's mode and worth that he be raised above what he is according to nature. Therefore it would seem that man's soul is not carried away to things divine.

Objection 3: Further, rapture denotes violence of some kind. But God rules us not by violence or force, as Damascene says [*De Fide Orth. ii, 30]. Therefore man's soul is not carried away to things divine.

On the contrary, The Apostle says (2 Cor. 12:2): "I know a man in Christ . . . rapt even to the third heaven." On which words a gloss says: "Rapt, that is to say, uplifted contrary to nature."

I answer that, Rapture denotes violence of a kind as stated above (OBJ[3]); and "the violent is that which has its principle without, and in which he that suffers violence concurs not at all" (Ethic. iii, 1). Now everything concurs in that to which it tends in accordance with its proper inclination, whether voluntary or natural. Wherefore he who is carried away by some external agent, must be carried to something different from that to which his inclination tends. This difference arises in two ways: in one way from the end of the inclination—for instance a stone, which is naturally inclined to be borne downwards, may be thrown upwards; in another way from the manner of tending—for instance a stone may be thrown downwards with greater velocity than consistent with its natural movement.

Accordingly man's soul also is said to be carried away, in a twofold manner, to that which is contrary to its nature: in one way, as regards the term of transport—as when it is carried away to punishment, according to Ps. 49:22, "Lest He snatch you away, and there be none to deliver you"; in another way, as regards the manner connatural to man, which is that he should understand the truth through sensible things. Hence when he is withdrawn from the apprehension of sensibles, he is said to be carried away, even though he be uplifted to things whereunto he is directed naturally: provided this be not done intentionally, as when a man betakes himself to sleep which is in accordance with nature, wherefore sleep cannot be called rapture, properly speaking.

This withdrawal, whatever its term may be, may arise from a threefold cause. First, from a bodily cause, as happens to those who suffer abstraction from the senses through weakness: secondly, by the power of the demons, as in those who are possessed: thirdly, by the power of God. In this last sense we are now speaking of rapture, whereby a man is uplifted by the spirit of God to things supernatural, and withdrawn from his senses, according to Ezech. 8:3, "The spirit lifted me up between the earth and the heaven, and brought me in the vision of God into Jerusalem."

It must be observed, however, that sometimes a person is said to be carried away, not only through being withdrawn from his senses, but also through being withdrawn from the things to which he was attending, as when a person's mind wanders contrary to his purpose. But this is to use the expression in a less proper signification.

Reply to Objection 1: It is natural to man to tend to divine things through the apprehension of things sensible, according to Rom. 1:20, "The invisible things of God . . . are clearly seen, being understood by the things that are made." But the mode, whereby a man is uplifted to divine things and withdrawn from his senses, is not natural to man.

Reply to Objection 2: It belongs to man's mode and dignity that he be uplifted to divine things, from the very fact that he is made to God's image. And since a divine good infinitely surpasses the faculty of man in order to attain that good, he needs the divine assistance which is bestowed on him in every gift of grace. Hence it is not contrary to nature, but above the faculty of nature that man's mind be thus uplifted in rapture by God.

Reply to Objection 3: The saying of Damascene refers to those things which a man does by himself. But as to those things which are beyond the scope of the free-will, man needs to be uplifted by a stronger operation, which in a certain respect may be called force if we consider the mode of operation, but not if we consider its term to which man is directed both by nature and by his intention.

Whether rapture pertains to the cognitive rather than to the appetitive power?

Objection 1: It would seem that rapture pertains to the appetitive rather than to the cognitive power. For Dionysius says (Div. Nom. iv): "The Divine love causes ecstasy." Now love pertains to the appetitive power. Therefore so does ecstasy or rapture.

Objection 2: Further, Gregory says (Dial. ii, 3) that "he who fed the swine debased himself by a dissipated mind and an unclean life; whereas Peter, when the angel delivered him and carried him into ecstasy, was not beside himself, but above himself." Now the prodigal son sank into the depths by his appetite. Therefore in those also who are carried up into the heights it is the appetite that is affected.

Objection 3: Further, a gloss on Ps. 30:1, "In Thee, O Lord, have I hoped, let me never be confounded," says in explaining the title [*Unto the end, a psalm for David, in an ecstasy]: "{Ekstasis} in Greek signifies in Latin 'excessus mentis,' an aberration of the mind. This happens in two ways, either through dread of earthly things or through the mind being rapt in heavenly things and forgetful of this lower world." Now dread of earthly things pertains to the appetite. Therefore rapture of the mind in heavenly things, being placed in opposition to this dread, also pertains to the appetite.

On the contrary, A gloss on Ps. 115:2, "I said in my excess: Every man is a liar," says: "We speak of ecstasy, not when the mind wanders through fear, but when it is carried aloft on the wings of revelation." Now revelation pertains to the intellective power. Therefore ecstasy or rapture does also.

I answer that, We can speak of rapture in two ways. First, with regard to the term of rapture, and thus, properly speaking, rapture cannot pertain to the appetitive, but only to the cognitive power. For it was stated [3693](A[1]) that rapture is outside the inclination of the person who is rapt; whereas the movement of the appetitive power is an inclination to an appetible good. Wherefore, properly speaking, in desiring something, a man is not rapt, but is moved by himself.

Secondly, rapture may be considered with regard to its cause, and thus it may have a cause on the part of the appetitive power. For from the very fact that the appetite is strongly affected towards something, it may happen, owing to the violence of his affection, that a man is carried away from everything else. Moreover, it has an effect on the appetitive power, when for instance a man delights in the things to which he is rapt. Hence the Apostle said that he was rapt, not only "to the third heaven"—which pertains to the contemplation of the intellect—but also into "paradise," which pertains to the appetite.

Reply to Objection 1: Rapture adds something to ecstasy. For ecstasy means simply a going out of oneself by being placed outside one's proper order [*Cf. [3694]FS, Q[28], A[3]]; while rapture denotes a certain violence in addition. Accordingly ecstasy may pertain to the appetitive power, as when a man's appetite tends to something outside him, and in this sense Dionysius says that "the Divine love causes ecstasy," inasmuch as it makes man's appetite tend to the object loved. Hence he says afterwards that "even God Himself, the cause of all things, through the overflow of His loving goodness, goes outside Himself in His providence for all beings." But even if this were said expressly of rapture, it would merely signify that love is the cause of rapture.

Reply to Objection 2: There is a twofold appetite in man; to wit, the intellective appetite which is called the will, and the sensitive appetite known as the sensuality. Now it is proper to man that his lower appetite be subject to the higher appetite, and that the higher move the lower. Hence man may become outside himself as regards the appetite, in two ways. In one way, when a man's intellective appetite tends wholly to divine things, and takes no account of those things whereto the sensitive appetite inclines him; thus Dionysius says (Div. Nom. iv) that "Paul being in ecstasy through the vehemence of Divine love" exclaimed: "I live, now not I, but Christ liveth in me."

In another way, when a man tends wholly to things pertaining to the lower appetite, and takes no account of his higher appetite. It is thus that "he who fed the swine debased himself"; and this latter kind of going out of oneself, or being beside oneself, is more akin than the former to the nature of rapture because the higher appetite is more proper to man. Hence when through the violence of his lower appetite a man is withdrawn from the movement of his higher appetite, it is more a case of being withdrawn from that which is proper to him. Yet, because there is no violence therein, since the will is able to resist the passion, it falls short of the true nature of rapture, unless perchance the passion be so strong that it takes away entirely the use of reason, as happens to those who are mad with anger or love.

It must be observed. however, that both these excesses affecting the appetite may cause an excess in the cognitive power, either because the mind is carried away to certain intelligible objects, through being drawn away from objects of sense, or because it is caught up into some imaginary vision or fanciful apparition.

Reply to Objection 3: Just as love is a movement of the appetite with regard to good, so fear is a movement of the appetite with regard to evil. Wherefore either of them may equally cause an aberration of mind; and all the more since fear arises from love, as Augustine says (De Civ. Dei xiv, 7,9).

Whether Paul, when in rapture, saw the essence of God?

Objection 1: It would seem that Paul, when in rapture, did not see the essence of God. For just as we read of Paul that he was rapt to the third heaven, so we read of Peter (Acts 10:10) that "there came upon him an ecstasy of mind." Now Peter, in his ecstasy, saw not God's essence but an imaginary vision. Therefore it would seem that neither did Paul see the essence of God.

Objection 2: Further, the vision of God is beatific. But Paul, in his rapture, was not beatified; else he would never have returned to the unhappiness of this life, but his body would have been glorified by the overflow from his soul, as will happen to the saints after the resurrection, and this clearly was not the case. Therefore Paul when in rapture saw not the essence of God.

Objection 3: Further, according to 1 Cor. 13:10–12, faith and hope are incompatible with the vision of the Divine essence. But Paul when in this state had faith and hope. Therefore he saw not the essence of God.

Objection 4: Further, as Augustine states (Gen. ad lit. xii, 6,7), "pictures of bodies are seen in the imaginary vision." Now Paul is stated (2 Cor. 12:2, 4) to have seen certain pictures in his rapture, for instance of the "third heaven" and of "paradise."

Therefore he would seem to have been rapt to an imaginary vision rather than to the vision of the Divine essence.

On the contrary, Augustine (Ep. CXLVII, 13; ad Paulin., de videndo Deum) concludes that "possibly God's very substance was seen by some while yet in this life: for instance by Moses, and by Paul who in rapture heard unspeakable words, which it is not granted unto man to utter."

I answer that, Some have said that Paul, when in rapture, saw "not the very essence of God, but a certain reflection of His clarity." But Augustine clearly comes to an opposite decision, not only in his book (De videndo Deum), but also in Gen. ad lit. xii, 28 (quoted in a gloss on 2 Cor. 12:2). Indeed the words themselves of the Apostle indicate this. For he says that "he heard secret words, which it is not granted unto man to utter": and such would seem to be words pertaining to the vision of the blessed, which transcends the state of the wayfarer, according to Is. 64:4, "Eye hath not seen, O God, besides Thee, what things Thou hast prepared for them that love [Vulg.: 'wait for'] Thee" [*1 Cor. 2:9]. Therefore it is more becoming to hold that he saw God in His essence.

Reply to Objection 1: Man's mind is rapt by God to the contemplation of divine truth in three ways. First, so that he contemplates it through certain imaginary pictures, and such was the ecstasy that came upon Peter. Secondly, so that he contemplates the divine truth through its intelligible effects; such was the ecstasy of David, who said (Ps. 115:11): "I said in my excess: Every man is a liar." Thirdly, so that he contemplates it in its essence. Such was the rapture of Paul, as also of Moses [*Cf. Q[174], A[4]]; and not without reason, since as Moses was the first Teacher of the Jews, so was Paul the first "Teacher of the gentiles" [*Cf. [3695]FP, Q[68], A[4]].

Reply to Objection 2: The Divine essence cannot be seen by a created intellect save through the light of glory, of which it is written (Ps. 35:10): "In Thy light we shall see light." But this light can be shared in two ways. First by way of an abiding form, and thus it beatifies the saints in heaven. Secondly, by way of a transitory passion, as stated above ([3696]Q[171] , A[2]) of the light of prophecy; and in this way that light was in Paul when he was in rapture. Hence this vision did not beatify him simply, so as to overflow into his body, but only in a restricted sense. Consequently this rapture pertains somewhat to prophecy.

Reply to Objection 3: Since, in his rapture, Paul was beatified not as to the habit, but only as to the act of the blessed, it follows that he had not the act of faith at the same time, although he had the habit.

Reply to Objection 4: In one way by the third heaven we may understand something corporeal, and thus the third heaven denotes the empyrean [*1 Tim. 2:7; Cf. [3697]FP, Q[12], A[11], ad 2], which is described as the "third," in relation to the aerial and starry heavens, or better still, in relation to the aqueous and crystalline heavens. Moreover Paul is stated to be rapt to the "third heaven," not as though his rapture consisted in the vision of something corporeal, but because this place is appointed for the contemplation of the blessed. Hence the gloss on 2 Cor. 12 says that the "third heaven is a spiritual heaven, where the angels and the holy souls enjoy the contemplation of God: and when Paul says that he was rapt to this heaven he means that God showed him the life wherein He is to be seen forevermore."

In another way the third heaven may signify a supra-mundane vision. Such a vision may be called the third heaven in three ways. First, according to the order of the cognitive powers. In this way the first heaven would indicate a supramundane bodily vision, conveyed through the senses; thus was seen the hand of one writing on the wall (Dan. 5:5); the second heaven would be an imaginary vision such as Isaias saw, and John in the Apocalypse; and the third heaven would denote an intellectual vision according to Augustine's explanation (Gen. ad lit. xii, 26,28,34). Secondly, the third heaven may be taken according to the order of things knowable, the first heaven being "the knowledge of heavenly bodies, the second the knowledge of heavenly spirits, the third the knowledge of God Himself." Thirdly, the third heaven may denote the contemplation of God according to the degrees of knowledge whereby God is seen. The first of these degrees belongs to the angels of the lowest hierarchy [*Cf. [3698]FP, Q[108], A[1]], the second to the angels of the middle hierarchy, the third to the angels of the highest hierarchy, according to the gloss on 2 Cor. 12.

And since the vision of God cannot be without delight, he says that he was not only "rapt to the third heaven" by reason of his contemplation, but also into "Paradise" by reason of the consequent delight.

Whether Paul, when in rapture, was withdrawn from his senses?

Objection 1: It would seem that Paul, when in rapture, was not withdrawn from his senses. For Augustine says (Gen. ad lit. xii, 28): "Why should we not believe that when so great an apostle, the teacher of the gentiles, was rapt to this most sublime vision, God was willing to vouchsafe him a glimpse of that eternal life which is to take the place of the present life?" Now in that future life after the resurrection the saints will see the Divine essence without being withdrawn from the senses of the body. Therefore neither did such a withdrawal take place in Paul.

Objection 2: Further, Christ was truly a wayfarer, and also enjoyed an uninterrupted vision of the Divine essence, without, however, being withdrawn from His senses. Therefore there was no need for Paul to be withdrawn from his senses in order for him to see the essence of God.

Objection 3: Further, after seeing God in His essence, Paul remembered what he had seen in that vision; hence he said (2 Cor. 12:4): "He heard secret words, which it is not granted to man to utter." Now the memory belongs to the sensitive faculty according to the Philosopher (De Mem. et Remin. i). Therefore it seems that Paul, while seeing the essence of God, was not withdrawn from his senses.

On the contrary, Augustine says (Gen. ad lit. xii, 27): "Unless a man in some way depart this life, whether by going altogether out of his body or by turning away and withdrawing from his carnal senses, so that he truly knows not as the Apostle said, whether he be in the body or out of the body, he is not rapt and caught up into that vision.*" [*The text of St. Augustine reads: "when he is rapt," etc.]

I answer that, The Divine essence cannot be seen by man through any cognitive power other than the intellect. Now the human intellect does not turn to intelligible objects except by means of the phantasms [*Cf. [3699]FP, Q[84], A[7]] which it takes from the senses through the intelligible species; and it is in considering these phantasms that the intellect judges of and coordinates sensible objects. Hence in any operation that requires abstraction of the intellect from phantasms, there must be also withdrawal of the intellect from the senses. Now in the state of the wayfarer it is necessary for man's intellect, if it see God's essence, to be withdrawn from phantasms. For God's essence cannot be seen by means of a phantasm, nor indeed by any created intelligible species [*Cf. [3700]FP, Q[12], A[2]], since God's essence infinitely transcends not only all bodies, which are represented by phantasms, but also all intelligible creatures. Now when man's intellect is uplifted to the sublime vision of God's essence, it is necessary that his mind's whole attention should be summoned to that purpose in such a way that he understand naught else by phantasms, and be absorbed entirely in God. Therefore it is impossible for man while a wayfarer to see God in His essence without being withdrawn from his senses.

Reply to Objection 1: As stated above (A[3], OBJ[2]), after the resurrection, in the blessed who see God in His essence, there will be an overflow from the intellect to the lower powers and even to the body. Hence it is in keeping with the rule itself of the divine vision that the soul will turn towards phantasms and sensible objects. But there is no such overflow in those who are raptured, as stated (A[3], OBJ[2], ad 2), and consequently the comparison fails.

Reply to Objection 2: The intellect of Christ's soul was glorified by the habit of the light of glory, whereby He saw the Divine essence much more fully than an angel or a man. He was, however, a wayfarer on account of the passibility of His body, in respect of which He was "made a little lower than the angels" (Heb. 2:9), by dispensation, and not on account of any defect on the part of His intellect. Hence there is no comparison between Him and other wayfarers.

Reply to Objection 3: Paul, after seeing God in His essence, remembered what he had known in that vision, by means of certain intelligible species that remained in his intellect by way of habit; even as in the absence of the sensible object, certain impressions remain in the soul which it recollects when it turns to the phantasms. And so this was the knowledge that he was unable wholly to think over or express in words.

Whether, while in this state, Paul's soul was wholly separated from his body?

Objection 1: It would seem that, while in this state, Paul's soul was wholly separated from his body. For the Apostle says (2 Cor. 5:6,7): "While we are in the body we are absent from the Lord. For we walk by faith, and not by sight" [*'Per speciem,' i.e. by an intelligible species]. Now, while in that state, Paul was not absent from the Lord, for he saw Him by a species, as stated above [3701](A[3]). Therefore he was not in the body.

Objection 2: Further, a power of the soul cannot be uplifted above the soul's essence wherein it is rooted. Now in this rapture the intellect, which is a power of the soul, was withdrawn from its bodily surroundings through being uplifted to divine contemplation. Much more therefore was the essence of the soul separated from the body.

Objection 3: Further, the forces of the vegetative soul are more material than those of the sensitive soul. Now in order for him to be rapt to the vision of God, it was necessary for him to be withdrawn from the forces of the sensitive soul, as stated above [3702](A[4]). Much more, therefore, was it necessary for him to be withdrawn from the forces of the vegetative soul. Now when these forces cease to operate, the soul is no longer in any way united to the body. Therefore it would seem that in Paul's rapture it was necessary for the soul to be wholly separated from the body.

On the contrary, Augustine says (Ep. CXLVII, 13, ad Paulin.; de videndo Deum): "It is not incredible that this sublime revelation" (namely, that they should see God in His essence) "was vouchsafed certain saints, without their departing this life so completely as to leave nothing but a corpse for burial." Therefore it was not necessary for Paul's soul, when in rapture, to be wholly separated from his body.

I answer that, As stated above (A[1], OBJ[1]), in the rapture of which we are speaking now, man is uplifted by God's power, "from that which is according to nature to that which is above nature." Wherefore two things have to be considered: first, what pertains to man according to nature; secondly, what has to be done by God in man above his nature. Now, since the soul is united to the body as its natural form, it belongs to the soul to have a natural disposition to understand by turning to phantasms; and this is not withdrawn by the divine power from the soul in rapture, since its state undergoes no change, as stated above (A[3], ad 2,3). Yet, this state remaining, actual conversion to phantasms and sensible objects is withdrawn from the soul, lest it be hindered from being uplifted to that which transcends all phantasms, as stated above [3703](A[4]). Therefore it was not necessary that his soul in rapture should be so separated from the body as to cease to be united thereto as its form; and yet it was necessary for his intellect to be withdrawn from phantasms and the perception of sensible objects.

Reply to Objection 1: In this rapture Paul was absent from the Lord as regards his state, since he was still in the state of a wayfarer, but not as regards the act by which he saw God by a species, as stated above (A[3], ad 2,3).

Reply to Objection 2: A faculty of the soul is not uplifted by the natural power above the mode becoming the essence of the soul; but it can be uplifted by the divine power to something higher, even as a body by the violence of a stronger power is lifted up above the place befitting it according to its specific nature.

Reply to Objection 3: The forces of the vegetative soul do not operate through the soul being intent thereon, as do the sensitive forces, but by way of nature. Hence in the case of rapture there is no need for withdrawal from them, as from the sensitive powers, whose operations would lessen the intentness of the soul on intellective knowledge.

Did Paul know whether his soul were separated from his body?

Objection 1: It would seem that Paul was not ignorant whether his soul were separated from his body. For he says (2 Cor. 12:2): "I know a man in Christ rapt even to the third heaven." Now man denotes something composed of soul and body; and rapture differs from death. Seemingly therefore he knew that his soul was not separated from his body by death, which is the more probable seeing that this is the common opinion of the Doctors.

Objection 2: Further, it appears from the same words of the Apostle that he knew whither he was rapt, since it was "to the third heaven." Now this shows that he knew whether he was in the body or not, for if he knew the third heaven to be something corporeal, he must have known that his soul was not separated from his body, since a corporeal thing cannot be an object of sight save through the body. Therefore it would seem that he was not ignorant whether his soul were separated from his body.

Objection 3: Further, Augustine says (Gen. ad lit. xii, 28) that "when in rapture, he saw God with the same vision as the saints see Him in heaven." Now from the very fact that the saints see God, they know whether their soul is separated from their body. Therefore Paul too knew this.

On the contrary, It is written (2 Cor. 12:3): "Whether in the body, or out of the body, I know not, God knoweth."

I answer that, The true answer to this question must be gathered from the Apostle's very words, whereby he says he knew something, namely that he was "rapt even to the third heaven," and that something he knew not, namely "whether" he were "in the body or out of the body." This may be understood in two ways. First, the words "whether in the body or out of the body" may refer not to the very being of the man who was rapt (as though he knew not whether his soul were in his body or not), but to the mode of rapture, so that he ignored whether his body besides his soul, or, on the other hand, his soul alone, were rapt to the third heaven. Thus Ezechiel is stated (Ezech. 8:3) to have been "brought in the vision of God into Jerusalem." This was the explanation of a certain Jew according to Jerome (Prolog. super Daniel.), where he says that "lastly our Apostle" (thus said the Jew) "durst not assert that he was rapt in his body, but said: 'Whether in the body or out of the body, I know not.'"

Augustine, however, disapproves of this explanation (Gen. ad lit. xii, 3 seqq.) for this reason that the Apostle states that he knew he was rapt even to the third heaven. Wherefore he knew it to be really the third heaven to which he was rapt, and not an imaginary likeness of the third heaven: otherwise if he gave the name of third heaven to an imaginary third heaven, in the same way he might state that he was rapt in the body, meaning, by body, an image of his body, such as appears in one's dreams. Now if he knew it to be really the third heaven, it follows that either he knew it to be something spiritual and incorporeal, and then his body could not be rapt thither; or he knew it to be something corporeal, and then his soul could not be rapt thither without his body, unless it were separated from his body. Consequently we must explain the matter otherwise, by saying that the Apostle knew himself to be rapt both in soul and body, but that he ignored how his soul stood in relation to his body, to wit, whether it were accompanied by his body or not.

Here we find a diversity of opinions. For some say that the Apostle knew his soul to be united to his body as its form, but ignored whether it were abstracted from its senses, or again whether it were abstracted from the operations of the vegetative soul. But he could not but know that it was abstracted from the senses, seeing that he knew himself to be rapt; and as to his being abstracted from the operation of the vegetative soul, this was not of such importance as to require him to be so careful in mentioning it. It follows, then, that the Apostle ignored whether his soul were united to his body as its form, or separated from it by death. Some, however, granting this say that the Apostle did not consider the matter while he was in rapture, because he was wholly intent upon God, but that afterwards he questioned the point, when taking cognizance of what he had seen. But this also is contrary to the Apostle's words, for he there distinguishes between the past and what happened subsequently, since he states that at the present time he knows that he was rapt "fourteen years ago," and that at the present time he knows not "whether he was in the body or out of the body."

Consequently we must assert that both before and after he ignored whether his soul were separated from his body. Wherefore Augustine (Gen. ad lit. xii, 5), after discussing the question at length, concludes: "Perhaps then we must infer that he ignored whether, when he was rapt to the third heaven, his soul was in his body (in the same way as the soul is in the body, when we speak of a living body either of a waking or of a sleeping man, or of one that is withdrawn from his bodily senses during ecstasy), or whether his soul went out of his body altogether, so that his body lay dead."

Reply to Objection 1: Sometimes by the figure of synecdoche a part of man, especially the soul which is the principal part, denotes a man. or again we might take this to mean that he whom he states to have been rapt was a man not at the time of his rapture, but fourteen years afterwards: for he says "I know a man," not "I know a rapt man." Again nothing hinders death brought about by God being called rapture; and thus Augustine says (Gen. ad lit. xii, 3): "If the Apostle doubted the matter, who of us will dare to be certain about it?" Wherefore those who have something to say on this subject speak with more conjecture than certainty.

Reply to Objection 2: The Apostle knew that either the heaven in question was something incorporeal, or that he saw something incorporeal in that heaven; yet this could be done by his intellect, even without his soul being separated from his body.

Reply to Objection 3: Paul's vision, while he was in rapture, was like the vision of the blessed in one respect, namely as to the thing seen; and, unlike, in another respect, namely as to the mode of seeing, because he saw not so perfectly as do the saints in heaven. Hence Augustine says (Gen. ad lit. xii, 36): "Although, when the Apostle was rapt from his carnal senses to the third heaven, he lacked that full and perfect knowledge of things which is in the angels, in that he knew not whether he was in the body, or out of the body, this will surely not be lacking after reunion with the body in the resurrection of the dead, when this corruptible will put on incorruption."

OF THE GRACE OF TONGUES (TWO ARTICLES)

We must now consider those gratuitous graces that pertain to speech, and (1) the grace of tongues; (2) the grace of the word of wisdom and knowledge. Under the first head there are two points of inquiry:

(1) Whether by the grace of tongues a man acquires the knowledge of all languages?

(2) Of the comparison between this gift and the grace of prophecy.

Whether those who received the gift of tongues spoke in every language?

Objection 1: It seems that those who received the gift of tongues did not speak in every language. For that which is granted to certain persons by the divine power is the best of its kind: thus our Lord turned the water into good wine, as stated in Jn. 2:10. Now those who had the gift of tongues spoke better in their own language; since a gloss on Heb. 1, says that "it is not surprising that the epistle to the Hebrews is more graceful in style than the other epistles, since it is natural for a man to have more command over his own than over a strange language. For the Apostle wrote the other epistles in a foreign, namely the Greek, idiom; whereas he wrote this in the Hebrew tongue." Therefore the apostles did not receive the knowledge of all languages by a gratuitous grace.

Objection 2: Further, nature does not employ many means where one is sufficient; and much less does God Whose work is more orderly than nature's. Now God could make His disciples to be understood by all, while speaking one tongue: hence a gloss on Acts 2:6, "Every man heard them speak in his own tongue," says that "they spoke in every tongue, or speaking in their own, namely the Hebrew language, were understood by all, as though they spoke the language proper to each." Therefore it would seem that they had not the knowledge to speak in all languages.

Objection 3: Further, all graces flow from Christ to His body, which is the Church, according to Jn. 1:16, "Of His fullness we all have received." Now we do not read that Christ spoke more than one language, nor does each one of the faithful now speak save in one tongue. Therefore it would seem that Christ's disciples did not receive the grace to the extent of speaking in all languages.

On the contrary, It is written (Acts 2:4) that "they were all filled with the Holy Ghost, and they began to speak with divers tongues, according as the Holy Ghost gave them to speak"; on which passage a gloss of Gregory [*Hom. xxx in Ev.] says that "the Holy Ghost appeared over the disciples under the form of fiery tongues, and gave them the knowledge of all tongues."

I answer that, Christ's first disciples were chosen by Him in order that they might disperse throughout the whole world, and preach His faith everywhere, according to Mat. 28:19, "Going . . . teach ye all nations." Now it was not fitting that they who were being sent to teach others should need to be taught by others, either as to how they should speak to other people, or as to how they were to understand those who spoke to them; and all the more seeing that those who were being sent were of one nation, that of Judea, according to Is. 27:6, "When they shall rush out from Jacob [*Vulg.: 'When they shall rush in unto Jacob,' etc.] . . . they shall fill the face of the world with seed." Moreover those who were being sent were poor and powerless; nor at the outset could they have easily found someone to interpret their words faithfully to others, or to explain what others said to them, especially as they were sent to unbelievers. Consequently it was necessary, in this respect, that God should provide them with the gift of tongues; in order that, as the diversity of tongues was brought upon the nations when they fell away to idolatry, according to Gn. 11, so when the nations were to be recalled to the worship of one God a remedy to this diversity might be applied by the gift of tongues.

Reply to Objection 1: As it is written (1 Cor. 12:7), "the manifestation of the Spirit is given to every man unto profit"; and consequently both Paul and the other apostles were divinely instructed in the languages of all nations sufficiently for the requirements of the teaching of the faith. But as regards the grace and elegance of style which human art adds to a language, the Apostle was instructed in his own, but not in a foreign tongue. Even so they were sufficiently instructed in wisdom and scientific knowledge, as required for teaching the faith, but not as to all things known by acquired science, for instance the conclusions of arithmetic and geometry.

Reply to Objection 2: Although either was possible, namely that, while speaking in one tongue they should be understood by all, or that they should speak in all tongues, it was more fitting that they should speak in all tongues, because this pertained to the perfection of their knowledge, whereby they were able not only to speak, but also to understand what was said by others. Whereas if their one language were intelligible to all, this would either have been due to the knowledge of those who understood their speech, or it would have amounted to an illusion, since a man's words would have had a different sound in another's ears, from that with which they were uttered. Hence a gloss says on Acts 2:6 that "it was a greater miracle that they should speak all kinds of tongues"; and Paul says (1 Cor. 14:18): "I thank my God I speak with all your tongues."

Reply to Objection 3: Christ in His own person purposed preaching to only one nation, namely the Jews. Consequently, although without any doubt He possessed most perfectly the knowledge of all languages, there was no need for Him to speak in every tongue. And therefore, as Augustine says (Tract. xxxii in Joan.), "whereas even now the Holy Ghost is received, yet no one speaks in the tongues of all nations, because the Church herself already speaks the languages of all nations: since whoever is not in the Church, receives not the Holy Ghost."

Whether the gift of tongues is more excellent than the grace of prophecy?

Objection 1: It would seem that the gift of tongues is more excellent than the grace of prophecy. For, seemingly, better things are proper to better persons, according to the Philosopher (Topic. iii, 1). Now the gift of tongues is proper to the New Testament, hence we sing in the sequence of Pentecost [*The sequence: 'Sancti Spiritus adsit nobis gratia' ascribed to King Robert of France, the reputed author of the 'Veni Sancte Spiritus.' Cf. Migne, Patr. Lat. tom. CXLI]: "On this day Thou gavest Christ's apostles an unwonted gift, a marvel to all time": whereas prophecy is more pertinent to the Old Testament, according to Heb. 1:1, "God Who at sundry times and in divers manners spoke in times past to the fathers by the prophets." Therefore it would seem that the gift of tongues is more excellent than the gift of prophecy.

Objection 2: Further, that whereby we are directed to God is seemingly more excellent than that whereby we are directed to men. Now, by the gift of tongues, man is directed to God, whereas by prophecy he is directed to man; for it is written (1 Cor. 14:2,3): "He that speaketh in a tongue, speaketh not unto men, but unto God . . . but he that prophesieth, speaketh unto men unto edification." Therefore it would seem that the gift of tongues is more excellent than the gift of prophecy.

Objection 3: Further, the gift of tongues abides like a habit in the person who has it, and "he can use it when he will"; wherefore it is written (1 Cor. 14:18): "I thank my God I speak with all your tongues." But it is not so with the gift of prophecy, as stated above ([3704]Q[171], A[2]). Therefore the gift of tongues would seem to be more excellent than the gift of prophecy.

Objection 4: Further, the "interpretation of speeches" would seem to be contained under prophecy, because the Scriptures are expounded by the same Spirit from Whom they originated. Now the interpretation of speeches is placed after "divers kinds of tongues" (1 Cor. 12:10). Therefore it seems that the gift of tongues is more excellent than the gift of prophecy, particularly as regards a part of the latter.

On the contrary, The Apostle says (1 Cor. 14:5): "Greater is he that prophesieth than he that speaketh with tongues."

I answer that, The gift of prophecy surpasses the gift of tongues, in three ways. First, because the gift of tongues regards the utterance of certain words, which signify an intelligible truth, and this again is signified by the phantasms which appear in an imaginary vision; wherefore Augustine compares (Gen. ad lit. xii, 8) the gift of tongues to an imaginary vision. On the other hand, it has been stated above ([3705]Q[173], A[2]) that the gift of prophecy consists in the mind itself being enlightened so as to know an intelligible truth. Wherefore, as the prophetic enlightenment is more excellent than the imaginary vision, as stated above ([3706]Q[174], A[2]), so also is prophecy more excellent than the gift of tongues considered in itself. Secondly, because the gift of prophecy regards the knowledge of things, which is more excellent than the knowledge of words, to which the gift of tongues pertains.

Thirdly, because the gift of prophecy is more profitable. The Apostle proves this in three ways (1 Cor. 14); first, because prophecy is more profitable to the edification of the Church, for which purpose he that speaketh in tongues profiteth nothing, unless interpretation follow (1 Cor. 14:4,5). Secondly, as regards the speaker himself, for if he be enabled to speak in divers tongues without understanding them, which pertains to the gift of prophecy, his own mind would not be edified (1 Cor. 14:7–14). Thirdly, as to unbelievers for whose especial benefit the gift of tongues seems to have been given; since perchance they might think those who speak in tongues to be mad (1 Cor. 14:23), for instance the Jews deemed the apostles drunk when the latter spoke in various tongues (Acts 2:13): whereas by prophecies the unbeliever is convinced, because the secrets of his heart are made manifest (Acts 2:25).

Reply to Objection 1: As stated above ([3707]Q[174], A[3], ad 1), it belongs to the excellence of prophecy that a man is not only enlightened by an intelligible light, but also that he should perceive an imaginary vision: and so again it belongs to the perfection of the Holy Ghost's operation, not only to fill the mind with the prophetic light, and the imagination with the imaginary vision, as happened in the Old Testament, but also to endow the tongue with external erudition, in the utterance of various signs of speech. All this is done in the New Testament, according to 1 Cor. 14:26, "Every one of you hath a psalm, hath a doctrine, hath a tongue, hath a revelation," i.e. a prophetic revelation.

Reply to Objection 2: By the gift of prophecy man is directed to God in his mind, which is more excellent than being directed to Him in his tongue. "He that speaketh in a tongue "is said to speak "not unto men," i.e. to men's understanding or profit, but unto God's understanding and praise. On the other hand, by prophecy a man is directed both to God and to man; wherefore it is the more perfect gift.

Reply to Objection 3: Prophetic revelation extends to the knowledge of all things supernatural; wherefore from its very perfection it results that in this imperfect state of life it cannot be had perfectly by way of habit, but only imperfectly by way of passion. on the other hand, the gift of tongues is confined to a certain particular knowledge, namely of human words; wherefore it is not inconsistent with the imperfection of this life, that it should be had perfectly and by way of habit.

Reply to Objection 4: The interpretation of speeches is reducible to the gift of prophecy, inasmuch as the mind is enlightened so as to understand and explain any obscurities of speech arising either from a difficulty in the things signified, or from the words uttered being unknown, or from the figures of speech employed, according to Dan. 5:16, "I have heard of thee, that thou canst interpret obscure things, and resolve difficult things." Hence the interpretation of speeches is more excellent than the gift of tongues, as appears from the saying of the Apostle (1 Cor. 14:5), "Greater is he that prophesieth than he that speaketh with tongues; unless perhaps he interpret." Yet the interpretation of speeches is placed after the gift of tongues, because the interpretation of speeches extends even to the interpretation of divers kinds of tongues.

OF THE GRATUITOUS GRACE CONSISTING IN WORDS (TWO ARTICLES)

We must now consider the gratuitous grace that attaches to words; of which the Apostle says (1 Cor. 12:8): "To one . . . by the Spirit is given the word of wisdom, and to another the word of knowledge." Under this head there are two points of inquiry:

(1) Whether any gratuitous grace attaches to words?

(2) To whom is the grace becoming?

Whether any gratuitous grace attaches to words?

Objection 1: It would seem that a gratuitous grace does not attach to words. For grace is given for that which surpasses the faculty of nature. But natural reason has devised the art of rhetoric whereby a man is able to speak so as to teach, please, and persuade, as Augustine says (De Doctr. Christ. iv, 12). Now this belongs to the grace of words. Therefore it would seem that the grace of words is not a gratuitous grace.

Objection 2: Further, all grace pertains to the kingdom of God. But the Apostle says (1 Cor. 4:20): "The kingdom of God is not in speech, but in power." Therefore there is no gratuitous grace connected with words.

Objection 3: Further, no grace is given through merit, since "if by grace, it is not now of works" (Rom. 11:6). But the word is sometimes given to a man on his merits. For Gregory says (Moral. xi, 15) in explanation of Ps. 118:43, "Take not Thou the word of truth utterly out of my mouth" that "the word of truth is that which Almighty God gives to them that do it, and takes away from them that do it not." Therefore it would seem that the gift of the word is not a gratuitous grace.

Objection 4: Further, it behooves man to declare in words things pertaining to the virtue of faith, no less than those pertaining to the gift of wisdom or of knowledge.

Therefore if the word of wisdom and the word of knowledge are reckoned gratuitous graces, the word of faith should likewise be placed among the gratuitous graces.

On the contrary, It is written (Ecclus. 6:5): "A gracious tongue in a good man shall abound [Vulg.: 'aboundeth']." Now man's goodness is by grace. Therefore graciousness in words is also by grace.

I answer that, The gratuitous graces are given for the profit of others, as stated above ([3708]FS, Q[111], AA[1],4). Now the knowledge a man receives from God cannot be turned to another's profit, except by means of speech. And since the Holy Ghost does not fail in anything that pertains to the profit of the Church, He provides also the members of the Church with speech; to the effect that a man not only speaks so as to be understood by different people, which pertains to the gift of tongues, but also speaks with effect, and this pertains to the grace "of the word."

This happens in three ways. First, in order to instruct the intellect, and this is the case when a man speaks so as "to teach." Secondly, in order to move the affections, so that a man willingly hearkens to the word of God. This is the case when a man speaks so as "to please" his hearers, not indeed with a view to his own favor, but in order to draw them to listen to God's word. Thirdly, in order that men may love that which is signified by the word, and desire to fulfill it, and this is the case when a man so speaks as "to sway" his hearers. In order to effect this the Holy Ghost makes use of the human tongue as of an instrument; but He it is Who perfects the work within. Hence Gregory says in a homily for Pentecost (Hom. xxx in Ev.): "Unless the Holy Ghost fill the hearts of the hearers, in vain does the voice of the teacher resound in the ears of the body."

Reply to Objection 1: Even as by a miracle God sometimes works in a more excellent way those things which nature also can work, so too the Holy Ghost effects more excellently by the grace of words that which art can effect in a less efficient manner.

Reply to Objection 2: The Apostle is speaking there of the word that relies on human eloquence without the power of the Holy Ghost. Wherefore he says just before (1 Cor. 4:19): "I . . . will know, not the speech of them that are puffed up, but the power": and of himself he had already said (1 Cor. 2:4): "My speech and my preaching was not in the persuasive words of human wisdom, but in the showing of the spirit and power."

Reply to Objection 3: As stated above, the grace of the word is given to a man for the profit of others. Hence it is withdrawn sometimes through the fault of the hearer, and sometimes through the fault of the speaker. The good works of either of them do not merit this grace directly, but only remove the obstacles thereto. For sanctifying grace also is withdrawn on account of a person's fault, and yet he does not merit it by his good works, which, however, remove the obstacles to grace.

Reply to Objection 4: As stated above, the grace of the word is directed to the profit of others. Now if a man communicates his faith to others this is by the word of knowledge or of wisdom. Hence Augustine says (De Trin. xiv, 1) that "to know how faith may profit the godly and be defended against the ungodly, is apparently what the Apostle means by knowledge." Hence it was not necessary for him to mention the word of faith, but it was sufficient for him to mention the word of knowledge and of wisdom.

Whether the grace of the word of wisdom and knowledge is becoming to women?

Objection 1: It would seem that the grace of the word of wisdom and knowledge is becoming even to women. For teaching is pertinent to this grace, as stated in the foregoing Article. Now it is becoming to a woman to teach; for it is written (Prov. 4:3,4): "I was an only son in the sight of my mother, and she taught me [*Vulg.: 'I was my father's son, tender, and as an only son in the sight of my mother. And he taught me.']." Therefore this grace is becoming to women.

Objection 2: Further, the grace of prophecy is greater than the grace of the word, even as the contemplation of truth is greater than its utterance. But prophecy is granted to women, as we read of Deborah (Judges 4:4), and of Holda the prophetess, the wife of Sellum (4 Kings 22:14), and of the four daughters of Philip (Acts 21:9). Moreover the Apostle says (1 Cor. 11:5): "Every woman praying or prophesying," etc. Much more therefore would it seem that the grace of the word is becoming to a woman.

Objection 3: Further, it is written (1 Pet. 4:10): "As every man hath received grace ministering the same one to another." Now some women receive the grace of wisdom and knowledge, which they cannot minister to others except by the grace of the word. Therefore the grace of the word is becoming to women.

On the contrary, The Apostle says (1 Cor. 14:34): "Let women keep silence in the churches," and (1 Tim. 2:12): "I suffer not a woman to teach." Now this pertains especially to the grace of the word. Therefore the grace of the word is not becoming to women.

I answer that, Speech may be employed in two ways: in one way privately, to one or a few, in familiar conversation, and in this respect the grace of the word may be becoming to women; in another way, publicly, addressing oneself to the whole church, and this is not permitted to women. First and chiefly, on account of the condition attaching to the female sex, whereby woman should be subject to man, as appears from Gn. 3:16. Now teaching and persuading publicly in the church belong not to subjects but to the prelates (although men who are subjects may do these things if they be so commissioned, because their subjection is not a result of their natural sex, as it is with women, but of some thing supervening by accident). Secondly, lest men's minds be enticed to lust, for it is written (Ecclus. 9:11): "Her conversation burneth as fire." Thirdly, because as a rule women are not perfected in wisdom, so as to be fit to be intrusted with public teaching.

Reply to Objection 1: The passage quoted speaks of private teaching whereby a father instructs his son.

Reply to Objection 2: The grace of prophecy consists in God enlightening the mind, on the part of which there is no difference of sex among men, according to Col. 3:10,11, "Putting on the new" man, "him who is renewed unto knowledge, according to the image of Him that created him, where there is neither male nor female [*Vulg.: 'Neither Gentile nor Jew, circumcision nor uncircumcision, Barbarian nor Scythian, bond nor free.' Cf. [3709]FP, Q[93], A[6], ad 2 footnote]." Now the grace of the word pertains to the instruction of men among whom the difference of sex is found. Hence the comparison fails.

Reply to Objection 3: The recipients of a divinely conferred grace administer it in different ways according to their various conditions. Hence women, if they have the grace of wisdom or of knowledge, can administer it by teaching privately but not publicly.

OF THE GRACE OF MIRACLES (TWO ARTICLES)

We must next consider the grace of miracles, under which head there are two points of inquiry:

(1) Whether there is a gratuitous grace of working miracles?

(2) To whom is it becoming?

Whether there is a gratuitous grace of working miracles?

Objection 1: It would seem that no gratuitous grace is directed to the working of miracles. For every grace puts something in the one to whom it is given (Cf. [3710]FS, Q[90], A[1]). Now the working of miracles puts nothing in the soul of the man who receives it since miracles are wrought at the touch even of a dead body. Thus we read (4 Kings 13:21) that "some . . . cast the body into the sepulchre of Eliseus. And when it had touched the bones of Eliseus, the man came to life, and stood upon his feet." Therefore the working of miracles does not belong to a gratuitous grace.

Objection 2: Further, the gratuitous graces are from the Holy Ghost, according to 1 Cor. 12:4, "There are diversities of graces, but the same Spirit." Now the working of miracles is effected even by the unclean spirit, according to Mat. 24:24, "There shall arise false Christs and false prophets, and shall show great signs and wonders." Therefore it would seem that the working of miracles does not belong to a gratuitous grace.

Objection 3: Further, miracles are divided into "signs," "wonders" or "portents," and "virtues." [*Cf. 2 Thess. 2:9, where the Douay version renders 'virtus' by 'power.' The use of the word 'virtue' in the sense of a miracle is now obsolete, and the generic term 'miracle' is elsewhere used in its stead: Cf. 1 Cor. 12:10, 28; Heb. 2:4; Acts 2:22]. Therefore it is unreasonable to reckon the "working of miracles" a gratuitous grace, any more than the "working of signs" and "wonders."

Objection 4: Further, the miraculous restoring to health is done by the power of God. Therefore the grace of healing should not be distinguished from the working of miracles.

Objection 5: Further, the working of miracles results from faith—either of the worker, according to 1 Cor. 13:2, "If I should have all faith, so that I could remove mountains," or of other persons for whose sake miracles are wrought, according to Mat. 13:58, "And He wrought not many miracles there, because of their unbelief." Therefore, if faith be reckoned a gratuitous grace, it is superfluous to reckon in addition the working of signs as another gratuitous grace.

On the contrary, The Apostle (1 Cor. 12:9,10) says that among other gratuitous graces, "to another" is given "the grace of healing . . . to another, the working of miracles."

I answer that, As stated above ([3711]Q[177], A[1]), the Holy Ghost provides sufficiently for the Church in matters profitable unto salvation, to which purpose the gratuitous graces are directed. Now just as the knowledge which a man receives from God needs to be brought to the knowledge of others through the gift of tongues and the grace of the word, so too the word uttered needs to be confirmed in order that it be rendered credible. This is done by the working of miracles, according to Mk. 16:20, "And confirming the word with signs that followed": and reasonably so. For it is natural to man to arrive at the intelligible truth through its sensible effects. Wherefore just as man led by his natural reason is able to arrive at some knowledge of God through His natural effects, so is he brought to a certain degree of supernatural knowledge of the objects of faith by certain supernatural effects which are called miracles. Therefore the working of miracles belongs to a gratuitous grace.

Reply to Objection 1: Just as prophecy extends to whatever can be known supernaturally, so the working of miracles extends to all things that can be done supernaturally; the cause whereof is the divine omnipotence which cannot be communicated to any creature. Hence it is impossible for the principle of working miracles to be a quality abiding as a habit in the soul. On the other hand, just as the prophet's mind is moved by divine inspiration to know something supernaturally, so too is it possible for the mind of the miracle worker to be moved to do something resulting in the miraculous effect which God causes by His power. Sometimes this takes place after prayer, as when Peter raised to life the dead Tabitha (Acts 9:40): sometimes without any previous prayer being expressed, as when Peter by upbraiding the lying Ananias and Saphira delivered them to death (Acts 5:4, 9). Hence Gregory says (Dial. ii, 30) that "the saints work miracles, sometimes by authority, sometimes by prayer." In either case, however, God is the principal worker, for He uses instrumentally either man's inward movement, or his speech, or some outward action, or again the bodily contact of even a dead body. Thus when Josue had said as though authoritatively (Josh. 10:12): "Move not, O sun, toward Gabaon," it is said afterwards (Josh. 10:14): "There was not before or after so long a day, the Lord obeying the voice of a man."

Reply to Objection 2: Our Lord is speaking there of the miracles to be wrought at the time of Antichrist, of which the Apostle says (2 Thess. 2:9) that the coming of Antichrist will be "according to the working of Satan, in all power, and signs, and lying wonders." To quote the words of Augustine (De Civ. Dei xx, 19), "it is a matter of debate whether they are called signs and lying wonders, because he will deceive the senses of mortals by imaginary visions, in that he will seem to do what he does not, or because, though they be real wonders, they will seduce into falsehood them that believe." They are said to be real, because the things themselves will be real, just as Pharaoh's magicians made real frogs and real serpents; but they will not be real miracles, because they will be done by the power of natural causes, as stated in the [3712]FP, Q[114], A[4]; whereas the working of miracles which is ascribed to a gratuitous grace, is done by God's power for man's profit.

Reply to Objection 3: Two things may be considered in miracles. One is that which is done: this is something surpassing the faculty of nature, and in this respect miracles are called "virtues." The other thing is the purpose for which miracles are wrought, namely the manifestation of something supernatural, and in this respect they are commonly called "signs": but on account of some excellence they receive the name of "wonder" or "prodigy," as showing something from afar [procul].

Reply to Objection 4: The "grace of healing" is mentioned separately, because by its means a benefit, namely bodily health, is conferred on man in addition to the common benefit bestowed in all miracles, namely the bringing of men to the knowledge of God.

Reply to Objection 5: The working of miracles is ascribed to faith for two reasons. First, because it is directed to the confirmation of faith, secondly, because it proceeds from God's omnipotence on which faith relies. Nevertheless, just as besides the grace of faith, the grace of the word is necessary that people may be instructed in the faith, so too is the grace of miracles necessary that people may be confirmed in their faith.

Whether the wicked can work miracles?

Objection 1: It would seem that the wicked cannot work miracles. For miracles are wrought through prayer, as stated above (A[1], ad 1). Now the prayer of a sinner is not granted, according to Jn. 9:31, "We know that God doth not hear sinners," and Prov. 28:9, "He that turneth away his ear from hearing the law, his prayer shall be an abomination." Therefore it would seem that the wicked cannot work miracles.

Objection 2: Further, miracles are ascribed to faith, according to Mat. 17:19, "If you have faith as a grain of mustard seed you shall say to this mountain: Remove from hence hither, and it shall remove." Now "faith without works is dead," according to James 2:20, so that, seemingly, it is devoid of its proper operation. Therefore it would seem that the wicked, since they do not good works, cannot work miracles.

Objection 3: Further, miracles are divine attestations, according to Heb. 2:4, "God also bearing them witness by signs and wonders and divers miracles": wherefore in the Church the canonization of certain persons is based on the attestation of miracles. Now God cannot bear witness to a falsehood. Therefore it would seem that wicked men cannot work miracles.

Objection 4: Further, the good are more closely united to God than the wicked. But the good do not all work miracles. Much less therefore do the wicked.

On the contrary, The Apostle says (1 Cor. 13:2): "If I should have all faith, so that I could remove mountains, and have not charity, I am nothing." Now whosoever has not charity is wicked, because "this gift alone of the Holy Ghost distinguishes the children of the kingdom from the children of perdition," as Augustine says (De Trin. xv, 18). Therefore it would seem that even the wicked can work miracles.

I answer that, Some miracles are not true but imaginary deeds, because they delude man by the appearance of that which is not; while others are true deeds, yet they have not the character of a true miracle, because they are done by the power of some natural cause. Both of these can be done by the demons, as stated above (A[1], ad 2).

True miracles cannot be wrought save by the power of God, because God works them for man's benefit, and this in two ways: in one way for the confirmation of truth declared, in another way in proof of a person's holiness, which God desires to propose as an example of virtue. In the first way miracles can be wrought by any one who preaches the true faith and calls upon Christ's name, as even the wicked do sometimes. In this way even the wicked can work miracles. Hence Jerome commenting on Mat. 7:22, "Have not we prophesied in Thy name?" says: "Sometimes prophesying, the working of miracles, and the casting out of demons are accorded not to the merit of those who do these things, but to the invoking of Christ's name, that men may honor God, by invoking Whom such great miracles are wrought."

In the second way miracles are not wrought except by the saints, since it is in proof of their holiness that miracles are wrought during their lifetime or after death, either by themselves or by others. For we read (Acts 19:11,12) that "God wrought by the hand of Paul . . . miracles" and "even there were brought from his body to the sick, handkerchiefs . . . and the diseases departed from them." In this way indeed there is nothing to prevent a sinner from working miracles by invoking a saint; but the miracle is ascribed not to him, but to the one in proof of whose holiness such things are done.

Reply to Objection 1: As stated above ([3713]Q[83], A[16]) when we were treating of prayer, the prayer of impetration relies not on merit but on God's mercy, which extends even to the wicked, wherefore the prayers even of sinners are sometimes granted by God. Hence Augustine says (Tract. xliv in Joan.) that "the blind man spoke these words before he was anointed," that is, before he was perfectly enlightened; "since God does hear sinners." When it is said that the prayer of one who hears not the law is an abomination, this must be understood so far as the sinner's merit is concerned; yet it is sometimes granted, either for the spiritual welfare of the one who prays—as the publican was heard (Lk. 18:14)—or for the good of others and for God's glory.

Reply to Objection 2: Faith without works is said to be dead, as regards the believer, who lives not, by faith, with the life of grace. But nothing hinders a living thing from working through a dead instrument, as a man through a stick. It is thus that God works while employing instrumentally the faith of a sinner.

Reply to Objection 3: Miracles are always true witnesses to the purpose for which they are wrought. Hence wicked men who teach a false doctrine never work true miracles in confirmation of their teaching, although sometimes they may do so in praise of Christ's name which they invoke, and by the power of the sacraments which they administer. If they teach a true doctrine, sometimes they work true miracles as confirming their teaching, but not as an attestation of holiness. Hence Augustine says (QQ. lxxxiii, qu. 79): "Magicians work miracles in one way, good Christians in another, wicked Christians in another. Magicians by private compact with the demons, good Christians by their manifest righteousness, evil Christians by the outward signs of righteousness."

Reply to Objection 4: As Augustine says (QQ. lxxxiii, qu. 79), "the reason why these are not granted to all holy men is lest by a most baneful error the weak be deceived into thinking such deeds to imply greater gifts than the deeds of righteousness whereby eternal life is obtained."

OF THE DIVISION OF LIFE INTO ACTIVE AND CONTEMPLATIVE (TWO ARTICLES)

We must next consider active and contemplative life. This consideration will be fourfold: (1) Of the division of life into active and contemplative; (2) Of the contemplative life; (3) Of the active life; (4) Of the comparison between the active and the contemplative life.

Under the first head there are two points of inquiry:

(1) Whether life is fittingly divided into active and contemplative?

(2) Whether this is an adequate division?

Whether life is fittingly divided into active and contemplative?

Objection 1: It would seem that life is not fittingly divided into active and contemplative. For the soul is the principle of life by its essence: since the Philosopher says (De Anima ii, 4) that "in living things to live is to be." Now the soul is the principle of action and contemplation by its powers. Therefore it would seem that life is not fittingly divided into active and contemplative.

Objection 2: Further, the division of that which comes afterwards is unfittingly applied to that which comes first. Now active and contemplative, or "speculative" and "practical," are differences of the intellect (De Anima iii, 10); while "to live" comes before "to understand," since "to live" comes first to living things through the vegetative soul, as the Philosopher states (De Anima ii, 4). Therefore life is unfittingly divided into active and contemplative.

Objection 3: Further, the word "life" implies movement, according to Dionysius (Div. Nom. vi): whereas contemplation consists rather in rest, according to Wis. 8:16: "When I enter into my house, I shall repose myself with her." Therefore it would seem that life is unfittingly divided into active and contemplative.

On the contrary, Gregory says (Hom. xiv super Ezech.): "There is a twofold life wherein Almighty God instructs us by His holy word, the active life and the contemplative."

I answer that, Properly speaking, those things are said to live whose movement or operation is from within themselves. Now that which is proper to a thing and to which it is most inclined is that which is most becoming to it from itself; wherefore every living thing gives proof of its life by that operation which is most proper to it, and to which it is most inclined. Thus the life of plants is said to consist in nourishment and generation; the life of animals in sensation and movement; and the life of men in their understanding and acting according to reason. Wherefore also in men the life of every man would seem to be that wherein he delights most, and on which he is most intent; thus especially does he wish "to associate with his friends" (Ethic. ix, 12).

Accordingly since certain men are especially intent on the contemplation of truth, while others are especially intent on external actions, it follows that man's life is fittingly divided into active and contemplative.

Reply to Objection 1: Each thing's proper form that makes it actually "to be" is properly that thing's principle of operation. Hence "to live" is, in living things, "to be," because living things through having "being" from their form, act in such and such a way.

Reply to Objection 2: Life in general is not divided into active and contemplative, but the life of man, who derives his species from having an intellect, wherefore the same division applies to intellect and human life.

Reply to Objection 3: It is true that contemplation enjoys rest from external movements. Nevertheless to contemplate is itself a movement of the intellect, in so far as every operation is described as a movement; in which sense the Philosopher says (De Anima iii, 7) that sensation and understanding are movements of a kind, in so far as movement is defined "the act of a perfect thing." In this way Dionysius (Div. Nom. iv) ascribes three movements to the soul in contemplation, namely, "straight," "circular," and "oblique" [*Cf.[3714] Q[180], A[6]].

Whether life is adequately divided into active and contemplative?

Objection 1: It would seem that life is not adequately divided into active and contemplative. For the Philosopher says (Ethic. i, 5) that there are three most prominent kinds of life, the life of "pleasure," the "civil" which would seem to be the same as the active, and the "contemplative" life. Therefore the division of life into active and contemplative would seem to be inadequate.

Objection 2: Further, Augustine (De Civ. Dei xix, 1,2,3,19) mentions three kinds of life, namely the life of "leisure" which pertains to the contemplative, the "busy" life which pertains to the active, and a third "composed of both." Therefore it would seem that life is inadequately divided into active and contemplative.

Objection 3: Further, man's life is diversified according to the divers actions in which men are occupied. Now there are more than two occupations of human actions. Therefore it would seem that life should be divided into more kinds than the active and the contemplative.

On the contrary, These two lives are signified by the two wives of Jacob; the active by Lia, and the contemplative by Rachel: and by the two hostesses of our Lord; the contemplative life by Mary, and the active life by Martha, as Gregory declares (Moral. vi, 37 [*Hom. xiv in Ezech.]). Now this signification would not be fitting if there were more than two lives. Therefore life is adequately divided into active and contemplative.

I answer that, As stated above (A[1], ad 2), this division applies to the human life as derived from the intellect. Now the intellect is divided into active and contemplative, since the end of intellective knowledge is either the knowledge itself of truth, which pertains to the contemplative intellect, or some external action, which pertains to the practical or active intellect. Therefore life too is adequately divided into active and contemplative.

Reply to Objection 1: The life of pleasure places its end in pleasures of the body, which are common to us and dumb animals; wherefore as the Philosopher says (Ethic. Ethic. i, 5), it is the life "of a beast." Hence it is not included in this division of the life of a man into active and contemplative.

Reply to Objection 2: A mean is a combination of extremes, wherefore it is virtually contained in them, as tepid in hot and cold, and pale in white and black. In like manner active and contemplative comprise that which is composed of both. Nevertheless as in every mixture one of the simples predominates, so too in the mean state of life sometimes the contemplative, sometimes the active element, abounds.

Reply to Objection 3: All the occupations of human actions, if directed to the requirements of the present life in accord with right reason, belong to the active life which provides for the necessities of the present life by means of well-ordered activity. If, on the other hand, they minister to any concupiscence whatever, they belong to the life of pleasure, which is not comprised under the active life. Those human occupations that are directed to the consideration of truth belong to the contemplative life.

OF THE CONTEMPLATIVE LIFE (EIGHT ARTICLES)

We must now consider the contemplative life, under which head there are eight points of inquiry:

(1) Whether the contemplative life pertains to the intellect only, or also to the affections?

(2) Whether the moral virtues pertain to the contemplative life?

(3) Whether the contemplative life consists in one action or in several?

(4) Whether the consideration of any truth whatever pertains to the contemplative life?

(5) Whether the contemplative life of man in this state can arise to the vision of God?

(6) Of the movements of contemplation assigned by Dionysius (Div. Nom. iv);

(7) Of the pleasure of contemplation;

(8) Of the duration of contemplation.

Whether the contemplative life has nothing to do with the affections, and pertains wholly to the intellect?

Objection 1: It would seem that the contemplative life has nothing to do with the affections and pertains wholly to the intellect. For the Philosopher says (Metaph. ii, text. 3 [*Ed Did. ia, 1]) that "the end of contemplation is truth." Now truth pertains wholly to the intellect. Therefore it would seem that the contemplative life wholly regards the intellect.

Objection 2: Further, Gregory says (Moral. vi, 37; Hom. xix in Ezech.) that "Rachel, which is interpreted 'vision of the principle' [*Or rather, 'One seeing the principle,' if derived from {rah} and {irzn}; Cf. Jerome, De Nom. Hebr.], signifies the contemplative life." Now the vision of a principle belongs properly to the intellect. Therefore the contemplative life belongs properly to the intellect.

Objection 3: Further, Gregory says (Hom. xiv in Ezech.) that it belongs to the contemplative life, "to rest from external action." Now the affective or appetitive power inclines to external actions. Therefore it would seem that the contemplative life has nothing to do with the appetitive power.

On the contrary, Gregory says (Hom. xiv in Ezech.) that "the contemplative life is to cling with our whole mind to the love of God and our neighbor, and to desire nothing beside our Creator." Now desire and love pertain to the affective or appetitive power, as stated above ([3715]FS, Q[25], A[2]; [3716]FS, Q[26], A[2]). Therefore the contemplative life has also something to do with the affective or appetitive power.

I answer that, As stated above (Q[179], A[1]) theirs is said to be the contemplative who are chiefly intent on the contemplation of truth. Now intention is an act of the will, as stated above ([3717]FS, Q[12], A[1]), because intention is of the end which is the object of the will. Consequently the contemplative life, as regards the essence of the action, pertains to the intellect, but as regards the motive cause of the exercise of that action it belongs to the will, which moves all the other powers, even the intellect, to their actions, as stated above ([3718]FP, Q[82], A[4]; [3719]FS, Q[9], A[1]).

Now the appetitive power moves one to observe things either with the senses or with the intellect, sometimes for love of the thing seen because, as it is written (Mat. 6:21), "where thy treasure is, there is thy heart also," sometimes for love of the very knowledge that one acquires by observation. Wherefore Gregory makes the contemplative life to consist in the "love of God," inasmuch as through loving God we are aflame to gaze on His beauty. And since everyone delights when he obtains what he loves, it follows that the contemplative life terminates in delight, which is seated in the affective power, the result being that love also becomes more intense.

Reply to Objection 1: From the very fact that truth is the end of contemplation, it has the aspect of an appetible good, both lovable and delightful, and in this respect it pertains to the appetitive power.

Reply to Objection 2: We are urged to the vision of the first principle, namely God, by the love thereof; wherefore Gregory says (Hom. xiv in Ezech.) that "the contemplative life tramples on all cares and longs to see the face of its Creator."

Reply to Objection 3: The appetitive power moves not only the bodily members to perform external actions, but also the intellect to practice the act of contemplation, as stated above.

Whether the moral virtues pertain to the contemplative life?

Objection 1: It would seem that the moral virtues pertain to the contemplative life. For Gregory says (Hom. xiv in Ezech.) that "the contemplative life is to cling to the love of God and our neighbor with the whole mind." Now all the moral virtues, since their acts are prescribed by the precepts of the Law, are reducible to the love of God and of our neighbor, for "love . . . is the fulfilling of the Law" (Rom. 13:10). Therefore it would seem that the moral virtues belong to the contemplative life.

Objection 2: Further, the contemplative life is chiefly directed to the contemplation of God; for Gregory says (Hom. xiv in Ezech.) that "the mind tramples on all cares and longs to gaze on the face of its Creator." Now no one can accomplish this without cleanness of heart, which is a result of moral virtue [*Cf.[3720] Q[8], A[7]]. For it is written (Mat. 5:8): "Blessed are the clean of heart, for they shall see God": and (Heb. 12:14): "Follow peace with all men, and holiness, without which no man shall see God." Therefore it would seem that the moral virtues pertain to the contemplative life.

Objection 3: Further, Gregory says (Hom. xiv in Ezech.) that "the contemplative life gives beauty to the soul," wherefore it is signified by Rachel, of whom it is said (Gn. 29:17) that she was "of a beautiful countenance." Now the beauty of the soul consists in the moral virtues, especially temperance, as Ambrose says (De Offic. i, 43,45,46). Therefore it seems that the moral virtues pertain to the contemplative life.

On the contrary, The moral virtues are directed to external actions. Now Gregory says (Moral. vi [*Hom. xiv in Ezech.; Cf. A[1], OBJ[3]]) that it belongs to the contemplative life "to rest from external action." Therefore the moral virtues do not pertain to the contemplative life.

I answer that, A thing may belong to the contemplative life in two ways, essentially or dispositively. The moral virtues do not belong to the contemplative life essentially, because the end of the contemplative life is the consideration of truth: and as the Philosopher states (Ethic. ii, 4), "knowledge," which pertains to the consideration of truth, "has little influence on the moral virtues": wherefore he declares (Ethic. x, 8) that the moral virtues pertain to active but not to contemplative happiness.

On the other hand, the moral virtues belong to the contemplative life dispositively. For the act of contemplation, wherein the contemplative life essentially consists, is hindered both by the impetuosity of the passions which withdraw the soul's intention from intelligible to sensible things, and by outward disturbances. Now the moral virtues curb the impetuosity of the passions, and quell the disturbance of outward occupations. Hence moral virtues belong dispositively to the contemplative life.

Reply to Objection 1: As stated above [3721](A[1]), the contemplative life has its motive cause on the part of the affections, and in this respect the love of God and our neighbor is requisite to the contemplative life. Now motive causes do not enter into the essence of a thing, but dispose and perfect it. Wherefore it does not follow that the moral virtues belong essentially to the contemplative life.

Reply to Objection 2: Holiness or cleanness of heart is caused by the virtues that are concerned with the passions which hinder the purity of the reason; and peace is caused by justice which is about operations, according to Is. 32:17, "The work of justice shall be peace": since he who refrains from wronging others lessens the occasions of quarrels and disturbances. Hence the moral virtues dispose one to the contemplative life by causing peace and cleanness of heart.

Reply to Objection 3: Beauty, as stated above ([3722]Q[145], A[2]), consists in a certain clarity and due proportion. Now each of these is found radically in the reason; because both the light that makes beauty seen, and the establishing of due proportion among things belong to reason. Hence since the contemplative life consists in an act of the reason, there is beauty in it by its very nature and essence; wherefore it is written (Wis. 8:2) of the contemplation of wisdom: "I became a lover of her beauty."

On the other hand, beauty is in the moral virtues by participation, in so far as they participate in the order of reason; and especially is it in temperance, which restrains the concupiscences which especially darken the light of reason. Hence it is that the virtue of chastity most of all makes man apt for contemplation, since venereal pleasures most of all weigh the mind down to sensible objects, as Augustine says (Soliloq. i, 10).

Whether there are various actions pertaining to the contemplative life?

Objection 1: It would seem that there are various actions pertaining to the contemplative life. For Richard of St. Victor [*De Grat. Contempl. i, 3,4] distinguishes between "contemplation," "meditation," and "cogitation." Yet all these apparently pertain to contemplation. Therefore it would seem that there are various actions pertaining to the contemplative life.

Objection 2: Further, the Apostle says (2 Cor. 3:18): "But we . . . beholding [speculantes] the glory of the Lord with open face, are transformed into the same clarity [*Vulg.: 'into the same image from glory to glory.']." Now this belongs to the contemplative life. Therefore in addition to the three aforesaid, vision [speculatio] belongs to the contemplative life.

Objection 3: Further, Bernard says (De Consid. v, 14) that "the first and greatest contemplation is admiration of the Majesty." Now according to Damascene (De Fide Orth. ii, 15) admiration is a kind of fear. Therefore it would seem that several acts are requisite for the contemplative life.

Objection 4: Further, "Prayer," "reading," and "meditation" [*Hugh of St. Victor, Alleg. in N.T. iii, 4] are said to belong to the contemplative life. Again, "hearing" belongs to the contemplative life: since it is stated that Mary (by whom the contemplative life is signified) "sitting . . . at the Lord's feet, heard His word" (Lk. 10:39). Therefore it would seem that several acts are requisite for the contemplative life.

On the contrary, Life signifies here the operation on which a man is chiefly intent. Wherefore if there are several operations of the contemplative life, there will be, not one, but several contemplative lives.

I answer that, We are now speaking of the contemplative life as applicable to man. Now according to Dionysius (Div. Nom. vii) between man and angel there is this difference, that an angel perceives the truth by simple apprehension, whereas man arrives at the perception of a simple truth by a process from several premises. Accordingly, then, the contemplative life has one act wherein it is finally completed, namely the contemplation of truth, and from this act it derives its unity. Yet it has many acts whereby it arrives at this final act. Some of these pertain to the reception of principles, from which it proceeds to the contemplation of truth; others are concerned with deducing from the principles, the truth, the knowledge of which is sought; and the last and crowning act is the contemplation itself of the truth.

Reply to Objection 1: According to Richard of St. Victor "cogitation" would seem to regard the consideration of the many things from which a person intends to gather one simple truth. Hence cogitation may comprise not only the perceptions of the senses in taking cognizance of certain effects, but also the imaginations. and again the reason's discussion of the various signs or of anything that conduces to the truth in view: although, according to Augustine (De Trin. xiv, 7), cogitation may signify any actual operation of the intellect. "Meditation" would seem to be the process of reason from certain principles that lead to the contemplation of some truth: and "consideration" has the same meaning, according to Bernard (De Consid. ii, 2), although, according to the Philosopher (De Anima ii, 1), every operation of the intellect may be called "consideration." But "contemplation" regards the simple act of gazing on the truth; wherefore Richard says again (De Grat. Contempl. i, 4) that "contemplation is the soul's clear and free dwelling upon the object of its gaze; meditation is the survey of the mind while occupied in searching for the truth: and cogitation is the mind's glance which is prone to wander."

Reply to Objection 2: According to a gloss [*Cf. De Trin. xv, 8] of Augustine on this passage, "beholding" [speculatio] denotes "seeing in a mirror [speculo], not from a watch-tower [specula]." Now to see a thing in a mirror is to see a cause in its effect wherein its likeness is reflected. Hence "beholding" would seem to be reducible to meditation.

Reply to Objection 3: Admiration is a kind of fear resulting from the apprehension of a thing that surpasses our faculties: hence it results from the contemplation of the sublime truth. For it was stated above [3723](A[1]) that contemplation terminates in the affections.

Reply to Objection 4: Man reaches the knowledge of truth in two ways. First, by means of things received from another. In this way, as regards the things he receives from God, he needs "prayer," according to Wis. 7:7, "I called upon" God, "and the spirit of wisdom came upon me": while as regards the things he receives from man, he needs "hearing," in so far as he receives from the spoken word, and "reading," in so far as he receives from the tradition of Holy Writ. Secondly, he needs to apply himself by his personal study, and thus he requires "meditation."

Whether the contemplative life consists in the mere contemplation of God, or also in the consideration of any truth whatever?

Objection 1: It would seem that the contemplative life consists not only in the contemplation of God, but also in the consideration of any truth. For it is written (Ps. 138:14): "Wonderful are Thy works, and my soul knoweth right well." Now the knowledge of God's works is effected by any contemplation of the truth. Therefore it would seem that it pertains to the contemplative life to contemplate not only the divine truth, but also any other.

Objection 2: Further, Bernard says (De Consid. v, 14) that "contemplation consists in admiration first of God's majesty, secondly of His judgments, thirdly of

His benefits, fourthly of His promises." Now of these four the first alone regards the divine truth, and the other three pertain to His effects. Therefore the contemplative life consists not only in the contemplation of the divine truth, but also in the consideration of truth regarding the divine effects.

Objection 3: Further, Richard of St. Victor [*De Grat. Contempl. i, 6] distinguishes six species of contemplation. The first belongs to "the imagination alone," and consists in thinking of corporeal things. The second is in "the imagination guided by reason," and consists in considering the order and disposition of sensible objects. The third is in "the reason based on the imagination"; when, to wit, from the consideration of the visible we rise to the invisible. The fourth is in "the reason and conducted by the reason," when the mind is intent on things invisible of which the imagination has no cognizance. The fifth is "above the reason," but not contrary to reason, when by divine revelation we become cognizant of things that cannot be comprehended by the human reason. The sixth is "above reason and contrary to reason"; when, to wit, by the divine enlightening we know things that seem contrary to human reason, such as the doctrine of the mystery of the Trinity. Now only the last of these would seem to pertain to the divine truth. Therefore the contemplation of truth regards not only the divine truth, but also that which is considered in creatures.

Objection 4: Further, in the contemplative life the contemplation of truth is sought as being the perfection of man. Now any truth is a perfection of the human intellect. Therefore the contemplative life consists in the contemplation of any truth.

On the contrary, Gregory says (Moral. vi, 37) that "in contemplation we seek the principle which is God."

I answer that, As stated above [3724](A[2]), a thing may belong to the contemplative life in two ways: principally, and secondarily, or dispositively. That which belongs principally to the contemplative life is the contemplation of the divine truth, because this contemplation is the end of the whole human life. Hence Augustine says (De Trin. i, 8) that "the contemplation of God is promised us as being the goal of all our actions and the everlasting perfection of our joys." This contemplation will be perfect in the life to come, when we shall see God face to face, wherefore it will make us perfectly happy: whereas now the contemplation of the divine truth is competent to us imperfectly, namely "through a glass" and "in a dark manner" (1 Cor. 13:12). Hence it bestows on us a certain inchoate beatitude, which begins now and will be continued in the life to come; wherefore the Philosopher (Ethic. x, 7) places man's ultimate happiness in the contemplation of the supreme intelligible good.

Since, however, God's effects show us the way to the contemplation of God Himself, according to Rom. 1:20, "The invisible things of God . . . are clearly seen, being understood by the things that are made," it follows that the contemplation of the divine effects also belongs to the contemplative life, inasmuch as man is guided thereby to the knowledge of God. Hence Augustine says (De Vera Relig. xxix) that "in the study of creatures we must not exercise an empty and futile curiosity, but should make them the stepping-stone to things unperishable and everlasting."

Accordingly it is clear from what has been said ([3725]AA[1],2,3) that four things pertain, in a certain order, to the contemplative life; first, the moral virtues; secondly, other acts exclusive of contemplation; thirdly, contemplation of the divine effects; fourthly, the complement of all which is the contemplation of the divine truth itself.

Reply to Objection 1: David sought the knowledge of God's works, so that he might be led by them to God; wherefore he says elsewhere (Ps. 142:5,6): "I meditated on all Thy works: I meditated upon the works of Thy hands: I stretched forth my hands to Thee."

Reply to Objection 2: By considering the divine judgments man is guided to the consideration of the divine justice; and by considering the divine benefits and promises, man is led to the knowledge of God's mercy or goodness, as by effects already manifested or yet to be vouchsafed.

Reply to Objection 3: These six denote the steps whereby we ascend by means of creatures to the contemplation of God. For the first step consists in the mere consideration of sensible objects; the second step consists in going forward from sensible to intelligible objects; the third step is to judge of sensible objects according to intelligible things; the fourth is the absolute consideration of the intelligible objects to which one has attained by means of sensibles; the fifth is the contemplation of those intelligible objects that are unattainable by means of sensibles, but which the reason is able to grasp; the sixth step is the consideration of such intelligible things as the reason can neither discover nor grasp, which pertain to the sublime contemplation of divine truth, wherein contemplation is ultimately perfected.

Reply to Objection 4: The ultimate perfection of the human intellect is the divine truth: and other truths perfect the intellect in relation to the divine truth.

Whether in the present state of life the contemplative life can reach to the vision of the Divine essence?

Objection 1: It would seem that in the present state of life the contemplative life can reach to the vision of the Divine essence. For, as stated in Gn. 32:30, Jacob said: "I have seen God face to face, and my soul has been saved." Now the vision of God's face is the vision of the Divine essence. Therefore it would seem that in the present life one may come, by means of contemplation, to see God in His essence.

Objection 2: Further, Gregory says (Moral. vi, 37) that "contemplative men withdraw within themselves in order to explore spiritual things, nor do they ever carry with them the shadows of things corporeal, or if these follow them they prudently drive them away: but being desirous of seeing the incomprehensible light, they suppress all the images of their limited comprehension, and through longing to reach what is above them, they overcome that which they are." Now man is not hindered from seeing the Divine essence, which is the incomprehensible light, save by the necessity of turning to corporeal phantasms. Therefore it would seem that the contemplation of the present life can extend to the vision of the incomprehensible light in its essence.

Objection 3: Further, Gregory says (Dial. ii, 35): "All creatures are small to the soul that sees its Creator: wherefore when the man of God," the blessed Benedict, to wit, "saw a fiery globe in the tower and angels returning to heaven, without doubt he could only see such things by the light of God." Now the blessed Benedict was still in this life. Therefore the contemplation of the present life can extend to the vision of the essence of God.

On the contrary, Gregory says (Hom. xiv in Ezech.): "As long as we live in this mortal flesh, no one reaches such a height of contemplation as to fix the eyes of his mind on the ray itself of incomprehensible light."

I answer that, As Augustine says (Gen. ad lit. xii, 27), "no one seeing God lives this mortal life wherein the bodily senses have their play: and unless in some way he depart this life, whether by going altogether out of his body, or by withdrawing from his carnal senses, he is not caught up into that vision." This has been carefully discussed above (Q[175], AA[4],5), where we spoke of rapture, and in the [3726]FP, Q[12], A[2], where we treated of the vision of God.

Accordingly we must state that one may be in this life in two ways. First, with regard to act, that is to say by actually making use of the bodily senses, and thus contemplation in the present life can nowise attain to the vision of God's essence.

Secondly, one may be in this life potentially and not with regard to act, that is to say, when the soul is united to the mortal body as its form, yet so as to make use neither of the bodily senses, nor even of the imagination, as happens in rapture; and in this way the contemplation of the present life can attain to the vision of the Divine essence. Consequently the highest degree of contemplation in the present life is that which Paul had in rapture, whereby he was in a middle state between the present life and the life to come.

Reply to Objection 1: As Dionysius says (Ep. i ad Caium. Monach.), "if anyone seeing God, understood what he saw, he saw not God Himself, but something belonging to God." And Gregory says (Hom. xiv in Ezech.): "By no means is God seen now in His glory; but the soul sees something of lower degree, and is thereby refreshed so that afterwards it may attain to the glory of vision." Accordingly the words of Jacob, "I saw God face to face" do not imply that he saw God's essence, but that he saw some shape [*Cf. [3727]FP, Q[12], A[11], ad 1], imaginary of course, wherein God spoke to him. Or, "since we know a man by his face, by the face of God he signified his knowledge of Him," according to a gloss of Gregory on the same passage.

Reply to Objection 2: In the present state of life human contemplation is impossible without phantasms, because it is connatural to man to see the intelligible species in the phantasms, as the Philosopher states (De Anima iii, 7). Yet intellectual knowledge does not consist in the phantasms themselves, but in our contemplating in them the purity of the intelligible truth: and this not only in natural knowledge, but also in that which we obtain by revelation. For Dionysius says (Coel. Hier. i) that "the Divine glory shows us the angelic hierarchies under certain symbolic figures, and by its power we are brought back to the single ray of light," i.e. to the simple knowledge of the intelligible truth. It is in this sense that we must understand the statement of Gregory that "contemplatives do not carry along with them the shadows of things corporeal," since their contemplation is not fixed on them, but on the consideration of the intelligible truth.

Reply to Objection 3: By these words Gregory does not imply that the blessed Benedict, in that vision, saw God in His essence, but he wishes to show that because "all creatures are small to him that sees God," it follows that all things can easily be seen through the enlightenment of the Divine light. Wherefore he adds: "For however little he may see of the Creator's light, all created things become petty to him."

Whether the operation of contemplation is fittingly divided into a threefold movement, circular, straight and oblique?

Objection 1: It would seem that the operation of contemplation is unfittingly divided into a threefold movement, "circular," "straight," and "oblique" (Div. Nom. iv). For contemplation pertains exclusively to rest, according to Wis. 8:16, "When I go into my house, I shall repose myself with her." Now movement is opposed to rest. Therefore the operations of the contemplative life should not be described as movements.

Objection 2: Further, the action of the contemplative life pertains to the intellect, whereby man is like the angels. Now Dionysius describes these movements as being different in the angels from what they are in the soul. For he says (Div. Nom. iv) that the "circular" movement in the angel is "according to his enlightenment by the beautiful and the good." On the other hand, he assigns the circular movement of the soul to several things: the first of which is the "withdrawal of the soul into itself from externals"; the second is "a certain concentration of its powers, whereby it is rendered free of error and of outward occupation"; and the third is "union with those things that are above it." Again, he describes differently their respective straight movements. For he says that the straight movement of the angel is that by which he proceeds to the care of those things that are beneath him. On the other hand, he describes the straight movement of the soul as being twofold: first, "its progress towards things that are near it"; secondly, "its uplifting from external things to simple contemplation." Further, he assigns a different oblique movement to each. For he assigns the oblique movement of the angels to the fact that "while providing for those who have less they remain unchanged in relation to God": whereas he assigns the oblique movement of the soul to the fact that "the soul is enlightened in Divine knowledge by reasoning and discoursing." Therefore it would seem that the operations of contemplation are unfittingly assigned according to the ways mentioned above.

Objection 3: Further, Richard of St. Victor (De Contempl. i, 5) mentions many other different movements in likeness to the birds of the air. "For some of these rise at one time to a great height, at another swoop down to earth, and they do so repeatedly; others fly now to the right, now to the left again and again; others go forwards or lag behind many times; others fly in a circle now more now less extended; and others remain suspended almost immovably in one place." Therefore it would seem that there are only three movements of contemplation.

On the contrary, stands the authority of Dionysius (Div. Nom. iv).

I answer that, As stated above ([3728]Q[119], A[1], ad 3), the operation of the intellect, wherein contemplation essentially consists, is called a movement, in so far as movement is the act of a perfect thing, according to the Philosopher (De Anima iii, 1). Since, however, it is through sensible objects that we come to the knowledge of intelligible things, and since sensible operations do not take place without movement, the result is that even intelligible operations are described as movements, and are differentiated in likeness to various movements. Now of bodily movements, local movements are the most perfect and come first, as proved in Phys. viii, 7; wherefore the foremost among intelligible operations are described by being likened to them. These movements are of three kinds; for there is the "circular" movement, by which a thing moves uniformly round one point as center, another is the "straight" movement, by which a thing goes from one point to another; the third is "oblique," being composed as it were of both the others. Consequently, in intelligible operations, that which is simply uniform is compared to circular movement; the intelligible operation by which one proceeds from one point to another is compared to the straight movement; while the intelligible operation which unites something of uniformity with progress to various points is compared to the oblique movement.

Reply to Objection 1: External bodily movements are opposed to the quiet of contemplation, which consists in rest from outward occupations: but the movements of intellectual operations belong to the quiet of contemplation.

Reply to Objection 2: Man is like the angels in intellect generically, but the intellective power is much higher in the angel than in man. Consequently these movements must be ascribed to souls and angels in different ways, according as they are differently related to uniformity. For the angelic intellect has uniform knowledge in two respects. First, because it does not acquire intelligible truth from the variety of composite objects; secondly, because it understands the truth of intelligible objects not discursively, but by simple intuition. On the other hand, the intellect of the soul acquires intelligible truth from sensible objects, and understands it by a certain discoursing of the reason.

Wherefore Dionysius assigns the "circular" movement of the angels to the fact that their intuition of God is uniform and unceasing, having neither beginning nor end: even as a circular movement having neither beginning nor end is uniformly around the one same center. But on the part of the soul, ere it arrive at this uniformity, its twofold lack of uniformity needs to be removed. First, that which arises from the variety of external things: this is removed by the soul withdrawing from externals, and so the first thing he mentions regarding the circular movement of the soul is "the soul's withdrawal into itself from external objects." Secondly, another lack of uniformity requires to be removed from the soul, and this is owing to the discoursing of reason. This is done by directing all the soul's operations to the simple contemplation of the intelligible truth, and this is indicated by his saying in the second place that "the soul's intellectual powers must be uniformly concentrated," in other words that discoursing must be laid aside and the soul's gaze fixed on the contemplation of the one simple truth. In this operation of the soul there is no error, even as there is clearly no error in the understanding of first principles which we know by simple intuition. Afterwards these two things being done, he mentions thirdly the uniformity which is like that of the angels, for then all things being laid aside, the soul continues in the contemplation of God alone. This he expresses by saying: "Then being thus made uniform unitedly," i.e. conformably, "by the union of its powers, it is conducted to the good and the beautiful." The "straight" movement of the angel cannot apply to his proceeding from one thing to another by considering them, but only to the order of his providence, namely to the fact that the higher angel enlightens the lower angels through the angels that are intermediate. He indicates this when he says: "The angel's movement takes a straight line when he proceeds to the care of things subject to him, taking in his course whatever things are direct," i.e. in keeping with the dispositions of the direct order. Whereas he ascribes the "straight" movement in the soul to the soul's proceeding from exterior sensibles to the knowledge of intelligible objects. The "oblique" movement in the angels he describes as being composed of the straight and circular movements, inasmuch as their care for those beneath them is in accordance with their contemplation of God: while the "oblique" movement in the soul he also declares to be partly straight and partly circular, in so far as in reasoning it makes use of the light received from God.

Reply to Objection 3: These varieties of movement that are taken from the distinction between above and below, right and left, forwards and backwards, and from varying circles, are all comprised under either straight and oblique movement, because they all denote discursions of reason. For if the reason pass from the genus to the species, or from the part to the whole, it will be, as he explains, from above to below: if from one opposite to another, it will be from right to left; if from the cause to the effect, it will be backwards and forwards; if it be about accidents that surround a thing near at hand or far remote, the movement will be circular. The discoursing of reason from sensible to intelligible objects, if it be according to the order of natural reason, belongs to the straight movement; but if it be according to the Divine enlightenment, it will belong to the oblique movement as explained above (ad 2). That alone which he describes as immobility belongs to the circular movement.

Wherefore it is evident that Dionysius describes the movement of contemplation with much greater fulness and depth.

Whether there is delight in contemplation?

Objection 1: It would seem that there is no delight in contemplation. For delight belongs to the appetitive power; whereas contemplation resides chiefly in the intellect. Therefore it would seem that there is no delight in contemplation.

Objection 2: Further, all strife and struggle is a hindrance to delight. Now there is strife and struggle in contemplation. For Gregory says (Hom. xiv in Ezech.) that "when the soul strives to contemplate God, it is in a state of struggle; at one time it almost overcomes, because by understanding and feeling it tastes something of the incomprehensible light, and at another time it almost succumbs, because even while tasting, it fails." Therefore there is no delight in contemplation.

Objection 3: Further, delight is the result of a perfect operation, as stated in Ethic. x, 4. Now the contemplation of wayfarers is imperfect, according to 1 Cor. 13:12, "We see now through a glass in a dark manner." Therefore seemingly there is no delight in the contemplative life.

Objection 4: Further, a lesion of the body is an obstacle to delight. Now contemplation causes a lesion of the body; wherefore it is stated (Gn. 32) that after Jacob had said (Gn. 32:30), "'I have seen God face to face' . . . he halted on his foot (Gn. 32:31) . . . because he touched the sinew of his thigh and it shrank" (Gn. 32:32). Therefore seemingly there is no delight in contemplation.

On the contrary, It is written of the contemplation of wisdom (Wis. 8:16): "Her conversation hath no bitterness, nor her company any tediousness, but joy and gladness": and Gregory says (Hom. xiv in Ezech.) that "the contemplative life is sweetness exceedingly lovable."

I answer that, There may be delight in any particular contemplation in two ways. First by reason of the operation itself [*Cf. [3729]FS, Q[3], A[5]], because each individual delights in the operation which befits him according to his own nature or habit. Now contemplation of the truth befits a man according to his nature as a rational animal: the result being that "all men naturally desire to know," so that consequently they delight in the knowledge of truth. And more delightful still does this become to one who has the habit of wisdom and knowledge, the result of which is that he contemplates without difficulty. Secondly, contemplation may be delightful on the part of its object, in so far as one contemplates that which one loves; even as bodily vision gives pleasure, not only because to see is pleasurable in itself, but because one sees a person whom one loves. Since, then, the contemplative life consists chiefly in the contemplation of God, of which charity is the motive, as stated above ([3730]AA[1],2, ad 1), it follows that there is delight in the contemplative life, not only by reason of the contemplation itself, but also by reason of the Divine love.

In both respects the delight thereof surpasses all human delight, both because spiritual delight is greater than carnal pleasure, as stated above ([3731]FS, Q[31], A[5]), when we were treating of the passions, and because the love whereby God is loved out of charity surpasses all love. Hence it is written (Ps. 33:9): "O taste and see that the Lord is sweet."

Reply to Objection 1: Although the contemplative life consists chiefly in an act of the intellect, it has its beginning in the appetite, since it is through charity that one is urged to the contemplation of God. And since the end corresponds to the beginning, it follows that the term also and the end of the contemplative life has its being in the appetite, since one delights in seeing the object loved, and the very delight in the object seen arouses a yet greater love. Wherefore Gregory says (Hom. xiv in Ezech.) that "when we see one whom we love, we are so aflame as to love him more." And this is the ultimate perfection of the contemplative life, namely that the Divine truth be not only seen but also loved.

Reply to Objection 2: Strife or struggle arising from the opposition of an external thing, hinders delight in that thing. For a man delights not in a thing against which he strives: but in that for which he strives; when he has obtained it, other things being equal, he delights yet more: wherefore Augustine says (Confess. viii, 3) that "the more peril there was in the battle, the greater the joy in the triumph." But there is no strife or struggle in contemplation on the part of the truth which we contemplate, though there is on the part of our defective understanding and our corruptible body which drags us down to lower things, according to Wis. 9:15, "The corruptible body ss a load upon the soul, and the earthly habitation presseth down the mind that museth upon many things." Hence it is that when man attains to the contemplation of truth, he loves it yet more, while he hates the more his own deficiency and the weight of his corruptible body, so as to say with the Apostle (Rom. 7:24): "Unhappy man that I am, who shall deliver me from the body of this death?" Wherefore Gregory say (Hom. xiv in Ezech.): "When God is once known by desire and understanding, He withers all carnal pleasure in us."

Reply to Objection 3: The contemplation of God in this life is imperfect in comparison with the contemplation in heaven; and in like manner the delight of the wayfarer's contemplation is imperfect as compared with the delight of contemplation in heaven, of which it is written (Ps. 35:9): "Thou shalt make them drink of the torrent of Thy pleasure." Yet, though the contemplation of Divine things which is to be had by wayfarers is imperfect, it is more delightful than all other contemplation however perfect, on account of the excellence of that which is contemplated. Hence the Philosopher says (De Part. Animal. i, 5): "We may happen to have our own little theories about those sublime beings and godlike substances, and though we grasp them but feebly, nevertheless so elevating is the knowledge that they give us more delight than any of those things that are round about us": and Gregory says in the same sense (Hom. xiv in Ezech.): "The contemplative life is sweetness exceedingly lovable; for it carries the soul away above itself, it opens heaven and discovers the spiritual world to the eyes of the mind."

Reply to Objection 4: After contemplation Jacob halted with one foot, "because we need to grow weak in the love of the world ere we wax strong in the love of God," as Gregory says (Hom. xiv in Ezech.). "Thus when we have known the sweetness of God, we have one foot sound while the other halts; since every one who halts on one foot leans only on that foot which is sound."

Whether the contemplative life is continuous?

Objection 1: It would seem that the contemplative life is not continuous. For the contemplative life consists essentially in things pertaining to the intellect. Now all the intellectual perfections of this life will be made void, according to 1 Cor. 13:8, "Whether prophecies shall be made void, or tongues shall cease, or knowledge shall be destroyed." Therefore the contemplative life is made void.

Objection 2: Further, a man tastes the sweetness of contemplation by snatches and for a short time only: wherefore Augustine says (Confess. x, 40), "Thou admittest me to a most unwonted affection in my inmost soul, to a strange sweetness . . . yet through my grievous weight I sink down again." Again, Gregory commenting on the words of Job 4:15, "When a spirit passed before me," says (Moral. v, 33): "The mind does not remain long at rest in the sweetness of inward contemplation, for it is recalled to itself and beaten back by the very immensity of the light." Therefore the contemplative life is not continuous.

Objection 3: Further, that which is not connatural to man cannot be continuous. Now the contemplative life, according to the Philosopher (Ethic. x, 7), "is better than the life which is according to man." Therefore seemingly the contemplative life is not continuous.

On the contrary, our Lord said (Lk. 10:42): "Mary hath chosen the best part, which shall not be taken away from her," since as Gregory says (Hom. xiv in Ezech.), "the contemplative life begins here so that it may be perfected in our heavenly home."

I answer that, A thing may be described as continuous in two ways: first, in regard to its nature; secondly, in regard to us. It is evident that in regard to itself contemplative life is continuous for two reasons: first, because it is about incorruptible and unchangeable things; secondly, because it has no contrary, for there is nothing contrary to the pleasure of contemplation, as stated in Topic. i, 13. But even in our regard contemplative life is continuous—both because it is competent to us in respect of the incorruptible part of the soul, namely the intellect, wherefore it can endure after this life—and because in the works of the contemplative life we work not with our bodies, so that we are the more able to persevere in the works thereof, as the Philosopher observes (Ethic. x, 7).

Reply to Objection 1: The manner of contemplation is not the same here as in heaven: yet the contemplative life is said to remain by reason of charity, wherein it has both its beginning and its end. Gregory speaks in this sense (Hom. xiv in Ezech.): "The contemplative life begins here, so as to be perfected in our heavenly home, because the fire of love which begins to burn here is aflame with a yet greater love when we see Him Whom we love."

Reply to Objection 2: No action can last long at its highest pitch. Now the highest point of contemplation is to reach the uniformity of Divine contemplation, according to Dionysius [*Cf. Coel. Hier. iii], and as we have stated above (A[6], ad 2). Hence although contemplation cannot last long in this respect, it can be of long duration as regards the other contemplative acts.

Reply to Objection 3: The Philosopher declares the contemplative life to be above man, because it befits us "so far as there is in us something divine" (Ethic. x, 7), namely the intellect, which is incorruptible and impassible in itself, wherefore its act can endure longer.

OF THE ACTIVE LIFE (FOUR ARTICLES)

We must now consider the active life, under which head there are four points of inquiry:

(1) Whether all the works of the moral virtues pertain to the active life?

(2) Whether prudence pertains to the active life?

(3) Whether teaching pertains to the active life?

(4) Of the duration of the active life.

Whether all the actions of the moral virtues pertain to the active life?

Objection 1: It would seem that the acts of the moral virtues do not all pertain to the active life. For seemingly the active life regards only our relations with other persons: hence Gregory says (Hom. xiv in Ezech.) that "the active life is to give bread to the hungry," and after mentioning many things that regard our relations with other people he adds finally, "and to give to each and every one whatever he needs." Now we are directed in our relations to others, not by all the acts of moral virtues, but only by those of justice and its parts, as stated above (Q[58], AA[2],8; [3732]FS, Q[60], AA[2],3). Therefore the acts of the moral virtues do not all pertain to the active life.

Objection 2: Further, Gregory says (Hom. xiv in Ezech.) that Lia who was blear-eyed but fruitful signifies the active life: which "being occupied with work, sees less, and yet since it urges one's neighbor both by word and example to its imitation it begets a numerous offspring of good deeds." Now this would seem to belong to charity, whereby we love our neighbor, rather than to the moral virtues. Therefore seemingly the acts of moral virtue do not pertain to the active life.

Objection 3: Further, as stated above ([3733]Q[180], A[2]), the moral virtues dispose one to the contemplative life. Now disposition and perfection belong to the same thing. Therefore it would seem that the moral virtues do not pertain to the active life.

On the contrary, Isidore says (De Summo Bono iii, 15): "In the active life all vices must first of all be extirpated by the practice of good works, in order that in the contemplative life the mind's eye being purified one may advance to the contemplation of the Divine light." Now all vices are not extirpated save by acts of the moral virtues. Therefore the acts of the moral virtues pertain to the active life.

I answer that, As stated above ([3734]Q[179], A[1]) the active and the contemplative life differ according to the different occupations of men intent on different ends: one of which occupations is the consideration of the truth; and this is the end of the contemplative life, while the other is external work to which the active life is directed.

Now it is evident that the moral virtues are directed chiefly, not to the contemplation of truth but to operation. Wherefore the Philosopher says (Ethic. ii, 4) that "for virtue knowledge is of little or no avail." Hence it is clear that the moral virtues belong essentially to the active life; for which reason the Philosopher (Ethic. x, 8) subordinates the moral virtues to active happiness.

Reply to Objection 1: The chief of the moral virtues is justice by which one man is directed in his relations towards another, as the Philosopher proves (Ethic. v, 1). Hence the active life is described with reference to our relations with other people, because it consists in these things, not exclusively, but principally.

Reply to Objection 2: It is possible, by the acts of all the moral virtues, for one to direct one's neighbor to good by example: and this is what Gregory here ascribes to the active life.

Reply to Objection 3: Even as the virtue that is directed to the end of another virtue passes, as it were, into the species of the latter virtue, so again when a man makes use of things pertaining to the active life, merely as dispositions to contemplation, such things are comprised under the contemplative life. On the other hand, when we practice the works of the moral virtues, as being good in themselves, and not as dispositions to the contemplative life, the moral virtues belong to the active life.

It may also be replied, however, that the active life is a disposition to the contemplative life.

Whether prudence pertains to the active life?

Objection 1: It would seem that prudence does not pertain to the active life. For just as the contemplative life belongs to the cognitive power, so the active life belongs to the appetitive power. Now prudence belongs not to the appetitive but to the cognitive power. Therefore prudence does not belong to the active life.

Objection 2: Further, Gregory says (Hom. xiv in Ezech.) that the "active life being occupied with work, sees less," wherefore it is signified by Lia who was blear-eyed. But prudence requires clear eyes, so that one may judge aright of what has to be done. Therefore it seems that prudence does not pertain to the active life.

Objection 3: Further, prudence stands between the moral and the intellectual virtues. Now just as the moral virtues belong to the active life, as stated above [3735](A[1]), so do the intellectual virtues pertain to the contemplative life. Therefore it would seem that prudence pertains neither to the active nor to the contemplative life, but to an intermediate kind of life, of which Augustine makes mention (De Civ. Dei xix, 2,3,19).

On the contrary, The Philosopher says (Ethic. x, 8) that prudence pertains to active happiness, to which the moral virtues belong.

I answer that, As stated above (A[1], ad 3; [3736]FS, Q[18], A[6]), if one thing be directed to another as its end, it is drawn, especially in moral matters, to the species of the thing to which it is directed: for instance "he who commits adultery that he may steal, is a thief rather than an adulterer," according to the Philosopher (Ethic. v, 2). Now it is evident that the knowledge of prudence is directed to the works of the moral virtues as its end, since it is "right reason applied to action" (Ethic. vi, 5); so that the ends of the moral virtues are the principles of prudence, as the Philosopher says in the same book. Accordingly, as it was stated above (A[1], ad 3) that the moral virtues in one who directs them to the quiet of contemplation belong to the contemplative life, so the knowledge of prudence, which is of itself directed to the works of the moral virtues, belongs directly to the active life, provided we take prudence in its proper sense as the Philosopher speaks of it.

If, however, we take it in a more general sense, as comprising any kind of human knowledge, then prudence, as regards a certain part thereof, belongs to the contemplative life. In this sense Tully (De Offic. i, 5) says that "the man who is able most clearly and quickly to grasp the truth and to unfold his reasons, is wont to be considered most prudent and wise."

Reply to Objection 1: Moral works take their species from their end, as stated above ([3737]FS, Q[18], AA[4],6), wherefore the knowledge pertaining to the contemplative life is that which has its end in the very knowledge of truth; whereas the knowledge of prudence, through having its end in an act of the appetitive power, belongs to the active life.

Reply to Objection 2: External occupation makes a man see less in intelligible things, which are separated from sensible objects with which the works of the active life are concerned. Nevertheless the external occupation of the active life enables a man to see more clearly in judging of what is to be done, which belongs to prudence, both on account of experience, and on account of the mind's attention, since "brains avail when the mind is attentive" as Sallust observes [*Bell. Catilin., LI].

Reply to Objection 3: Prudence is said to be intermediate between the intellectual and the moral virtues because it resides in the same subject as the intellectual virtues, and has absolutely the same matter as the moral virtues. But this third kind of life is intermediate between the active and the contemplative life as regards the things about which it is occupied, because it is occupied sometimes with the contemplation of the truth, sometimes with eternal things.

Whether teaching is a work of the active or of the contemplative life?

Objection 1: It would seem that teaching is a work not of the active but of the contemplative life. For Gregory says (Hom. v in Ezech.) that "the perfect who have been able to contemplate heavenly goods, at least through a glass, proclaim them to their brethren, whose minds they inflame with love for their hidden beauty." But this pertains to teaching. Therefore teaching is a work of the contemplative life.

Objection 2: Further, act and habit would seem to be referable to the same kind of life. Now teaching is an act of wisdom: for the Philosopher says (Metaph. i, 1) that "to be able to teach is an indication of knowledge." Therefore since wisdom or knowledge pertain to the contemplative life, it would seem that teaching also belongs to the contemplative life.

Objection 3: Further, prayer, no less than contemplation, is an act of the contemplative life. Now prayer, even when one prays for another, belongs to the contemplative life. Therefore it would seem that it belongs also to the contemplative life to acquaint another, by teaching him, of the truth we have meditated.

On the contrary, Gregory says (Hom. xiv in Ezech.): "The active life is to give bread to the hungry, to teach the ignorant the words of wisdom."

I answer that, The act of teaching has a twofold object. For teaching is conveyed by speech, and speech is the audible sign of the interior concept. Accordingly one object of teaching is the matter or object of the interior concept; and as to this object teaching belongs sometimes to the active, sometimes to the contemplative life. It belongs to the active life, when a man conceives a truth inwardly, so as to be directed thereby in his outward action; but it belongs to the contemplative life when a man conceives an intelligible truth, in the consideration and love whereof he delights. Hence Augustine says (De Verb. Dom. Serm. civ, 1): "Let them choose for themselves the better part," namely the contemplative life, "let them be busy with the word, long for the sweetness of teaching, occupy themselves with salutary knowledge," thus stating clearly that teaching belongs to the contemplative life.

The other object of teaching is on the part of the speech heard, and thus the object of teaching is the hearer. As to this object all doctrine belongs to the active life to which external actions pertain.

Reply to Objection 1: The authority quoted speaks expressly of doctrine as to its matter, in so far as it is concerned with the consideration and love of truth.

Reply to Objection 2: Habit and act have a common object. Hence this argument clearly considers the matter of the interior concept. For it pertains to the man having wisdom and knowledge to be able to teach, in so far as he is able to express his interior concept in words, so as to bring another man to understand the truth.

Reply to Objection 3: He who prays for another does nothing towards the man for whom he prays, but only towards God Who is the intelligible truth; whereas he who teaches another does something in his regard by external action. Hence the comparison fails.

Whether the active life remains after this life?

Objection 1: It would seem that the active life remains after this life. For the acts of the moral virtues belong to the active life, as stated above [3738](A[1]). But the moral virtues endure after this life according to Augustine (De Trin. xiv, 9). Therefore the active life remains after this life.

Objection 2: Further, teaching others belongs to the active life, as stated above [3739](A[3]). But in the life to come when "we shall be like the angels," teaching will be possible: even as apparently it is in the angels of whom one "enlightens, cleanses, and perfects" [*Coel. Hier. iii, viii] another, which refers to the "receiving of knowledge," according to Dionysius (Coel. Hier. vii). Therefore it would seem that the active life remains after this life.

Objection 3: Further, the more lasting a thing is in itself, the more is it able to endure after this life. But the active life is seemingly more lasting in itself: for Gregory says (Hom. v in Ezech.) that "we can remain fixed in the active life, whereas we are nowise able to maintain an attentive mind in the contemplative life." Therefore the active life is much more able than the contemplative to endure after this life.

On the contrary, Gregory says (Hom. xiv in Ezech.): "The active life ends with this world, but the contemplative life begins here, to be perfected in our heavenly home."

I answer that, As stated above [3740](A[1]), the active life has its end in external actions: and if these be referred to the quiet of contemplation, for that very reason they belong to the contemplative life. But in the future life of the blessed the occupation of external actions will cease, and if there be any external actions at all, these will be referred to contemplation as their end. For, as Augustine says at the end of De Civitate Dei xxii, 30, "there we shall rest and we shall see, we shall see and love, we shall love and praise." And he had said before (De Civ. Dei xxii, 30) that "there God will be seen without end, loved without wearying, praised without tiring: such will be the occupation of all, the common love, the universal activity."

Reply to Objection 1: As stated above ([3741]Q[136], A[1], ad 1), the moral virtues will remain not as to those actions which are about the means, but as to the actions which are about the end. Such acts are those that conduce to the quiet of contemplation, which in the words quoted above Augustine denotes by "rest," and this rest excludes not only outward disturbances but also the inward disturbance of the passions.

Reply to Objection 2: The contemplative life, as stated above ([3742]Q[180], A[4]), consists chiefly in the contemplation of God, and as to this, one angel does not teach another, since according to Mat. 18:10, "the little ones' angels," who belong to the lower order, "always see the face of the Father"; and so, in the life to come, no man will teach another of God, but "we shall" all "see Him as He is" (1 Jn. 3:2). This is in keeping with the saying of Jeremiah 31:34: "They shall teach no more every man his neighbor . . . saying: Know the Lord: for all shall know me, from the least of them even to the greatest."

But as regards things pertaining to the "dispensation of the mysteries of God," one angel teaches another by cleansing, enlightening, and perfecting him: and thus they have something of the active life so long as the world lasts, from the fact that they are occupied in administering to the creatures below them. This is signified by the fact that Jacob saw angels "ascending" the ladder—which refers to contemplation—and "descending"—which refers to action. Nevertheless, as Gregory remarks (Moral. ii, 3), "they do not wander abroad from the Divine vision, so as to be deprived of the joys of inward contemplation." Hence in them the active life does not differ from the contemplative life as it does in us for whom the works of the active life are a hindrance to contemplation.

Nor is the likeness to the angels promised to us as regards the administering to lower creatures, for this is competent to us not by reason of our natural order, as it is to the angels, but by reason of our seeing God.

Reply to Objection 3: That the durability of the active life in the present state surpasses the durability of the contemplative life arises not from any property of either life considered in itself, but from our own deficiency, since we are withheld from the heights of contemplation by the weight of the body. Hence Gregory adds (Moral. ii, 3) that "the mind through its very weakness being repelled from that immense height recoils on itself."

OF THE ACTIVE LIFE IN COMPARISON WITH THE CONTEMPLATIVE LIFE (FOUR ARTICLES)

We must now consider the active life in comparison with the contemplative life, under which head there are four points of inquiry:

(1) Which of them is of greater import or excellence?

(2) Which of them has the greater merit?

(3) Whether the contemplative life is hindered by the active life?

(4) Of their order.

Whether the active life is more excellent than the contemplative?

Objection 1: It would seem that the active life is more excellent than the contemplative. For "that which belongs to better men would seem to be worthier and better," as the Philosopher says (Top. iii, 1). Now the active life belongs to persons of higher rank, namely prelates, who are placed in a position of honor and power; wherefore Augustine says (De Civ. Dei xix, 19) that "in our actions we must not love honor or power in this life." Therefore it would seem that the active life is more excellent than the contemplative.

Objection 2: Further, in all habits and acts, direction belongs to the more important; thus the military art, being the more important, directs the art of the bridle-maker [*Ethic. i, 1]. Now it belongs to the active life to direct and command the contemplative, as appears from the words addressed to Moses (Ex. 19:21), "Go down and charge the people, lest they should have a mind to pass the" fixed "limits to see the Lord." Therefore the active life is more excellent than the contemplative.

Objection 3: Further, no man should be taken away from a greater thing in order to be occupied with lesser things: for the Apostle says (1 Cor. 12:31): "Be zealous for the better gifts." Now some are taken away from the state of the contemplative life to the occupations of the active life, as in the case of those who are transferred to the state of prelacy. Therefore it would seem that the active life is more excellent than the contemplative.

On the contrary, Our Lord said (Lk. 10:42): "Mary hath chosen the best part, which shall not be taken away from her." Now Mary figures the contemplative life. Therefore the contemplative life is more excellent than the active.

I answer that, Nothing prevents certain things being more excellent in themselves, whereas they are surpassed by another in some respect. Accordingly we must reply that the contemplative life is simply more excellent than the active: and the Philosopher proves this by eight reasons (Ethic. x, 7,8). The first is, because the contemplative life becomes man according to that which is best in him, namely the intellect, and according to its proper objects, namely things intelligible; whereas the active life is occupied with externals. Hence Rachael, by whom the contemplative life is signified, is interpreted "the vision of the principle," [*Or rather, 'One seeing the principle,' if derived from {rah} and {irzn}; Cf. Jerome, De Nom. Hebr.] whereas as Gregory says (Moral. vi, 37) the active life is signified by Lia who was blear-eyed. The second reason is because the contemplative life can be more continuous, although not as regards the highest degree of contemplation, as stated above ([3743]Q[180], A[8], ad 2;[3744] Q[181], A[4], ad 3), wherefore Mary, by whom the contemplative life is signified, is described as "sitting" all the time "at the Lord's feet." Thirdly, because the contemplative life is more delightful than the active; wherefore Augustine says (De Verb. Dom. Serm. ciii) that "Martha was troubled, but Mary feasted." Fourthly, because in the contemplative life man is more self-sufficient, since he needs fewer things for that purpose; wherefore it was said (Lk. 10:41): "Martha, Martha, thou art careful and art troubled about many things." Fifthly, because the contemplative life is loved more for its own sake, while the active life is directed to something else. Hence it is written (Ps. 36:4): "One thing I have asked of the Lord, this will I seek after, that I may dwell in the house of the Lord all the days of my life, that I may see the delight of the Lord." Sixthly, because the contemplative life consists in leisure and rest, according to Ps. 45:11, "Be still and see that I am God." Seventhly, because the contemplative life is according to Divine things, whereas active life is according to human things; wherefore Augustine says (De Verb. Dom. Serm. civ): "'In the beginning was the Word': to Him was Mary hearkening: 'The Word was made flesh': Him was Martha serving." Eighthly, because the contemplative life is according to that which is most proper to man, namely his intellect; whereas in the works of the active life the lower powers also, which are common to us and brutes, have their part; wherefore (Ps. 35:7) after the words, "Men and beasts Thou wilt preserve, O

Lord," that which is special to man is added (Ps. 35:10): "In Thy light we shall see light."

Our Lord adds a ninth reason (Lk. 10:42) when He says: "Mary hath chosen the best part, which shall not be taken away from her," which words Augustine (De Verb. Dom. Serm. ciii) expounds thus: "Not—Thou hast chosen badly but—She has chosen better. Why better? Listen—because it shall not be taken away from her. But the burden of necessity shall at length be taken from thee: whereas the sweetness of truth is eternal."

Yet in a restricted sense and in a particular case one should prefer the active life on account of the needs of the present life. Thus too the Philosopher says (Topic. iii, 2): "It is better to be wise than to be rich, yet for one who is in need, it is better to be rich . . ."

Reply to Objection 1: Not only the active life concerns prelates, they should also excel in the contemplative life; hence Gregory says (Pastor. ii, 1): "A prelate should be foremost in action, more uplifted than others in contemplation."

Reply to Objection 2: The contemplative life consists in a certain liberty of mind. For Gregory says (Hom. iii in Ezech.) that "the contemplative life obtains a certain freedom of mind, for it thinks not of temporal but of eternal things." And Boethius says (De Consol. v, 2): "The soul of man must needs be more free while it continues to gaze on the Divine mind, and less so when it stoops to bodily things." Wherefore it is evident that the active life does not directly command the contemplative life, but prescribes certain works of the active life as dispositions to the contemplative life; which it accordingly serves rather than commands. Gregory refers to this when he says (Hom. iii in Ezech.) that "the active life is bondage, whereas the contemplative life is freedom."

Reply to Objection 3: Sometimes a man is called away from the contemplative life to the works of the active life, on account of some necessity of the present life, yet not so as to be compelled to forsake contemplation altogether. Hence Augustine says (De Civ. Dei xix, 19): "The love of truth seeks a holy leisure, the demands of charity undertake an honest toil," the work namely of the active life. "If no one imposes this burden upon us we must devote ourselves to the research and contemplation of truth, but if it be imposed on us, we must bear it because charity demands it of us. Yet even then we must not altogether forsake the delights of truth, lest we deprive ourselves of its sweetness, and this burden overwhelm us." Hence it is clear that when a person is called from the contemplative life to the active life, this is done by way not of subtraction but of addition.

Whether the active life is of greater merit than the contemplative?

Objection 1: It would seem that the active life is of greater merit than the contemplative. For merit implies relation to meed; and meed is due to labor, according to 1 Cor. 3:8, "Every man shall receive his own reward according to his own labor." Now labor is ascribed to the active life, and rest to the contemplative life; for Gregory says (Hom. xiv in Ezech.): "Whosoever is converted to God must first of all sweat from labor, i.e. he must take Lia, that afterwards he may rest in the embraces of Rachel so as to see the principle." Therefore the active life is of greater merit than the contemplative.

Objection 2: Further, the contemplative life is a beginning of the happiness to come; wherefore Augustine commenting on Jn. 21:22, "So I will have him to remain till I come," says (Tract. cxxiv in Joan.): "This may be expressed more clearly: Let perfect works follow Me conformed to the example of My passion, and let contemplation begun here remain until I come, that it may be perfected when I shall come." And Gregory says (Hom. xiv in Ezech.) that "contemplation begins here, so as to be perfected in our heavenly home." Now the life to come will be a state not of meriting but of receiving the reward of our merits. Therefore the contemplative life would seem to have less of the character of merit than the active, but more of the character of reward.

Objection 3: Further, Gregory says (Hom. xii in Ezech.) that "no sacrifice is more acceptable to God than zeal for souls." Now by the zeal for souls a man turns to the occupations of the active life. Therefore it would seem that the contemplative life is not of greater merit than the active.

On the contrary, Gregory says (Moral. vi, 37): "Great are the merits of the active life, but greater still those of the contemplative."

I answer that, As stated above ([3745]FS, Q[114], A[4]), the root of merit is charity; and, while, as stated above (Q[25], A[1]), charity consists in the love of God and our neighbor, the love of God is by itself more meritorious than the love of our neighbor, as stated above (Q[27], A[8]). Wherefore that which pertains more directly to the love of God is generically more meritorious than that which pertains directly to the love of our neighbor for God's sake. Now the contemplative life pertains directly and immediately to the love of God; for Augustine says (De Civ. Dei xix, 19) that "the love of" the Divine "truth seeks a holy leisure," namely of the contemplative life, for it is that truth above all which the contemplative life seeks, as stated above (Q[181], A[4], ad 2). On the other hand, the active life is more directly concerned with the love of our neighbor, because it is "busy about much serving" (Lk. 10:40). Wherefore the contemplative life is generically of greater merit than the active life. This is moreover asserted by Gregory (Hom. iii in Ezech.): "The contemplative life surpasses in merit the active life, because the latter labors under the stress of present work," by reason of the necessity of assisting our neighbor, "while the former with heartfelt relish has a foretaste of the coming rest," i.e. the contemplation of God.

Nevertheless it may happen that one man merits more by the works of the active life than another by the works of the contemplative life. For instance through excess of Divine love a man may now and then suffer separation from the sweetness of Divine contemplation for the time being, that God's will may be done and for His glory's sake. Thus the Apostle says (Rom. 9:3): "I wished myself to be an anathema from Christ, for my brethren"; which words Chrysostom expounds as follows (De Compunct. i, 7 [*Ad Demetr. de Compunct. Cordis.]): "His mind was so steeped in the love of Christ that, although he desired above all to be with Christ, he despised even this, because thus he pleased Christ."

Reply to Objection 1: External labor conduces to the increase of the accidental reward; but the increase of merit with regard to the essential reward consists chiefly in charity, whereof external labor borne for Christ's sake is a sign. Yet a much more expressive sign thereof is shown when a man, renouncing whatsoever pertains to this life, delights to occupy himself entirely with Divine contemplation.

Reply to Objection 2: In the state of future happiness man has arrived at perfection, wherefore there is no room for advancement by merit; and if there were, the merit would be more efficacious by reason of the greater charity. But in the present life contemplation is not without some imperfection, and can always become more perfect; wherefore it does not remove the idea of merit, but causes a yet greater merit on account of the practice of greater Divine charity.

Reply to Objection 3: A sacrifice is rendered to God spiritually when something is offered to Him; and of all man's goods, God specially accepts that of the human soul when it is offered to Him in sacrifice. Now a man ought to offer to God, in the first place, his soul, according to Ecclus. 30:24, "Have pity on thy own soul, pleasing God"; in the second place, the souls of others, according to Apoc. 22:17, "He that heareth, let him say: Come." And the more closely a man unites his own or another's soul to God, the more acceptable is his sacrifice to God; wherefore it is more acceptable to God that one apply one's own soul and the souls of others to contemplation than to action. Consequently the statement that "no sacrifice is more acceptable to God than zeal for souls," does not mean that the merit of the active life is preferable to the merit of the contemplative life, but that it is more meritorious to offer to God one's own soul and the souls of others, than any other external gifts.

Whether the contemplative life is hindered by the active life?

Objection 1: It would seem that the contemplative life is hindered by the active life. For the contemplative life requires a certain stillness of mind, according to Ps. 45:11, "Be still, and see that I am God"; whereas the active life involves restlessness, according to Lk. 10:41, "Martha, Martha, thou art careful and troubled about many things." Therefore the active life hinders the contemplative.

Objection 2: Further, clearness of vision is a requisite for the contemplative life. Now active life is a hindrance to clear vision; for Gregory says (Hom. xiv in Ezech.) that it "is blear-eyed and fruitful, because the active life, being occupied with work, sees less." Therefore the active life hinders the contemplative.

Objection 3: Further, one contrary hinders the other. Now the active and the contemplative life are apparently contrary to one another, since the active life is busy about many things, while the contemplative life attends to the contemplation of one; wherefore they differ in opposition to one another. Therefore it would seem that the contemplative life is hindered by the active.

On the contrary, Gregory says (Moral. vi, 37): "Those who wish to hold the fortress of contemplation, must first of all train in the camp of action."

I answer that, The active life may be considered from two points of view. First, as regards the attention to and practice of external works: and thus it is evident that the active life hinders the contemplative, in so far as it is impossible for one to be busy with external action, and at the same time give oneself to Divine contemplation. Secondly, active life may be considered as quieting and directing the internal passions of the soul; and from this point of view the active life is a help to the contemplative, since the latter is hindered by the inordinateness of the internal passions. Hence Gregory says (Moral. vi, 37): "Those who wish to hold the fortress of contemplation must first of all train in the camp of action. Thus after careful study they will learn whether they no longer wrong their neighbor, whether they bear with equanimity the wrongs their neighbors do to them, whether their soul is neither overcome with joy in the presence of temporal goods, nor cast down with too great a sorrow when those goods are withdrawn. In this way they will known when they withdraw within themselves, in order to explore spiritual things, whether they no longer carry with them the shadows of the things corporeal, or, if these follow them, whether they prudently drive them away." Hence the work of the active life conduces to the contemplative, by quelling the interior passions which give rise to the phantasms whereby contemplation is hindered.

This suffices for the Replies to the Objections; for these arguments consider the occupation itself of external actions, and not the effect which is the quelling of the passions.

Whether the active life precedes the contemplative?

Objection 1: It would seem that the active life does not precede the contemplative. For the contemplative life pertains directly to the love of God; while the active life pertains to the love of our neighbor. Now the love of God precedes the love of our neighbor, since we love our neighbor for God's sake. Seemingly therefore the contemplative life also precedes the active life.

Objection 2: Further, Gregory says (Hom. xiv in Ezech.): "It should be observed that while a well-ordered life proceeds from action to contemplation, sometimes it is useful for the soul to turn from the contemplative to the active life." Therefore the active is not simply prior to the contemplative.

Objection 3: Further, it would seem that there is not necessarily any order between things that are suitable to different subjects. Now the active and the contemplative life are suitable to different subjects; for Gregory says (Moral. vi, 37): "Often those who were able to contemplate God so long as they were undisturbed have fallen when pressed with occupation; and frequently they who might live advantageously occupied with the service of their fellow-creatures are killed by the sword of their inaction."

I answer that, A thing is said to precede in two ways. First, with regard to its nature; and in this way the contemplative life precedes the active, inasmuch as it applies itself to things which precede and are better than others, wherefore it moves and directs the active life. For the higher reason which is assigned to contemplation is compared to the lower reason which is assigned to action, and the husband is compared to his wife, who should be ruled by her husband, as Augustine says (De Trin. xii, 3,7,12).

Secondly, a thing precedes with regard to us, because it comes first in the order of generation. In this way the active precedes the contemplative life, because it disposes one to it, as stated above [3746](A[1]; Q[181], A[1], ad 3); and, in the order of generation, disposition precedes form, although the latter precedes simply and according to its nature.

Reply to Objection 1: The contemplative life is directed to the love of God, not of any degree, but to that which is perfect; whereas the active life is necessary for any degree of the love of our neighbor. Hence Gregory says (Hom. iii in Ezech.):

"Without the contemplative life it is possible to enter the heavenly kingdom, provided one omit not the good actions we are able to do; but we cannot enter therein without the active life, if we neglect to do the good we can do."

From this it is also evident that the active precedes the contemplative life, as that which is common to all precedes, in the order of generation, that which is proper to the perfect.

Reply to Objection 2: Progress from the active to the contemplative life is according to the order of generation; whereas the return from the contemplative life to the active is according to the order of direction, in so far as the active life is directed by the contemplative. Even thus habit is acquired by acts, and by the acquired habit one acts yet more perfectly, as stated in Ethic. ii, 7.

Reply to Objection 3: He that is prone to yield to his passions on account of his impulse to action is simply more apt for the active life by reason of his restless spirit. Hence Gregory says (Moral. vi, 37) that "there be some so restless that when they are free from labor they labor all the more, because the more leisure they have for thought, the worse interior turmoil they have to bear." Others, on the contrary, have the mind naturally pure and restful, so that they are apt for contemplation, and if they were to apply themselves wholly to action, this would be detrimental to them. Wherefore Gregory says (Moral. vi, 37) that "some are so slothful of mind that if they chance to have any hard work to do they give way at the very outset." Yet, as he adds further on, "often . . . love stimulates slothful souls to work, and fear restrains souls that are disturbed in contemplation." Consequently those who are more adapted to the active life can prepare themselves for the contemplative by the practice of the active life; while none the less, those who are more adapted to the contemplative life can take upon themselves the works of the active life, so as to become yet more apt for contemplation.

TREATISE ON THE STATES OF LIFE (QQ[183]-189)

OF MAN'S VARIOUS DUTIES AND STATES IN GENERAL (FOUR ARTICLES)

We must next consider man's various states and duties. We shall consider (1) man's duties and states in general; (2) the state of the perfect in particular.

Under the first head there are four points of inquiry:

(1) What constitutes a state among men?

(2) Whether among men there should be various states and duties?

(3) Of the diversity of duties;

(4) Of the diversity of states.

Whether the notion of a state denotes a condition of freedom or servitude?

Objection 1: It would seem that the notion of a state does not denote a condition of freedom or servitude. For "state" takes its name from "standing." Now a person is said to stand on account of his being upright; and Gregory says (Moral. vii, 17): "To fall by speaking harmful words is to forfeit entirely the state of righteousness." But a man acquires spiritual uprightness by submitting his will to God; wherefore a gloss on Ps. 32:1, "Praise becometh the upright," says: "The upright are those who direct their heart according to God's will." Therefore it would seem that obedience to the Divine commandments suffices alone for the notion of a state.

Objection 2: Further, the word "state" seems to denote immobility according to 1 Cor. 15:48, "Be ye steadfast [stabiles] and immovable"; wherefore Gregory says (Hom. xxi in Ezech.): "The stone is foursquare, and is stable on all sides, if no disturbance will make it fall." Now it is virtue that enables us "to act with immobility," according to Ethic. ii, 4. Therefore it would seem that a state is acquired by every virtuous action.

Objection 3: Further, the word "state" seems to indicate height of a kind; because to stand is to be raised upwards. Now one man is made higher than another by various duties; and in like manner men are raised upwards in various ways by various grades and orders. Therefore the mere difference of grades, orders, or duties suffices for a difference of states.

On the contrary, It is thus laid down in the Decretals (II, qu. vi, can. Si Quando): "Whenever anyone intervene in a cause where life or state is at stake he must do so, not by a proxy, but in his own person"; and "state" here has reference to freedom or servitude. Therefore it would seem that nothing differentiates a man's state, except that which refers to freedom or servitude.

I answer that, "State," properly speaking, denotes a kind of position, whereby a thing is disposed with a certain immobility in a manner according with its nature. For it is natural to man that his head should be directed upwards, his feet set firmly on the ground, and his other intermediate members disposed in becoming order; and this is not the case if he lie down, sit, or recline, but only when he stands upright: nor again is he said to stand, if he move, but only when he is still. Hence it is again that even in human acts, a matter is said to have stability [statum] in reference to its own disposition in the point of a certain immobility or restfulness. Consequently matters which easily change and are extrinsic to them do not constitute a state among men, for instance that a man be rich or poor, of high or low rank, and so forth. Wherefore in the civil law [*Dig. I, IX, De Senatoribus] (Lib. Cassius ff. De Senatoribus) it is said that if a man be removed from the senate, he is deprived of his dignity rather than of his state. But that alone seemingly pertains to a man's state, which regards an obligation binding his person, in so far, to wit, as a man is his own master or subject to another, not indeed from any slight or unstable cause, but from one that is firmly established; and this is something pertaining to the nature of freedom or servitude. Therefore state properly regards freedom or servitude whether in spiritual or in civil matters.

Reply to Objection 1: Uprightness as such does not pertain to the notion of state, except in so far as it is connatural to man with the addition of a certain restfulness. Hence other animals are said to stand without its being required that they should be upright; nor again are men said to stand, however upright their position be, unless they be still.

Reply to Objection 2: Immobility does not suffice for the notion of state; since even one who sits or lies down is still, and yet he is not said to stand.

Reply to Objection 3: Duty implies relation to act; while grades denote an order of superiority and inferiority. But state requires immobility in that which regards a condition of the person himself.

Whether there should be different duties or states in the Church?

Objection 1: It would seem that there should not be different duties or states in the Church. For distinction is opposed to unity. Now the faithful of Christ are called to unity according to Jn. 17:21,22: "That they . . . may be one in Us . . . as We also are one." Therefore there should not be a distinction of duties and states in the Church.

Objection 2: Further, nature does not employ many means where one suffices. But the working of grace is much more orderly than the working of nature. Therefore it were more fitting for things pertaining to the operations of grace to be administered by the same persons, so that there would not be a distinction of duties and states in the Church.

Objection 3: Further, the good of the Church seemingly consists chiefly in peace, according to Ps. 147:3, "Who hath placed peace in thy borders," and 2 Cor. 13:11, "Have peace, and the God of peace . . . shall be with you." Now distinction is a hindrance to peace, for peace would seem to result from likeness, according to Ecclus. 13:19, "Every beast loveth its like," while the Philosopher says (Polit. vii, 5) that "a little difference causes dissension in a state." Therefore it would seem that there ought not to be a distinction of states and duties in the Church.

On the contrary, It is written in praise of the Church (Ps. 44:10) that she is "surrounded with variety": and a gloss on these words says that "the Queen," namely the Church, "is bedecked with the teaching of the apostles, the confession of martyrs, the purity of virgins, the sorrowings of penitents."

I answer that, The difference of states and duties in the Church regards three things. In the first place it regards the perfection of the Church. For even as in the order of natural things, perfection, which in God is simple and uniform, is not to be found in the created universe except in a multiform and manifold manner, so too, the fulness of grace, which is centered in Christ as head, flows forth to His members in various ways, for the perfecting of the body of the Church. This is the meaning of the Apostle's words (Eph. 4:11,12): "He gave some apostles, and some prophets, and other some evangelists, and other some pastors and doctors for the perfecting of the saints." Secondly, it regards the need of those actions which are necessary in the Church. For a diversity of actions requires a diversity of men appointed to them, in order that all things may be accomplished without delay or confusion; and this is indicated by the Apostle (Rom. 12:4,5), "As in one body we have many members, but all the members have not the same office, so we being many are one body in Christ." Thirdly, this belongs to the dignity and beauty of the Church, which consist in a certain order; wherefore it is written (3 Kings 10:4,5) that "when the queen of Saba saw all the wisdom of Solomon . . . and the apartments of his servants, and the order of his ministers . . . she had no longer any spirit in her." Hence the Apostle says (2 Tim. 2:20) that "in a great house there are not only vessels of gold and silver, but also of wood and of earth."

Reply to Objection 1: The distinction of states and duties is not an obstacle to the unity of the Church, for this results from the unity of faith, charity, and mutual service, according to the saying of the Apostle (Eph. 4:16): "From whom the whole body being compacted," namely by faith, "and fitly joined together," namely by charity, "by what every joint supplieth," namely by one man serving another.

Reply to Objection 2: Just as nature does not employ many means where one suffices, so neither does it confine itself to one where many are required, according to the saying of the Apostle (1 Cor. 12:17), "If the whole body were the eye, where would be the hearing?" Hence there was need in the Church, which is Christ's body, for the members to be differentiated by various duties, states, and grades.

Reply to Objection 3: Just as in the natural body the various members are held together in unity by the power of the quickening spirit, and are dissociated from one another as soon as that spirit departs, so too in the Church's body the peace of the various members is preserved by the power of the Holy Spirit, Who quickens the body of the Church, as stated in Jn. 6:64. Hence the Apostle says (Eph. 4:3): "Careful to keep the unity of the Spirit in the bond of peace." Now a man departs from this unity of spirit when he seeks his own; just as in an earthly kingdom peace ceases when the citizens seek each man his own. Besides, the peace both of mind and of an earthly commonwealth is the better preserved by a distinction of duties and states, since thereby the greater number have a share in public actions. Wherefore the Apostle says (1 Cor. 12:24,25) that "God hath tempered [the body] together that there might be no schism in the body, but the members might be mutually careful one for another."

Whether duties differ according to their actions?

Objection 1: It would seem that duties do not differ according to their actions. For there are infinite varieties of human acts both in spirituals and in temporals. Now there can be no certain distinction among things that are infinite in number. Therefore human duties cannot be differentiated according to a difference of acts.

Objection 2: Further, the active and the contemplative life differ according to their acts, as stated above ([3747]Q[179], A[1]). But the distinction of duties seems to be other than the distinction of lives. Therefore duties do not differ according to their acts.

Objection 3: Further, even ecclesiastical orders, states, and grades seemingly differ according to their acts. If, then, duties differ according to their acts it would seem that duties, grades, and states differ in the same way. Yet this is not true, since they are divided into their respective parts in different ways. Therefore duties do not differ according to their acts.

On the contrary, Isidore says (Etym. vi, 19) that "officium [duty] takes its name from 'efficere' [to effect], as though it were instead of 'efficium,' by the change of one letter for the sake of the sound." But effecting pertains to action. Therefore duties differ according to their acts.

I answer that, As stated above [3748](A[2]), difference among the members of the Church is directed to three things: perfection, action, and beauty; and according to these three we may distinguish a threefold distinction among the faithful. One, with regard to perfection, and thus we have the difference of states, in reference to which some persons are more perfect than others. Another distinction regards action and this is the distinction of duties: for persons are said to have various duties when they are appointed to various actions. A third distinction regards the order of ecclesiastical beauty: and thus we distinguish various grades according as in the same state or duty one person is above another. Hence according to a variant text [*The Septuagint] it is written (Ps. 47:4): "In her grades shall God be known."

Reply to Objection 1: The material diversity of human acts is infinite. It is not thus that duties differ, but by their formal diversity which results from diverse species of acts, and in this way human acts are not infinite.

Reply to Objection 2: Life is predicated of a thing absolutely: wherefore diversity of acts which are becoming to man considered in himself. But efficiency, whence we have the word "office" (as stated above), denotes action tending to something else according to Metaph. ix, text. 16 [*Ed. Did. viii, 8]. Hence offices differ properly in respect of acts that are referred to other persons; thus a teacher is said to have an office, and so is a judge, and so forth. Wherefore Isidore says (Etym. vi, 19) that "to have an office is to be officious," i.e. harmful "to no one, but to be useful to all."

Reply to Objection 3: Differences of state, offices and grades are taken from different things, as stated above (A[1], ad 3). Yet these three things may concur in the same subject: thus when a person is appointed to a higher action, he attains thereby both office and grade, and sometimes, besides this, a state of perfection, on account of the sublimity of the act, as in the case of a bishop. The ecclesiastical orders are particularly distinct according to divine offices. For Isidore says (Etym. vi): "There are various kinds of offices; but the foremost is that which relates to sacred and Divine things."

Whether the difference of states applies to those who are beginning, progressing, or perfect?

Objection 1: It would seem that the difference of states does not apply to those who are beginning, progressing, or perfect. For "diverse genera have diverse species and differences" [*Aristotle, Categ. ii]. Now this difference of beginning, progress, and perfection is applied to the degrees of charity, as stated above ([3749]Q[24], A[9]), where we were treating of charity. Therefore it would seem that the differences of states should not be assigned in this manner.

Objection 2: Further, as stated above [3750](A[1]), state regards a condition of servitude or freedom, which apparently has no connection with the aforesaid difference of beginning, progress, and perfection. Therefore it is unfitting to divide state in this way.

Objection 3: Further, the distinction of beginning, progress, and perfection seems to refer to "more" and "less," and this seemingly implies the notion of grades. But the distinction of grades differs from that of states, as we have said above ([3751]AA[2],3). Therefore state is unfittingly divided according to beginning, progress, and perfection.

On the contrary, Gregory says (Moral. xxiv, 11): "There are three states of the converted, the beginning, the middle, and the perfection"; and (Hom. xv in Ezech.): "Other is the beginning of virtue, other its progress, and other still its perfection."

I answer that, As stated above [3752](A[1]) state regards freedom or servitude. Now in spiritual things there is a twofold servitude and a twofold freedom: for there is the servitude of sin and the servitude of justice; and there is likewise a twofold freedom, from sin, and from justice, as appears from the words of the Apostle (Rom. 6:20, 22), "When you were the servants of sin, you were free men to justice . . . but now being made free from sin," you are . . ."become servants to God."

Now the servitude of sin or justice consists in being inclined to evil by a habit of sin, or inclined to good by a habit of justice: and in like manner freedom from sin is not to be overcome by the inclination to sin, and freedom from justice is not to be held back from evil for the love of justice. Nevertheless, since man, by his natural reason, is inclined to justice, while sin is contrary to natural reason, it follows that freedom from sin is true freedom which is united to the servitude of justice, since they both incline man to that which is becoming to him. In like manner true servitude is the servitude of sin, which is connected with freedom from justice, because man is thereby hindered from attaining that which is proper to him. That a man become the servant of justice or sin results from his efforts, as the Apostle declares (Rom. 6:16): "To whom you yield yourselves servants to obey, his servants you are whom you obey, whether it be of sin unto death, or of obedience unto justice." Now in every human effort we can distinguish a beginning, a middle, and a term; and consequently the state of spiritual servitude and freedom is differentiated according to these things, namely, the beginning—to which pertains the state of beginners—the middle, to which pertains the state of the proficient—and the term, to which belongs the state of the perfect.

Reply to Objection 1: Freedom from sin results from charity which "is poured forth in our hearts by the Holy Ghost, Who is given to us" (Rom. 5:5). Hence it is written (2 Cor. 3:17): "Where the Spirit of the Lord is, there is liberty." Wherefore the same division applies to charity as to the state of those who enjoy spiritual freedom.

Reply to Objection 2: Men are said to be beginners, proficient, and perfect (so far as these terms indicate different states), not in relation to any occupation whatever, but in relation to such occupations as pertain to spiritual freedom or servitude, as stated above [3753](A[1]).

Reply to Objection 3: As already observed (A[3], ad 3), nothing hinders grade and state from concurring in the same subject. For even in earthly affairs those who are free, not only belong to a different state from those who are in service, but are also of a different grade.

OF THE STATE OF PERFECTION IN GENERAL (EIGHT ARTICLES)

We must now consider those things that pertain to the state of perfection whereto the other states are directed. For the consideration of offices in relation to other acts belongs to the legislator; and in relation to the sacred ministry it comes under the consideration of orders of which we shall treat in the Third Part [*XP, Q[34]].

Concerning the state of the perfect, a three-fold consideration presents itself: (1) The state of perfection in general; (2) Things relating to the perfection of bishops; (3) Things relating to the perfection of religious.

Under the first head there are eight points of inquiry:

(1) Whether perfection bears any relation to charity?

(2) Whether one can be perfect in this life?

(3) Whether the perfection of this life consists chiefly in observing the counsels or the commandments?

(4) Whether whoever is perfect is in the state of perfection?

(5) Whether especially prelates and religious are in the state of perfection?

(6) Whether all prelates are in the state of perfection?

(7) Which is the more perfect, the episcopal or the religious state?

(8) The comparison between religious and parish priests and archdeacons.

Whether the perfection of the Christian life consists chiefly in charity?

Objection 1: It would seem that the perfection of the Christian life does not consist chiefly in charity. For the Apostle says (1 Cor. 14:20): "In malice be children, but in sense be perfect." But charity regards not the senses but the affections. Therefore it would seem that the perfection of the Christian life does not chiefly consist in charity.

Objection 2: Further,'it is written (Eph. 6:13): "Take unto you the armor of God, that you may be able to resist in the evil day, and to stand in all things perfect"; and the text continues (Eph. 6:14, 16), speaking of the armor of God: "Stand therefore having your loins girt about with truth, and having on the breast-plate of justice . . . in all things taking the shield of faith." Therefore the perfection of the Christian life consists not only in charity, but also in other virtues.

Objection 3: Further, virtues like other habits, are specified by their acts. Now it is written (James 1:4) that "patience hath a perfect work." Therefore seemingly the state of perfection consists more specially in patience.

On the contrary, It is written (Col. 3:14): "Above all things have charity, which is the bond of perfection," because it binds, as it were, all the other virtues together in perfect unity.

I answer that, A thing is said to be perfect in so far as it attains its proper end, which is the ultimate perfection thereof. Now it is charity that unites us to God, Who is the last end of the human mind, since "he that abideth in charity abideth in God, and God in him" (1 Jn. 4:16). Therefore the perfection of the Christian life consists radically in charity.

Reply to Objection 1: The perfection of the human senses would seem to consist chiefly in their concurring together in the unity of truth, according to 1 Cor. 1:10, "That you be perfect in the same mind [sensu], and in the same judgment." Now this is effected by charity which operates consent in us men. Wherefore even the perfection of the senses consists radically in the perfection of charity.

Reply to Objection 2: A man may be said to be perfect in two ways. First, simply: and this perfection regards that which belongs to a thing's nature, for instance an animal may be said to be perfect when it lacks nothing in the disposition of its members and in such things as are necessary for an animal's life. Secondly, a thing is said to be perfect relatively: and this perfection regards something connected with the thing externally, such as whiteness or blackness or something of the kind. Now the Christian life consists chiefly in charity whereby the soul is united to God; wherefore it is written (1 Jn. 3:14): "He that loveth not abideth in death." Hence the perfection of the Christian life consists simply in charity, but in the other virtues relatively. And since that which is simply, is paramount and greatest in comparison with other things, it follows that the perfection of charity is paramount in relation to the perfection that regards the other virtues.

Reply to Objection 3: Patience is stated to have a perfect work in relation to charity, in so far as it is an effect of the abundance of charity that a man bears hardships patiently, according to Rom. 8:35, "Who . . . shall separate us from the love of Christ? Shall tribulation? Or distress?" etc.

Whether any one can be perfect in this life?

Objection 1: It would seem that none can be perfect in this life. For the Apostle says (1 Cor. 13:10): "When that which is perfect is come, that which is in part shall be done away." Now in this life that which is in part is not done away; for in this life faith and hope, which are in part, remain. Therefore none can be perfect in this life.

Objection 2: Further, "The perfect is that which lacks nothing" (Phys. iii, 6). Now there is no one in this life who lacks nothing; for it is written (James 3:2): "In many things we all offend"; and (Ps. 138:16): "Thy eyes did see my imperfect being." Therefore none is perfect in this life.

Objection 3: Further, the perfection of the Christian life, as stated [3754](A[1]), relates to charity, which comprises the love of God and of our neighbor. Now, neither as to the love of God can one have perfect charity in this life, since according to Gregory (Hom. xiv in Ezech.) "the furnace of love which begins to burn here, will burn more fiercely when we see Him Whom we love"; nor as to the love of our neighbor, since in this life we cannot love all our neighbors actually, even though we love them habitually; and habitual love is imperfect. Therefore it seems that no one can be perfect in this life.

On the contrary, The Divine law does not prescribe the impossible. Yet it prescribes perfection according to Mat. 5:48, "Be you . . . perfect, as also your heavenly Father is perfect." Therefore seemingly one can be perfect in this life.

I answer that, As stated above [3755](A[1]), the perfection of the Christian life consists in charity. Now perfection implies a certain universality because according to Phys. iii, 6, "the perfect is that which lacks nothing." Hence we may consider a threefold perfection. One is absolute, and answers to a totality not only on the part of the lover, but also on the part of the object loved, so that God be loved as much as He is lovable. Such perfection as this is not possible to any creature, but is competent to God alone, in Whom good is wholly and essentially.

Another perfection answers to an absolute totality on the part of the lover, so that the affective faculty always actually tends to God as much as it possibly can; and such perfection as this is not possible so long as we are on the way, but we shall have it in heaven.

The third perfection answers to a totality neither on the part of the object served, nor on the part of the lover as regards his always actually tending to God, but on the part of the lover as regards the removal of obstacles to the movement of love towards God, in which sense Augustine says (QQ. LXXXIII, qu. 36) that "carnal desire is the bane of charity; to have no carnal desires is the perfection of charity." Such perfection as this can be had in this life, and in two ways. First, by the removal from man's affections of all that is contrary to charity, such as mortal sin; and there can be no charity apart from this perfection, wherefore it is necessary for salvation. Secondly, by the removal from man's affections not only of whatever is contrary to charity, but also of whatever hinders the mind's affections from tending wholly to God. Charity is possible apart from this perfection, for instance in those who are beginners and in those who are proficient.

Reply to Objection 1: The Apostle is speaking there of heavenly perfection which is not possible to those who are on the way.

Reply to Objection 2: Those who are perfect in this life are said to "offend in many things" with regard to venial sins, which result from the weakness of the present life: and in this respect they have an "imperfect being" in comparison with the perfection of heaven.

Reply to Objection 3: As the conditions of the present life do not allow of a man always tending actually to God, so neither does it allow of his tending actually to each individual neighbor; but it suffices for him to tend to all in common and collectively, and to each individual habitually and according to the preparedness of his mind. Now in the love of our neighbor, as in the love of God we may observe a twofold perfection: one without which charity is impossible, and consisting in one's having in one's affections nothing that is contrary to the love of one's neighbor; and another without which it is possible to have charity. The latter perfection may be considered in three ways. First, as to the extent of love, through a man loving not only his friends and acquaintances but also strangers and even his enemies, for as Augustine says (Enchiridion lxxiii) this is a mark of the perfect children of God. Secondly, as to the intensity of love, which is shown by the things which man despises for his neighbor's sake, through his despising not only external goods for the sake of his neighbor, but also bodily hardships and even death, according to Jn. 15:13, "Greater love than this no man hath, that a man lay down his life for his friends." Thirdly, as to the effect of love, so that a man will surrender not only temporal but also spiritual goods and even himself, for his neighbor's sake, according to the words of the Apostle (2 Cor. 12:15), "But I most gladly will spend and be spent myself for your souls."

Whether, in this life, perfection consists in the observance of the commandments or of the counsels?

Objection 1: It would seem that, in this life, perfection consists in the observance not of the commandments but of the counsels. For our Lord said (Mat. 19:21): "If thou wilt be perfect, go sell all [Vulg.: 'what'] thou hast, and give to the poor . . . and come, follow Me." Now this is a counsel. Therefore perfection regards the counsels and not the precepts.

Objection 2: Further, all are bound to the observance of the commandments, since this is necessary for salvation. Therefore, if the perfection of the Christian life consists in observing the commandments, it follows that perfection is necessary for salvation, and that all are bound thereto; and this is evidently false.

Objection 3: Further, the perfection of the Christian life is gauged according to charity, as stated above [3756](A[1]). Now the perfection of charity, seemingly, does not consist in the observance of the commandments, since the perfection of charity is preceded both by its increase and by its beginning, as Augustine says (Super Canonic. Joan. Tract. ix). But the beginning of charity cannot precede the observance of the commandments, since according to Jn. 14:23, "If any one love Me, he will keep My word." Therefore the perfection of life regards not the commandments but the counsels.

On the contrary, It is written (Dt. 6:5): "Thou shalt love the Lord thy God with thy whole heart," and (Lev. 19:18): "Thou shalt love thy neighbor [Vulg.: 'friend'] as thyself"; and these are the commandments of which our Lord said (Mat. 22:40): "On these two commandments dependeth the whole law and the prophets." Now the perfection of charity, in respect of which the Christian life is said to be perfect, consists in our loving God with our whole heart, and our neighbor as ourselves. Therefore it would seem that perfection consists in the observance of the precepts.

I answer that, Perfection is said to consist in a thing in two ways: in one way, primarily and essentially; in another, secondarily and accidentally. Primarily and essentially the perfection of the Christian life consists in charity, principally as to the love of God, secondarily as to the love of our neighbor, both of which are the matter of the chief commandments of the Divine law, as stated above. Now the love of God and of our neighbor is not commanded according to a measure, so that what is in excess of the measure be a matter of counsel. This is evident from the very form of the commandment, pointing, as it does, to perfection—for instance in the words, "Thou shalt love the Lord thy God with thy whole heart": since "the whole" is the same as "the perfect," according to the Philosopher (Phys. iii, 6), and in the words, "Thou shalt love thy neighbor as thyself," since every one loves himself most. The reason of this is that "the end of the commandment is charity," according to the Apostle (1 Tim. 1:5); and the end is not subject to a measure, but only such things as are directed to the end, as the Philosopher observes (Polit. i, 3); thus a physician does not measure the amount of his healing, but how much medicine or diet he shall employ for the purpose of healing. Consequently it is evident that perfection consists essentially in the observance of the commandments; wherefore Augustine says (De Perf. Justit. viii): "Why then should not this perfection be prescribed to man, although no man has it in this life?"

Secondarily and instrumentally, however, perfection consists in the observance of the counsels, all of which, like the commandments, are directed to charity; yet not in the same way. For the commandments, other than the precepts of charity, are directed to the removal of things contrary to charity, with which, namely, charity is incompatible, whereas the counsels are directed to the removal of things that hinder the act of charity, and yet are not contrary to charity, such as marriage, the occupation of worldly business, and so forth. Hence Augustine says (Enchiridion cxxi): "Whatever things God commands, for instance, 'Thou shalt not commit adultery,' and whatever are not commanded, yet suggested by a special counsel, for instance, 'It is good for a man not to touch a woman,' are then done aright when they are referred to the love of God, and of our neighbor for God's sake, both in this world and in the world to come." Hence it is that in the Conferences of the Fathers (Coll. i, cap. vii) the abbot Moses says: "Fastings, watchings, meditating on the Scriptures, penury and loss of all one's wealth, these are not perfection but means to perfection, since not in them does the school of perfection find its end, but through them it achieves its end," and he had already said that "we endeavor to ascend by these steps to the perfection of charity."

Reply to Objection 1: In this saying of our Lord something is indicated as being the way to perfection by the words, "Go, sell all thou hast, and give to the poor"; and something else is added wherein perfection consists, when He said, "And follow Me." Hence Jerome in his commentary on Mat. 19:27, says that "since it is not enough merely to leave, Peter added that which is perfect: 'And have followed Thee'"; and Ambrose, commenting on Lk. 5:27, "Follow Me," says: "He commands him to follow, not with steps of the body, but with devotion of the soul, which is the effect of charity." Wherefore it is evident from the very way of speaking that the counsels are means of attaining to perfection, since it is thus expressed: "If thou wilt be perfect, go, sell," etc., as though He said: "By so doing thou shalt accomplish this end."

Reply to Objection 2: As Augustine says (De Perf. Justit. viii) "the perfection of charity is prescribed to man in this life, because one runs not right unless one knows whither to run. And how shall we know this if no commandment declares it to us?" And since that which is a matter of precept can be fulfilled variously, one does not break a commandment through not fulfilling it in the best way, but it is enough to fulfil it in any way whatever. Now the perfection of Divine love is a matter of precept for all without exception, so that even the perfection of heaven is not excepted from this precept, as Augustine says (De Perf. Justit. viii [*Cf. De Spir. et Lit. XXXVI]), and one escapes transgressing the precept, in whatever measure one attains to the perfection of Divine love. The lowest degree of Divine love is to love nothing more than God, or contrary to God, or equally with God, and whoever fails from this degree of perfection nowise fulfils the precept. There is another degree of the Divine love, which cannot be fulfilled so long as we are on the way, as stated above [3757](A[2]), and it is evident that to fail from this is not to be a transgressor of the precept; and in like manner one does not transgress the precept, if one does not attain to the intermediate degrees of perfection, provided one attain to the lowest.

Reply to Objection 3: Just as man has a certain perfection of his nature as soon as he is born, which perfection belongs to the very essence of his species, while there is another perfection which he acquires by growth, so again there is a perfection of charity which belongs to the very essence of charity, namely that man love God above all things, and love nothing contrary to God, while there is another perfection of charity even in this life, whereto a man attains by a kind of spiritual growth, for instance when a man refrains even from lawful things, in order more freely to give himself to the service of God.

Whether whoever is perfect is in the state of perfection?

Objection 1: It would seem that whoever is perfect is in the state of perfection. For, as stated above (A[3], ad 3), just as bodily perfection is reached by bodily growth, so spiritual perfection is acquired by spiritual growth. Now after bodily growth one is said to have reached the state of perfect age. Therefore seemingly also after spiritual growth, when one has already reached spiritual perfection, one is in the state of perfection.

Objection 2: Further, according to Phys. v, 2, movement "from one contrary to another" has the same aspect as "movement from less to more." Now when a man is changed from sin to grace, he is said to change his state, in so far as the state of sin differs from the state of grace. Therefore it would seem that in the same manner, when one progresses from a lesser to a greater grace, so as to reach the perfect degree, one is in the state of perfection.

Objection 3: Further, a man acquires a state by being freed from servitude. But one is freed from the servitude of sin by charity, because "charity covereth all sins" (Prov. 10:12). Now one is said to be perfect on account of charity, as stated above [3758](A[1]). Therefore, seemingly, whoever has perfection, for this very reason has the state of perfection.

On the contrary, Some are in the state of perfection, who are wholly lacking in charity and grace, for instance wicked bishops or religious. Therefore it would seem that on the other hand some have the perfection of life, who nevertheless have not the state of perfection.

I answer that, As stated above ([3759]Q[183], A[1]), state properly regards a condition of freedom or servitude. Now spiritual freedom or servitude may be considered in man in two ways: first, with respect to his internal actions; secondly, with respect to his external actions. And since according to 1 Kings 16:7, "man seeth those things that appear, but the Lord beholdeth the heart," it follows that with regard to man's internal disposition we consider his spiritual state in relation to the Divine judgment, while with regard to his external actions we consider man's spiritual state in relation to the Church. It is in this latter sense that we are now speaking of states, namely in so far as the Church derives a certain beauty from the variety of states [*Cf.[3760] Q[183], A[2]].

Now it must be observed, that so far as men are concerned, in order that any one attain to a state of freedom or servitude there is required first of all an obligation or a release. For the mere fact of serving someone does not make a man a slave, since even the free serve, according to Gal. 5:13, "By charity of the spirit serve one another": nor again does the mere fact of ceasing to serve make a man free, as in the case of a runaway slave; but properly speaking a man is a slave if he be bound to serve, and a man is free if he be released from service. Secondly, it is required that the aforesaid obligation be imposed with a certain solemnity; even as a certain solemnity is observed in other matters which among men obtain a settlement in perpetuity.

Accordingly, properly speaking, one is said to be in the state of perfection, not through having the act of perfect love, but through binding himself in perpetuity and with a certain solemnity to those things that pertain to perfection. Moreover it happens that some persons bind themselves to that which they do not keep, and some fulfil that to which they have not bound themselves, as in the case of the two sons (Mat. 21:28, 30), one of whom when his father said: "Work in my vineyard," answered: "I will not," and "afterwards . . . he went," while the other "answering said: I go . . . and he went not." Wherefore nothing hinders some from being perfect without being in the state of perfection, and some in the state of perfection without being perfect.

Reply to Objection 1: By bodily growth a man progresses in things pertaining to nature, wherefore he attains to the state of nature; especially since "what is according to nature is," in a way, "unchangeable" [*Ethic. v, 7], inasmuch as nature is determinate to one thing. In like manner by inward spiritual growth a man reaches the state of perfection in relation to the Divine judgment. But as regards the distinctions of ecclesiastical states, a man does not reach the state of perfection except by growth in respect of external actions.

Reply to Objection 2: This argument also regards the interior state. Yet when a man passes from sin to grace, he passes from servitude to freedom; and this does not result from a mere progress in grace, except when a man binds himself to things pertaining to grace.

Reply to Objection 3: Again this argument considers the interior state. Nevertheless, although charity causes the change of condition from spiritual servitude to spiritual freedom, an increase of charity has not the same effect.

Whether religious and prelates are in the state of perfection?

Objection 1: It would seem that prelates and religious are not in the state of perfection. For the state of perfection differs from the state of the beginners and the proficient. Now no class of men is specially assigned to the state of the proficient or of the beginners. Therefore it would seem that neither should any class of men be assigned to the state of perfection.

Objection 2: Further, the outward state should answer to the inward, else one is guilty of lying, "which consists not only in false words, but also in deceitful deeds," according to Ambrose in one of his sermons (xxx de Tempore). Now there are many prelates and religious who have not the inward perfection of charity. Therefore, if all religious and prelates are in the state of perfection, it would follow that all of them that are not perfect are in mortal sin, as deceivers and liars.

Objection 3: Further, as stated above [3761](A[1]), perfection is measured according to charity. Now the most perfect charity would seem to be in the martyrs, according to Jn. 15:13, "Greater love than this no man hath, that a man lay down his life for his friends": and a gloss on Heb. 12:4, "For you have not yet resisted unto blood," says: "In this life no love is more perfect than that to which the holy martyrs attained, who strove against sin even unto blood." Therefore it would seem that the state of perfection should be ascribed to the martyrs rather than to religious and bishops.

On the contrary, Dionysius (Eccl. Hier. v) ascribes perfection to bishops as being perfecters, and (Eccl. Hier. vi) to religious (whom he calls monks or {therapeutai}, i.e. servants of God) as being perfected.

I answer that, As stated above [3762](A[4]), there is required for the state of perfection a perpetual obligation to things pertaining to perfection, together with a certain solemnity. Now both these conditions are competent to religious and bishops. For religious bind themselves by vow to refrain from worldly affairs, which they might lawfully use, in order more freely to give themselves to God, wherein consists the perfection of the present life. Hence Dionysius says (Eccl. Hier. vi), speaking of religious: "Some call them {therapeutai}," i.e. servants, "on account of their rendering pure service and homage to God; others call them {monachoi}" [*i.e. solitaries; whence the English word 'monk'], "on account of the indivisible and single-minded life which by their being wrapped in," i.e. contemplating, "indivisible things, unites them in a Godlike union and a perfection beloved of God" [*Cf. Q[180], A[6]]. Moreover, the obligation in both cases is undertaken with a certain solemnity of profession and consecration; wherefore Dionysius adds (Eccl. Hier. vi): "Hence the holy legislation in bestowing perfect grace on them accords them a hallowing invocation."

In like manner bishops bind themselves to things pertaining to perfection when they take up the pastoral duty, to which it belongs that a shepherd "lay down his life for his sheep," according to Jn. 10:15. Wherefore the Apostle says (1 Tim. 6:12): "Thou . . . hast confessed a good confession before many witnesses," that is to say, "when he was ordained," as a gloss says on this passage. Again, a certain solemnity of consecration is employed together with the aforesaid profession, according to 2 Tim. 1:6: "Stir up the grace of God which is in thee by the imposition of my hands," which the gloss ascribes to the grace of the episcopate. And Dionysius says (Eccl. Hier. v) that "when the high priest," i.e. the bishop, "is ordained, he receives on his head the most holy imposition of the sacred oracles, whereby it is signified that he is a participator in the whole and entire hierarchical power, and that not only is he the enlightener in all things pertaining to his holy discourses and actions, but that he also confers this on others."

Reply to Objection 1: Beginning and increase are sought not for their own sake, but for the sake of perfection; hence it is only to the state of perfection that some are admitted under certain obligations and with solemnity.

Reply to Objection 2: Those who enter the state of perfection do not profess to be perfect, but to tend to perfection. Hence the Apostle says (Phil. 3:12): "Not as though I had already attained, or were already perfect; but I follow after, if I may by any means apprehend": and afterwards (Phil. 3:15): "Let us therefore as many as are perfect, be thus minded." Hence a man who takes up the state of perfection is not guilty of lying or deceit through not being perfect, but through withdrawing his mind from the intention of reaching perfection.

Reply to Objection 3: Martyrdom is the most perfect act of charity. But an act of perfection does not suffice to make the state of perfection, as stated above [3763](A[4]).

Whether all ecclesiastical prelates are in the state of perfection?

Objection 1: It would seem that all ecclesiastical prelates are in a state of perfection. For Jerome commenting on Titus 1:5, "Ordain . . . in every city," etc. says: "Formerly priest was the same as bishop," and afterwards he adds: "Just as priests know that by the custom of the Church they are subject to the one who is placed over them, so too, bishops should recognize that, by custom rather than by the very ordinance of our Lord, they are above the priests, and are together the rightful governors of the Church." Now bishops are in the state of perfection. Therefore those priests also are who have the cure of souls.

Objection 2: Further, just as bishops together with their consecration receive the cure of souls, so also do parish priests and archdeacons, of whom a gloss on Acts 6:3, "Brethren, look ye out . . . seven men of good reputation," says: "The apostles decided here to appoint throughout the Church seven deacons, who were to be of a higher degree, and as it were the supports of that which is nearest to the altar." Therefore it would seem that these also are in the state of perfection.

Objection 3: Further, just as bishops are bound to "lay down their life for their sheep," so too are parish priests and archdeacons. But this belongs to the perfection of charity, as stated above (A[2], ad 3). Therefore it would seem that parish priests and archdeacons also are in the state of perfection.

On the contrary, Dionysius says (Eccl. Hier. v): "The order of pontiffs is consummative and perfecting, that of the priests is illuminative and light-giving, that of the ministers is cleansing and discretive." Hence it is evident that perfection is ascribed to bishops only.

I answer that, In priests and deacons having cure of souls two things may be considered, namely their order and their cure. Their order is directed to some act in the Divine offices. Wherefore it has been stated above ([3764]Q[183], A[3], ad 3) that the distinction of orders is comprised under the distinction of offices. Hence by receiving a certain order a man receives the power of exercising certain sacred acts, but he is not bound on this account to things pertaining to perfection, except in so far as in the Western Church the receiving of a sacred order includes the taking of a vow of continence, which is one of the things pertaining to perfection, as we shall state further on ([3765]Q[186], A[4]). Therefore it is clear that from the fact that a man receives a sacred order a man is not placed simply in the state of perfection, although inward perfection is required in order that one exercise such acts worthily.

In like manner, neither are they placed in the state of perfection on the part of the cure which they take upon themselves. For they are not bound by this very fact under the obligation of a perpetual vow to retain the cure of souls; but they can surrender it—either by entering religion, even without their bishop's permission (cf. Decret. xix, qu. 2, can. Duae sunt)—or again an archdeacon may with his bishop's permission resign his arch-deaconry or parish, and accept a simple prebend without cure, which would be nowise lawful, if he were in the state of perfection; for "no man putting his hand to the plough and looking back is fit for the kingdom of God" (Lk. 9:62). On the other hand bishops, since they are in the state of perfection, cannot abandon the episcopal cure, save by the authority of the Sovereign Pontiff (to whom alone it belongs also to dispense from perpetual vows), and this for certain causes, as we shall state further on ([3766]Q[185], A[4]). Wherefore it is manifest that not all prelates are in the state of perfection, but only bishops.

Reply to Objection 1: We may speak of priest and bishop in two ways. First, with regard to the name: and thus formerly bishops and priests were not distinct. For bishops are so called "because they watch over others," as Augustine observes (De Civ. Dei xix, 19); while the priests according to the Greek are "elders." [*Referring to the Greek {episkopos} and {presbyteros} from which the English 'bishop' and 'priest' are derived.] Hence the Apostle employs the term "priests" in reference to both, when he says (1 Tim. 5:17): "Let the priests that rule well be esteemed worthy of double honor"; and again he uses the term "bishops" in the same way, wherefore addressing the priests of the Church of Ephesus he says (Acts 20:28): "Take heed to yourselves" and "to the whole flock, wherein the Holy Ghost hath placed you bishops, to rule the church of God."

But as regards the thing signified by these terms, there was always a difference between them, even at the time of the apostles. This is clear on the authority of Dionysius (Eccl. Hier. v), and of a gloss on Lk. 10:1, "After these things the Lord appointed," etc. which says: "Just as the apostles were made bishops, so the seventy-two disciples were made priests of the second order." Subsequently, however, in order to avoid schism, it became necessary to distinguish even the terms, by calling the higher ones bishops and the lower ones priests. But to assert that priests nowise differ from bishops is reckoned by Augustine among heretical doctrines (De Heres. liii), where he says that the Arians maintained that "no distinction existed between a priest and a bishop."

Reply to Objection 2: Bishops have the chief cure of the sheep of their diocese, while parish priests and archdeacons exercise an inferior ministry under the bishops. Hence a gloss on 1 Cor. 12:28, "to one, helps, to another, governments [*Vulg.: 'God hath set some in the church . . . helps, governments,' etc.]," says: "Helps, namely assistants to those who are in authority," as Titus was to the Apostle, or as archdeacons to the bishop; "governments, namely persons of lesser authority, such as priests who have to instruct the people": and Dionysius says (Eccl. Hier. v) that "just as we see the whole hierarchy culminating in Jesus, so each office culminates in its respective godlike hierarch or bishop." Also it is said (XVI, qu. i, can. Cunctis): "Priests and deacons must all take care not to do anything without their bishop's permission." Wherefore it is evident that they stand in relation to their bishop as wardens or mayors to the king; and for this reason, just as in earthly governments the king alone receives a solemn blessing, while others are appointed by simple commission, so too in the Church the episcopal cure is conferred with the solemnity of consecration, while the archdeacon or parish priest receives his cure by simple appointment; although they are consecrated by receiving orders before having a cure.

Reply to Objection 3: As parish priests and archdeacons have not the chief cure, but a certain ministry as committed to them by the bishop, so the pastoral office does not belong to them in chief, nor are they bound to lay down their life for the sheep, except in so far as they have a share in their cure. Hence we should say that they have an office pertaining to perfection rather than that they attain the state of perfection.

Whether the religious state is more perfect than that of prelates?

Objection 1: It would seem that the religious state is more perfect than that of prelates. For our Lord said (Mat. 19:21): "If thou wilt be perfect, go" and "sell" all [Vulg.: 'what'] "thou hast, and give to the poor"; and religious do this. But bishops are not bound to do so; for it is said (XII, qu. i, can. Episcopi de rebus): "Bishops, if they wish, may bequeath to their heirs their personal or acquired property, and whatever belongs to them personally." Therefore religious are in a more perfect state than bishops.

Objection 2: Further, perfection consists more especially in the love of God than in the love of our neighbor. Now the religious state is directly ordered to the love of God, wherefore it takes its name from "service and homage to God," as Dionysius says (Eccl. Hier. vi); [*Quoted above A[5]] whereas the bishop's state would seem to be ordered to the love of our neighbor, of whose cure he is the "warden," and from this he takes his name, as Augustine observes (De Civ. Dei. xix, 19). Therefore it would seem that the religious state is more perfect than that of bishops.

Objection 3: Further, the religious state is directed to the contemplative life, which is more excellent than the active life to which the episcopal state is directed. For Gregory says (Pastor. i, 7) that "Isaias wishing to be of profit to his neighbor by means of the active life desired the office of preaching, whereas Jeremias, who was fain to hold fast to the love of his Creator, exclaimed against being sent to preach." Therefore it would seem that the religious state is more perfect than the episcopal state.

On the contrary, It is not lawful for anyone to pass from a more excellent to a less excellent state; for this would be to look back [*Cf. Lk. 9:62]. Yet a man may pass from the religious to the episcopal state, for it is said (XVIII, qu. i, can. Statutum) that "the holy ordination makes a monk to be a bishop." Therefore the episcopal state is more perfect than the religious.

I answer that, As Augustine says (Gen. ad lit. xii, 16), "the agent is ever more excellent than the patient." Now in the genus of perfection according to Dionysius (Eccl. Hier. v, vi), bishops are in the position of "perfecters," whereas religious are in the position of being "perfected"; the former of which pertains to action, and the latter to passion. Whence it is evident that the state of perfection is more excellent in bishops than in religious.

Reply to Objection 1: Renunciation of one's possessions may be considered in two ways. First, as being actual: and thus it is not essential, but a means, to perfection, as stated above [3767](A[3]). Hence nothing hinders the state of perfection from being without renunciation of one's possessions, and the same applies to other outward practices. Secondly, it may be considered in relation to one's preparedness, in the sense of being prepared to renounce or give away all: and this belongs directly to perfection. Hence Augustine says (De QQ. Evang. ii, qu. 11): "Our Lord shows that the children of wisdom understand righteousness to consist neither in eating nor in abstaining, but in bearing want patiently." Wherefore the Apostle says (Phil. 4:12): "I know . . . both to abound and to suffer need." Now bishops especially are bound to despise all things for the honor of God and the spiritual welfare of their flock, when it is necessary for them to do so, either by giving to the poor of their flock, or by suffering "with joy the being stripped of" their "own goods" [*Heb. 10:34].

Reply to Objection 2: That bishops are busy about things pertaining to the love of their neighbor, arises out of the abundance of their love of God. Hence our Lord asked Peter first of all whether he loved Him, and afterwards committed the care of His flock to him. And Gregory says (Pastor. i, 5): "If the pastoral care is a proof of love, he who refuses to feed God's flock, though having the means to do so, is convicted of not loving the supreme Pastor." And it is a sign of greater love if a man devotes himself to others for his friend's sake, than if he be willing only to serve his friend.

Reply to Objection 3: As Gregory says (Pastor. ii, 1), "a prelate should be foremost in action, and more uplifted than others in contemplation," because it is incumbent on him to contemplate, not only for his own sake, but also for the purpose of instructing others. Hence Gregory applies (Hom. v in Ezech.) the words of Ps. 144:7, "They shall publish the memory . . . of Thy sweetness," to perfect men returning after their contemplation.

Whether parish priests and archdeacons are more perfect than religious?

Objection 1: It would seem that also parish priests and archdeacons are more perfect than religious. For Chrysostom says in his Dialogue (De Sacerdot. vi): "Take for example a monk, such as Elias, if I may exaggerate somewhat, he is not to be compared with one who, cast among the people and compelled to carry the sins of many, remains firm and strong." A little further on he says: "If I were given the choice, where would I prefer to please, in the priestly office, or in the monastic solitude, without hesitation I should choose the former." Again in the same book (ch. 5) he says: "If you compare the toils of this project, namely of the monastic life, with a well-employed priesthood, you will find them as far distant from one another as a common citizen is from a king." Therefore it would seem that priests who have the cure of souls are more perfect than religious.

Objection 2: Further, Augustine says (ad Valerium, Ep. xxi): "Let thy religious prudence observe that in this life, and especially at these times, there is nothing so difficult, so onerous, so perilous as the office of bishop, priest, or deacon; while in God's sight there is no greater blessing, if one engage in the fight as ordered by our Commander-in-chief." Therefore religious are not more perfect than priests or deacons.

Objection 3: Further, Augustine says (Ep. lx, ad Aurel.): "It would be most regrettable, were we to exalt monks to such a disastrous degree of pride, and deem the clergy deserving of such a grievous insult," as to assert that 'a bad monk is a good clerk,' "since sometimes even a good monk makes a bad clerk." And a little before this he says that "God's servants," i.e. monks, "must not be allowed to think that they may easily be chosen for something better," namely the clerical state, "if they should become worse thereby," namely by leaving the monastic state. Therefore it would seem that those who are in the clerical state are more perfect than religious.

Objection 4: Further, it is not lawful to pass from a more perfect to a less perfect state. Yet it is lawful to pass from the monastic state to a priestly office with a cure attached, as appears (XVI, qu. i, can. Si quis monachus) from a decree of Pope Gelasius, who says: "If there be a monk, who by the merit of his exemplary life is worthy of the priesthood, and the abbot under whose authority he fights for Christ his King, ask that he be made a priest, the bishop shall take him and ordain him in such place as he shall choose fitting." And Jerome says (Ad Rustic. Monach., Ep. cxxv): "In the monastery so live as to deserve to be a clerk." Therefore parish priests and archdeacons are more perfect than religious.

Objection 5: Further, bishops are in a more perfect state than religious, as shown above [3768](A[7]). But parish priests and archdeacons. through having cure of souls, are more like bishops than religious are. Therefore they are more perfect.

Objection 6: Further, virtue "is concerned with the difficult and the good" (Ethic. ii, 3). Now it is more difficult to lead a good life in the office of parish priest or archdeacon than in the religious state. Therefore parish priests and archdeacons have more perfect virtue than religious.

On the contrary, It is stated (XIX, qu. ii, cap. Duce): "If a man while governing the people in his church under the bishop and leading a secular life is inspired by the Holy Ghost to desire to work out his salvation in a monastery or under some canonical rule, since he is led by a private law, there is no reason why he should be constrained by a public law." Now a man is not led by the law of the Holy Ghost, which is here called a "private law," except to something more perfect. Therefore it would seem that religious are more perfect than archdeacons or parish priests.

I answer that, When we compare things in the point of super-eminence, we look not at that in which they agree, but at that wherein they differ. Now in parish priests and archdeacons three things may be considered, their state, their order, and their office. It belongs to their state that they are seculars, to their order that they are priests or deacons, to their office that they have the cure of souls committed to them.

Accordingly, if we compare these with one who is a religious by state, a deacon or priest by order, having the cure of souls by office, as many monks and canons regular have, this one will excel in the first point, and in the other points he will be equal. But if the latter differ from the former in state and office, but agree in order, such as religious priests and deacons not having the cure of souls, it is evident that the latter will be more excellent than the former in state, less excellent in office, and equal in order.

We must therefore consider which is the greater, preeminence of state or of office; and here, seemingly, we should take note of two things, goodness and difficulty. Accordingly, if we make the comparison with a view to goodness, the religious state surpasses the office of parish priest or archdeacon, because a religious pledges his whole life to the quest of perfection, whereas the parish priest or archdeacon does not pledge his whole life to the cure of souls, as a bishop does, nor is it competent to him, as it is to a bishop, to exercise the cure of souls in chief, but only in certain particulars regarding the cure of souls committed to his charge, as stated above (A[6], ad 2). Wherefore the comparison of their religious state with their office is like the comparisons of the universal with the particular, and of a holocaust with a sacrifice which is less than a holocaust according to Gregory (Hom. xx in Ezech.). Hence it is said (XIX, qu. i, can. Clerici qui monachorum.): "Clerics who wish to take the monastic vows through being desirous of a better life must be allowed by their bishops the free entrance into the monastery."

This comparison, however, must be considered as regarding the genus of the deed; for as regards the charity of the doer it happens sometimes that a deed which is of less account in its genus is of greater merit if it be done out of greater charity.

On the other hand, if we consider the difficulty of leading a good life in religion, and in the office of one having the cure of souls, in this way it is more difficult to lead a good life together with the exercise of the cure of souls, on account of outward dangers: although the religious life is more difficult as regards the genus of the deed, by reason of the strictness of religious observance. If, however, the religious is also without orders, as in the case of religious lay brethren, then it is evident that the pre-eminence of order excels in the point of dignity, since by holy orders a man is appointed to the most august ministry of serving Christ Himself in the sacrament of the altar. For this requires a greater inward holiness than that which is requisite for the religious state, since as Dionysius says (Eccl. Hier. vi) the monastic order must follow the priestly orders, and ascend to Divine things in imitation of them. Hence, other things being equal, a cleric who is in holy orders, sins more grievously if he do something contrary to holiness than a religious who is not in holy orders: although a religious who is not in orders is bound to regular observance to which persons in holy orders are not bound.

Reply to Objection 1: We might answer briefly these quotations from Chrysostom by saying that he speaks not of a priest of lesser order who has the cure of souls, but of a bishop, who is called a high-priest; and this agrees with the purpose of that book wherein he consoles himself and Basil in that they were chosen to be bishops. We may, however, pass this over and reply that he speaks in view of the difficulty. For he had already said: "When the pilot is surrounded by the stormy sea and is able to bring the ship safely out of the tempest, then he deserves to be acknowledged by all as a perfect pilot"; and afterwards he concludes, as quoted, with regard to the monk, "who is not to be compared with one who, cast among the people . . . remains firm"; and he gives the reason why, because "both in the calm end in the storm he piloted himself to safety." This proves nothing more than that the state of one who has the cure of souls is fraught with more danger than the monastic state; and to keep oneself innocent in face of a greater peril is proof of greater virtue. on the other hand, it also indicates greatness of virtue if a man avoid dangers by entering religion; hence he does not say that "he would prefer the priestly office to the monastic solitude," but that "he would rather please" in the former than in the latter, since this is a proof of greater virtue.

Reply to Objection 2: This passage quoted from Augustine also clearly refers to the question of difficulty which proves the greatness of virtue in those who lead a good life, as stated above (ad 1).

Reply to Objection 3: Augustine there compares monks with clerics as regards the pre-eminence of order, not as regards the distinction between religious and secular life.

Reply to Objection 4: Those who are taken from the religious state to receive the cure of souls, being already in sacred orders, attain to something they had not hitherto, namely the office of the cure, yet they do not put aside what they had already. For it is said in the Decretals (XVI, qu. i, can. De Monachis): "With regard to those monks who after long residence in a monastery attain to the order of clerics, we bid them not to lay aside their former purpose."

On the other hand, parish priests and archdeacons, when they enter religion, resign their cure, in order to enter the state of perfection. This very fact shows the excellence of the religious life. When religious who are not in orders are admitted to the clerical state and to the sacred orders, they are clearly promoted to something better, as stated: this is indicated by the very way in which Jerome expresses himself: "So live in the monastery as to deserve to be a clerk."

Reply to Objection 5: Parish priests and archdeacons are more like bishops than religious are, in a certain respect, namely as regards the cure of souls which they have subordinately; but as regards the obligation in perpetuity, religious are more like a bishop, as appears from what we have said above ([3769]AA[5],6).

Reply to Objection 6: The difficulty that arises from the arduousness of the deed adds to the perfection of virtue; but the difficulty that results from outward obstacles sometimes lessens the perfection of virtue—for instance, when a man loves not virtue so much as to wish to avoid the obstacles to virtue, according to the saying of the Apostle (1 Cor. 9:25), "Everyone that striveth for the mastery refraineth himself from all things": and sometimes it is a sign of perfect virtue—for instance, when a man forsakes not virtue, although he is hindered in the practice of virtue unawares or by some unavoidable cause. In the religious state there is greater difficulty arising from the arduousness of deeds; whereas for those who in any way at all live in the world, there is greater difficulty resulting from obstacles to virtue, which obstacles the religious has had the foresight to avoid.

OF THINGS PERTAINING TO THE EPISCOPAL STATE (EIGHT ARTICLES)

We must now consider things pertaining to the episcopal state. Under this head there are eight points of inquiry:

(1) Whether it is lawful to desire the office of a bishop?

(2) Whether it is lawful to refuse the office of bishop definitively?

(3) Whether the better man should be chosen for the episcopal office?

(4) Whether a bishop may pass over to the religious state?

(5) Whether he may lawfully abandon his subjects in a bodily manner?

(6) Whether he can have anything of his own?

(7) Whether he sins mortally by not distributing ecclesiastical goods to the poor?

(8) Whether religious who are appointed to the episcopal office are bound to religious observances?

Whether it is lawful to desire the office of a bishop?

Objection 1: It would seem that it is lawful to desire the office of a bishop. For the Apostle says (1 Tim. 3:1): "He that desires [Vulg.: 'If a man desire'] the office of a bishop, he desireth a good work." Now it is lawful and praiseworthy to desire a good work. Therefore it is even praiseworthy to desire the office of a bishop.

Objection 2: Further, the episcopal state is more perfect than the religious, as we have said above ([3770]Q[184], A[7]). But it is praiseworthy to desire to enter the religious state. Therefore it is also praiseworthy to desire promotion to the episcopal state.

Objection 3: Further, it is written (Prov. 11:26): "He that hideth up corn shall be cursed among the people; but a blessing upon the head of them that sell." Now a man who is apt, both in manner of life and by knowledge, for the episcopal office, would seem to hide up the spiritual corn, if he shun the episcopal state, whereas by accepting the episcopal office he enters the state of a dispenser of spiritual corn. Therefore it would seem praiseworthy to desire the office of a bishop, and blameworthy to refuse it.

Objection 4: Further, the deeds of the saints related in Holy Writ are set before us as an example, according to Rom. 15:4, "What things soever were written, were written for our learning." Now we read (Is. 6:8) that Isaias offered himself for the office of preacher, which belongs chiefly to bishops. Therefore it would seem praiseworthy to desire the office of a bishop.

On the contrary, Augustine says (De Civ. Dei xix, 19): "The higher place, without which the people cannot be ruled, though it be filled becomingly, is unbecomingly desired."

I answer that, Three things may be considered in the episcopal office. One is principal and final, namely the bishop's work, whereby the good of our neighbor is intended, according to Jn. 21:17, "Feed My sheep." Another thing is the height of degree, for a bishop is placed above others, according to Mat. 24:45, "A faithful and a wise servant, whom his lord hath appointed over his family." The third is something resulting from these, namely reverence, honor, and a sufficiency of temporalities, according to 1 Tim. 5:17, "Let the priests that rule well be esteemed worthy of double honor." Accordingly, to desire the episcopal office on account of these incidental goods is manifestly unlawful, and pertains to covetousness or ambition. Wherefore our Lord said against the Pharisees (Mat. 23:6,7): "They love the first places at feasts, and the first chairs in the synagogues, and salutations in the market-place, and to be called by men, Rabbi." As regards the second, namely the height of degree, it is presumptuous to desire the episcopal office. Hence our Lord reproved His disciples for seeking precedence, by saying to them (Mat. 20:25): "You know that the princes of the gentiles lord it over them." Here Chrysostom says (Hom. lxv in Matth.) that in these words "He points out that it is heathenish to seek precedence; and thus by comparing them to the gentiles He converted their impetuous soul."

On the other hand, to desire to do good to one's neighbor is in itself praiseworthy, and virtuous. Nevertheless, since considered as an episcopal act it has the height of degree attached to it, it would seem that, unless there be manifest and urgent reason for it, it would be presumptuous for any man to desire to be set over others in order to do them good. Thus Gregory says (Pastor. i, 8) that "it was praiseworthy to seek the office of a bishop when it was certain to bring one into graver dangers." Wherefore it was not easy to find a person to accept this burden, especially seeing that it is through the zeal of charity that one divinely instigated to do so, according to Gregory, who says (Pastor. i, 7) that "Isaias being desirous of profiting his neighbor, commendably desired the office of preacher."

Nevertheless, anyone may, without presumption, desire to do such like works if he should happen to be in that office, or to be worthy of doing them; so that the object of his desire is the good work and not the precedence in dignity. Hence Chrysostom* says: "It is indeed good to desire a good work, but to desire the primacy of honor is vanity. For primacy seeks one that shuns it, and abhors one that desires it." [*The quotation is from the Opus Imperfectum in Matth. (Hom. xxxv), falsely ascribed to St. John Chrysostom.]

Reply to Objection 1: As Gregory says (Pastor. i, 8), "when the Apostle said this he who was set over the people was the first to be dragged to the torments of martyrdom," so that there was nothing to be desired in the episcopal office, save the good work. Wherefore Augustine says (De Civ. Dei xix, 19) that when the Apostle said, "'Whoever desireth the office of bishop, desireth a good work,' he wished to explain what the episcopacy is: for it denotes work and not honor: since {skopos} signifies 'watching.' Wherefore if we like we may render {episkopein} by the Latin 'superintendere' [to watch over]: thus a man may know himself to be no bishop if he loves to precede rather than to profit others." For, as he observed shortly before, "in our actions we should seek, not honor nor power in this life, since all things beneath the sun are vanity, but the work itself which that honor or power enables us to do." Nevertheless, as Gregory says (Pastor. i, 8), "while praising the desire" (namely of the good work) "he forthwith turns this object of praise into one of fear, when he adds: It behooveth . . . a bishop to be blameless," as though to say: "I praise what you seek, but learn first what it is you seek."

Reply to Objection 2: There is no parity between the religious and the episcopal state, for two reasons. First, because perfection of life is a prerequisite of the episcopal state, as appears from our Lord asking Peter if he loved Him more than the others, before committing the pastoral office to him, whereas perfection is not a prerequisite of the religious state, since the latter is the way to perfection. Hence our Lord did not say (Mat. 19:21): "If thou art perfect, go, sell all [Vulg.: 'what'] thou hast," but "If thou wilt be perfect." The reason for this difference is because, according to Dionysius (Eccl. Hier. vi), perfection pertains actively to the bishop, as the "perfecter," but to the monk passively as one who is "perfected": and one needs to be perfect in order to bring others to perfection, but not in order to be brought to perfection. Now it is presumptuous to think oneself perfect, but it is not presumptuous to tend to perfection. Secondly, because he who enters the religious state subjects himself to others for the sake of a spiritual profit, and anyone may lawfully do this. Wherefore Augustine says (De Civ. Dei xix, 19): "No man is debarred from striving for the knowledge of truth, since this pertains to a praiseworthy ease." On the other hand, he who enters the episcopal state is raised up in order to watch over others, and no man should seek to be raised thus, according to Heb. 5:4, "Neither doth any man take the honor to himself, but he that is called by God": and Chrysostom says: "To desire supremacy in the Church is neither just nor useful. For what wise man seeks of his own accord to submit to such servitude and peril, as to have to render an account of the whole Church? None save him who fears not God's judgment, and makes a secular abuse of his ecclesiastical authority, by turning it to secular uses."

Reply to Objection 3: The dispensing of spiritual corn is not to be carried on in an arbitrary fashion, but chiefly according to the appointment and disposition of God, and in the second place according to the appointment of the higher prelates, in whose person it is said (1 Cor. 4:1): "Let a man so account of us as of the ministers of Christ, and the dispensers of the mysteries of God." Wherefore a man is not deemed to hide spiritual corn if he avoids governing or correcting others, and is not competent to do so, neither in virtue of his office nor of his superior's command; thus alone is he deemed to hide it, when he neglects to dispense it while under obligation to do so in virtue of his office, or obstinately refuses to accept the office when it is imposed on him. Hence Augustine says (De Civ. Dei xix, 19): "The love of truth seeks a holy leisure, the demands of charity undertake an honest labor. If no one imposes this burden upon us, we must devote ourselves to the research and contemplation of truth, but if it be imposed on us, we must bear it because charity demands it of us."

Reply to Objection 4: As Gregory says (Pastor. i, 7), "Isaias, who wishing to be sent, knew himself to be already cleansed by the live coal taken from the altar, shows us that no one should dare uncleansed to approach the sacred ministry. Since, then, it is very difficult for anyone to be able to know that he is cleansed, it is safer to decline the office of preacher."

Whether it is lawful for a man to refuse absolutely an appointment to the episcopate?

Objection 1: It would seem that it is lawful to refuse absolutely an appointment to the episcopate. For as Gregory says (Pastor. i, 7), "Isaias wishing to be of profit to his neighbor by means of the active life, desired the office of preaching, whereas Jeremias who was fain to hold fast to the love of his Creator by contemplation exclaimed against being sent to preach." Now no man sins by being unwilling to forgo better things in order to adhere to things that are not so good. Since then the love of God surpasses the love of our neighbor, and the contemplative life is preferable to the active, as shown above ([3771]Q[25], A[1];[3772] Q[26], A[2];[3773] Q[182], A[1]) it would seem that a man sins not if he refuse absolutely the episcopal office.

Objection 2: Further, as Gregory says (Pastor. i, 7), "it is very difficult for anyone to be able to know that he is cleansed: nor should anyone uncleansed approach the sacred ministry." Therefore if a man perceives that he is not cleansed, however urgently the episcopal office be enjoined him, he ought not to accept it.

Objection 3: Further, Jerome (Prologue, super Marc.) says that "it is related of the Blessed Mark* that after receiving the faith he cut off his thumb that he might be excluded from the priesthood." [*This prologue was falsely ascribed to St. Jerome, and the passage quoted refers, not to St. Mark the Evangelist, but to a hermit of that name. (Cf. Baronius, Anno Christi, 45, num. XLIV)] Likewise some take a vow never to accept a bishopric. Now to place an obstacle to a thing amounts to the same as refusing it altogether. Therefore it would seem that one may, without sin, refuse the episcopal office absolutely.

On the contrary, Augustine says (Ep. xlviii ad Eudox.): "If Mother Church requires your service, neither accept with greedy conceit, nor refuse with fawning indolence"; and afterwards he adds: "Nor prefer your ease to the needs of the Church: for if no good men were willing to assist her in her labor, you would seek in vain how we could be born of her."

I answer that, Two things have to be considered in the acceptance of the episcopal office: first, what a man may fittingly desire according to his own will; secondly, what it behooves a man to do according to the will of another. As regards his own will it becomes a man to look chiefly to his own spiritual welfare, whereas that he look to the spiritual welfare of others becomes a man according to the appointment of another having authority, as stated above (A[1], ad 3). Hence just as it is a mark of an inordinate will that a man of his own choice incline to be appointed to the government of others, so too it indicates an inordinate will if a man definitively refuse the aforesaid office of government in direct opposition to the appointment of his superior: and this for two reasons.

First, because this is contrary to the love of our neighbor, for whose good a man should offer himself according as place and time demand: hence Augustine says (De Civ. Dei xix, 19) that "the demands of charity undertake an honest labor." Secondly, because this is contrary to humility, whereby a man submits to his superior's commands: hence Gregory says (Pastor. i, 6): "In God's sight humility is genuine when it does not obstinately refuse to submit to what is usefully prescribed."

Reply to Objection 1: Although simply and absolutely speaking the contemplative life is more excellent than the active, and the love of God better than the love of our neighbor, yet, on the other hand, the good of the many should be preferred to the good of the individual. Wherefore Augustine says in the passage quoted above: "Nor prefer your own ease to the needs of the Church," and all the more since it belongs to the love of God that a man undertake the pastoral care of Christ's sheep. Hence Augustine, commenting on Jn. 21:17, "Feed My sheep," says (Tract. cxxiii in Joan.): "Be it the task of love to feed the Lord's flock, even as it was the mark of fear to deny the Shepherd."

Moreover prelates are not transferred to the active life, so as to forsake the contemplative; wherefore Augustine says (De Civ. Dei xix, 19) that "if the burden of the pastoral office be imposed, we must not abandon the delights of truth," which are derived from contemplation.

Reply to Objection 2: No one is bound to obey his superior by doing what is unlawful, as appears from what was said above concerning obedience ([3774]Q[104], A[5]). Accordingly it may happen that he who is appointed to the office of prelate perceive something in himself on account of which it is unlawful for him to accept a prelacy. But this obstacle may sometimes be removed by the very person who is appointed to the pastoral cure—for instance, if he have a purpose to sin, he may abandon it—and for this reason he is not excused from being bound to obey definitely the superior who has appointed him. Sometimes, however, he is unable himself to remove the impediment that makes the pastoral office unlawful to him, yet the prelate who appoints him can do so—for instance, if he be irregular or excommunicate. In such a case he ought to make known his defect to the prelate who has appointed him; and if the latter be willing to remove the impediment, he is bound humbly to obey. Hence when Moses had said (Ex. 4:10): "I beseech thee, Lord, I am not eloquent from yesterday, and the day before," the Lord answered (Ex. 4:12): "I will be in thy mouth, and I will teach thee what thou shalt speak." At other times the impediment cannot be removed, neither by the person appointing nor by the one appointed—for instance, if an archbishop be unable to dispense from an irregularity; wherefore a subject, if irregular, would not be bound to obey him by accepting the episcopate or even sacred orders.

Reply to Objection 3: It is not in itself necessary for salvation to accept the episcopal office, but it becomes necessary by reason of the superior's command. Now one may lawfully place an obstacle to things thus necessary for salvation, before the command is given; else it would not be lawful to marry a second time, lest one should thus incur an impediment to the episcopate or holy orders. But this would not be lawful in things necessary for salvation. Hence the Blessed Mark did not act against a precept by cutting off his finger, although it is credible that he did this by the instigation of the Holy Ghost, without which it would be unlawful for anyone to lay hands on himself. If a man take a vow not to accept the bishop's office, and by this intend to bind himself not even to accept it in obedience to his superior prelate, his vow is unlawful; but if he intend to bind himself, so far as it lies with him, not to seek the episcopal office, nor to accept it except under urgent necessity, his vow is lawful, because he vows to do what it becomes a man to do.

Whether he that is appointed to the episcopate ought to be better than others?

Objection 1: It would seem that one who is appointed to the episcopate ought to be better than others. For our Lord, when about to commit the pastoral office to Peter, asked him if he loved Him more than the others. Now a man is the better through loving God the more. Therefore it would seem that one ought not to be appointed to the episcopal office except he be better than others.

Objection 2: Further, Pope Symmachus says (can. Vilissimus I, qu. 1): "A man is of very little worth who though excelling in dignity, excels not in knowledge and holiness." Now he who excels in knowledge and holiness is better. Therefore a man ought not to be appointed to the episcopate unless he be better than others.

Objection 3: Further, in every genus the lesser are governed by the greater, as corporeal things are governed by things spiritual, and the lower bodies by the higher, as Augustine says (De Trin. iii, 3). Now a bishop is appointed to govern others. Therefore he should be better than others.

On the contrary, The Decretal [*Can. Cum dilectus, de Electione] says that "it suffices to choose a good man, nor is it necessary to choose the better man."

I answer that, In designating a man for the episcopal office, something has to be considered on the part of the person designate, and something on the part of the designator. For on the part of the designator, whether by election or by appointment, it is required that he choose such a one as will dispense the divine mysteries faithfully. These should be dispensed for the good of the Church, according to 1 Cor. 14:12, "Seek to abound unto the edifying of the Church"; and the divine mysteries are not committed to men for their own meed, which they should await in the life to come. Consequently he who has to choose or appoint one for a bishop is not bound to take one who is best simply, i.e. according to charity, but one who is best for governing the Church, one namely who is able to instruct, defend, and govern the Church peacefully. Hence Jerome, commenting on Titus 1:5, says against certain persons that "some seek to erect as pillars of the Church, not those whom they know to be more useful to the Church, but those whom they love more, or those by whose obsequiousness they have been cajoled or undone, or for whom some person in authority has spoken, and, not to say worse than this, have succeeded by means of gifts in being made clerics."

Now this pertains to the respect of persons, which in such matters is a grave sin. Wherefore a gloss of Augustine [*Ep. clxvii ad Hieron.] on James 2:1, "Brethren, have not . . . with respect of persons," says: "If this distinction of sitting and standing be referred to ecclesiastical honors, we must not deem it a slight sin to 'have the faith of the Lord of glory with respect of persons.' For who would suffer a rich man to be chosen for the Church's seat of honor, in despite of a poor man who is better instructed and holier?"

On the part of the person appointed, it is not required that he esteem himself better than others, for this would be proud and presumptuous; but it suffices that he perceive nothing in himself which would make it unlawful for him to take up the office of prelate. Hence although Peter was asked by our Lord if he loved Him more than the others, he did not, in his reply, set himself before the others, but answered simply that he loved Christ.

Reply to Objection 1: Our Lord knew that, by His own bestowal, Peter was in other respects fitted to govern the Church: wherefore He questioned him about his greater love, to show that when we find a man otherwise fitted for the government of the Church, we must look chiefly to his pre-eminence in the love of God.

Reply to Objection 2: This statement refers to the pursuits of the man who is placed in authority. For he should aim at showing himself to be more excellent than others in both knowledge and holiness. Wherefore Gregory says (Pastor. ii, 1) "the occupations of a prelate ought to excel those of the people, as much as the shepherd's life excels that of his flock." But he is not to be blamed and looked upon as worthless if he excelled not before being raised to the prelacy.

Reply to Objection 3: According to 1 Cor. 12:4 seqq., "there are diversities of graces . . . and . . . of ministries . . . and . . . of operations." Hence nothing hinders one from being more fitted for the office of governing, who does not excel in the grace of holiness. It is otherwise in the government of the natural order, where that which is higher in the natural order is for that very reason more fitted to dispose of those that are lower.

Whether a bishop may lawfully forsake the episcopal cure, in order to enter religion?

Objection 1: It seems that a bishop cannot lawfully forsake his episcopal cure in order to enter religion. For no one can lawfully pass from a more perfect to a less perfect state; since this is "to look back," which is condemned by the words of our Lord (Lk. 9:62), "No man putting his hand to the plough, and looking back, is fit for the kingdom of God." Now the episcopal state is more perfect than the religious, as shown above ([3775]Q[184], A[7]). Therefore just as it is unlawful to return to the world from the religious state, so is it unlawful to pass from the episcopal to the religious state.

Objection 2: Further, the order of grace is more congruous than the order of nature. Now according to nature a thing is not moved in contrary directions; thus if a stone be naturally moved downwards, it cannot naturally return upwards from below. But according to the order of grace it is lawful to pass from the religious to the episcopal state. Therefore it is not lawful to pass contrariwise from the episcopal to the religious state.

Objection 3: Further, in the works of grace nothing should be inoperative. Now when once a man is consecrated bishop he retains in perpetuity the spiritual power of giving orders and doing like things that pertain to the episcopal office: and this power would seemingly remain inoperative in one who gives up the episcopal cure. Therefore it would seem that a bishop may not forsake the episcopal cure and enter religion.

On the contrary, No man is compelled to do what is in itself unlawful. Now those who seek to resign their episcopal cure are compelled to resign (Extra, de Renunt. cap. Quidam). Therefore apparently it is not unlawful to give up the episcopal cure.

I answer that, The perfection of the episcopal state consists in this that for love of God a man binds himself to work for the salvation of his neighbor, wherefore he is bound to retain the pastoral cure so long as he is able to procure the spiritual welfare of the subjects entrusted to his care: a matter which he must not neglect—neither for the sake of the quiet of divine contemplation, since the Apostle, on account of the needs of his subjects, suffered patiently to be delayed even from the contemplation of the life to come, according to Phil. 1:22–25, "What I shall choose I know not, but I am straitened between two, having a desire to be dissolved, and to be with Christ, a thing by far better. But to abide still in the flesh is needful for you. And having this confidence, I know that I shall abide"; nor for the sake of avoiding any hardships or of acquiring any gain whatsoever, because as it is written (Jn. 10:11), "the good shepherd giveth his life for his sheep."

At times, however, it happens in several ways that a bishop is hindered from procuring the spiritual welfare of his subjects. Sometimes on account of his own defect, either of conscience (for instance if he be guilty of murder or simony), or of body (for example if he be old or infirm), or of irregularity arising, for instance, from bigamy. Sometimes he is hindered through some defect in his subjects, whom he is unable to profit. Hence Gregory says (Dial. ii, 3): "The wicked must be borne patiently, when there are some good who can be succored, but when there is no profit at all for the good, it is sometimes useless to labor for the wicked. Wherefore the perfect when they find that they labor in vain are often minded to go elsewhere in order to labor with fruit." Sometimes again this hindrance arises on the part of others, as when scandal results from a certain person being in authority: for the Apostle says (1 Cor. 8:13): "If meat scandalize my brother, I will never eat flesh": provided, however, the scandal is not caused by the wickedness of persons desirous of subverting the faith or the righteousness of the Church; because the pastoral cure is not to be laid aside on account of scandal of this kind, according to Mat. 15:14, "Let them alone," those namely who were scandalized at the truth of Christ's teaching, "they are blind, and leaders of the blind."

Nevertheless just as a man takes upon himself the charge of authority at the appointment of a higher superior, so too it behooves him to be subject to the latter's authority in laying aside the accepted charge for the reasons given above. Hence Innocent III says (Extra, de Renunt., cap. Nisi cum pridem): "Though thou hast wings wherewith thou art anxious to fly away into solitude, they are so tied by the bonds of authority, that thou art not free to fly without our permission." For the Pope alone can dispense from the perpetual vow, by which a man binds himself to the care of his subjects, when he took upon himself the episcopal office.

Reply to Objection 1: The perfection of religious and that of bishops are regarded from different standpoints. For it belongs to the perfection of a religious to occupy oneself in working out one's own salvation, whereas it belongs to the perfection of a bishop to occupy oneself in working for the salvation of others. Hence so long as a man can be useful to the salvation of his neighbor, he would be going back, if he wished to pass to the religious state, to busy himself only with his own salvation, since he has bound himself to work not only for his own but also for others' salvation. Wherefore Innocent III says in the Decretal quoted above that "it is more easily allowable for a monk to ascend to the episcopacy, than for a bishop to descend to the monastic life. If, however, he be unable to procure the salvation of others it is meet he should seek his own."

Reply to Objection 2: On account of no obstacle should a man forego the work of his own salvation, which pertains to the religious state. But there may be an obstacle to the procuring of another's salvation; wherefore a monk may be raised to the episcopal state wherein he is able also to work out his own salvation. And a bishop, if he be hindered from procuring the salvation of others, may enter the religious life, and may return to his bishopric should the obstacle cease, for instance by the correction of his subjects, cessation of the scandal, healing of his infirmity, removal of his ignorance by sufficient instruction. Again, if he owed his promotion to simony of which he was in ignorance, and resigning his episcopate entered the religious life, he can be reappointed to another bishopric [*Cap. Post translat., de Renunt.]. On the other hand, if a man be deposed from the episcopal office for some sin, and confined in a monastery that he may do penance, he cannot be reappointed to a bishopric. Hence it is stated (VII, qu. i, can. Hoc nequaquam): "The holy synod orders that any man who has been degraded from the episcopal dignity to the monastic life and a place of repentance, should by no means rise again to the episcopate."

Reply to Objection 3: Even in natural things power remains inactive on account of a supervening obstacle, for instance the act of sight ceases through an affliction of the eye. So neither is it unreasonable if, through the occurrence of some obstacle from without, the episcopal power remain without the exercise of its act.

Whether it is lawful for a bishop on account of bodily persecution to abandon the flock committed to his care?

Objection 1: It would seem that it is unlawful for a bishop, on account of some temporal persecution, to withdraw his bodily presence from the flock committed to his care. For our Lord said (Jn. 10:12) that he is a hireling and no true shepherd, who "seeth the wolf coming, and leaveth the sheep and flieth": and Gregory says (Hom. xiv in Ev.) that "the wolf comes upon the sheep when any man by his injustice and robbery oppresses the faithful and the humble." Therefore if, on account of the persecution of a tyrant, a bishop withdraws his bodily presence from the flock entrusted to his care, it would seem that he is a hireling and not a shepherd.

Objection 2: Further, it is written (Prov. 6:1): "My son, if thou be surety for thy friend, thou hast engaged fast thy hand to a stranger," and afterwards (Prov. 6:3): "Run about, make haste, stir up thy friend." Gregory expounds these words and says (Pastor. iii, 4): "To be surety for a friend, is to vouch for his good conduct by engaging oneself to a stranger. And whoever is put forward as an example to the lives of others, is warned not only to watch but even to rouse his friend." Now he cannot do this if he withdraw his bodily presence from his flock. Therefore it would seem that a bishop should not on account of persecution withdraw his bodily presence from his flock.

Objection 3: Further, it belongs to the perfection of the bishop's state that he devote himself to the care of his neighbor. Now it is unlawful for one who has professed the state of perfection to forsake altogether the things that pertain to perfection. Therefore it would seem unlawful for a bishop to withdraw his bodily presence from the execution of his office, except perhaps for the purpose of devoting himself to works of perfection in a monastery.

On the contrary, our Lord commanded the apostles, whose successors bishops are (Mat. 10:23): "When they shall persecute you in this city, flee into another."

I answer that, In any obligation the chief thing to be considered is the end of the obligation. Now bishops bind themselves to fulfil the pastoral office for the sake of the salvation of their subjects. Consequently when the salvation of his subjects demands the personal presence of the pastor, the pastor should not withdraw his personal presence from his flock, neither for the sake of some temporal advantage, nor even on account of some impending danger to his person, since the good shepherd is bound to lay down his life for his sheep.

On the other hand, if the salvation of his subjects can be sufficiently provided for by another person in the absence of the pastor, it is lawful for the pastor to withdraw his bodily presence from his flock, either for the sake of some advantage to the Church, or on account of some danger to his person. Hence Augustine says (Ep. ccxxviii ad Honorat.): "Christ's servants may flee from one city to another, when one of them is specially sought out by persecutors: in order that the Church be not abandoned by others who are not so sought for. When, however, the same danger threatens all, those who stand in need of others must not be abandoned by those whom they need." For "if it is dangerous for the helmsman to leave the ship when the sea is calm, how much more so when it is stormy," as Pope Nicholas I says (cf. VII, qu. i, can. Sciscitaris).

Reply to Objection 1: To flee as a hireling is to prefer temporal advantage or one's bodily welfare to the spiritual welfare of one's neighbor. Hence Gregory says (Hom. xiv in Ev.): "A man cannot endanger himself for the sake of his sheep, if he uses his authority over them not through love of them but for the sake of earthly gain: wherefore he fears to stand in the way of danger lest he lose what he loves." But he who, in order to avoid danger, leaves the flock without endangering the flock, does not flee as a hireling.

Reply to Objection 2: If he who is surety for another be unable to fulfil his engagement, it suffices that he fulfil it through another. Hence if a superior is hindered from attending personally to the care of his subjects, he fulfils his obligation if he do so through another.

Reply to Objection 3: When a man is appointed to a bishopric, he embraces the state of perfection as regards one kind of perfection; and if he be hindered from the practice thereof, he is not bound to another kind of perfection, so as to be obliged to enter the religious state. Yet he is under the obligation of retaining the intention of devoting himself to his neighbor's salvation, should an opportunity offer, and necessity require it of him.

Whether it is lawful for a bishop to have property of his own?

Objection 1: It would seem that it is not lawful for a bishop to have property of his own. For our Lord said (Mat. 19:21): "If thou wilt be perfect, go sell all [Vulg.: 'what] thou hast, and give to the poor . . . and come, follow Me"; whence it would seem to follow that voluntary poverty is requisite for perfection. Now bishops are in the state of perfection. Therefore it would seem unlawful for them to possess anything as their own.

Objection 2: Further, bishops take the place of the apostles in the Church, according to a gloss on Lk. 10:1. Now our Lord commanded the apostles to possess nothing of their own, according to Mat. 10:9, "Do not possess gold, nor silver, nor money in your purses"; wherefore Peter said for himself and the other apostles (Mat. 19:27): "Behold we have left all things and have followed Thee." Therefore it would seem that bishops are bound to keep this command, and to possess nothing of their own.

Objection 3: Further, Jerome says (Ep. lii ad Nepotian.): "The Greek {kleros} denotes the Latin 'sors.' Hence clerics are so called either because they are of the Lord's estate, or because the Lord Himself is the estate, i.e. portion of clerics. Now he that possesses the Lord, can have nothing besides God; and if he have gold and silver, possessions, and chattels of all kinds, with such a portion the Lord does not vouchsafe to be his portion also." Therefore it would seem that not only bishops but even clerics should have nothing of their own.

On the contrary, It is stated (XII, qu. i, can. Episcopi de rebus): "Bishops, if they wish, may bequeath to their heirs their personal or acquired property, and whatever belongs to them personally."

I answer that, No one is bound to works of supererogation, unless he binds himself specially thereto by vow. Hence Augustine says (Ep. cxxvii ad Paulin. et Arment.): "Since you have taken the vow, you have already bound yourself, you can no longer do otherwise. Before you were bound by the vow, you were free to submit." Now it is evident that to live without possessing anything is a work of supererogation, for it is a matter not of precept but of counsel. Wherefore our Lord after saying to the young man: "If thou wilt enter into life, keep the commandments," said afterwards by way of addition: "If thou wilt be perfect go sell" all "that thou hast, and give to the poor" (Mat. 19:17, 21). Bishops, however, do not bind themselves at their ordination to live without possessions of their own; nor indeed does the pastoral office, to which they bind themselves, make it necessary for them to live without anything of their own. Therefore bishops are not bound to live without possessions of their own.

Reply to Objection 1: As stated above ([3776]Q[184], A[3], ad 1) the perfection of the Christian life does not essentially consist in voluntary poverty, but voluntary poverty conduces instrumentally to the perfection of life. Hence it does not follow that where there is greater poverty there is greater perfection; indeed the highest perfection is compatible with great wealth, since Abraham, to whom it was said (Gn. 17:1): "Walk before Me and be perfect," is stated to have been rich (Gn. 13:2).

Reply to Objection 2: This saying of our Lord can be understood in three ways. First, mystically, that we should possess neither gold nor silver means that the preacher should not rely chiefly on temporal wisdom and eloquence; thus Jerome expounds the passage.

Secondly, according to Augustine's explanation (De Consens. Ev. ii, 30), we are to understand that our Lord said this not in command but in permission. For he permitted them to go preaching without gold or silver or other means, since they were to receive the means of livelihood from those to whom they preached; wherefore He added: "For the workman is worthy of his meat." And yet if anyone were to use his own means in preaching the Gospel, this would be a work of supererogation, as Paul says in reference to himself (1 Cor. 9:12, 15).

Thirdly, according to the exposition of Chrysostom [*Hom. ii in Rom. xvi, 3], we are to understand that our Lord laid these commands on His disciples in reference to the mission on which they were sent to preach to the Jews, so that they might be encouraged to trust in His power, seeing that He provided for their wants without their having means of their own. But it does not follow from this that they, or their successors, were obliged to preach the Gospel without having means of their own: since we read of Paul (2 Cor. 11:8) that he "received wages" of other churches for preaching to the Corinthians, wherefore it is clear that he possessed something sent to him by others. And it seems foolish to say that so many holy bishops as Athanasius, Ambrose, and Augustine would have disobeyed these commandments if they believed themselves bound to observe them.

Reply to Objection 3: Every part is less than the whole. Accordingly a man has other portions together with God, if he becomes less intent on things pertaining to God by occupying himself with things of the world. Now neither bishops nor clerics ought thus to possess means of their own, that while busy with their own they neglect those that concern the worship of God.

Whether bishops sin mortally if they distribute not to the poor the ecclesiastical goods which accrue to them?

Objection 1: It would seem that bishops sin mortally if they distribute not to the poor the ecclesiastical goods which they acquire. For Ambrose [*Basil, Serm. lxiv, de Temp., among the supposititious works of St. Jerome] expounding Lk. 12:16, "The land of a certain . . . man brought forth plenty of fruits," says: "Let no man claim as his own that which he has taken and obtained by violence from the common property in excess of his requirements"; and afterwards he adds: "It is not less criminal to take from him who has, than, when you are able and have plenty to refuse him who has not." Now it is a mortal sin to take another's property by violence. Therefore bishops sin mortally if they give not to the poor that which they have in excess.

Objection 2: Further, a gloss of Jerome on Is. 3:14, "The spoil of the poor is in your house," says that "ecclesiastical goods belong to the poor." Now whoever keeps for himself or gives to others that which belongs to another, sins mortally and is bound to restitution. Therefore if bishops keep for themselves, or give to their relations or friends, their surplus of ecclesiastical goods, it would seem that they are bound to restitution.

Objection 3: Further, much more may one take what is necessary for oneself from the goods of the Church, than accumulate a surplus therefrom. Yet Jerome says in a letter to Pope Damasus [*Cf. Can. Clericos, cause. i, qu. 2; Can. Quoniam; cause. xvi, qu. 1; Regul. Monach. iv, among the supposititious works of St. Jerome]: "It is right that those clerics who receive no goods from their parents and relations should be supported from the funds of the Church. But those who have sufficient income from their parents and their own possessions, if they take what belongs to the poor, they commit and incur the guilt of sacrilege." Wherefore the Apostle says (1 Tim. 5:16): "If any of the faithful have widows, let him minister to them, and let not the Church be charged, that there may be sufficient for them that are widows indeed." Much more therefore do bishops sin mortally if they give not to the poor the surplus of their ecclesiastical goods.

On the contrary, Many bishops do not give their surplus to the poor, but would seem commendably to lay it out so as to increase the revenue of the Church.

I answer that, The same is not to be said of their own goods which bishops may possess, and of ecclesiastical goods. For they have real dominion over their own goods; wherefore from the very nature of the case they are not bound to give these things to others, and may either keep them for themselves or bestow them on others at will. Nevertheless they may sin in this disposal by inordinate affection, which leads them either to accumulate more than they should, or not to assist others, in accordance with the demands of charity; yet they are not bound to restitution, because such things are entrusted to their ownership.

On the other hand, they hold ecclesiastical goods as dispensers or trustees. For Augustine says (Ep. clxxxv ad Bonif.): "If we possess privately what is enough for us, other things belong not to us but to the poor, and we have the dispensing of them; but we can claim ownership of them only by wicked theft." Now dispensing requires good faith, according to 1 Cor. 4:2, "Here now it is required among the dispensers that a man be found faithful." Moreover ecclesiastical goods are to be applied not only to the good of the poor, but also to the divine worship and the needs of its ministers. Hence it is said (XII, qu. ii, can. de reditibus): "Of the Church's revenues or the offerings of the faithful only one part is to be assigned to the bishop, two parts are to be used by the priest, under pain of suspension, for the ecclesiastical fabric, and for the benefit of the poor; the remaining part is to be divided among the clergy according to their respective merits." Accordingly if the goods which are assigned to the use of the bishop are distinct from those which are appointed for the use of the poor, or the ministers, or for the ecclesiastical worship, and if the bishop keeps back for himself part of that which should be given to the poor, or to the ministers for their use, or expended on the divine worship, without doubt he is an unfaithful dispenser, sins mortally, and is bound to restitution.

But as regards those goods which are deputed to his private use, the same apparently applies as to his own property, namely that he sins through immoderate attachment thereto or use thereof, if he exceeds moderation in what he keeps for himself, and fails to assist others according to the demands of charity.

On the other hand, if no distinction is made in the aforesaid goods, their distribution is entrusted to his good faith; and if he fail or exceed in a slight degree, this may happen without prejudice to his good faith, because in such matters a man cannot possibly decide precisely what ought to be done. On the other hand, if the excess be very great he cannot be ignorant of the fact; consequently he would seem to be lacking in good faith, and is guilty of mortal sin. For it is written (Mat. 24:48–51) that "if that evil servant shall say in his heart: My lord is long a-coming," which shows contempt of God's judgment, "and shall begin to strike his fellow-servants," which is a sign of pride, "and shall eat and drink with drunkards," which proceeds from lust, "the lord of that servant shall come in a day that he hopeth not . . . and shall separate him," namely from the fellowship of good men, "and appoint his portion with hypocrites," namely in hell.

Reply to Objection 1: This saying of Ambrose refers to the administration not only of ecclesiastical things but also of any goods whatever from which a man is bound, as a duty of charity, to provide for those who are in need. But it is not possible to state definitely when this need is such as to impose an obligation under pain of mortal sin, as is the case in other points of detail that have to be considered in human acts: for the decision in such matters is left to human prudence.

Reply to Objection 2: As stated above the goods of the Church have to be employed not only for the use of the poor, but also for other purposes. Hence if a bishop or cleric wish to deprive himself of that which is assigned to his own use, and give it to his relations or others, he sins not so long as he observes moderation, so, to wit, that they cease to be in want without becoming the richer thereby. Hence Ambrose says (De Offic. i, 30): "It is a commendable liberality if you overlook not your kindred when you know them to be in want; yet not so as to wish to make them rich with what you can give to the poor."

Reply to Objection 3: The goods of churches should not all be given to the poor, except in a case of necessity: for then, as Ambrose says (De Offic. ii, 28), even the vessels consecrated to the divine worship are to be sold for the ransom of prisoners, and other needs of the poor. In such a case of necessity a cleric would sin if he chose to maintain himself on the goods of the Church, always supposing him to have a patrimony of his own on which to support himself.

Reply to Objection 4: The goods of the churches should be employed for the good of the poor. Consequently a man is to be commended if, there being no present necessity for helping the poor, he spends the surplus from the Church revenue, in buying property, or lays it by for some future use connected with the Church or the needs of the poor. But if there be a pressing need for helping the poor, to lay by for the future is a superfluous and inordinate saving, and is forbidden by our Lord Who said (Mat. 6:34): "Be . . . not solicitous for the morrow."

Whether religious who are raised to the episcopate are bound to religious observances?

Objection 1: It would seem that religious who are raised to the episcopate are not bound to religious observances. For it is said (XVIII, qu. i, can. Statutum) that a "canonical election loosens a monk from the yoke imposed by the rule of the monastic profession, and the holy ordination makes of a monk a bishop." Now the regular observances pertain to the yoke of the rule. Therefore religious who are appointed bishops are not bound to religious observances.

Objection 2: Further, he who ascends from a lower to a higher degree is seemingly not bound to those things which pertain to the lower degree: thus it was stated above ([3777]Q[88], A[12], ad 1) that a religious is not bound to keep the vows he made in the world. But a religious who is appointed to the episcopate ascends to something greater, as stated above (Q[84], A[7]). Therefore it would seem that a bishop is not bound to those things whereto he was bound in the state of religion.

Objection 3: Further, religious would seem to be bound above all to obedience, and to live without property of their own. But religious who are appointed bishops, are not bound to obey the superiors of their order, since they are above them; nor apparently are they bound to poverty, since according to the decree quoted above (OBJ[1]) "when the holy ordination has made of a monk a bishop he enjoys the right, as the lawful heir, of claiming his paternal inheritance." Moreover they are sometimes allowed to make a will. Much less therefore are they bound to other regular observances.

On the contrary, It is said in the Decretals (XVI, qu. i, can. De Monachis): "With regard to those who after long residence in a monastery attain to the order of clerics, we bid them not to lay aside their former purpose."

I answer that, As stated above (A[1], ad 2) the religious state pertains to perfection, as a way of tending to perfection, while the episcopal state pertains to perfection, as a professorship of perfection. Hence the religious state is compared to the episcopal state, as the school to the professorial chair, and as disposition to perfection. Now the disposition is not voided at the advent of perfection, except as regards what perchance is incompatible with perfection, whereas as to that wherein it is in accord with perfection, it is confirmed the more. Thus when the scholar has become a professor it no longer becomes him to be a listener, but it becomes him to read and meditate even more than before. Accordingly we must assert that if there be among religious observances any that instead of being an obstacle to the episcopal office, are a safeguard of perfection, such as continence, poverty, and so forth, a religious, even after he has been made a bishop, remains bound to observe these, and consequently to wear the habit of his order, which is a sign of this obligation.

On the other hand, a man is not bound to keep such religious observances as may be incompatible with the episcopal office, for instance solitude, silence, and certain severe abstinences or watchings and such as would render him bodily unable to exercise the episcopal office. For the rest he may dispense himself from them, according to the needs of his person or office, and the manner of life of those among whom he dwells, in the same way as religious superiors dispense themselves in such matters.

Reply to Objection 1: He who from being a monk becomes a bishop is loosened from the yoke of the monastic profession, not in everything, but in those that are incompatible with the episcopal office, as stated above.

Reply to Objection 2: The vows of those who are living in the world are compared to the vows of religion as the particular to the universal, as stated above ([3778]Q[88], A[12], ad 1). But the vows of religion are compared to the episcopal dignity as disposition to perfection. Now the particular is superfluous when one has the universal, whereas the disposition is still necessary when perfection has been attained.

Reply to Objection 3: It is accidental that religious who are bishops are not bound to obey the superiors of their order, because, to wit, they have ceased to be their subjects; even as those same religious superiors. Nevertheless the obligation of the vow remains virtually, so that if any person be lawfully set above them, they would be bound to obey them, inasmuch as they are bound to obey both the statutes of their rule in the way mentioned above, and their superiors if they have any.

As to property they can nowise have it. For they claim their paternal inheritance not as their own, but as due to the Church. Hence it is added (XVIII, qu. i, can. Statutum) that after he has been ordained bishop at the altar to which he is consecrated and appointed according to the holy canons, he must restore whatever he may acquire.

Nor can he make any testament at all, because he is entrusted with the sole administration of things ecclesiastical, and this ends with his death, after which a testament comes into force according to the Apostle (Heb. 9:17). If, however, by the Pope's permission he make a will, he is not to be understood to bequeath property of his own, but we are to understand that by apostolic authority the power of his administration has been prolonged so as to remain in force after his death.

OF THOSE THINGS IN WHICH THE RELIGIOUS STATE PROPERLY CONSISTS (TEN ARTICLES)

We must now consider things pertaining to the religious state: which consideration will be fourfold. In the first place we shall consider those things in which the religious state consists chiefly; secondly, those things which are lawfully befitting to religious; thirdly, the different kinds of religious orders; fourthly, the entrance into the religious state.

Under the first head there are ten points of inquiry:

(1) Whether the religious state is perfect?

(2) Whether religious are bound to all the counsels?

(3) Whether voluntary poverty is required for the religious state?

(4) Whether continency is necessary?

(5) Whether obedience is necessary?

(6) Whether it is necessary that these should be the matter of a vow?

(7) Of the sufficiency of these vows;

(8) Of their comparison one with another;

(9) Whether a religious sins mortally whenever he transgresses a statute of his rule?

(10) Whether, other things being equal, a religious sins more grievously by the same kind of sin than a secular person?

Whether religion implies a state of perfection?

Objection 1: It would seem that religion does not imply a state of perfection. For that which is necessary for salvation does not seemingly pertain to perfection. But religion is necessary for salvation, whether because "thereby we are bound [religamur] to the one almighty God," as Augustine says (De Vera Relig. 55), or because it takes its name from "our returning [religimus] to God Whom we had lost by neglecting Him" [*Cf.[3779] Q[81], A[1]], according to Augustine (De Civ. Dei x, 3). Therefore it would seem that religion does not denote the state of perfection.

Objection 2: Further, religion according to Tully (De Invent. Rhet. ii, 53) is that "which offers worship and ceremony to the Divine nature." Now the offering of worship and ceremony to God would seem to pertain to the ministry of holy orders rather than to the diversity of states, as stated above ([3780]Q[40], A[2];[3781] Q[183], A[3]). Therefore it would seem that religion does not denote the state of perfection.

Objection 3: Further, the state of perfection is distinct from the state of beginners and that of the proficient. But in religion also some are beginners, and some are proficient. Therefore religion does not denote the state of perfection.

Objection 4: Further, religion would seem a place of repentance; for it is said in the Decrees (VII, qu. i, can. Hoc nequaquam): "The holy synod orders that any man who has been degraded from the episcopal dignity to the monastic life and a place of repentance, should by no means rise again to the episcopate." Now a place of repentance is opposed to the state of perfection; hence Dionysius (Eccl. Hier. vi) places penitents in the lowest place, namely among those who are to be cleansed. Therefore it would seem that religion is not the state of perfection.

On the contrary, In the Conferences of the Fathers (Collat. i, 7) abbot Moses speaking of religious says: "We must recognize that we have to undertake the hunger of fasting, watchings, bodily toil, privation, reading, and other acts of virtue, in order by these degrees to mount to the perfection of charity." Now things pertaining to human acts are specified and denominated from the intention of the end. Therefore religious belong to the state of perfection.

Moreover Dionysius says (Eccl. Hier. vi) that those who are called servants of God, by reason of their rendering pure service and subjection to God, are united to the perfection beloved of Him.

I answer that, As stated above ([3782]Q[141], A[2]) that which is applicable to many things in common is ascribed antonomastically to that to which it is applicable by way of excellence. Thus the name of "fortitude" is claimed by the virtue which preserves the firmness of the mind in regard to most difficult things, and the name of "temperance," by that virtue which tempers the greatest pleasures. Now religion as stated above ([3783]Q[81] , A[2]; A[3], ad 2) is a virtue whereby a man offers something to the service and worship of God. Wherefore those are called religious antonomastically, who give themselves up entirely to the divine service, as offering a holocaust to God. Hence Gregory says (Hom. xx in Ezech.): "Some there are who keep nothing for themselves, but sacrifice to almighty God their tongue, their senses, their life, and the property they possess." Now the perfection of man consists in adhering wholly to God, as stated above ([3784]Q[184], A[2]), and in this sense religion denotes the state of perfection.

Reply to Objection 1: To offer something to the worship of God is necessary for salvation, but to offer oneself wholly, and one's possessions to the worship of God belongs to perfection.

Reply to Objection 2: As stated above ([3785]Q[81], A[1], ad 1; A[4], ad 1,2;[3786] Q[85], A[3]) when we were treating of the virtue of religion, religion has reference not only to the offering of sacrifices and other like things that are proper to religion, but also to the acts of all the virtues which in so far as these are referred to God's service and honor become acts of religion. Accordingly if a man devotes his whole life to the divine service, his whole life belongs to religion, and thus by reason of the religious life that they lead, those who are in the state of perfection are called religious.

Reply to Objection 3: As stated above ([3787]Q[184], AA[4],6) religion denotes the state of perfection by reason of the end intended. Hence it does not follow that whoever is in the state of perfection is already perfect, but that he tends to perfection. Hence Origen commenting on Mat. 19:21, "If thou wilt be perfect," etc., says (Tract. viii in Matth.) that "he who has exchanged riches for poverty in order to become perfect does not become perfect at the very moment of giving his goods to the poor; but from that day the contemplation of God will begin to lead him to all the virtues." Thus all are not perfect in religion, but some are beginners, some proficient.

Reply to Objection 4: The religious state was instituted chiefly that we might obtain perfection by means of certain exercises, whereby the obstacles to perfect charity are removed. By the removal of the obstacles of perfect charity, much more are the occasions of sin cut off, for sin destroys charity altogether. Wherefore since it belongs to penance to cut out the causes of sin, it follows that the religious state is a most fitting place for penance. Hence (XXXIII, qu. ii, cap. Admonere) a man who had killed his wife is counseled to enter a monastery which is described as "better and lighter," rather than to do public penance while remaining in the world.

Whether every religious is bound to keep all the counsels?

Objection 1: It would seem that every religious is bound to keep all the counsels. For whoever professes a certain state of life is bound to observe whatever belongs to that state. Now each religious professes the state of perfection. Therefore every religious is bound to keep all the counsels that pertain to the state of perfection.

Objection 2: Further, Gregory says (Hom. xx in Ezech.) that "he who renounces this world, and does all the good he can, is like one who has gone out of Egypt and offers sacrifice in the wilderness." Now it belongs specially to religious to renounce the world. Therefore it belongs to them also to do all the good they can. and so it would seem that each of them is bound to fulfil all the counsels.

Objection 3: Further, if it is not requisite for the state of perfection to fulfil all the counsels, it would seem enough to fulfil some of them. But this is false, since some who lead a secular life fulfil some of the counsels, for instance those who observe continence. Therefore it would seem that every religious who is in the state of perfection is bound to fulfil whatever pertains to perfection: and such are the counsels.

On the contrary, one is not bound, unless one bind oneself, to do works of supererogation. But every religious does not bind himself to keep all the counsels, but to certain definite ones, some to some, others to others. Therefore all are not bound to keep all of them.

I answer that, A thing pertains to perfection in three ways. First, essentially, and thus, as stated above ([3788]Q[184], A[3]) the perfect observance of the precepts of charity belongs to perfection. Secondly, a thing belongs to perfection consequently: such are those things that result from the perfection of charity, for instance to bless them that curse you (Lk. 6:27), and to keep counsels of a like kind, which though they be binding as regards the preparedness of the mind, so that one has to fulfil them when necessity requires; yet are sometimes fulfilled, without there being any necessity, through superabundance of charity. Thirdly, a thing belongs to perfection instrumentally and dispositively, as poverty, continence, abstinence, and the like.

Now it has been stated [3789](A[1]) that the perfection of charity is the end of the religious state. And the religious state is a school or exercise for the attainment of perfection, which men strive to reach by various practices, just as a physician may use various remedies in order to heal. But it is evident that for him who works for an end it is not necessary that he should already have attained the end, but it is requisite that he should by some means tend thereto. Hence he who enters the religious state is not bound to have perfect charity, but he is bound to tend to this, and use his endeavors to have perfect charity.

For the same reason he is not bound to fulfil those things that result from the perfection of charity, although he is bound to intend to fulfil them: against which intention he acts if he contemns them, wherefore he sins not by omitting them but by contempt of them.

In like manner he is not bound to observe all the practices whereby perfection may be attained, but only those which are definitely prescribed to him by the rule which he has professed.

Reply to Objection 1: He who enters religion does not make profession to be perfect, but he professes to endeavor to attain perfection; even as he who enters the schools does not profess to have knowledge, but to study in order to acquire knowledge. Wherefore as Augustine says (De Civ. Dei viii, 2), Pythagoras was unwilling to profess to be a wise man, but acknowledged himself, "a lover of wisdom." Hence a religious does not violate his profession if he be not perfect, but only if he despises to tend to perfection.

Reply to Objection 2: Just as, though all are bound to love God with their whole heart, yet there is a certain wholeness of perfection which cannot be omitted without sin, and another wholeness which can be omitted without sin ([3790]Q[184], A[2], ad 3), provided there be no contempt, as stated above (ad 1), so too, all, both religious and seculars, are bound, in a certain measure, to do whatever good they can, for to all without exception it is said (Eccles. 9:10): "Whatsoever thy hand is able to do, do it earnestly." Yet there is a way of fulfilling this precept, so as to avoid sin, namely if one do what one can as required by the conditions of one's state of life: provided there be no contempt of doing better things, which contempt sets the mind against spiritual progress.

Reply to Objection 3: There are some counsels such that if they be omitted, man's whole life would be taken up with secular business; for instance if he have property of his own, or enter the married state, or do something of the kind that regards the essential vows of religion themselves; wherefore religious are bound to keep all such like counsels. Other counsels there are, however, about certain particular better actions, which can be omitted without one's life being taken up with secular actions; wherefore there is no need for religious to be bound to fulfil all of them.

Whether poverty is required for religious perfection?

Objection 1: It would seem that poverty is not required for religious perfection. For that which it is unlawful to do does not apparently belong to the state of perfection. But it would seem to be unlawful for a man to give up all he possesses; since the Apostle (2 Cor. 8:12) lays down the way in which the faithful are to give alms saying: "If the will be forward, it is accepted according to that which a man hath," i.e. "you should keep back what you need," and afterwards he adds (2 Cor. 8:13): "For I mean not that others should be eased, and you burthened," i.e. "with poverty," according to a gloss. Moreover a gloss on 1 Tim. 6:8, "Having food, and wherewith to be covered," says: "Though we brought nothing, and will carry nothing away, we must not give up these temporal things altogether." Therefore it seems that voluntary poverty is not requisite for religious perfection.

Objection 2: Further, whosoever exposes himself to danger sins. But he who renounces all he has and embraces voluntary poverty exposes himself to danger—not only spiritual, according to Prov. 30:9, "Lest perhaps . . . being compelled by poverty, I should steal and forswear the name of my God," and Ecclus. 27:1, "Through poverty many have sinned"—but also corporal, for it is written (Eccles. 7:13): "As wisdom is a defense, so money is a defense," and the Philosopher says (Ethic. iv, 1) that "the waste of property appears to be a sort of ruining of one's self, since thereby man lives." Therefore it would seem that voluntary poverty is not requisite for the perfection of religious life.

Objection 3: Further, "Virtue observes the mean," as stated in Ethic. ii, 6. But he who renounces all by voluntary poverty seems to go to the extreme rather than to observe the mean. Therefore he does not act virtuously: and so this does not pertain to the perfection of life.

Objection 4: Further, the ultimate perfection of man consists in happiness. Now riches conduce to happiness; for it is written (Ecclus. 31:8): "Blessed is the rich man that is found without blemish," and the Philosopher says (Ethic. i, 8) that "riches contribute instrumentally to happiness." Therefore voluntary poverty is not requisite for religious perfection.

Objection 5: Further, the episcopal state is more perfect than the religious state. But bishops may have property, as stated above ([3791]Q[185], A[6]). Therefore religious may also.

Objection 6: Further, almsgiving is a work most acceptable to God, and as Chrysostom says (Hom. ix in Ep. ad Hebr.) "is a most effective remedy in repentance." Now poverty excludes almsgiving. Therefore it would seem that poverty does not pertain to religious perfection.

On the contrary, Gregory says (Moral. viii, 26): "There are some of the righteous who bracing themselves up to lay hold of the very height of perfection, while they aim at higher objects within, abandon all things without." Now, as stated above, ([3792]AA[1],2), it belongs properly to religious to brace themselves up in order to lay hold of the very height of perfection. Therefore it belongs to them to abandon all outward things by voluntary poverty.

I answer that, As stated above [3793](A[2]), the religious state is an exercise and a school for attaining to the perfection of charity. For this it is necessary that a man wholly withdraw his affections from worldly things; since Augustine says (Confess. x, 29), speaking to God: "Too little doth he love Thee, who loves anything with Thee, which he loveth not for Thee." Wherefore he says (QQ. lxxxiii, qu. 36) that "greater charity means less cupidity, perfect charity means no cupidity." Now the possession of worldly things draws a man's mind to the love of them: hence Augustine says (Ep. xxxi ad Paulin. et Theras.) that "we are more firmly attached to earthly things when we have them than when we desire them: since why did that young man go away sad, save because he had great wealth? For it is one thing not to wish to lay hold of what one has not, and another to renounce what one already has; the former are rejected as foreign to us, the latter are cut off as a limb." And Chrysostom says (Hom. lxiii in Matth.) that "the possession of wealth kindles a greater flame and the desire for it becomes stronger."

Hence it is that in the attainment of the perfection of charity the first foundation is voluntary poverty, whereby a man lives without property of his own, according to the saying of our Lord (Mat. 19:21), "If thou wilt be perfect, go, sell all [Vulg.: 'what'] thou hast, and give to the poor . . . and come, follow Me."

Reply to Objection 1: As the gloss adds, "when the Apostle said this (namely "not that you should be burthened," i.e. with poverty)," he did not mean that "it were better not to give: but he feared for the weak, whom he admonished so to give as not to suffer privation." Hence in like manner the other gloss means not that it is unlawful to renounce all one's temporal goods, but that this is not required of necessity. Wherefore Ambrose says (De Offic. i, 30): "Our Lord does not wish," namely does not command us "to pour out our wealth all at once, but to dispense it; or perhaps to do as did Eliseus who slew his oxen, and fed the poor with that which was his own so that no household care might hold him back."

Reply to Objection 2: He who renounces all his possessions for Christ's sake exposes himself to no danger, neither spiritual nor corporal. For spiritual danger ensues from poverty when the latter is not voluntary; because those who are unwillingly poor, through the desire of money-getting, fall into many sins, according to 1 Tim. 6:9, "They that will become rich, fall into temptation and into the snare of the devil." This attachment is put away by those who embrace voluntary poverty, but it gathers strength in those who have wealth, as stated above. Again bodily danger does not threaten those who, intent on following Christ, renounce all their possessions and entrust themselves to divine providence. Hence Augustine says (De Serm. Dom. in Monte ii, 17): "Those who seek first the kingdom of God and His justice are not weighed down by anxiety lest they lack what is necessary."

Reply to Objection 3: According to the Philosopher (Ethic. ii, 6), the mean of virtue is taken according to right reason, not according to the quantity of a thing. Consequently whatever may be done in accordance with right reason is not rendered sinful by the greatness of the quantity, but all the more virtuous. It would, however, be against right reason to throw away all one's possessions through intemperance, or without any useful purpose; whereas it is in accordance with right reason to renounce wealth in order to devote oneself to the contemplation of wisdom. Even certain philosophers are said to have done this; for Jerome says (Ep. xlviii ad Paulin.): "The famous Theban, Crates, once a very wealthy man, when he was going to Athens to study philosophy, cast away a large amount of gold; for he considered that he could not possess both gold and virtue at the same time." Much more therefore is it according to right reason for a man to renounce all he has, in order perfectly to follow Christ. Wherefore Jerome says (Ep. cxxv ad Rust. Monach.): "Poor thyself, follow Christ poor."

Reply to Objection 4: Happiness or felicity is twofold. One is perfect, to which we look forward in the life to come; the other is imperfect, in respect of which some are said to be happy in this life. The happiness of this life is twofold, one is according to the active life, the other according to the contemplative life, as the Philosopher asserts (Ethic. x, 7,8). Now wealth conduces instrumentally to the happiness of the active life which consists in external actions, because as the Philosopher says (Ethic. i, 8) "we do many things by friends, by riches, by political influence, as it were by instruments." On the other hand, it does not conduce to the happiness of the contemplative life, rather is it an obstacle thereto, inasmuch as the anxiety it involves disturbs the quiet of the soul, which is most necessary to one who contemplates. Hence it is that the Philosopher asserts (Ethic. x, 8) that "for actions many things are needed, but the contemplative man needs no such things," namely external goods, "for his operation; in fact they are obstacles to his contemplation."

Man is directed to future happiness by charity; and since voluntary poverty is an efficient exercise for the attaining of perfect charity, it follows that it is of great avail in acquiring the happiness of heaven. Wherefore our Lord said (Mat. 19:21): "Go, sell all [Vulg.: 'what'] thou hast, and give to the poor, and thou shalt have treasure in heaven." Now riches once they are possessed are in themselves of a nature to hinder the perfection of charity, especially by enticing and distracting the mind. Hence it is written (Mat. 13:22) that "the care of this world and the deceitfulness of riches choketh up the word" of God, for as Gregory says (Hom. xv in Ev.) by "preventing the good desire from entering into the heart, they destroy life at its very outset." Consequently it is difficult to safeguard charity amidst riches: wherefore our Lord said (Mat. 19:23) that "a rich man shall hardly enter into the kingdom of heaven," which we must understand as referring to one who actually has wealth, since He says that this is impossible for him who places his affection in riches, according to the explanation of Chrysostom (Hom. lxiii in Matth.), for He adds (Mat. 19:24): "It is easier for a camel to pass through the eye of a needle, than for a rich man to enter into the kingdom of heaven." Hence it is not said simply that the "rich man" is blessed, but "the rich man that is found without blemish, and that hath not gone after gold," and this because he has done a difficult thing, wherefore the text continues (Mat. 19:9): "Who is he? and we will praise him; for he hath done wonderful things in his life," namely by not loving riches though placed in the midst of them.

Reply to Objection 5: The episcopal state is not directed to the attainment of perfection, but rather to the effect that, in virtue of the perfection which he already has, a man may govern others, by administering not only spiritual but also temporal things. This belongs to the active life, wherein many things occur that may be done by means of wealth as an instrument, as stated (ad 4). Wherefore it is not required of bishops, who make profession of governing Christ's flock, that they have nothing of their own, whereas it is required of religious who make profession of learning to obtain perfection.

Reply to Objection 6: The renouncement of one's own wealth is compared to almsgiving as the universal to the particular, and as the holocaust to the sacrifice. Hence Gregory says (Hom. xx in Ezech.) that those who assist "the needy with the things they possess, by their good deeds offer sacrifice, since they offer up something to God and keep back something for themselves; whereas those who keep nothing for themselves offer a holocaust which is greater than a sacrifice." Wherefore Jerome also says (Contra Vigilant.): "When you declare that those do better who retain the use of their possessions, and dole out the fruits of their possessions to the poor, it is not I but the Lord Who answers you; If thou wilt be perfect," etc., and afterwards he goes on to say: "This man whom you praise belongs to the second and third degree, and we too commend him: provided we acknowledge the first as to be preferred to the second and third." For this reason in order to exclude the error of Vigilantius it is said (De Eccl. Dogm. xxxviii): "It is a good thing to give away one's goods by dispensing them to the poor: it is better to give them away once for all with the intention of following the Lord, and, free of solicitude, to be poor with Christ."

Whether perpetual continence is required for religious perfection?

Objection 1: It would seem that perpetual continence is not required for religious perfection. For all perfection of the Christian life began with Christ's apostles. Now the apostles do not appear to have observed continence, as evidenced by Peter, of whose mother-in-law we read Mat. 8:14. Therefore it would seem that perpetual continence is not requisite for religious perfection.

Objection 2: Further, the first example of perfection is shown to us in the person of Abraham, to whom the Lord said (Gn. 17:1): "Walk before Me, and be perfect." Now the copy should not surpass the example. Therefore perpetual continence is not requisite for religious perfection.

Objection 3: Further, that which is required for religious perfection is to be found in every religious order. Now there are some religious who lead a married life. Therefore religious perfection does not require perpetual continence.

On the contrary, The Apostle says (2 Cor. 7:1): "Let us cleanse ourselves from all defilement of the flesh and of the spirit, perfecting sanctification in the fear of God." Now cleanness of flesh and spirit is safeguarded by continence, for it is said (1 Cor. 7:34): "The unmarried woman and the virgin thinketh on the things of the Lord that she may be holy both in spirit and in body [Vulg.: 'both in body and in spirit']." Therefore religious perfection requires continence.

I answer that, The religious state requires the removal of whatever hinders man from devoting himself entirely to God's service. Now the use of sexual union hinders the mind from giving itself wholly to the service of God, and this for two reasons. First, on account of its vehement delectation, which by frequent repetition increases concupiscence, as also the Philosopher observes (Ethic. iii, 12): and hence it is that the use of venery withdraws the mind from that perfect intentness on tending to God. Augustine expresses this when he says (Solil. i, 10): "I consider that nothing so casts down the manly mind from its height as the fondling of women, and those bodily contacts which belong to the married state." Secondly, because it involves man in solicitude for the control of his wife, his children, and his temporalities which serve for their upkeep. Hence the Apostle says (1 Cor. 7:32,33): "He that is without a wife is solicitous for the things that belong to the Lord, how he may please God: but he that is with a wife is solicitous for the things of the world, how he may please his wife."

Therefore perpetual continence, as well as voluntary poverty, is requisite for religious perfection. Wherefore just as Vigilantius was condemned for equaling riches to poverty, so was Jovinian condemned for equaling marriage to virginity.

Reply to Objection 1: The perfection not only of poverty but also of continence was introduced by Christ Who said (Mat. 19:12): "There are eunuchs who have made themselves eunuchs, for the kingdom of heaven," and then added: "He that can take, let him take it." And lest anyone should be deprived of the hope of attaining perfection, he admitted to the state of perfection those even who were married. Now the husbands could not without committing an injustice forsake their wives, whereas men could without injustice renounce riches. Wherefore Peter whom He found married, He severed not from his wife, while "He withheld from marriage John who wished to marry" [*Prolog. in Joan. among the supposititious works of St. Jerome].

Reply to Objection 2: As Augustine says (De Bono Conjug. xxii), "the chastity of celibacy is better than the chastity of marriage, one of which Abraham had in use, both of them in habit. For he lived chastely, and he might have been chaste without marrying, but it was not requisite then." Nevertheless if the patriarchs of old had perfection of mind together with wealth and marriage, which is a mark of the greatness of their virtue, this is no reason why any weaker person should presume to have such great virtue that he can attain to perfection though rich and married; as neither does a man unarmed presume to attack his enemy, because Samson slew many foes with the jaw-bone of an ass. For those fathers, had it been seasonable to observe continence and poverty, would have been most careful to observe them.

Reply to Objection 3: Such ways of living as admit of the use of marriage are not the religious life simply and absolutely speaking, but in a restricted sense, in so far as they have a certain share in those things that belong to the religious state.

Whether obedience belongs to religious perfection?

Objection 1: It would seem that obedience does not belong to religious perfection. For those things seemingly belong to religious perfection, which are works of supererogation and are not binding upon all. But all are bound to obey their superiors, according to the saying of the Apostle (Heb. 13:17), "Obey your prelates, and be subject to them." Therefore it would seem that obedience does not belong to religious perfection.

Objection 2: Further, obedience would seem to belong properly to those who have to be guided by the sense of others, and such persons are lacking in discernment. Now the Apostle says (Heb. 5:14) that "strong meat is for the perfect, for them who by custom have their senses exercised to the discerning of good and evil." Therefore it would seem that obedience does not belong to the state of the perfect.

Objection 3: Further, if obedience were requisite for religious perfection, it would follow that it is befitting to all religious. But it is not becoming to all; since some religious lead a solitary life, and have no superior whom they obey. Again religious superiors apparently are not bound to obedience. Therefore obedience would seem not to pertain to religious perfection.

Objection 4: Further, if the vow of obedience were requisite for religion, it would follow that religious are bound to obey their superiors in all things, just as they are bound to abstain from all venery by their vow of continence. But they are not bound to obey them in all things, as stated above ([3794]Q[104], A[5]), when we were treating of the virtue of obedience. Therefore the vow of obedience is not requisite for religion.

Objection 5: Further, those services are most acceptable to God which are done freely and not of necessity, according to 2 Cor. 9:7, "Not with sadness or of necessity." Now that which is done out of obedience is done of necessity of precept. Therefore those good works are more deserving of praise which are done of one's own accord. Therefore the vow of obedience is unbecoming to religion whereby men seek to attain to that which is better.

On the contrary, Religious perfection consists chiefly in the imitation of Christ, according to Mat. 19:21, "If thou wilt be perfect, go sell all [Vulg.: 'what'] thou hast, and give to the poor, and follow Me." Now in Christ obedience is commended above all according to Phil. 2:8, "He became [Vulg.: 'becoming'] obedient unto death." Therefore seemingly obedience belongs to religious perfection.

I answer that, As stated above ([3795]AA[2],3) the religious state is a school and exercise for tending to perfection. Now those who are being instructed or exercised in order to attain a certain end must needs follow the direction of someone under whose control they are instructed or exercised so as to attain that end as disciples under a master. Hence religious need to be placed under the instruction and command of someone as regards things pertaining to the religious life; wherefore it is said (VII, qu. i, can. Hoc nequaquam): "The monastic life denotes subjection and discipleship." Now one man is subjected to another's command and instruction by obedience: and consequently obedience is requisite for religious perfection.

Reply to Objection 1: To obey one's superiors in matters that are essential to virtue is not a work of supererogation, but is common to all: whereas to obey in matters pertaining to the practice of perfection belongs properly to religious. This latter obedience is compared to the former as the universal to the particular. For those who live in the world, keep something for themselves, and offer something to God; and in the latter respect they are under obedience to their superiors:

whereas those who live in religion give themselves wholly and their possessions to God, as stated above ([3796]AA[1],3). Hence their obedience is universal.

Reply to Objection 2: As the Philosopher says (Ethic. ii, 1,2), by performing actions we contract certain habits, and when we have acquired the habit we are best able to perform the actions. Accordingly those who have not attained to perfection, acquire perfection by obeying, while those who have already acquired perfection are most ready to obey, not as though they need to be directed to the acquisition of perfection, but as maintaining themselves by this means in that which belongs to perfection.

Reply to Objection 3: The subjection of religious is chiefly in reference to bishops, who are compared to them as perfecters to perfected, as Dionysius states (Eccl. Hier. vi), where he also says that the "monastic order is subjected to the perfecting virtues of the bishops, and is taught by their godlike enlightenment." Hence neither hermits nor religious superiors are exempt from obedience to bishops; and if they be wholly or partly exempt from obedience to the bishop of the diocese, they are nevertheless bound to obey the Sovereign Pontiff, not only in matters affecting all in common, but also in those which pertain specially to religious discipline.

Reply to Objection 4: The vow of obedience taken by religious, extends to the disposition of a man's whole life, and in this way it has a certain universality, although it does not extend to all individual acts. For some of these do not belong to religion, through not being of those things that concern the love of God and of our neighbor, such as rubbing one's beard, lifting a stick from the ground and so forth, which do not come under a vow nor under obedience; and some are contrary to religion. Nor is there any comparison with continence whereby acts are excluded which are altogether contrary to religion.

Reply to Objection 5: The necessity of coercion makes an act involuntary and consequently deprives it of the character of praise or merit; whereas the necessity which is consequent upon obedience is a necessity not of coercion but of a free will, inasmuch as a man is willing to obey, although perhaps he would not be willing to do the thing commanded considered in itself. Wherefore since by the vow of obedience a man lays himself under the necessity of doing for God's sake certain things that are not pleasing in themselves, for this very reason that which he does is the more acceptable to God, though it be of less account, because man can give nothing greater to God, than by subjecting his will to another man's for God's sake. Hence in the Conferences of the Fathers (Coll. xviii, 7) it is stated that "the Sarabaitae are the worst class of monks, because through providing for their own needs without being subject to superiors, they are free to do as they will; and yet day and night they are more busily occupied in work than those who live in monasteries."

Whether it is requisite for religious perfection that poverty, continence, and obedience should come under a vow?

Objection 1: It would seem that it is not requisite for religious perfection that the three aforesaid, namely poverty, continence, and obedience, should come under a vow. For the school of perfection is founded on the principles laid down by our Lord. Now our Lord in formulating perfection (Mat. 19:21) said: "If thou wilt be perfect, go, sell all [Vulg.: 'what'] thou hast, and give to the poor," without any mention of a vow. Therefore it would seem that a vow is not necessary for the school of religion.

Objection 2: Further, a vow is a promise made to God, wherefore (Eccles. 5:3) the wise man after saying: "If thou hast vowed anything to God, defer not to pay it," adds at once, "for an unfaithful and foolish promise displeaseth Him." But when a thing is being actually given there is no need for a promise. Therefore it suffices for religious perfection that one keep poverty, continence, and obedience without. vowing them.

Objection 3: Further, Augustine says (Ad Pollent., de Adult. Conjug. i, 14): "The services we render are more pleasing when we might lawfully not render them, yet do so out of love." Now it is lawful not to render a service which we have not vowed, whereas it is unlawful if we have vowed to render it. Therefore seemingly it is more pleasing to God to keep poverty, continence, and obedience without a vow. Therefore a vow is not requisite for religious perfection.

On the contrary, In the Old Law the Nazareans were consecrated by vow according to Num. 6:2, "When a man or woman shall make a vow to be sanctified and will consecrate themselves to the Lord," etc. Now these were a figure of those "who attain the summit of perfection," as a gloss [*Cf. Moral. ii] of Gregory states. Therefore a vow is requisite for religious perfection.

I answer that, It belongs to religious to be in the state of perfection, as shown above (Q[174], A[5]). Now the state of perfection requires an obligation to whatever belongs to perfection: and this obligation consists in binding oneself to God by means of a vow. But it is evident from what has been said ([3797]AA[3],4,5) that poverty, continence, and obedience belong to the perfection of the Christian life. Consequently the religious state requires that one be bound to these three by vow. Hence Gregory says (Hom. xx in Ezech.): "When a man vows to God all his possessions, all his life, all his knowledge, it is a holocaust"; and afterwards he says that this refers to those who renounce the present world.

Reply to Objection 1: Our Lord declared that it belongs to the perfection of life that a man follow Him, not anyhow, but in such a way as not to turn back. Wherefore He says again (Lk. 9:62): "No man putting his hand to the plough, and looking back, is fit for the kingdom of God." And though some of His disciples went back, yet when our Lord asked (Jn. 6:68,69), "Will you also go away?" Peter answered for the others: "Lord, to whom shall we go?" Hence Augustine says (De Consensu Ev. ii, 17) that "as Matthew and Mark relate, Peter and Andrew followed Him after drawing their boats on to the beach, not as though they purposed to return, but as following Him at His command." Now this unwavering following of Christ is made fast by a vow: wherefore a vow is requisite for religious perfection.

Reply to Objection 2: As Gregory says (Moral. ii) religious perfection requires that a man give "his whole life" to God. But a man cannot actually give God his whole life, because that life taken as a whole is not simultaneous but successive. Hence a man cannot give his whole life to God otherwise than by the obligation of a vow.

Reply to Objection 3: Among other services that we can lawfully give, is our liberty, which is dearer to man than aught else. Consequently when a man of his own accord deprives himself by vow of the liberty of abstaining from things pertaining to God's service, this is most acceptable to God. Hence Augustine says (Ep. cxxvii ad Paulin. et Arment.): "Repent not of thy vow; rejoice rather that thou canst no longer do lawfully, what thou mightest have done lawfully but to thy own cost. Happy the obligation that compels to better things."

Whether it is right to say that religious perfection consists in these three vows?

Objection 1: It would seem that it is not right to say that religious perfection consists in these three vows. For the perfection of life consists of inward rather than of outward acts, according to Rom. 14:17, "The Kingdom of God is not meat and drink, but justice and peace and joy in the Holy Ghost." Now the religious vow binds a man to things belonging to perfection. Therefore vows of inward actions, such as contemplation, love of God and our neighbor, and so forth, should pertain to the religious state, rather than the vows of poverty, continence, and obedience which refer to outward actions.

Objection 2: Further, the three aforesaid come under the religious vow, in so far as they belong to the practice of tending to perfection. But there are many other things that religious practice, such as abstinence, watchings, and the like. Therefore it would seem that these three vows are incorrectly described as pertaining to the state of perfection.

Objection 3: Further, by the vow of obedience a man is bound to do according to his superior's command whatever pertains to the practice of perfection. Therefore the vow of obedience suffices without the two other vows.

Objection 4: Further, external goods comprise not only riches but also honors. Therefore, if religious, by the vow of poverty, renounce earthly riches, there should be another vow whereby they may despise worldly honors.

On the contrary, It is stated (Extra, de Statu Monach., cap. Cum ad monasterium) that "the keeping of chastity and the renouncing of property are affixed to the monastic rule."

I answer that, The religious state may be considered in three ways. First, as being a practice of tending to the perfection of charity: secondly, as quieting the human mind from outward solicitude, according to 1 Cor. 7:32: "I would have you to be without solicitude": thirdly, as a holocaust whereby a man offers himself and his possessions wholly to God; and in corresponding manner the religious state is constituted by these three vows.

First, as regards the practice of perfection a man is required to remove from himself whatever may hinder his affections from tending wholly to God, for it is in this that the perfection of charity consists. Such hindrances are of three kinds. First, the attachment to external goods, which is removed by the vow of poverty; secondly, the concupiscence of sensible pleasures, chief among which are venereal pleasures, and these are removed by the vow of continence; thirdly, the inordinateness of the human will, and this is removed by the vow of obedience. In like manner the disquiet of worldly solicitude is aroused in man in reference especially to three things. First, as regards the dispensing of external things, and this solicitude is removed from man by the vow of poverty; secondly, as regards the control of wife and children, which is cut away by the vow of continence; thirdly, as regards the disposal of one's own actions, which is eliminated by the vow of obedience, whereby a man commits himself to the disposal of another.

Again, "a holocaust is the offering to God of all that one has," according to Gregory (Hom. xx in Ezech.). Now man has a threefold good, according to the Philosopher (Ethic. i, 8). First, the good of external things, which he wholly offers to God by the vow of voluntary poverty: secondly, the good of his own body, and this good he offers to God especially by the vow of continence, whereby he renounces the greatest bodily pleasures. the third is the good of the soul, which man wholly offers to God by the vow of obedience, whereby he offers God his own will by which he makes use of all the powers and habits of the soul. Therefore the religious state is fittingly constituted by the three vows.

Reply to Objection 1: As stated above [3798](A[1]), the end whereunto the religious vow is directed is the perfection of charity, since all the interior acts of virtue belong to charity as to their mother, according to 1 Cor. 13:4, "Charity is patient, is kind," etc. Hence the interior acts of virtue, for instance humility, patience, and so forth, do not come under the religious vow, but this is directed to them as its end.

Reply to Objection 2: All other religious observances are directed to the three aforesaid principal vows; for if any of them are ordained for the purpose of procuring a livelihood, such as labor, questing, and so on, they are to be referred to poverty; for the safeguarding of which religious seek a livelihood by these means. Other observances whereby the body is chastised, such as watching, fasting, and the like, are directly ordained for the observance of the vow of continence. And such religious observances as regard human actions whereby a man is directed to the end of religion, namely the love of God and his neighbor (such as reading, prayer, visiting the sick, and the like), are comprised under the vow of obedience that applies to the will, which directs its actions to the end according to the ordering of another person. The distinction of habit belongs to all three vows, as a sign of being bound by them: wherefore the religious habit is given or blessed at the time of profession.

Reply to Objection 3: By obedience a man offers to God his will, to which though all human affairs are subject, yet some are subject to it alone in a special manner, namely human actions, since passions belong also to the sensitive appetite. Wherefore in order to restrain the passions of carnal pleasures and of external objects of appetite, which hinder the perfection of life, there was need for the vows of continence and poverty; but for the ordering of one's own actions accordingly as the state of perfection requires, there was need for the vow of obedience.

Reply to Objection 4: As the Philosopher says (Ethic. iv, 3), strictly and truly speaking honor is not due save to virtue. Since, however, external goods serve instrumentally for certain acts of virtue, the consequence is that a certain honor is given to their excellence especially by the common people who acknowledge none but outward excellence. Therefore since religious tend to the perfection of virtue it becomes them not to renounce the honor which God and all holy men accord to virtue, according to Ps. 138:17, "But to me Thy friends, O God, are made exceedingly honorable." On the other hand, they renounce the honor that is given to outward excellence, by the very fact that they withdraw from a worldly life: hence no special vow is needed for this.

Whether the vow of obedience is the chief of the three religious vows?

Objection 1: It would seem that the vow of obedience is not the chief of the three religious vows. For the perfection of the religious life was inaugurated by Christ. Now Christ gave a special counsel of poverty; whereas He is not stated to have given a special counsel of obedience. Therefore the vow of poverty is greater than the vow of obedience.

Objection 2: Further, it is written (Ecclus. 26:20) that "no price is worthy of a continent soul." Now the vow of that which is more worthy is itself more excellent. Therefore the vow of continence is more excellent than the vow of obedience.

Objection 3: Further, the greater a vow the more indispensable it would seem to be. Now the vows of poverty and continence "are so inseparable from the monastic rule, that not even the Sovereign Pontiff can allow them to be broken," according to a Decretal (De Statu Monach., cap. Cum ad monasterium): yet he can dispense a religious from obeying his superior. Therefore it would seem that the vow of obedience is less than the vow of poverty and continence.

On the contrary, Gregory says (Moral. xxxv, 14): "Obedience is rightly placed before victims, since by victims another's flesh, but by obedience one's own will, is sacrificed." Now the religious vows are holocausts, as stated above ([3799]AA[1],3, ad 6). Therefore the vow of obedience is the chief of all religious vows.

I answer that, The vow of obedience is the chief of the three religious vows, and this for three reasons.

First, because by the vow of obedience man offers God something greater, namely his own will; for this is of more account than his own body, which he offers God by continence, and than external things, which he offers God by the vow of poverty. Wherefore that which is done out of obedience is more acceptable to God than that which is done of one's own will, according to the saying of Jerome (Ep. cxxv ad Rustic Monach.): "My words are intended to teach you not to rely on your own judgment": and a little further on he says: "You may not do what you will; you must eat what you are bidden to eat, you may possess as much as you receive, clothe yourself with what is given to you." Hence fasting is not acceptable to God if it is done of one's own will, according to Is. 58:3, "Behold in the day of your fast your own will is found."

Secondly, because the vow of obedience includes the other vows, but not vice versa: for a religious, though bound by vow to observe continence and poverty, yet these also come under obedience, as well as many other things besides the keeping of continence and poverty.

Thirdly, because the vow of obedience extends properly to those acts that are closely connected with the end of religion; and the more closely a thing is connected with the end, the better it is.

It follows from this that the vow of obedience is more essential to the religious life. For if a man without taking a vow of obedience were to observe, even by vow, voluntary poverty and continence, he would not therefore belong to the religious state, which is to be preferred to virginity observed even by vow; for Augustine says (De Virgin. xlvi): "No one, methinks, would prefer virginity to the monastic life." [*St. Augustine wrote not 'monasterio' but 'martyrio'—to 'martyrdom'; and St. Thomas quotes the passage correctly above[3800], Q[124], A[3] and[3801] Q[152], A[5]].

Reply to Objection 1: The counsel of obedience was included in the very following of Christ, since to obey is to follow another's will. Consequently it is more pertinent to perfection than the vow of poverty, because as Jerome, commenting on Mat. 19:27, "Behold we have left all things," observes, "Peter added that which is perfect when he said: And have followed Thee."

Reply to Objection 2: The words quoted mean that continence is to be preferred, not to all other acts of virtue, but to conjugal chastity, or to external riches of gold and silver which are measured by weight [*'Pondere,' referring to the Latin 'ponderatio' in the Vulgate, which the Douay version renders 'price.']. Or again continence is taken in a general sense for abstinence from ali evil, as stated above ([3802]Q[155], A[4], ad 1).

Reply to Objection 3: The Pope cannot dispense a religious from his vow of obedience so as to release him from obedience to every superior in matters relating to the perfection of life, for he cannot exempt him from obedience to himself. He can, however, exempt him from subjection to a lower superior, but this is not to dispense him from his vow of obedience.

Whether a religious sins mortally whenever he transgresses the things contained in his rule?

Objection 1: It would seem that a religious sins mortally whenever he transgresses the things contained in his rule. For to break a vow is a sin worthy of condemnation, as appears from 1 Tim. 5:11,12, where the Apostle says that widows who "will marry have [Vulg.: 'having'] damnation, because they have made void their first faith." But religious are bound to a rule by the vows of their profession. Therefore they sin mortally by transgressing the things contained in their rule.

Objection 2: Further, the rule is enjoined upon a religious in the same way as a law. Now he who transgresses a precept of law sins mortally. Therefore it would seem that a monk sins mortally if he transgresses the things contained in his rule.

Objection 3: Further, contempt involves a mortal sin. Now whoever repeatedly does what he ought not to do seems to sin from contempt. Therefore it would seem that a religious sins mortally by frequently transgressing the things contained in his rule.

On the contrary, The religious state is safer than the secular state; wherefore Gregory at the beginning of his Morals [*Epist. Missoria, ad Leand. Episc. i] compares the secular life to the stormy sea, and the religious life to the calm port. But if every transgression of the things contained in his rule were to involve a religious in mortal sin, the religious life would be fraught with danger of account of its multitude of observances. Therefore not every transgression of the things contained in the rule is a mortal sin.

I answer that, As stated above (A[1], ad 1,2), a thing is contained in the rule in two ways. First, as the end of the rule, for instance things that pertain to the acts of the virtues; and the transgression of these, as regards those which come under a common precept, involves a mortal sin; but as regards those which are not included in the common obligation of a precept, the transgression thereof does not involve a mortal sin, except by reason of contempt, because, as stated above [3803](A[2]), a religious is not bound to be perfect, but to tend to perfection, to which the contempt of perfection is opposed.

Secondly, a thing is contained in the rule through pertaining to the outward practice, such as all external observances, to some of which a religious is bound by the vow of his profession. Now the vow of profession regards chiefly the three things aforesaid, namely poverty, continence, and obedience, while all others are directed to these. Consequently the transgression of these three involves a mortal sin, while the transgression of the others does not involve a mortal sin, except either by reason of contempt of the rule (since this is directly contrary to the profession whereby a man vows to live according to the rule), or by reason of a precept, whether given orally by a superior, or expressed in the rule, since this would be to act contrary to the vow of obedience.

Reply to Objection 1: He who professes a rule does not vow to observe all the things contained in the rule, but he vows the regular life which consists essentially in the three aforesaid things. Hence in certain religious orders precaution is taken to profess, not the rule, but to live according to the rule, i.e. to tend to form one's conduct in accordance with the rule as a kind of model; and this is set aside by contempt. Yet greater precaution is observed in some religious orders by professing obedience according to the rule, so that only that which is contrary to a precept of the rule is contrary to the profession, while the transgression or omission of other things binds only under pain of venial sin, because, as stated above (A[7], ad 2), such things are dispositions to the chief vows. And venial sin is a disposition to mortal, as stated above ([3804]FS, Q[88], A[3]), inasmuch as it hinders those things whereby a man is disposed to keep the chief precepts of Christ's law, namely the precepts of charity.

There is also a religious order, that of the Friars Preachers, where such like transgressions or omissions do not, by their very nature, involve sin, either mortal or venial; but they bind one to suffer the punishment affixed thereto, because it is in this way that they are bound to observe such things. Nevertheless they may sin venially or mortally through neglect, concupiscence, or contempt.

Reply to Objection 2: Not all the contents of the law are set forth by way of precept; for some are expressed under the form of ordinance or statute binding under pain of a fixed punishment. Accordingly, just as in the civil law the transgression of a legal statute does not always render a man deserving of bodily death, so neither in the law of the Church does every ordinance or statute bind under mortal sin; and the same applies to the statutes of the rule.

Reply to Objection 3: An action or transgression proceeds from contempt when a man's will refuses to submit to the ordinance of the law or rule, and from this he proceeds to act against the law or rule. on the other hand, he does not sin from contempt, but from some other cause, when he is led to do something against the ordinance of the law or rule through some particular cause such as concupiscence or anger, even though he often repeat the same kind of sin through the same or some other cause. Thus Augustine says (De Nat. et Grat. xxix) that "not all sins are committed through proud contempt." Nevertheless the frequent repetition of a sin leads dispositively to contempt, according to the words of Prov. 18:3, "The wicked man, when he is come into the depth of sins, contemneth."

Whether a religious sins more grievously than a secular by the same kind of sin?

Objection 1: It would seem that a religious does not sin more grievously than a secular by the same kind of sin. For it is written (2 Paralip 30:18,19): "The Lord Who is good will show mercy to all them who with their whole heart seek the Lord the God of their fathers, and will not impute it to them that they are not sanctified." Now religious apparently follow the Lord the God of their fathers with their whole heart rather than seculars, who partly give themselves and their possessions to God and reserve part for themselves, as Gregory says (Hom. xx in Ezech.).

Therefore it would seem that it is less imputed to them if they fall short somewhat of their sanctification.

Objection 2: Further, God is less angered at a man's sins if he does some good deeds, according to 2 Paralip 19:2,3, "Thou helpest the ungodly, and thou art joined in friendship with them that hate the Lord, and therefore thou didst deserve indeed the wrath of the Lord: but good works are found in thee." Now religious do more good works than seculars. Therefore if they commit any sins, God is less angry with them.

Objection 3: Further, this present life is not carried through without sin, according to James 3:2, "In many things we all offend." Therefore if the sins of religious were more grievous than those of seculars it would follow that religious are worse off than seculars: and consequently it would not be a wholesome counsel to enter religion.

On the contrary, The greater the evil the more it would seem to be deplored. But seemingly the sins of those who are in the state of holiness and perfection are the most deplorable, for it is written (Jer. 23:9): "My heart is broken within me," and afterwards (Jer. 23:11): "For the prophet and the priest are defiled; and in My house I have found their wickedness." Therefore religious and others who are in the state of perfection, other things being equal, sin more grievously.

I answer that, A sin committed by a religious may be in three ways more grievous than a like sin committed by a secular. First, if it be against his religious vow; for instance if he be guilty of fornication or theft, because by fornication he acts against the vow of continence, and by theft against the vow of poverty; and not merely against a precept of the divine law. Secondly, if he sin out of contempt, because thereby he would seem to be the more ungrateful for the divine favors which have raised him to the state of perfection. Thus the Apostle says (Heb. 10:29) that the believer "deserveth worse punishments" who through contempt tramples under foot the Son of God. Hence the Lord complains (Jer. 11:15): "What is the meaning that My beloved hath wrought much wickedness in My house?" Thirdly, the sin of a religious may be greater on account of scandal, because many take note of his manner of life: wherefore it is written (Jer. 23:14): "I have seen the likeness of adulterers, and the way of lying in the Prophets of Jerusalem; and they strengthened the hands of the wicked, that no man should return from his evil doings."

On the other hand, if a religious, not out of contempt, but out of weakness or ignorance, commit a sin that is not against the vow of his profession, without giving scandal (for instance if he commit it in secret) he sins less grievously in the same kind of sin than a secular, because his sin if slight is absorbed as it were by his many good works, and if it be mortal, he more easily recovers from it. First, because he has a right intention towards God, and though it be intercepted for the moment, it is easily restored to its former object. Hence Origen commenting on Ps. 36:24, "When he shall fall he shall not be bruised," says (Hom. iv in Ps. 36): "The wicked man, if he sin, repents not, and fails to make amends for his sin. But the just man knows how to make amends and recover himself; even as he who had said: 'I know not the man,' shortly afterwards when the Lord had looked on him, knew to shed most bitter tears, and he who from the roof had seen a woman and desired her knew to say: 'I have sinned and done evil before Thee.'" Secondly, he is assisted by his fellow-religious to rise again, according to Eccles. 4:10, "If one fall he shall be supported by the other: woe to him that is alone, for when he falleth he hath none to lift him up."

Reply to Objection 1: The words quoted refer to things done through weakness or ignorance, but not to those that are done out of contempt.

Reply to Objection 2: Josaphat also, to whom these words were addressed, sinned not out of contempt, but out of a certain weakness of human affection.

Reply to Objection 3: The just sin not easily out of contempt; but sometimes they fall into a sin through ignorance or weakness from which they easily arise. If, however, they go so far as to sin out of contempt, they become most wicked and incorrigible, according to the word of Jer. 2:20: "Thou hast broken My yoke, thou hast burst My bands, and thou hast said: 'I will not serve.' For on every high hill and under every green tree thou didst prostitute thyself." Hence Augustine says (Ep. lxxviii ad Pleb. Hippon.): "From the time I began to serve God, even as I scarcely found better men than those who made progress in monasteries, so have I not found worse than those who in the monastery have fallen."

OF THOSE THINGS THAT ARE COMPETENT TO RELIGIOUS (SIX ARTICLES)

We must now consider the things that are competent to religious; and under this head there are six points of inquiry:

(1) Whether it is lawful for them to teach, preach, and do like things?

(2) Whether it is lawful for them to meddle in secular business?

(3) Whether they are bound to manual labor?

(4) Whether it is lawful for them to live on alms?

(5) Whether it is lawful for them to quest?

(6) Whether it is lawful for them to wear coarser clothes than other persons?

Whether it is lawful for religious to teach, preach, and the like?

Objection 1: It would seem unlawful for religious to teach, preach, and the like. For it is said (VII, qu. i, can. Hoc nequaquam) in an ordinance of a synod of Constantinople [*Pseudosynod held by Photius in the year 879]: "The monastic life is one of subjection and discipleship, not of teaching, authority, or pastoral care." And Jerome says (ad Ripar. et Desider. [*Contra Vigilant. xvi]): "A monk's duty is not to teach but to lament." Again Pope Leo [*Leo I, Ep. cxx ad Theodoret., 6, cf. XVI, qu. i, can. Adjicimus]: says "Let none dare to preach save the priests of the Lord, be he monk or layman, and no matter what knowledge he may boast of having." Now it is not lawful to exceed the bounds of one's office or transgress the ordinance of the Church. Therefore seemingly it is unlawful for religious to teach, preach, and the like.

Objection 2: Further, in an ordinance of the Council of Nicea (cf. XVI, qu. i, can. Placuit) it is laid down as follows: "It is our absolute and peremptory command addressed to all that monks shall not hear confessions except of one another, as is right, that they shall not bury the dead except those dwelling with them in the monastery, or if by chance a brother happen to die while on a visit." But just as the above belong to the duty of clerics, so also do preaching and teaching. Therefore since "the business of a monk differs from that of a cleric," as Jerome says (Ep. xiv ad Heliod.), it would seem unlawful for religious to preach, teach, and the like.

Objection 3: Further, Gregory says (Regist. v, Ep. 1): "No man can fulfil ecclesiastical duties, and keep consistently to the monastic rule": and this is quoted XVI, qu. i, can. Nemo potest. Now monks are bound to keep consistently to the monastic rule. Therefore it would seem that they cannot fulfil ecclesiastical duties, whereof teaching and preaching are a part. Therefore seemingly it is unlawful for them to preach, teach, and do similar things.

On the contrary, Gregory is quoted (XVI, qu. i, can. Ex auctoritate) as saying: "By authority of this decree framed in virtue of our apostolic power and the duty of our office, be it lawful to monk priests who are configured to the apostles, to preach, baptize, give communion, pray for sinners, impose penance, and absolve from sin."

I answer that, A thing is declared to be unlawful to a person in two ways. First, because there is something in him contrary to that which is declared unlawful to him: thus to no man is it lawful to sin, because each man has in himself reason and an obligation to God's law, to which things sin is contrary. And in this way it is said to be unlawful for a person to preach, teach, or do like things, because there is in him something incompatible with these things, either by reason of a precept—thus those who are irregular by ordinance of the Church may not be raised to the sacred orders—or by reason of sin, according to Ps. 49:16, "But to the sinner God hath said: Why dost thou declare My justice?"

In this way it is not unlawful for religious to preach, teach, and do like things, both because they are bound neither by vow nor by precept of their rule to abstain from these things, and because they are not rendered less apt for these things by any sin committed, but on the contrary they are the more apt through having taken upon themselves the practice of holiness. For it is foolish to say that a man is rendered less fit for spiritual duties through advancing himself in holiness; and consequently it is foolish to declare that the religious state is an obstacle to the fulfilment of such like duties. This error is rejected by Pope Boniface [*Boniface IV] for the reasons given above. His words which are quoted (XVI, qu. i, can. Sunt. nonnulli) are these: "There are some who without any dogmatic proof, and with extreme daring, inspired with a zeal rather of bitterness than of love, assert that monks though they be dead to the world and live to God, are unworthy of the power of the priestly office, and that they cannot confer penance, nor christen, nor absolve in virtue of the power divinely bestowed on them in the priestly office. But they are altogether wrong." He proves this first because it is not contrary to the rule; thus he continues: "For neither did the Blessed Benedict the saintly teacher of monks forbid this in any way," nor is it forbidden in other rules. Secondly, he refutes the above error from the usefulness of the monks, when he adds at the end of the same chapter: "The more perfect a man is, the more effective is he in these, namely in spiritual works."

Secondly, a thing is said to be unlawful for a man, not on account of there being in him something contrary thereto, but because he lacks that which enables him to do it: thus it is unlawful for a deacon to say mass, because he is not in priestly orders; and it is unlawful for a priest to deliver judgment because he lacks the episcopal authority. Here, however, a distinction must be made. Because those things which are a matter of an order, cannot be deputed to one who has not the order, whereas matters of jurisdiction can be deputed to those who have not ordinary jurisdiction: thus the delivery of a judgment is deputed by the bishop to a simple priest. In this sense it is said to be unlawful for monks and other religious to preach, teach, and so forth, because the religious state does not give them the power to do these things. They can, however, do them if they receive orders, or ordinary jurisdiction, or if matters of jurisdiction be delegated to them.

Reply to Objection 1: It results from the words quoted that the fact of their being monks does not give monks the power to do these things, yet it does not involve in them anything contrary to the performance of these acts.

Reply to Objection 2: Again, this ordinance of the Council of Nicea forbids monks to claim the power of exercising those acts on the ground of their being monks, but it does not forbid those acts being delegated to them.

Reply to Objection 3: These two things are incompatible, namely, the ordinary cure of ecclesiastical duties, and the observance of the monastic rule in a monastery. But this does not prevent monks and other religious from being sometimes occupied with ecclesiastical duties through being deputed thereto by superiors having ordinary cure; especially members of religious orders that are especially instituted for that purpose, as we shall say further on ([3805]Q[188], A[4]).

Whether it is lawful for religious to occupy themselves with secular business?

Objection 1: It would seem unlawful for religious to occupy themselves with secular business. For in the decree quoted above [3806](A[1]) of Pope Boniface it is said that the "Blessed Benedict bade them to be altogether free from secular business; and this is most explicitly prescribed by the apostolic doctrine and the teaching of all the Fathers, not only to religious, but also to all the canonical clergy," according to 2 Tim. 2:4, "No man being a soldier to God, entangleth himself with secular business." Now it is the duty of all religious to be soldiers of God. Therefore it is unlawful for them to occupy themselves with secular business.

Objection 2: Further, the Apostle says (1 Thess. 4:11): "That you use your endeavor to be quiet, and that you do your own business," which a gloss explains thus—"by refraining from other people's affairs, so as to be the better able to attend to the amendment of your own life." Now religious devote themselves in a special way to the amendment of their life. Therefore they should not occupy themselves with secular business.

Objection 3: Further, Jerome, commenting on Mat. 11:8, "Behold they that are clothed in soft garments are in the houses of kings," says: "Hence we gather that an austere life and severe preaching should avoid the palaces of kings and the mansions of the voluptuous." But the needs of secular business induce men to frequent the palaces of kings. Therefore it is unlawful for religious to occupy themselves with secular business.

On the contrary, The Apostle says (Rom. 16:1): "I commend to you Phoebe our Sister," and further on (Rom. 16:2), "that you assist her in whatsoever business she shall have need of you."

I answer that, As stated above ([3807]Q[186], AA[1],7, ad 1), the religious state is directed to the attainment of the perfection of charity, consisting principally in the love of God and secondarily in the love of our neighbor. Consequently that which religious intend chiefly and for its own sake is to give themselves to God. Yet if their neighbor be in need, they should attend to his affairs out of charity, according to Gal. 6:2, "Bear ye one another's burthens: and so you shall fulfil the law of Christ," since through serving their neighbor for God's sake, they are obedient to the divine love. Hence it is written (James 1:27): "Religion clean and undefiled before God and the Father, is this: to visit the fatherless and widows in their tribulation," which means, according to a gloss, to assist the helpless in their time of need.

We must conclude therefore that it is unlawful for either monks or clerics to carry on secular business from motives of avarice; but from motives of charity, and with their superior's permission, they may occupy themselves with due moderation in the administration and direction of secular business. Wherefore it is said in the Decretals (Dist. xxxviii, can. Decrevit): "The holy synod decrees that henceforth no cleric shall buy property or occupy himself with secular business, save with a view to the care of the fatherless, orphans, or widows, or when the bishop of the city commands him to take charge of the business connected with the Church." And the same applies to religious as to clerics, because they are both debarred from secular business on the same grounds, as stated above.

Reply to Objection 1: Monks are forbidden to occupy themselves with secular business from motives of avarice, but not from motives of charity.

Reply to Objection 2: To occupy oneself with secular business on account of another's need is not officiousness but charity.

Reply to Objection 3: To haunt the palaces of kings from motives of pleasure, glory, or avarice is not becoming to religious, but there is nothing unseemly in their visiting them from motives of piety. Hence it is written (4 Kings 4:13): "Hast thou any business, and wilt thou that I speak to the king or to the general of the army?" Likewise it becomes religious to go to the palaces of kings to rebuke and guide them, even as John the Baptist rebuked Herod, as related in Mat. 14:4.

Whether religious are bound to manual labor?

Objection 1: It would seem that religious are bound to manual labor. For religious are not exempt from the observance of precepts. Now manual labor is a matter of precept according to 1 Thess. 4:11, "Work with your own hands as we commanded you"; wherefore Augustine says (De oper. Monach. xxx): "But who can allow these insolent men," namely religious that do no work, of whom he is speaking there, "who disregard the most salutary admonishment of the Apostle, not merely to be borne with as being weaker than others, but even to preach as though they were holier than others." Therefore it would seem that religious are bound to manual labor.

Objection 2: Further, a gloss [*St. Augustine, (De oper. Monach. xxi)] on 2 Thess. 3:10, "If any man will not work, neither let him eat," says: "Some say that this command of the Apostle refers to spiritual works, and not to the bodily labor of the farmer or craftsman"; and further on: "But it is useless for them to try to hide from themselves and from others the fact that they are unwilling not only to fulfil, but even to understand the useful admonishments of charity"; and again: "He wishes God's servants to make a living by working with their bodies." Now religious especially are called servants of God, because they give themselves entirely to the service of God, as Dionysius asserts (Eccl. Hier. vi). Therefore it would seem that they are bound to manual labor.

Objection 3: Further, Augustine says (De oper. Monach. xvii): "I would fain know how they would occupy themselves, who are unwilling to work with their body. We occupy our time, say they, with prayers, psalms, reading, and the word of God." Yet these things are no excuse, and he proves this, as regards each in particular. For in the first place, as to prayer, he says: "One prayer of the obedient man is sooner granted than ten thousand prayers of the contemptuous": meaning that those are contemptuous and unworthy to be heard who work not with their hands. Secondly, as to the divine praises he adds: "Even while working with their hands they can easily sing hymns to God." Thirdly, with regard to reading, he goes on to say: "Those who say they are occupied in reading, do they not find there what the Apostle commanded? What sort of perverseness is this, to wish to read but not to obey what one reads?" Fourthly, he adds in reference to preaching [*Cap. xviii]: "If one has to speak, and is so busy that he cannot spare time for manual work, can all in the monastery do this? And since all cannot do this, why should all make this a pretext for being exempt? And even if all were able, they should do so by turns, not only so that the others may be occupied in other works, but also because it suffices that one speak while many listen." Therefore it would seem that religious should not desist from manual labor on account of such like spiritual works to which they devote themselves.

Objection 4: Further, a gloss on Lk. 12:33, "Sell what you possess," says: "Not only give your clothes to the poor, but sell what you possess, that having once for all renounced all your possessions for the Lord's sake, you may henceforth work with the labor of your hands, so as to have wherewith to live or to give alms." Now it belongs properly to religious to renounce all they have. Therefore it would seem likewise to belong to them to live and give alms through the labor of their hands.

Objection 5: Further, religious especially would seem to be bound to imitate the life of the apostles, since they profess the state of perfection. Now the apostles worked with their own hands, according to 1 Cor. 4:12: "We labor, working with our own hands." Therefore it would seem that religious are bound to manual labor.

On the contrary, Those precepts that are commonly enjoined upon all are equally binding on religious and seculars. But the precept of manual labor is enjoined upon all in common, as appears from 2 Thess. 3:6, "Withdraw yourselves from every brother walking disorderly," etc. (for by brother he signifies every Christian, according to 1 Cor. 7:12, "If any brother have a wife that believeth not"). Now it is written in the same passage (2 Thess. 3:10): "If any man will not work, neither let him eat." Therefore religious are not bound to manual labor any more than seculars are.

I answer that, Manual labor is directed to four things. First and principally to obtain food; wherefore it was said to the first man (Gn. 3:19): "In the sweat of thy face shalt thou eat bread," and it is written (Ps. 127:2): "For thou shalt eat the labors of thy hands." Secondly, it is directed to the removal of idleness whence arise many evils; hence it is written (Ecclus. 33:28,29): "Send" thy slave "to work, that he be not idle, for idleness hath taught much evil." Thirdly, it is directed to the curbing of concupiscence, inasmuch as it is a means of afflicting the body; hence it is written (2 Cor. 6:5,6): "In labors, in watchings, in fastings, in chastity." Fourthly, it is directed to almsgiving, wherefore it is written (Eph. 4:28): "He that stole, let him now steal no more; but rather let him labor, working with his hands the thing which is good, that he may have something to give to him that suffereth need." Accordingly, in so far as manual labor is directed to obtaining food, it comes under a necessity of precept in so far as it is necessary for that end: since that which is directed to an end derives its necessity from that end, being, in effect, so far necessary as the end cannot be obtained without it. Consequently he who has no other means of livelihood is bound to work with his hands, whatever his condition may be. This is signified by the words of the Apostle: "If any man will not work, neither let him eat," as though to say: "The necessity of manual labor is the necessity of meat." So that if one could live without eating, one would not be bound to work with one's hands. The same applies to those who have no other lawful means of livelihood: since a man is understood to be unable to do what he cannot do lawfully. Wherefore we find that the Apostle prescribed manual labor merely as a remedy for the sin of those who gained their livelihood by unlawful means. For the Apostle ordered manual labor first of all in order to avoid theft, as appears from Eph. 4:28, "He that stole, let him now steal no more; but rather let him labor, working with his hands." Secondly, to avoid the coveting of others' property, wherefore it is written (1 Thess. 4:11): "Work with your own hands, as we commanded you, and that you walk honestly towards them that are without." Thirdly, to avoid the discreditable pursuits whereby some seek a livelihood. Hence he says (2 Thess. 3:10–12): "When we were with you, this we declared to you: that if any man will not work, neither let him eat. For we have heard that there are some among you who walk disorderly, working not at all, but curiously meddling" (namely, as a gloss explains it, "who make a living by meddling in unlawful things). Now we charge them that are such, and beseech them . . . that working with silence, they would eat their own bread." Hence Jerome states (Super epist. ad Galat. [*Preface to Bk. ii of Commentary]) that the Apostle said this "not so much in his capacity of teacher as on account of the faults of the people."

It must, however, be observed that under manual labor are comprised all those human occupations whereby man can lawfully gain a livelihood, whether by using his hands, his feet, or his tongue. For watchmen, couriers, and such like who live by their labor, are understood to live by their handiwork: because, since the hand is "the organ of organs" [*De Anima iii, 8], handiwork denotes all kinds of work, whereby a man may lawfully gain a livelihood.

In so far as manual labor is directed to the removal of idleness, or the affliction of the body, it does not come under a necessity of precept if we consider it in itself, since there are many other means besides manual labor of afflicting the body or of removing idleness: for the flesh is afflicted by fastings and watchings, and idleness is removed by meditation on the Holy Scriptures and by the divine praises. Hence a gloss on Ps. 118:82, "My eyes have failed for Thy word," says: "He is not idle who meditates only on God's word; nor is he who works abroad any better than he who devotes himself to the study of knowing the truth." Consequently for these reasons religious are not bound to manual labor, as neither are seculars, except when they are so bound by the statutes of their order. Thus Jerome says (Ep. cxxv ad Rustic Monach.): "The Egyptian monasteries are wont to admit none unless they work or labor, not so much for the necessities of life, as for the welfare of the soul, lest it be led astray by wicked thoughts." But in so far as manual labor is directed to almsgiving, it does not come under the necessity of precept, save perchance in some particular case, when a man is under an obligation to give alms, and has no other means of having the wherewithal to assist the poor: for in such a case religious would be bound as well as seculars to do manual labor.

Reply to Objection 1: This command of the Apostle is of natural law: wherefore a gloss on 2 Thess. 3:6, "That you withdraw yourselves from every brother walking disorderly," says, "otherwise than the natural order requires," and he is speaking of those who abstained from manual labor. Hence nature has provided man with hands instead of arms and clothes, with which she has provided other animals, in order that with his hands he may obtain these and all other necessaries. Hence it is clear that this precept, even as all the precepts of the natural law, is binding on both religious and seculars alike. Yet not everyone sins that works not with his hands, because those precepts of the natural law which regard the good of the many are not binding on each individual, but it suffices that one person apply himself to this business and another to that; for instance, that some be craftsmen, others husbandmen, others judges, and others teachers, and so forth, according to the words of the Apostle (1 Cor. 12:17), "If the whole body were the eye, where would be the hearing? If the whole were the hearing, where would be the smelling?"

Reply to Objection 2: This gloss is taken from Augustine's De operibus Monachorum, cap. 21, where he speaks against certain monks who declared it to be unlawful for the servants of God to work with their hands, on account of our Lord's saying (Mat. 6:25): "Be not solicitous for your life, what you shall eat." Nevertheless his words do not imply that religious are bound to work with their hands, if they have other means of livelihood. This is clear from his adding: "He wishes the servants of God to make a living by working with their bodies." Now this does not apply to religious any more than to seculars, which is evident for two reasons. First, on account of the way in which the Apostle expresses himself, by saying: "That you withdraw yourselves from every brother walking disorderly." For he calls all Christians brothers, since at that time religious orders were not as yet founded. Secondly, because religious have no other obligations than what seculars have, except as required by the rule they profess: wherefore if their rule contain nothing about manual labor, religious are not otherwise bound to manual labor than seculars are.

Reply to Objection 3: A man may devote himself in two ways to all the spiritual works mentioned by Augustine in the passage quoted: in one way with a view to the common good, in another with a view to his private advantage. Accordingly those who devote themselves publicly to the aforesaid spiritual works are thereby exempt from manual labor for two reasons: first, because it behooves them to be occupied exclusively with such like works; secondly, because those who devote themselves to such works have a claim to be supported by those for whose advantage they work.

On the other hand, those who devote themselves to such works not publicly but privately as it were, ought not on that account to be exempt from manual labor, nor have they a claim to be supported by the offerings of the faithful, and it is of these that Augustine is speaking. For when he says: "They can sing hymns to God even while working with their hands; like the craftsmen who give tongue to fable telling without withdrawing their hands from their work," it is clear that he cannot refer to those who sing the canonical hours in the church, but to those who tell psalms or hymns as private prayers. Likewise what he says of reading and prayer is to be referred to the private prayer and reading which even lay people do at times, and not to those who perform public prayers in the church, or give public lectures in the schools. Hence he does not say: "Those who say they are occupied in teaching and instructing," but: "Those who say they are occupied in reading." Again he speaks of that preaching which is addressed, not publicly to the people, but to one or a few in particular by way of private admonishment. Hence he says expressly: "If one has to speak." For according to a gloss on 1 Cor. 2:4, "Speech is addressed privately, preaching to many."

Reply to Objection 4: Those who despise all for God's sake are bound to work with their hands, when they have no other means of livelihood, or of almsgiving (should the case occur where almsgiving were a matter of precept), but not otherwise, as stated in the Article. It is in this sense that the gloss quoted is to be understood.

Reply to Objection 5: That the apostles worked with their hands was sometimes a matter of necessity, sometimes a work of supererogation. It was of necessity when they failed to receive a livelihood from others. Hence a gloss on 1 Cor. 4:12, "We labor, working with our own hands," adds, "because no man giveth to us." It was supererogation, as appears from 1 Cor. 9:12, where the Apostle says that he did not use the power he had of living by the Gospel. The Apostle had recourse to this supererogation for three motives. First, in order to deprive the false apostles of the pretext for preaching, for they preached merely for a temporal advantage; hence he says (2 Cor. 11:12): "But what I do, that I will do that I may cut off the occasion from them," etc. Secondly, in order to avoid burdening those to whom he preached; hence he says (2 Cor. 12:13): "What is there that you have had less than the other churches, but that I myself was not burthensome to you?" Thirdly, in order to give an example of work to the idle; hence he says (2 Thess. 3:8,9): "We worked night and day . . . that we might give ourselves a pattern unto you, to imitate us." However, the Apostle did not do this in places like Athens where he had facilities for preaching daily, as Augustine observes (De oper. Monach. xviii). Yet religious are not for this reason bound to imitate the Apostle in this matter, since they are not bound to all works of supererogation: wherefore neither did the other apostles work with their hands.

Whether it is lawful for religious to live on alms?

Objection 1: It would seem unlawful for religious to live on alms. For the Apostle (1 Tim. 5:16) forbids those widows who have other means of livelihood to live on the alms of the Church, so that the Church may have "sufficient for them that are widows indeed." And Jerome says to Pope Damasus [*Cf. Cf. Can. Clericos, cause. i, qu. 2; Can. Quoniam, cause xvi, qu. 1; Regul. Monach. iv among the supposititious works of St. Jerome] that "those who have sufficient income from their parents and their own possessions, if they take what belongs to the poor they commit and incur the guilt of sacrilege, and by the abuse of such things they eat and drink judgment to themselves." Now religious if they be able-bodied can support themselves by the work of their hands. Therefore it would seem that they sin if they consume the alms belonging to the poor.

Objection 2: Further, to live at the expense of the faithful is the stipend appointed to those who preach the Gospel in payment of their labor or work, according to Mat. 10:10: "The workman is worthy of his meat." Now it belongs not to religious to preach the Gospel, but chiefly to prelates who are pastors and teachers. Therefore religious cannot lawfully live on the alms of the faithful.

Objection 3: Further, religious are in the state of perfection. But it is more perfect to give than to receive alms; for it is written (Acts 20:35): "It is a more blessed thing to give, rather than to receive." Therefore they should not live on alms, but rather should they give alms of their handiwork.

Objection 4: Further, it belongs to religious to avoid obstacles to virtue and occasions of sin. Now the receiving of alms offers an occasion of sin, and hinders an act of virtue; hence a gloss on 2 Thess. 3:9, "That we might give ourselves a pattern unto you," says: "He who through idleness eats often at another's table, must needs flatter the one who feeds him." It is also written (Ex. 23:8): "Neither shalt thou take bribes which . . . blind the wise, and pervert the words of the just," and (Prov. 22:7): "The borrower is servant to him that lendeth." This is contrary to religion, wherefore a gloss on 2 Thess. 3:9, "That we might give ourselves a pattern," etc., says, "our religion calls men to liberty." Therefore it would seem that religious should not live on alms.

Objection 5: Further, religious especially are bound to imitate the perfection of the apostles; wherefore the Apostle says (Phil. 3:15): "Let us . . . as many as are perfect, be thus minded." But the Apostle was unwilling to live at the expense of the faithful, either in order to cut off the occasion from the false apostles as he himself says (2 Cor. 11:12), or to avoid giving scandal to the weak, as appears from 1 Cor. 9:12. It would seem therefore that religious ought for the same reasons to refrain from living on alms. Hence Augustine says (De oper. Monach. 28): "Cut off the occasion of disgraceful marketing whereby you lower yourselves in the esteem of others, and give scandal to the weak: and show men that you seek not an easy livelihood in idleness, but the kingdom of God by the narrow and strait way."

On the contrary, Gregory says (Dial. ii, 1): The Blessed Benedict after leaving his home and parents dwelt for three years in a cave, and while there lived on the food brought to him by a monk from Rome. Nevertheless, although he was able-bodied, we do not read that he sought to live by the labor of his hands. Therefore religious may lawfully live on alms.

I answer that, A man may lawfully live on what is his or due to him. Now that which is given out of liberality becomes the property of the person to whom it is given. Wherefore religious and clerics whose monasteries or churches have received from the munificence of princes or of any of the faithful any endowment whatsoever for their support, can lawfully live on such endowment without working with their hands, and yet without doubt they live on alms. Wherefore in like manner if religious receive movable goods from the faithful they can lawfully live on them. For it is absurd to say that a person may accept an alms of some great property but not bread or some small sum of money. Nevertheless since these gifts would seem to be bestowed on religious in order that they may have more leisure for religious works, in which the donors of temporal goods wish to have a share, the use of such gifts would become unlawful for them if they abstained from religious works, because in that case, so far as they are concerned, they would be thwarting the intention of those who bestowed those gifts.

A thing is due to a person in two ways. First, on account of necessity, which makes all things common, as Ambrose [*Basil, Serm. de Temp. lxiv, among the supposititious works of St. Ambrose] asserts. Consequently if religious be in need they can lawfully live on alms. Such necessity may occur in three ways. First, through weakness of body, the result being that they are unable to make a living by working with their hands. Secondly, because that which they gain by their handiwork is insufficient for their livelihood: wherefore Augustine says (De oper. Monach. xvii) that "the good works of the faithful should not leave God's servants who work with their hands without a supply of necessaries, that when the hour comes for them to nourish their souls, so as to make it impossible for them to do these corporal works, they be not oppressed by want." Thirdly, because of the former mode of life of those who were unwont to work with their hands: wherefore Augustine says (De oper. Monach. xxi) that "if they had in the world the wherewithal easily to support this life without working, and gave it to the needy when they were converted to God, we must credit their weakness and bear with it." For those who have thus been delicately brought up are wont to be unable to bear the toil of bodily labor.

In another way a thing becomes due to a person through his affording others something whether temporal or spiritual, according to 1 Cor. 9:11, "If we have sown unto you spiritual things, is it a great matter if we reap your carnal things?" And in this sense religious may live on alms as being due to them in four ways. First, if they preach by the authority of the prelates. Secondly, if they be ministers of the altar, according to 1 Cor. 9:13,14, "They that serve the altar partake with the altar. So also the lord ordained that they who preach the Gospel should live by the Gospel." Hence Augustine says (De oper. Monach. xxi): "If they be gospelers, I allow, they have" (a claim to live at the charge of the faithful): "if they be ministers of the altar and dispensers of the sacraments, they need not insist on it, but it is theirs by perfect right." The reason for this is because the sacrament of the altar wherever it be offered is common to all the faithful. Thirdly, if they devote themselves to the study of Holy Writ to the common profit of the whole Church. Wherefore Jerome says (Contra Vigil. xiii): "It is still the custom in Judea, not only among us but also among the Hebrews, for those who meditate on the law of the Lord day and night, end have no other share on earth but God alone, to be supported by the subscriptions of the synagogues and of the whole world." Fourthly, if they have endowed the monastery with the goods they possessed, they may live on the alms given to the monastery. Hence Augustine says (De oper. Monach. xxv) that "those who renouncing or distributing their means, whether ample or of any amount whatever, have desired with pious and salutary humility to be numbered among the poor of Christ, have a claim on the community and on brotherly love to receive a livelihood in return. They are to be commended indeed if they work with their hands, but if they be unwilling, who will dare to force them? Nor does it matter, as he goes on to say, to which monasteries, or in what place any one of them has bestowed his goods on his needy brethren; for all Christians belong to one commonwealth."

On the other hand, in the default of any necessity, or of their affording any profit to others, it is unlawful for religious to wish to live in idleness on the alms given to the poor. Hence Augustine says (De oper. Monach. xxii): "Sometimes those who enter the profession of God's service come from a servile condition of life, from tilling the soil or working at some trade or lowly occupation. In their case it is not so clear whether they came with the purpose of serving God, or of evading a life of want and toil with a view to being fed and clothed in idleness, and furthermore to being honored by those by whom they were wont to be despised and downtrodden. Such persons surely cannot excuse themselves from work on the score of bodily weakness, for their former mode of life is evidence against them." And he adds further on (De oper. Monach. xxv): "If they be unwilling to work, neither let them eat. For if the rich humble themselves to piety, it is not that the poor may be exalted to pride; since it is altogether unseemly that in a life wherein senators become laborers, laborers should become idle, and that where the lords of the manor have come after renouncing their ease, the serfs should live in comfort."

Reply to Objection 1: These authorities must be understood as referring to cases of necessity, that is to say, when there is no other means of succoring the poor: for then they would be bound not only to refrain from accepting alms, but also to give what they have for the support of the needy.

Reply to Objection 2: Prelates are competent to preach in virtue of their office, but religious may be competent to do so in virtue of delegation; and thus when they work in the field of the Lord, they may make their living thereby, according to 2 Tim. 2:6, "The husbandman that laboreth must first partake of the fruits," which a gloss explains thus, "that is to say, the preacher, who in the field of the Church tills the hearts of his hearers with the plough of God's word." Those also who minister to the preachers may live on alms. Hence a gloss on Rom. 15:27, "If the Gentiles have been made partakers of their spiritual things, they ought also in carnal things to minister to them," says, "namely, to the Jews who sent preachers from Jerusalem." There are moreover other reasons for which a person has a claim to live at the charge of the faithful, as stated above.

Reply to Objection 3: Other things being equal, it is more perfect to give than to receive. Nevertheless to give or to give up all one's possessions for Christ's sake, and to receive a little for one's livelihood is better than to give to the poor part by part, as stated above ([3808]Q[186], A[3], ad 6).

Reply to Objection 4: To receive gifts so as to increase one's wealth, or to accept a livelihood from another without having a claim to it, and without profit to others or being in need oneself, affords an occasion of sin. But this does not apply to religious, as stated above.

Reply to Objection 5: Whenever there is evident necessity for religious living on alms without doing any manual work, as well as an evident profit to be derived by others, it is not the weak who are scandalized, but those who are full of malice like the Pharisees, whose scandal our Lord teaches us to despise (Mat. 15:12–14). If, however, these motives of necessity and profit be lacking, the weak might possibly be scandalized thereby; and this should be avoided. Yet the same scandal might be occasioned through those who live in idleness on the common revenues.

Whether it is lawful for religious to beg?

Objection 1: It would seem unlawful for religious to beg. For Augustine says (De oper. Monach. xxviii): "The most cunning foe has scattered on all sides a great number of hypocrites wearing the monastic habit, who go wandering about the country," and afterwards he adds: "They all ask, they all demand to be supported in their profitable penury, or to be paid for a pretended holiness." Therefore it would seem that the life of mendicant religious is to be condemned.

Objection 2: Further, it is written (1 Thess. 4:11): "That you . . . work with your own hands as we commanded you, and that you walk honestly towards them that are without: and that you want nothing of any man's": and a gloss on this passage says: "You must work and not be idle, because work is both honorable and a light to the unbeliever: and you must not covet that which belongs to another and much less beg or take anything." Again a gloss [*St. Augustine, (De oper. Monach. iii)] on 2 Thess. 3:10, "If any man will not work," etc. says: "He wishes the servants of God to work with the body, so as to gain a livelihood, and not be compelled by want to ask for necessaries." Now this is to beg. Therefore it would seem unlawful to beg while omitting to work with one's hands.

Objection 3: Further, that which is forbidden by law and contrary to justice, is unbecoming to religious. Now begging is forbidden in the divine law; for it is written (Dt. 15:4): "There shall be no poor nor beggar among you," and (Ps. 36:25): "I have not seen the just forsaken, nor his seed seeking bread." Moreover an able-bodied mendicant is punished by civil law, according to the law (XI, xxvi, de Valid. Mendicant.). Therefore it is unfitting for religious to beg.

Objection 4: Further, "Shame is about that which is disgraceful," as Damascene says (De Fide Orth. ii, 15). Now Ambrose says (De Offic. i, 30) that "to be ashamed to beg is a sign of good birth." Therefore it is disgraceful to beg: and consequently this is unbecoming to religious.

Objection 5: Further, according to our Lord's command it is especially becoming to preachers of the Gospel to live on alms, as stated above [3809](A[4]). Yet it is not becoming that they should beg, since a gloss on 2 Tim. 2:6, "The husbandman, that laboreth," etc. says: "The Apostle wishes the gospeler to understand that to accept necessaries from those among whom he labors is not mendicancy but a right." Therefore it would seem unbecoming for religious to beg.

On the contrary, It becomes religious to live in imitation of Christ. Now Christ was a mendicant, according to Ps. 39:18, "But I am a beggar and poor"; where a gloss says: "Christ said this of Himself as bearing the 'form of a servant,'" and further on: "A beggar is one who entreats another, and a poor man is one who has not enough for himself." Again it is written (Ps. 69:6): "I am needy and poor"; where a gloss says: "'Needy,' that is a suppliant; 'and poor,' that is, not having enough for myself, because I have no worldly wealth." And Jerome says in a letter [*Reference unknown]: "Beware lest whereas thy Lord," i.e. Christ, "begged, thou amass other people's wealth." Therefore it becomes religious to beg.

I answer that, Two things may be considered in reference to mendicancy. The first is on the part of the act itself of begging, which has a certain abasement attaching to it; since of all men those would seem most abased who are not only poor, but are so needy that they have to receive their meat from others. In this way some deserve praise for begging out of humility, just as they abase themselves in other ways, as being the most efficacious remedy against pride which they desire to quench either in themselves or in others by their example. For just as a disease that arises from excessive heat is most efficaciously healed by things that excel in cold, so proneness to pride is most efficaciously healed by those things which savor most of abasement. Hence it is said in the Decretals (II, cap. Si quis semel, de Paenitentia): "To condescend to the humblest duties, and to devote oneself to the lowliest service is an exercise of humility; for thus one is able to heal the disease of pride and human glory." Hence Jerome praises Fabiola (Ep. lxxvii ad ocean.) for that she desired "to receive alms, having poured forth all her wealth for Christ's sake." The Blessed Alexis acted in like manner, for, having renounced all his possessions for Christ's sake he rejoiced in receiving alms even from his own servants. It is also related of the Blessed Arsenius in the Lives of the Fathers (v, 6) that he gave thanks because he was forced by necessity to ask for alms. Hence it is enjoined to some people as a penance for grievous sins to go on a pilgrimage begging. Since, however, humility like the other virtues should not be without discretion, it behooves one to be discreet in becoming a mendicant for the purpose of humiliation, lest a man thereby incur the mark of covetousness or of anything else unbecoming. Secondly, mendicancy may be considered on the part of that which one gets by begging: and thus a man may be led to beg by a twofold motive. First, by the desire to have wealth or meat without working for it, and such like mendicancy is unlawful; secondly, by a motive of necessity or usefulness. The motive is one of necessity if a man has no other means of livelihood save begging; and it is a motive of usefulness if he wishes to accomplish something useful, and is unable to do so without the alms of the faithful. Thus alms are besought for the building of a bridge, or church, or for any other work whatever that is conducive to the common good: thus scholars may seek alms that they may devote themselves to the study of wisdom. In this way mendicancy is lawful to religious no less than to seculars.

Reply to Objection 1: Augustine is speaking there explicitly of those who beg from motives of covetousness.

Reply to Objection 2: The first gloss speaks of begging from motives of covetousness, as appears from the words of the Apostle; while the second gloss speaks of those who without effecting any useful purpose, beg their livelihood in order to live in idleness. on the other hand, he lives not idly who in any way lives usefully.

Reply to Objection 3: This precept of the divine law does not forbid anyone to beg, but it forbids the rich to be so stingy that some are compelled by necessity to beg. The civil law imposes a penalty on able-bodied mendicants who beg from motives neither of utility nor of necessity.

Reply to Objection 4: Disgrace is twofold; one arises from lack of honesty [*Cf.[3810] Q[145], A[1]], the other from an external defect, thus it is disgraceful for a man to be sick or poor. Such like uncomeliness of mendicancy does not pertain to sin, but it may pertain to humility, as stated above.

Reply to Objection 5: Preachers have the right to be fed by those to whom they preach: yet if they wish to seek this by begging so as to receive it as a free gift and not as a right this will be a mark of greater humility.

Whether it is lawful for religious to wear coarser clothes than others?

Objection 1: It would seem unlawful for religious to wear coarser clothes than others. For according to the Apostle (1 Thess. 5:22) we ought to "refrain from all appearance of evil." Now coarseness of clothes has an appearance of evil; for our Lord said (Mat. 7:15): "Beware of false prophets who come to you in the clothing of sheep": and a gloss on Apoc. 6:8, "Behold a pale horse," says: "The devil finding that he cannot succeed, neither by outward afflictions nor by manifest heresies, sends in advance false brethren, who under the guise of religion assume the characteristics of the black and red horses by corrupting the faith." Therefore it would seem that religious should not wear coarse clothes.

Objection 2: Further, Jerome says (Ep. lii ad Nepotian.): "Avoid somber," i.e. black, "equally with glittering apparel. Fine and coarse clothes are equally to be shunned, for the one exhales pleasure, the other vainglory." Therefore, since vainglory is a graver sin than the use of pleasure, it would seem that religious who should aim at what is more perfect ought to avoid coarse rather than fine clothes.

Objection 3: Further, religious should aim especially at doing works of penance. Now in works of penance we should use, not outward signs of sorrow, but rather signs of joy; for our Lord said (Mat. 6:16): "When you fast, be not, as the hypocrites, sad," and afterwards He added: "But thou, when thou fastest, anoint thy head and wash thy face." Augustine commenting on these words (De Serm. Dom. in Monte ii, 12): "In this chapter we must observe that not only the glare and pomp of outward things, but even the weeds of mourning may be a subject of ostentation, all the more dangerous as being a decoy under the guise of God's service." Therefore seemingly religious ought not to wear coarse clothes.

On the contrary, The Apostle says (Heb. 11:37): "They wandered about in sheepskins in goat-skins," and a gloss adds—"as Elias and others." Moreover it is said in the Decretal XXI, qu. iv, can. Omnis jactantia: "If any persons be found to deride those who wear coarse and religious apparel they must be reproved. For in the early times all those who were consecrated to God went about in common and coarse apparel."

I answer that, As Augustine says (De Doctr. Christ. iii, 12), "in all external things, it is not the use but the intention of the user that is at fault." In order to judge of this it is necessary to observe that coarse and homely apparel may be considered in two ways. First, as being a sign of a man's disposition or condition, because according to Ecclus. 19:27, "the attire . . . of the man" shows "what he is." In this way coarseness of attire is sometimes a sign of sorrow: wherefore those who are beset with sorrow are wont to wear coarser clothes, just as on the other hand in times of festivity and joy they wear finer clothes. Hence penitents make use of coarse apparel, for example, the king (Jonah 3:6) who "was clothed with sack-cloth," and Achab (3 Kings 21:27) who "put hair-cloth upon his flesh." Sometimes, however, it is a sign of the contempt of riches and worldly ostentation. Wherefore Jerome says (Ep. cxxv ad Rustico Monach.): "Let your somber attire indicate your purity of mind, your coarse robe prove your contempt of the world, yet so that your mind be not inflated withal, lest your speech belie your habit." In both these ways it is becoming for religious to wear coarse attire, since religion is a state of penance and of contempt of worldly glory.

But that a person wish to signify this to others arises from three motives. First, in order to humble himself: for just as a man's mind is uplifted by fine clothes, so is it humbled by lowly apparel. Hence speaking of Achab who "put hair-cloth on his flesh," the Lord said to Elias: "Hast thou not seen Achab humbled before Me?" (3 Kings 21:29). Secondly, in order to set an example to others; wherefore a gloss on Mat. 3:4, "(John) had his garments of camel's hair," says: "He who preaches penance is clothed in the habit of penance." Thirdly, on account of vainglory; thus Augustine says (cf. OBJ[3]) that "even the weeds of mourning may be a subject of ostentation."

Accordingly in the first two ways it is praiseworthy to wear humble apparel, but in the third way it is sinful.

Secondly, coarse and homely attire may be considered as the result of covetousness or negligence, and thus also it is sinful.

Reply to Objection 1: Coarseness of attire has not of itself the appearance of evil, indeed it has more the appearance of good, namely of the contempt of worldly glory. Hence it is that wicked persons hide their wickedness under coarse clothing. Hence Augustine says (De Serm. Dom. in Monte ii, 24) that "the sheep should not dislike their clothing for the reason that the wolves sometimes hide themselves under it."

Reply to Objection 2: Jerome is speaking there of the coarse attire that is worn on account of human glory.

Reply to Objection 3: According to our Lord's teaching men should do no deeds of holiness for the sake of show: and this is especially the case when one does something strange. Hence Chrysostom [*Hom. xiii in Matth. in the Opus Imperfectum, falsely ascribed to St. John Chrysostom] says: "While praying a man should do nothing strange, so as to draw the gaze of others, either by shouting or striking his breast, or casting up his hands," because the very strangeness draws people's attention to him. Yet blame does not attach to all strange behavior that draws people's attention, for it may be done well or ill. Hence Augustine says (De Serm. Dom. in Monte ii, 12) that "in the practice of the Christian religion when a man draws attention to himself by unwonted squalor and shabbiness, since he acts thus voluntarily and not of necessity, we can gather from his other deeds whether his behavior is motivated by contempt of excessive dress or by affectation." Religious, however, would especially seem not to act thus from affectation, since they wear a coarse habit as a sign of their profession whereby they profess contempt of the world.

OF THE DIFFERENT KINDS OF RELIGIOUS LIFE (EIGHT ARTICLES)

We must now consider the different kinds of religious life, and under this head there are eight points of inquiry:

(1) Whether there are different kinds of religious life or only one?

(2) Whether a religious order can be established for the works of the active life?

(3) Whether a religious order can be directed to soldiering?

(4) Whether a religious order can be established for preaching and the exercise of like works?

(5) Whether a religious order can be established for the study of science?

(6) Whether a religious order that is directed to the contemplative life is more excellent than one that is directed to the active life?

(7) Whether religious perfection is diminished by possessing something in common?

(8) Whether the religious life of solitaries is to be preferred to the religious life of those who live in community?

Whether there is only one religious order?

Objection 1: It would seem that there is but one religious order. For there can be no diversity in that which is possessed wholly and perfectly; wherefore there can be only one sovereign good, as stated in the [3811]FP, Q[6] , AA[2],3,4. Now as Gregory says (Hom. xx in Ezech.), "when a man vows to Almighty God all that he has, all his life, all his knowledge, it is a holocaust," without which there is no religious life. Therefore it would seem that there are not many religious orders but only one.

Objection 2: Further, things which agree in essentials differ only accidentally. Now there is no religious order without the three essential vows of religion, as stated above ([3812]Q[186], AA[6],7). Therefore it would seem that religious orders differ not specifically, but only accidentally.

Objection 3: Further, the state of perfection is competent both to religious and to bishops, as stated above ([3813]Q[185], AA[5],7). Now the episcopate is not diversified specifically, but is one wherever it may be; wherefore Jerome says (Ep. cxlvi ad Evan.): "Wherever a bishop is, whether at Rome, or Gubbio, or Constantinople, or Reggio, he has the same excellence, the same priesthood." Therefore in like manner there is but one religious order.

Objection 4: Further, anything that may lead to confusion should be removed from the Church. Now it would seem that a diversity of religious orders might confuse the Christian people, as stated in the Decretal de Statu Monach. et Canon. Reg. [*Cap. Ne Nimia, de Relig. Dom.]. Therefore seemingly there ought not to be different religious orders.

On the contrary, It is written (Ps. 44:10) that it pertains to the adornment of the queen that she is "surrounded with variety."

I answer that, As stated above (Q[186], A, 7;[3814] Q[187], A[2]), the religious state is a training school wherein one aims by practice at the perfection of charity. Now there are various works of charity to which a man may devote himself; and there are also various kinds of exercise. Wherefore religious orders may be differentiated in two ways. First, according to the different things to which they may be directed: thus one may be directed to the lodging of pilgrims, another to visiting or ransoming captives. Secondly, there may be various religious orders according to the diversity of practices; thus in one religious order the body is chastised by abstinence in food, in another by the practice of manual labor, scantiness of clothes, or the like.

Since, however, the end imports most in every matter, [*Arist., Topic. vi 8] religious orders differ more especially according to their various ends than according to their various practices.

Reply to Objection 1: The obligation to devote oneself wholly to God's service is common to every religious order; hence religious do not differ in this respect, as though in one religious order a person retained some one thing of his own, and in another order some other thing. But the difference is in respect of the different things wherein one may serve God, and whereby a man may dispose himself to the service of God.

Reply to Objection 2: The three essential vows of religion pertain to the practice of religion as principles to which all other matters are reduced, as stated above ([3815]Q[186], A[7]). But there are various ways of disposing oneself to the observance of each of them. For instance one disposes oneself to observe the vow of continence, by solitude of place, by abstinence, by mutual fellowship, and by many like means. Accordingly it is evident that the community of the essential vows is compatible with diversity of religious life, both on account of the different dispositions and on account of the different ends, as explained above.

Reply to Objection 3: In matters relating to perfection, the bishop stands in the position of agent, and the religious as passive, as stated above ([3816]Q[184], A[7]). Now the agent, even in natural things, the higher it is, is so much the more one, whereas the things that are passive are various. Hence with reason the episcopal state is one, while religious orders are many.

Reply to Objection 4: Confusion is opposed to distinction and order. Accordingly the multitude of religious orders would lead to confusion, if different religious orders were directed to the same end and in the same way, without necessity or utility. Wherefore to prevent this happening it has been wholesomely forbidden to establish a new religious order without the authority of the Sovereign Pontiff.

Whether a religious order should be established for the works of the active life?

Objection 1: It would seem that no religious order should be established for the works of the active life. For every religious order belongs to the state of perfection, as stated above ([3817]Q[184], A[5];[3818] Q[186], A[1]). Now the perfection of the religious state consists in the contemplation of divine things. For Dionysius says (Eccl. Hier. vi) that they are "called servants of God by reason of their rendering pure service and subjection to God, and on account of the indivisible and singular life which unites them by holy reflections," i.e. contemplations, "on invisible things, to the Godlike unity and the perfection beloved of God." Therefore seemingly no religious order should be established for the works of the active life.

Objection 2: Further, seemingly the same judgment applies to canons regular as to monks, according to Extra, De Postul., cap. Ex parte; and De Statu Monach., cap. Quod Dei timorem: for it is stated that "they are not considered to be separated from the fellowship of monks": and the same would seem to apply to all other religious. Now the monastic rule was established for the purpose of the contemplative life; wherefore Jerome says (Ep. lviii ad Paulin.): "If you wish to be what you are called, a monk," i.e. a solitary, "what business have you in a city?" The same is found stated in Extra, De Renuntiatione, cap. Nisi cum pridem; and De Regular., cap. Licet quibusdam. Therefore it would seem that every religious order is directed to the contemplative life, and none to the active life.

Objection 3: Further, the active life is concerned with the present world. Now all religious are said to renounce the world; wherefore Gregory says (Hom. xx in Ezech.): "He who renounces this world, and does all the good he can, is like one who has gone out of Egypt and offers sacrifice in the wilderness." Therefore it would seem that no religious order can be directed to the active life.

On the contrary, It is written (James 1:27): "Religion clean and undefiled before God and the Father, is this: to visit the fatherless and widows in their tribulation." Now this belongs to the active life. Therefore religious life can be fittingly directed to the active life.

I answer that, As stated above [3819](A[1]), the religious state is directed to the perfection of charity, which extends to the love of God and of our neighbor. Now the contemplative life which seeks to devote itself to God alone belongs directly to the love of God, while the active life, which ministers to our neighbor's needs, belongs directly to the love of one's neighbor. And just as out of charity we love our neighbor for God's sake, so the services we render our neighbor redound to God, according to Mat. 25:40, "What you have done [Vulg.: 'As long as you did it'] to one of these My least brethren, you did it to Me." Consequently those services which we render our neighbor, in so far as we refer them to God, are described as sacrifices, according to Heb. 13:16, "Do not forget to do good and to impart, for by such sacrifices God's favor is obtained." And since it belongs properly to religion to offer sacrifice to God, as stated above (Q[81], A[1], ad 1; A[4], ad 1), it follows that certain religious orders are fittingly directed to the works of the active life. Wherefore in the Conferences of the Fathers (Coll. xiv, 4) the Abbot Nesteros in distinguishing the various aims of religious orders says: "Some direct their intention exclusively to the hidden life of the desert and purity of heart; some are occupied with the instruction of the brethren and the care of the monasteries; while others delight in the service of the guesthouse," i.e. in hospitality.

Reply to Objection 1: Service and subjection rendered to God are not precluded by the works of the active life, whereby a man serves his neighbor for God's sake, as stated in the Article. Nor do these works preclude singularity of life; not that they involve man's living apart from his fellow-men, but in the sense that each man individually devotes himself to things pertaining to the service of God; and since religious occupy themselves with the works of the active life for God's sake, it follows that their action results from their contemplation of divine things. Hence they are not entirely deprived of the fruit of the contemplative life.

Reply to Objection 2: The same judgment applies to monks and to all other religious, as regards things common to all religious orders: for instance as regards their devoting themselves wholly to the divine service, their observance of the essential vows of religion, and their refraining from worldly business. But it does not follow that this likeness extends to other things that are proper to the monastic profession, and are directed especially to the contemplative life. Hence in the aforesaid Decretal, De Postulando, it is not simply stated that "the same judgment applies to canons regular" as "to monks," but that it applies "in matters already mentioned," namely that "they are not to act as advocates in lawsuits." Again the Decretal quoted, De Statu Monach., after the statement that "canons regular are not considered to be separated from the fellowship of monks," goes on to say: "Nevertheless they obey an easier rule." Hence it is evident that they are not bound to all that monks are bound.

Reply to Objection 3: A man may be in the world in two ways: in one way by his bodily presence, in another way by the bent of his mind. Hence our Lord said to His disciples (Jn. 15:19): "I have chosen you out of the world," and yet speaking of them to His Father He said (Jn. 17:11): "These are in the world, and I come to Thee." Although, then, religious who are occupied with the works of the active life are in the world as to the presence of the body, they are not in the world as regards their bent of mind, because they are occupied with external things, not as seeking anything of the world, but merely for the sake of serving God: for "they . . . use this world, as if they used it not," to quote 1 Cor. 7:31. Hence (James 1:27) after it is stated that "religion clean and undefiled . . . is . . . to visit the fatherless and widows in their tribulation," it is added, "and to keep one's self unspotted from this world," namely to avoid being attached to worldly things.

Whether a religious order can be directed to soldiering?

Objection 1: It would seem that no religious order can be directed to soldiering. For all religious orders belong to the state of perfection. Now our Lord said with reference to the perfection of Christian life (Mat. 5:39): "I say to you not to resist evil; but if one strike thee on the right cheek, turn to him also the other," which is inconsistent with the duties of a soldier. Therefore no religious order can be established for soldiering.

Objection 2: Further, the bodily encounter of the battlefield is more grievous than the encounter in words that takes place between counsel at law. Yet religious are forbidden to plead at law, as appears from the Decretal De Postulando quoted above (A[2], OBJ[2]). Therefore it is much less seemly for a religious order to be established for soldiering.

Objection 3: Further, the religious state is a state of penance, as we have said above ([3820]Q[187], A[6]). Now according to the code of laws soldiering is forbidden to penitents. for it is said in the Decretal De Poenit., Dist. v, cap. 3: "It is altogether opposed to the rules of the Church, to return to worldly soldiering after doing penance." Therefore it is unfitting for any religious order to be established for soldiering.

Objection 4: Further, no religious order may be established for an unjust object. But as Isidore says (Etym. xviii, 1), "A just war is one that is waged by order of the emperor." Since then religious are private individuals, it would seem unlawful for them to wage war; and consequently no religious order may be established for this purpose.

On the contrary, Augustine says (Ep. clxxxix; ad Bonifac.), "Beware of thinking that none of those can please God who handle war-like weapons. Of such was holy David to whom the Lord gave great testimony." Now religious orders are established in order that men may please God. Therefore nothing hinders the establishing of a religious order for the purpose of soldiering.

I answer that, As stated above [3821](A[2]), a religious order may be established not only for the works of the contemplative life, but also for the works of the active life, in so far as they are concerned in helping our neighbor and in the service of God, but not in so far as they are directed to a worldly object. Now the occupation of soldiering may be directed to the assistance of our neighbor, not only as regards private individuals, but also as regards the defense of the whole commonwealth. Hence it is said of Judas Machabeus (1 Macc. 3:2,3) that "he [Vulg.: 'they'] fought with cheerfulness the battle of Israel, and he got his people great honor." It can also be directed to the upkeep of divine worship, wherefore (1 Macc. 3:21) Judas is stated to have said: "We will fight for our lives and our laws," and further on (1 Macc. 13:3) Simon said: "You know what great battles I and my brethren, and the house of my father, have fought for the laws and the sanctuary."

Hence a religious order may be fittingly established for soldiering, not indeed for any worldly purpose, but for the defense of divine worship and public safety, or also of the poor and oppressed, according to Ps. 81:4: "Rescue the poor, and deliver the needy out of the hand of the sinner."

Reply to Objection 1: Not to resist evil may be understood in two ways. First, in the sense of forgiving the wrong done to oneself, and thus it may pertain to perfection, when it is expedient to act thus for the spiritual welfare of others. Secondly, in the sense of tolerating patiently the wrongs done to others: and this pertains to imperfection, or even to vice, if one be able to resist the wrongdoer in a becoming manner. Hence Ambrose says (De Offic. i, 27): "The courage whereby a man in battle defends his country against barbarians, or protects the weak at home, or his friends against robbers is full of justice": even so our Lord says in the passage quoted [*Lk. 6:30 "Of him that taketh away thy goods, ask them not again"; Cf. Mat. 5:40], " . . . thy goods, ask them not again." If, however, a man were not to demand the return of that which belongs to another, he would sin if it were his business to do so: for it is praiseworthy to give away one's own, but not another's property. And much less should the things of God be neglected, for as Chrysostom [*Hom. v in Matth. in the Opus Imperfectum, falsely ascribed to St. John Chrysostom] says, "it is most wicked to overlook the wrongs done to God."

Reply to Objection 2: It is inconsistent with any religious order to act as counsel at law for a worldly object, but it is not inconsistent to do so at the orders of one's superior and in favor of one's monastery, as stated in the same Decretal, or for the defense of the poor and widows. Wherefore it is said in the Decretals (Dist. lxxxviii, cap. 1): "The holy synod has decreed that henceforth no cleric is to buy property or occupy himself with secular business, save with a view to the care of the fatherless . . . and widows." Likewise to be a soldier for the sake of some worldly object is contrary to all religious life, but this does not apply to those who are soldiers for the sake of God's service.

Reply to Objection 3: Worldly soldiering is forbidden to penitents, but the soldiering which is directed to the service of God is imposed as a penance on some people, as in the case of those upon whom it is enjoined to take arms in defense of the Holy Land.

Reply to Objection 4: The establishment of a religious order for the purpose of soldiering does not imply that the religious can wage war on their own authority; but they can do so only on the authority of the sovereign or of the Church.

Whether a religious order can be established for preaching or hearing confessions?

Objection 1: It would seem that no religious order may be established for preaching, or hearing confessions. For it is said (VII, qu. i [*Cap. Hoc nequaquam; Cf.[3822] Q[187], A[1], OBJ[1]]): "The monastic life is one of subjection and discipleship, not of teaching, authority, or pastoral care," and the same apparently applies to religious. Now preaching and hearing confessions are the actions of a pastor and teacher. Therefore a religious order should not be established for this purpose.

Objection 2: Further, the purpose for which a religious order is established would seem to be something most proper to the religious life, as stated above

[3823](A[1]). Now the aforesaid actions are not proper to religious but to bishops. Therefore a religious order should not be established for the purpose of such actions.

Objection 3: Further, it seems unfitting that the authority to preach and hear confessions should be committed to an unlimited number of men; and there is no fixed number of those who are received into a religious order. Therefore it is unfitting for a religious order to be established for the purpose of the aforesaid actions.

Objection 4: Further, preachers have a right to receive their livelihood from the faithful of Christ, according to 1 Cor. 9. If then the office of preaching be committed to a religious order established for that purpose, it follows that the faithful of Christ are bound to support an unlimited number of persons, which would be a heavy burden on them. Therefore a religious order should not be established for the exercise of these actions.

Objection 5: Further, the organization of the Church should be in accordance with Christ's institution. Now Christ sent first the twelve apostles to preach, as related in Luke 9, and afterwards He sent the seventy-two disciples, as stated in Luke 10. Moreover, according to the gloss of Bede on "And after these things" (Lk. 10:1), "the apostles are represented by the bishops, the seventy-two disciples by the lesser priests," i.e. the parish priests. Therefore in addition to bishops and parish priests, no religious order should be established for the purpose of preaching and hearing confessions.

On the contrary, In the Conferences of the Fathers (Coll. xiv, 4), Abbot Nesteros, speaking of the various kinds of religious orders, says: "Some choosing the care of the sick, others devoting themselves to the relief of the afflicted and oppressed, or applying themselves to teaching, or giving alms to the poor, have been most highly esteemed on account of their devotion and piety." Therefore just as a religious order may be established for the care of the sick, so also may one be established for teaching the people by preaching and like works.

I answer that, As stated above [3824](A[2]), it is fitting for a religious order to be established for the works of the active life, in so far as they are directed to the good of our neighbor, the service of God, and the upkeep of divine worship. Now the good of our neighbor is advanced by things pertaining to the spiritual welfare of the soul rather than by things pertaining to the supplying of bodily needs, in proportion to the excellence of spiritual over corporal things. Hence it was stated above (Q[32], A[3]) that spiritual works of mercy surpass corporal works of mercy. Moreover this is more pertinent to the service of God, to Whom no sacrifice is more acceptable than zeal for souls, as Gregory says (Hom. xii in Ezech.). Furthermore, it is a greater thing to employ spiritual arms in defending the faithful against the errors of heretics and the temptations of the devil, than to protect the faithful by means of bodily weapons. Therefore it is most fitting for a religious order to be established for preaching and similar works pertaining to the salvation of souls.

Reply to Objection 1: He who works by virtue of another, acts as an instrument. And a minister is like an "animated instrument," as the Philosopher says (Polit. i, 2 [*Cf. Ethic. viii, 11]). Hence if a man preach or do something similar by the authority of his superiors, he does not rise above the degree of "discipleship" or "subjection," which is competent to religious.

Reply to Objection 2: Some religious orders are established for soldiering, to wage war, not indeed on their own authority, but on that of the sovereign or of the Church who are competent to wage war by virtue of their office, as stated above (A[3], ad 4). In the same way certain religious orders are established for preaching and hearing confessions, not indeed by their own authority, but by the authority of the higher and lower superiors, to whom these things belong by virtue of their office. Consequently to assist one's superiors in such a ministry is proper to a religious order of this kind.

Reply to Objection 3: Bishops do not allow these religious severally and indiscriminately to preach or hear confessions, but according to the discretion of the religious superiors, or according to their own appointment.

Reply to Objection 4: The faithful are not bound by law to contribute to the support of other than their ordinary prelates, who receive the tithes and offerings of the faithful for that purpose, as well as other ecclesiastical revenues. But if some men are willing to minister to the faithful by exercising the aforesaid acts gratuitously, and without demanding payment as of right, the faithful are not burdened thereby because their temporal contributions can be liberally repaid by those men, nor are they bound by law to contribute, but by charity, and yet not so that they be burdened thereby and others eased, as stated in 2 Cor. 8:13. If, however, none be found to devote themselves gratuitously to services of this kind, the ordinary prelate is bound, if he cannot suffice by himself, to seek other suitable persons and support them himself.

Reply to Objection 5: The seventy-two disciples are represented not only by the parish priests, but by all those of lower order who in any way assist the bishops in their office. For we do not read that our Lord appointed the seventy-two disciples to certain fixed parishes, but that "He sent them two and two before His face into every city and place whither He Himself was to come." It was fitting, however, that in addition to the ordinary prelates others should be chosen for these duties on account of the multitude of the faithful, and the difficulty of finding a sufficient number of persons to be appointed to each locality, just as it was necessary to establish religious orders for military service, on account of the secular princes being unable to cope with unbelievers in certain countries.

Whether a religious order should be established for the purpose of study?

Objection 1: It would seem that a religious order should not be established for the purpose of study. For it is written (Ps. 70:15,16): "Because I have not known letters [Douay: 'learning'], I will enter into the powers of the Lord," i.e. "Christian virtue," according to a gloss. Now the perfection of Christian virtue, seemingly, pertains especially to religious. Therefore it is not for them to apply themselves to the study of letters.

Objection 2: Further, that which is a source of dissent is unbecoming to religious, who are gathered together in the unity of peace. Now study leads to dissent: wherefore different schools of thought arose among the philosophers. Hence Jerome (Super Epist. ad Tit. 1:5) says: "Before a diabolical instinct brought study into religion, and people said: I am of Paul, I of Apollo, I of Cephas," etc. Therefore it would seem that no religious order should be established for the purpose of study.

Objection 3: Further, those who profess the Christian religion should profess nothing in common with the Gentiles. Now among the Gentiles were some who professed philosophy, and even now some secular persons are known as professors of certain sciences. Therefore the study of letters does not become religious.

On the contrary, Jerome (Ep. liii ad Paulin.) urges him to acquire learning in the monastic state, saying: "Let us learn on earth those things the knowledge of which will remain in heaven," and further on: "Whatever you seek to know, I will endeavor to know with you."

I answer that As stated above [3825](A[2]), religion may be ordained to the active and to the contemplative life. Now chief among the works of the active life are those which are directly ordained to the salvation of souls, such as preaching and the like. Accordingly the study of letters is becoming to the religious life in three ways. First, as regards that which is proper to the contemplative life, to which the study of letters helps in a twofold manner. In one way by helping directly to contemplate, namely by enlightening the intellect. For the contemplative life of which we are now speaking is directed chiefly to the consideration of divine things, as stated above (Q[180], A[4]), to which consideration man is directed by study; for which reason it is said in praise of the righteous (Ps. 1:2) that "he shall meditate day and night" on the law of the Lord, and (Ecclus. 39:1): "The wise man will seek out the wisdom of all the ancients, and will be occupied in the prophets." In another way the study of letters is a help to the contemplative life indirectly, by removing the obstacles to contemplation, namely the errors which in the contemplation of divine things frequently beset those who are ignorant of the scriptures. Thus we read in the Conferences of the Fathers (Coll. x, 3) that the Abbot Serapion through simplicity fell into the error of the Anthropomorphites, who thought that God had a human shape. Hence Gregory says (Moral. vi) that "some through seeking in contemplation more than they are able to grasp, fall away into perverse doctrines, and by failing to be the humble disciples of truth become the masters of error." Hence it is written (Eccles. 2:3): "I thought in my heart to withdraw my flesh from wine, that I might turn my mind to wisdom and might avoid folly."

Secondly, the study of letters is necessary in those religious orders that are founded for preaching and other like works; wherefore the Apostle (Titus 1:9), speaking of bishops to whose office these acts belong, says: "Embracing that faithful word which is according to doctrine, that he may be able to exhort in sound doctrine and to convince the gainsayers." Nor does it matter that the apostles were sent to preach without having studied letters, because, as Jerome says (Ep. liii ad Paulin.), "whatever others acquire by exercise and daily meditation in God's law, was taught them by the Holy Ghost."

Thirdly, the study of letters is becoming to religious as regards that which is common to all religious orders. For it helps us to avoid the lusts of the flesh; wherefore Jerome says (Ep. cxxv ad Rust. Monach.): "Love the science of the Scriptures and thou shalt have no love for carnal vice." For it turns the mind away from lustful thoughts, and tames the flesh on account of the toil that study entails according to Ecclus. 31:1, "Watching for riches* consumeth the flesh." [*Vigilia honestatis St. Thomas would seem to have taken 'honestas' in the sense of virtue]. It also helps to remove the desire of riches, wherefore it is written (Wis. 7:8): "I . . . esteemed riches nothing in comparison with her," and (1 Macc. 12:9): "We needed none of these things," namely assistance from without, "having for our comfort the holy books that are in our hands." It also helps to teach obedience, wherefore Augustine says (De oper. Monach. xvii): "What sort of perverseness is this, to wish to read, but not to obey what one reads?" Hence it is clearly fitting that a religious order be established for the study of letters.

Reply to Objection 1: This commentary of the gloss is an exposition of the Old Law of which the Apostle says (2 Cor. 3:6): "The letter killeth." Hence not to know letters is to disapprove of the circumcision of the "letter" and other carnal observances.

Reply to Objection 2: Study is directed to knowledge which, without charity, "puffeth up," and consequently leads to dissent, according to Prov. 13:10, "Among the proud there are always dissensions": whereas, with charity, it "edifieth and begets concord." Hence the Apostle after saying (1 Cor. 1:5): "You are made rich . . . in all utterance and in all knowledge," adds (1 Cor. 1:10): "That you all speak the same thing, and that there be no schisms among you." But Jerome is not speaking here of the study of letters, but of the study of dissensions which heretics and schismatics have brought into the Christian religion.

Reply to Objection 3: The philosophers professed the study of letters in the matter of secular learning: whereas it becomes religious to devote themselves chiefly to the study of letters in reference to the doctrine that is "according to godliness" (Titus 1:1). It becomes not religious, whose whole life is devoted to the service of God, to seek for other learning, save in so far as it is referred to the sacred doctrine. Hence Augustine says at the end of De Musica vi, 17: "Whilst we think that we should not overlook those whom heretics delude by the deceitful assurance of reason and knowledge, we are slow to advance in the consideration of their methods. Yet we should not be praised for doing this, were it not that many holy sons of their most loving mother the Catholic Church had done the same under the necessity of confounding heretics."

Whether a religious order that is devoted to the contemplative life is more excellent than on that is given to the active life?

Objection 1: It would seem that a religious order which is devoted to the contemplative life is not more excellent than one which is given to the active life. For it is said (Extra, de Regular. et Transeunt. ad Relig., cap. Licet), quoting the words of Innocent III: "Even as a greater good is preferred to a lesser, so the common profit takes precedence of private profit: and in this case teaching is rightly preferred to silence, responsibility to contemplation, work to rest." Now the religious order which is directed to the greater good is better. Therefore it would seem that those religious orders that are directed to the active life are more excellent than those which are directed to the contemplative life.

Objection 2: Further, every religious order is directed to the perfection of charity, as stated above ([3826]AA[1],2). Now a gloss on Heb. 12:4, "For you have not yet resisted unto blood," says: "In this life there is no more perfect love than that to which the holy martyrs attained, who fought against sin unto blood." Now to fight unto blood is becoming those religious who are directed to military service, and yet this pertains to the active life. Therefore it would seem that religious orders of this kind are the most excellent.

Objection 3: Further, seemingly the stricter a religious order is, the more excellent it is. But there is no reason why certain religious orders directed to the active life should not be of stricter observance than those directed to the contemplative life. Therefore they are more excellent.

On the contrary, our Lord said (Lk. 10:42) that the "best part" was Mary's, by whom the contemplative life is signified.

I answer that, As stated above [3827](A[1]), the difference between one religious order and another depends chiefly on the end, and secondarily on the exercise. And since one thing cannot be said to be more excellent than another save in respect of that in which it differs therefrom, it follows that the excellence of one religious order over another depends chiefly on their ends, and secondarily on their respective exercises. Nevertheless each of these comparisons is considered in a different way. For the comparison with respect to the end is absolute, since the end is sought for its own sake; whereas the comparison with respect to exercise is relative, since exercise is sought not for its own sake, but for the sake of the end. Hence a religious order is preferable to another, if it be directed to an end that is absolutely more excellent either because it is a greater good or because it is directed to more goods. If, however, the end be the same, the excellence of one religious order over another depends secondarily, not on the amount of exercise, but on the proportion of the exercise to the end in view. Wherefore in the Conferences of the Fathers (Coll. ii, 2) Blessed Antony is quoted, as preferring discretion whereby a man moderates all his actions, to fastings, watchings, and all such observances.

Accordingly we must say that the work of the active life is twofold. one proceeds from the fulness of contemplation, such as teaching and preaching. Wherefore Gregory says (Hom. v in Ezech.) that the words of Ps. 144:7, "They shall publish the memory of . . . Thy sweetness," refer "to perfect men returning from their contemplation." And this work is more excellent than simple contemplation. For even as it is better to enlighten than merely to shine, so is it better to give to others the fruits of one's contemplation than merely to contemplate. The other work of the active life consists entirely in outward occupation, for instance almsgiving, receiving guests, and the like, which are less excellent than the works of contemplation, except in cases of necessity, as stated above ([3828]Q[182], A[1]). Accordingly the highest place in religious orders is held by those which are directed to teaching and preaching, which, moreover, are nearest to the episcopal perfection, even as in other things "the end of that which is first is in conjunction with the beginning of that which is second," as Dionysius states (Div. Nom. vii). The second place belongs to those which are directed to contemplation, and the third to those which are occupied with external actions.

Moreover, in each of these degrees it may be noted that one religious order excels another through being directed to higher action in the same genus; thus among the works of the active life it is better to ransom captives than to receive guests, and among the works of the contemplative life prayer is better than study. Again one will excel another if it be directed to more of these actions than another, or if it have statutes more adapted to the attainment of the end in view.

Reply to Objection 1: This Decretal refers to the active life as directed to the salvation of souls.

Reply to Objection 2: Those religious orders that are established for the purpose of military service aim more directly at shedding the enemy's blood than at the shedding of their own, which latter is more properly competent to martyrs. Yet there is no reason why religious of this description should not acquire the merit of martyrdom in certain cases, and in this respect stand higher than other religious; even as in some cases the works of the active life take precedence of contemplation.

Reply to Objection 3: Strictness of observances, as the Blessed Antony remarks (Conferences of the Fathers; Coll. ii, 2), is not the chief object of commendation in a religious order; and it is written (Is. 58:5): "Is this such a fast as I have chosen, for a man to afflict his soul for a day?" Nevertheless it is adopted in religious life as being necessary for taming the flesh, "which if done without discretion, is liable to make us fail altogether," as the Blessed Antony observes. Wherefore a religious order is not more excellent through having stricter observances, but because its observances are directed by greater discretion to the end of religion. Thus the taming of the flesh is more efficaciously directed to continence by means of abstinence in meat and drink, which pertain to hunger and thirst, than by the privation of clothing, which pertains to cold and nakedness, or by bodily labor.

Whether religious perfection is diminished by possessing something in common?

Objection 1: It would seem that religious perfection is diminished by possessing something in common. For our Lord said (Mat. 19:21): "If thou wilt be perfect, go sell all [Vulg.: 'what'] thou hast and give to the poor." Hence it is clear that to lack worldly wealth belongs to the perfection of Christian life. Now those who possess something in common do not lack worldly wealth. Therefore it would seem that they do not quite reach to the perfection of Christian life.

Objection 2: Further, the perfection of the counsels requires that one should be without worldly solicitude; wherefore the Apostle in giving the counsel of virginity said (1 Cor. 7:32): "I would have you to be without solicitude." Now it belongs to the solicitude of the present life that certain people keep something to themselves for the morrow; and this solicitude was forbidden His disciples by our Lord (Mat. 6:34) saying: "Be not . . . solicitous for tomorrow." Therefore it would seem that the perfection of Christian life is diminished by having something in common.

Objection 3: Further, possessions held in common belong in some way to each member of the community; wherefore Jerome (Ep. lx ad Heliod. Episc.) says in reference to certain people: "They are richer in the monastery than they had been in the world; though serving the poor Christ they have wealth which they had not while serving the rich devil; the Church rejects them now that they are rich, who in the world were beggars." But it is derogatory to religious perfection that one should possess wealth of one's own. Therefore it is also derogatory to religious perfection to possess anything in common.

Objection 4: Further, Gregory (Dial. iii, 14) relates of a very holy man named Isaac, that "when his disciples humbly signified that he should accept the possessions offered to him for the use of the monastery, he being solicitous for the safeguarding of his poverty, held firmly to his opinion, saying: A monk who seeks earthly possessions is no monk at all": and this refers to possessions held in common, and which were offered him for the common use of the monastery. Therefore it would seem destructive of religious perfection to possess anything in common.

Objection 5: Further, our Lord in prescribing religious perfection to His disciples, said (Mat. 10:9,10): "Do not possess gold, nor silver, nor money in your purses, nor script for your journey." By these words, as Jerome says in his commentary, "He reproves those philosophers who are commonly called Bactroperatae [*i.e. staff and scrip bearers], who as despising the world and valuing all things at naught carried their pantry about with them." Therefore it would seem derogatory to religious perfection that one should keep something whether for oneself or for the common use.

On the contrary, Prosper [*Julianus Pomerius, among the works of Prosper] says (De Vita Contempl. ix) and his words are quoted (XII, qu. 1, can. Expedit): "It is sufficiently clear both that for the sake of perfection one should renounce having anything of one's own, and that the possession of revenues, which are of course common property, is no hindrance to the perfection of the Church."

I answer that, As stated above ([3829]Q[184], A[3], ad 1;[3830] Q[185], A[6], ad 1), perfection consists, essentially, not in poverty, but in following Christ, according to the saying of Jerome (Super Matth. xix, 27): "Since it is not enough to leave all, Peter adds that which is perfect, namely, 'We have followed Thee,'" while poverty is like an instrument or exercise for the attainment of perfection. Hence in the Conferences of the Fathers (Coll. i, 7) the abbot Moses says: "Fastings, watchings, meditating on the Scriptures, poverty, and privation of all one's possessions are not perfection, but means of perfection."

Now the privation of one's possessions, or poverty, is a means of perfection, inasmuch as by doing away with riches we remove certain obstacles to charity; and these are chiefly three. The first is the cares which riches bring with them; wherefore our Lord said (Mat. 13:22): "That which was sown [Vulg.: 'He that received the seed'] among thorns, is he that heareth the word, and the care of this world, and the deceitfulness of riches, choketh up the word." The second is the love of riches, which increases with the possession of wealth; wherefore Jerome says (Super Matth. xix, 23) that "since it is difficult to despise riches when we have them, our Lord did not say: 'It is impossible for a rich man to enter the kingdom of heaven,' but: 'It is difficult.'" The third is vainglory or elation which results from riches, according to Ps. 48:7, "They that trust in their own strength, and glory in the multitude of their riches."

Accordingly the first of these three cannot be altogether separated from riches whether great or small. For man must needs take a certain amount of care in acquiring or keeping external things. But so long as external things are sought or possessed only in a small quantity, and as much as is required for a mere livelihood, such like care does not hinder one much; and consequently is not inconsistent with the perfection of Christian life. For our Lord did not forbid all care, but only such as is excessive and hurtful; wherefore Augustine, commenting on Mat. 6:25, "Be not solicitous for your life, what you shall eat," says (De Serm. in Monte [*The words quoted are from De Operibus Monach. xxvi]): "In saying this He does not forbid them to procure these things in so far as they needed them, but to be intent on them, and for their sake to do whatever they are bidden to do in preaching the Gospel." Yet the possession of much wealth increases the weight of care, which is a great distraction to man's mind and hinders him from giving himself wholly to God's service. The other two, however, namely the love of riches and taking pride or glorying in riches, result only from an abundance of wealth.

Nevertheless it makes a difference in this matter if riches, whether abundant or moderate, be possessed in private or in common. For the care that one takes of one's own wealth, pertains to love of self, whereby a man loves himself in temporal matters; whereas the care that is given to things held in common pertains to the love of charity which "seeketh not her own," but looks to the common good. And since religion is directed to the perfection of charity, and charity is perfected in "the love of God extending to contempt of self" [*Augustine, De Civ. Dei xiv, 28], it is contrary to religious perfection to possess anything in private. But the care that is given to common goods may pertain to charity, although it may prove an obstacle to some higher act of charity, such as divine contemplation or the instructing of one's neighbor. Hence it is evident that to have excessive riches in common, whether in movable or in immovable property, is an obstacle to perfection, though not absolutely incompatible with it; while it is not an obstacle to religious perfection to have enough external things, whether movables or immovables, as suffice for a livelihood, if we consider poverty in relation to the common end of religious orders, which is to devote oneself to the service of God. But if we consider poverty in relation to the special end of any religious order, then this end being presupposed, a greater or lesser degree of poverty is adapted to that religious order; and each religious order will be the more perfect in respect of poverty, according as it professes a poverty more adapted to its end. For it is evident that for the purpose of the outward and bodily works of the active life a man needs the assistance of outward things, whereas few are required for contemplation. Hence the Philosopher says (Ethic. x, 8) that "many things are needed for action, and the more so, the greater and nobler the actions are. But the contemplative man requires no such things for the exercise of his act: he needs only the necessaries; other things are an obstacle to his contemplation." Accordingly it is clear that a religious order directed to the bodily actions of the active life, such as soldiering or the lodging of guests, would be imperfect if it lacked common riches; whereas those religious orders which are directed to the contemplative life are the more perfect, according as the poverty they profess burdens them with less care for temporal things. And the care of temporal things is so much a greater obstacle to religious life as the religious life requires a greater care of spiritual things.

Now it is manifest that a religious order established for the purpose of contemplating and of giving to others the fruits of one's contemplation by teaching and preaching, requires greater care of spiritual things than one that is established for contemplation only. Wherefore it becomes a religious order of this kind to embrace a poverty that burdens one with the least amount of care. Again it is clear that to keep what one has acquired at a fitting time for one's necessary use involves the least burden of care. Wherefore a threefold degree of poverty corresponds to the three aforesaid degrees of religious life. For it is fitting that a religious order which is directed to the bodily actions of the active life should have an abundance of riches in common; that the common possession of a religious order directed to contemplation should be more moderate, unless the said religious be bound, either themselves or through others, to give hospitality or to assist the poor; and that those who aim at giving the fruits of their contemplation to others should have their life most exempt from external cares; this being accomplished by their laying up the necessaries of life procured at a fitting time. This, our Lord, the Founder of poverty, taught by His example. For He had a purse which He entrusted to Judas, and in which were kept the things that were offered to Him, as related in Jn. 12:6.

Nor should it be argued that Jerome (Super Matth. xvii, 26) says: "If anyone object that Judas carried money in the purse, we answer that He deemed it unlawful to spend the property of the poor on His own uses," namely by paying the tax—because among those poor His disciples held a foremost place, and the money in Christ's purse was spent chiefly on their needs. For it is stated (Jn. 4:8) that "His disciples were gone into the city to buy meats," and (Jn. 13:29) that the disciples "thought, because Judas had the purse, that Jesus had said to him: But those things which we have need of for the festival day, or that he should give something to the poor." From this it is evident that to keep money by, or any other common property for the support of religious of the same order, or of any other poor, is in accordance with the perfection which Christ taught by His example. Moreover, after the resurrection, the disciples from whom all religious orders took their origin kept the price of the lands, and distributed it according as each one had need (Acts 4:34,35).

Reply to Objection 1: As stated above ([3831]Q[184], A[3], ad 1), this saying of our Lord does not mean that poverty itself is perfection, but that it is the means of perfection. Indeed, as shown above ([3832]Q[186], A[8]), it is the least of the three chief means of perfection; since the vow of continence excels the vow of poverty, and the vow of obedience excels them both. Since, however, the means are sought not for their own sake, but for the sake of the end, a thing is better, not for being a greater instrument, but for being more adapted to the end. Thus a physician does not heal the more the more medicine he gives, but the more the medicine is adapted to the disease. Accordingly it does not follow that a religious order is the more perfect, according as the poverty it professes is more perfect, but according as its poverty is more adapted to the end both common and special. Granted even that the religious order which exceeds others in poverty be more perfect in so far as it is poorer, this would not make it more perfect simply. For possibly some other religious order might surpass it in matters relating to continence, or obedience, and thus be more perfect simply, since to excel in better things is to be better simply.

Reply to Objection 2: Our Lord's words (Mat. 6:34), "Be not solicitous for tomorrow," do not mean that we are to keep nothing for the morrow; for the Blessed Antony shows the danger of so doing, in the Conferences of the Fathers (Coll. ii, 2), where he says: "It has been our experience that those who have attempted to practice the privation of all means of livelihood, so as not to have the wherewithal to procure themselves food for one day, have been deceived so unawares that they were unable to finish properly the work they had undertaken." And, as Augustine says (De oper. Monach. xxiii), "if this saying of our Lord, 'Be not solicitous for tomorrow,' means that we are to lay nothing by for the morrow, those who shut themselves up for many days from the sight of men, and apply their whole mind to a life of prayer, will be unable to provide themselves with these things." Again he adds afterwards: "Are we to suppose that the more holy they are, the less do they resemble the birds?" And further on (De oper. Monach. xxiv): "For if it be argued from the Gospel that they should lay nothing by, they answer rightly: Why then did our Lord have a purse, wherein He kept the money that was collected? Why, in days long gone by, when famine was imminent, was grain sent to the holy fathers? Why did the apostles thus provide for the needs of the saints?"

Accordingly the saying: "Be not solicitous for tomorrow," according to Jerome (Super Matth.) is to be rendered thus: "It is enough that we think of the present; the future being uncertain, let us leave it to God": according to Chrysostom [*Hom. xvi in the Opus Imperfectum, falsely ascribed to St. John Chrysostom], "It is enough to endure the toil for necessary things, labor not in excess for unnecessary things": according to Augustine (De Serm. Dom. in Monte ii, 17): "When we do any good action, we should bear in mind not temporal things which are denoted by the morrow, but eternal things."

Reply to Objection 3: The saying of Jerome applies where there are excessive riches, possessed in private as it were, or by the abuse of which even the individual members of a community wax proud and wanton. But they do not apply to moderate wealth, set by for the common use, merely as a means of livelihood of which each one stands in need. For it amounts to the same that each one makes use of things pertaining to the necessaries of life, and that these things be set by for the common use.

Reply to Objection 4: Isaac refused to accept the offer of possessions, because he feared lest this should lead him to have excessive wealth, the abuse of which would be an obstacle to religious perfection. Hence Gregory adds (Dial. iii, 14): "He was as afraid of forfeiting the security of his poverty, as the rich miser is careful of his perishable wealth." It is not, however, related that he refused to accept such things as are commonly necessary for the upkeep of life.

Reply to Objection 5: The Philosopher says (Polit. i, 5,6) that bread, wine, and the like are natural riches, while money is artificial riches. Hence it is that certain philosophers declined to make use of money, and employed other things, living according to nature. Wherefore Jerome shows by the words of our Lord, Who equally forbade both, that it comes to the same to have money and to possess other things necessary for life. And though our Lord commanded those who were sent to preach not to carry these things on the way, He did not forbid them to be possessed in common. How these words of our Lord should be understood has been shown above (Q[185], A[6] , ad 2; [3833]FS, Q[108], A[2], ad 3).

Whether the religious life of those who live in community is more perfect than that of those who lead a solitary life?

Objection 1: It would seem that the religious life of those who live in community is more perfect than that of those who lead a solitary life. For it is written (Eccles. 4:9): "It is better . . . that two should be together, than one; for they have the advantage of their society." Therefore the religious life of those who live in community would seem to be more perfect.

Objection 2: Further, it is written (Mat. 18:20): "Where there are two or three gathered together in My name, there am I in the midst of them." But nothing can be better than the fellowship of Christ. Therefore it would seem better to live in community than in solitude.

Objection 3: Further, the vow of obedience is more excellent than the other religious vows; and humility is most acceptable to God. Now obedience and humility are better observed in company than in solitude; for Jerome says (Ep. cxxv ad Rustic. Monach.): "In solitude pride quickly takes man unawares, he sleeps as much as he will, he does what he likes"; whereas when instructing one who lives in community, he says: "You may not do what you will, you must eat what you are bidden to eat, you may possess so much as you receive, you must obey one you prefer not to obey, you must be a servant to your brethren, you must fear the superior of the monastery as God, love him as a father." Therefore it would seem that the religious life of those who live in community is more perfect than that of those who lead a solitary life.

Objection 4: Further, our Lord said (Lk. 11:33): "No man lighteth a candle and putteth it in a hidden place, nor under a bushel." Now those who lead a solitary life are seemingly in a hidden place, and to be doing no good to any man. Therefore it would seem that their religious life is not more perfect.

Objection 5: Further, that which is in accord with man's nature is apparently more pertinent to the perfection of virtue. But man is naturally a social animal, as the Philosopher says (Polit. i, 1). Therefore it would seem that to lead a solitary life is not more perfect than to lead a community life.

On the contrary, Augustine says (De oper. Monach. xxiii) that "those are holier who keep themselves aloof from the approach of all, and give their whole mind to a life of prayer."

I answer that, Solitude, like poverty, is not the essence of perfection, but a means thereto. Hence in the Conferences of the Fathers (Coll. i, 7) the Abbot Moses says that "solitude," even as fasting and other like things, is "a sure means of acquiring purity of heart." Now it is evident that solitude is a means adapted not to action but to contemplation, according to Osee 2:14, "I . . . will lead her into solitude [Douay: 'the wilderness']; and I will speak to her heart." Wherefore it is not suitable to those religious orders that are directed to the works whether corporal or spiritual of the active life; except perhaps for a time, after the example of Christ, Who as Luke relates (6:12), "went out into a mountain to pray; and He passed the whole night in the prayer of God." On the other hand, it is suitable to those religious orders that are directed to contemplation.

It must, however, be observed that what is solitary should be self-sufficing by itself. Now such a thing is one "that lacks nothing," and this belongs to the idea of a perfect thing [*Aristotle, Phys. iii, 6]. Wherefore solitude befits the contemplative who has already attained to perfection. This happens in two ways: in one way by the gift only of God, as in the case of John the Baptist, who was "filled with the Holy Ghost even from his mother's womb" (Lk. 1:11), so that he was in the desert even as a boy; in another way by the practice of virtuous action, according to Heb. 5:14: "Strong meat is for the perfect; for them who by custom have their senses exercised to the discerning of good and evil."

Now man is assisted in this practice by the fellowship of others in two ways. First, as regards his intellect, to the effect of his being instructed in that which he has to contemplate; wherefore Jerome says (ad Rustic. Monach., Ep. cxxv): "It pleases me that you have the fellowship of holy men, and teach not yourself. Secondly, as regards the affections, seeing that man's noisome affections are restrained by the example and reproof which he receives from others; for as Gregory says (Moral. xxx, 23), commenting on the words, "To whom I have given a house in the wilderness" (Job 39:6), "What profits solitude of the body, if solitude of the heart be lacking?" Hence a social life is necessary for the practice of perfection. Now solitude befits those who are already perfect; wherefore Jerome says (ad Rustic. Monach., Ep. cxxv): "Far from condemning the solitary life, we have often commended it. But we wish the soldiers who pass from the monastic school to be such as not to be deterred by the hard noviciate of the desert, and such as have given proof of their conduct for a considerable time.

Accordingly, just as that which is already perfect surpasses that which is being schooled in perfection, so the life of the solitaries, if duly practiced, surpasses the community life. But if it be undertaken without the aforesaid practice, it is fraught with very great danger, unless the grace of God supply that which others acquire by practice, as in the case of the Blessed Antony and the Blessed Benedict.

Reply to Objection 1: Solomon shows that two are better than one, on account of the help which one affords the other either by "lifting him" up, or by "warming him," i.e. giving him spiritual heat (Eccles. 4:10,11). But those who have already attained to perfection do not require this help.

Reply to Objection 2: According to 1 Jn. 4:16, "He that abideth in charity abideth in God and God in him." Wherefore just as Christ is in the midst of those who are united together in the fellowship of brotherly love, so does He dwell in the heart of the man who devotes himself to divine contemplation through love of God.

Reply to Objection 3: Actual obedience is required of those who need to be schooled according to the direction of others in the attainment of perfection; but those who are already perfect are sufficiently "led by the spirit of God" so that they need not to obey others actually. Nevertheless they have obedience in the preparedness of the mind.

Reply to Objection 4: As Augustine says (De Civ. Dei xix, 19), "no one is forbidden to seek the knowledge of truth, for this pertains to a praiseworthy leisure." That a man be placed "on a candlestick," does not concern him but his superiors, and "if this burden is not placed on us," as Augustine goes on to say (De Civ. Dei xix, 19), "we must devote ourselves to the contemplation of truth," for which purpose solitude is most helpful. Nevertheless, those who lead a solitary life are most useful to mankind. Hence, referring to them, Augustine says (De Morib. Eccl. xxxi): "They dwell in the most lonely places, content to live on water and the bread that is brought to them from time to time, enjoying colloquy with God to whom they have adhered with a pure mind. To some they seem to have renounced human intercourse more than is right: but these understand not how much such men profit us by the spirit of their prayers, what an example to us is the life of those whom we are forbidden to see in the body."

Reply to Objection 5: A man may lead a solitary life for two motives. one is because he is unable, as it were, to bear with human fellowship on account of his uncouthness of mind; and this is beast-like. The other is with a view to adhering wholly to divine things; and this is superhuman. Hence the Philosopher says (Polit. i, 1) that "he who associates not with others is either a beast or a god," i.e. a godly man.

OF THE ENTRANCE INTO RELIGIOUS LIFE (TEN ARTICLES)

We must now consider the entrance into religious life. Under this head there are ten points of inquiry:

(1) Whether those who are not practiced in the observance of the commandments should enter religion?

(2) Whether it is lawful for a person to be bound by vow to enter religion?

(3) Whether those who are bound by vow to enter religion are bound to fulfil their vow?

(4) Whether those who vow to enter religion are bound to remain there in perpetuity?

(5) Whether children should be received into religion?

(6) Whether one should be withheld from entering religion through deference to one's parents?

(7) Whether parish priests or archdeacons may enter religion?

(8) Whether one may pass from one religious order to another?

(9) Whether one ought to induce others to enter religion?

(10) Whether serious deliberation with one's relations and friends is requisite for entrance into religion?

Whether those who are not practiced in keeping the commandments should enter religion?

Objection 1: It would seem that none should enter religion but those who are practiced in the observance of the commandments. For our Lord gave the counsel of perfection to the young man who said that he had kept the commandments "from his youth." Now all religious orders originate from Christ. Therefore it would seem that none should be allowed to enter religion but those who are practiced in the observance of the commandments.

Objection 2: Further, Gregory says (Hom. xv in Ezech., and Moral. xxii): "No one comes suddenly to the summit; but he must make a beginning of a good life in the smallest matters, so as to accomplish great things." Now the great things are the counsels which pertain to the perfection of life, while the lesser things are the commandments which belong to common righteousness. Therefore it would seem that one ought not to enter religion for the purpose of keeping the counsels, unless one be already practiced in the observance of the precepts.

Objection 3: Further, the religious state, like the holy orders, has a place of eminence in the Church. Now, as Gregory writes to the bishop Siagrius [*Regist. ix, Ep. 106], "order should be observed in ascending to orders. For he seeks a fall who aspires to mount to the summit by overpassing the steps." [*The rest of the quotation is from Regist. v, Ep. 53, ad Virgil. Episc.]. "For we are well aware that walls when built receive not the weight of the beams until the new fabric is rid of its moisture, lest if they should be burdened with weight before they are seasoned they bring down the whole building" (Dist. xlviii, can. Sicut neophytus). Therefore it would seem that one should not enter religion unless one be practiced in the observance of the precepts.

Objection 4: Further, a gloss on Ps. 130:2, "As a child that is weaned is towards his mother," says: "First we are conceived in the womb of Mother Church, by being taught the rudiments of faith. Then we are nourished as it were in her womb, by progressing in those same elements. Afterwards we are brought forth to the light by being regenerated in baptism. Then the Church bears us as it were in her hands and feeds us with milk, when after baptism we are instructed in good works and are nourished with the milk of simple doctrine while we progress; until having grown out of infancy we leave our mother's milk for a father's control, that is to say, we pass from simple doctrine, by which we are taught the Word made flesh, to the Word that was in the beginning with God." Afterwards it goes on to say: "For those who are just baptized on Holy Saturday are borne in the hands of the Church as it were and fed with milk until Pentecost, during which time nothing arduous is prescribed, no fasts, no rising at midnight. Afterwards they are confirmed by the Paraclete Spirit, and being weaned so to speak, begin to fast and keep other difficult observances. Many, like the heretics and schismatics, have perverted this order by being weaned before the time. Hence they have come to naught." Now this order is apparently perverted by those who enter religion, or induce others to enter religion, before they are practiced in the easier observance of the commandments. Therefore they would seem to be heretics or schismatics.

Objection 5: Further, one should proceed from that which precedes to that which follows after. Now the commandments precede the counsels, because they are more universal, for "the implication of the one by the other is not convertible" [*Categor. ix], since whoever keeps the counsels keeps the commandments, but the converse does not hold. Seeing then that the right order requires one to pass from that which comes first to that which comes after, it follows that one ought not to pass to the observance of the counsels in religion, without being first of all practiced in the observance of the commandments.

On the contrary, Matthew the publican who was not practiced in the observance of the commandments was called by our Lord to the observance of the counsels. For it is stated (Lk. 5:28) that "leaving all things he . . . followed Him." Therefore it is not necessary for a person to be practiced in the observance of the commandments before passing to the perfection of the counsels.

I answer that, As shown above ([3834]Q[188], A[1]), the religious state is a spiritual schooling for the attainment of the perfection of charity. This is accomplished through the removal of the obstacles to perfect charity by religious observances; and these obstacles are those things which attach man's affections to earthly things. Now the attachment of man's affections to earthly things is not only an obstacle to the perfection of charity, but sometimes leads to the loss of charity, when through turning inordinately to temporal goods man turns away from the immutable good by sinning mortally. Hence it is evident that the observances of the religious state, while removing the obstacles to perfect charity, remove also the occasions of sin: for instance, it is clear that fasting, watching, obedience, and the like withdraw man from sins of gluttony and lust and all other manner of sins.

Consequently it is right that not only those who are practiced in the observance of the commandments should enter religion in order to attain to yet greater perfection, but also those who are not practiced, in order the more easily to avoid sin and attain to perfection.

Reply to Objection 1: Jerome (Super Matth. xix, 20) says: "The young man lies when he says: 'All these have I kept from my youth.' For if he had fulfilled this commandment, 'Thou shalt love thy neighbor as thyself,' why did he go away sad when he heard: Go, sell all thou hast and give to the poor?" But this means that he lied as to the perfect observance of this commandment. Hence Origen says (Tract. viii super Matth.) that "it is written in the Gospel according to the Hebrews that when our Lord had said to him: 'Go, sell all thou hast,' the rich man began to scratch his head; and that our Lord said to him: How sayest thou: I have fulfilled the law and the prophets, seeing that it is written in the law: Thou shalt love thy neighbor as thyself? Behold many of thy brethren, children of Abraham, are clothed in filth, and die of hunger, whilst thy house is full of all manner of good things, and nothing whatever hath passed thence to them. And thus our Lord reproves him saying: If thou wilt be perfect, go, etc. For it is impossible to fulfil the commandment which says, Thou shalt love thy neighbor as thyself, and to be rich, especially to have such great wealth." This also refers to the perfect fulfilment of this precept. on the other hand, it is true that he kept the commandments imperfectly and in a general way. For perfection consists chiefly in the observance of the precepts of charity, as stated above ([3835]Q[184], A[3]). Wherefore in order to show that the perfection of the counsels is useful both to the innocent and to sinners, our Lord called not only the innocent youth but also the sinner Matthew. Yet Matthew obeyed His call, and the youth obeyed not, because sinners are converted to the religious life more easily than those who presume on their innocency. It is to the former that our Lord says (Mat. 21:31): "The publicans and the harlots shall go into the kingdom of God before you."

Reply to Objection 2: The highest and the lowest place can be taken in three ways. First, in reference to the same state and the same man; and thus it is evident that no one comes to the summit suddenly, since every man that lives aright, progresses during the whole course of his life, so as to arrive at the summit. Secondly, in comparison with various states; and thus he who desires to reach to a higher state need not begin from a lower state: for instance, if a man wish to be a cleric he need not first of all be practiced in the life of a layman. Thirdly, in comparison with different persons; and in this way it is clear that one man begins straightway not only from a higher state, but even from a higher degree of holiness, than the highest degree to which another man attains throughout his whole life. Hence Gregory says (Dial. ii, 1): "All are agreed that the boy Benedict began at a high degree of grace and perfection in his daily life."

Reply to Objection 3: As stated above ([3836]Q[184], A[6]) the holy orders prerequire holiness, whereas the religious state is a school for the attainment of holiness. Hence the burden of orders should be laid on the walls when these are already seasoned with holiness, whereas the burden of religion seasons the walls, i.e. men, by drawing out the damp of vice.

Reply to Objection 4: It is manifest from the words of this gloss that it is chiefly a question of the order of doctrine, in so far as one has to pass from easy matter to that which is more difficult. Hence it is clear from what follows that the statement that certain "heretics" and "schismatics have perverted this order" refers to the order of doctrine. For it continues thus: "But he says that he has kept these things, namely the aforesaid order, binding himself by an oath [*Referring to the last words of the verse, and taking 'retributio,' which Douay renders 'reward,' as meaning 'punishment']. Thus I was humble not only in other things but also in knowledge, for 'I was humbly minded'; because I was first of all fed with milk, which is the Word made flesh, so that I grew up to partake of the bread of angels, namely the Word that is in the beginning with God." The example which is given in proof, of the newly baptized not being commanded to fast until Pentecost, shows that no difficult things are to be laid on them as an obligation before the Holy Ghost inspires them inwardly to take upon themselves difficult things of their own choice. Hence after Pentecost and the receiving of the Holy Ghost the Church observes a fast. Now the Holy Ghost, according to Ambrose (Super Luc. 1:15), "is not confined to any particular age; He ceases not when men die, He is not excluded from the maternal womb." Gregory also in a homily for Pentecost (xxx in Ev.) says: "He fills the boy harpist and makes him a psalmist: He fills the boy abstainer and makes him a wise judge [*Dan. 1:8–17]," and afterwards he adds: "No time is needed to learn whatsoever He will, for He teaches the mind by the merest touch." Again it is written (Eccles. 8:8), "It is not in man's power to stop the Spirit," and the Apostle admonishes us (1 Thess. 5:19): "Extinguish not the Spirit," and (Acts 7:51) it is said against certain persons: "You always resist the Holy Ghost."

Reply to Objection 5: There are certain chief precepts which are the ends, so to say, of the commandments and counsels. These are the precepts of charity, and the counsels are directed to them, not that these precepts cannot be observed without keeping the counsels, but that the keeping of the counsels conduces to the better observance of the precepts. The other precepts are secondary and are directed to the precepts of charity; in such a way that unless one observe them it is altogether impossible to keep the precepts of charity. Accordingly in the intention the perfect observance of the precepts of charity precedes the counsels, and yet sometimes it follows them in point of time. For such is the order of the end in relation to things directed to the end. But the observance in a general way of the precepts of charity together with the other precepts, is compared to the counsels as the common to the proper, because one can observe the precepts without observing the counsels, but not vice versa. Hence the common observance of the precepts precedes the counsels in the order of nature; but it does not follow that it precedes them in point of time, for a thing is not in the genus before being in one of the species. But the observance of the precepts apart from the counsels is directed to the observance of the precepts together with the counsels; as an imperfect to a perfect species, even as the irrational to the rational animal. Now the perfect is naturally prior to the imperfect, since "nature," as Boethius says (De Consol. iii, 10), "begins with perfect things." And yet it is not necessary for the precepts first of all to be observed without the counsels, and afterwards with the counsels, just as it is not necessary for one to be an ass before being a man, or married before being a virgin. In like manner it is not necessary for a person first of all to keep the commandments in the world before entering religion; especially as the worldly life does not dispose one to religious perfection, but is more an obstacle thereto.

Whether one ought to be bound by vow to enter religion?

Objection 1: It would seem that one ought not to be bound by vow to enter religion. For in making his profession a man is bound by the religious vow. Now before profession a year of probation is allowed, according to the rule of the Blessed Benedict (lviii) and according to the decree of Innocent IV [*Sext. Decret., cap. Non solum., de Regular. et Transeunt, ad Relig.] who moreover forbade anyone to be bound to the religious life by profession before completing the year of probation. Therefore it would seem that much less ought anyone while yet in the world to be bound by vow to enter religion.

Objection 2: Further, Gregory says (Regist. xi, Ep. 15): Jews "should be persuaded to be converted, not by compulsion but of their own free will" (Dist. xlv, can. De Judaeis). Now one is compelled to fulfil what one has vowed. Therefore no one should be bound by vow to enter religion.

Objection 3: Further, no one should give another an occasion of falling; wherefore it is written (Ex. 21:33,34): "If a man open a pit . . . and an ox or an ass fall into it, the owner of the pit shall pay the price of the beasts." Now through being bound by vow to enter religion it often happens that people fall into despair and various sins. Therefore it would seem that one ought not to be bound by vow to enter religion.

On the contrary, It is written, (Ps. 75:12): "Vow ye, and pay to the Lord your God"; and a gloss of Augustine says that "some vows concern the individual, such as vows of chastity, virginity, and the like." Consequently Holy Scripture invites us to vow these things. But Holy Scripture invites us only to that which is better. Therefore it is better to bind oneself by vow to enter religion.

I answer that, As stated above ([3837]Q[88], A[6]), when we were treating of vows, one and the same work done in fulfilment of a vow is more praiseworthy than if it be done apart from a vow, both because to vow is an act of religion, which has a certain pre-eminence among the virtues, and because a vow strengthens a man's will to do good; and just as a sin is more grievous through proceeding from a will obstinate in evil, so a good work is the more praiseworthy through proceeding from a will confirmed in good by means of a vow. Therefore it is in itself praiseworthy to bind oneself by vow to enter religion.

Reply to Objection 1: The religious vow is twofold. One is the solemn vow which makes a man a monk or a brother in some other religious order. This is called the profession, and such a vow should be preceded by a year's probation, as the objection proves. The other is the simple vow which does not make a man a monk or a religious, but only binds him to enter religion, and such a vow need not be preceded by a year's probation.

Reply to Objection 2: The words quoted from Gregory must be understood as referring to absolute violence. But the compulsion arising from the obligation of a vow is not absolute necessity, but a necessity of end, because after such a vow one cannot attain to the end of salvation unless one fulfil that vow. Such a necessity is not to be avoided; indeed, as Augustine says (Ep. cxxvii ad Armentar. et Paulin.), "happy is the necessity that compels us to better things."

Reply to Objection 3: The vow to enter religion is a strengthening of the will for better things, and consequently, considered in itself, instead of giving a man an occasion of falling, withdraws him from it. But if one who breaks a vow falls more grievously, this does not derogate from the goodness of the vow, as neither does it derogate from the goodness of Baptism that some sin more grievously after being baptized.

Whether one who is bound by a vow to enter religion is under an obligation of entering religion?

Objection 1: It would seem that one who is bound by the vow to enter religion is not under an obligation of entering religion. For it is said in the Decretals (XVII, qu. ii, can. Consaldus): "Consaldus, a priest under pressure of sickness and emotional fervour, promised to become a monk. He did not, however, bind himself to a monastery or abbot; nor did he commit his promise to writing, but he renounced his benefice in the hands of a notary; and when he was restored to health he refused to become a monk." And afterwards it is added: "We adjudge and by apostolic authority we command that the aforesaid priest be admitted to his benefice and sacred duties, and that he be allowed to retain them in peace." Now this would not be if he were bound to enter religion. Therefore it would seem that one is not bound to keep one's vow of entering religion.

Objection 2: Further, no one is bound to do what is not in his power. Now it is not in a person's power to enter religion, since this depends on the consent of those whom he wishes to join. Therefore it would seem that a man is not obliged to fulfil the vow by which he bound himself to enter religion.

Objection 3: Further, a less useful vow cannot remit a more useful one. Now the fulfilment of a vow to enter religion might hinder the fulfilment of a vow to take up the cross in defense of the Holy Land; and the latter apparently is the more useful vow, since thereby a man obtains the forgiveness of his sins. Therefore it would seem that the vow by which a man has bound himself to enter religion is not necessarily to be fulfilled.

On the contrary, It is written (Eccles. 5:3): "If thou hast vowed anything to God, defer not to pay it, for an unfaithful and foolish promise displeaseth him"; and a gloss on Ps. 75:12, "Vow ye, and pay to the Lord your God," says: "To vow depends on the will: but after the vow has been taken the fulfilment is of obligation."

I answer that, As stated above ([3838]Q[88], A[1]), when we were treating of vows, a vow is a promise made to God in matters concerning God. Now, as Gregory says in a letter to Boniface [*Innoc. I, Epist. ii, Victricio Epo. Rotomag., cap. 14; Cf. can. Viduas: cause. xxvii, qu. 1]: "If among men of good faith contracts are wont to be absolutely irrevocable, how much more shall the breaking of this promise given to God be deserving of punishment!" Therefore a man is under an obligation to fulfil what he has vowed, provided this be something pertaining to God.

Now it is evident that entrance into religion pertains very much to God, since thereby man devotes himself entirely to the divine service, as stated above ([3839]Q[186], A[1]). Hence it follows that he who binds himself to enter religion is under an obligation to enter religion according as he intends to bind himself by his vow: so that if he intend to bind himself absolutely, he is obliged to enter as soon as he can, through the cessation of a lawful impediment; whereas if he intend to bind himself to a certain fixed time, or under a certain fixed condition, he is bound to enter religion when the time comes or the condition is fulfilled.

Reply to Objection 1: This priest had made, not a solemn, but a simple vow. Hence he was not a monk in effect, so as to be bound by law to dwell in a monastery and renounce his cure. However, in the court of conscience one ought to advise him to renounce all and enter religion. Hence (Extra, De Voto et Voti

Redemptione, cap. Per tuas) the Bishop of Grenoble, who had accepted the episcopate after vowing to enter religion, without having fulfilled his vow, is counseled that if "he wish to heal his conscience he should renounce the government of his see and pay his vows to the Most High."

Reply to Objection 2: As stated above ([3840]Q[88], A[3], ad 2), when we were treating of vows, he who has bound himself by vow to enter a certain religious order is bound to do what is in his power in order to be received in that order; and if he intend to bind himself simply to enter the religious life, if he be not admitted to one, he is bound to go to another; whereas if he intend to bind himself only to one particular order, he is bound only according to the measure of the obligation to which he has engaged himself.

Reply to Objection 3: The vow to enter religion being perpetual is greater than the vow of pilgrimage to the Holy Land, which is a temporal vow; and as Alexander III says (Extra, De Voto et Voti Redemptione, cap. Scripturae), "he who exchanges a temporary service for the perpetual service of religion is in no way guilty of breaking his vow."

Moreover it may be reasonably stated that also by entrance into religion a man obtains remission of all his sins. For if by giving alms a man may forthwith satisfy for his sins, according to Dan. 4:24, "Redeem thou thy sins with alms," much more does it suffice to satisfy for all his sins that a man devote himself wholly to the divine service by entering religion, for this surpasses all manner of satisfaction, even that of public penance, according to the Decretals (XXXIII, qu. i, cap. Admonere) just as a holocaust exceeds a sacrifice, as Gregory declares (Hom. xx in Ezech.). Hence we read in the Lives of the Fathers (vi, 1) that by entering religion one receives the same grace as by being baptized. And yet even if one were not thereby absolved from all debt of punishment, nevertheless the entrance into religion is more profitable than a pilgrimage to the Holy Land, as regards the advancement in good, which is preferable to absolution from punishment.

Whether he who has vowed to enter religion is bound to remain in religion in perpetuity?

Objection 1: It would seem that he who has vowed to enter religion, is bound in perpetuity to remain in religion. For it is better not to enter religion than to leave after entering, according to 2 Pet. 2:21, "It had been better for them not to have known the way of justice, than after they have known it to turn back," and Lk. 9:62, "No man putting his hand to the plough, and looking back, is fit for the kingdom of God." But he who bound himself by the vow to enter religion, is under the obligation to enter, as stated above [3841](A[3]). Therefore he is also bound to remain for always.

Objection 2: Further, everyone is bound to avoid that which gives rise to scandal, and is a bad example to others. Now by leaving after entering religion a man gives a bad example and is an occasion of scandal to others, who are thereby withdrawn from entering or incited to leave. Therefore it seems that he who enters religion in order to fulfil a vow which he had previously taken, is bound to remain evermore.

Objection 3: Further, the vow to enter religion is accounted a perpetual vow: wherefore it is preferred to temporal vows, as stated above (A[3], ad 3;[3842] Q[88], A[12], ad 1). But this would not be so if a person after vowing to enter religion were to enter with the intention of leaving. It seems, therefore, that he who vows to enter religion is bound also to remain in perpetuity.

On the contrary, The vow of religious profession, for the reason that it binds a man to remain in religion for evermore, has to be preceded by a year of probation; whereas this is not required before the simple vow whereby a man binds himself to enter religion. Therefore it seems that he who vows to enter religion is not for that reason bound to remain there in perpetuity.

I answer that, The obligation of a vow proceeds from the will: because "to vow is an act of the will" according to Augustine [*Gloss of Peter Lombard on Ps. 75:12]. Consequently the obligation of a vow extends as far as the will and intention of the person who takes the vow. Accordingly if in vowing he intend to bind himself not only to enter religion, but also to remain there evermore, he is bound to remain in perpetuity. If, on the other hand, he intend to bind himself to enter religion for the purpose of trial, while retaining the freedom to remain or not remain, it is clear that he is not bound to remain. If, however, in vowing he thought merely of entering religion, without thinking of being free to leave, or of remaining in perpetuity, it would seem that he is bound to enter religion according to the form prescribed by common law, which is that those who enter should be given a year's probation. Wherefore he is not bound to remain for ever.

Reply to Objection 1: It is better to enter religion with the purpose of making a trial than not to enter at all, because by so doing one disposes oneself to remain always. Nor is a person accounted to turn or to look back, save when he omits to do that which he engaged to do: else whoever does a good work for a time, would be unfit for the kingdom of God, unless he did it always, which is evidently false.

Reply to Objection 2: A man who has entered religion gives neither scandal nor bad example by leaving, especially if he do so for a reasonable motive; and if others are scandalized, it will be passive scandal on their part, and not active scandal on the part of the person leaving, since in doing so, he has done what was lawful, and expedient on account of some reasonable motive, such as sickness, weakness, and the like.

Reply to Objection 3: He who enters with the purpose of leaving forthwith, does not seem to fulfil his vow, since this was not his intention in vowing. Hence he must change that purpose, at least so as to wish to try whether it is good for him to remain in religion, but he is not bound to remain for evermore.

Whether children should be received in religion?

Objection 1: It would seem that children ought not to be received in religion. Because it is said (Extra, De Regular. et Transeunt. ad Relig., cap. Nullus): "No one should be tonsured unless he be of legal age and willing." But children, seemingly, are not of legal age; nor have they a will of their own, not having perfect use of reason. Therefore it seems that they ought not to be received in religion.

Objection 2: Further, the state of religion would seem to be a state of repentance; wherefore religion is derived [*Cf.[3843] Q[81], A[1]] from "religare" [to bind] or from "re-eligere" [to choose again], as Augustine says (De Civ. Dei x, 3 [*Cf. De Vera Relig. lv]). But repentance does not become children. Therefore it seems that they should not enter religion.

Objection 3: Further, the obligation of a vow is like that of an oath. But children under the age of fourteen ought not to be bound by oath (Decret. XXII, qu. v, cap. Pueri and cap. Honestum.). Therefore it would seem that neither should they be bound by vow.

Objection 4: Further, it is seemingly unlawful to bind a person to an obligation that can be justly canceled. Now if any persons of unripe age bind themselves to religion, they can be withdrawn by their parents or guardians. For it is written in the Decretals (XX, qu. ii, can. Puella) that "if a maid under twelve years of age shall take the sacred veil of her own accord, her parents or guardians, if they choose, can at once declare the deed null and void." It is therefore unlawful for children, especially of unripe age, to be admitted or bound to religion.

On the contrary, our Lord said (Mat. 19:14): "Suffer the little children, and forbid them not to come to Me." Expounding these words Origen says (Tract. vii in Matth.) that "the disciples of Jesus before they have been taught the conditions of righteousness [*Cf. Mat. 19:16–30], rebuke those who offer children and babes to Christ: but our Lord urges His disciples to stoop to the service of children. We must therefore take note of this, lest deeming ourselves to excel in wisdom we despise the Church's little ones, as though we were great, and forbid the children to come to Jesus."

I answer that, As stated above (A[2], ad 1), the religious vow is twofold. One is the simple vow consisting in a mere promise made to God, and proceeding from the interior deliberation of the mind. Such a vow derives its efficacy from the divine law. Nevertheless it may encounter a twofold obstacle. First, through lack of deliberation, as in the case of the insane, whose vows are not binding [*Extra, De Regular. et Transeunt. ad Relig., cap. Sicut tenor]. The same applies to children who have not reached the required use of reason, so as to be capable of guile, which use boys attain, as a rule, at about the age of fourteen, and girls at the age of twelve, this being what is called "the age of puberty," although in some it comes earlier and in others it is delayed, according to the various dispositions of nature. Secondly, the efficacy of a simple vow encounters an obstacle, if the person who makes a vow to God is not his own master; for instance, if a slave, though having the use of reason, vows to enter religion, or even is ordained, without the knowledge of his master: for his master can annul this, as stated in the Decretals (Dist. LIV, cap. Si servus). And since boys and girls under the age of puberty are naturally in their father's power as regards the disposal of their manner of life, their father may either cancel or approve their vow, if it please him to do so, as it is expressly said with regard to a woman (Num. 30:4).

Accordingly if before reaching the age of puberty a child makes a simple vow, not yet having full use of reason, he is not bound in virtue of the vow; but if he has the use of reason before reaching the age of puberty, he is bound, so far as he is concerned, by his vow; yet this obligation may be removed by his father's authority, under whose control he still remains, because the ordinance of the law whereby one man is subject to another considers what happens in the majority of cases. If, however, the

child has passed the age of puberty, his vow cannot be annulled by the authority of his parents; though if he has not the full use of reason, he would not be bound in the sight of God.

The other is the solemn vow which makes a man a monk or a religious. Such a vow is subject to the ordinance of the Church, on account of the solemnity attached to it. And since the Church considers what happens in the majority of cases, a profession made before the age of puberty, however much the person who makes profession may have the use of reason, or be capable of guile, does not take effect so as to make him a religious (Extra, De Regular., etc. cap. Significatum est.).

Nevertheless, although they cannot be professed before the age of puberty, they can, with the consent of their parents, be received into religion to be educated there: thus it is related of John the Baptist (Lk. 1:80) that "the child grew and was strengthened in spirit, and was in the deserts." Hence, as Gregory states (Dial. ii, 3), "the Roman nobles began to give their sons to the blessed Benedict to be nurtured for Almighty God"; and this is most fitting, according to Lam. 3:27, "It is good for a man when he has borne the yoke from his youth." It is for this reason that by common custom children are made to apply themselves to those duties or arts with which they are to pass their lives.

Reply to Objection 1: The legal age for receiving the tonsure and taking the solemn vow of religion is the age of puberty, when a man is able to make use of his own will; but before the age of puberty it is possible to have reached the lawful age to receive the tonsure and be educated in a religious house.

Reply to Objection 2: The religious state is chiefly directed to the attachment of perfection, as stated above ([3844]Q[186], A[1], ad 4); and accordingly it is becoming to children, who are easily drawn to it. But as a consequence it is called a state of repentance, inasmuch as occasions of sin are removed by religious observances, as stated above ([3845]Q[186], A[1], ad 4).

Reply to Objection 3: Even as children are not bound to take oaths (as the canon states), so are they not bound to take vows. If, however, they bind themselves by vow or oath to do something, they are bound in God's sight, if they have the use of reason, but they are not bound in the sight of the Church before reaching the age of fourteen.

Reply to Objection 4: A woman who has not reached the age of puberty is not rebuked (Num. 30:4) for taking a vow without her parents' consent: but the vow can be made void by her parents. Hence it is evident that she does not sin in vowing. But we are given to understand that she binds herself by vow, so far as she may, without prejudice to her parents' authority.

Whether one ought to be withdrawn from entering religion through deference to one's parents?

Objection 1: It would seem that one ought to be withdrawn from entering religion through deference to one's parents. For it is not lawful to omit that which is of obligation in order to do that which is optional. Now deference to one's parents comes under an obligation of the precept concerning the honoring of our parents (Ex. 20:12); wherefore the Apostle says (1 Tim. 5:4): "If any widow have children or grandchildren, let her learn first to govern her own house, and to make a return of duty to her parents." But the entrance to religion is optional. Therefore it would seem that one ought not to omit deference to one's parents for the sake of entering religion.

Objection 2: Further, seemingly the subjection of a son to his father is greater than that of a slave to his master, since sonship is natural, while slavery results from the curse of sin, as appears from Gn. 9:25. Now a slave cannot set aside the service of his master in order to enter religion or take holy orders, as stated in the Decretals (Dist. LIV, cap. Si servus). Much less therefore can a son set aside the deference due to his father in order to enter religion.

Objection 3: Further, a man is more indebted to his parents than to those to whom he owes money. Now persons who owe money to anyone cannot enter religion. For Gregory says (Regist. viii, Ep. 5) that "those who are engaged in trade must by no means be admitted into a monastery, when they seek admittance, unless first of all they withdraw from public business" (Dist. liii, can. Legem.). Therefore seemingly much less may children enter religion in despite of their duty to their parents.

On the contrary, It is related (Mat. 4:22) that James and John "left their nets and father, and followed our Lord." By this, says Hilary (Can. iii in Matth.), "we learn that we who intend to follow Christ are not bound by the cares of the secular life, and by the ties of home."

I answer that, As stated above ([3846]Q[101], A[2], ad 2) when we were treating of piety, parents as such have the character of a principle, wherefore it is competent to them as such to have the care of their children. Hence it is unlawful for a person having children to enter religion so as altogether to set aside the care for their children, namely without providing for their education. For it is written (1 Tim. 5:8) that "if any man have not care of his own . . . he hath denied the faith, and is worse than an infidel."

Nevertheless it is accidentally competent to parents to be assisted by their children, in so far, to wit, as they are placed in a condition of necessity. Consequently we must say that when their parents are in such need that they cannot fittingly be supported otherwise than by the help of their children, these latter may not lawfully enter religion in despite of their duty to their parents. If, however, the parents' necessity be not such as to stand in great need of their children's assistance, the latter may, in despite of the duty they owe their parents, enter religion even against their parents' command, because after the age of puberty every freeman enjoys freedom in things concerning the ordering of his state of life, especially in such as belong to the service of God, and "we should more obey the Father of spirits that we may live [*'Shall we not much more obey the Father of Spirits, and live?'']," as says the Apostle (Heb. 12:9), than obey our parents. Hence as we read (Mat. 8:22; Lk. 9:62) our Lord rebuked the disciple who was unwilling to follow him forthwith on account of his father's burial: for there were others who could see to this, as Chrysostom remarks [*Hom. xxvii in Matth.].

Reply to Objection 1: The commandment of honoring our parents extends not only to bodily but also to spiritual service, and to the paying of deference. Hence even those who are in religion can fulfil the commandment of honoring their parents, by praying for them and by revering and assisting them, as becomes religious, since even those who live in the world honor their parents in different ways as befits their condition.

Reply to Objection 2: Since slavery was imposed in punishment of sin, it follows that by slavery man forfeits something which otherwise he would be competent to have, namely the free disposal of his person, for "a slave belongs wholly to his master" [*Aristotle, Polit. i, 2]. On the other hand, the son, through being subject to his father, is not hindered from freely disposing of his person by transferring himself to the service of God; which is most conducive to man's good.

Reply to Objection 3: He who is under a certain fixed obligation cannot lawfully set it aside so long as he is able to fulfil it. Wherefore if a person is under an obligation to give an account to someone or to pay a certain fixed debt, he cannot lawfully evade this obligation in order to enter religion. If, however, he owes a sum of money, and has not wherewithal to pay the debt, he must do what he can, namely by surrendering his goods to his creditor. According to civil law [*Cod. IV, x, de Oblig. et Action, 12] money lays an obligation not on the person of a freeman, but on his property, because the person of a freeman "is above all pecuniary consideration" [*Dig. L, xvii, de div. reg. Jur. ant. 106,176]. Hence, after surrendering his property, he may lawfully enter religion, nor is he bound to remain in the world in order to earn the means of paying the debt.

On the other hand, he does not owe his father a special debt, except as may arise in a case of necessity, as stated above.

Whether parish priests may lawfully enter religion?

Objection 1: It would seem that parish priests cannot lawfully enter religion. For Gregory says (Past. iii, 4) that "he who undertakes the cure of souls, receives an awful warning in the words: 'My son, if thou be surety for thy friend, thou hast engaged fast thy hand to a stranger'" (Prov. 6:1); and he goes on to say, "because to be surety for a friend is to take charge of the soul of another on the surety of one's own behavior." Now he who is under an obligation to a man for a debt, cannot enter religion, unless he pay what he owes, if he can. Since then a priest is able to fulfil the cure of souls, to which obligation he has pledged his soul, it would seem unlawful for him to lay aside the cure of souls in order to enter religion.

Objection 2: Further, what is lawful to one is likewise lawful to all. But if all priests having cure of souls were to enter religion, the people would be left without a pastor's care, which would be unfitting. Therefore it seems that parish priests cannot lawfully enter religion.

Objection 3: Further, chief among the acts to which religious orders are directed are those whereby a man gives to others the fruit of his contemplation. Now such acts are competent to parish priests and archdeacons, whom it becomes by virtue of their office to preach and hear confessions. Therefore it would seem unlawful for a parish priest or archdeacon to pass over to religion.

On the contrary, It is said in the Decretals (XIX, qu. ii, cap. Duce sunt leges.): "If a man, while governing the people in his church under the bishop and leading a secular life, is inspired by the Holy Ghost to desire to work out his salvation in a monastery or under some canonical rule, even though his bishop withstand him, we authorize him to go freely."

I answer that, As stated above (A[3], ad 3;[3847] Q[88], A[12], ad 1), the obligation of a perpetual vow stands before every other obligation. Now it belongs properly to bishops and religious to be bound by perpetual vow to devote themselves to the divine service [*Cf.[3848] Q[184], A[5]], while parish priests and archdeacons are not, as bishops are, bound by a perpetual and solemn vow to retain the cure of souls. Wherefore bishops "cannot lay aside their bishopric for any pretext whatever, without the authority of the Roman Pontiff" (Extra, De Regular. et Transeunt. ad Relig., cap. Licet.): whereas archdeacons and parish priests are free to renounce in the hands of the bishop the cure entrusted to them, without the Pope's special permission, who alone can dispense from perpetual vows. Therefore it is evident that archdeacons and parish priests may lawfully enter religion.

Reply to Objection 1: Parish priests and archdeacons have bound themselves to the care of their subjects, as long as they retain their archdeaconry or parish, but they did not bind themselves to retain their archdeaconry or parish for ever.

Reply to Objection 2: As Jerome says (Contra Vigil.): "Although they," namely religious, "are sorely smitten by thy poisonous tongue, about whom you argue, saying; 'If all shut themselves up and live in solitude, who will go to church? who will convert worldlings? who will be able to urge sinners to virtue?' If this holds true, if all are fools with thee, who can be wise? Nor will virginity be commendable, for if all be virgins, and none marry, the human race will perish. Virtue is rare, and is not desired by many." It is therefore evident that this is a foolish alarm; thus might a man fear to draw water lest the river run dry. [*St. Thomas gives no reply to the third objection, which is sufficiently solved in the body of the article.]

Whether it is lawful to pass from one religious order to another?

Objection 1: It seems unlawful to pass from one religious order to another, even a stricter one. For the Apostle says (Heb. 10:25): "Not forsaking our assembly, as some are accustomed"; and a gloss observes: "Those namely who yield through fear of persecution, or who presuming on themselves withdraw from the company of sinners or of the imperfect, that they may appear to be righteous." Now those who pass from one religious order to another more perfect one would seem to do this. Therefore this is seemingly unlawful.

Objection 2: Further, the profession of monks is stricter than that of canons regular (Extra, De Statu Monach. et Canonic. Reg., cap. Quod Dei timorem). But it is unlawful for anyone to pass from the state of canon regular to the monastic state. For it is said in the Decretals (XIX, qu. iii, can. Mandamus): "We ordain and without any exception forbid any professed canon regular to become a monk, unless (which God forbid) he have fallen into public sin." Therefore it would seem unlawful for anyone to pass from one religious order to another of higher rank.

Objection 3: Further, a person is bound to fulfil what he has vowed, as long as he is able lawfully to do so; thus if a man has vowed to observe continence, he is bound, even after contracting marriage by words in the present tense, to fulfil his vow so long as the marriage is not consummated, because he can fulfil the vow by entering religion. Therefore if a person may lawfully pass from one religious order to another, he will be bound to do so if he vowed it previously while in the world. But this would seem objectionable, since in many cases it might give rise to scandal. Therefore a religious may not pass from one religious order to another stricter one.

On the contrary, It is said in the Decretals (XX, qu. iv, can. Virgines): "If sacred virgins design for the good of their soul to pass to another monastery on account of a stricter life, and decide to remain there, the holy synod allows them to do so": and the same would seem to apply to any religious. Therefore one may lawfully pass from one religious order to another.

I answer that, It is not commendable to pass from one religious order to another: both because this frequently gives scandal to those who remain; and because, other things being equal, it is easier to make progress in a religious order to which one is accustomed than in one to which one is not habituated. Hence in the Conferences of the Fathers (Coll. xiv, 5) Abbot Nesteros says: "It is best for each one that he should, according to the resolve he has made, hasten with the greatest zeal and care to reach the perfection of the work he has undertaken, and nowise forsake the profession he has chosen." And further on he adds (cap. 6) by way of reason: "For it is impossible that one and the same man should excel in all the virtues at once, since if he endeavor to practice them equally, he will of necessity, while trying to attain them all, end in acquiring none of them perfectly": because the various religious orders excel in respect of various works of virtue.

Nevertheless one may commendably pass from one religious order to another for three reasons. First, through zeal for a more perfect religious life, which excellence depends, as stated above ([3849]Q[188], A[6]), not merely on severity, but chiefly on the end to which a religious order is directed, and secondarily on the discretion whereby the observances are proportionate to the due end. Secondly, on account of a religious order falling away from the perfection it ought to have: for instance, if in a more severe religious order, the religious begin to live less strictly, it is commendable for one to pass even to a less severe religious order if the observance is better. Hence in the Conferences of the Fathers (Coll. xix, 3,5,6) Abbot John says of himself that he had passed from the solitary life, in which he was professed, to a less severe life, namely of those who lived in community, because the hermetical life had fallen into decline and laxity. Thirdly, on account of sickness or weakness, the result of which sometimes is that one is unable to keep the ordinances of a more severe religious order, though able to observe those of a less strict religion.

There is, however, a difference in these three cases. For in the first case one ought, on account of humility, to seek permission: yet this cannot be denied, provided it be certain that this other religion is more severe. "And if there be a probable doubt about this, one should ask one's superior to decide" (Extra, De Regular. et Transeunt. ad Relig., cap. Licet.). In like manner the superior's decision should be sought in the second case. In the third case it is also necessary to have a dispensation.

Reply to Objection 1: Those who pass to a stricter religious order, do so not out of presumption that they may appear righteous, but out of devotion, that they may become more righteous.

Reply to Objection 2: Religious orders whether of monks or of canons regular are destined to the works of the contemplative life. Chief among these are those which are performed in the divine mysteries, and these are the direct object of the orders of canons regular, the members of which are essentially religious clerics. On the other hand, monastic religious are not essentially clerics, according to the Decretals (XVI, qu. i, cap. Alia causa). Hence although monastic orders are more severe, it would be lawful, supposing the members to be lay monks, to pass from the monastic order to an order of canons regular, according to the statement of Jerome (Ep. cxxv, ad Rustic. Monach.): "So live in the monastery as to deserve to become a cleric"; but not conversely, as expressed in the Decretal quoted (XIX, qu. iii). If, however, the monks be clerics devoting themselves to the sacred ministry, they have this in common with canons regular coupled with greater severity, and consequently it will be lawful to pass from an order of canons regular to a monastic order, provided withal that one seek the superior's permission (XIX, qu. iii; cap. Statuimus).

Reply to Objection 3: The solemn vow whereby a person is bound to a less strict order, is more binding than the simple vow whereby a person is bound to a stricter order. For if after taking a simple vow a person were to be married, his marriage would not be invalid, as it would be after his taking a solemn vow. Consequently a person who is professed in a less severe order is not bound to fulfil a simple vow he has taken on entering a more severe order.

Whether one ought to induce others to enter religion?

Objection 1: It would seem that no one ought to induce others to enter religion. For the blessed Benedict prescribes in his Rule (lviii) that "those who seek to enter religion must not easily be admitted, but spirits must be tested whether they be of God"; and Cassian has the same instruction (De Inst. Caenob. iv, 3). Much less therefore is it lawful to induce anyone to enter religion.

Objection 2: Further, our Lord said (Mat. 23:15): "Woe to you . . . because you go round about the sea and the land to make one proselyte, and when he is made you make him the child of hell twofold more than yourselves." Now thus would seem to do those who induce persons to enter religion. Therefore this would seem blameworthy.

Objection 3: Further, no one should induce another to do what is to his prejudice. But those who are induced to enter religion, sometimes take harm therefrom, for sometimes they are under obligation to enter a stricter religion. Therefore it would not seem praiseworthy to induce others to enter religion.

On the contrary, It is written (Ex. 26:3, seqq. [*St. Thomas quotes the sense, not the words]): "Let one curtain draw the other." Therefore one man should draw another to God's service.

I answer that, Those who induce others to enter religion not only do not sin, but merit a great reward. For it is written (James 5:20): "He who causeth a sinner to be converted from the error of his way, shall save his soul from death, and shall cover a multitude of sins"; and (Dan. 12:3): "They that instruct many to justice shall be as stars for all eternity."

Nevertheless such inducement may be affected by a threefold inordinateness. First, if one person force another by violence to enter religion: and this is forbidden in the Decretals (XX, qu. iii, cap. Praesens). Secondly, if one person persuade another simoniacally to enter religion, by giving him presents: and this is forbidden in the Decretal (I, qu. ii, cap. Quam pio). But this does not apply to the case where one provides a poor person with necessaries by educating him in the world for the religious life; or when without any compact one gives a person little presents for the sake of good fellowship. Thirdly, if one person entices another by lies: for it is to be feared that the person thus enticed may turn back on finding himself deceived, and thus "the last state of that man" may become "worse than the first" (Lk. 11:26).

Reply to Objection 1: Those who are induced to enter religion have still a time of probation wherein they make a trial of the hardships of religion, so that they are not easily admitted to the religious life.

Reply to Objection 2: According to Hilary (Can. xxiv in Matth.) this saying of our Lord was a forecast of the wicked endeavors of the Jews, after the preaching of Christ, to draw Gentiles or even Christians to observe the Jewish ritual, thereby making them doubly children of hell, because, to wit, they were not forgiven the former sins which they committed while adherents of Judaism, and furthermore they incurred the guilt of Jewish perfidy; and thus interpreted these words have nothing to do with the case in point.

According to Jerome, however, in his commentary on this passage of Matthew, the reference is to the Jews even at the time when it was yet lawful to keep the legal observances, in so far as he whom they converted to Judaism "from paganism, was merely misled; but when he saw the wickedness of his teachers, he returned to his vomit, and becoming a pagan deserved greater punishment for his treachery." Hence it is manifest that it is not blameworthy to draw others to the service of God or to the religious life, but only when one gives a bad example to the person converted, whence he becomes worse.

Reply to Objection 3: The lesser is included in the greater. Wherefore a person who is bound by vow or oath to enter a lesser order, may be lawfully induced to enter a greater one. unless there be some special obstacle, such as ill-health, or the hope of making greater progress in the lesser order. On the other hand, one who is bound by vow or oath to enter a greater order, cannot be lawfully induced to enter a lesser order, except for some special and evident motive, and then with the superior's dispensation.

Whether it is praiseworthy to enter religion without taking counsel of many, and previously deliberating for a long time?

Objection 1: It would not seem praiseworthy to enter religion without taking counsel of many, and previously deliberating for a long time. For it is written (1 Jn. 4:1): "Believe not every spirit, but try the spirits if they be of God." Now sometimes a man's purpose of entering religion is not of God, since it often comes to naught through his leaving the religious life; for it is written (Acts 5:38,39): "If this counsel or this work be of God, you cannot overthrow it." Therefore it would seem that one ought to make a searching inquiry before entering religion.

Objection 2: Further, it is written (Prov. 25:9): "Treat thy cause with thy friend." Now a man's cause would seem to be especially one that concerns a change in his state of life. Therefore seemingly one ought not to enter religion without discussing the matter with one's friends.

Objection 3: Further, our Lord (Lk. 14:28) in making a comparison with a man who has a mind to build a tower, says that he doth "first sit down and reckon the charges that are necessary, whether he have wherewithal to finish it," lest he become an object of mockery, for that "this man began to build and was not able to finish." Now the wherewithal to build the tower, as Augustine says (Ep. ad Laetum ccxliii), is nothing less than that "each one should renounce all his possessions." Yet it happens sometimes that many cannot do this, nor keep other religious observances; and in signification of this it is stated (1 Kings 17:39) that David could not walk in Saul's armor, for he was not used to it. Therefore it would seem that one ought not to enter religion without long deliberation beforehand and taking counsel of many.

On the contrary, It is stated (Mat. 4:20) that upon our Lord's calling them, Peter and Andrew "immediately leaving their nets, followed Him." Here Chrysostom says (Hom. xiv in Matth.): "Such obedience as this does Christ require of us, that we delay not even for a moment."

I answer that, Long deliberation and the advice of many are required in great matters of doubt, as the Philosopher says (Ethic. iii, 3); while advice is unnecessary in matters that are certain and fixed. Now with regard to entering religion three points may be considered. First, the entrance itself into religion, considered by itself; and thus it is certain that entrance into religion is a greater good, and to doubt about this is to disparage Christ Who gave this counsel. Hence Augustine says (De Verb. Dom., Serm. c, 2): "The East," that is Christ, "calleth thee, and thou turnest to the West," namely mortal and fallible man. Secondly, the entrance into religion may be considered in relation to the strength of the person who intends to enter. And here again there is no room for doubt about the entrance to religion, since those who enter religion trust not to be able to stay by their own power, but by the assistance of the divine power, according to Is. 40:31, "They that hope in the Lord shall renew their strength, they shall take wings as eagles, they shall run and not be weary, they shall walk and not faint." Yet if there be some special obstacle (such as bodily weakness, a burden of debts, or the like) in such cases a man must deliberate and take counsel with such as are likely to help and not hinder him. Hence it is written (Ecclus. 37:12): "Treat with a man without religion concerning holiness [*The Douay version supplies the negative: 'Treat not . . . nor with . . . '], with an unjust man concerning justice," meaning that one should not do so, wherefore the text goes on (Ecclus. 37:14,15), "Give no heed to these in any matter of counsel, but be continually with a holy man." In these matters, however, one should not take long deliberation. Wherefore Jerome says (Ep. and Paulin. liii): "Hasten, I pray thee, cut off rather than loosen the rope that holds the boat to the shore." Thirdly, we may consider the way of entering religion, and which order one ought to enter, and about such matters also one may take counsel of those who will not stand in one's way.

Reply to Objection 1: The saying: "Try the spirits, if they be of God," applies to matters admitting of doubt whether the spirits be of God; thus those who are already in religion may doubt whether he who offers himself to religion be led by the spirit of God, or be moved by hypocrisy. Wherefore they must try the postulant whether he be moved by the divine spirit. But for him who seeks to enter religion there can be no doubt but that the purpose of entering religion to which his heart has given birth is from the spirit of God, for it is His spirit "that leads" man "into the land of uprightness" (Ps. 142:10).

Nor does this prove that it is not of God that some turn back; since not all that is of God is incorruptible: else corruptible creatures would not be of God, as the Manicheans hold, nor could some who have grace from God lose it, which is also heretical. But God's "counsel" whereby He makes even things corruptible and changeable, is imperishable according to Is. 46:10, "My counsel shall stand and all My will shall be done." Hence the purpose of entering religion needs not to be tried whether it be of God, because "it requires no further demonstration," as a gloss says on 1 Thess. 5:21, "Prove all things."

Reply to Objection 2: Even as "the flesh lusteth against the spirit" (Gal. 5:17), so too carnal friends often thwart our spiritual progress, according to Mic. 7:6, "A man's enemies are they of his own household." Wherefore Cyril expounding Lk. 9:61, "Let me first take my leave of them that are at my house," says [*Cf. St. Thomas's Catena Aurea]: "By asking first to take his leave of them that were at his house, he shows he was somewhat of two minds. For to communicate with his neighbors, and consult those who are unwilling to relish righteousness, is an indication of weakness and turning back. Hence he hears our Lord say: 'No man putting his hand to the plough, and looking back, is fit for the kingdom of God,' because he looks back who seeks delay in order to go home and confer with his kinsfolk."

Reply to Objection 3: The building of the tower signifies the perfection of Christian life; and the renunciation of one's possessions is the wherewithal to build this tower. Now no one doubts or deliberates about wishing to have the wherewithal, or whether he is able to build the tower if he have the wherewithal, but what does come under deliberation is whether one has the wherewithal. Again it need not be a matter of deliberation whether one ought to renounce all that one has, or whether by so doing one may be able to attain to perfection; whereas it is a matter of deliberation whether that which one is doing amounts to the renunciation of all that he has, since unless he does renounce (which is to have the wherewithal) he cannot, as the text goes on to state, be Christ's disciple, and this is to build the tower.

The misgiving of those who hesitate as to whether they may be able to attain to perfection by entering religion is shown by many examples to be unreasonable. Hence Augustine says (Confess. viii, 11): "On that side whither I had set my face, and whither I trembled to go, there appeared to me the chaste dignity of continency . . . honestly alluring me to come and doubt not, and stretching forth to receive and embrace me, her holy hands full of multitudes of good examples. There were so many young men and maidens here, a multitude of youth and every age, grave widows and aged virgins . . . And she smiled at me with a persuasive mockery as though to say: Canst not thou what these youths and these maidens can? Or can they either in themselves, and not rather in the Lord their God? . . . Why standest thou in thyself, and so standest not? Cast thyself upon Him; fear not, He will not withdraw Himself that thou shouldst fall. Cast thyself fearlessly upon Him: He will receive and will heal thee."

The example quoted of David is not to the point, because "the arms of Saul," as a gloss on the passage observes, "are the sacraments of the Law, as being burdensome": whereas religion is the sweet yoke of Christ, for as Gregory says (Moral. iv, 33), "what burden does He lay on the shoulders of the mind, Who commands us to shun all troublesome desires, Who warns us to turn aside from the rough paths of this world?"

To those indeed who take this sweet yoke upon themselves He promises the refreshment of the divine fruition and the eternal rest of their souls.

To which may He Who made this promise bring us, Jesus Christ our Lord, "Who is over all things God blessed for ever. Amen."

Made in the USA
Columbia, SC
12 April 2025

56512073R00339